Praise for Julia Lovell's

Maoism

"[Maoism's] history has not been adequately told in one sweeping, accessible book—until now. . . . [Lovell's] new book covers a vast amount of ground. . . . The book's greatest strength is its scope. Lovell traveled widely, used archives and conducted interviews in many countries and synthesized the work of scholars in the growing field of global Cold War studies. She demonstrates how Maoism was more than an amorphous idea, but a strategy pushed by China."
                                                        —Ian Johnson,
                                        The New York Times Book Review

"Julia Lovell has given us a masterful corrective to the greatest misconception about today's China. For too long, visitors who marveled at China's new luxuries and capitalist zeal assumed that Maoism had gone the way of its creator. That was a mistake. Lovell's account—eloquent, engrossing, intelligent—not only explains why Xi Jinping has revived some of Mao's techniques, but also why Mao's playbook for the 'People's War' retains an intoxicating and tragic appeal to marginalized people the world over."
                                                        —Evan Osnos,
                    National Book Award–winning author of *Age of Ambition*

"Surprisingly, the story of Maoism outside China has never been told. Now, at last, we have this scintillating, sweeping narrative. It is a book packed with jaw-dropping stories, told with the pace and punch of a thriller. Chilling, but exhilaratingly readable, as a warning from history. This book could not be more timely."
                                        —Michael Wood, historian and broadcaster

Julia Lovell

Maoism

Julia Lovell is professor of modern China at Birkbeck College, University of London. Her two most recent books are *The Great Wall* and *The Opium War* (which won the 2012 Jan Michalski Prize). Her many translations of modern Chinese fiction into English include Lu Xun's *The Real Story of Ah-Q and Other Tales of China*. She is currently completing a new translation of *Journey to the West* by Wu Cheng'en. She writes about China for several newspapers, including *The Guardian*, *Financial Times*, *The New York Times*, and *The Wall Street Journal*.

Maoism

JULIA LOVELL

Maoism

A Global History

VINTAGE BOOKS
A DIVISION OF PENGUIN RANDOM HOUSE LLC
NEW YORK

FIRST VINTAGE BOOKS EDITION, AUGUST 2020

Copyright © 2019 by Julia Lovell

All rights reserved. Published in the United States by Vintage Books,
a division of Penguin Random House LLC, New York. Originally published in hardcover
in Great Britain by The Bodley Head, an imprint of Vintage Publishing, a division of Penguin
Random House Ltd., London, and subsequently published in the United States by Alfred A.
Knopf, a division of Penguin Random House LLC, New York, in 2019.

The Library of Congress has cataloged the Knopf edition as follows:
Name: Lovell, Julia, author.
Title: Maoism : a global history / Julia Lovell.
Description: First United States edition. | New York : Alfred A. Knopf, 2019. | Includes
bibliographical references
(pages 495–588) and index.
Identifiers: LCCN 2019010428
Subjects: LCSH: Communism—China—History. | Mao, Zedong, 1893–1976. | BISAC: HISTORY /
Asia / China. | HISTORY / Modern / 20th Century. | POLITICAL SCIENCE / Political
Ideologies / General.
Classification: LCC HX418 .L68 2019 | DDC 335.43/45—dc23
LC record available at https://lccn.loc.gov/2019010428

Vintage Books Trade Paperback ISBN: 978-0-525-56590-1
eBook ISBN: 978-0-525-65605-0

Author photograph © Dominic Mifsud
Book design by M. Kristen Bearse

www.vintagebooks.com

Printed in the United States of America
10 9 8 7 6 5 4 3 2 1

To my father, William (Bill) Lovell,
1946–2014

CONTENTS

Maoism

INTRODUCTION

Beijing, autumn 1936. A spacious courtyard house, the residence of the American journalists Helen and Edgar Snow. Helen – in her late twenties, boyishly slim, Hollywood good looks – settles down to a morning's writing. The front door opens; Edgar enters. She has not seen her husband for four months. Since June, he has been almost incommunicado on a trip to the Chinese Communist state in the north-west. He is, in Helen's characteristically sharp description, 'grinning foolishly behind a grizzled beard and looking like the cat that had swallowed the canary'. Dancing jubilantly around the room in a 'grey cap with a red star on its faded front', he orders from their Chinese cook a hearty American breakfast – eggs, coffee, milk.[1] His bag is laden with notebooks, photographic films and the text of 20,000 of Mao's transcribed words. Over the coming months, he will write up this material into a book he calls *Red Star Over China*. It will become a world bestseller. *Red Star* will not only determine Snow's career as a chronicler of the Chinese Communist revolution and as a mediator between the Chinese Communists and international audiences, but will also turn Mao into a political celebrity. The book will translate Mao and his revolution to Indian nationalists, Chinese intellectuals, Soviet partisans, American presidents, Malayan insurgents, anti-apartheid fighters, Western radicals, Nepali rebels and many others. *Red Star* is the beginning of global Maoism.

The jungle in Perak, Malaya, late 1940s. Soldiers in the British colonial army (British, Malay, Australian, Gurkhas) pick over the remnants of abandoned Malayan Communist Party (MCP) camps. They find dozens of copies of Edgar Snow's *Red Star* in its Chinese translation. In 1948, the MCP – dominated by ethnic Chinese – has launched an anti-British insurgency that Malaya's colonial rulers have dubbed the 'Emergency'. It is one of the earliest decolonising rebellions against the old European empires in the wake of the Second World War. Mao and his revolution are inspirational to these rebels: for his devotion to protracted, guerrilla warfare; for his creation of a tightly indoctrinated party and army; and for his defiance of European, American and Japanese imperialism.

Washington, November 1950. Cold War jitters in the State Department building. News of Chinese Communist intervention in the Korean War is confirmed; fears of global Maoist insurrection breed. Senator Joe McCarthy – 'the great national intimidator'[2] – rides high on popular panic about Communist infiltration of the United States, ousting two liberal senators through accusations of 'red' associations. For America's leaders, the Malayan Emergency is part of the Cold War, not an anti-colonial struggle; its root cause is declared to be transnational Chinese subversion and it must be defeated to prevent the global victory of Communism. The 'domino theory' – the idea that, without US intervention, the territories of South East Asia will one by one fall to Chinese Communism – is born. As the Korean War turns for the worse that winter and some 7,000 GIs are captured when human waves of Chinese soldiers push through their lines and on to Seoul, America is gripped by stories of a new-style Maoist psy-war trialled on its POWs in Korea. An American journalist (and perhaps sometime CIA agent) called Edward Hunter publishes allegations of Mao's terrifying new weapon against humanity: 'brainwashing'. CIA officers, journalists, behavioural scientists, novelists and film-makers will collude through the 1950s to imagine a powerful machinery of Maoist thought control. This dread of Chinese 'brainwashing' – building on pre-existing terror of Soviet mind manipulations – will balloon America's 'covert sphere', justifying the existence of a secret state within the state and the CIA's vast psychological operations programme. Through a series of code-named initiatives in the 1950s and '60s – Bluebird, Artichoke, MK-Ultra – the CIA will seek to reverse-engineer the Soviet and Chinese techniques of mind control it has deemed so dangerous. Eventually, this project will morph into the 'enhanced interrogations' of the present War on Terror, undermining the foundations of US democracy.

★

The Bronx, New York, 1969. A young American radical called Dennis O'Neil has a contretemps with a friend. Like many of his generation, O'Neil is a passionate admirer of Mao Zedong and of his Cultural Revolution. His friend favours Trotsky. They devise a scientific trial to settle whose political strategy is superior. For a set period of time every day, they will each read from their idol's selected works to different marijuana plants on the balcony of their fourteenth-floor apartment. 'My plant flourished and his withered,' O'Neil later remembers. 'Proof positive.' Meanwhile, in a San Francisco bookstore called China Books and Periodicals – the West Coast's main outlet for Mao's words – further eccentricity plays out. Amid the stacks of Little Red Books, a group of self-styled 'ultra-democrats' called the Seven Diggers sit in the lotus position, their energies sustained by cannabis-infused brownies, reading Mao on the Chinese revolution and guerrilla warfare. A pair of trench-coated FBI officers browse Chinese postage stamps to one side of the store as they monitor the situation.[3]

The CIA's experiments with LSD in devising their own mind-control programme play a key part in the drug-fuelled youth rebellions of the 1960s and '70s. By 1969, the quantities of LSD in CIA-funded research labs in universities have leaked into recreational use by students. The burgeoning drug scene helps unleash a noisy protest culture, which identifies with the Cultural Revolution. Mao-ish hippydom – instanced on Dennis O'Neil's balcony and in Seven Diggers seances – results. Mao fever spreads across the West: 'big character posters' are pasted over French campuses, Mao badges are pinned on West German student lapels, Little Red Book quotations are daubed on walls of Italian lecture halls. Maoist-anarchists scramble to the top of a church in West Berlin and bombard passers-by with hundreds of Little Red Books. But there are toughs as well as flakes. Aspiring revolutionaries travel to China or Albania, for political and military training designed and funded by the People's Republic of China (PRC). After 1968, the militancy of Cultural Revolution Maoism inspires the urban terrorism of West Germany's Red Army Faction and the Red Brigades in Italy that attacks these fragile European democracies struggling for legitimacy in the wake of fascism.

Nanjing, 1965. As enthusiasm for Mao's revolution sweeps global left-wing politics, a Peruvian professor of philosophy attends a military

training school in Nanjing. It is later speculated that here he met
Saloth Sar – subsequently Pol Pot, architect of Khmer Rouge genocide
in Cambodia – who also attends classes that year at Beijing's Yafeila
peixun zhongxin (the Asian, African and Latin American training centre
just outside the marble precincts of the imperial Summer Palace) for
revolutionaries from those regions. 'We picked up a pen,' Abimael
Guzmán says later, remembering an explosives training class, 'and it
blew up, and when we took a seat it blew up, too. It was a kind of
general fireworks display ... perfectly calculated to show us that
anything could be blown up if you figure out how to do it ... That
school contributed greatly to my development and helped me begin
to gain an appreciation for Chairman Mao Zedong.'[4] In 1979, as leader
of the Communist Party of Peru – Shining Path, Guzmán embarks on
his Maoist People's War – a brutal campaign that over the next two
decades will claim some 70,000 lives and cost Peru some 10 billion
pounds' worth of economic damage. After twelve years of protracted
guerrilla war, Guzmán – as a final Maoist flourish – sets as the date
for his ultimate, power-seizing offensive the ninety-ninth anniversary
of Mao's birthday: 26 December 1992.[5] The revolution, he forecasts,
will cost 'a million deaths'.[6] Some predict that if the Shining Path's
revolution succeeds – a realistic prospect in early 1990s Peru – its
aftermath will generate bloodshed dwarfing that perpetrated by the
Khmer Rouge.

In addition to Pol Pot, Guzmán may have encountered another
aspiring revolutionary while in Nanjing: a towering, intense, serious
Southern Rhodesian, with close-cropped hair, and green eyes deep-
set in a light brown, pockmarked face, called Josiah Tongogara. He
is usually sunk in thought about the liberation of Southern Rhodesia
from white rule; if pushed to make small talk, he discourses only
on his willingness to die 'through the barrel of a gun' (in fact, he
will die in an ill-judged overtaking manoeuvre on a highway). As
with Guzmán, Tongogara's time in China makes a dedicated Maoist
of him. At the Nanjing military academy, he comes to worship the
Chinese as 'mentors in morality as well as in military skills and
strategies'.[7] In the late 1960s, Tongogara returns to the Southern
Rhodesian border where the Zimbabwean African National Liberation Army (ZANLA), the armed wing of the Zimbabwe African

National Union (ZANU), is preparing for its guerrilla war against Southern Rhodesia. He abandons ZANLA's old, failing, hit-and-run tactics, and remakes the army's struggle along patient, protracted Maoist lines. He translates Mao into Shona: his guerrilla troops must depend on the people as *simba rehove riri mumvura* – as a fish has its strength in water. Meanwhile, Chinese instructors train ZANLA recruits in nearby Tanzania; in the late 1970s, 5,000 cadets are schooled for an offensive dubbed *Sasa tunamaliza* (Now We Are Finishing).[8] Exhausted by ZANU's resistance, the white rulers of Southern Rhodesia are forced to negotiate. As a child, Tongogara odd-jobbed by retrieving tennis balls dropped by a young white boy called Ian Smith. In 1979, as ZANLA's representative at the peace talks, he shares coffee breaks with Smith – now prime minister of the white-majority Southern Rhodesian government – at Lancaster House in London.[9]

Deep in central India's jungles today, Naxalite guerrillas in olive fatigues and bright saris dance in lines before a photograph of Chairman Mao and declare war on the government's 'uniformed goons' who have confiscated local land for its precious bauxite reserves. In these beautiful, brutal jungles, the still-militant Indian Maoist movement traces its origins back to its Cultural Revolution–inspired incarnation in 1967, when its leaders were also in Beijing, alongside men like Guzmán and Tongogara. In 2006, India's rulers consider this Maoist insurgency the 'biggest internal security threat to the Indian state'.[10] While intellectuals in New Delhi argue about whether the insurgents are tribal terrorists led by high-caste manipulators or desperate rebels with a cause, Maoists and police engage in reciprocal murdering sprees: one week, a dozen police are slaughtered by Maoist landmines; the next, the police rape and kill civilians with alleged Maoist connections. Unlike the Maoist rebels in Nepal, who in 2006 abandoned their insurgency to participate in parliamentary democracy, the Indian comrades are stalwarts of purist Maoist doctrine and refuse to take part in elections. The Naxalites give Arundhati Roy – one of India's most famous writers and public intellectuals – exclusive access to their story, escorting her around their secret camps. On her return to literary Delhi, she publishes articles praising their simple, vibrant and comradely culture.[11] Is Roy a romantic intellectual in love with a ferocious revolutionary ideal that would (to paraphrase Nabokov on earlier foreign admirers of Soviet Russia) destroy her 'as naturally as rabbits are by ferrets and farmers', if it were to win control of India? Or has she acutely highlighted the appeal of anarchic Maoist liberation to a persecuted underclass left no alternative by a brutal, corrupt government?

In Chongqing, a metropolis on the banks of the Yangtze River that is officially 'China's happiest city', thousands of identically scarlet-shirted civilians gather in a public square to sing and dance Maoist hymns: 'Without the Communist Party, There Would Be No New China', 'Heaven and Earth Are Small Compared with the Party's Benevolence', 'The Communist Party Is Wonderful, the Communist Party Is Wonderful, the Communist Party Is Wonderful'.[12] Stories abound in the press about the miraculously therapeutic properties of these anthems: about a woman who has recovered from crippling depression through listening; about the psychiatric patients whose symptoms 'suddenly disappeared' after they joined revolutionary choirs; of the prisoners cured of their criminality by singing 'red songs'.[13] Students are sent down to the countryside to learn from the peasants. Solemn-looking party cadres don shapeless blue Maoist uniforms and travel to a mountainous, isolated corner of south-east China 'to deepen their understanding and experience' of the revolution, and generally improve their 'red morals'.[14] 'There are some abominably sour and smelly literati around at the moment,' a People's Liberation Army elder observes, as critics of the regime disappear without trace into Communist prisons. 'They attack Chairman Mao and practise de-Maoification. We must fight to repel this reactionary counter-current.'[15] A young man petitions the government to prosecute writers who voice criticism of the Great Helmsman, and demands that neighbourhoods report to the police anyone suspected of disloyalty to the chairman.[16]

   This is not 1966 – the year in which Mao started his Cultural Revolution, the high point of his utopian fever that unleashed bands of Red Guards onto the streets of China's cities, that dislocated millions of educated urbanites to remote rural areas, and that left at least 1.5 million dead (following on from the 30 million death toll of the man-made famine of the early 1960s). This is 2011, and that is why these songs can also be heard in karaoke bars, why Chinese mobile phones – 13 million at a time – are being bombarded by Mao-quotation texts, why Mao's message can target audiences through TV schedules dominated by classic revolutionary films and why the government has launched 'Red Twitter' – delivering gobbets of laconic 1960s wisdom via a very twenty-first-century micro-medium.[17] Bo Xilai – architect of this neo-Maoist revival – is purged in spring 2012, for corruption and for his wife's poisoning of an Old Harrovian called Neil Heywood. Yet Xi Jinping, who becomes party secretary in November 2012, inherits and implements Bo's neo-Maoism on a national stage. In the first few months after he comes to power, Xi launches a 'mass line' (one of Mao's favourite catchphrases) website, to crack down on corruption and boost links between the Communist Party and the grass roots, and reintroduces Mao-style 'criticism and self-criticism' throughout the state bureaucracy. For the first time since the death of Mao in 1976, Xi Jinping has rehabilitated Maoist strategies into China's national, public culture.

These eight scenarios – ranging from the 1930s to the present, and across Asia, Africa, Europe and the Americas – suggest the chronological and geographic scope of Maoism, one of the most significant and complicated political forces of the modern world. A potent mix of party-building discipline, anti-colonial rebellion and 'continuous revolution', grafted onto the secular religion of Soviet Marxism, Maoism not only unlocks the contemporary history of China, but is also a key influence on global insurgency, insubordination and intolerance across the last eighty years. But beyond China, and especially in the West, the global spread and importance of Mao and his ideas in the contemporary history of radicalism are only dimly sensed, if at all. They have been effaced by the end of the Cold War, the apparent global victory of neo-liberal capitalism, and the resurgence of religious extremism. This book aims to bring Mao and his ideas out of the shadows, and recast Maoism as one of the major stories of the twentieth and twenty-first centuries.

In 1935, Mao manoeuvred his way into a position of leadership in the Chinese Communist Party (CCP). At the time, the authority was arguably not worth having. That year, around 8,000 exhausted revolutionaries on the run from encirclement and annihilation campaigns directed by the ruling Nationalist Party tramped into Yan'an, a small, impoverished town dug out of the hillsides of north-west China. But within ten years – a decade that saw the country scourged variously by floods, famine and Japanese invasion – Communist Party membership had surged to 1.2 million and its armies increased to more than 900,000.[18] After another four years, the Chinese Communists under Mao Zedong had expelled their rivals for China, the Nationalists under Chiang Kai-shek, from the mainland and onto Taiwan. Since its founding in 1949, the PRC has somehow managed to survive longer than any of the revolutionary regimes that preceded it in China – despite the convulsions of a vast man-made famine, and a civil war (the Cultural Revolution) that cost and disrupted the lives of tens of millions of Chinese people.

Today's PRC is held together by the legacies of Maoism. Although the Chinese Communist Party has long abandoned the utopian turmoil of Maoism in favour of an authoritarian capitalism that prizes prosperity and stability, the Great Helmsman has left a heavy mark on politics and society. His portrait – six by four and a half metres – still hangs in Tiananmen Square, the heartland of Chinese political power, in the centre of the capital. In the middle of the square, his waxen, embalmed body still lies in state, like a sleeping beauty awaiting the kiss of history to bring him back to life. 'Mao's invisible hand' (as one recent book puts it) remains omnipresent in China's polity: in the deep politicisation of its judiciary; the supremacy of the one-party state over all other interests; the fundamental intolerance of dissident voices.[19]

Maoism is a body of contradictory ideas that has distinguished itself from earlier guises of Marxism in several important ways. Giving centre stage to a non-Western, anti-colonial agenda, Mao declared to radicals in developing countries that Russian-style Communism should be adapted to local, national conditions; that the Soviet Union could go wrong. Diverging from Stalin, he told revolutionaries to take their struggle out of the cities and deep into the countryside. Although, like Lenin and Stalin, Mao was determined to build a one-party state with military discipline, he also (especially in his last decade) championed an anarchic democracy, telling the Chinese people that 'rebellion is justified': that when 'there is great chaos under Heaven, the situation is excellent'. He preached the doctrine of voluntarism: that by sheer audacity of belief the Chinese – and any other people with the necessary strength of will – could transform their country; revolutionary zeal, not weaponry, was the decisive factor. Perhaps most innovatively of all, Mao declared that 'women can hold up half the sky'. Although his own womanising practice fell far short of his rhetoric, none of his global peers voiced such an egalitarian agenda.

Born of an era in which China was held in contempt by the international system, Mao assembled a practical and theoretical toolkit for turning a fractious, failing empire into a defiant global power. He created a language that intellectuals and peasants, men and women could understand; a system of propaganda and thought control that has been described as 'one of the most ambitious attempts at human manipulation in history'; a disciplined army; and he gathered around him a company of unusually talented, ruthless comrades. His ideas elicited extraordinary levels of fervour. Millions entered into marriages of political convenience and abandoned their children to devote themselves to a utopian experiment. These children, in turn, denounced, humiliated and – in extreme cases – killed their parents in the 1960s and '70s, in the name of their Great Helmsman.

My first chapter will explore definitions of Maoism, a term that has been used both admiringly and pejoratively for several decades to signify a spectrum of political behaviour: ranging from anarchic mass democracy to Machiavellian brutality against political enemies. The English terms 'Maoist' and 'Maoism' gained currency in US Cold War analyses of China, intended to categorise and stereotype a 'Red China' that was the essence of alien threat. After Mao's death, they became catch-all words for dismissing what was perceived as the unitary repressive madness of China from 1949 to 1976. Here the term is not understood in this petrified form. 'Maoism' in this book is an umbrella word for the wide range of theory and practice attributed to Mao and his influence over the past eighty years. In other words, this term is useful only if we accept that the ideas and experiences it describes are living and changing, have been translated and mistranslated, both during and after Mao's lifetime, and on their journeys within and without China.

As the People's Republic of China is reasserting its global ambitions for the first time since the Mao era, the imperative to understand the political legacy that unifies the country becomes ever more urgent. But there is also a pressing need to evaluate the power and appeal of Maoism beyond China, where it has enjoyed a long afterlife in revolutionary movements based on Mao's theories of class struggle and guerrilla warfare. Maoism contains within it ideas that have exerted an extraordinary tenacity and ability to travel, that have put down roots in terrains culturally and geographically far removed from that of China: the tea plantations of northern India, the sierras of the Andes, Paris's fifth arrondissement, the fields of Tanzania, the rice paddies of Cambodia and the terraces of Brixton. My book is a history both of this Chinese movement, and of its global legacies: it analyses Maoism's ambivalent history and enduring appeal to power-hungry dreamers and to dispossessed rebels all over the world.

Yet global Maoism remains one of the missed – or misunderstood – stories of the twentieth and twenty-first centuries. One has only to compare the quantities of books about Hitler and Stalin and their international consequences with the lack of studies that synthesise and explain the legacies of Maoism throughout the world. Why do we tend not to see Maoism globally? Why does this book not already exist?[20]

Since the 1980s, readers in the European languages (and especially English) that dominate international publishing have been able to access dozens of eyewitness accounts of Mao-era China, in the form of memoirs written by victims of the Cultural Revolution. These present a compelling narrative of horror: of violence and persecution stemming from Mao's abuse of his personality cult, and of mindless xenophobia. The dramatic contrast between our picture of a dysfunctional, disastrous Mao's China drawn from these works, on the one hand, and of contemporary China – a land of functional state-building and pragmatic consumerism – on the other, seems to signal that Maoism has been relegated to the dustbin of history. Kitsch enhances the sense of detachment. Even while a broad swathe of Western readers now equate Mao with Stalin or Hitler for the destructiveness of his policies, tourists to China snap up red vinyl-covered copies of the Little Red Book or Mao-emblazoned lighters playing the Maoist anthem 'The East Is Red'. Visitors to contemporary Germany would not dream of buying copies of *Mein Kampf* or novelty alarm clocks depicting Hitler Youth performing the Nazi salute. Joke books for British children blithely crack lame puns: Q: Who was the most powerful cat in China? A: Chairman Miaow. Again, an analogous joke built around Stalin or Hitler is unthinkable.

All this suggests that, to Western eyes, Mao has been safely consigned to 'the past', with no risk that his ideas or heirs will make a comeback. So much about Communism, and especially about Communism during the era of high Maoism in the 1960s and '70s, now seems alien and superannuated, not least its doctrinal dialects and acronyms (to cite just a handful of West German Maoist groupuscules from this epoch: the MLPD, KBW, KPD/ML, KABD ...). But the truth is that many of the ongoing tragedies of underdevelopment and conflict that trouble Africa, Asia, Latin America and the Middle East today are hangovers from conflicts in which the Cold War superpowers – the US, the USSR *and* Mao's China – were once enmeshed. And Maoist ideology helped shape the Cold War in these regions.

Yet the sidelining of global Maoism is not only down to our own inattention. It is also a consequence of post-Mao China's success in communicating a particular narrative of its past. In 1978, Mao's successor Deng Xiaoping told the world that China would 'never seek hegemony' and almost every foreign policy PR campaign since then has been devoted to arguing China's status as victim, not activist or aggressor, in international politics. For the past ten years, as China has ascended to superpower status, its rulers have advanced the theory of China's 'peaceful rise', insisting that its new strength and influence will be a force for international harmony rather than militant nationalism. The writing of history is an important corroborating part of this narrative: government publicity repeats that China has never interfered in the sovereign affairs of other countries. The idea of a virtuously neutral China thus contrasts with the actions of the hawkish West. Modern China's own history of victimisation by imperialist nations between 1839 and 1945 encourages sympathy with this view.

The CCP's latest campaign for global influence is the 'China Dream', designed to market internationally the idea of a strong, successful China. Its book-length manifesto argues that 'China has a tradition of cherishing peace and harmony and it never seeks to pillage others or establish spheres of influence'.[21] When I was researching my first book, tracing post-Mao China's obsession with winning a Nobel Prize in

Literature, I encountered over and over – in documents and interviews –
a Great Wall of Denial that China had had any kind of contact with
the outside world between 1949 and 1976. In the received wisdom
of the 1990s and 2000s, the People's Republic of China made its first,
grand entrance to the international world in 1978, when Deng Xiaoping
took supreme power. Mao-era China therefore had no foreign policy,
this version of history upholds: it was isolated by and from the international community.

Under these circumstances, China does not want to illuminate its
desire for leadership of the world revolution during the Maoist period,
a time when it exported not only ideology, in the form of hundreds of
millions of copies of the Little Red Book, but also harder currencies
of revolution – money, weapons and training for global insurgencies,
especially in the developing world. Naturally, the story of CIA or KGB
interference abroad is no more edifying, but at least the history is
better known. A senior Chinese diplomatic historian has expressed
the embarrassment that this stretch of the past causes China's contemporary rulers. 'The CCP today doesn't want people to talk about this
history ... Their interference in foreign countries back then was truly
excessive.'[22] Given the intensity with which the contemporary PRC
yearns for global influence, it is an irony that memory of the period
during which China enjoyed arguably its greatest global soft power
in its entire recorded history has to be 'disappeared' for political
reasons. The party's treatment of this issue exemplifies the inconsistencies of Chinese politics today. The contemporary party state, which
owes its legitimacy and political stability to Mao, yearns for international 'face'. Yet because the history and legacy of the Mao era,
and especially the Cultural Revolution (the principal motor of global
Maoism), were so unstable, and the contemporary CCP fetishises
political and economic stability above any other governmental goal,
this same party state refuses ownership of the global influence
that this era seeded (including contemporary Maoist movements in
India and Nepal).

Due to the delicacy of these questions in contemporary China,
many historical materials remain out of reach. In an archival release
unprecedented in Communist history, China's Ministry of Foreign
Affairs (MFA) began opening its 1949–65 archives to researchers in 2003
(never before had a Communist state declassified the papers of a

government department while still in power). But this partial opening stopped short of the crucial Cultural Revolution years and most of the MFA materials were reclassified in 2012–13 during an IT 'systems upgrade'. In any case, the two most important organisations handling the export of Chinese revolutionary theory and practice were the International Liaison Department (ILD, Zhonglianbu) and military intelligence. The former handled party-to-party relations, and therefore dealt with ambitious Communist groups (posing varying levels of threat to their governments) in, say, Burma, Cambodia, Malaysia, France, West Germany, Peru and elsewhere. Within China the organisation was, and remains, so secretive that knowledge of its exact location from the 1950s to the 1970s is, apparently, still not in the public domain. Needless to say, there is no prospect of either organisation opening its archives, unless the CCP itself falls from power. As a result, global Maoism is not an easy subject to research: there is no unified archive for the topic, and primary sources are scattered across speeches, telegrams and minutes of meetings (many of which remain classified), as well as memoirs and oral histories in a wide variety of languages. The sensitivity of the topic within China has further intensified with the accession to power of Xi Jinping, son of a first-generation revolutionary leader, Xi Zhongxun. Since Xi owes much of his own political prestige to the sanctity of the revolution's image, it has become more important than ever to bury any embarrassing historical details from the Mao era, and particularly those that contradict the doctrine of Chinese non-interference in foreign affairs.

The perception of Maoism as a system of ideas and practices relevant only to China has also kept it on the edges of global history. General histories of the Cold War have often underestimated the importance of Maoist China as offering a genuine alternative to Soviet Communism, providing intellectual and practical support to rebels throughout the world. Recent scholarship has increasingly acknowledged the Asian and specifically Chinese influence. Odd Arne Westad's two important histories of the Cold War since 2005 have globalised study of this conflict. A cohort of excellent historians inside and outside China – Westad, Chen Jian, Li Danhui, Lorenz Lüthi, Sergey Radchenko, Shen Zhihua, Yang Kuisong, Yafeng Xia – took advantage of widening PRC declassification through the 2000s, before the clawback began in 2011.[23] But it is still the case that, perhaps stemming from a more general neglect (beyond specialists) of the global role of China in the twentieth century, Maoist China's influence on the radical political upsurge during the 1960s and '70s remains curiously sidelined in anglophone histories of the period. There is, for example, no English-language book on the spread and impact of Maoist ideas in either post-war Italy or West Germany. There is certainly no synoptic, detailed history of China's involvement in a wide range of conflict and unrest erupting since the Second World War in Asia, Africa, the Americas, Europe and the Middle East.

The pentagonic Moscow–Berlin–Prague–London–Washington plots in John le Carré's novels urged anglophone readers to think of the great crises of the Cold War as overwhelmingly American, Soviet and European stories. But this is not how it looked in the 1960s and 1970s, when territories across Asia seemed set to topple before Chinese Communism's messages of militant rebellion; and when European, American and Australian politicians accused China of a 'programme for Maoist world domination' reminiscent 'of *Mein Kampf*', of leading 'a worldwide subversive movement ... in Latin America, in Africa, in Asia'. 'Should Australia fall,' one Antipodean commentator phlegmatically remarked, 'historians will not pause to reflect too deeply on the fate of this handful of white men who thought they could live under the shadow of the Chinese phallus.'[24] The stilted international voice of China – the Beijing-published magazine *Peking Review* – encouraged this sense of alarm in editions across dozens of languages: 'Chairman Mao ... is the great leader of the revolutionary people of the world ... lighting the hearts of the revolutionary people of the world and indicating the road to victory in the revolution.'[25] Internal documents reported Mao proclaiming that 'China is not only the political centre of world revolution, it must also be the centre of world revolution militarily and technically'.[26] Westerners and Soviets alike quailed at Mao's breezy arithmetic concerning the possible outcome of a nuclear war: 'If the worst came to the worst and half of mankind died, the other half would remain while imperialism would be razed to the ground and the whole world would become socialist.'[27]

Without taking China into account, it is impossible to understand US actions during the Cold War in Asia, where American presidents created and propped up states to stymie Mao. The publication of the Pentagon Papers in 1971 revealed that America's war in Vietnam was not 'to help [a] friend' (South Vietnam) but to 'contain China'. Looking afresh at the global role of Mao's China also helps us reconsider one of the defining analyses of the Cold War in Asia: Washington's 'domino theory', the logic of which dictated US political and military intervention in South East Asia. For good reasons, analysts since at least the 1970s have been intensely critical of this set of assumptions, for it led to the enormities committed by the US Army in Vietnam between 1965 and 1973, and to overt and covert operations that destabilised newly independent nations, and facilitated or propped up dictatorships (for example, in Indonesia, Burma and Cambodia). Intellectually, also, the idea of the domino theory is unsatisfying because it suggests that the diverse states of South East Asia were helplessly passive actors before the subversion of Mao's China. But understandable moral revulsion at and rejection of the US foreign policy results of the domino theory have helped foster a neglect (particularly since the 1980s) of Mao-era China's influence on Cold War South East Asia. This book suggests revisiting and reworking these ideas. It argues that the domino theory did have some purchase on reality: that Mao and his lieutenants *did* want to spread their blueprint for revolution through South East Asia and beyond. Almost every country in the region – Vietnam, the Philippines, Indonesia, Malaya/Malaysia, Cambodia and Burma – had strong, capable Communist movements (often predating the founding of the PRC), influenced and for the most part materially supported by Mao's China after 1949. For these countries had long suffered at the hands of colonial, extractive regimes – little surprise that first Lenin's and then Mao's militant attacks on imperialism appealed to some of South East Asia's brightest minds. Without a huge influx of British and then American materiel and boots on the ground, it is far from clear that the local opponents of Communism in South East Asia would have been able to withstand these insurgencies in the ways that they did, if at all.

Studying the global travels of Maoism requires us not only to reconsider this set of ideas from the perspective of a recent, ideological past when the doctrines of Communism governed, and mattered to, vast swathes of humanity, but also to think our way into very different geographical vantage points. For many growing up in the developing world between the 1950s and 1970s, Mao-era China did not (and still does not) represent a basket case, but rather an admirable, independent alternative to the political models of the US and USSR.[28] It provided an example of a poor, agrarian country persecuted by Western or Japanese expansionism standing up for itself in the world. In Nepal today, many ordinary consumers idealise China as an economic paradise, and believe it is so prosperous because, not in spite, of Mao. From Paris to Phnom Penh, from Beijing to Berlin, from Lima to London, from Dar es Salaam to Derby, Mao offered not only rhetorical defiance, but also practical strategies for empowering impoverished states marginalised or dominated by global powers; for training low-tech peasant insurgencies against state-funded, colonial militaries.

During and after the Cold War, Maoism exercised a particular attraction for underdeveloped, colonised or recently decolonised states such as Tanzania, Nepal, India, Cambodia and Indonesia, which at least superficially seemed to resemble pre-1949 China. It exercised this appeal often without much material aid from the PRC, certainly in comparison with the budget dispensed by the Soviet-sponsored Comintern through the 1920s and '30s. In true guerrilla style, Mao's ideas and sayings have captivated the developed world too, percolating through the best French arrondissements and elite US campuses – 'Dig deep tunnels, store grain everywhere,' declaimed radical Harvard students in the 1970s. Maoism has also taken root in parts of the developing world that bear no solid resemblance to pre-revolutionary China – such as Peru. Without a proper understanding of Maoism's global appeal and travels, it is hard to make sense of events as geographically and chronologically disparate as the Malayan Emergency, the 1965 massacres in Indonesia, the cultural revolutions of Western Europe and the US of 1968, the Vietnam War and the Khmer Rouge genocide, the end of white rule in Southern Rhodesia and the rise of Robert Mugabe's ZANU, Shining Path's insurgency in Peru, the civil war in Nepal that ended centuries of monarchy, and contemporary insurrection in India's jungles. Conflicts and crises influenced by Mao are not only major historical events; several are still with us, in India, Peru, Nepal and Zimbabwe.

Mao's own internationalism is worth a book in itself, for what it tells us about the variousness – *not* homogeneity – of PRC foreign policy. Mao combined dreams of world revolution with nationalist ambition and a Chinese imperialism of much older vintage. He veered between imperious acquisitiveness – reasserting imperial China's claims over parts of the Soviet Union – and free-handed generosity to 'fraternal' parties whom he saw as part of a Sino-/Mao-centric civilisation. He carelessly gifted strips of the Sino-Korean border to his 'fraternal ally' Kim Il-sung, and promised, when meeting members of the radical pro-China Indian Communist Party, to make over to a future Communist Indian government *all* the border territory that India and China bloodily disputed through the 1960s.[29] Mao's lofty socialist solidarity – and massive financial aid – to Vietnam was tinged with domineering imperialism; two years after his death, Sino-Vietnamese tensions escalated into a vile border war. Mao was steeped in an older Middle Kingdom mentality: in attempting leadership of the global revolution, he also wanted to reassert China's claims to occupy the centre of the world.[30] Emphasis on China's global mission had an important role to play at home, too. As the headquarters of revolution, Mao argued, China was peculiarly vulnerable to attack by the reactionary world. He harked constantly on China's international insecurity to mobilise domestic campaigns against potential opponents who were attacked as 'spies' and 'enemies of the revolutionary masses'.

Many of global Maoism's actual consequences were unintended. For example, Mao-era China threw money, time and expertise at Africa in the hope of winning sympathy for and converts to its political cause, but not one lookalike Maoist regime took power. There was only piecemeal uptake of Mao's strategy and symbols in Tanzania and Southern Rhodesia, home to his most fervent African admirers. In Nepal, India and Peru, by contrast, the PRC's investment was more muted: glossy magazines, translations and radio in local languages, the occasional invitation to China – little more. Yet in those countries, Mao's ideas found passionate adherents who deployed his strategies in wars that transformed their countries' contemporary history. The story of global Maoism exemplifies the unpredictable course of Communist China's ongoing quest for soft power. However closely the party state has tried to mould and direct its global image, its initiatives forever spin off in unexpected, uncontrollable directions. For Maoism is an unstable political creed that simultaneously reveres a centralised party and mass leadership, collective obedience and anti-state rebellion. In its global journeys, Maoism has served causes that questioned or attacked existing governments; in its country of origin, it has created an omnipotent party state. It has lionised peasant revolution, while winning many of its followers or sympathisers from educated elites (Louis Althusser, Jean-Paul Sartre, Michel Foucault, Baburam Bhattarai, Abimael Guzmán) – it has been a revolution spread through books. Cerebral global Maoists have often turned the idealised 'masses' into cannon fodder for their doctrinal revolutions, combining sympathy with brutality towards those suffering at the bottom of society.

The close of the Cold War – with its disintegration of old US and Soviet alliances, and the rise of ever more fluid global cultures of travel and transmission – has, if anything, only strengthened the validity of Mao's guerrilla tactics and strategies. Analysts of Daesh claim that the group came to power by deploying Mao's ideas about asymmetric warfare against an established state; there is certainly a paper trail of influence from Cultural Revolution doctrines of 'People's War' to insurgencies in the Middle East. China gave the PLO, in the words of one satisfied Palestinian visitor, 'everything that we asked for', and several Palestinian militants made the transition from Maoism to jihadism in the 1980s.[31]

Moreover, once you write Maoism back into the global history of the twentieth century, you start to get a very different narrative from the standard one in which the Soviet Union loses the Cold War to neoliberalism. A quarter of a century since Communism collapsed in Europe and then in the USSR, China's Communist Party continues – seemingly – to flourish. Under its direction, China has become a world economic and political force. The CCP – its practice and legitimacy still dominated by Mao – has, with quite extraordinary success, recast itself as a champion of the market economy, while remaining an essentially secretive, Leninist organisation. If the CCP is still in charge in 2024, the Chinese Communist revolution will have exceeded the 74-year lifespan of its Soviet older brother. China's leaders feel a nervous pride at this prospect: the causes of the Soviet collapse in 1991 fascinate past and present members of the politburo. If the CCP survives much beyond this point, historians may come to see October 1949, rather than October 1917, as the game-changing revolution of the last century.

Study of the history and fallout of global Maoism holds lessons highly relevant to contemporary challenges across the world. This book argues that exploring global Maoism is vital to comprehending not only Chinese history, but also radical politics in many parts of the globe – the politics of disenfranchisement, discontent and impoverishment. In India today, the Maoist Naxalite movement recruits most strongly from the least privileged members of society. Maoism became an international force in the era of decolonisation. In the developing world, its message of anti-imperialist confrontation appealed to peoples who had been repressed economically, politically and culturally; who aspired to the living standards of the industrialised West and to international dignity. Although the Cold War has ended, problems of poverty and inequality persist. As Europe contends with a migration crisis that results from impoverishment and political turmoil, the past and present of global Maoism are important reminders of the radicalism that can spring from material and political desperation, and of its consequences.

Over the last two years, the election of Donald Trump and the rise of European populist politics have brought questions of sovereignty under new scrutiny. In the UK, for example, does it reside with 'the people' (as a demagogue like Nigel Farage argues), or with Parliament? What is the relationship between the 'will of the people' and the specialist elite who legislate in the capital? These are questions with which Maoism has grappled – often with violent results – in its oscillations between 'democratic centralism' (Lenin's veneration of an all-powerful, secretive party core), the 'mass line' (Mao's proposition that grass-roots ideas should shape party policy) and the 'mass democracy' (manipulated, in reality, by the party-authored cult of Mao) of the Cultural Revolution. In theory, Mao and Maoism agitated to give voice to the marginalised, and to prevent the inevitable flow of power to technocratic metropolitan elites (though the reality has been very different). Intriguingly, the rebellious repertoires of Leninism and Maoism seem to appeal to the architects of Trumpolitics. Steve Bannon sees himself as a 'tsar of agitation', as (in his own words) a Leninist plotting to bring the political system crashing down.[32] The Australian sinologist Geremie Barmé has compared Trump ('the Great Disrupter') with Mao: for his erratic populism, his scorn for the bureaucratic establishment, his predilection for brief, earthy statements (albeit in early-morning tweets, rather than compendia of quotations), his rhetorical obsession with national autarky.[33] In a development emblematic of the US alt-right's political confusion (and the ductility of Maoism), Trump's administration was roiled by yet more turmoil in August 2017 when a paranoid memo circulating around Trump supporters in the National Security Council was leaked to the press: it described a 'deep-state' conspiracy against the president conducted according to the strategies and tactics of the 'Maoist insurgency model'.[34]

The history of global Maoism also offers important but neglected case studies of radicalisation – one of the preoccupations of contemporary sociology. The analytical literature on this subject currently focuses almost exclusively on religion (especially Islam), overlooking examples of Maoist-inspired political violence and indoctrination in South East Asia, Western Europe and Latin America. The recent jailing in the UK of Aravindan Balakrishnan, leader of a Brixton Maoist party of the 1970s, for 'brainwashing' and holding captive for decades several women reminds us forcefully (and close to home) of the potency of such indoctrination. Veteran radicals on the FBI's watch list during the War on Terror were, back in the 1960s and '70s, adherents of Maoist-inflected groups; their opposition to the American government was forged through engagement with Maoism. International rebels still with us today learned their subversion from Maoist texts.[35] At the other end of the political spectrum, the US Army remains hung up on Maoist military strategy, which is still the textbook model of insurgency to be tackled in their counter-insurgency manuals. Although radicalisation by political ideology, especially Communist ideology, has come to seem old hat in the post–Cold War world, it is similar in process to radicalisation by religion – in its deployment of close-tie relationships to gain recruits, its use of simple, confident explanations and its exploitation of socio-economic crises. Indeed, the global history of Maoism – inside and outside China – is notable for the religious overtones of its leadership cults. In China, Mao was depicted as the sun illuminating his people, who performed their veneration through loyalty dances. Peru's Mao, Abimael Guzmán (aka Gonzalo, his *nom de guerre*), was also outlined in golden effulgence on Shining Path posters, and cadres compelled peasants under their rule to exclaim 'Ay, Gonzalo', instead of 'Ay, Jesús'. The past and ongoing stories of global Maoism pose questions about radicalisation that resonate loudly today. What kind of socio-economic circumstances, belief systems and social structures incubate political violence? What happens to such programmes as they struggle for and capture power? How can societies battered by insurgency and counter-insurgency mend themselves?

Finally, a note about coverage. This book aims to recount a global history of Maoism, but it is impossible to tell every story. Other examples abound: the Caribbean, Icelandic, Mexican, Swiss Maoists; the Maoism of the Philippine and Burmese Communist parties; the members of the Palestinian Liberation Organisation euphemistically hosted in Mao's China on scholarships to study modern Chinese literature. Nor can every episode relevant to this history be told in the detail that it demands: the Southern Rhodesian War, Peruvian land reform, Indonesian independence, second-wave feminism, the West German Green movement will only be sketched in outline. Neither is this a linear biography of Mao and of his impact on China, although both stories weave in and out of the book's pages. I have tried to select episodes that evoked the trajectory, the variety and (what seemed to me) the most significant afterlives of global Maoism. As I researched and wrote, I was unable to find a book that juxtaposes these histories to give a unified sense of their diversity and significance. This is an attempt to fill that space.

My story of international Maoism begins, like so many extraordinary stories of modern Asia, in 1930s Shanghai, an interlocking world of gangsters, revolutionaries, intellectuals and society hostesses. In 1936, Song Qingling, the beautiful widow of the first president of the republic, Sun Yat-sen, sister-in-law of Chiang Kai-shek (the scourge of China's left wing) and pre-eminent fellow traveller to Mao's Communists, introduced Edgar Snow, an ambitious journalist from the American Midwest on the hunt for an international scoop, to an underground network that would escort him to Mao's new headquarters in dusty north-west China. Over the weeks that the American spent in the Communist base, Mao and his closest lieutenants gave Snow a world exclusive, immersing him in a doctored account of their past and present that photoshopped the violence and purges, and portrayed them as persecuted patriots and democrats. At the end of his stay in the north-west, Snow had 20,000 words of transcribed interviews, all checked and corrected by Mao.

Mao and his comrades had chosen their man well. Snow – a non-Communist foreigner with impeccable media connections – was the ideal mouthpiece for taking their story to the international world. *Red Star* turned Mao into a political leader with global name recognition. Its Chinese edition won educated young urbanites over to Mao's revolution at a time when Chinese Communism was on the point of annihilation. Since 1937, the book has created rebels and guerrillas: from the jungles of Malaysia to the freezing fields of west Russia, from the alternative lifestyles of West Germany's 1960s counterculture to the training camps of high-caste Nepali Maoists.

I move chronologically through the political, diplomatic and cultural history of international Maoism: through the lives, texts and material objects – *Red Star Over China*, the Little Red Book (in its dozens of languages and translations), rubbery pink 45s of 'The East Is Red' – that communicated the Maoist credo across China and the globe. Ranging between the 1930s and the present day, the pages of this book are peopled by politicians, professors, poets, revolutionaries, transla-tors, misfits, Machiavels, fanatics and flakes – some of whom ended up ruling one of the largest, most powerful countries in the world. Communism presents itself as an impersonal political science, demanding that the individual submit to abstract ideological authority. Yet the story of Mao's global travels is full of human drama. It is challenging to find anyone less socially conformist than Mao himself: a rebel who hated his father, who aged thirty-four declared war on the Chinese state, who serially philandered, who wore patched pyjamas to state functions and regularly dragged both Chinese and foreign leaders to audiences with him in the earliest hours of the morning, who purged (often to death) most of his closest comrades; who refused to brush his teeth, ever. The ranks of Mao's acolytes and imitators are filled with similar eccentrics and misfits: the brother of a Mumbai ice-cream magnate who trained as an accountant before declaring war on the Indian state; a Colombian armchair guerrilla who chose whisky over the revolution; a Peruvian philosophy prof who adored Beethoven alongside Mao; a future president of that renowned bureaucracy the European Union. Maoism, with its preaching of 'protracted warfare', seems particularly suited to oddballs, to those determined both to set themselves in conflict with society, and to control it.

I will describe the apocalyptic fears of the early Cold War, when China's 1950 treaty with the Soviet Union sent shivers up the spines of Western governments. The alliance was, Odd Arne Westad has written, 'the greatest power to challenge the political supremacy of the Western capitals since the final expansion of the Ottoman empire in the sixteenth century'.[36] Yet a decade later, China's potentially world-dominating friendship with the USSR unravelled at speed. Denouncing the Soviets as 'revisionists' anxious to appease the Americans, Mao and his lieutenants seized every opportunity to sledge the USSR in public and to assert themselves as the true leaders of the world revolution. Maoism's travels through the 1960s and '70s – the decades in which Mao bid for supremacy in global Communism – are the centrepiece of the book. I will track the conflagration of Mao fever: the Mao badges that seeped through China's borders to Nepal, India and Cambodia, becoming radical chic among Kathmandu, Kolkata and Phnom Penh youth; the well-thumbed issues of *Peking Review* declaring Mao 'the great helmsman of the world revolution' and 'the never-setting sun'; the crackling, nasal broadcasts of Peking Radio beamed into the African savannah; the Americans and Europeans who worshipped Mao's China from afar (hippies, civil rights campaigners, philosophers, terrorists and Shirley MacLaine).[37]

Maoism had an important place in the hot conflicts of the Cold War, mixed up in Communist movements in Indonesia, Cambodia and Vietnam – movements that transformed the destinies of these countries. To the Vietnamese Communists, Maoist China supplied moral and material support. It schooled Pol Pot and gave him over $1 billion in aid, free military assistance and medical check-ups. On the brink of committing genocide, Pol lounged by Mao's swimming pool as the moribund chairman lauded the Cambodian's emptying of the country's cities into forced labour projects and killing fields: 'Your experience is better than ours ... You are basically right.'[38]

The final chapters will describe Maoism's long, bloody afterlives in Peru, Nepal and India, with their confused mix of empathy for, and ruthlessness towards, those who suffer at the bottom of their societies. In 1996, only four years after Abimael Guzmán was captured directing his revolution from a respectable barrio of Lima, Nepalese Maoists declared a 'People's War' – trained by the resurgent Indian

Naxalites – on the government's long-term, systematic neglect of the country's rural majority. By the close of the conflict in 2006, some 17,000 Nepalis had died. In an ironic twist, the Nepalese borrowing of Mao's tactics of guerrilla warfare has been not only a security threat but also a source of intense embarrassment to China's contemporary rulers, who claim that Mao's ideas have been grossly misinterpreted. Far more than a Cold War aftershock, Indian and Nepali Maoism are part of the current inflammation of global radicalisation. The conflagration of Maoism across South Asia raises fundamental questions about development, social justice, environmentalism and international exploitation.

The story concludes, as it begins, in China. Even as it strives to suppress memory of Mao's chaotic Cultural Revolution, the government revives Mao-era songs, films and language in an attempt to generate nostalgic affection for a regime that has long become more capitalist than Communist. Angry young men denounce the profiteering compradors of the current Communist Party and call for a return to Mao's radical egalitarianism. Laid-off workers, waving Little Red Books, demonstrate against their fat-cat bosses. In villages up and down the country, farmers battle – with knives, bricks and sticks – their corrupt local officials. They are all heirs to Mao's strange legacy of party discipline, political puritanism and People's War. To understand the volatile legacy that is still shaping political practice today, we need to track the history of Maoism in China, but also its uses and reinterpretations far beyond China's borders.

I

WHAT IS MAOISM?

In the first week of January 2016, a vast golden statue of Mao was unveiled in the middle of the Henan countryside in central China, looming out of frozen brown fields under grey skies. Over thirty-six metres high, it cost £312,000 to build, and was paid for by local people and businessmen. For forty-eight hours tourists gathered to take selfies with this curious effigy (apart from the swept-back, receding hairline, the statue's head barely resembled Mao). The statue was, word had it, the brainchild of one Mr Sun Qingxin, a local food-processing entrepreneur crazy for the Helmsman. 'His factory is full of Maos,' testified a local potato farmer.[1] Commentators in the Chinese cyber-sphere had divergent responses. 'Eternal life to Mao Zedong!', 'He is our legend, our god – we should worship him!', 'Crazy', 'Pull it down', 'It doesn't look like him … he should have been sitting on a sofa.' Use the money to build roads or clinics instead, others argued.[2] Then, on 7 January, a black cloth was draped over Mao's head and the statue was destroyed by Public Security officials, leaving behind only rubble and rumours that it had violated planning regulations. Even the usually authoritative *People's Daily* was puzzled by the whole business, confessing that 'the reasons for the demolition are not clear'.[3] Several locals wept as the statue came down, among them probably descen-dants of the multitudes – one analyst puts the figure at 7.8 million – who died in Henan during the 1960s famine caused by Mao's policies.[4]

The mysterious rise and fall of the golden Mao colossus of Henan evokes the elusive quality of Mao and Maoism, both in and beyond China. The term 'Maoism' became popular in the 1950s to denote Anglo-American summaries of the system of political thought and practice instituted across the new People's Republic of China. Since then, it has had a fractious history. Its Chinese translation, *Mao zhuyi*, has never been endorsed by CCP ideologues. It is a dismissive term used by liberals to describe adulation for Mao among contemporary China's alt-left, or by government analysts to describe and disavow 'Maoist' politics in India or Nepal today. 'This group,' sniffed the Chinese Ministry of Foreign Affairs when protesting the use of the tag by the Communist Party of Nepal (Maoist), '[has] nothing to do with China, and we [feel] indignant that they usurped the name of Mao Zedong, the great leader of the Chinese people.'[5] Orthodox Chinese analysts use the more cerebral term 'Mao Zedong Thought'.

Yet for all its imperfections it will be used here because it has become the most commonly used term for a successful Chinese Communist programme from the 1930s to the present day. It has validity only on the understanding that the Maoist programme – despite possessing a solid symbolic core, in the shape of Mao himself – has taken various (and often contradictory) forms over decades and continents, according to context. It comes into formal existence in the early 1940s, though builds on antecedents from earlier in Mao's life and thought. This chapter sets out the core features of this programme, as Mao and his later disciples (in China and beyond) saw them, organising them – in the style of that ubiquitous badge of high, 1960s Maoism, the Little Red Book – by a series of key quotations. It sorts between the derivative and the original in Mao's ideas: where they overlap with, and differ from, Mao's Soviet predecessors.[6] Some of these differences are in kind, others in degree. In the former category there is Mao's veneration of the peasantry as a revolutionary force and his lifelong tenderness for anarchic rebellion against authority. In the latter category belong central elements of the Leninist–Stalinist project, with its veneration of political violence, its championing of anti-colonial resistance, and its use of thought-control techniques to forge a disciplined, increasingly repressive party and society.[7]

1. 'Power comes out of the barrel of a gun.'

Shanghai, 12 April 1927, 4 a.m. A bugle call from the headquarters of the Nationalist Party on Route Ghisi, in the far south of the French concession, was answered by the siren from a gunboat moored on the city's east side. Members of Shanghai's most powerful triad, the

Green Gang – disguised in blue factory workers' uniforms, with white armbands – converged on Communist strongholds scattered through the low-rise Chinese quarters of the city. Sunrise was still an hour and a half away when machine-gun fire rattled through the darkness. Every worker who resisted was shot down. Others were lashed together and marched away for execution. A general strike was called for the following day but those who turned out for a protest demonstration were brought down by Nationalist machine-gun fire, rifle butts and bayonets. The protesters had put women and children at the front of the march, assuming that Nationalist troops would not open fire. More than three hundred were killed that day, witnesses reckoned, and a far larger number wounded, some of whom were buried alive with the dead.

Three weeks earlier, Communist prospects in the city had looked very different. In the last ten days of March, Shanghai's warlord ruler had surrendered the metropolis to a coalition of armed pickets organised by the young Chinese Communist Party (CCP). Strikers had first shut down the city and then – initially armed with only 100 rifles, 250 pistols and 200 hand grenades, plus propaganda leaflets, posters and newspapers – had fought for shipyards, police stations and the railway.[8] The taking of the city was crucial to the uprising launched in 1926 – the so-called Northern Expedition, China's second revolution in fifteen years – against army strongmen who had carved the country into regional kingdoms.

The 1911 Revolution had brought to an end some 2,000 years of dynastic rule. Within five years, central authority had disintegrated with the rise of 'warlords', provincial commanders. The young republic still had a president in the capital Beijing, but his authority over the localities was nominal. Nonetheless, faith in the idea of a unified China persisted. Urban China in particular periodically erupted with discontent at the new status quo, for political paralysis under fragmented military rule made China domestically and internationally vulnerable. On 4 May 1919, patriotic protests in Beijing and Shanghai broke out after China's warlord rulers agreed at the Versailles Conference to sign away a large slice of north-east China to Japan. By 1923, Sun Yat-sen – the republic's first, briefly incumbent president (in early 1912) and a man obsessed with the idea of reunifying China – forged an alliance between his Nationalist Party (the Guomindang or GMD) and the

Communist Party, all funded, trained and armed by the Soviet Union and its Communist International (Comintern). Sun's death in 1925 notwithstanding, his successor as Nationalist leader, Chiang Kai-shek, launched the Northern Expedition, a military campaign to reunite the country, the following year. Soviet-trained Chinese troops pushed up from the south, fighting or bribing warlords into submission. The forces were a united front of the conservative GMD and more radical CCP: the GMD controlled the formal, standing army, but everywhere they fought, their task was made easier by striking workers and peasant activists (organised by Communists), who disrupted the communications, materiel and authority of the old regime.

This was an uneasy alliance, however. The aims and power base of the two parties were fundamentally at odds: the GMD had always relied on the moneyed classes for funds, while the Communists were devoted to organising rebellion by China's urban workers and poor farmers. Chiang Kai-shek, leader of the Nationalists, marched into Shanghai at the end of March 1927 and – behind public reassurances to the labour unions and to Shanghai's foreigners – made a secret deal with Shanghai's Green Ganglander-in-chief, Du Yuesheng, to break the city's Communists. Then, on 11 April, Du invited Wang Shouhua, the Communist leader of the General Labour Union, to a quiet dinner in his French-style villa, where one of Du's Green Gang underlings strangled him. A few hours later, early on 12 April, Du's thugs – paid and armed by Chinese and foreign businessmen – eliminated unsuspecting, unprepared Communist strongholds throughout the city.

The massacre of red Shanghai heralded months and years of horrific violence in China against those of proven or suspected Communist sympathies. Some estimate that millions died: disembowelled, decapitated, soaked in petrol and set alight, branded to death with hot irons, tied to trees with grit rubbed into their mutilations. Special efforts were made to brutalise female comrades. Nationalist troops suppressing peasant associations in one province 'cut open the breasts of the women comrades, pierced their bodies perpendicularly with iron wires and paraded them naked through the streets'.[9]

Of all the lessons learned by the Chinese Communist Party in its history, the one taught by the bloody spring of 1927 left arguably the deepest impression. To stand a chance of survival, the party needed an army. In 1927, Mao Zedong – one of several party leaders who began to endorse violence at the time – turned the moral of the tale into his best-known aphorism, one that subsequently migrated from Chinese propaganda posters to Black Panther flyers, from hand-copied Parisian student rags to Indian jungle-rallies: 'Political power comes out of the barrel of a gun.' Eleven years later, he added the crucial refinement: 'The Party commands the gun, and the gun must never be allowed to command the Party.'[10] This affection for political violence underpinned the cult that Mao would create over the next half-century. In the context of modern political movements, respect for the power of the gun was not remotely exceptional – indeed, fascism celebrated violence more avidly than Communism. But within Chinese Communism, Mao's rhetorical intervention was decisive.

In the recriminations that followed the disaster of 1927, Chinese Communists blamed the Comintern for insisting that they keep working with the Nationalists, for forcing upon them a deal that made them the subordinate partner in the united front and that forbade them from forming an independent army. In reality, though, it had not occurred to them that they might need to arm themselves seriously, beyond the local workers' and farmers' militias that supported the Nationalists' standing army. The first seven years of Communism in China – Comintern representatives properly began work in China in 1920 – were dominated by intellectuals and bookworms, who consistently refused to acknowledge the violence inherent in the theory and practice of Communism. Mao too was a bookworm, albeit of peasant origin, but one who cherished violence; so were many of his later global followers.

Communism was just one of the political solutions to China's ills – political chaos, chronic poverty, injustice and gender inequality – with which young radicals toyed in the late 1910s. They were little interested in the military ruthlessness of Lenin's victory in Russia; they preferred the vague, romantic image of the October Revolution as a spontaneous national upsurge to its reality (a brutal, drawn-out civil war). Representatives of the Comintern sent to China drew these disparate rebels together into the first congress of the CCP in a Shanghai town house in 1921. However, the early CCP was not a tight, Leninist party structure, but rather a loose network of earnest if often dilettante-ish study cells.

Although present at the first congress, the 27-year-old Mao was at that point far from an iron man of the Communist Party, or a particular enthusiast of the Soviet Union. His view in December 1920 – when he took his first Communist turn – was that 'a Russian-style revolution is a last resort when all other means have been exhausted'.[11] Mao had done his best to turn his back on his peasant origins through his teens and early twenties. He had spent years in Changsha, the provincial capital of his native Hunan, studying and reading widely, developing his capacity for philosophical abstraction, indulging in long, wordy musings with friends. One meeting of the New People's Study Society – a radical cell co-organised by Mao in Hunan – spent much of its time deliberating whether the society's aim ought to be 'to transform the world' or to 'transform China and the world'. The associates then came up with the following list of hell-raising measures to achieve their goal: 'Study; propaganda; a savings society; vegetable gardens.' Once those key decisions had been taken, the society turned its attention to the all-important programme of 'recreational activities': river cruises, mountain excursions, spring outings to visit graves, dinner meetings, frolics in the snow (arrangements to be made whenever it snowed).[12] China's early Communists had great difficulty committing themselves in practice to the sort of charismatic 'military organisation of agents all lending their attention to the same cause' that Lenin conceptualised in *What Is to be Done?*[13] Scattered through a network of cells and study societies in China and Europe, and taking in a good sprinkle of renegade anarchists, they were distinctly insubordinate. 'Party members', Chen Duxiu – the first leader of the CCP, between 1921 and 1927 – commented plaintively in 1923, 'often do not have complete faith in the party.'[14]

It took the horror of the 1927 crackdown, and the subsequent rise within the party of men like Mao from outside the first generation of elite intellectual leaders, to assert the primacy of the military and of violence. Mao made his first intervention on this subject in 1927, and would fixate upon it for the rest of his life. 'Only with guns', he wrote in the 1930s, 'can the whole world be transformed.'[15] In the 1940s, war carried him to absolute power. In the 1950s, he imposed military discipline on Chinese society and agriculture to achieve crash-industrialisation and finance his nuclear programme. He led a revolution in which political violence against 'counter-revolutionaries' was perfectly normalised. In 1968, after the first two anarchic years of Cultural Revolution, he turned China into an army dictatorship. By this point, aspiring insurgents from California to Kolkata worshipped him as the military colossus of the revolution.

Mao's attachment to political violence was not in itself original within global Communism. Lenin and Stalin also venerated it: it is written into Marx's tumultuous visions of world revolution and in any case suited the two Soviet leaders' own ruthless temperaments. However, although Lenin and Stalin were appreciative of violence (the civil war, during which Stalin put in plenty of time as a front-line enforcer, was a formative experience for many Bolsheviks), the two Soviet leaders were ideologues and organisers by trade – not men of the army, as Mao fully became in the late 1920s. Mao was a winning strategist, on and off the battlefield; much of his power and prestige within the party derived from this. After his ideas began to go global, legitimisation of violence for political purposes was associated closely with Mao: partly thanks to Mao's talent for sound bites, and partly thanks to the CCP's PR manipulations in the 1960s and '70s. Through these decades, Mao and his lieutenants portrayed Khrushchev and the Soviet Union as bourgeois appeasers of capitalism, while painting themselves as heroic foot soldiers in a global People's War. This vision of Mao and Maoism crossed continents, turning him into the architect of defiant, protracted, guerrilla warfare against the nuclear arsenals of the superpowers and the professional armies of established states. An anti-apartheid militia in South Africa in the early 1960s, for example, called itself Yu Chin Chan, in a mis-romanisation of Mao's guerrilla warfare (*youji zhan* in Chinese).[16] Again, the style of warfare that Mao prioritised in his own writing was distinct from the Soviet model. In the Soviet Union, despite the contributions of partisans to anti-Nazi resistance in the Second World War, the Red Army – not guerrilla warfare – was the paradigmatic tool of war. (Though it is also worth pointing out that, in practice, Mao's recipe for guerrilla manoeuvres played a limited role in Chinese revolutionary wars during the 1930s and '40s. Nationalist armies carried most of the resistance to the Japanese during the Second World War, and Chinese Communist victory in the final years of the civil war up to 1949 was won through field battles that the Soviets taught the CCP how to fight.)[17]

2. '*In a very short time, several hundred million peasants in China's central, southern and northern provinces will rise like a fierce wind or tempest, a force so swift and violent that no power, however great, will be able to suppress it . . . Revolution is not a dinner party.*'

The day-to-day intensity of organisational work in the CCP changed after May 1925. That summer, Shanghai saw spontaneous demonstrations and strikes against the foreign presence in the city, after Sikh constables opened fire on a crowd protesting the arrest of six Chinese students by the British. Eleven Chinese people were killed, and at least twenty wounded. Activists in the city organised solidarity strikes in Shanghai, in Canton and in Hong Kong. There was a steep hike in CCP membership: from 994 in 1925, to just under 60,000 in April 1927.[18] This wave of recruitment created the workers' militias that shut down the city on behalf of the Northern Expedition in March 1927.

Meanwhile, Mao was more interested in the countryside. During the radical upsurge of 1925–27, Communist-run peasant associations – initially tolerated by the Guomindang in its desire to become a party with a mass following – also increased in number. As the Northern Expedition moved up the country, Communist cadres seized the opportunity to remake rural society: they redistributed land, and humiliated and expelled rich landlords. In January 1927 Mao returned to Hunan where he completed a report registering, for his native province alone, an increase in membership of peasant associations from 300,000 to 10 million in just one year.[19] It is worth quoting at some length from the report – later, a text beloved by Italian factory workers and Indian undergraduates – because it gives a flavour of the rhetorical elan that would make Mao a global Communist celebrity.

[The peasants] will break through all the trammels that bind them and rush forward along the road to liberation. They will, *in the end*, send all the imperialists, warlords, corrupt officials, local bullies, and bad gentry to their graves. All revolutionary parties and all revolutionary comrades will stand before them to be tested, to be accepted or rejected as they decide. To march at their head and lead them? To stand behind them, gesticulating and criticising them? Or to stand opposite them and oppose them? . . . [T]hose who submit to it survive, and those who resist perish . . . A revolution is not a dinner party, or writing an essay, or painting a picture, or doing embroidery; it cannot be so refined, so leisurely and gentle ... A revolution is an uprising, an act of violence whereby one class overthrows the power of another ... They, who used to rank below everyone else, now rank above everybody else.[20]

This was a watershed moment for Mao's Chinese version of Communism. Marx infamously likened peasants to 'potatoes in a sack' – he believed that the urban, not the rural, proletariat would carry the revolution. Lenin and Stalin adapted this view only to turn the peasantry into the key source of 'primitive capital accumulation', the springboard for rapid industrialisation and modernisation to catch up with Europe. For over half a century, exploitation of the peasantry was the norm for Soviet Communism – from ruthless civil war requisitions, via Stalin's brutal collectivisation in the late 1920s, to Khrushchev's long-standing war on private plots. The gross inequalities inflicted on the countryside did not begin to come to an end until 1974, when peasants previously tied to their collectives were granted the internal passport, giving them in theory freedom of movement. Between the 1950s and 1970s, Mao proved capable of a similar, if not greater, cruelty towards the Chinese peasantry: his pursuit of industrialisation was principally responsible for a famine that cost some 30 million lives. But Soviet distrust towards the peasantry did not translate directly into Maoism: although in both states the Communist Party was determined to maintain iron control, the CCP under Mao stressed and attained a saturation of the rural grass roots that the Soviets never rivalled. Compare the power bases of the Bolshevik and Maoist parties on the eve of taking power, in 1917 and 1949 respectively: the fingers of one hand would not be required to count the number of villages that the Soviets controlled before seizing power in 1917, whereas peasant militias formed the logistical backbone to CCP victory in the civil war in 1949.

Mao was himself, of course, a peasant by origin, and he always spoke, dressed and ate like one. He regularly produced earthy, sometimes foul analogies – underscoring time and again his refusal to be planed into a smooth, establishment statesman. Long articles reminded him of 'the foot-bindings of a slattern, long and stinky'. Despite the cult of infallibility being built up around Mao through the 1950s and '60s, he was – with the ingenuousness of an autodidact – unafraid of showing his ignorance. While once speaking with a Brazilian delegation, he revealed that he had no idea where Brazil was. He met world leaders in patched pyjamas and socks (and sometimes in a bathrobe) and favoured one dish above all others – Hunan-style fatty pork, with a bowl of whole chillies on the side, all washed down with a tin mug of tea (as a postprandial *digestif*, Mao would chew squeakily on the sodden tea leaves in the bottom of the cup). Maoism, from its beginnings in the 1930s through to today, has styled itself as a rural religion that represents and fights for toiling farmers.

In his 'Report from Hunan', Mao particularly celebrated the violent tyranny exercised by the rural lumpenproletariat against local land-owners. 'The only effective way of suppressing the reactionaries is to execute at least one or two in each county ... it is necessary to bring about a brief reign of terror in every rural area ... to exceed the proper limits.'[21] Parts of the report seemed almost ecstatic at the violence witnessed. 'It is wonderful! It is wonderful!'[22] By 1927, Mao – to the horror of his intellectual bosses such as Chen Duxiu, who was deeply unhappy about the levels of violence approved and encouraged by Mao in Hunan – had championed both the military and the rural turn in CCP history.

Over the next seven years of fierce Nationalist suppression of the CCP, Mao dug into a poor, remote mountain range – Jinggangshan – on the border between Hunan and Jiangxi provinces. Here he honed his talent for guerrilla warfare, the principles of which he condensed to a sixteen-syllable jingle for his illiterate peasant troops: *Di jin, wo tui; di zhu, wo rao; Di pi, wo da; Di tui, wo zhui* (when the enemy advances, retreat; when the enemy rests, harass; when the enemy grows tired, attack; when the enemy retreats, pursue).[23] Strict rules for army discipline were laid down: 'Obey orders'; 'Don't take as much as a sweet potato from the masses'; 'Anything confiscated from land-lords and local bullies to be handed in for public distribution'. Military victories would clear the way for setting up red bases in remote parts of the countryside. In advocating and conducting guerrilla warfare, Mao began, for the first time, to set policy, rather than simply follow it. Commanded in 1929 by the Central Committee in Shanghai to disperse the army, he robustly refused: the order was 'unreal' and 'liquidationist'. The Central Committee responded by accusing him of 'roving bandit ideology'. No matter: on 4 October 1930, Communist forces under Mao took their first major city in Jiangxi – Ji'an, the province's third-largest settlement.[24]

3. *'Practice is the sole criterion of truth.'*

In the spring of 1930, Mao toured a county called Xunwu in deep southern Jiangxi. Everything interested him: its waterways, its postal services, the derelict state of the umbrella-manufacturing business, the seaweed trade, the eight different kinds of sugar sold and their relative popularity, the vogue for a hairstyle called the 'Thai pomelo'; and, of course, the different economic classes – landlords (large, middle and small), peasants (rich and poor), and the progress of land redistribution. This was a very different Mao from the one whose blood had been set racing by revolutionary carnage in Hunan. Here was the careful, methodical analyst and architect of revolution, fixated on empirical observation and putting 'practice' above political formulas. An intricately detailed report – hundreds of pages long – resulted.[25]

Almost as a companion piece to his *Report from Xunwu*, in May 1930 Mao also published an essay entitled 'Opposing Bookism'. 'Many of our comrades keep their eyes shut all day long and go around talking nonsense,' he claimed. 'This is disgraceful for a Communist ... You can't solve that problem? Well, go and investigate its present situation and its history!'[26] By the late 1930s, his rhetoric matched his message, when addressing those overfond of theories. 'Your dogma', he told them, 'is less use than dogshit ... Books cannot walk and you can open and close a book at will; this is the easiest thing in the world to do, a great deal easier than it is for the cook to prepare a meal, and much easier than it is for him to slaughter a pig. He has to catch the pig ... the pig can run ... he slaughters it ... the pig squeals. A book placed on a desk cannot run, nor can it squeal. You can dispose of it in any manner you wish. Is there anything easier to do?'[27]

Although, as he reached his dotage, Mao presented himself increasingly as the gnomic sage of the world revolution, it was an earlier Mao – Mao the common-sense Communist – who appealed to millions of non-Chinese acolytes. In the late 1960s and early 1970s, thousands of educated French Maoists devoted themselves to 'serving the people' (another of Mao's favourite slogans) as *établis*, working in factories or in the countryside. Others undertook 'long marches' (in imitation of the Chinese Communists' mythologised trek to the north-west between 1934 and 1935) through the countryside, in order to understand better the conditions of the French proletariat. They repeated Mao's terse dictum 'no investigation, no right to speak' as a litany. 'I've always kept in mind a quotation from President Mao, which I still like and say a lot,' recalled Tiennot Grumbach, once a prominent Maoist from the elite École Normale Supérieure, in 2008. '"There are those who cross the field without seeing the roses, there are those who stop their horse to look at the roses, and there are those who get off their horse to smell the roses." That was our idea: to smell the roses. And for us, the roses were the workers.'[28]

Mao's insistence on the primacy of practice explains another aspect of his appeal: his call to mould Soviet Communism to Chinese reality. Beginning in the 1930s, Mao became a living advertisement for the flexible adaptation of Communism to national context. 'China's revolutionary war', he wrote in 1936, 'is waged in the specific environment of China and has its own specific circumstances and nature [and] specific laws of its own ... Some people ... say that it is enough merely to study the experience of revolutionary war in Russia [and the] laws by which the civil war in the Soviet Union was directed. [But] if we copy and apply them ... without allowing any changes, we shall ... be "cutting the feet to fit the shoes" and be defeated.'[29] Or as the peasant Mao also put it: 'We must plant our backsides on the body of China.'[30] During Japan's brutal occupation of China, he cleverly took the patriotic high ground, reminding all who would listen that 'we want to form a national liberation front, and success for it will mean victory in the anti-Japanese struggle, and a victory, ultimately, for world peace ... Our most urgent problem is national liberation. At present, our objective cannot be Communism, nor even socialism; what we demand and hope for is the establishment of a national people's democratic republic.'[31] Mao is often credited with creating – or at least nurturing – Communist nationalism, through his 'sinicising' of Marxism. His self-confident split with the Soviet Union's vision of global revolution (which became openly rancorous after the 1950s) inspired many other Communist nationalisms, in both Eastern Europe and South East Asia. These nationalisms would culminate in the toxic Indochinese triangle of China–Cambodia–Vietnam conflict.

4. *'Women can hold up half the sky.'*

In February 1935, a slim, handsome Chinese woman with long black hair lay in a thatched hut in Guizhou, south-west China, amid steep, forested mountainsides. The shack was leaking water, for the rain outside was torrential. After hours of labour, she gave birth to a baby girl: her fourth child. She was attended by her sister-in-law, who showed her the baby and asked what she would be called. The woman shook her head. The following day, the army that had brought her here was to move on, and she must travel with them; the baby could not come with her. Her sister-in-law left the child, a few dollars and some opium with a local family. Though nearby, the mother's husband was absent; he had other things to attend to. Two months later, the mother was caught in an enemy air raid; shrapnel sliced into her skull and spine. A month after that, the baby died; the local woman who had taken her in had no milk.

The mother was He Zizhen, Mao's second wife. She would give him two more children; but only one – her fifth, a daughter – would survive into adulthood. The rest died of illness, or were given away after birth and became untraceable. 'Why are women so afraid of giving birth?' Mao used to joke to other women. 'Look at [Zizhen], giving birth for her is as easy as a hen dropping an egg.'[32] Mao's carelessness about procreation was not unique in the Communist Party. Back in the 1920s, when China's feminist movement was in its infancy, radical women had pushed for birth control to become a front-line party issue, to address at least some of the biologically determined inequality that hampered their participation in the revolution. Their male counterparts buried the question: women would be expected to bear children whenever their men made them pregnant *and* devote maximum energies to politics.[33]

He Zizhen's childbirth at Guizhou took place midway through the CCP's Long March. The previous autumn, Communist troops broke out of the south-west corner of Jiangxi, to escape Chiang Kai-shek's military campaign to destroy the CCP. The Long March traced a massive, reverse L-shape across some of the country's wildest terrain – the freezing peaks of Tibet, the boggy plains of the far north-west, finally ending in the bleak, crumbly landscapes of Shaanxi – all the while fighting running battles with a pursuing Nationalist army. Of the 80,000 who began the trek, only 8,000 are said to have completed it, settling in a new base area around the town of Yan'an. But Mao – who, at the start of the Long March, was only the lowest-ranking member of the politburo – emerged resurgent from the ordeal. During the military crises of the Long March, Mao took over leadership of the army; this transition was a key staging post in Mao's rise to power in the CCP. In the course of the twelve years that Yan'an served as the capital of the CCP state in north-west China, Mao would attain supreme political as well as military authority; the CCP's experience of state-building during this period left a deep imprint on future Communist governance.

He Zizhen's physical and psychological traumas notwithstanding, in 1937 Mao would begin a semi-public dalliance with a beautiful actress, Wu Lili, the only Chinese woman in the vicinity with permed hair and lipstick, and a recent urban recruit to the Communist state in north-west China. After Zizhen caught Mao sneaking into Lili's cave one summer evening, she had a screaming fight with the two of them, and with the American left-wing journalist Agnes Smedley, who had organised the dance parties at which Mao and Lili flirted. That year, not long after Lili was sent away, Zizhen – pregnant again – opted to travel to the Soviet Union to have her shrapnel injuries treated. Mao quickly took up with another actress of far more dubious background: a former star of Shanghai B-movies called Lan Ping – Blue Apple – who restyled herself as Comrade Jiang Qing. (In 1966, she would become the chief, vindictive crusader of the Cultural Revolution, in her own words 'biting whomsoever Chairman Mao told me to bite' – as well as settling a number of her own scores.) In Moscow, Zizhen suffered a mental breakdown when her new baby died of pneumonia at six months; Mao seems to have sent no response to the news. She only learned that she had been summarily divorced and replaced by Jiang Qing two years later when she heard a translation of an article in the Soviet press referring to 'Mao and his wife'.[34]

Mao's treatment of Zizhen was not the only instance of his irresponsibility towards women. His first wife was Yang Kaihui, the daughter of his beloved teacher Yang Changji; Kaihui – an educated political activist – bore him three sons. In November 1930, she was arrested in Hunan by a Nationalist commander for her connection with Mao, and shot; she would have been spared, had she been willing to denounce him. Mao rewarded her loyalty with infidelity. Almost two years before her execution, he had taken up with Zizhen in Jiangxi; he had not even bothered to tell Kaihui, who was tormented by rumours of his new romance.

And yet the young Mao of the 1910s was positively feminist in his rhetoric. He reviled old-style arranged marriages as 'indirect rape' and declared that its perpetrators – the parents – should be imprisoned for it.[35] He railed against women's lack of a public position in society: the way in which they could not enter shops, stay in hotels, work in business. 'Smash parental arrangements', 'smash matchmaking', he called.[36] Much later on, in 1968, he famously proclaimed that 'women can hold up half the sky': 'Men and women are the same. What men can do women can also do.'[37] The second law implemented by the new People's Republic in 1950 was a marriage law, enabling women to divorce their husbands and to hold land.

The imputation of feminism to Mao helped push his ideas across the world. 'The idea of women holding up half the sky was all part of the influence of Mao,' considered Dennis O'Neil, a radical student swept up in the US counterculture of the 1960s, who subsequently devoted his life to Maoist-infused politics. 'The Cuban revolution was very macho ... The Maoist revolution had a very different feel: of social relations being transformed, not by diktat but from the ground up, by the participants themselves. Women modeled a lot of consciousness-raising groups on [China's] "speak bitterness" meetings, with people denouncing the old ways, speaking out about the ways in which they're oppressed.'[38] By the late 1960s, however, Mao had for years also been indulging his taste for pretty young women, taking advantage of their hero worship on his vast plank-bed in Zhongnanhai, an old imperial palace west of the Forbidden City and the cloistered residence of the Communist leadership after 1949. According to his doctor, he knowingly infected his paramours with venereal disease: 'I wash myself inside the bodies of my women,' he declared.[39] Mao's inconsistency towards women speaks of his hypocrisy, his split personality, the chasm between his speech and action – or, put more indulgently, his deep-seated capacity for pragmatism.

This pragmatism could manifest itself also in his economic policy. Despite his exhortations to the army against confiscations from ordinary people, in February 1929 he wrote the following 'fundraising

letter' to the merchants of south Jiangxi: 'we are writing to you now
to request that you kindly collect on our behalf 5,000 big foreign
dollars for the soldiers' pay, 7,000 pairs of straw sandals and 7,000
pairs of socks [and] 300 bolts of white cloth ... It is urgent that these
be delivered ... before eight o'clock this evening ... If you ignore
our requests, it will be proof that [you] merchants are collaborating
with the reactionaries ... In that case we will be obliged to burn
down all the reactionary shops ... Do not say that we have not fore-
warned you!'[40]

In the early 1940s, in north-west China, Mao's government found
itself once more in dire economic need, this time in a province
whose principal industry was opium. 'Since opium entered China,'
a Communist editorial of 1941 sternly explained, 'it has become the
greatest source of harm to the Chinese people, inseparable from
imperialist invasion and from the process of China becoming a
semi-colony. Imperialism has used opium to enslave and oppress
the Chinese people. As the Chinese people have become ever
weaker, ever poorer, opium has played a most detestable and
poisonous destructive role.'[41] But the Communist state's account
books for the period are scattered with references to a 'special
product' that rescued the Communists from their trade deficit, and
that by 1945 was generating more than 40 per cent of the state's
budget. This was opium, processed in 'Special Factories' and transported south and west to generate export revenue for Communist
armies. In 1945, as an American mission flew in to inspect Mao's
kingdom, it found itself gazing over nothing more controversial
than swaying fields of sorghum and wheat. The opium poppies
had been uprooted just in time to maintain – for the next forty
years at least – the propriety of the Chinese Communist wartime
image.[42]

Brute force, patriotism, above all pragmatism – a powerful
toolbox for any aspiring prince. But none of it would have held
together without ideological control: the ability to assemble and
assert a single authoritative party line (even if there was always a
gap between high-flown rhetoric and reality). And this was forged
by Mao (and his ghostwriters) in the north-west between 1936
and 1945.

5. *'Expose errors and criticise shortcomings.'*

In the Central Research Institute at Yan'an, in early summer 1942, the great and the good of the Chinese Communist Party gathered for a forum: 'Democracy and Discipline in the Party'. Somewhere between a rally and a show trial, it was convened not in a stuffy seminar room but at a sports ground, and would last for sixteen days. The assembled audience contemplated a pale man in his mid-thirties, a writer called Wang Shiwei. Too ill to stand – he was suffering from tuberculosis – he was sunk into a canvas reclining chair. Mao's secretary and ghostwriter Chen Boda – a bookish, bespectacled man with a squashy face and a noticeable stammer – overcame his speech impediment to deliver a ferocious oration. 'This kind of person ... is like a spineless leech! ... he is as minute as a mosquito; like the kind that sneak in silently to bite you.' He punned vulgarly on Wang's given name (literally, the smell of truth), changing one of the tones, so that it became instead 'the stench of shit'. Ai Qing – Ai Weiwei's father, and one of twentieth-century China's most renowned poets – weighed in too: Wang Shiwei's 'viewpoint is reactionary and his remedies are poisonous. This "individual" does not deserve to be described as "human" let alone as a "comrade".' On the final day of the conference, Ding Ling, one of Yan'an's brightest literary stars – a once feisty individualist who shot to fame in the 1920s for her tell-all fictions about the modern woman's sexual fantasies – turned on Wang too, denouncing him as an 'insult' to literature and art.[43] Wang would spend the rest of his life a prisoner. In the spring of 1947, he was dragged out of his cell and told to kneel on the yellow-brown soil of Shaanxi. A young Communist cadre took out a hatchet and hacked off his head.

Wang's trial has since become one of the most notorious events in the 'Rectification Campaign' of 1942–43. This was by no means Mao's first attempt at a purge. In early 1930, amid military disasters and likely infiltration by the GMD, Mao identified 'a severe crisis in the Party in western and southern Jiangxi ... the local leading organs of the Party at all levels are filled with landlords and rich peasants'. Six years before Stalin began his own great purges, Mao cracked down. 'The most merciless torture' was ordered to expose 'Anti-Bolshevik' conspirators: burning skin with incense sticks, bone-breaking beatings, nailing palms to a table and jabbing bamboo splints under fingernails. The wives of suspects suffered more: their breasts were slashed open, their genitals burnt. In one week alone, 2,000 army members were shot. By 1931, the purge fanned out to include 'those who complained about the Party in their sleep, those who refused to help carry provisions ... those who stayed away from mass rallies, those who failed to show up for Party meetings'. At the end of it all, tens of thousands were dead. Even as the purge wound down between 1932 and 1934, perhaps a hundred people were still being shot every month.[44] 'Comrades,' some Jiangxi Communists pleaded, 'is our Party going to be forever so black and lightless?'[45]

But the Rectification of 1942 – Mao's first disciplining of the party since becoming pre-eminent leader in 1941 – was more considered, more thorough and more sophisticated. There are many different ways to characterise and explain this campaign, within and beyond the framework of Communist terror. As the treatment of Wang reveals, it united the classic ingredients of a Stalinist witch-hunt: the isolation of the target; the 'persuasion' of former allies to join the attack; the rally (or 'struggle meeting', in the militarised Chinese terminology), turning the purge into mass spectacle; the public humiliation of the 'enemy', warning others against similar behaviour; the audience's coercive, collective mockery of the target. Rectification marked the initiation of what has been named 'one of the most ambitious attempts at human manipulation in history'.[46] In 1950s America, this project would be named brainwashing; in China, it came to be known as 'thought reform', and was the organisational and disciplinary foundation on which the ideological legitimacy and authority of Mao's political project rested. As with other ingredients in the Maoist formula, thought reform was not original in itself – both the Soviets and the Nazis had made use of similar techniques – but its comprehensiveness arguably was. Its techniques were copied with varying degrees of intensity throughout Maoism's global travels. Peru's Shining Path and Japan's far-left United Red Army and Revolutionary Left Faction were particularly devoted to criticism/self-criticism. In the winter of 1971–72, these last two groups – while training in a mountain hideout in central Japan – lynched twelve of their comrades deemed insufficiently committed to revolutionary introspection.

What had Wang Shiwei done, to bring the full weight of Mao's censure down upon him? In February and March 1942, he had published in the Yan'an press a brief series of essays criticising the way in which the Communist state was organised. He reported grumblings among Yan'an Communist youth about excessive hierarchy: about cadres who mouthed platitudes concerning 'class friendship', but only cared about how much chicken they got to eat. 'I am not an egalitarian,' Wang wrote, 'but the three classes of clothing and five grades of food are not necessarily reasonable and needed ... If, on the one hand, the ill can't get a bowl of noodles ... while, on the other hand, there are some ... healthy "big shots" who receive unnecessary and unreasonable perks ... this cannot but result in trouble.' He readily admitted that 'Yan'an is superior to the "outside world", but Yan'an can and must become even better.'[47] Wang was asserting something very simple: the right of the individual to independent criticism of Communist politics. On reading these essays, Mao is said to have immediately decided to purge him.

Mao's treatment of Wang Shiwei showcased the careful combination of manipulation and brute force that Mao and the party exercised to create uniformity of thought. By 1942, the Communist movement had grown substantially after the human disaster of the Long March – the ranks had been swollen, in particular, by idealistic educated urban youth intoxicated with Edgar Snow's loving 1937 portrait of the Communist north-west in *Red Star Over China*. These were emotional but mostly ill-disciplined recruits to Communism. They were children of the May Fourth era: educated in the liberal, questioning values of China's patriotic but cosmopolitan Enlightenment of the 1910s and early 1920s, disgusted by the arbitrary brutality of Nationalist or warlord China. Wang Shiwei was inspired to become a Communist by the fate of his first sweetheart, a fearless young Communist killed by the Nationalist army in 1928. Wang's future attacker Ding Ling had fled to Yan'an in 1936 after three years under Nationalist arrest – having secretly joined the Communist Party in 1932, she was suspect for her left-wing literary output and for her common-law marriage to a Communist activist executed by the Nationalists in 1931. But both Wang and Ding were unable instantly to switch off their critical faculties when they reached Yan'an. In essays and bitterly sad stories, Ding Ling pointed out the incompetence and prejudice prevalent in Yan'an: the way that talents were misused by underqualified cadres; the compound of traditional and revolutionary sexism that sniped both at women who didn't marry, and at those who stayed at home to look after their babies.[48]

As Mao unleashed his onslaught on Wang Shiwei, he presented his own answer to his contrarian literary critics, spelling out the role of culture in revolutionary war. Writers and artists must keep to 'the stand of the Party', for 'our stand is that of the proletariat and of the masses'. 'Since the audience for our literature and art consists of workers, peasants and soldiers and of their cadres', writers must repair to villages and factories, to spend time with peasants and workers: 'even though their hands [are] soiled and their feet smeared with cow dung, they [are] really cleaner than the bourgeois and petit-bourgeois intellectuals … Without such a change, without such remolding, [writers and artists] can do nothing well and will be misfits.' Yan'an did not need criticism or satire, he wrote. 'If you are a proletarian writer or artist, you will eulogize … the proletariat and working people.' It was time for writers to 'go among the masses'; otherwise 'difficulties will arise for them'.[49]

In addition to defining a line on cultural and 'thought' work, Rectification implemented it through imposing study and 'discussion' – both in small groups and individual interrogations – of orthodox articles, speeches and ideas. Those suspected of deviation from Mao's line were arrested and 'screened': in fact, by July 1943, 70 per cent of new recruits had been deemed unreliable.[50] Torture and intimidation became commonplace; satire was outlawed. The success of the programme can be judged by the effects on some of its most conspicuous victims. Within a year of his public humiliation, Wang Shiwei was dramatically changed. In late summer 1943, Mao invited a gaggle of journalists, Chinese and foreign, to visit Yan'an. When they asked to see Wang Shiwei, one witness was struck by his 'grey deadly look. He said over and over: "I'm a Trotskyite. I attacked Mao. So I deserve to be executed. I should have been executed a thousand times. But Mao is so magnanimous. He doesn't want me to die. He allows me to work. I am working diligently and have realised the great principle that labour is holy. I am extremely grateful for his mercy."'[51] A few days into the 'Forum on Democracy and Discipline in the Party' in summer 1942, Wang's former celebrity allies – most notably, Ding Ling and Ai Qing – had abandoned him, completed grovelling self-criticisms and launched vicious attacks on Wang's 'Trotskyism'. After the events of May 1942, Ding Ling – the famous literary starlet, formerly prone to moody portraits, her shoulders draped in furs, her hair waved and set – cocooned herself in shapeless padded cotton clothes and banished herself to villages where she devoted her energies to staging folky plays newly infused with Communist propaganda.

Rectification left hundreds, perhaps thousands, incarcerated in yellow, dusty caves dug into the crumbly hillsides of Yan'an. It was the prototype for every subsequent movement of thought reform launched under Mao: the mass meetings designed to humiliate and isolate targets; the repeated writing of confessions; the discussion groups where silence was not an option; the honing of self-criticism. In China, it came to be widely seen as a rehearsal for the purges of the Cultural Revolution; not coincidentally, Mao brought his key mobiliser for Rectification – Kang Sheng, also known as 'Mao's pistol' – back to the political centre stage to galvanise the Cultural Revolution. Kang lived the part of Mao's secret police chief, dressing and accessorising all in black: lustrous, Soviet-style leather jacket, breeches, boots, moustache, horse, riding crop and Alsatian. His two weaknesses were Song-dynasty pots and good food (his personal chef in Yan'an had previously cooked for Puyi, the last emperor of the Qing dynasty); otherwise, he was 'obsessed with power but totally lacking in beliefs'. Kang Sheng's work also made possible the globalisation of Maoism through the 1960s and early 1970s. As head of the CCP's secretive International Liaison Department (in charge of relations with foreign Communist parties, and therefore more important than the Ministry of Foreign Affairs), Kang Sheng oversaw the export of revolutionary ideas, strategies, money and weapons to Communist insurgencies; he hosted worshipful Western Maoists in Beijing and funnelled cash and intelligence to the Khmer Rouge in Cambodia.[52]

For sure, Rectification and the early 1940s in the Communist northwest were frightening times if you were a highly educated, liberal intellectual, inclined to question the need for absolute party discipline. If, by contrast, you were a local farmer, you might have had a different perspective, for Rectification coincided roughly with the 'cooperative movement', a renewed push for socio-economic levelling, rolled out across local villages. Such individuals often found their rents being reduced and their interest rate on loans cut; they benefited from schemes to share animals, tools and seeds; some were even able to

choose village officials in local elections; many enjoyed a boost to
local productivity, as soldiers and Communist cadres pitched in to help
with farming and crafts; and there were opportunities to learn to read
and write, as urban intellectuals descended on villages to spread education.[53] Communist recruits in Yan'an from poor backgrounds spoke
in the 1980s of appreciating Mao because of his understanding of
Chinese society and organisation of political work.[54] Rectification was
both a terrifying ordeal and the process through which Mao created
a disciplined party and bureaucracy – in contrast with the corrupt
lassitude of the Guomindang.

In 1943 Mao (with the help of Kang Sheng) intensified Rectification
into the badly named 'Rescue Campaign', a witch-hunt for 'spies' and
'traitors' in which so many were arrested 'that the caves could not
hold them all', and in which more than 90 per cent of accusations
were later deemed groundless.[55] He also coined another of his key
policy ideas: the 'mass line'.

> [A]ll correct leadership must come from the masses and go to the
> masses. This means to take the ideas of the masses (scattered and
> unsystematic ideas) and ... turn them into concentrated and systematic
> ideas by means of study, then propagandize and explain these ideas to
> the masses until the masses embrace them as their own ... testing
> [their] correctness [in action]. Then, once again concentrate ideas from
> the masses and persevere in sending them back to the masses. In such
> an endless cycle, the ideas will become ever more correct, vital, and
> abundant each time.[56]

This policy idea installed a slippery relationship between dictatorship and democracy at the heart of Mao's polity. True to his peasant
origins, Mao acclaimed the brilliance of the (rural) masses, for only
their ideas were 'correct'. (The following year he exhorted his followers
to 'serve the people', further laying claim to the populist benevolence
of his regime; this slogan travelled the world during the Cultural
Revolution, winning Mao particularly fervent followers among African
and Asian American communities.) Yet only he (and the party) could
concentrate, systematise and apply the brilliance of their ideas. One
of contemporary China's most outspoken critics of Mao, an academic
who almost died twice under Mao's policies (of starvation in the Great

Leap Forward, of violent persecution in the Cultural Revolution), has put it this way: 'Mao's great talent lay in turning the Chinese people into slaves, while making them feel like they were the masters of the country ... All the world's dictators have studied Mao.' Rectification and the mass line provided the framework for ideological unity and 'thought work' in Mao's party. It formed a basis for mass mobilisation – and theoretical justification for the CCP to claim that its methods were 'democratic' – that would be followed in the Malayan jungles, in the black neighbourhoods of California, on the Peruvian sierra and in the mountains of Nepal.

> 6. 'The East is Red, the sun rises.
> In China a Mao Zedong is born.
> He seeks the people's happiness.
> He is the people's Great Saviour.'

In the early 1940s in Yan'an, Mao was enthroned as the philosopher-king of Chinese Communism, and the Maoist anthem 'The East is Red' was written.[57] Until the late 1930s Mao was famed as a military man: his doctrinal skills in Marxism–Leninism lagged far behind those of his rivals for power – the party members who had recently returned from study in the dark arts of Stalinism in Moscow. Their leader, a pudgy-faced theoretician called Wang Ming, was well trained in both theory and practice: he had sent several of his compatriots to the Gulag during Stalin's purges. Mao, by contrast, was – even in the late 1930s, almost two decades after his conversion to Communism – still a rudimentary Marxist. He had almost no time for Marx's more careful historical and economic analyses, condensing the message of *The Communist Manifesto* down to: 'Class struggle, class struggle, class struggle!'[58] Some of Mao's closest colleagues listening to his lectures were embarrassed by his *bêtises* and blatant plagiarism from Chinese translations of Marxist texts. Perhaps as a result of all this, Mao long harboured a sense of inferiority towards intellectuals that no doubt shaped his harshness towards them once in power.

From the late 1930s on, however, Mao launched his own claims to doctrinal originality and to a leadership cult. On 22 June 1937, a key CCP publication, *Liberation*, published Mao's portrait for the first time. The message of the iconography was unmistakable: marching columns in the background lent the portrait movement and dynamism; Mao's face was lit up by the sun's rays from behind; space was made for a quotation.[59] Mao's writings and speeches began to be collected and canonised. His secretary Chen Boda, a former professor of ancient history, edited a new version of the CCP's history that turned Mao into the presiding party genius, and helped him formulate most of his key essays: 'On Guerrilla Warfare' (1937), 'On Contradiction' (1937), 'On Practice' (1937), 'On Protracted War' (1938), 'On New Democracy' (1940).[60] In 1939, *Liberation* acclaimed Mao as the 'leader of the people who is esteemed by the masses both at home and abroad'.[61] '[T]he leading, most typical person in applying creative Marxism to Chinese problems', enthused a young theoretician in 1941, 'is our party leader, Comrade Mao Zedong. He is our party's great revolutionary, a talented theorist, a strategist, and one of the most creative Marxist-Leninists in China.'[62] In January 1942, as Yan'an geared up for Rectification, Mao's writings were recommended for study *above* those of Marx, Engels, Lenin and Stalin.[63] At the cult's apogee – in the early years of the Cultural Revolution – Chinese citizens abroad would weep with emotion in front of customs officials when declaring their Chinese-language editions of Mao's words.[64]

Mao's direction of the 1942–43 Rectification Campaign marginalised those in the party with lingering doubts about his prowess as a theoretician. According to Wang Ming, Mao's nearest rival at the time, Mao launched Rectification 'to replace Leninism by Maoism, to write the history of the Chinese Communist Party as the history of Mao Zedong alone; to elevate the personality of Mao Zedong above the Central Committee and the entire Party [so as to] capture the chief leading place in the Party leadership and all power in the Party in his own hands'.[65] Ai Qing lionised him in verse ('Mao Zedong'), and a cartoon in the party daily lined up Mao's portrait next to those of Marx, Engels, Lenin and Stalin.[66] Zhu De – founder of the Red Army and a former equal in the party – offered him glowing encomia: 'our party now has its own most talented leader in Comrade Mao Zedong. He has genuinely comprehended Marxist-Leninist theory, and moreover is adept at using this theory to guide the Chinese revolution step by step to victory. Not only is he the most authoritative person in our entire party, but he also enjoys the greatest political confidence among the people throughout the country. In addition, a large number of sincere and courageous party cadres, fully experienced in struggle and having close relations with the masses, have been nurtured for the party and the revolution under his education and care.'[67] Mao was transitioning from machinating warlord to revolutionary sage.

In addition to its Stalinist terror tactics (Mao adored Stalin's 1938 potted guide to managing the Bolsheviks, *History of the Communist Party of the Soviet Union: Short Course*, and made it required reading for the CCP leadership), Yan'an projected a reverence for culture. Soon after Mao arrived, this impoverished corner of China began to teem with schools, universities, research institutes – the Lu Xun Academy, the Resistance University, the Central Research Institute. Yan'an Communists devoted themselves to study: cavefuls of earnest revolutionaries – eight to each cave – were woken at six in the morning, attended lectures until lunchtime, then conducted private study or production work until bed at nine. There was, quite simply, not much else to do but read and talk: there were no private radios and few film projectors. They were allowed free time on Sundays to wash in the river.[68] In this 'republic of caves', Mao was Socrates, Plato and – as a practising romantic poet – Byron, transforming an army camp into the 'Tantric centre of the Chinese revolution'.[69] It was a place of testing pilgrimage – the journey there through the Nationalist blockade was perilous – in which the business of revolution was infused with religious fervour. It was no coincidence, perhaps, that the centre of propaganda operations (a printing press heaved up and down the Long March on the backs of the rank and file) was rebuilt and installed in Yan'an's highest point: the Cave of the 10,000 Buddhas. There, thronged by these myriad Buddhas, it became the textual loudspeaker for Mao's authority.[70] After Yan'an became a Communist stronghold, the caves occupied by the leadership – Mao, Zhu De, Liu Shaoqi and Zhou Enlai – were clustered together, physically embodying the cohesive intimacy of this ideological community.

'[Mao] dressed simply and could speak like a peasant, but he was really a teacher,' remembered one Yan'an veteran. 'I knew by looking that he was a presence and not a simple teacher.'[71] Of course, Mao was assisted by skilled ghostwriters and secretaries; but in his essays of the late 1930s and early 1940s he took discursive control of China's past and present. To be sure, his power did not stem from his oratory. When he announced the founding of the People's Republic from the rostrum at Tiananmen Square in 1949, his cadences were almost squeakily high-pitched and his Hunan accent thick almost to the point of incomprehensibility. But his essays are disciplined pieces of work. In his writings on China's modern history, in particular, he marshalled the dispiriting anarchy of the previous century into a tidy teleology that explained cause and effect, that identified his revolution as the logical saviour of the Chinese nation. By insisting on the malevolence of China's foreign antagonists from the nineteenth century onwards, Mao legitimised his own use of violence, against both imperialists and their alleged Chinese allies – Nationalists, capitalists, compradors, landlords, and anyone suspected of sympathising with them. 'In the face of such enemies,' Mao wrote, 'the Chinese revolution cannot be other than protracted and ruthless ... In the face of such enemies, the principal means or form of the Chinese revolution must be armed struggle.'[72] Mao's ability to create compelling, comprehensible narratives of human history, both ancient and modern, was much admired by global Maoists, and especially coveted by Shining Path's Abimael Guzmán, whose followers named him 'Shampoo' for his ability to 'wash brains' with his easy-to-grasp philosophical certitudes.

And Mao's stories were far more effective than Marxist tracts: they were scattered with surprising, coarse humour and classical references – testament to Mao's background as autodidact peasant. Rectification was experienced both as a terrifying purge and as a cult-like bonding ritual, in which some 20,000 individuals were divided into small, monitored groups and set to study the same texts, to debate the same questions.[73] In Yan'an, Mao became much more than an army man: he was revered as a poet, theorist and calligrapher; as a political philosopher able to slot the confusing elements, forces and ideas with which China had been contending for the previous century into a blueprint for success.[74] As a devoted Chinese collector of Mao memorabilia told me in 2014 (in a turn of phrase that is perhaps my favourite in the thousands of conversations that I have had on Mao): 'Mao was better than Genghis Khan because he was a poet.' It was his apparent ability to multitask, and often using simple language, that won Mao the hearts of so many foreign acolytes, from West German undergraduates to Indian farmers.

In 1944, after years of seclusion, Yan'an reopened to journalists from the outside. They were struck by its intellectual homogeneity. '[I]f you ask the same question of twenty or thirty people, from intellectuals to workers, their replies are always more or less the same,' observed one reporter. 'Even questions about love, there seems to be a point of view that has been decided by meetings.' The 'air of nervous intensity [was stifling] ... Most people had very earnest faces and serious expressions. Among the big chiefs, apart from Mr Mao Zedong who often has a sense of humour, and Mr Zhou Enlai who is very good at chatting, the others rarely crack a joke.'[75] That same year, the American journalists Annalee Jacoby and Theodore White – sworn enemies of the corruption and censorship of Chiang Kai-shek's Nationalists – observed a curious obsequiousness on the part of Mao's lieutenants towards their dear leader: the way in which they made 'ostentatious notes on his free-running speeches as if drinking from the fountain of knowledge. Nor were panegyrics of the most high-flown, almost nauseatingly slavish eloquence unusual.'[76]

In 1940, Liu Shaoqi had remarked (doubtless to Mao's considerable annoyance) that Chinese Communism had not yet produced 'a great work'.[77] Within another three years, Liu changed his mind: the history of the CCP had developed 'with Comrade Mao Zedong at the centre ... All cadres and party members ... should diligently study and master Comrade Mao Zedong's doctrines on the Chinese revolution and other subjects. They should arm themselves with Comrade Mao Zedong's thought.'[78] This same essay, published on 6 July 1943, gave birth to the religion of Maoism – Mao Zedong Thought (*Mao Zedong sixiang*, originally *Mao Zedong tongzhi di sixiang*, Comrade Mao Zedong Thought). 'Our Comrade Mao Zedong,' Liu summarised in 1945 at the 7th Party Congress (which enshrined Mao Zedong Thought as 'the guide' for all the CCP's work), 'is not only the greatest revolutionary and statesman in Chinese history, but also the greatest theoretician and scientist in Chinese history.'[79] This sanctification of party control under an absolutist, infallible helmsman inspired other 'dear leaders' such as Peru's Abimael Guzmán, who witnessed the Mao cult at its Cultural Revolution apogee.

7. 'Imperialism is a paper tiger.'

In 1917, Lenin identified imperialism as 'the highest stage of capitalism' and began bringing non-European socialists to Moscow. Two years later, with Bolshevik power far from established in Russia, Lenin hosted the founding Congress of a 'Communist International' (Comintern): over fifty delegates attended, representing some twenty-five countries. Lenin was receptive to the ideas of M. N. Roy, a globetrotting Indian Communist who had already helped found the Mexican Communist Party (one of the first Communist parties founded outside Russia). Roy urged Lenin to sponsor Communist parties and insurrections throughout the colonial world; accordingly, by the early 1920s, China, India, Indonesia, Turkey and Iran all had Communist parties. In 1921, Lenin concluded that 'the destiny of all Western civilization now largely depends on drawing the masses of the East into political activities'.[80] The Comintern gave military or political training to young men picked out for high office. The Communist University for the Toilers of the East, placed under the direction of the Comintern in 1923, trained activists from China, India, Indonesia, Korea and Indochina (its most glittering South East Asian alumnus was arguably Ho Chi Minh), but several dozen Africans and Arabs who would later hold important positions were also graduates: Albert Nzula, secretary of the Communist Party of South Africa; Jomo Kenyatta, Kenya's first president; and the influential pan-Africanist George Padmore, adviser to Ghana's President Nkrumah.[81]

For two reasons, Mao and his lieutenants appeared to champion the anti-imperialist programme even more fiercely than the Soviets. First, Mao had a flair for creating catchy sound bites. In 1946, in his cave at Yan'an he invited another carefully chosen American to dinner: a radical journalist called Anna Louise Strong who, after a two-decade dalliance, was falling out of love with the Soviet Union and under the spell of Mao and the CCP. There, he produced another of his best-known aphorisms: American 'reactionaries', he pronounced, 'are paper tigers'.[82] He was clearly pleased with the image, for he returned to it in 1956 and 1957, in more explicitly anti-colonial terms, addressing Latin Americans and an international gathering of Communists in Moscow:

'the countries of the Americas, Asia and Africa will have to go on quarrelling with the United States till the very end, till the paper tiger is destroyed by the wind and the rain'.[83]

Second, the apparent fervour of Mao's anti-imperialism was also a matter of historical contingency. The consolidation of the PRC coincided with a global upsurge in decolonisation across Africa, Asia and the Middle East in the wake of the Second World War. That context did not exist for the Soviet Union's own anti-imperial ventures in the 1920s. Even though nationalists in, for example, Indonesia had already authored their own strongly anti-colonial movements in the 1920s and '30s, and even though at no point in its history did the CCP contribute as much materially to global anti-colonial rebellions as the Soviet Union – which also funnelled millions of roubles per year, in addition to military aid and training, to the Chinese revolution during the 1920s alone – this historical coincidence enabled the PRC under Mao to present itself as the global headquarters of anti-imperialism. In the 1950s, China under Mao bid for leadership in the decolonising world through prominent interventions in the Geneva Conference of 1954 (which deliberated the status of post-colonial Cambodia, Laos and Vietnam) and in the Bandung Conference of 1955. The crowning moment of Mao's anti-colonial reputation was his defence minister Lin Biao's promotion of Maoist revolution in his globally publicised 1965 essay, 'Long Live the Victory of People's War!':

> Comrade Mao Zedong's theory of the establishment of rural revolutionary base areas and the encirclement of the cities from the countryside is of outstanding and universal practical importance for the present revolutionary struggles of all the oppressed nations and peoples ... if North America and Western Europe can be called 'the cities of the world', then Asia, Africa and Latin America constitute 'the rural areas of the world' ... the contemporary world revolution also presents a picture of the encirclement of cities by the rural areas.[84]

This defiance of colonialism through 'People's War' gave Mao and his programme a global moral glamour. Throughout the 1960s, cheerleaders inside and outside China promoted Mao's theories as the key to launching successful revolutionary wars against US imperialism. West German radicals presumptuously identified with an oppressed 'third world', and American anti-Vietnam War protesters acclaimed Mao the theoretical genius behind the Vietcong's independence struggle. Indian and Latin American insurrectionists dogmatically applied Mao's signature analysis of 1930s China as 'semi-colonial, semi-feudal' to their own societies, and his methods of uncompromising warfare to their governments and populations.

8. 'To rebel is justified.'

Mao spent the year building up to the start of the Cultural Revolution (summer 1966) in retreat, away from Beijing. He was planning an event unprecedented (and unrepeated) in Communist history: an attack launched by the supreme leader on his own party. Between 1966 and his death in 1976, Mao subjected the CCP to waves of purges and wilful doctrinal purification. International politics – in particular, the Soviet Union's retreat from advocating violent revolution – provided a global justification. But Mao's immediate aim was to topple domestic critics of his radical politics and economics: men like Liu Shaoqi and Deng Xiaoping, who had begun to dismantle collectivisation.

As he plotted his imminent onslaught on the party establishment, he turned to one of his favourite books from the Chinese popular canon: *The Journey to the West*. One of the masterworks of classical Chinese writing, it recounts a Tang dynasty monk's quest for Buddhist scriptures in the seventh century AD, aided by one of the most memorable reprobates of world literature: an omni-talented, kung fu–practising Monkey King called Sun Wukong. A cornerstone text of Chinese rebelliousness, the novel commences with a spirited prologue – seven chapters long – recounting the Monkey King's irreverence for earthly and heavenly authority, and his limitless appetite for mischief. After taking up a bureaucratic sinecure in the heavenly government of the Jade Emperor, he gorges himself on the peaches, wine and elixirs of immortality, wages war on the heavenly government and army of the Jade Emperor, and urinates on the hand of the Buddha. To Mao – an anarchist in his early twenties – the havoc-wreaking instincts of the Monkey King were a lifelong inspiration, and he repeatedly referenced Sun Wukong throughout his time as paramount leader of China. In 1961, he devoted the last stanza of a poem to this inveterate troublemaker:

The Golden Monkey swung his enormous cudgel
And cleansed the universe of a myriad miles of dust.
Today, with the return of evil miasmal mists,
We acclaim Sun Wukong, the great sage.[85]

In seeking to incite Red Guard attacks on the party establishment early in the Cultural Revolution, Mao once more invoked the Monkey King: 'We need more Sun Wukongs ... to disrupt the heavenly palace.'[86] Red Guards readily picked up the cue on their own protest posters: 'Revolutionaries are like the Monkey King: their golden staff is powerful, their supernatural powers are sweeping ... we use our sorcery to turn the old world on its head, crush it into pieces, turn it into dust, create chaos and great disorder, the bigger the better!'[87] In 1967, Mao relaunched his idea of 'continuous revolution' (jixu geming): the need for ceaseless, violent shake-ups of the political establishment – the Cultural Revolution was only the beginning.[88] This concept grew from his disdain since the late 1950s for the USSR's privileging of economic growth over radical revolutionary turmoil, and from his fear that his own comrades were Soviet epigones. (His paranoia about this may also have been stoked by the plots of Journey to the West, whose pages are populated by man-eating demons artfully disguised as kindly old people, beautiful young women and adorable children.)

Even though Mao was a profoundly autocratic man of the party and the army, and although that party and army were in power for the last three decades of his life, he never ceased to see himself also as an outlier. As he aged, he cut himself off increasingly from (indeed, worked to destroy) party structures and comrades. Although his contemporary Khrushchev was capable of unstatesmanlike behaviour – brandishing his shoe at the UN in New York; getting drunk and openly calling Mao 'a pair of torn galoshes' at a diplomatic banquet – Mao was easily his superior for unconventionality. 'I graduated from the University of Outlaws,' he told his long-suffering doctor more than once.[89] In conversations with foreign notables, Mao consistently presented himself as the perennial outsider, as a rebel against the establishment, 'without law, without god': 'we are really in the minority ... we are not afraid of criticism ... we the Chinese fight like roosters ... we, the Chinese, are militant, and especially me'.[90]

Mao's militancy in turn generated his yearnings for a violent world revolution. 'We are in favour of a revolutionary war whose goal is to overthrow imperialism and its adherents,' he told the Soviet premier Aleksei Kosygin in 1965. 'One must create a revolutionary war situation ... Precisely, truth is born due to [quarrels] – blade against blade.'[91] In two increasingly peculiar exchanges from the early 1970s, he exhorted Nicolae Ceauşescu and then the Japanese prime minister, Tanaka Kakuei, to have a fight with his second in command Zhou Enlai.[92] Mao turned this world view into state policy in 1966 when propelling the Cultural Revolution's assault on party and government authorities, but the spirit of devil-may-care rebellion had been present all his conscious life. It manifested itself both in rows with his father as a young adult, and in his unleashing of chaos during the Cultural Revolution: 'Bombard the headquarters ... Don't be afraid of making trouble. The bigger the trouble we make, the better ... There is great chaos under heaven; the situation is excellent.'[93]

Rebels and insurgents all over the world picked up on the radical rhetoric of high, Cultural Revolution Maoism (and it is notable that mature Communist parties in power – in Vietnam, North Korea and of course the Soviet Union – were horrified by it). Across the protests of the late 1960s, rebellious students imitated the political behaviour of the Cultural Revolution to rebel against their national establishments. They reproduced translations of Chinese big-character posters, and wrote their own; they recited Cultural Revolution speeches during their occupations of university buildings. In November 1966, student representatives rushed into a meeting with the president of West Berlin's Freie Universität wearing Mao badges and calling themselves 'Red Guards'.[94] On a blackboard behind the students gathered at one meeting of the West Berlin Socialist Student Union (SDS) in 1967, someone had scrawled the Maoist dictum: 'To rebel is justified.'[95] During the Cultural Revolution, Mao's championing of the 'global peasantry' taking on the developed world and his encouragement of youthful rebellion turned him, in the eyes of hopeful insurgents and student protesters, into a revolutionary messiah.

Mao's love of rebellion fed also into his passionate belief in voluntarism: that as long as you believed you could do something, you could accomplish it – regardless of material obstacles. This idea permeates his writing and policies: in his unwavering revolt against the

Chinese state between 1927 and 1949; and in his intoxication with mobilising the Chinese people to work day and night through the Great Leap Forward to achieve – through sheer self-belief – 'sputnik targets' in agricultural and industrial growth (by melting down woks and fertilising fields with broken glass). His global disciples – inveterate rebels and outsiders themselves – eagerly imbibed Mao's messages that individuals can triumph through simple audacity or force of will: 'A single spark can start a prairie fire'; 'Dare to struggle, dare to win'; 'Whoever is not afraid of being drawn and quartered, can dare to pull the emperor from his horse'; 'A weak nation can defeat a strong, a small nation can defeat a big [if only it dares] to rise in struggle, to take up arms ... This is a law of history.' Young Maoists in Norway after 1968 – some of them avid science-fiction readers – imagined that their reading of Mao gave them and their rebellion against the Norwegian state superpowers; the strongest Maoist movement in the Western world grew through the 1970s out of this belief.

Again, there was little here that was purely original: Stalin, for example, had launched an attack on his own bureaucracy in his 'Great Break' of 1928–32; unleashing workers against bosses was an ingredient of his purges, too. The difference from Soviet precedents lay in the degree to which Mao was willing to pursue this policy, and also in its chronology. The Cultural Revolution was Mao's last campaign, and hence became his political testament; Stalin's Terror was succeeded by some fifteen years of 'Great Retreat', of re-entrenchment of the *nomenklatura*. And, as always with Mao, there was little consistency. He rapidly backtracked from the Shanghai commune, the experimental political model that emerged from the first eight months of violence and disorder of the Cultural Revolution. 'If everything were changed into a commune, then what about the party?' he asked. 'There must be a party somehow! There must be a nucleus, no matter what we call it. Be it called the Communist Party, or Social Democratic Party, or Guomindang ... there must be a party.'[96]

9. *'On contradiction: the struggle of opposites is ceaseless.'*

In contemplating Mao and his ideas, we are left principally with inconsistency. Mao was an army man, an arch political manipulator and centraliser, the architect of his own personality cult, a fetishiser of party discipline; and a glorifier of mass rebellion who continually saw himself as an outsider. He was a rhetorical feminist, who serially impregnated, abandoned, sexually abused and infected women. The wife of a close associate from the Yan'an days up until Mao's death remembered him thus: 'I really admired him. He was so clever. He was very humorous. I was afraid of him. I avoided him. He didn't say much, he'd ask you your view ... You'd ask him what he thought and he wouldn't say.' This conversational assessment, lacking the analytical cogency of a scripted answer, condenses Mao's mutability: his informality; his guardedness; the reverence and fear he inspired; his savvy manipulations.

In 1937, amid the yellow dust of Yan'an, Mao delivered a lecture on one of his very favourite subjects: 'Contradiction'. He was brimming with words and ideas: it took him fifteen years to edit them down into a form sufficiently concise for his *Selected Works*.[97] When finally complete, the essay was thick with doctrinal name-dropping: Marx, Engels, Lenin, dialectics. But the concluding message – which Mao lived and breathed – was glibly simple: 'The law of contradiction in things, that is, the law of the unity of opposites, is the fundamental law of nature and of society ... the struggle of opposites is ceaseless, it goes on both when the opposites are coexisting and when they are transforming themselves into each other ... this again is the universality and absoluteness of contradiction.'[98] Marx contended that history would ultimately sublate all contradictions into synthesis, with an iron logic, direction and end point. Mao, meanwhile, introduced and embraced a greater instability into his analysis of the interplay of contradictions; different forces and factors could play and exchange leading roles in different times and circumstances. Mao possessed a genius for devising political theories – veneered with Marxism – that defined chaotic inconsistency as dynamism. This doctrinal justification of capriciousness is the final element that propelled Mao's ideas across the world: he told rebels and subversives impatient for change that internal contradictions in thought and action were not to be feared. Quite the opposite: they were a wellspring of energy. As Mao consolidated his absolute personal authority over the party, he delivered his strategy of the 'mass line'. He mobilised his dictator's personality cult to tell his Red Guards that it was right to rebel, inspiring insurgents the world over with his theory of 'continuous revolution' against authority.

It is perhaps this perplexing, inconsistent mutability, in combination with memory of the political and military success of Mao, that has given the political line which carries his name its potency, persuasiveness and mobility. Somehow, Maoism is the creed of winners and insiders, of losers and outsiders, of leaders and underdogs, of absolute rulers, vast, disciplined bureaucracies, and oppressed masses. Frustrated with its contradictions, its muddying of tidy disciplines, Christophe Bourseiller, an authority on Maoism's journey to Europe, goes so far as to say: 'Maoism doesn't exist. It never has done. That, without doubt, explains its success.'[99]

2

THE RED STAR –
REVOLUTION BY THE BOOK

Late one summer's night in 1936, in a cave gouged out of a yellow loess cliff in north-west China, two men – one Chinese, one American – talked. The American – slim, dark-haired, bearded – was perched on a stool; his Chinese interlocutor – tall, slightly gaunt, with a mop of black hair – lolled jovially over a brick bed, occasionally removing his trousers to cool himself down or pick lice out of his crotch.[1]

For the Chinese man – Mao Zedong – a good deal was at stake in getting his self-presentation just so. Aged forty-four, Mao had only recently gained a position of relative strength in the Chinese Communist Party, and was still facing off challenges from rivals with large armies and greater fluency in the Marxist classics. The entire Communist state in north-west China was facing imminent extinction by China's official government, the Nationalists under Chiang Kai-shek. While Chiang limbered up for one last assault to eliminate Mao and his comrades, Chiang's subordinates were building a military blockade around the area. 'The remnant Communists,' he confidently told his army that autumn, 'are now encompassed in a few scattered regions and can be exterminated without much difficulty. At present, Communism is no longer a real menace to China.'[2] With the military cordon had come a news blackout: no information about the Communist movement independent of Nationalist censorship had broken through for months; the Nationalists took advantage of this vacuum to spread rumours that the leadership had been killed on their 'Long March' from south-east to north-west China in 1934–35.

The presence of Mao's American visitor thus offered a crucial opportunity for Mao to address the outside world. The man was Edgar Snow, a young, ambitious journalist from Kansas City in search of the scoop that would secure both his reputation and personal finances. Snow – a well-disposed but non-Communist foreigner with media reach both in China and beyond – had been carefully selected by the underground Communist Party as the perfect mouthpiece to take Mao's story beyond the Communist base area and win it friends. Accordingly, Mao worked hard to create as favourable and approachable an impression as possible, making himself available to Snow in multiple private interviews, most of them lasting deep into the night.[3]

Mao's nonchalance was misleading. In reality, very little was being left to chance in this encounter. Throughout every one of Snow's interviews with Mao, another Chinese man sat to one side, interpreting between the two, to ensure that the correct version of Mao's story was recorded. After Snow had completed his English-language transcript of the conversation, it would then be translated back into Chinese for Mao to check and revise, then translated one last time back into English.[4] Every one of Mao's 20,000 words that Snow took away with him from the north-west went through this editing process. Details about CCP plans for and response to Snow's visit remain inaccessible, locked in the Archive of the Central Committee of the CCP in the centre of Beijing, off-limits to all but the most trusted servants of the party. But we can guess a little at the stringent preparations that lay behind Mao's casual affability, from the four succinct instructions he gave for the visit in advance of Snow's arrival at Communist headquarters: 'Security, secrecy, warmth and red carpet.'[5]

The efforts paid off. The following year, a charmed Snow wrote up his painstakingly edited impressions of the Communist state and interviews with its leaders into *Red Star Over China*, portraying Mao and his comrades as idealistic patriots and egalitarian democrats with a sense of humour. Mao's aims, Snow declared, were 'to awaken [China's millions] to a belief in human rights, to combat the timidity, passiveness, and static faiths of Taoism and Confucianism, to educate, to persuade … them … to fight for a life of justice, equality, freedom, and human dignity'.[6] The book became a surprise bestseller on publication – in Britain alone it sold over 100,000 copies in a matter of weeks – and garnered ecstatic reviews. Pearl S. Buck, perhaps America's

most influential writer on matters Chinese at the time, called it
'intensely readable ... extraordinary ... every page of it is significant'.[7]
It was, John K. Fairbank (the founder of modern Chinese studies at
Harvard) later commented, 'an event in modern Chinese history'.[8] Its
success turned Snow into an authority on Chinese politics. Five years
later, Roosevelt consulted him as the president worked out a China
policy. In the mid-1940s, an American State Department official who
had absorbed Snow's portrait of Maoism would help leak Chiang
Kai-shek's battle plans to Communist sympathisers.

But *Red Star*'s reach was wider still. Translated into Chinese, it
convinced crowds of young, educated liberals and patriots – in the
mainland and across the Chinese diaspora – to abandon their bourgeois urban existences and trek to the north-west to serve Mao's
revolution as organisers, administrators and propagandists. The
book's Chinese translator and editor, a brilliant young linguist called
Hu Yuzhi, was posted as an undercover CCP agent to South East
Asia during the Second World War. There, the book was read by
future leaders of the Malaysian Communist Party. During the twelve
years of the Malayan Emergency – in which some 8,000 Malayan
and British soldiers and civilians would die – hundreds of copies of
Red Star Over China were found in Communist training camps.[9]
Snow's record of Chinese guerrilla warfare became a handbook for
anti-Nazi partisans in wartime Russia, for Huk guerrillas in the
Philippines, and for anti-British revolutionaries in India.[10] Mao's relationship with Snow – which he would continue to milk, when it
suited him, for international publicity up until Snow's death of
pancreatic cancer at the age of sixty-six – became the first emblematic example of the importance of the international factor in Mao's
political vision.

Edgar Snow is the first main character in this global history of
Maoism because without him both a domestic and an international
cult of Mao would be hard to imagine. It is difficult to overestimate
the influence, across space and time, of *Red Star Over China*. Acclaimed
as one of the greatest American journalistic accounts of the twentieth
century, it created a figurehead (Mao) to humanise the Chinese
Communist movement, and a constellation of principles and loyalists
around him. Snow's starring role in fashioning Maoism highlights,
from its very beginning, the border-crossing quality of a doctrine that

is often seen as the most Chinese – and most rural – of political reli-
gions. Snow illuminates the international PR genius of the CCP from
its early days, and the way Mao's ideas and persona traversed territories, languages and classes, and attracted international cheerleaders.
Snow's part in this process also foreshadows the way in which Mao
and his lieutenants built and manipulated international networks of
support from the 1930s to the present day – networks that changed
the course of China's civil war and the Cold War, and influenced
Mao's own political thought and practice.

And to understand why a former frat boy from Missouri became
the international vector for the Maoist creed, we have to travel far
from the impoverished dust bowl of north-west China to the high
societies of 1930s Shanghai and Beijing.

There was little in Snow's background to suggest that he would come
to play a major role in a world-changing revolutionary movement
such as Maoism. On the contrary, he grew up a happy-go-lucky son
of the American Midwest, brimming with establishment confidence.
Until McCarthyism made his life professionally impossible in the US,
he was blessed by good luck and conventional approbation. As a
child, he was an Eagle Scout, at college he was president of his
fraternity. He had an amiable personality and refined good looks –
delicately cast features, dark, closely curled hair, an easy smile. He
moved to New York in his early twenties with his older brother
Howard, to make a career in advertising. 'I went to New York with
the firm intention of making a hundred thousand dollars before I
was thirty,' Snow later remembered, so as to have the leisure 'to
produce great masterpieces for which I felt the literary world was
waiting'.[11] When, a year or two later, he decided to take a round-the-
world trip before settling down, he made a smooth career switch to
journalism. On reaching Hawai'i, he managed to sell a travel article
to finance a vacation there; he then scammed his way on to Japan,
by successfully stowing away on a liner. A jovial article about the
escapade sold well, but was less auspicious for the cabin boy who
had failed to report his presence: he was dismissed by the shipping
company and reduced to beggary.[12]

In 1928, Snow landed in Shanghai. China held him for the next
thirteen years, as he made the transition from head of advertising for

a local newspaper to fully accredited correspondent, with opportunities to travel around China's railways and to rub shoulders with the great and the good of China's new Nationalist government, including its generalissimo-president, Chiang Kai-shek himself. 'Thus your brother enters into the field of Far Eastern journalism,' he wrote cheerfully to Howard, back in America. 'Huzzahs and banzais!' In 1930s Shanghai, luxury seemed ludicrously cheap to an American with a handful of dollars. 'One can live in such style over here on so little,' he told his mother in a letter. 'For instance, I can have a rickshaw available day or night for $24 a month – $12 in our money ... Such are the allurements of the Orient.' He obtained an excellent personal cook-orderly for only $10 a month – a tenth of the cost in New York.[13]

But there was a restlessness to Edgar Snow, too. He had abandoned a conventional American path to success (aspiring to partnership in a New York firm, early marriage, children) for the far less certain career of freelance writer, halfway across the world. In China, he was regularly offered respectable office jobs: editorships, advertising directorships, consular posts. He turned them all down to protect his freedom to travel and write. In 1930, not long after his arrival in Shanghai, he wrote a sharp article satirising the smug, caged existence of Shanghai expatriates that riled many of his fellow Shanghailanders. While most Westerners lived existences rich in marmalade and breaded cutlets, and low on Chinese reality, Snow was horrified by the poverty and famine that he witnessed on his trips around China. By the early 1930s, therefore, he craved something more than the world of foreign privilege that he inhabited in Shanghai – even though he gladly returned to it (in need of razors, coffee and milk) after one of his journeys on China's wild side. Fortunately for Snow, the ideal intermediary to introduce him to the 'real China' lived on his doorstep: Song Qingling, the Chinese Communist Party's most alluringly brilliant fellow traveller.

Song Qingling was a curious combination of privilege and steel. She was the daughter of Charlie Song, an ordained Methodist minister turned Shanghai comprador who had grown rich supplying needy Western businessmen in Shanghai. Thanks to her father's cosmopolitanism, Qingling enjoyed a childhood of gilded freedom exceptional even for the daughters of similarly wealthy Chinese. Charlie Song was

unusual in being determined to give his daughters as good an education as his sons; Qingling first attended Shanghai's best foreign
missionary school, and later Wesleyan College in Georgia. She and her
two sisters, Ailing and Meiling, thus became the first Chinese girls to
study in the United States. This triumvirate were taught from a young
age a sense of entitlement, but also independence and self-reliance. If
they suffered from homesickness, it was expunged from their reminiscences, which told only of accomplishment and fun: all three not only
graduated *summa cum laude* but also threw themselves into midnight
feasts and extracurriculars such as student journalism. Qingling penned
earnest essays about China's need for reform ('Chinese politics, for
many hundred years, have been characterised by nepotism and dishon-
esty'); her younger sister Meiling, who later married Chiang Kai-shek,
founded a society newspaper (the profits were spent on ice cream and
salted peanuts).[14]

Qingling returned to Asia in 1913, a year after the conclusion of the
republican revolution that had brought some 2,000 years of dynastic
history to an end. The Song family became, in many ways, the aristocracy of the revolution. Charlie Song was a long-time supporter of
Sun Yat-sen, the mercurial leader of the revolutionary movement.
During Sun's long, hard years in political exile between 1895 and 1911,
while uprising after uprising failed, Charlie served as Sun's backer and
secretary: he poured money into Sun's revolutionary organisations;
he chaired midnight meetings for insurrectionists. After the victory
of the revolution and founding of the Republic in 1912, Qingling
became Sun's personal secretary. The consequences were the stuff of
cliché. When the two fell in love and her parents refused to allow her
to marry Sun (he was twenty-six years her senior), Qingling escaped
from her room down a ladder positioned by a sympathetic maidservant
and ran off to join her beloved in Tokyo. Following a legally sketchy
divorce (for almost three decades, Sun had been married to a girl from
his village, who had borne him a son and two daughters), the two of
them were married the day after she arrived in Japan.

Song Qingling's marriage turned her into a key political player.
Until Sun's untimely death from cancer in 1925, she devoted herself
to his causes, serving as his interpreter, secretary and tireless supporter;
she miscarried her one pregnancy while escaping from an assassination
attempt on him. In widowhood, she was dedicated to protecting his

legacy. For two years, from 1925 to 1927, she worked with Sun's self-appointed successor, Chiang Kai-shek, during his revolutionary alliance with the Chinese Communist Party. After Chiang brutally purged the Communists in early 1927, she leaned strongly leftwards. On returning from a year's exile in Moscow in 1928, she put her energies and talents – her cosmopolitanism, her charm, her beauty, her political untouchability (she was one of the few left-wing public figures whom Chiang Kai-shek did not dare terrorise; his wife, Qingling's adoring younger sister, would have given him hell for it) – into burnishing the image of Communism. Qingling was a living advertisement of the movement's ability to recruit physically and intellectually glamorous individuals. But she was also a skilled recruiter herself. Time and again she directed towards the Communists the educated Chinese whom the party needed to run its state. And always with an eye to international image, she drew to the cause useful, impressionable foreigners. Edgar Snow was one of her best-known finds; another was Sidney Rittenberg. A former American GI who stayed on in China for thirty years after 1949, Rittenberg masterminded English-language propaganda broadcasts for the People's Republic and translated Mao's works into English, despite spending two periods (six and ten years, respectively) in solitary confinement during that time, both times on Mao's orders. He remains an internationally influential advocate for China today.

Edgar Snow first encountered Qingling in 1932, when he was dispatched to write a newspaper profile of her. The woman he met was approaching forty; retaining the figure and complexion of a woman in her early twenties, she was intellectually and socially at the peak of her powers. Although painfully shy as a young woman, she had acquired through her decade as Sun's wife impressive social assurance. Despite her Communist sympathies, Qingling remained reassuringly cosmopolitan and pleasure-loving: she kept her house in Shanghai's French concession immaculate, decorated with paintings, scrolls and flowers. Until it became politically incorrect after 1949, she preferred to speak English even with Chinese friends. She kept an extensive record collection (she was particularly fond of European opera), and hosted dance parties. She liked to be called Suzy – the sobriquet she had picked up at school – rather than the Chinese Qingling, or the redoubtable Madame Sun Yat-sen. Her lunch and dinner parties brought together Chinese intellectual glitterati, travel-ling foreign celebrities and probable, prestigious leftist sympathisers. A photograph taken during one such gathering in 1933 speaks of her skills as a society hostess. There are the writers Lu Xun (the founding figure in Chinese modernism) and Lin Yutang (for decades, the best-known literary ambassador of Chinese culture into English); the educa-tionalist Cai Yuanpei (president of China's first modern university, Beida, and patron of China's cultural renaissance, the New Culture movement of the 1910s); George Bernard Shaw, passing through Shanghai; Harold Isaacs, a left-leaning American journalist; and Agnes Smedley, a radical bohemian American novelist and Comintern agent who, partly under Song Qingling's influence, would later travel out to Mao's state and become a devoted biographer of Chinese Communism. Soon after meeting Qingling, Rewi Alley, a New Zealand educationalist who after 1949 became one of the loudest foreign cheer-leaders for Mao's China, agreed to keep a secret radio receiver in his house so that she could contact Mao's Central Committee whenever necessary.[15] Beneath her cultured sophistication, though, Qingling was tough and, some have alleged, a paid-up Comintern spy.

Snow and Song Qingling's first meeting took place in the Chocolate Shop, one of the favourite haunts of Shanghai's International Settlement, at 883 Bubbling Well Road – the hub of expatriate society. They started with lunch then, as Snow fell increasingly under her spell, stayed for afternoon tea and cakes, until dinnertime. He admired her 'modesty', her 'conscience', her 'moral and physical courage', her 'sharp scalpel for hypocrites' and 'her youthfulness and beauty'.[16] She was, he summarised in a letter to his sister, a 'radiant personality ... an extraordinary woman, warmly human, indisputably sincere, intel-lectually brilliant, a hater of deceit and hypocrisy, but magnanimous as a Gandhi'.[17] She was idealistic but also fun, camping up her pronun-ciation of Chiang Kai-shek's title: the Gen-eral-issssimo, she called him. She managed to seem both passionately engaged in improving China, and disarmingly sceptical about all of China's political actors. 'I have never trusted any Chinese politicians except Dr Sun Yat-sen ... I distrust Mao Zedong less than the others.'[18] She entranced Snow in a maternal way – his own mother had died just two years earlier – and Qingling became both a godmother in his personal life, and a political mentor. When he decided in 1932 to marry Helen Foster,

a good-looking and ambitious young American, Qingling was the first
to know of it – in parental fashion, she hosted a wedding banquet for
them and gifted them a silver American percolator (which they never
worked out how to use). Qingling told him all about the 'Guomindang,
about Sun Yat-sen and his unwritten hopes ... and many other facts
I could never have learned from books', Snow recalled. Over the
coming years, 'she would introduce me to young writers and artists
and fighters who were to make history'.[19] Some of these contacts led
directly to Mao Zedong.

Song Qingling was, in other words, one of the Chinese
Communists' greatest assets: both of the movement, but also
outside it. To preserve her value as a fellow traveller, the CCP did
not permit her to join the party until she was on her deathbed, at
which point she was granted membership as extreme unction. Her
skill was to present herself as a humane, objective democrat, leaving
charmed audiences to assume that the political cause she supported –
the Chinese Communists – must espouse the same goals. In reality,
she did not tread such an impartial path. Although she told Snow
that she distrusted all politicians, Mao Zedong included, by 1937
she had become a covert stakeholder in Mao's revolution, sending
him $50,000 of her savings – almost $750,000 by today's rates.[20]

In 1933, Edgar Snow moved from Shanghai to begin his married
life in Beijing, after a honeymoon on Bali (among other places). When
the newlyweds reached Beijing they continued their radical chic life –
through the worst years of the American Depression – in bourgeois-
bohemian luxury. They rented a small compound (with room for three
servants, whom they paid collectively $40 a month), complete with
'authentic red gates, a moon door, a high compound wall ... and
inside a little courtyard where flowers bloom and some fruit trees that
are a cloud of blossom'.[21] Helen befriended the Dakotan proprietor
of a designer clothing and jewellery store, Helen Burton, enabling
her to satisfy her appetite for luxury by working as an out-of-hours
fashion model for Burton's furs, ball gowns and jewellery. She would
twirl about Beijing's ballrooms to Viennese tunes ('the orchestra always
played waltzes when I appeared'), to encourage envious onlookers to
order similar gowns. A few pieces she could not resist acquiring herself:
a leopard-skin coat, a cape made of delicate ermine belly fur. In 1930s

Beijing, she later reminisced with regret, the two best waltzers (and incidentally the two most attractive men) were an Italian Fascist and an aristocratic Nazi. Helen had no choice but to suspend her political principles: 'An apolitical bridge came down when the Viennese waltz began, and we maintained a silent truce till it was over.'[22] The Snows' beloved white greyhound, Gobi, was a gift from another Nazi sympathiser, the Swedish explorer Sven Hedin (Edgar's own politics were assuredly anti-Nazi and anti-Fascist). For further diversion, the couple bought 'a sleek Mongol racing pony' and became regulars at the Beijing races. A whirl of social teas, dinner parties and polo filled in any remaining time; when Beijing became too hot or dusty, the Snows repaired at the weekend to temples in the cooler western hills (still a favoured haunt for champagne-soaked expatriate weekend picnics today).[23]

At the same time, the Snows ventured into leftist politics (their activities sometimes financed by their racing pony's wins): their compound became a haven for radical artists and for demonstrating students from nearby Yenching University, where Snow taught journalism. Several were, unbeknown to the Snows, card-carrying Communists who allowed the couple to imagine that they were the American dynamos behind an upsurge of patriotic student protest in late 1935. One of these, an enigmatic 25-year-old party member called David (Qiwei) Yu left Beijing in 1936 to continue his underground work in north-east China disguised in one of Edgar's English tailored tweed suits – to avoid, the rather questionable assumption went, drawing too much attention to himself.[24] This David Yu would have an unexpected long-range impact on the Chinese Communist revolution. His first, common-law wife was a library clerk called Li Yunhe. Although the relationship dissolved within a year or two, she – at least partly under his tutelage – later also made her way out to the Communist north-west, after a brief career interlude in Shanghai as a B-movie actress called Lan Ping. In Yan'an, she changed her name one more time, to Jiang Qing, on becoming Mao's fourth and final wife. In 1966, she would help him launch his last great purge: the Cultural Revolution.

When Snow expressed his desire to visit the new Communist state in north-west China, David Yu and Song Qingling set about making it possible. As it turned out, Mao had earlier sent a request to the party in Shanghai for a foreign personal doctor, and a friendly journalist to help with international PR. When Snow visited Shanghai in early May of 1936, Song Qingling appointed him to the latter vacancy; a Lebanese-American medic called George Hatem would accompany him.[25] Liu Shaoqi – the head of the Communist underground in the north-east, and David Yu's immediate superior, who would in the early 1940s become Mao's second in command and play a central role in the creation of Mao's personality cult – approved the trip. A Beijing professor (and secret Communist agent) gave Snow his passport to the north-west: a letter of introduction to Mao written in invisible ink.[26]

On 15 June, febrile from eleventh-hour jabs – smallpox, typhoid, typhus, cholera – Snow departed his comfortable Beijing expatriate life for an adventure in the north-west. Helen described a cheerful farewell:

> Ed petted the bouncing puppies ... Our dear sweet Mongol coolie, Ch'en, was in a third rickshaw with the luggage, and Gobi rode in the seat with me as always ... we almost missed the train bound for [Xi'an]. I put [his] nasal oil in Ed's pocket as he climbed aboard. He stood on the steps, grinning as if he were Caesar at one of his triumphs, and saluted: 'Heil, Hitler!'[27]

She would hear almost nothing more from him until he wrote in September, from the Communist base, requesting milk chocolate, coffee and *Reader's Digest*. A month later he turned up back on their doorstep, with a jovial 'Mrs Livingstone, I presume?'[28]

How to account for the success of *Red Star Over China*? For one, it was a classic adventure story, playing out on two levels: Snow's own danger-packed quest for the Communist state, and the story of the Chinese Communists' battle for survival. But its genius went beyond that. It humanised the Chinese Communists, giving remote revolutionaries characteristics that seemed comfortably familiar to Anglo-American readers: humour, candour, approachability, statesmanship, patriotism.[29]

The entire book was a fantastic scoop: Edgar Snow was the first journalist (Chinese or foreign) to gain this level of access to what would become arguably the biggest story of twentieth-century Asia: the

Chinese Communist state. He drew attention to his derring-do in the book's opening: 'Such was the strength of years of anti-Communist propaganda in a country whose press is as rigidly censored and regimented as that of Italy or Germany [that] there had been perhaps no greater mystery among nations, no more confused an epic, than the story of Red China ... isolated by a news blockade as effective as a stone fortress ... more inaccessible than Tibet.'[30] 'I do not know', he told one of his editors, 'that anything of the sort has occurred elsewhere in modern journalistic history, for the situation is so unusual that it can scarcely have had a counterpart.'[31]

The journey out alone was fraught with exhilaration and danger as Snow passed through the iniquities of Nationalist China to break his story about the 'real' Red China. The peril was heightened by the melodramatic excitement – leavened by ironic self-awareness – of passing through a network of Communist agents. Underground party activity in Shanghai, where the CCP's organisation was strongest, was marked by brutality: the CCP's assassination team, the Red Brigade (sometimes called the 'dog killers' squad'), murdered and buried dozens of 'rebellious elements' under a pleasant grassy area in residential Shanghai.[32] Those activists encountered by Snow, by contrast, were larkish cosmopolitans. In Xi'an – the north-western city from which Snow set out for the Communist area – his contact was a Pastor Wang, a tubby Communist theologian educated at St John's University in Shanghai (one of China's most prestigious universities, with an anglophone curriculum). The two men identified each other by producing matching halves of a card containing English verses. Next, Snow encountered an underground agent named Liu Ding ('call me Charles'), with a fondness for golfing tweeds. Then, while on a visit to some ancient ruins, Snow was importuned by a man dressed as a Nationalist official. 'Look at me! Look at me!' he smirked with Cat-in-the-Hat-ish elan, winking at Snow, before revealing that he was Deng Fa, the Red Army's chief of secret police – a man with a $50,000 price on his head. He 'danced with pleasure ... He was irrepressible ... he literally hugged me repeatedly', while offering Snow his pictures, his diary, his horse. 'What a Chinese! What a Red-bandit!' Snow whooped to himself.[33] (Deng Fa was notorious within Chinese Communist circles for the sadistic relish with which he carried out the Chinese Communists' first internal bloodletting in 1930, in which thousands were accused of being 'anti-Bolshevik elements' and tortured; at least several hundred were executed.)

The landscape – which Snow describes as almost lunar in its strangeness – heightened his sense of adventure. He described 'an infinite variety of queer, embattled shapes – hills like great castles, like rows of mammoth, nicely rounded scones, like ranges torn by some giant hand, leaving behind the imprint of angry fingers. Fantastic, incredible, and sometimes frightening shapes, a world configurated by a mad god – and yet sometimes a world also of strange surrealist beauty.'[34] Politically and geographically, Snow felt the excitement of the first space travellers.

Throughout his four months in the Communist area, Snow was given apparently free access to the leadership and rank and file. He was bowled over first of all by Zhou Enlai, Mao's chief lieutenant (and a decent English-speaker): 'a pure intellectual ... a scholar turned insurrectionist'. Snow described Zhou's almost feminine good looks, with a figure once as 'willowy as a girl's' and 'large, warm, deep-set eyes'; but he spoke mildly, leaving an impression 'of a cool, logical and empirical mind', bereft of fanaticism. Peng Dehuai, one of the top Communist generals (later put in charge of Chinese intervention in the Korean War, then purged in the late 1950s for criticising the famine-producing Great Leap Forward, and maltreated to death during the Cultural Revolution), was 'a gay, laughter-loving man, in excellent health' with a great fondness for children. Zhu De, another general, 'plays a good game of table tennis and a wistful game of basketball'. Snow nicknamed the commissioner of education, Xu Deli, Santa Claus.[35] The lower orders, Snow found, 'were wonderful ... I had never before seen so much personal dignity in any Chinese youngsters ... cheerful, gay, energetic and loyal – the living spirit of an astonishing crusade of youth'.[36] They were disciplined (over half the Red Army, Snow estimated, were virgins), industrious, temperate, self-reliant (Snow noted only a handful of Russian rifles, all of which dated from the 1917 revolution).[37] And they were beloved by non-Communist locals. 'Tactics are important,' observed Peng Dehuai, 'but we could not exist if the majority of the people did not support us. We are nothing but the fist of the people beating their oppressors!'[38] The Red Army, Snow was told, 'is a revolutionary army ... is anti-Japanese ... helps the peasants

... Here we are all equals ... In the White [Nationalist] Army the soldiers are treated like slaves.'[39] These disarmingly informal but puritanical patriots, fighting for liberty, equality and self-determin-ation, resembled nothing more than the Chinese incarnation of the American dream.

The centrepiece of Snow's book – and the main source of biograph-ical narrative to future Maoist movements – was the portrait of Mao himself: relaxed, accessible (despite the $250,000 price that Chiang Kai-shek had put on his head) and dignified:

> a gaunt, rather Lincolnesque figure [with] an intellectual face of great shrewdness ... undeniably you feel a certain force of destiny in him ... a kind of solid elemental vitality [but with] no ritual of hero-worship built up around him. I never met a Chinese Red who drivelled 'our-great-leader' phrases ... He had the simplicity and naturalness of the Chinese peasant, with a lively sense of humour and a love of rustic laughter ... And yet Mao is an accomplished scholar of Classical Chinese, an omnivorous reader, a deep student of philosophy and history, a good speaker, a man with an unusual memory and extraor-dinary powers of concentration, an able writer, careless in his personal habits and appearance but astonishingly meticulous about details of duty, a man of tireless energy, and a military and political strategist of considerable genius ... You feel that whatever extraordinary there is in this man grows out of the uncanny degree to which he synthesises and expresses the urgent demands of millions of Chinese, and especially the peasantry ... If these demands and the movement which is pressing them forward are the dynamics which can regenerate China, then in this deeply historical sense Mao Zedong may possibly become a very great man.[40]

Snow found no thuggery to Mao – only rational, thoughtful discipline: 'class hatred is for him probably fundamentally a mechanism in the bulwark of his philosophy, rather than a basic impulse to action ... Mao impressed me as a man of considerable depth of feeling. I remember that his eyes moistened once or twice when speaking of dead comrades, or recalling incidents in his youth ... when some starving peasants were beheaded in his province for demanding food from the yamen.'[41] 'We don't kill captured [enemies],' Snow was told.

'We educate them and give them a chance to repent.'[42] Snow was also careful to remind readers that Mao was the new father of a baby girl; that his only luxury was a mosquito net and that he barely cared what he ate, as long as it contained chilli, or what he wore – his trousers were riddled with cigarette burns.

In *Red Star*, Snow seemed to take Mao's every utterance on trust. 'He appears to be quite free from symptoms of megalomania ... to be sincere, honest, and truthful.'[43] For nights on end, Snow crouched on a stool in Mao's cave, taking down his story word for word: his thirst for education, his appealing rebelliousness, his love of physical fitness, his creative contribution to Marxism (recognising the peasants as a revolutionary force). Mao portrayed himself as both an ardent patriot ('the fundamental issue before the Chinese people today is the struggle against Japanese imperialism') and a sympathetic internationalist ('When China really wins her independence, then legitimate foreign trading interests will enjoy more opportunities than ever before').[44] Mao fed to Snow a neat teleology of recent Chinese and Chinese Communist history, running through the Revolution of 1911, the May Fourth Movement of 1919, the founding of the Communist Party in 1921, the White Terror of 1927, the creation of Communist base areas in the late 1920s, and a thrilling narrative of the Long March, including – most celebrated of all – the heroic crossing of the Dadu River in Sichuan where a single Red Army daredevil crawled across an iron-chain bridge and put the enemy to flight with a single, well-aimed hand grenade, permitting the rest of the force to follow safely. Snow's retelling shaped Mao's words into a third-person narrative that combined the authoritativeness of history with novelistic colour. 'Never before had the Sichuanese seen Chinese fighters like these – men for whom soldiering was not just a rice-bowl, but youths ready to commit suicide to win! ... Suddenly, on the southern shore, their comrades began to scream with joy. "Long live the Red Army! Long live the revolution! Long live the thirty heroes of Dadu River!" For the Whites were withdrawing, were in pell-mell flight!'[45] Oral histories over the past ten years have cast doubt on Mao/Snow's heroic centrepiece, but for decades it transferred through English- and Chinese-language accounts, turning the Long March into an epic Communist triumph against adversity. The final flourish in Snow's account portrayed Mao as an intellectual and a poet: 'a rebel who can write verse as well as lead a crusade'. 'Could such people really be thinking seriously of war?' Snow asked rhetorically, implicitly denying any streak of ruthless totalitarianism.[46]

Skilfully guided by Mao and his comrades, Snow presented the Chinese Communists as persecuted innocents, as appealing underdogs: as patriots first and Communists second, willing and able to fight the Japanese, constrained only by Nationalist repression. Throughout his time in the north-west, Snow failed to meet a single uncongenial individual: everywhere he was greeted by 'cheerful smiles' and 'kindly eyes'. The Communist state represented the most perfectly harmonious community: its inhabitants danced, acted and sang – sometimes hilarious ditties, such as one about a revolutionary chilli pepper – and 'what discipline they had seemed almost entirely self-imposed'. The only criticism he heard voiced was from a Communist engineer who complained that the workers in local industries 'spend entirely too much time *singing!*' 'I often had a queer feeling', Snow mused, 'among the Reds that I was in the midst of a host of schoolboys, engaged in a life of violence because some strange design of history had made this seem infinitely more important to them than football games, textbooks, love or the main concerns of youth in other countries ... It has been their sincere and sharply felt propagandist aim to shake, to arouse, the millions of rural China to their responsibilities in society'.[47] Thanks to the Communists, who had brought education, electricity and tax rebates, the peasantry were now 'standing erect in a state of consciousness, after two millenniums of sleep'.[48] In Yan'an, Snow wanted to see – and did see – a brand-new China, led by Mao.

By the end of Snow's account, Mao – this hitherto elusive Communist – was, as one analysis nicely put it, both 'humanised' and 'larger than life': the ideal springboard for a leadership cult.[49] Snow seems to have been at least a little in love with Mao, indicated by the range of affectionate nicknames by which he referred to him in letters: Maussy, Mausie, Mauzzie (Helen Snow feminised him to Maizie).[50] In all, Snow concluded at the end, 'I lived a holiday life, riding, bathing, and playing tennis' with various commissars (described as 'interesting, lovable, good-looking') on a court mown close by goats and sheep. When night fell, he entertained himself by teaching the politburo and its wives rummy and poker. His hosts ensured he ate well, too: although living in one of the poorest regions of China, he gained weight during his stay. 'The Reds', summarised Snow, 'were direct, frank, simple, undevious, and scientific-minded. They rejected nearly all the old Chinese philosophy that was the basis of what was once Chinese civilization ... Most of the time I felt completely at ease in their company as if I were with some of my countrymen.' Little surprise, then, that Snow felt depressed as he left. 'I felt that I was not going home, but leaving it.'[51]

Let there be no doubt: Snow's work was groundbreaking. He was the first foreign journalist to risk the trek out to the forbidden 'Red' state; he invested much time and energy in bringing an untold story out into the world. Other encounters corroborate elements of Snow's portrait of Mao. Throughout his career the Helmsman was renowned for his informality in interviews: summoning his inter-locutors to his bedside, or swimming pools; dressing in patched clothes or trousers studded with cigarette burns, pyjamas or swim-ming trunks. Long after their deaths, both Mao and Zhou would be fondly remembered by nervous young interpreters for the efforts they made to set these functionaries at their ease. As Snow was repelled by his first-hand experience of the corruption, indiscipline and brutality of Nationalist China, his enthusiastic response to the orderly idealism he perceived in the Communist north-west is under-standable.

But the credibility of Red Star is compromised by the vested inter-ests of its author and its subjects. For different reasons, both sides needed the book to be a global smash. In 1936, Snow needed to write a book that would secure his financial future, that would generate royalties and earn him a reputation as a cutting-edge commentator on Far Eastern affairs. To achieve this, the book had to be both sensa-tional and likeable. He thus excised inconvenient details, for example omitting the tight controls to which Mao, Zhou and other leaders subjected his work. First, there was on-site censorship: Snow's English transcript of the translator's version of Mao's words being translated into Chinese, corrected by Mao, then translated back into English. Then, as Snow toiled on turning his notes into copy through the winter of 1936, his interviewees continued to send him a stream of amendments: telling him to remove any trace of dissent with Comintern policy, to expunge any praise for out-of-favour Chinese intellectuals, to tone down criticism of political enemies turned allies, to talk up anti-Japanese patriotism.[52]

The CCP also needed to seem as congenial as possible, for the sake of the international PR they anticipated and indeed received through *Red Star*. Snow's account of the north-western Chinese state turned out to be deeply formative of favourable international perceptions of wartime Communism, and of Mao more generally, over the coming decades. This positive impression of the Communists at a particular historical juncture merged into longer-range assumptions about Mao's revolution and state. Snow's judgements seem imprinted on Mark Selden's *The Yenan Way* (1971), a classic work of late-1960s–early-1970s left-wing US scholarship that argued (in the context of widespread disgust at US foreign policy in Vietnam and China) forcefully for the democratic, cooperative nature of the wartime CCP state, and by implicit extension for the regime that Mao founded in 1949.

It should be recalled that Snow's visit in 1936 took place years before knowledge of events that removed so much of the shine from the 'golden age' of Chinese Communism: the Communist state's reliance on secret opium cultivation and trade starting in the early 1940s and which, as we have seen, by 1945 provided more than 40 per cent of state revenue; the 'Rectification' of 1942, the first centrally coordinated campaign using public terror and humiliation to suppress intellectual dissent, in which Mao demonstrated his mastery of Stalin's own techniques of manipulating internal party struggles. Nonetheless, Snow's seductively jaunty account also excised or obscured clear instances of ruthlessness or brutality from the CCP's recent past. Mao was depicted as a doting husband and father (recall that his relationship with He Zizhen had begun adulterously in 1928, while he was still married to his second wife, Yang Kaihui). Omitted was the bloody 'Anti-Bolshevik' purge orchestrated by Mao in south-east China in 1930. Unmentioned was the CCP's recent maltreatment of non-useful foreigners: between 1932 and 1936, at least three foreign missionaries captured by CCP units were either killed or died of maltreatment; several more were captured, publicly vilified as 'big-nose imperialists' and held for ransom.[53]

In another strange turn of events, *Red Star* created Mao as a national and global political personality before there was such a thing in the Chinese Communist Party as Maoism (or, in the party's preferred phrase, Mao Zedong Thought). For when Snow visited Yan'an, Mao was only recently installed in a position of significant leadership, but he was not even first among equals. He was a practical man of military strategy; ideologically, he was weak, derivative and deferred to Moscow-educated ideologues. In 1937, the year after Snow's visit, Mao's path to power would be even more strongly challenged by the arrival in Yan'an of Moscow's choice for leader, Wang Ming.

Between 1949 and 1976, the CCP created a lavish and exhaustively orchestrated hospitality machine, designed to distract from or conceal discordant realities, and to cater to the whims of carefully chosen foreign guests, in the hope and expectation that, on leaving the Chinese state, they would proselytise the virtues of the Communists and their government. In this, they drew but also elaborated on the machinery built through the 1920s and '30s by the Soviet Union. Although the leaders of the Communist state in north-west China could not offer the same luxuries as the post-1949 PRC – the flower-laden welcoming party at Beijing airport, the invitation to the rostrum at Tiananmen Square, the fireworks displays, the five-star accommodation – they did their best. On arriving at the walled capital of the Communist base area, Snow was treated like a head of state, greeted by welcoming banners, a military band, and the highest-ranking leaders in residence. 'It was the first time I had been greeted by the entire cabinet of a government, the first time a whole city had been turned out to welcome me,' Snow recalled. 'The effect produced on me was highly emotional.'[54] Although Snow's diet was dominated by standard-issue millet rations, he was provided with freshly baked bread, clean towels, hot water, soap – and at a moment of intense caffeine craving, 'rich brown coffee and sugar'. His benefactor, Snow openly admitted, 'had won my heart'.[55] While in the north-west, Snow was only rarely allowed to pay for what he consumed: when he later filed his expense claims to one of his newspapers, he revealed that he had managed to spend well under $100 over four months. 'You are a foreign guest,' one cook explained, when Snow tried to pay for a feast of scrambled eggs, steamed rolls, boiled millet, cabbage and roast pork, 'and you have business with our Chairman, Mao.'[56]

There was, moreover, substantial continuity between the personnel masterminding Snow's trip and those who would handle foreigners in the PRC after 1949. Chief of staff was Zhou Enlai, who through the 1930s effected a remarkable transformation in image, from underground party hatchet man to chief of 'United Front' work, charming almost everyone he encountered: Henry Kissinger, Richard Nixon, Ho Chi Minh, Prince Norodom Sihanouk of Cambodia. Martha Gellhorn, who encountered him as the CCP representative in the Nationalist wartime capital of Chongqing, confessed 'she would have followed Zhou to the ends of the world had he beckoned'. (Her more sceptical husband, Ernest Hemingway, observed that 'he does a fine job of selling the Communist standpoint on anything that comes up'.) During the Marshall Mission, the failed negotiations between the Communists, Nationalists and Americans at the end of the Second World War, the always affable Zhou – a favourite cocktail-party guest at the US embassy – convinced the Americans that he was their 'kind of guy': that Mao wanted an American-style democracy and, given the choice, would prefer America to Moscow as a holiday destination. By the end of this charm offensive, General Marshall had leaked substantial intelligence to Zhou and threatened to stop funding Chiang Kai-shek's preparations for civil war against Mao.[57] At the epochal Bandung Conference of 1955, Zhou quelled fears of Chinese Communist imperialism before an audience of dignitaries from almost thirty Asian, African and Middle Eastern countries, in a soothing speech written during a lunch break (to replace the stiff set piece that he had prepared). His successful address massively enhanced the PRC's prestige in the Non-Aligned Movement and decolonising world. When foreign pilgrims visited China between the 1950s and 1970s, all craved an audience with the handsome, Paris-educated Zhou. An infatuated Nixon fully wanted to *be* Zhou: the two of them, he told Kissinger on the eve of his 1972 rapprochement with China, were quite remarkably alike. Both had 'strong convictions, came up through adversity. [Are] cool. Unflappable … tough and bold … willing to take chances [and] subtle.'[58]

Behind these triumphs stood an operation of military discipline (although the workings of the system remain opaque, many of Communist China's most trusted diplomats and foreign affairs operatives came up through the army). Zhou was obsessed with diplomatic precision, coining catchphrases that reflected his preoccupation. 'In diplomacy,' he once famously said, 'there's no such thing as a small detail', and he urged his operatives to maintain the 'five diligences': diligent eyes, ears, mouth, hands and feet. 'Establish friendly feelings with the foreign media, make friends with every single one of them, and form close friendships ... know the enemy and know oneself ... do things gradually and make use of every bit of time and space.'[59] Already by the late 1930s, Zhou was running a complex network of operatives in political and cultural circles across China and Asia. One of his great success stories was Hu Yuzhi, who helped translate *Red Star Over China* into Chinese in the autumn–winter of 1937. Directed by Zhou, Hu concealed his underground party membership until he was on his deathbed in 1986, and for decades maintained a useful cover as a prestigious, but non-aligned, intellectual, who deployed his cultural capital as an independent to introduce key Mao-infused texts to those outside the party (in addition to *Red Star*, Mao's 'On Protracted War').[60] Again following Zhou's direction, Hu (according to one British colonial official, 'a little homunculus of a man with bright eyes like a marmoset') served as a Communist plant in the Nationalist propaganda bureau in China, and then went to Singapore, to promote the patriotism of the CCP to rich and influential Overseas Chinese (ethnic Chinese migrants and their descendants) such as the left-wing pineapple mogul Tan Kah-kee.[61] The latter's support vastly increased the CCP's credibility among the Chinese diaspora, before and after 1949 and, more practically, their foreign currency remittances back to the motherland.

Snow's path towards CCP sympathiser was facilitated not only by Song Qingling but also by friendship with Huang Hua, one of his students at Yenching University. In the 1930s, as an activist in student politics – and underground CCP member – Huang had got friendly with the Snows in Beijing. On the eve of organising a student demonstration, Edgar had gifted him a box of chocolates, joking that they had tear gas for centres, in case the students needed to defend themselves from police attack. In 1936, when Song Qingling engineered that fateful invitation to the north-west, Snow quickly asked for Huang to accompany him as a translator. Although not accredited as such, the charming, jovial Huang became a key collaborator in the making of *Red Star*. In the abundant photographs that survive of Huang's public career at Yan'an and across subsequent decades, he is easily recognisable by his beaming smile. Snow was constitutionally somewhat earnest, so it is quite plausible that the disarming good humour of many of the conversations reported in *Red Star* was seeded by the amiable Huang's translations. After Snow headed back to Beijing with his bag of redacted notes, Huang stayed in the north-west and became an indispensable part of the CCP's international PR machine. He served as the go-to translator for leadership encounters with VIPP (Very Important Potential Propagandists): journalists, academics, as well as the US military observer group to Yan'an in 1944. His role – as a tough patriot with an affable, cosmopolitan veneer – was always to sell the idea of the CCP without seeming to sell it, and he did it well. In May 1949, he was entrusted with one of the most sensitive missions in PRC history: making contact with John Leighton Stuart, the US ambassador to Nationalist China, to discuss possible relations between the CCP and the US and an aid package to a future Chinese Communist state. Huang Hua deployed his personal contacts to the maximum, as an alumnus of Yenching, at which Stuart had been president. (This particular overture foundered, however, when the Americans refused Mao's demand that they abandon entirely Chiang Kai-shek and his Nationalist government.)[62] Later, during the Cultural Revolution, Huang was the only Chinese ambassador left in post, in Cairo. At every point of his extraordinary career through seventy years of turbulent CCP history, he remained on-message, never diverting from whichever party mission he was executing.

In Communist China in 1936, therefore, Snow encountered some of China's most brilliant, determined and, when necessary, charming politicians and strategists. History would prove them many times more politically effective than the Nationalist politicians with whom Snow had become familiar during his Shanghai years.

When in 1938 Zhou Sufei, a strikingly beautiful left-leaning Shanghai movie actress, well schooled in the classic progressive texts of the time, left Shanghai for Yan'an, she was familiar with Snow's articles about the north-west in pictorials: 'about the caves, the lessons, the study. Oh, Snow's propaganda was very powerful. Yan'an turned out to be much harder than I expected from Snow's reports. Mao got on so well with Snow and with George Hatem [whom she married, with strong encouragement from Mao and Zhou Enlai for it would keep the useful medic at their side] because he needed them. And he trusted them because Song Qingling had sent them.'

Zhou Sufei's remark about the propaganda value of Snow's book, if anything, underestimates its importance. There is a thriving heritage industry in China built around preserving and propagating the memory of 'friends of China' such as Snow: the 'Three S Society' was founded in the 1980s to celebrate Edgar Snow, Agnes Smedley and Anna Louise Strong, three Americans credited with great achievements in promoting Communist China abroad. *Red Star* in China today retains an almost talismanic quality: entire volumes of essays are dedicated to recounting its impact on international perceptions of Chinese Communism. On a visit to a Mao-era memorabilia flea market in Beijing in 2014, I was quickly approached on my arrival by an excitable Chinese man holding a Chinese-language first edition of *Red Star*, anxious to have his photograph taken with me – apparently the only Caucasian foreigner in the vicinity – as a marker of Sino-Western friendship.

There can be no uncertainty about *Red Star*'s impact since publication. It won Snow a channel of direct communication with President Roosevelt. (Snow had drawn the US government's attention to the book by sending the ambassador to China the transcripts of his interviews with Mao.)[63] Among rebels in Japan, South Korea, India, Nepal, Western Europe and the US during the 1950s, 1960s and 1970s, it remained core reading on China and the Chinese revolution. The professional study of China polarised in the 1960s and '70s: between the 'establishment' represented by men like John K. Fairbank, Harvard's hugely influential first professor of modern Chinese history, and young radicals like Jonathan Mirsky and Mark Selden. The latter reviled US foreign policy in South East Asia and China and saw older scholarly generations as propping up American assumptions about the region that had led to the Vietnam War and US refusal to recognise the PRC. *Red Star Over China* remained one of the few books that had credibility on both sides of this divide. Fairbank affirmed it as a 'classic', while Selden cited it in his own 1971 analysis (*The Yenan Way*) of 1940s Yan'an as a mass democracy.[64] In 1968, *Red Star* changed the life of a young Chinese-American called Alex Hing, then a 22-year-old petty criminal and karate fan in San Francisco's Chinatown.

> Youth in general in the US were starting to come of age, starting to oppose the US's sterile culture. But in Chinatown the situation was worse than elsewhere: we grew up in a very repressive atmosphere, controlled by the Guomindang and Confucianism. I read *The Autobiography of Malcolm X* and *Red Star*, probably back to back. And

then I became a revolutionary ... It was fascinating how a very small force that believed in a better society, in socialism, would be able to take on the Guomindang under Mao's leadership. He had utter confidence, there was not one doubt in this man's mind that he was going to win. [I thought that] if you implement the revolution scientifically, you can achieve not just the liberation of the country but liberation of the whole world from US oppression.

For Hing, reading *Red Star* began two decades of political agitation in Asian-American radical parties built on Mao's theory and practice of revolution. Although he now devotes himself to less militant disciplines – he is a professional chef and t'ai chi instructor – he remains a devotee of Maoist techniques. 'I moved into a condo a year ago,' he told me in 2015. 'I'm already on the organising committee. I can analyse contradictions straight away. That's what Maoism has done for me.'[65]

From Burma, to Malaya, to India, to Russia, to South Africa, insurgents, nationalists and revolutionaries drew lessons from Snow on partisan warfare and patriotism. In 1942, a group of Indian Communist rebels imprisoned by the British in Agra smuggled into custody a copy of *Red Star* and held daily conferences discussing the book. As one of them remembered almost half a century later, Edgar Snow's Mao was an ordinary, flesh-and-blood man but also 'the most dazzling star of all mankind'.[66] Through the 1960s and '70s, Snow's *Red Star* was a core text for the thousands of educated Indians who went underground to join a Maoist insurgency; the book played the same role in Nepal between the 1970s and 1990s. The instinctive sympathy for Mao and his revolution among parts of the Indian and Nepali left wing today is at least in part a legacy of Snow's 1937 write-up. In 1939, one primary-school teacher in Thailand was sufficiently galvanised by *Red Star* to abandon his family, travel solo to Yan'an (along dangerous clandestine networks via Hong Kong) and devote the rest of his life to the Chinese revolution. '*Red Star Over China* commanded me to come to Yan'an,' he recalled.[67] Reporting from the western Soviet Union in 1943, Edgar Snow encountered three female partisans, still in their teens. He asked them how they had learned to fight the Nazis. 'We bought a book called *Red Star Over China* in Smolensk,' they replied. 'Just about everyone in our squad has read it.'[68] Nelson Mandela, as he prepared to embrace armed struggle in the fight against apartheid in 1961, took copious notes on Snow's 'brilliant' book, concluding that 'it was Mao's determination and non-traditional thinking that had led him to victory'.[69] Snow's account persuaded doctors besides George Hatem, men like Norman Bethune, to travel out to Chinese Communist areas to offer their medical services. It drew to Yan'an sympathetic scholars and writers such as Owen Lattimore and Seymour Topping, and inspired later volumes of reportage, including Jack Belden's *China Shakes the World*.[70]

Yet the most tangible impact of the book was within China. Hu Yuzhi probably risked his life to get the book out in Chinese. With the help of a team of translators, he cranked it through press in late 1937 amid a blaze of war, as Guomindang and Japanese soldiers fought for control of the city in the first battle of the conflict that would become the Second World War.[71] The target audience of the 1937 translation were educated, urban, patriotic youth, and memoir upon memoir attests the reach of the book within the perilous political context of Japanese-occupied Shanghai. Student political groups were mesmerised by *Red Star* and its author; it circulated secretly across universities and high schools in Shanghai, where 50,000 copies were printed; pirate versions spread over China and sinophone Asia. Readers were so avid that some copies were ripped into individual chapters, to enable Snow's words to travel more rapidly. 'Young people loved this red book,' remembered Chen Yiming, seventeen in 1937 and the son of a Shanghai educationalist. 'It pushed them onto the road of resistance and revolution … it entrenched me in my Communist outlook. I threw myself into the revolution … *Red Star Over China* was an essential textbook for [underground party members].'[72]

Journalists extended its reach: the editor of one of Shanghai's biggest cultural newspapers in 1938 penned a pseudonymous article exhorting young people to go to Yan'an, then became a travel agent for the many who responded to his call.[73] Writers, artists, journalists and actors seemed particularly susceptible to its vivid evocation of cheery utopia, citing it as model and inspiration. Hua Junwu, who would become one of the great cartoonists of twentieth-century China, was working as a bank clerk in Shanghai in 1938, when a close friend passed him a copy of the Chinese translation of *Red Star*. 'I read on, and on. The book had me in its grip,' he recalled. '[The north-west] was a pure land, completely different from the old, Nationalist society that I hated so much ... There, the air was fresh, everyone was equal, you could breathe freely, and the CCP and Red Army were speaking out for patriotism and resistance ... When Shanghai was occupied [by the Japanese], Snow and *Red Star Over China* were torches in the darkness. Without telling family, friends or relatives ... I fled Shanghai, embarking on the three-month journey [north-west]. This was the strength that *Red Star Over China* gave me.'[74] In Yan'an, Hua became a cartoonist for the chief Communist newspaper, *Liberation Daily*; after 1949, he became artistic director of the *People's Daily*. (He was denounced in mass-criticism rallies during the Cultural Revolution for his gently satirical cartoons.) Dai Ailian, a Trinidad-born dancer who would become one of the founding figures of modern Chinese ballet, read *Red Star* in the late 1930s while a student in London; it persuaded her to migrate to China after the Communist revolution, despite speaking no Chinese. (She, like Hua, paid a price for her patriotic decision: ostracised during the Cultural Revolution for her foreign origins, she was exiled to labour in the countryside; her husband divorced her.)

Red Star won friends for the CCP all over China; some went to Yan'an, others descended into the party underground. The book was an important weapon in the party's battle for hearts and minds; more important – some readers say – than Mao's own works.[75] As one devoted reader observed: 'I've read the works of Chairman Mao and other leaders, but I've never read a book that described the Chinese revolution as vividly ... and systematically as *Red Star Over China*.'[76] After the Communist takeover, it was deployed once more, to nail the resolve of People's Liberation Army soldiers sent to bring the far south-west under Communist control in 1949.[77]

In Chinese memoirs, the work is somewhat paradoxically acclaimed both for its truth-telling (reporting, for the first time, the 'real' CCP) and for depicting an aspirational model for a future society. In this way, *Red Star* passed out of Snow's control and became a work of idealised socialist realism. The book, recalled one reader, inspired a 'generation of hot-blooded youth ... What was Yan'an like? Was there really a new world there? How were the people there planning and creating a model for a future China? Before *Red Star Over China*, we didn't have a ... vivid, concrete answer to this ... *Red Star* was a shaft of fierce light, illuminating the way forward for young people struggling in the dark.' Far beyond the Mao era, it evolved into a self-help manual: in 1989, one young man wrote an essay about how *Red Star Over China* had helped him through a diagnosis of colon cancer, and to realise his dream of becoming a writer.[78]

The depiction of strong women in *Red Star* was a particular inspiration to the second wave of Chinese feminism in the 1930s, encouraging young women to abandon their conventional domestic lives and head north-west. The younger daughter from a patriarchal Shanghai clan told of how she and her sisters – abandoned by feckless menfolk – were passed a copy of the book by a patriotic teacher. 'I read it over and over; I couldn't put it down. It told me about the Soviet area in China, where men and women lived equally; it opened new horizons for me ... Because Snow was a foreign friend, we trusted that his reporting was the truth. Thanks to this, my and my sisters' minds broke out of the apolitical prison of feudalism. We became patriots [and] CCP members.'[79]

After 1949, the book's message would come full circle. Even though Mao himself never showed any desire to go back to Yan'an, the symbolic birthplace of Maoism, he was so enamoured of his idealised vision – expressed in *Red Star* – of a cooperative, self-reliant Communist utopia in the north-west run on military lines that he tried to impose it across the whole of the country.[80] Having originally been a polycentric phenomenon that was pragmatically adapted to suit each region of China in which it took root, Chinese Communism now became dangerously dogmatic. It was this loss of flexibility – the 'one size fits all' approach – that led to many of the tragedies from the 1950s onwards: the Great Leap Forward and its subsequent famine; and Mao's attempt to resurrect this model in the Cultural Revolution. In designing his international PR, therefore, he also defined himself and his politics. Mao's revolution ate many of those originally persuaded by *Red Star*'s Maoism: many of those seduced by the book's rosy aura of democracy and patriotism would be persecuted and imprisoned during the Cultural Revolution.[81]

And still Mao was not yet done with Snow: after the founding of the People's Republic in 1949 and before his death in 1972, Snow would be permitted periodic, intensively regulated visits back to China, which in turn generated further influential books (one of which refuted reports of a famine that we now know killed tens of millions).[82] These accounts had a disproportionate impact in a context of very limited foreign reporting on China, owing to the CCP's stringent restrictions on access. In 1970, Mao deployed him (ineffectually, as it turned out) as intermediary to Henry Kissinger and Richard Nixon, while planning the sensational US–China détente of 1972 – a mere handful of years after the two countries had been on the brink of nuclear war. In public at least, Snow was the archetypal 'friend of China': a foreigner assiduously courted by the regime in the hope and expectation that, on his return home, he would speak for the merits of Mao's revolution. On 15 February 1972, Snow died at the age of sixty-six, of pancreatic cancer, in Switzerland – the country in which he had taken refuge after McCarthyism made it impossible for him to earn a living in the US. Mao and Zhou had sent a delegation of doctors and officials – including his old friend Huang Hua – to stay with him, while he slipped into a coma and out of this world.

Given what we now know about the Chinese revolution, Snow and his book should perhaps have been treated more sceptically across the decades – *Red Star*'s significance as a document of a particular historical moment notwithstanding. Examined from a contemporary perspective, Snow is an awkward, compromised figure, both happy-go-lucky *Boys' Own* adventurer and defender of implacable revolutionaries. Often read as a paean to simple, pure idealism, his most famous book was ensnared in murkier motivations: his own need to manufacture a global hit, his left-wing leanings, the ambitions and manipulations of his hosts. Nonetheless, he remains acclaimed by Chinese and Western commentators, as the 'masterful' author of 'probably the greatest book of reporting by an American foreign correspondent in [the twentieth] century'.[83]

Red Star is a powerful emblem of the international Mao cult: of the translatability of Mao and his ideas, both within, on the periphery of and far beyond China. To those suffering violent occupation by militarily superior foes (Soviet partisans, for example, or Malayan Chinese during the Second World War), it offered a populist military and political strategy, and the inspiring example of a self-made man (Mao). Young European, American and Indian students and subversives of the 1960s fell in love with Mao the rebel – earthy, poetic, statesman-like. The book and its afterlives exemplify the way that Maoism has always been defined by its global travels.

3

THE BRAINWASH — CHINA AND
THE WORLD IN THE 1950S

In 1951, Edward Hunter, a foreign correspondent and sometime CIA stringer, published *Brain-washing in Red China: The Calculated Destruction of Men's Minds*.[1] The book promised to expose the 'new and horrifying extremes in ... psychological warfare being waged against the free world and against the very concept of freedom'. Hunter claimed that he had discovered an entirely new form of thought control unleashed on the world by the Chinese Communist Party after taking power in 1949. It was anti-American, fiercely coercive and ambitious for a total change in mental state – menticide, as it was sometimes termed; mind murder.[2] The Chinese, Hunter declared, had achieved 'psychological warfare on a scale incalculably more immense than any militarist of the past has ever envisaged'.[3] In 1956, he made another bid for royalties with a follow-up tome, *Brainwashing: The Story of Men Who Defied It*.

> The intent is to change a mind radically so that its owner becomes a living puppet – a human robot – without the atrocity being visible from the outside. The aim is to create a mechanism in flesh and blood, with new beliefs and new thought processes inserted into a captive body. What that amounts to is the search for a slave race that, unlike the slaves of olden times, can be trusted never to revolt, always to be amenable to orders, like an insect to its instincts.[4]

Hunter had found his vocation: propagating the idea of a global conspiracy by the Chinese Communists to 'brainwash' anyone who fell into their power. Through the 1950s, he would repackage his ideas in books, lectures, articles and testimonies to Congress. By the end of the decade, the US government and intelligence agencies would be devoting billions of dollars and myriads of hours into researching these techniques of mind control and reverse-engineering them for use by the US military-industrial complex.

Outwardly, Hunter enjoyed a successful career in American journalism. But with hindsight his life's work represents calamitous failure – the ability of rank amateurism and ignorance to sway opinion at the highest levels of Cold War policymaking in a nervy US. Hunter was neither psychiatrist nor psychologist, and he did not speak or read Chinese. His position as journalist-spook raised – to put it mildly – some ethical issues. And yet in only a handful of years, his views on China and its psy-war against the 'free world' helped mould percep-tions of Chinese Communism under Mao as an irresistibly expansionist doctrine. With the help of government officials, some opportunistic psychiatrists and a suggestible media, Hunter's ideas about brain-washing became orthodoxy. The United States might possess – for the time being at least – the most advanced military weapons, but Mao's China had something more menacing: the ability to bend the human mind to its will. And after China's involvement in two hot conflicts of the early Cold War – the Korean War and the Malayan Emergency – had brought Mao's revolution into overt and covert conflict with the United States and Britain, these suppositions appeared eminently plausible.

Bemusement, fear, loathing, and at times an alarmed respect – these were the emotions that Communist China generated in 1950s America. For much of the previous decade the US government had poured billions into China's Nationalist, Guomindang, government. A political and military debacle had resulted. Chiang Kai-shek had refused to crack down on the Guomindang's notorious levels of corruption until he had defeated his rivals for control of China: the Japanese and the Communists. In August 1945, following years of stubborn Nationalist resistance and two atomic bombs, Japan had surrendered. But in the final showdown with the Communists – in the civil war that almost immediately followed Japanese capitulation – Chiang's commanders and armies proved inadequate for the military task. They became trapped in defensive manoeuvres or made a hash of their offensives; they scrapped and bickered; they lost their nerve. Meanwhile, Mao's commanders (stints at Soviet military crammers in the early 1940s had enabled them to graduate from guerrilla raids to set-piece field battles) trained their troops into disciplined fighting units. Communist armies swept south in pursuit of Chiang Kai-shek who, in December 1949, fled to Taiwan, singing the national anthem as he drove out to his escape plane.[5]

The Communist takeover of China constituted a major American trauma of the early Cold War. For a few weeks in spring 1949, Mao seemed to dally with the possibility of an American friendship. But on 30 June, in the first substantial document outlining the future People's Republic, he declared that revolutionary China would 'lean to one side' – to the Soviet Union.[6] This officially subscribed the new PRC to the expansive designs of Soviet Russia, as defined by George Kennan's famous 1946 Long Telegram, which pushed American foreign policy towards antagonistic containment of the USSR. The alliance immediately pressed the domino-theory panic button in the United States. 'Asia is lost,' noted Eisenhower in 1950, 'with ... even Australia under threat. India itself is not safe!'[7]

The first year of the Korean War seemed to show what kind of a threat to US interests Mao's China would be. The initial attack, launched by North Korean forces ambitious to reunify the peninsula, on 25 June 1950 across the 38th parallel – the dividing line that Americans and Soviets had traced across Korea in 1945, the north allying with the Soviets, the south with the US – had taken the South Korean Army and post-war American occupying forces by surprise, pushing them out of Seoul and into a pocket of territory in the far south-east. (Only days earlier, Syngman Rhee, the US-supported ruler of South Korea, had himself advocated an attack on the north; if he had acted sooner, the Korean War could also plausibly have been started by the South.[8]) General MacArthur, ebullient from his successes in reconstructing Japan as a docile US ally in East Asia, had responded with an audacious counter-attack on Inchon, the nearest port to Seoul. A combined UN and US force of 13,000 soldiers landed on the beaches of Inchon, then pushed on to the South Korean capital. It went, as the US journalist David Halberstam later pronounced, 'not merely as MacArthur had planned, but as he had dreamed'.[9] After UN forces drove North Korean armies back up beyond the 38th parallel, restoring the status quo ante, MacArthur decided that he had a mandate to push further: to oust North Korea's Communist rulers and to head for the border with China and the Soviet Union.

In late November, to celebrate Thanksgiving, tens of thousands of frozen turkeys were shipped as far as the front line of the UN offensive, some 800 kilometres north of Pyongyang (another 800 kilometres short of the border with China). There, in already freezing conditions, they were thawed, roasted and served up to the troops. The day before the feast, MacArthur had boasted that 'the war will be finished by the end of the year'.[10] Seventy-two hours later, on 24 November, a 400,000-strong Chinese People's Volunteers army attacked and turned MacArthur's triumph into a rout. On 4 January 1951, Seoul was again in Communist hands.

The strike was a devastating shock. And in the course of the offensive, Chinese forces took some 7,000 Americans prisoner. Their first months of captivity were brutally hard. The winter of 1950–51 was one of the toughest on record and the POWs endured long marches to camps in the bitter cold with minimal food, clothing and bedding, and no medicine; many perished. But opinion back in America feared psychological more than physical damage to the POWs. Until an armistice was signed in July 1953, and an agreement reached for the repatriation of POWs, a series of media revelations suggested that the prisoners had been 'remoulded' in enemy captivity. A Chinese information broadcast entitled 'Oppose Bacteriological Warfare!' presented half a dozen captured American airmen testifying that they had unleashed germ warfare on North Korea (which the US has always denied). 'I voluntarily admitted my part,' confessed one. 'At no point have I been treated anything but kindly.'[11] Back home in the US, populists and specialists created a picture of inexorable Communist Chinese brainwashing: a depatterning and then repatterning of the human mind.

As armistice talks finally made progress, an advance guard of 149 American prisoners were released in spring 1953, but twenty of these were quarantined in California. 'GIs Tell of Their Brainwashing Ordeal', ran the headline of an article in *Life* magazine, which elaborated a Chinese plan to 'capture the minds of American prisoners and send them back to the US to spread Communist doctrine'.[12] In summer 1953, another 3,597 American POWs were released in a deal that permitted prisoners to choose between Communist and non-Communist China (the PRC or the ROC, the Nationalists' Republic of China on Taiwan) and North or South Korea. While negotiators doubtless anticipated only East Asian POWs would exercise this choice (around 22,000 soldiers in Communist armies refused repatriation), to the shock of US public opinion twenty-three Americans opted for the PRC. The scandal triggered a national campaign of persuasion to change their minds, with tens of thousands of American schoolchildren mobilised to write letters begging the twenty-three to come home; in the end just two relented.

After almost three years in Chinese-run POW camps, the majority of American POWs who did choose to return home were not sent back immediately to their families. They were brought back by ship, which took a fortnight to reach the US. Officially, the army wanted to give them 'good food and plenty of rest'. In fact, Washington generals used these fourteen days for intensive psychological profiling to detect Communist mind-moulding. Psychiatrists, spies and detectives swarmed around the prisoners, shoving booklets of questionnaires into their faces. The interrogations – which could go on for eight hours at a time – did not end on the boat home. Not satisfied with the two feet of dossiers that they had put together, FBI agents visited and revisited so-called RECAP-Ks (Returned and Exchanged Captured American Personnel in Korea) for years.[13]

It was in substantial part Edward Hunter's publications throughout the period of US POW incarceration in Korea that created such an atmosphere of suggestibility towards Chinese brainwashing in the US. And Hunter was not willing to limit his ideas to the Chinese menace in the Korean theatre: the threat he diagnosed was global in scope. *Brain-washing in Red China* followed what he called 'the trail' of Chinese influence and brainwashing deep into the post-war anti-colonial conflicts of the Malayan jungle and Vietnam. For Hunter, the Malayan Emergency – an insurgency launched in 1948 by the Malayan Communist Party against British rule – was not an anti-colonial struggle for independence, but 'actually an invasion, every bit as much of an aggression as the Chinese Communist participation in the fighting in Korea ... many of the leaders of the guerrilla warfare in Malaya had been imported into that country from China by the British and the Americans during World War II. Those thus brought in were practically all adherents of Mao Tse-tung.' Indeed, any country in South East Asia that hosted an Overseas Chinese population was vulnerable to 'Chinese Communist imperialism'.[14] Although we have come to associate the US administration's domino theory – the idea that if one country in a region fell to the Communists, others would soon topple too – with Vietnam, these fears began with the Malayan Emergency in 1948. If territories in South East Asia such as Malaya were to be 'swept by communism', worried Secretary of State Dean Acheson in 1949, 'we shall have suffered a major political rout the repercussions of which will be felt throughout the rest of the world'.[15]

Hunter tapped into a rich seam of anxiety about the expansion of Chinese Communism. Through the early Emergency period, British and American officials in Malaya, Singapore and at home jumped to conclusions about mainland interference in the Malayan Communists' actions. But while contemporary documents are rich in speculation about mainland involvement, they are sparse on corroboration; 'may', 'suggest', 'appear' are the favoured verbs.[16] In UK government documents of the 1950s, the 'Overseas Chinese' represented a clear security concern. The Cabinet decided that they were a 'militant force ... inasmuch as their loyalty to and interest in being protected by a Chinese government makes them almost automatic agencies of the Peking Government in areas where that Government's influence is predominant'.[17] 'The large numbers of Chinese scattered over every country in South East Asia,' agreed British intelligence, 'often organised as in Siam and Malaya in active Communist parties, form exceedingly dangerous fifth-columns.'[18]

Hunter's allegations of brainwashing became ever more outlandish. In his 1956 recapitulation of the theme, he likened

Chinese mind control to 'witchcraft, with its incantations, trances, poisons and potions, with a strange flair of science about it all, like a devil dancer in a tuxedo, carrying his magic brew in a test tube'.[19] In 1958 he took the limelight in a three-and-a-half-hour testimony before the congressional Committee on Un-American Activities:

> In the jungles of Malaya, I came across the diaries taken from the bodies of slain Chinese guerrilla fighters. I had a number translated. To my amazement, I read exactly what I had heard from ... people who had fled from China ... Brainwashing was the new procedure, built up out of all earlier processes of persuasion ... it was a strategy for the conquest of the world by communism.[20]

'You, the American people, against aggression,' summarised a US Army broadcast to the nation at the close of the Korean War. 'This is the Big Picture.'[21]

The spectre of brainwashing cast a long shadow over US society. Building on earlier Cold War terrors of Stalinist indoctrination, men like Hunter outlined an even more powerful, Chinese-authored version of Soviet-style thought control. By 1956, psychologists given special access to military files on the US POWs in Korea had concluded that brainwashing did not exist, or at least that there was nothing particularly new in the thought reform that American prisoners had undergone: it was just repetitive persuasive coercion, under conditions of extreme physical stress (bitter cold and hunger). 'There is nothing mysterious about personality changes resulting from the brainwashing process ... the techniques used in producing confessions ... have been used, especially by police states, for centuries.'[22] US intelligence was nonetheless determined to deploy the spectre of brainwashing as a pretext for MK-Ultra, the CIA's massive programme of psy-war through the 1950s and '60s. Historians of torture now draw direct links between Hunter's blueprint for 'brainwashing', the CIA's attempts to reverse-engineer this process for American purposes, and the 'enhanced interrogation' techniques unleashed during George W. Bush's War on Terror.[23]

In the search for ways to understand and counter Communist interrogation, MK-Ultra experimented with truth drugs (mostly LSD, but also a speculative toxin extracted from the gall bladder of the Tanganyikan crocodile), hypnosis, brain concussion, lip-reading, jolting monkey brains with radio waves, and a remote-controlled cat.[24] The fear of Chinese brainwashing thus provided a justification for MK-Ultra's years of peak crazy, during which the CIA – according to two of the sharpest historians of the US brainwashing terror – threw 'untold excrescences' of cash at 'black psychiatry'.[25] In the early 1950s, the CIA bought up the world's supply of LSD, in order to carry out clinical experiments concerning its effects on a variety of human and non-human subjects. It placed stockpiles of the drug in hospitals attached to America's top universities, and once word got around about the trials, swarms of students volunteered as guinea pigs. Researchers began taking the drug home to give to friends or sell on the black market. The CIA's open-handedness with the drug also had far more tragic consequences. In late November 1953, Frank Olson – a microbiologist in the CIA – killed himself ten days after his boss secretly spiked his glass of Cointreau with LSD, triggering psychosis and a nervous breakdown.[26]

None of this would have been possible without the conviction, sunk deep into the intelligence professions, that brainwashing – total mind control – was possible. Through the 1950s, the CIA financed the work of Scottish-Canadian psychiatrist Dr Ewen Cameron at McGill University, who pioneered radical methods that aimed to break his patients down to nothing, then rebuild them. Cameron's assistant recalled his boss investigating 'brainwashing among soldiers who had been in Korea. We, in Montreal, started to use some of the techniques.' Experimenting on more than a hundred human guinea pigs, Cameron gave them a daily dozen of electric shocks; kept them in comas for up to eighty-six days continuously; and forced them to listen, for fifteen hours at a time, to simple negative or positive messages about their personalities. One woman came out of the treatment unable to remember her three children.[27] A middle-aged depressive would only drink milk from a bottle and forgot how to talk. 'In the past two years,' Cameron crowed in 1955, 'more than a hundred persons have thus been successfully brainwashed – Canadian style.' The CIA was enchanted, and ploughed cash into his work, via the 'Society for the Investigation of Human Ecology' – a front organisation for funding experiments not always within the ethically acceptable.[28]

The wisdom supposedly gleaned from these studies soaked down into the army's interrogation defence programmes. These included SERE, the US military's training in 'Survival, Evasion, Resistance, Escape', designed by psychiatrists who had studied closely analyses of returned POWs from Korea. It was to prepare personnel for Communist 'brainwashing' by toughening them up through exposure to mental and physical torture – isolation, stress positions and listening to recordings of Yoko Ono singing.[29] After 9/11, the CIA made SERE an offensive weapon, turning its exposure therapy into interrogation techniques and mainstreaming the agency's application of torture, clearly contravening the Geneva Convention and the US-authored and -ratified 1984 Convention Against Torture, which defined torture as 'severe pain or suffering, whether physical or mental'.[30] The enhanced interrogations of the War on Terror – or what one CIA psychologist euphemistically described as 'doing special things to special people in special places' – sprang from SERE; SERE sprang from the 1950s experiments in brainwashing.[31]

The perceived threat of Chinese 'thought reform' thus empowered one of the more powerful and anti-democratic institutions of post-war American government and society: counter-intelligence. By the 2010s, the machinery of America's covert state was costing $75 billion, spread between sixteen intelligence agencies, all devoted to 'the state of exception': 'the paradoxical suspension of democracy as a means of saving democracy'.[32]

The Anglo-American obsession with brainwashing – as part of an imagined Mao-inspired plan for Communist world domination – rested on a particular reading of the People's Republic's influence in the world by a roll-call of unreliable witnesses. It included not just obvious Cold War partisans like Edward Hunter, but also diplomats with first-hand expertise who should have known better. The idea of the Malayan Emergency being a 'Peking conspiracy' came from British diplomats and politicians desperate for American support in their struggles to contain what was more an anti-colonial insurgency than an attempted Communist revolution. The fact that the political make-up of the British-ruled Federation of Malaya newly inaugurated in February 1948 had disenfranchised ethnic Chinese in favour of the Malay majority, and had thereby pushed the former towards the Chinese-dominated Malayan Communist Party, was conveniently forgotten. The British got their message through to US policymakers: in 1949, Dean Acheson declared that 'the only alternative to British rule visible at this time is Chinese domination, which would be unacceptable not only to Malaya but also to us'. In 1951, the State Department's lead on South East Asia portrayed China as an omnivorous menace. 'Malaya is likely to be invaded whenever the Chinese feel that they have digested Indo-China and Thailand.'[33] The Americans came good for their British allies: although the US government eventually decided not to send troops to Malaya, it stumped up $1.5 million in 'technical assistance, information services, and educational exchange'.[34]

In creating an image of all-powerful Chinese 'brainwashing', professional propagandists masquerading as serious political analysts supposed an ideologically unified Maoist front stretching from China to Korea and Malaya. Recent declassifications, however, provide a more nuanced narrative about Mao's international ambitions, the CCP's relationship with Malayan and North Korean Communists, and the large Chinese diaspora in South East Asia, and the party's own view of the 'brainwashing' project.

Mao was always eager to take a leading role in the world revolution. In early 1949, almost a year before he had consolidated his control of the mainland, he was keen to build an 'Asian Cominform' in China to direct the revolution in that continent. By the end of July 1949 (and three months before the founding of the PRC), Mao's very own Marxism-Leninism Academy had opened for business, hosting Asian Communist leaders on a one-year course in Mao's revolution taught by veteran Communists, including Zhu De, Deng Xiaoping and Mao's Yan'an secretary Chen Boda. In November 1949, Mao's second in command Liu Shaoqi (encouraged by Stalin) declared that armed struggle 'is the road of Mao Zedong [and an] inevitable path toward the liberation of other people in the colonial and semi-colonial countries'. The following year, Liu remade the point more explicitly:

After the victory of the revolution, the CCP should use all means to
help the Communist parties and people among the oppressed peoples
of Asia to fight for liberation ... to consolidate the victory of the
Chinese Revolution worldwide ... We should provide fraternal assistance and warm hospitality to the Communist parties and revolutionaries
from all countries ... introduce them to details of the experiences of
the Chinese Revolution [and] answer their questions carefully.[35]

In 1950, some four hundred trainees gathered at the academy in
Beijing, to begin their apprenticeships in insurgency before being sent
back to lead the revolution in their respective Asian countries. That
year, the CCP took another important step in organising the world
revolution by setting up the International Liaison Department, which
took responsibility for coordinating interactions with other Communist
parties.[36] The ILD had a broad portfolio: managing relations with
international Communist insurgencies, arranging explosives training
for Latin American revolutionaries like Abimael Guzmán and sched-
uling dentist appointments for Pol Pot.

The first cohort of trainees came from Vietnam, Thailand, the
Philippines, Indonesia, Burma, Malaya and India. One of them was
Mohit Sen, who in subsequent decades would become a lynchpin
Indian Communist leader. His backstory was an extraordinary expression of the type of cultured privilege that nurtured high-caste Indian
Communists. His father was a leading judge, but also a skilled flautist,
boxer and sure rifle shot; his mother, an accomplished singer, pianist
and cellist. Their Kolkata household was so Anglophile that his parents
insisted on speaking English at home – Sen had to pick up his Bengali
elsewhere. He was well schooled at a Jesuit College before – like his
high-flying brother – going on to Cambridge; 'I never thought of
taking up a job,' he recalled.[37] Sen was an obsessive for Bach and
Beethoven, for English and Russian literature, for *Battleship Potemkin*,
The Grapes of Wrath, *Brief Encounter* and *Gone with the Wind*. At
Cambridge, he ate muffins with E. M. Forster, joined the Communist
Party of India, and fell in love with a brilliant mathematician (and
comrade). In 1950, he found his way to China, via an invitation issued
at the World Congress of the International Union of Students in
Prague (one of the many nodes in the tourist itinerary of international
Communism in the 1950s and '60s). When after a long, lovesick slog

along the Trans-Siberian Railway – he was missing his fiancée desperately – Sen crossed the border into China, he instantly encountered Mao's personality cult: a performance of 'The East Is Red'. (The first verse runs: 'The sun rises, in China a Mao Zedong is born'.) 'It was all very overwhelming,' he observed. On reaching Beijing, he saw Mao for himself. 'He was taller and bulkier than I imagined he would be. My image of him was that of the gaunt revolutionary with a concentrated gaze that I had seen in the illustrations of Edgar Snow's *Red Star Over China*.' But Sen still found him 'Olympian'. 'There was no speech that did not eulogise him with every reference greeted with deafening applause ... the Chinese people have stood up! ... millions felt free as a people.' Two months into Sen's stay, Mao personally invited him to join the inaugural class of the CCP's school of revolution, the Marxism-Leninism Academy.[38]

Despite its name, the academy's curriculum was all about Mao. After a crash course in Chinese – set text: Mao – and now disguised in the blue cotton uniform of a CCP cadre, Sen was dispatched with his two hundred classmates (half of them were Vietnamese; the rest came from the Philippines, Australia, Japan, Thailand and Burma) to Guangdong in the south to witness land reform. The campaign – the CCP's top priority for the countryside in the early 1950s – redistributed some 43 per cent of land to 60 per cent of the farming population, though at considerable human cost (at least one million landlords are estimated to have been killed).[39] 'All through, the unceasing refrain was the power and the glory of the Chinese Communist Party and Chairman Mao,' Sen recalled. A final 'victory meeting' was held against the backdrop of a massive portrait of Mao, and to the soundtrack of pledges of eternal loyalty to the chairman and yet more renditions of 'The East Is Red'. The rookie Maoists then returned to their Beijing campus, which had been erected in a matter of weeks: 'a huge compound enclosed by high walls [with] dormitories, lecture halls, dining rooms, cinema and dance room'. A swimming pool was under way and the trainee revolutionaries volunteered to help dig it. It did not take long before the construction workers tactfully asked the 'foreign student comrades' to 'kindly do their work, i.e., study and let them do theirs, i.e., build the swimming pool'. Guest of honour at the complex's inauguration, Mao urged the tourists 'to be better revolutionaries'.[40]

Looking back in 2003, Sen still remembered the exhilaration of learning about the Chinese revolution, and 'the courage and originality of Mao'. The students were taught about Mao's 'three magic wands' – 'armed struggle, the united front and the CPC' – and underwent bouts of self-criticism lasting weeks at a time (and leading to the suicide of two Vietnamese comrades). The party also encouraged ballroom dancing 'to overcome the inhibitions of the feudal days of interaction between men and women'. Mao turned up most Saturdays for a dinner-dance: he 'used to lumber about [and] smile gently ... Many of the women cadres wanted to dance with him.'[41] (Years later, Mao's doctor would describe the bedroom that Mao maintained next to the ballroom, to which he would periodically retire with his dance partners.) After two years, Sen graduated and returned to India, where he became a career Communist.

Malayan Communist insurgents also travelled to China for guidance from Mao's Asian Cominform. Chin Peng – future secretary general of the Malayan Communist Party and architect of the emergency – was an early convert to Mao. While in his early teens in the late 1930s he discovered a Chinese edition of *Red Star Over China* on the school library shelves. He spent the summer of 1938 poring over Mao's words. '[*On Protracted War*] was ... a handbook on how to win the war against the Japanese. In it [Mao] called for the mobilisation of the people and the adoption of guerrilla war tactics.'[42] On the point of travelling to China 'to join Mao', Chin was recruited by the MCP, which had been founded in 1930 under instructions from the Far East Bureau of the Comintern in Shanghai. It was under the command of the Nanyang (South Seas) Provisional Committee of the CCP.[43]

When Japanese invasion prevented his pilgrimage to Yan'an, Chin Peng became a Maoist guerrilla commander during the Second World War, carrying with him from jungle hideout to jungle hideout his 'travelling library' of Mao's works. He threw himself into the South East Asian Communist underground: secret meetings with Vietnamese, Burmese and Thai counterparts, all officiated by the Chinese Communist Party; double, triple agents; constant intrigue and betrayal. Later, he cheered Mao's defiance of colonialism, and especially his catchphrase 'Imperialists are paper tigers': it fitted his hatred of both Japanese invaders and the '"No Asians Allowed" attitude to social intercourse'

of Malaya's British rulers.[44] Throughout the Japanese occupation of
Malaya, Chin Peng led the Malayan People's Anti-Japanese Army in
collaboration with British soldiers; the British government awarded
him the Order of the British Empire for it. But when the Japanese
surrendered in August 1945, he was determined to translate Mao's
theories of guerrilla warfare into Malaya's fight for independence. 'Now
with the Japanese defeated, it was Britain's turn again.'[45] Chin Peng
OBE (soon to become 'Public Enemy No. 1' of the Malayan government) and the MCP led hundreds of strikes against the returned British
rulers, who failed in the immediate post-war years to resolve the
economic crisis caused by Japanese occupation. The British declared
an emergency on 18 June 1948 after the MCP killed three Caucasian
plantation managers. Based in Malaya's jungles, the MCP hammered
the 40,000-strong British force with assassinations and ambushes. In
1951, the British high commissioner himself, Henry Gurney, was killed
in an MCP attack. Meanwhile, the new British colonial governor tried
to starve the insurgents into submission by creating 'New Villages' –
fortified settlements surrounded by barbed wire, in which civilians
could be monitored and prevented from passing food or intelligence
to the guerrillas.

By 1955, the British had fought the guerrillas into retreat. (Their
strategy would become a model for successful counter-insurgency in
the Western bloc, emulated by the Americans in Vietnam, and by the
Indian state when fighting the Maoist uprising in the eastern jungles
in the early twenty-first century.) The following year, Chin Peng
emerged from the jungle to negotiate peace with the British and the
future Malay ruler of the country (an aristocratic civil servant called
Tunku Abdul Rahman), in the northern town of Baling. But Chin
refused to accept the surrender that Abdul Rahman and the British
demanded of the MCP, and melted back into a clandestine existence.
By 1957, however, after the country had gained independence (and was
renamed Malaysia), the original rationale for the emergency had
evaporated. Debate still rages within Malaysia about the role of the
MCP in ending British rule. The party's supporters claim that
the MCP forced the hand of the British; its enemies accuse them of
terrorist thuggery that brought unnecessary suffering to civilians.

Like most local Communist leaders, Chin Peng was desperate not
to resemble a foreign puppet and played down Chinese assistance: he

received from China, he protested, 'not even a bullet'.[46] 'If the [MCP], since 1948, had been getting all this direct assistance from ... Peking in terms of weapons, equipment, finance and political direction, how come its armed struggle was in such a shambles ten years later?'[47] In practice, the contact was close and nurturing. In late 1948, even while the Chinese civil war was still ongoing, MCP cadres sick with TB were sent to the mainland for treatment.[48] In 1950, MCP members gathered round transistors to listen to Radio Peking; when they were starving in the jungle, they asked Beijing's advice as to whether there was a way to make rubber seeds edible.[49] Without CCP training in cyphers, the MCP's couriers would not have known how to encrypt their communications.

In 1951, MCP propaganda began to underline Mao's unique theoretical contributions to Communist revolution. 'We must study ... in a solemn manner ... the Mao Tse-tung ideology, because it is a Marxist-Leninist theory having very close bearing on our present revolutionary struggle.' (Some testy colonial official scribbled in the margins of an intercepted copy: 'It must be very tedious for the ... communists to have to read through this stodgy stuff ... I can't really believe that we have the technique to win the hearts and minds of chaps like this.')[50] Mao's name was conspicuously cited before Stalin's, including to validate insights such as 'It is ... important for us to make good use of our brains'.[51] Mao's image was worn by MCP members and sympathisers in ingeniously covert ways, concealed within girls' brooches with a flower design on the outside. If safely among comrades, they could press a little catch and reveal a picture of Mao. By the middle of the 1950s, British colonial operatives had intercepted MCP–CCP courier lines; these communications indicated extensive contact between the two parties. Two members (half) of the MCP politburo were in China and busy dispatching CCP directives back for adoption in Malaya. China reportedly provided training facilities for hundreds, if not thousands of Malayan revolutionaries, and devised plans to smuggle CCP-trained Malayan Chinese back into Malaya on opium boats.[52] And it was from Beijing that the MCP received the orders to 'fold up the flags and silence the drums' (*yanxi xigu*): to stop the armed struggle and negotiate with the British at the Baling talks.[53]

In June 1961, Chin Peng himself went into exile in China – disguised in dark glasses and a false moustache. Flying into Beijing airport, he was met by Liu Ningyi, deputy director of the ILD. 'I was given', Chin remembered,

> a substantial bungalow next to Peking's highly secret Liaison Department … The Liaison headquarters then comprised such a secret operation that it hid behind a high stone wall and there were no signs announcing its functions. Within the Liaison compound was a separate mini-compound of houses, enclosed behind yet another wall, for the families of those working for the department. Strict regulations forbade any family members strolling into the office section. All matters in the Liaison offices were handled on an appointment-only basis. My bungalow formed part of an accommodation section set aside to house officials of fraternal communist parties operating in Peking. It was located on a broad boulevard leading straight into Tiananmen Square in the heart of the Chinese capital.

His neighbours were a cosmopolitan lot. 'Burmese, Siamese, Lao, Cambodian and Indonesian comrades … all maintained important training facilities in China.'[54] This was China's own version of Moscow's Hotel Lux, the oddly chosen name that the Bolsheviks gave to the former Hotel France, which housed foreign revolutionaries (many of them later purged by the Terror) and a colony of rats through the 1920s and '30s.

One insider on the CCP–MCP relationship was Ah Cheng, one of Chin Peng's closest comrades in the MCP. Ah Cheng was a first-generation Malayan Chinese immigrant revolutionary. Born in 1919 in rural Guangdong (south China), he went to Malaya to study in the 1930s, and joined the MCP in 1938. In 1948, as a high-ranking party member, he was sent to China to get treatment for his tuberculosis but also to serve as a liaison in Beijing between the MCP and the CCP. He returned to Malaysia in around 1960; Chin Peng took his place in Beijing. Ah Cheng made a second official trip to China in 1965 and stayed until 1972.

Thanks to the five-volume memoir that he wrote of his life and times, Ah Cheng is an important source on the CCP–MCP relationship from the late 1940s to the early 1970s, revealing the ways in which the CCP sought to transmit their revolutionary model to Malayan and other South East Asian revolutionaries, as well as the nature of interactions between the two parties. Ah Cheng's emotions towards the CCP are interestingly mixed, combining reverence for Mao's revolutionary experience with mounting disillusionment on witnessing the failures of Maoism in power. While British government documents suggested covert coordinated movement between the MCP and the CCP from the late 1940s, Ah Cheng's experience tells a more chaotic story.

His first Chinese International Liaison contact, Qiao Guanhua (later the PRC's first delegate to the UN and future husband of Mao's English teacher; many of China's most trusted diplomats came up through, or double-jobbed in, far more secretive and sensitive party-to-party work), failed to make an assignation in a shadowy Kowloon alley. Ah Cheng spent the next few months trying and failing to make contact in Hong Kong. In the end, he slogged to Beijing on his own steam. There he was inducted – alongside a cohort of some thirty other South East Asian revolutionaries – into an elite 'study group' housed in Zhongnanhai, the former imperial residence at the centre of Beijing that CCP leaders took over as their private quarters in 1949. He enjoyed five-star party treatment: access to top officials, a German-trained doctor, leadership-standard food rations, and the now familiar course on Mao. Ah Cheng's recollections of the history classes that he and his fellow students had on the Chinese civil war communicate an almost childlike hero worship of the Maoist model. 'Wonderful! Wonderful!' they cried out, as Deng Xiaoping lectured them about the CCP's crossing of the Yangtze during the civil war.[55]

There were cracks in the relationship, however. Although the CCP was lavish in its theoretical support for Malayan comrades during the 1950s, that was (according to Ah Cheng) as far as it went. Ah Cheng recalled asking for material help from the CCP, when British repression during the First Emergency was near its peak. 'Our help to fraternal parties is mainly political or moral,' a CCP official primly replied. A disgruntled Ah Cheng bluntly pointed out that at the time China was lavishing non-repayable material aid on both North Korea and Ho Chi Minh's Democratic Republic of Vietnam in their reunification wars.[56]

China's own national self-interest or convenience always trumped revolutionary theory when it came to supporting the MCP. Mao and Zhou Enlai urged the Malayan Communists to negotiate with the

British in 1956 to fit the PRC's new self-projection as a non-interfering source of international harmony; this was to gain leadership kudos with the Afro-Asian and Non-Aligned movements. About a month after the collapse of the Baling talks, in early 1956, Ah Cheng was abruptly summoned late one night to talks with the top CCP leadership: with Mao, Zhou, Liu Shaoqi, Zhu De, Deng Xiaoping and director of International Liaison Wang Jiaxiang, all squeezed together on a single sofa. Mao began by praising Chin Peng's defiant response to Tunku Abdul Rahman's demand that the MCP surrender: 'we would prefer to fight to the last man'. Chin Peng, Mao flattered, was 'a hero ... the word surrender doesn't exist in the dictionary of us communists'. But then, in an abrupt change of tone, Zhou suggested a surprisingly non-Communist way forward for the struggling MCP. 'We'll help set you up in business. Why don't you get some of your cadres to open a shop in Malaya and we'll send some goods for you to sell?' The meeting left Ah Cheng bemused and disappointed; the CCP was clearly trying to give him an exit strategy from a revolution that they had encouraged and even designed in their image, but which no longer suited their geopolitical ambitions.[57] In July 1961 – as the CCP spurned Soviet 'peaceful coexistence' and yelled for global armed struggle, in a bid for leadership of the world revolution – the story changed again. Deng Xiaoping pulled Chin Peng out of revolutionary retirement and promised him generous Chinese backing if he and the MCP now resumed the armed struggle in Malaysia. Chin Peng, the obedient acolyte, complied. From bases on the border with Thailand, the MCP and its thousands of insurgents fought the Second Emergency against independent Malaysia and Singapore between the 1960s and '80s, through jungle battles, political subversion, arson and assassinations. Nineteen years later, in 1980, Deng would summon Chin Peng to another similarly imperious interview: this time the instructions were to shut the MCP down, in the interests of improving China's diplomatic and economic ties with Malaysia's and Singapore's governments.[58] Deng was only continuing Mao's own policy of growing detachment. In talks to re-establish Sino-Malaysian diplomatic relations in 1974, the Malaysian prime minister, Tun Abdul Razak, quickly broached the most sensitive issue between the two states, asking Mao to use his influence to shut down the MCP insurgency on the Thai border. 'Tricky,' Mao responded. 'We haven't had any contact with them for many years.

Anyway, they don't listen to us. Don't worry: they'll never beat you.'[59] With its Chinese backing gone and Communist governments collapsing across the Soviet bloc, the MCP finally signed a peace accord with the Malaysian government in December 1989.

I have dwelt here on the history of links between the Malayan Communist Party and Mao's Chinese Communist Party, because this connection became an integral part of Cold War narratives of Mao's global ambitions. I could equally have focused on the CCP's assistance to the Burmese Communist Party (BCP): it trained its leaders in China across decades (and deceived beautiful Chinese women into marrying them); it deliberately reactivated the BCP insurgency in the mid-1960s by bringing Burmese revolutionary refugees out of semi-retirement (they had earlier been put to grass in a mercury factory in China's south-west) and dispatching them back to Burma to make insurgency; it kept the BCP bases near China's southern border alive with electricity, food, clothing and weapons; it sent euphemistically named 'Greetings and Appreciations Teams' (in reality, military advisers) to direct battles. During the Cultural Revolution, fervent Red Guards from south and south-west China served as foot soldiers in the BCP uprising; many perished. The BCP repaid the debt with near-slavish devotion: morning and evening, its members bowed to Mao's portrait; Mao's works were mandatory pre-breakfast reading; at party meetings, comrades would wish eternal life to Mao before expressing the same sentiment for their own party; the BCP victimised those who suggested that Burma's context *might* be different from that of China and replicated the Cultural Revolution's bloody purge of the leadership, singing Maoist hymns at the rallies that condemned to death former comrades. China's encouragement of the BCP delivered the country a civil war. The head of state, Ne Win, expressed his frustration while inspecting a regional map displayed at an educational fair in 1970: he located then punched a hole through China.[60]

The Koreans were conspicuously absent from Mao's University of the Revolution – a signal perhaps that Stalin claimed them as his own. Nonetheless, the history of the Korean Workers' Party (KWP) was steeped in Chinese Communist influence. During the 1920s and '30s, Korean Communists took refuge in China, in response to the exceptional pressures of Japanese occupation; many joined the CCP and were responsible for turning it into a credible force in the north-east borderlands between China and Korea. A variety of radical organisations which would later feed into the KWP – the Korean Independence League (KIL), the North China Korean Youth Association, the North China Branch of the Korean Volunteer Corps – were founded under the sponsorship of the Chinese Communist Party and army. During the 1940s, the KIL was headquartered in Yan'an – its leaders were called the 'Yan'an faction' (*Yan'an pai*) on returning to North Korea, where they were purged by Kim Il-sung in the 1950s. Before Kim returned to Korea at the end of the Second World War, he had had most of his sketchy education and Communist career inside China and in Chinese, as a member of the Chinese Communist Party. The *nom de guerre* that he selected in 1935 was designed in Chinese characters: Jin Richeng, Jin (Kim, Gold, a surname) Becomes-the-Sun – Kim Il-sung in Korean pronunciation. But in the early 1940s, he had taken refuge in the Soviet Union, becoming fluent in Russian and Soviet military studies, and winning the trust of Lavrenty Beria and, by extension, Stalin. By the time he returned to Korea in 1945, as Stalin's chosen one, his Korean was scrappy.

Many Korean fighters stayed in China during the final years of the civil war between Communists and the Nationalist Party: almost 35,000 ethnic Koreans in Yanbian (the region bordering Korea and north-east China) fought for the CCP, while over 100,000 joined militias and police forces. Without a supply office in Pyongyang (where the CCP representative became a regular drinking buddy of Kim Il-sung), Mao would have had great difficulty running his armies in the crucial north-eastern theatre of war. In return, Kim received CCP help in constructing an army of Koreans who had cut their teeth fighting in China during the Second World War – including 800 trained, experienced military-school graduates. Before returning home, two Korean regiments wrote fulsome telegrams to Mao: the Chinese Revolution, they hymned, was 'the best model for the oppressed people in the East' and also 'a solid foundation for the victory of the Korean Revolution'. In summer 1950, almost 50,000 ethnic Korean People's Liberation Army officers and soldiers crossed the border into North Korea – a major boost in military personnel that would enable Kim Il-sung to begin the first hot conflict of the Cold War.[61]

But Mao's military support was not unconditional. Throughout 1949 Mao was ready and willing to help Kim in the event – which seemed probable at the time – of a strike by Syngman Rhee and South Korea north of the 38th parallel. Actually initiating a new international conflict, however, made no sense to Mao, who was still mired in the pacification of the mainland and in plans to 'liberate' Tibet and Taiwan. If Kim Il-sung himself began a war and China were to back him up, it would have a serious impact on Mao's own ambitions to unify the far-flung corners of the old Chinese empire (as indeed came to pass). American watchers of the Communist world were convinced that the Korean War was driven by a Chinese–Soviet–Korean alliance 'as close as lips and teeth', and avid to bring down the free world. A scene from the film *The Manchurian Candidate* (1962), in which this cabal of allies gathered in a brainwashing headquarters somewhere in north-east China to manipulate the minds of guileless Americans, pictured this seamless cooperation. But the reality of these 'fraternal' relations was (and, in the case of China and North Korea, remains) far more fractious.

After American troops left Korea in June 1949, Kim quickly began spoiling for an invasion of the south. At first, neither Soviet nor CCP leaders were keen to give the US a pretext for returning to the Korean peninsula. Stalin budged first. Buoyed by the USSR's first successful nuclear test, the CCP's victory against Chiang Kai-shek and Dean Acheson's declaration in January 1950 that South Korea was not within the US 'defensive perimeter', Stalin was swayed by Kim's ebullient assurance that 'the war will be won in three days'.[62] The Soviet leader saw a Korean war as a low-risk way of distracting the Americans from Europe and began manoeuvring to bring it about. While in Moscow over the winter of 1949–50 on his first ever trip outside China, Mao had asked for Stalin's help in the final chapter of China's civil war: defeating the Nationalists on their last refuge, the island of Taiwan. Stalin refused to commit Soviet forces. Unknown to Mao, Stalin at the same time summoned another high-level East Asian guest to town: Kim Il-sung, to whom he secretly promised support if he were to attack South Korea. Stalin covered himself by giving Kim one precondition: he had to get Chinese endorsement first. When a reluctant Kim Il-sung finally broached the subject in Beijing on 13 May 1950, the meeting presumably went badly, for no minutes have ever been made publicly available. All we know is that the discussion ended late, with a visit by Zhou Enlai to the Soviet embassy just before midnight, requesting the instant dispatch of a tight-lipped telegram to Stalin. 'Comrade Mao Zedong would appreciate Comrade Filippov's [Stalin's] personal explanation about this ... immediately.'[63]

Mao's lack of enthusiasm for a risky conflict in Korea is understandable: the CCP's military capacity was clustered around the south-east coast, perched for an invasion of Taiwan. A Cold War conflagration on the north-east border would require the shifting of all these offensive troops to defence in the north-east – from one end of the country to another. Drafts of telegrams and notes of conversations unearthed from archives make clear that Mao came within a whisker of refusing to help the Koreans. In autumn 1950, the Soviet ambassador reported that Mao did not want to be involved as rebuilding China was his priority. 'Korea, while temporarily suffering defeat, will change the form of struggle to partisan war.'[64] It was only after an all-night politburo meeting on 1 October – the first anniversary of the founding of the PRC – that Mao brought the rest of the leadership around to his view, that China should send troops. As the self-proclaimed leader of the Asian revolution he saw it as his duty.[65]

The Chinese war effort began badly when Mao's first choice of command – Lin Biao, the architect of the CCP's 1948 triumph in the north-east, the turning point of the civil war – declined the job. There were other difficulties, too. Mao counted on Soviet air support for his badly trained and equipped troops. Stalin refused – presumably to maintain plausible deniability regarding the Soviet involvement in the war – then relented only slightly, promising limited air cover over north-east China. Years later, Mao would continue to resent Stalin's slippery diplomacy over these issues – particularly after it became clear in wartime correspondence that the Soviet leader never intended to gift his assistance to the Chinese (who risked and lost hundreds of thousands of lives in Korea). At the end of it, the Soviets presented their bill for military materiel provided.

Mao was, therefore, bounced into the Korean War – not as part of a long-term conspiracy, but through Stalin's self-interested impulses and instinct for playing on Mao's status-conscious desire to claim leadership of the Asian revolution. Given that Mao and his immediate lieutenants had already committed themselves so publicly to leading

the world revolution – with their Beijing training courses, their proclamations about the relevance of China to oppressed people in Asia –
their international revolutionary credentials would have been shredded
had they not stepped into the war. Stalin and Kim, in short, created
a conflict that impinged not only on one of China's most sensitive,
complex frontiers – the Korean–Soviet–Chinese border – but also on
Mao's self-image. The Chinese were thus forced to rescue Kim when
the war turned against the North Koreans.

Far from representing a tight-knit alliance between Mao, Stalin and
Kim, then, the Korean War instead highlighted the fault lines in their
relationships. Kim resented Mao's unwillingness to assist with Korean
unification – China had had its revolution, so why should Korea have
to wait? In Mao's mind, China's revolution was not complete until
Taiwan had returned to mainland control – why could Kim not wait
until that had been achieved? 'They are our next-door neighbors,'
grumbled Mao, 'but they did not even consult with us before they
started the war.' The war was deeply costly to China: in manpower
(officially, 360,000 Chinese soldiers were killed or injured) and in equipment. In 1950, the CCP had to give up its campaign to recover Taiwan.
Although at the time it was seen as a temporary postponement, serious
military preparations never restarted. But Kim was never particularly
grateful to Mao for bailing him out. He felt that the thousands of
Koreans who had 'sacrificed for the Chinese Revolution' were
'commensurate with' the hundreds of thousands of Chinese troops
sent into the Korean War.[66]

The experience of the Korean War set a pattern for the Sino–North
Korean relationship, long after the UN, North Korea and China signed
in 1953 a temporary armistice which has never been superseded by a
'final peaceful settlement' (making the Korean War the world's longest,
continuous Cold War conflict). For almost seven decades, small, capri-
cious, ungracious North Korea has somehow managed to manipulate
its bigger, stronger, richer neighbour into being a lifeline of support.
This dynamic has made possible the contemporary geopolitical crisis
of the Korean peninsula.

With his doctrine of *juche* (self-sufficiency), Kim Il-sung told North
Korea and the world that the country would go its own way. 'Those
who returned from the Soviet Union advocate the Soviet method and
those who returned from China advocate the Chinese method.

This is a meaningless debate ... We are carrying out the Korean Revolution.'[67] Kim managed to have it both ways: he preached *juche* in Korea, but sucked aid from Moscow and Beijing. After 1953, 1.2 million 'Chinese People's Volunteers' stayed on in North Korea to reconstruct a ravaged country (at the end of the war, only one building – a colonial-era bank – was still standing in Pyongyang): rebuilding homes, dams, bridges and canals. Kim pointedly headquartered them in grim living conditions miles from Pyongyang and downplayed any mention of their contribution in the capital's War Museum.[68] Mao by contrast – eager for leadership of the revolution in Asia, aware of North Korean suspicion of imperial China's historical interference in the peninsula, in need of an ally against US-sponsored containment in South East Asia and Japan – was determined to buy Kim's friendship. Despite China's own desperate conditions, Mao provided almost as much aid to reconstruct North Korea in the 1950s as did the Soviet Union – 88 million metres of cotton here, 600,000 pairs of shoes there – and wrote off the country's trade deficit.[69] China was also magnanimous regarding its border with North Korea. In secret negotiations in 1962, it gave in to almost all Kim's demands – including for the mountain range encompassing Mount Paektu, a sacred mountain to the Koreans, and according to legend the birthplace of Kim Jong-il (who was born in the Soviet Union).[70]

Juche notwithstanding, there were large pockets of Chinese influence on Kim's revolution. For example, Kim admired Mao's Rectification Campaign and personality cult as a way of disciplining his Korean Workers' Party and silencing dissidents. His Ch'ollima (Flying Horse) movement enthusiastically plagiarised the voluntarism of the Great Leap Forward, with Kim instructing a North Korean delegation visiting China in 1958 to '[c]arefully learn and study the Chinese experiences and bring them back to Korea'. Launched in 1958, Ch'ollima had all the features of Mao's own programme of breakneck economic development: mass mobilisation of 'volunteer' workers; crazed industrial development; compression of cautious planning targets; feverish optimism about North Korea's ability to overtake the more developed economy of Japan and achieve universal prosperity; enhanced political oppression, as any failures were blamed on 'saboteurs' or 'hostile elements'. The North Koreans dutifully began killing spiders, flies and mice (deemed responsible for destroying useful crops); they planted rubber trees on mountainsides; and they strove to make 'every citizen a soldier', as Kim turned North Korea into a fortress nation obsessed with self-defence against external attack. Already by the close of the 1960s, North Korea's army was proportionally four times larger than its Soviet counterpart.[71] Without understanding this historical addiction to universal militarisation, it is hard to comprehend the country's contemporary attachment to a nuclear programme and its devotion of at least 20 per cent GDP to military spending. This proportion dwarfs that committed by the US to its own armed forces. Although in absolute monetary terms, the US spends far more (as its economy is many times larger than North Korea's), its military budget is 'only' 3.5 per cent of GDP.

Zhou Enlai underlined the similarities between Chinese and North Korean campaigns. 'We made a Great Leap Forward, and you mounted a flying horse.'[72] Ch'ollima's insistence on inevitable triumph – through political will – over material obstacles runs through the regime today, where construction has to proceed at vertiginous speed. Every six months, it seems, the Democratic People's Republic of Korea (DPRK) comes up with a new velocity for revolutionary construction: Ch'ollima speed, Masikryong speed, Pyongyang speed and, most recently, Kim Jong-un's very own Mallima speed (Mallima is another flying horse, but ten times faster than the sluggish Ch'ollima).

The Korean translation of 'mass line' (*kunjung noson*) was also borrowed from the Chinese (*qunzhong luxian*), as was the all-important principle of 'self-reliance' (*charyok gaengsaeng* – *zili gengsheng* in the Chinese, a key slogan from Yan'an days, and resurrected during the Great Leap Forward and the Cultural Revolution). Mao-style 'self-reliance' would, ironically, become the foundation stone of 'self-sufficient' *juche*, the official state ideology of North Korea and of Kimism, which Kim used to assert his originality and independence from China and to drive his campaign against 'flunkeyism', Korea's age-old subservience to things Chinese.[73] (One of Kim's first cultural interventions in North Korea was to ban the use of Hanja – Chinese characters used in Korean texts. From 1947, all government documents in North Korea were written in Hangul, the Korean alphabet. Anti-Communist South Korea took another two decades to push Chinese characters out of the education system.) Above all, Kim Il-sung cultivated a leadership cult that first echoed Mao's but ultimately made the latter cult seem almost self-effacing by comparison: Kim became the 'peerless patriot, national hero, ever-victorious iron-willed brilliant commander, outstanding leader of the international communist movement, ingenious thinker, sun of the nation, red sun of the oppressed people of the world, greatest leader of our time'. It can be little coincidence that the cult of Kim Il-sung (as the *suryong* – supreme leader) took off in the late 1960s – at the same time as Mao worship peaked during the Cultural Revolution. In April 1972, on the occasion of Kim's sixtieth birthday, the regime revealed a 240,000-square-metre monument overlooking Pyongyang, crowned by a 20-metre bronze-and-gold statue of the great leader.[74]

In 1970 Kim Il-sung began to compete directly with Mao as the supremo of global revolution: 'Kim Il-sung is not only the great leader of the DPRK,' his propaganda announced, 'but also the one who can lead the world.'[75] During the 1970s and '80s, Kim Il-sung went shopping for international influence, especially in Africa: he financed insurgency in Angola, built gymnasiums in Madagascar, treated the leader of Togo to a ginseng sauna. Kim enjoyed particularly warm relations with Guinea, which sycophantically declared Kim the 'leader of the Third World', and with Robert Mugabe (once presenting him with a gun as a gift). In the early 1980s, Mugabe commissioned the North Koreans to train up an elite force, the Fifth Brigade, which he deployed to crush Zimbabwean opponents. Today, North Korean art maintains a curiously high profile across the continent. Since the 1970s Mansudae Art Studio – the branch of North Korea's propaganda department founded to create godlike images of Kim Il-sung – has won a stream of lucrative commissions for African national monuments unmistakably in the socialist-realist mould, all rippling muscles and heroic poses: the Tiglachin Monument in Ethiopia, the African Renaissance in Senegal, Heroes' Acre in Zimbabwe, the Statue of the Unknown Soldier in Namibia.[76] These commissions have probably helped fund North Korea's nuclear programme: some of these projects generated tens of millions of foreign currency dollars.

Although there were diplomatic hiccups – among them, presenting a teetotal Muslim leader with a bottle of aged snake whiskey – Kim's ambitions for global domination looked plausible to some.[77] One

Vietnamese diplomat saw it this way: '[Mao Zedong's] role as a world leader is nearing its end ... Kim Il-sung is relatively young and has a strong personality. The Korean leadership is pursuing a long-term strategy to propagate Kim Il-sung as the leader of the Asian people.' But in bidding for leadership of the world revolution, Kim only revealed his indebtedness to Mao. For global Kimism adopted most of the techniques of its precursor, global Maoism. It threw money at publishing, and international 'study groups' discussing Kim Il-sung Thought; representatives of the latter were invited on all-expenses-paid trips to the DPRK and treated as national dignitaries.[78]

Mao summarised his view of Kim in the mid-1950s to Anastas Mikoyan, an old acquaintance in first Stalin's and then Khrushchev's administrations: 'You promoted Kim Il-sung. Just like a small tree, you planted it. The Americans pulled it up. We planted it in the same place. It is now extremely pompous.' Kim, for his part, was always riled by Mao's habit of referring to him in the Chinese diminutive: *Xiao Jin*, 'Little Kim'.[79] Through the 1950s, Kim machinated to rid himself of the 'Yan'an faction' of Sinophiles: one by one, they were blamed for the military failure of the war, sacked, arrested, exiled, executed. In 1960, Kim spat that Mao was plotting to 'turn Korea into a Chinese colony' and that Kim would 'never trust the Chinese or visit China again'.[80] Nevertheless, that same year – the worst of China's Great Leap Forward famine – he continued taking China's aid money (including a bonus 230,000 tons of grain).[81]

The rift between North Korea and China opened widest during the Cultural Revolution's years of greatest chaos (1966–69). Kim Il-sung told the Soviet president, Leonid Brezhnev, that Mao's unleashing of the Red Guards was 'massive idiocy' and 'Chinese wickedness'.[82] In conversation with East Germans, North Korean diplomats speculated as to whether Mao had gone senile and needed a stiff dose of Korean ginseng. Mao's Red Guards struck back in their newspapers. Kim was 'a fat revisionist' of the 'Korean revisionist clique, as well as a million-aire, an aristocrat, and a leading bourgeois element in Korea'.[83] Just in case the message was not getting through, Chinese radicals set up loudspeakers along the border to bellow insults (on twelve-hour loops) about the North Koreans' Dear Leader. Events took a horrific turn in the frontier town of Yanbian, where freight trains trundled from China into the DPRK, draped with the corpses of Koreans killed in the pitched battles of the Cultural Revolution, and daubed with threatening graffiti: 'This will be your fate also, you tiny revisionists!'[84] And yet, contradictorily, Chinese aid continued: 40,000 tons of granulated sugar poured into the country in 1967. Between 1968 and 1973, China postponed the building of its own metro in Beijing to build one for Pyongyang instead.[85]

Sino-North Korean conflict filtered all the way down to the grass roots. Throughout the 1950s and '60s, thousands of Koreans came to China to learn industrial trades in factories. The archives at Shanghai – as an industrial centre, a prime destination for many North Koreans on the apprentice programme – contain discordant reports produced by their Chinese minders. In particular, the North Koreans bitterly resented their minders' attempts to proselytise Mao Zedong Thought at them, and matched any claim about Mao with a rival encomium to Kim. Near the start of the Cultural Revolution, when their Shanghainese hosts redoubled their efforts to spread Mao Zedong Thought, the North Koreans responded by throwing away Mao badges as soon as they were given them, or by sneering at portraits of Mao pasted in the streets. They responded to news of China's first successful nuclear test with indifference. 'In twenty years, North Korea will achieve this too.' ('I don't know what their proof was,' spluttered one irked Chinese spy into his report.)[86]

The lore of brainwashing held that, in addition to overthrowing entire states through war and subverting vulnerable Americans, the Chinese Communists unquestionably controlled the loyalties of Chinese migrants and their descendants in South East Asia. According to Washington and London, mainland China was as expansionist as Hitler's Germany, and eyed its neighbouring states covetously, in search of *Lebensraum*. To Anglo-American security establishments, therefore, after 1949 Overseas Chinese were a security liability in these front-line territories of the Cold War. This assumption about the Overseas Chinese was not only a key ingredient of the domino theory, but also dictated US political and military backing for Taiwan as an alternative centre of Chinese allegiance; a policy that continues to shape East Asia today.[87] But for much of the 1950s, in the eyes of Mao and his lieutenants, the Overseas Chinese were less 'seeds of revolution' and more golden geese whose remittances back to relatives kept the country afloat. Between 1950 and

1957, they amounted to an estimated $1.17 billion, almost cancelling the country's trade deficit for this same period ($1.38 billion).[88]

With a view to maximising such remittances, the Bank of China set up 'bureaus' within their branches, where mainland Chinese could write letters to their overseas relatives asking for funds. Some were little more than ransom notes. Several Overseas Chinese in North America committed suicide on receiving letters demanding money to protect relatives in China imprisoned during land reform. One Chinese immigrant in San Francisco killed himself after a $4,000 'donation' on behalf of his 81-year-old mother failed to rescue her from execution. The US government estimated in 1951 that the 'ransom money already sent to Red China through Hong Kong by Overseas Chinese in the United States alone would be sufficient to support the population of Hong Kong for a year'.[89]

The conflicts between Overseas Chinese and the mainland were many, ranging from the financial to the sexual. One of the earliest sources of tension sprang from the early PRC's most enlightened piece of legislation: the 1950 marriage law, which gave men and women equal rights to sue for divorce. Many women left behind for years or even decades by Overseas Chinese husbands now filed. Even though the government's Overseas Chinese bureau tended to favour the distant husbands in such suits (in the interests of protecting the all-important remittances), it also tacitly condoned stay-behind wives' adultery. Worse still, some cadres had affairs with these wives themselves. One of them, according to a local report, divided his time between 'more than ten' of these spouses.[90]

Far from being true believers, the Overseas Chinese were more often victims of the revolution. As land reform spread across the country, the flash, mock-European mansions – Doric columns and all – built along the south-east coast by the families of Overseas Chinese became targets. Their residents were executed, and so their relatives abroad stopped sending cash. On seeing remittances plummet, the party often toned down its revolutionary zeal. For example, during land reform the luxurious Ancestral Hall of the Sino-Australian Guo brothers – directors of the Wing On chain, China's first department stores – was violently confiscated. Some five years later, though, the regime returned the hall to the family, revoked the clan's 'landlord' status and 'persuaded' a

Mao Zedong and Zhou Enlai in Yan'an, north-west China, *c*.1936. By this point, Mao was beginning to eclipse Zhou in authority within the Chinese Communist Party (CCP).

Mao with his third (fourth, if an arranged marriage is counted) and final wife, Jiang Qing, in Yan'an in the early 1940s.

The first portrait of Mao published in a CCP journal, *Liberation*, in 1937. Note the iconography: Mao's face is lit by the sun's rays from behind; marching columns in the background give the image movement and dynamism.

Song Qingling brings together the Shanghai cultural aristocracy and a famous literary tourist, in 1933. From left to right: Agnes Smedley, George Bernard Shaw, Song Qingling, Cai Yuanpei, Harold Isaacs, Lin Yutang and Lu Xun.

Helen and Edgar Snow around the time of their marriage in the early 1930s.

RANDOM HOUSE PUBLISHES

RED STAR OVER CHINA

BY EDGAR SNOW

The only foreign correspondent who penetrated deep into Northwest China and returned to tell the tale, describes with first-hand detail the amazing stories of:

★ The 6000-mile "Long March" of the army of Chu Teh, "The Red Napoleon."

★ The inside story of the kidnapping of Chiang Kai-shek, and its tremendous consequences.

★ China's united front against Japan, and its war tactics and objectives.

With the only pictures ever taken behind the lines of the Chinese Red Army.

Jacket of the first American edition of *Red Star Over China* (1938).

Edgar Snow with Mao during the former's visit to the Communist state in the northwest. During Snow's first visit in 1936, Mao made himself available for hours of interviews and the transcripts generated Snow's highly favourable write-up in *Red Star Over China*.

Hu Yuzhi oversaw the translation of *Red Star Over China* into Chinese during the war-torn autumn of 1937. This edition had a huge impact, especially on patriotic Chinese youth in China and South East Asia, many of whom were inspired to travel to Yan'an or join the underground Communist movement. Here, he is pictured in 1939 on the way to Singapore, where he did important 'united front' work winning support for the CCP.

Chin Peng, leader of the Malayan Communist Party (MCP) during the Malayan Emergency and beyond, pictured in June 1961. Chin's own comment reads: 'I am freshly arrived in Peking and standing in historical Tiananmen Square in my newly tailored Mao suit.' Chin was hosted by the secretive International Liaison Department. Early in his stay, the CCP leadership instructed him to resume armed struggle against the independent Malaysian state.

Two MCP guerrillas, photographed during the first Malayan Emergency.

Captured MCP guerrillas and activists aboard a steamer, being deported to China during the 1950s.

Mao welcomes
Kim Il-sung
to China in
October 1954.

Edward Hunter, a foreign
correspondent and sometime
CIA stringer who through the
1950s popularised in English
the idea of 'brain-washing'
as an inexorable project
for world domination by
Chinese Communists.

Clarence Adams, one of the twenty-one American POWs who chose to go to China in 1953
after release from captivity in Korea. He directly linked his decision to disgust at the racist
discrimination he had suffered in the United States and in the Korean War. In 1966, he
decided to bring his family back to the US.

A new Chinese edition of the map of the world published in spring 1966. Across the top runs a quotation from Mao: 'The socialist system will eventually replace the capitalist system; this is an objective law independent of man's will. However much the reactionaries try to hold back the wheel of history, eventually revolution will take place and will inevitably triumph.' To left and right, two lines from a 1963 poem by Mao: 'The four seas are rising, clouds and waters raging / The five continents are rocking, wind and thunder roaring.' The poem in full ends 'Away with all pests! / Our force is irresistible.'

A propaganda poster to celebrate the seventeenth anniversary of the founding of the PRC, showing people from around the world waving Little Red Books. The caption reads: 'Chairman Mao is the Red Sun in Our Hearts'.

Mao and Nikita Khrushchev review China's National Day celebrations in October 1959. By this point, relations between the two men had started to become openly rancorous.

A delegation of senior CCP leaders return in summer 1963, greeted by cheering crowds, from a confrontational set of meetings with Soviet counterparts in Moscow; this was a milestone in the conflict between the PRC and the USSR. Deng Xiaoping is first on the left, front line; after Mao's death, Deng would dismantle Mao's economic legacy, while preserving the Chairman's political legitimacy. Kang Sheng, wearing glasses, is third from the left, front line. In Yan'an in the 1940s, he became Mao's secret police chief. As head of the CCP's International Liaison Department in the 1960s, he played a key role in the Cultural Revolution and in vectoring Mao's revolutionary ideas across the world.

'Brave the wind and the waves, everything has remarkable abilities.' This 1958 poster – created near the start of the Great Leap Forward – visualised Mao's utopian belief in voluntarism: as long as you believe you can do something, you can. Note the man reading a book sitting on a missile: the Great Leap Forward also aimed to break down the divisions between intellectual, technical and manual labour.

'Hold high the great red banner of Mao Zedong Thought to wage the Great Proletarian Cultural Revolution to the end – revolution is no crime, to rebel is justified.' This early Cultural Revolution poster (*c*.1966) embodied one of the greatest contradictions of Maoism: its mixing of autocracy (reverence for the cultish leader) with Mao's rhetorical zeal for revolt.

relative from the ancestral village to write privately to the brothers about how good her life was on the mainland. In a counterproductive stunt, however, the party then published this 'private' letter in a left-wing Hong Kong newspaper, thereby fuelling rather than quietening overseas suspicions.[91] To keep in with the Overseas Chinese, the party created an entire programme of 'preferential treatment' (*youdai*): 'Overseas Chinese only' shops, where they could obtain food and goods rarely on sale elsewhere; even 'Overseas Chinese New Villages', pockets of bourgeois lifestyles eradicated in most other parts of China.[92]

After 1956, accelerated collectivisation and the mobilisations of the Great Leap Forward swept these double standards away: ancestral graves were dug over for irrigation and farming, and everyone – young and old – was put to labour round the clock. Families with Overseas Chinese connections left when they could – almost 1,500 fled the island of Hainan at the start of 1956.[93] Between 1959 and 1961, the PRC publicly welcomed – into the apex of the famine – some 130,000 ethnic Chinese from Indonesia, declaring that it recognised their 'suffering and hardship'; that no longer did they have to be 'overseas orphans'.[94] Real life was different. They returned to hard manual labour on the tea estates of south and south-east China.

Many ethnic Chinese members of the MCP exiled to the mainland by the British in the 1950s were denounced and purged during the Anti-Rightist Campaign (1957) or the Cultural Revolution, and had to wait decades for rehabilitation; the Chinese revolution thus ate its nieces and nephews, as well as children. Small wonder that when Chin Peng negotiated a surrender deal with the Malaysian government in 1989 (more than forty years after the emergency had begun), many Chinese exiles opted to return to Malaysia. C. C. Chin, a Malaysian Chinese writer who has dedicated his career to archiving the history of the MCP, observed that these exiles had 'always held their heads high when resisting British imperialism. But they had no idea how to handle ... the struggle sessions of the Anti-Rightist Campaign and the Cultural Revolution ... The psychological pressure was worse than prison or physical torture. Some, unable to bear it, broke down or killed themselves.' One survivor put it in Maoist jargon: 'We became fish without water.'[95] Paradoxically, during the Cultural Revolution – when any foreign connection was grounds for suspicion, and often

outright indictment – Overseas Chinese and their relatives on the mainland were persecuted as a capitalist 'fifth column', while their counterparts in South East Asia were monitored and hounded by local security
services under suspicion of being a Communist 'fifth column' for mainland China. (Indeed, from Yangon to Phnom Penh to Singapore, many
Chinese youth proselytised the Cultural Revolution's Mao cult, pushing
Little Red Books and Mao badges on locals.)[96]

Mao's China turned even career revolutionaries into sceptics. Ah
Cheng, back in China in the mid-1960s, was first confused and then
appalled by what he saw: by the dogmatism of the Cultural Revolution
(he was told that, since his name contained a politically inauspicious
character, he would have been purged if he had been a member of
the CCP); by the violent persecutions of the Red Guards; by the
political and economic hardship suffered by his immediate family (both
his father and parents-in-law remained in China after 1949). On a
private visit to his father in Guangdong, he learned that the famine
of the early 1960s had been caused by excessive state extractions and
that the communes had impoverished ordinary people. 'The Malayan
economy couldn't be run like this, I thought to myself ... Why should
everyone have to be poor?' He tried to make sense of the Cultural
Revolution by burying himself in Mao's works but ended up only
'uneasy and depressed', while his comrades exploited the rhetoric of
the Cultural Revolution to oust their own enemies.[97] In their camps
on the Thai border, MCP guerrillas purged and even executed emergency veterans as 'spies'.[98] Ah Cheng remained an emotional Maoist:
Mao was the grand old man of the revolution and the benefactor of
the MCP. When Mao airily gifted the MCP a radio station in Hunan
(the 'Voice of Revolution') from which to broadcast into Malaysia –
complete with dormitories, shops, clinics, ping-pong tables, basketball
and badminton courts, swimming pool, telephone exchange, hair-
dresser, baths, all ringed in bamboo and supposedly built to withstand
an anticipated Soviet nuclear strike – Mao Zedong Thought was the
keynote of every broadcast. 'Without Mao', Ah Cheng acknowledged,
'there would be no radio station!' But he also saw that Maoism-in-
power was costing the Chinese people dearly.[99]

The 1950s were fat years for psychiatrists in the US. As the perception of an 'extreme historical situation' took shape against the

backdrop of reports of 'brainwashed POWs' (even the fact-checking *New Yorker* called the effect of Chinese and Korean imprisonment on US prisoners 'something new in history'), a Washington merry-go-round of anxious symposia about this new Chinese psychological weapon gathered speed.[100] Amid all this, however, one important angle on 'brainwashing' went ignored. What did the Chinese themselves think they were doing? If expert, non-partisan American minds had been set to work on this problem, they would have found answers that complicated the American projection of a Maoist plot to 'brainwash' the world.

The US intelligence community did not have easy access to solid information about China. The debacle – from the US point of view – of Chinese Communist victory in 1949 led to a witch-hunt of the 'China Hands' in the State Departmant whom the US government had relied upon to craft its policy during the civil war. Almost an entire generation was purged from positions of influence and respectability, including John Service and Owen Lattimore, both of whom had been drawn to Yan'an and to the CCP at least in part by Edgar Snow's sympathetic account. Several of those at the centre of US policymaking on China before 1949 were hauled through government subcommittees challenging their 'loyalty'; none went to prison but many suffered intellectual-political exile. This traumatic phase for Chinese expertise in the US unbalanced American analysis and policy-making for decades – the US is arguably still suffering the consequences today.

Back in the 1950s, individuals with Chinese-language expertise and contacts were sidelined from the State Department – even treated as national traitors. 'Connection with China was so feared that even people who were probably giving the sanest, most lucid intelligence in the US about China were driven out of office,' remembered Ethan Young, a self-confessed third-generation 'red diaper' baby (namely, the offspring of a left-leaning family) who grew up in the 1950s, becoming a student radical in the 1960s; we will meet him again later. 'It was sort of on the level of child pornography. Every piece of material that came out of China was stamped by the government and the stamp basically said: beware what you're reading here, this is coming from a hostile country.'[101] Owen Lattimore took himself off to the University of Leeds, where he founded a superb East Asia department; John Service, after a career of non-promotion in the State Department, lived out his years as a librarian at Berkeley.

Consequently, those drafted to interrogate and analyse intelligence on 'brainwashing' – this defining idea about Maoist global ambitions through the 1950s – often had little or no independent East Asia expertise, and usually no East Asian languages. Many were suggestible or opportunistic Cold Warriors like Edward Hunter. The contrast with the expertise that the North Koreans and Chinese interrogators brought to bear on their handling of US POWs was striking: they spoke good (and sometimes beautiful) English, and several had studied at American universities. One POW noted that the Chinese re-educators were 'professors, editors, or top officials from various organisations ... they were friendly and personable'.[102] Americans at the time possessed, therefore, little insight into what Chinese Communists themselves thought they were doing.

Historians of the post-war US have been understandably critical of the collusion of psychological professionals with the American 'military-industrial complex', and therefore sceptical about the term 'brainwashing'. Analysts have identified it as a term cynically deployed by charlatans such as Edward Hunter to seed fear about the Communist enemy and justify the unbridled expansion of a 'covert sphere' empowered to employ any defensive or offensive means against this 'unprecedented threat' to the American way of life. According to this view, 'brainwashing' can tell us something about the anxieties of Cold War America, but very little about Mao-era political life.

Others disagree, however. Although in her research into Mao-era 'thought reform', the historian Aminda Smith has not found the term 'brainwashing' in Chinese documents from the 1950s, there is enough circumstantial evidence to suggest that it was not just a cynical creation by Hunter – that it *was* a term in informal circulation in the mainland; for it had linguistic roots both culturally deep (going back to ancient Daoist ideas of 'heart-' or 'mind-washing') and politically shallow (echoing rhetoric deployed in Maoist thought-reform movements). Moreover, thought reform was a project with universalising aspirations: the language and techniques deployed on domestic Chinese and American subjects (in Korea) were strikingly similar. But this political remoulding of individuals – though often brutal and manipulative – was not the all-conquering process US Cold Warriors imagined.

Re-education was a foundational ingredient in the Chinese Communist revolution. Without the ability to persuade ordinary people that the radical changes they were suggesting would transform their lives for the better, the CCP would not have been able to mobilise mass support. Those at the bottom of Chinese society had to be bounced out of a fatalistic mindset – blaming their appalling living conditions on 'fate' (ming) – and into articulating grievances against their oppressors through 'consciousness-raising' (qifa juewu). (This later became a key tool of 1960s countercultural rebels, including second-wave feminists, against establishments in the US and Western Europe.)[103] They needed to work out, as Mao's famous opening to his class analysis of Chinese society put it, 'who are our enemies? Who are our friends?'[104] After 1949, thought reform rolled out on a national level the techniques honed during Yan'an's Rectification Movement: small-group discussions and criticism/self-criticism, individual interrogations, the writing and rewriting of autobiographies and confessions.

America's brainwashing terror imagined implacable squads of Chinese indoctrinators. Lived experience was chaotic, however. When the CCP took over Beijing, the party even struggled to keep its own cadres under tight ideological control. Chinese political organisation in Korea could seem similarly unprepared. As one American POW recalled, 'when the Chinese first captured us, there was no place to keep us and no food to give us'.[105] Neither was discipline watertight – either for Chinese or foreign prisoners. A 1954 report on the thought reform of Beijing's underclasses found that 'Internees regularly use going to the doctor, getting water, or getting food as a chance to run away'. Many Chinese re-educatees put up a fight. One prostitute distracted a guard by flashing at him, while her interned former colleagues made a run for it (some of them throwing punches at their custodians as they fled). Others refused to work or study: 'they sleep all day and read fiction', went one report. 'Cadres are unable to do anything about it.'[106]

In the panic that followed the 'brainwashing' revelations in America and other Western countries, the deficiencies in the thought-reform programme unleashed on US POWs were too easily overlooked.

Chinese political commissars in the camps bored the Americans. One described how he and his peers became 'so confounded fed-up' with lectures, fighting sleep during 'all that political crap'. Where they thought they could get away with it, POWs yawned, joked and cheeked their way through indoctrination. The original Chinese lyrics of the anthem 'The East Is Red' were distorted into 'who flung dung at Mao Zedong'.[107] It was, for the most part, sheer physical hardship, not menticide, that led prisoners to cooperate: the frozen death marches, the lack of medical treatment for wounds, the inadequate food. James Veneris, one of the GIs who chose China in 1953, remembered on a Chinese chat show what originally caused him to surrender to the Chinese: the offer of a cigarette from the company that captured him. Veneris wanted to join the CCP and become a Chinese citizen, his widow and daughter recalled tearfully after his death, because the Chinese 'saved his life ... he never forgot that'.[108]

Edward Hunter accused Chinese thought reformers of psychological sorcery. They, by contrast, believed that they were 'unbrainwashing': undoing these POWs' capitalist brainwashing. Many re-educators in Korea saw their subjects as occupying the bottom stratum of US society, as being the puppets and victims of their rulers. 'We know that you are just little pawns in the great capitalist game,' one interrogator told a prisoner. 'Therefore, we are going to give you the chance of being re-educated.'[109] 'It's simple,' remembered another re-educator. 'At that time Western countries, and in particular the United States, were terrible places for ordinary working people like enlisted soldiers. We didn't have to use any special methods. Most of the prisoners were poor guys who hadn't had much choice but to become soldiers, and now they were stuck there, away from their families. It wasn't hard to convince them that they were getting a bad deal. And it wasn't hard to show them that the ordinary Koreans and Chinese they were fighting were getting the same bad deal ... We tried to show them that another kind of world, another kind of system was possible. That was really our main goal.'[110] The role that Maoism and Maoist China would play in the massive social and cultural rebellions of the 1960s vindicated this analysis – as did the story of a black American GI called Clarence Adams.

Like thousands of other US soldiers in North Korea that day, on 24 November 1950 Clarence Adams made his way through a second helping of Thanksgiving turkey. 'It would be three long years before I got another decent meal. Of course, for a lot of my buddies, that Thanksgiving dinner was their last supper.' The following day, he recalled, suddenly 'Chinese troops were everywhere – on the mountaintops, the hillsides, in the valleys – and thousands of American troops were trapped'. As his regiment tried to retreat, he did not sleep or even eat for days, moving from one frozen rice paddy to the next. His company was made up of black soldiers, and he realised after four days that, in direct contravention of conventional strategy, his heavy-gun company was being used to help white companies with only light arms escape. A couple of days later, he was taken prisoner in a ditch by Chinese soldiers. His first two meaningful contacts with his captors were broadly positive. One soldier gave him a handful of grain to eat – his first food in days. Another Chinese man, an interpreter, rushed up and said: 'You are not the exploiters! You are the exploited.'[111]

Adams almost died in captivity in Korea. His blood was sucked by 'hog lice as big as soybeans'; and he was forced to amputate his own gangrened toes.[112] 'More and more I asked myself, Who really benefits from this war? Is it the arms makers? The Chinese insisted it was a "rich man's war but a poor man's fight" ... When I thought about my life as a young black man, I had great difficulty in seeing what democracy and freedom had done for me.' Growing up in Memphis through the 1930s and '40s, Adams became used to stop-and-search, segregated spaces and white violence. He had originally joined up because he was on the run from police brutality. 'Why are the rich rich and the poor poor?' he began to ask himself. 'Why do blacks always get kicked around like animals? ... The more I thought about all this, the more I believed there was some truth in what the Chinese were telling us. Critics in America later called this brainwashing, but how can it be brainwashing if someone is telling you something you already know is true?'[113]

In 1953, Adams became one of the twenty-one GIs who chose China, where he married a Chinese woman and had two children. 'The Chinese didn't brainwash me,' Adams later protested. 'They un-brainwashed me ... I went to China because I was looking for freedom, a way out of poverty, and to be treated like a human being, instead of something subhuman. I never belonged to the Communist

Party, I never became a Chinese citizen, and in no way did I betray my country.'[114] It was, he insisted, 'racism at home rather than Chinese propaganda that inspired my decision'.[115]

Adams brought the same questioning rationality to bear on his decision to return to the US in 1966. Although Mao's China had given him an opportunity to go to university, to travel, to become a translator, he felt his career options were limited. He also missed his family back home and disliked the lack of individualism among Chinese acquaintances. David Hawkins, another American POW who opted for China, where he got a university education and drove trucks before returning to the US in 1957, made a similar point. 'The Chinese have a saying: think twice, speak once. And I fell into that same habit, I questioned everything that was said to me; I never took anything at face value ... I learned to be a better American.'[116]

4

WORLD REVOLUTION

In spring 1966, as the Cultural Revolution began, Ditu (Maps) Publishing House in Beijing issued a new edition of the map of the world. At its centre was the PRC, coloured salmon pink. Across the top ran a quotation from Mao: 'The socialist system will eventually replace the capitalist system; this is an objective law independent of man's will. However much the reactionaries try to hold back the wheel of history, eventually revolution will take place and will inevitably triumph.' Left and right, the world was framed by two lines from a 1963 poem by Mao: 'The four seas are rising, clouds and waters raging / The five continents are rocking, wind and thunder roaring.' (The poem in full ended 'Away with all pests! / Our force is irresistible.')

The map visualised the global hopes of Mao's revolution in its most expansive phase. Other publications chorused a similarly international message. *Peking Review* – the tedious, extraordinarily popular global mouthpiece of Maoist politics through the 1960s – reported on worship of Mao and his revolution across all continents of the world. 'Chairman Mao belongs to China and to the whole world,' one Malian craftsman was quoted. 'Like the sun, he belongs to all mankind.' At this point in the iconography of the Mao cult, the chairman was almost invariably haloed by saintly effulgence. One poster from 1969 has his radiant face overlooking crowds of multi-ethnic zealots: Africans, Turks, Arabs, Caucasians.[1] Beginning in the late 1950s and peaking in the first half of the Cultural Revolution (1966–71), Chinese propaganda portrayed Mao as the genius saviour of the world revolution: battling Western imperialists, treacherous Soviet revisionists and capitalist scabs in his own party.

High Maoism – as I call it here – showcased a peculiar form of internationalism: universal in theory, parochial in practice. It made a utopian case for the global relevance of Maoism, while engaging in petty doctrinal disputes with the Soviet Union. It bid for a world role while destroying China's diplomatic relations in almost every part of the world. It shouted about universal solidarity while asserting Mao's planetary leadership. It was often more about domestic *amour propre* than international realpolitik.

Yet for all its contradictions, high Maoism was deeply productive of history. Within China, it generated the energy and emotion that kept the Cultural Revolution – a unique instance of a Communist Party very deliberately tearing itself apart – spinning through the 1960s and 1970s. And it was the motor for the global cult of the chairman. In presenting Mao – in glossy magazines, technicolour posters and documentaries – as the genius of world revolution, it would sow the seeds of insurrection across Africa, Asia and Latin America, and sink billions of dollars of Chinese aid into these regions. It would help inspire the counterculture movement across Western Europe and the US, in the process merging with the culture of free love and drugs. It would stoke revolutionary wars across Indochina – revolutions that curdled into nationalist conflicts in the late 1970s. And in the slightly longer term, Mao's schemes for world revolution – built upon (often puzzlingly) ferocious rivalry with the Soviet Union – would hasten the end of the Cold War.

These days, the Sino-Soviet Split might sound like a transcultural dessert; the quarrels between Mao and the Soviets for leadership of the world revolution in the 1960s and '70s seem both arid and over-heated, veering bizarrely between the ideological and the infantile. (Even Nikita Khrushchev – the Soviet leader at the epicentre of the argument – often did not understand them.) Half a century ago, though, they transformed global history. The row with China pushed the Soviet Union towards imperial overreach, as it competed with the PRC for influence in the developing world. It wrecked the international socialist alliance, made possible Nixon's spectacular rapprochement with China in 1972, and fuelled bad-tempered, insubordinate national-isms across the Communist bloc – and especially in Cambodia and Vietnam. It was the beginning of the end of the Cold War, and the vector of global insurgencies that are still with us today.

And to unpick this story, we have to dive deep into the era of high Maoism: the Great Leap Forward, the Cultural Revolution and the row with the Soviet Union that drove both these epochal events.

★

The 18th of November 1957 was a stressful day for Li Yueran. The occasion was high profile: an unprecedented gathering of the leaders of sixty-four Communist parties from across the globe, lavishly hosted in Moscow. Li – an experienced interpreter between Chinese and Russian – had been detailed to translate Mao's address to the assembled delegates. The conference was a breakout moment for Mao and the CCP – the first international gathering at which the Chinese party began to approach parity with their Soviet big brother. As a sign of special respect to Mao, the Soviets had waived the requirement for him to submit his speech in writing in advance – the only speaker thus honoured. Mao had taken full advantage of their leniency and chosen to speak extempore. Li was to translate cold.

As soon as Mao began to speak, it was obvious that he was in troublemaking mode. He started by saying that he would remain seated – a 'stroke' a few years earlier, he told the delegates, made it hard for him to stand while speaking. It was an excuse for imperious body language. In May the following year, at the start of the fierce Beijing summer, he threw himself into showpiece labouring at a reservoir north of Beijing. Almost a decade later, he would be standing for hours viewing millions of hysterical Red Guards from the rostrum at Tiananmen Square. When Mao was in combative mood – and especially when dealing with the Soviets – he would frequently begin by feigning illness, to disarm a likely antagonist. 'Flu is my frequent guest,' he complained to the Soviet ambassador in 1963, 'and today I can only receive you lying in bed, and, moreover, it seems that I will die soon.'[2] Mao went on to debate for two and a half hours.

Now, in Moscow, Mao showed his translator no mercy. His speech veered between earthy Chinese idioms, ancient historical allusions and off-piste philosophising. This was Mao expecting, demanding a respectful international audience of peers for his idiosyncratically Chinese language of revolution.

There is a Chinese saying which goes, 'A snake without a head cannot proceed' ... another Chinese proverb says with all its beauty the lotus needs the green of its leaves to set it off. You, comrade Khrushchev, even though you are a beautiful lotus, you too need the leaves to set you off ... Still another Chinese proverb says three cobblers with their wits combined equal Zhuge Liang, the master mind.

The speech's content was confrontational. In the months preceding the conference, Mao had revealed himself as the alpha male of the Communist world, engaging Khrushchev in a boasting competition about who would first overtake the economic superpowers of the West. 'Can we not avoid the Soviet Union's detours and do things faster and better?' Mao had asked in party meetings.[3] In Moscow, Mao bragged that China would overtake Great Britain industrially within fifteen years. And it was at this moment that Mao decided – having tried these ideas out in private conversations – to air his views on the international balance of power in the inevitable nuclear Third World War.

> There are two winds in the world today, the east wind and the west wind. There is a Chinese saying, 'Either the east wind prevails over the west wind or the west wind prevails over the east wind'. It is characteristic of the situation today, I believe, that the east wind is prevailing over the west wind ... Let us imagine, how many people will die if [nuclear] war should break out? Out of the world's population of 2,700 million, one-third – or if more, half – may be lost ... if the worst came to the worst and half of mankind died, the other half would remain while imperialism would be razed to the ground and the whole world would become socialist; in a number of years there would be 2,700 million people again and definitely more.[4]

Khrushchev later remembered that (apart from Song Qingling laughing loyally at Mao's 'racy' reference to rapid Chinese procreation following nuclear holocaust) 'the audience was dead silent' after Mao completed his hour-long peroration. Mikoyan – Stalin's old envoy to Mao in China, and therefore familiar with the ways of the chairman – was sufficiently shocked that he rose to his feet and stood silently glowering at Mao.[5] After they had recovered themselves, the leaders of the Polish and Czech parties objected that although China was populous enough to survive a nuclear attack, Poland and Czechoslovakia would be obliterated.[6] When the Italian Communist leader, Palmiro Togliatti, voiced a similar reservation with regard to Italy, Mao smoothly responded: 'But who told you that Italy must survive? Three hundred million Chinese will be left, and that will be enough for the human race to continue.'[7] Mao, his doctor later remembered, 'was genuinely delighted with the outcome of the Moscow conference'.[8]

Mao's performance in Moscow was designed to antagonise the Soviets. He was on his worst behaviour throughout the visit, despite his hosts' generosity. When the Soviets sent two planes to transport the delegation, and lavished the travellers with caviar, fish and chips, sandwiches and vodka, Mao's response was: 'It's not to our liking.' While in Russia, he would touch only the Hunanese food cooked by his own chef. Khrushchev arranged for Mao to stay in the finest room of Catherine the Great's former palace, a luxurious labyrinth of corridors and vast reception rooms glittering with chandeliers. Mao expressed his disdain by eschewing the en suite bathroom in favour of a chamber pot (brought all the way from China). When Khrushchev invited him to a performance of *Swan Lake*, viewed from the Soviet leader's special box, Mao announced – by his doctor's account – that he was leaving at the end of the second act, grousing: 'Why don't they just dance normally?'[9]

Mao's treatment and response in 1957 contrasted starkly with his experiences in 1949–50. On his first visit, Stalin had snubbed and stalled him, before driving hard bargains at the negotiating table; in public, Mao had responded ingratiatingly. Now, on his second visit, Mao responded to Khrushchev's hospitality with scorn: Mao clearly felt that *he* was Khrushchev's senior and superior. The whole visit – his defiant rudeness, his one-upmanship with Khrushchev, his wilful, China-focused comments – marked the beginning of a new epoch in Mao's projection of his own revolution and status. I am the sovereign of the world revolution, he told his sixty-three fellow Communist leaders, and I say what I like about it.

There were many causes of the rift between China and the Soviet Union: from the personal and petty, to the geopolitical and historical.[10] As we have already seen, Mao was the sworn enemy of Russian food and toilets. In his more expansive quarrels, he told the Soviets that he still planned to get even with them over tsarist land grabs of the nineteenth century. The Chinese side recognised and resented profound inequalities in the relationship between the countries. Life was good for Soviet advisers across the socialist bloc, including in impoverished China – and many took advantage of the generosity of their hosts. Soviet advisers lived carelessly well in China, with their hosts covering expenses as well as salaries that were astronomical by local Chinese standards. In the 1950s, the CCP built, in a quiet rural suburb of west Beijing, in between the city and its universities, the 'Friendship Hotel'. There were leafy grounds in which white deer brought especially for the Russians grazed; a swimming pool; spacious apartments filled with good, heavily lacquered furniture. The hotel's 'Friendship Palace' offered breakfast and billiards. The Soviets, by contrast, overcharged Chinese students in the Soviet Union for substandard courses of study and living conditions.

But it was above all ideology that pushed these two powers apart.[11] Trouble began in February 1956, at the 20th Congress of the Communist Party of the Soviet Union. Here Khrushchev not only denounced Stalin's tyranny but also launched a new foreign policy direction, 'peaceful coexistence' with the USA and other capitalist countries. Two months later, the Cominform – successor organisation to the Comintern – was disbanded. 'Peaceful coexistence' broke with the Soviet past by arguing that the Communist bloc was not inexorably destined to clash with capitalism through violent revolution; instead, it would persuade other states through successful example.

Despite Mao's long history of snubs at the hands of Stalin, when Khrushchev began de-Stalinisation in 1956, Mao set his face against it. He was willing to admit that Stalin (who had been wayward in his support through the Anti-Japanese and civil wars: in 1944, he had told an American diplomat that the CCP under Mao were 'margarine' – phoney – Communists) had made bad mistakes, in particular with regard to China. But Mao was addicted to other aspects of the Stalinist project. For obvious reasons, he wanted to defend the need for a personality cult. Following on from his formative readings of Stalin's *Brief Course* in the 1930s, he also retained a deep attachment for the tenets of 'revolutionary Stalinism' of the 1920s: the belief that the population, especially the rural population, could be hectored and (where necessary) terrorised into generating the agrarian surpluses necessary to fund rapid industrial and above all military development. Khrushchev, Mao considered, was a bureaucrat turning his back on revolution through armed struggle. In November 1956, some nine months after Khrushchev's Secret Speech to the 20th Congress, Mao coined and defined for the first time the phrase that would drive in turn the split with the Soviet Union, the internal purges of the Cultural Revolution, and the confident global expansion of Maoism: 'de-Stalinization ... is revisionism'.[12] While Khrushchev pledged to do all possible to avoid a Third World War, Mao's camp proclaimed that war with the 'imperialists' was inevitable – any other view betrayed the revolution.

Throughout 1958, Mao deliberately manufactured global quarrels in a way that was explicitly designed to challenge 'peaceful coexistence' and to style himself the world supremo of revolutionary troublemaking. That year, the Central Committee enshrined Mao's slogan of 'continuous revolution' – a term designed to distinguish Mao's own tireless revolution from its stalled Soviet counterpart. The late 1950s broadcast most of the ideas that, in fully amplified form, would define high Maoism: 'politics and the masses decide everything' (rather than experts and planners); political struggle must be militarised ('Everybody should organise militias, each person should have a gun, in order to realise an entire nation in arms'); material reality (namely, China's abundant poverty) was no obstacle – all that mattered was 'communist spirit'. Mao simultaneously stoked his own cult: 'A team must worship its leader.'[13] These years also saw the resurgence of Lin Biao, an emotionally unstable military genius and calculating sycophant who replaced the more critical Peng Dehuai as defence minister in 1959. (According to Mao's doctor, Lin was phobic about light, wind and liquids; he kept hydrated only through eating bread that his wife had dipped in water.[14]) Lin ingratiated himself with the chairman through his proposal to use Mao Zedong Military Thought as the core pedagogy for the People's Liberation Army. His propaganda campaigns were fundamental to the creation of 'high Maoism'. This upsurge of confidence in Mao and the boundless possibilities of his revolution were the foundation of Mao's two flagship campaigns of the 1950s and '60s: the Great Leap Forward and the Cultural Revolution.

In both, Mao blurred foreign and domestic policy: the revolution abroad would stoke the revolution at home. He radicalised at home to boost his international profile (enabling him to boast that China was about to 'overtake the UK and catch up with the US', *chao Ying gan Mei*) and he radicalised foreign policy in order to place the Chinese in a state of permanent military readiness. This defied conventional political wisdom, namely that to achieve economic and political construction, a peaceful context was required. Mao took exactly the opposite view.

Between July and August 1958, Mao did his utmost to generate conflict with both the USSR and the US. In late July, Khrushchev rushed to China to patch up a quarrel that Mao had manufactured about a proposed joint submarine fleet. Throughout the visit – unthinkable during Stalin's time, when it was always the Man of Steel who ordered other Communist leaders to scuttle to Moscow – Mao concentrated on enraging Khrushchev. First, he accommodated the Russian in a mosquito-infested suburban guest house without air conditioning. Next, he forced Khrushchev to meet by the swimming pool in Zhongnanhai. Mao was a famed swimmer; Khrushchev got by with inflatable armbands. After a few preliminaries, Mao removed his bath-robe and proposed that the conversation – about the current political situation – continue in the water. Off Mao went, with Khrushchev – clad in satin trunks, a knotted handkerchief and inflated float aids – struggling in his wake; an interpreter delicately wove between the two leaders of the largest Communist powers in the world. Mao delighted in asking complex questions, in response to which Khrushchev could only splutter, having swallowed mouthfuls of water. 'It was an unfor-gettable picture,' remembered a Soviet witness.[15]

His work done with Khrushchev, Mao then ramped up international tensions with the US by ordering on 23 August an intense bombard-ment – hundreds of thousands of shells – of Jinmen, a set of Nationalist-controlled islands between the mainland and Taiwan. By early September 1958, President Eisenhower's Secretary of State, John Foster Dulles, hinted that nuclear weapons could be deployed to resolve the crisis; through their strategic alliance with the PRC, the Soviets had to be ready to respond in kind. Mao was not interested in actually retaking the islands. For him, this confrontation – potentially as serious as the Cuban Missile Crisis – was just power games, a way of pressurising (as he put it, placing a 'noose' over the neck of) the Americans.[16] A massive propaganda campaign explained the bombard-ment to the Chinese people as a righteous defence of victimised Chinese sovereignty against American imperialism. At the same time, it justified Mao marshalling the Chinese people into the economic radicalism of the Great Leap Forward. The drive to forge massive quantities of steel and the helter-skelter organisation of communes all depended on the imposition of military discipline on the Chinese population, warranted by a manufactured sense of international crisis. As Brezhnev later put it, Mao's aim was to convince his people that China was a 'besieged fortress' to create 'external conditions that could justify the use of extreme moral and physical measures to manipulate the workers' into superhuman levels of diligence.'[17] The risk – global nuclear war – that Mao was willing to take with a fragile international situation, in order to achieve these goals, was extraordinary.[18] Mao admitted to his doctor that he was spoiling for a massive fight, regardless of the human consequences. 'Maybe we can get the United States to drop an atom bomb on Fujian. Maybe ten or twenty million people will be killed.'[19]

For obvious reasons, historians of the Great Leap Forward have emphasised its appalling human costs within China. These began with the destruction of privacy, as the state deprived individuals of the right to cook family meals, to manage their own land and produce, to rest; even, in the case of some women, to wear clothes while they laboured. By 1959, it was clear that the state would not permit its rural citizens to carry out the most basic of bodily functions: eating. As its cadres presented fictionalised statistics of vast grain harvests, the state extracted its set quota of this illusory harvest to feed the cities and sell abroad to generate revenue for industrial development. But as the official statistics far exceeded the actual amount being produced, farmers were left with almost nothing. Historians inside and outside China have tracked the horrendous results: tens of millions of deaths from starvation and malnutrition-related disease, as well as from beatings administered by state thugs hoping to extract yet more food from 'hoarding' peasants.

While we must be attentive to the domestic horrors of the Great Leap and its ensuing famine, it is impossible to understand these enormities without outlining the global ambitions that drove them. Although Mao was inspired to imitate Stalin's roseate depiction of Soviet collectivisation in his 'Great Turn' of the late 1920s, the chairman was also desperate to surpass the Soviet Union and the West – to assert China's global supremacy. This was apparent in Mao's rhetoric:

the obsession with realising a fully Communist society before the USSR, with overtaking economically Britain, France and the USA. 'In the future,' he prophesied in 1957, predicting that China would increase grain production by 69 per cent and that of cotton by 100 per cent, 'we'll establish a global committee [and] make plans on global unification.'[20] Dizzy with the imagined successes of the Great Leap Forward, on National Day in 1959 Chen Yi – one of Mao's closest lieutenants – crowed that China's achievements were a 'tremendous encouragement to all the oppressed nations and people of the world fighting for their liberation. In the Chinese people they see their own tomorrow. They feel that everything Chinese people accomplished they too should be able to accomplish. They draw unlimited confidence and courage from the victory of the Chinese people ... The Chinese people see their yesterday in all the oppressed nations.'[21]

China's new self-styling as the granary of the world brought with it a profligate policy of international aid. The Republic of China, under Chiang Kai-shek, had always been a recipient of external assistance, most notably from the United States. To advertise his domestic and global successes – however chimerical they were – Mao was determined to be generous. As the famine reached its worst point in 1960–61, Mao remained uncompromisingly open-handed, with foreign aid growing by more than 50 per cent in this period. The year 1960 saw a dramatic increase in Chinese aid to Africa: in the case of Algeria alone, 50.6 million yuan, up from 600,000 the previous year.[22] In 1961, 660 million yuan was reserved for foreign aid – 260 million more than the annual average of the previous decade. Albania was a particular beneficiary – in two shipments, China provided one-fifth of the country's grain needs. 'The Chinese gave us everything,' recalled one Albanian diplomat. Famine was apparent to him even as a foreigner, even in Beijing (cities were shielded from the worst of the privations and the regime did its utmost to hide the famine from non-Chinese visitors). 'When we needed anything we just asked the Chinese ... I felt ashamed.'[23] Not ashamed enough to stop asking, however: through the 1950s and '60s, the Albanians developed a well-deserved reputation for begging from both the Soviets and the Chinese.[24]

In 1960, the rulers of the Soviet Union received a letter from a rank-and-file member of the CCP. Its message was blunt: the 'centre of world revolution has shifted to China, and Mao Zedong is the greatest contemporary Marxist'.²⁵ Early that year, Mao had appointed a committee of five ideologues to present a manifesto arguing for China's candidacy for leadership of the world revolution. 'Long Live Leninism' – a meandering paean to global class struggle against 'US imperialists in Asia, Africa and Latin America', and to Mao's strategy of 'protracted war' – hit the presses in April 1960. It publicly denounced the Soviet project of 'peaceful coexistence' with the USA. 'The modern revisionists, proceeding from their absurd arguments on the current world situation and from their absurd argument that the Marxist-Leninist theory of class analysis and class struggle is obsolete, attempt to totally overthrow the fundamental theories of Marxism-Leninism on a series of questions like violence, war, peaceful coexistence, etc.' The Central Committee of the CCP, by contrast, 'creatively set forth for the Chinese people, in accordance with Lenin's principles and in the light of conditions in China, the correct principles of the general line for building socialism, the great leap forward and the people's communes, which have inspired the initiative and revolutionary spirit of the masses throughout the country and are thus day after day bringing about new changes in the face of our country.' Nine further polemics followed in 1963–64.²⁶ Distribution was rapid: readers in Algiers could catch up, should they wish, on the latest Communist scholasticism only five days after it was first published in Beijing.²⁷ Partly in response to Chinese pomposity, Khrushchev pulled all Soviet advisers from China in July 1960. And as part of his preoccupation with international 'face', Mao insisted on repaying all outstanding debts to the Soviets at speed – within five short years. '[I]n Yan'an,' he glibly remarked, 'we also had ... difficulties, we ate hot peppers and nobody died, the current time is quite similar, we want to fasten our belts.'²⁸

The dispute descended into petty name-calling. Denouncing the Soviets as 'revisionists' anxious to appease the Americans, Mao and his lieutenants seized any opportunity to sledge the USSR in public and to assert themselves as the true leaders of the world revolution. 'Banging, trampling, hushing and shouting' became the standard soundtrack to international Communist congresses. A former propaganda chief in Vietnam, Xuan Vu, recalled that 'in 1960, the people in the North began to learn about the differences between China and the Soviet Union through loud street-corner radio speakers. From

8 till 8.30 each night, the loudspeakers would broadcast Radio Peking on a direct hookup. From 8.30 till 9 pm, it would be Radio Moscow. The two stations began to abuse each other. The Chinese would insult Khrushchev, and the Russians in turn would insult Mao.'[29] Chinese officials who picked unedifying fights with their Soviet counterparts were treated like heroes: one such delegation was met at the airport in Beijing by more than 5,000 cadres, plus a delighted Mao and Zhou Enlai.[30] Most parts of the Eastern bloc remained loyal to the USSR, however. In an attempt to bar the Chinese from a meeting of Communist parties in Budapest in 1962, for example, the Romanians lied that all flights between Bucharest and the Hungarian capital were full. At another congress in East Berlin, the German Communists switched off the Chinese delegation's microphones, literally to mute their abuse.[31]

Khrushchev's preference (especially when plenty of vodka was available) was to liken Mao to suboptimal footwear: 'an old boot', 'torn galoshes'.[32] Mao returned the compliment by calling Soviet policy programmes 'long and stinky'. Whenever Sino-Soviet relations had the faintest hope of improving, Mao was careful to re-sabotage. In 1964, when some border negotiations seemed to be going surprisingly well, Mao told a Japanese Socialist Party delegation that he still wanted to 'settle accounts' with the Soviet Union over Russian occupation of Chinese territory a century earlier, and raised the question of China recovering (Outer) Mongolia. The Soviet delegation, relaxing during a break in talks at the CCP seaside resort of Beidaihe, broke off their paddling and returned home in a fury. When in 1965 the Soviet premier Kosygin asked Mao whether he could consider a Sino-Soviet rapprochement, Mao replied that he had pledged to denounce the Soviets for 10,000 years. As a special concession, he would reduce that time period by a millennium, but further than that he could not go.

In June 1960, Zhou Enlai reported to the politburo 'two years of famines due to crop failures', resulting in a 'completely dangerous' domestic political outlook.[33] By the following year, Liu Shaoqi and Deng Xiaoping had backtracked from the Great Leap. In January 1962, Mao faced a challenge to his authority: speaking to 7,000 cadres at a conference in Beijing, Liu Shaoqi reported for three hours on China's economic cataclysm. The country was in the midst of a 'man-made disaster' and the central leadership was to blame. 'So many people have died of hunger!' he told Mao in private (again, at the swimming pool). 'History will judge you and me, even cannibalism will go into the books!'[34] Mao went into temporary retreat, as his close colleagues began to dissolve the communes and reintroduce private plots. Moderation in domestic economic policy had its counterpart in foreign policy: the so-called 'Three Reconciliations and One Reduction' advocated reconciliation with the US, USSR and India, and a reduction of revolutionary aid.

In 1962, the CCP, and Mao in particular, therefore faced an unprecedented domestic crisis of legitimacy. Mao manoeuvred his way out of it, engineering a return to the political centre, with a freshly grandstanding speech in September that year. He preached about the evergreen necessity for class struggle, and about his and China's leadership of the world revolution against imperialism and revisionism, especially in Asia, Africa and Latin America.[35] China, in Mao's new slogan, had a sacred responsibility to *fanxiu fangxiu* – to oppose (Soviet) revisionism abroad, and defend against it in China; it was the same fight to preserve the revolution, in different theatres. The ensuing propaganda campaign told the Chinese people – especially urban audiences – to wage revolution as both a Chinese and a global responsibility. A crime against the Chinese revolution became a crime against the world revolution. To save China from the threat of 'revisionism' was to save the world.

In 1965, Minister of Defence Lin Biao actively encouraged the global export of Maoist revolution in his puff piece, 'Long Live the Victory of People's War!': 'Mao Zedong's thought is a common asset of the revolutionary people of the whole world. This is the great international significance of the thought of Mao Zedong ... Hold aloft the just banner of people's war ... Victory will certainly go to the people of the world!'[36]

Upping his rhetoric in 1966, Lin Biao described the Little Red Book of quotations by Mao – of which more than a billion copies were printed, in dozens of languages, between 1966 and 1971 – as a 'spiritual atom bomb of infinite power'.[37] Across the 1960s, Mao's key allies in planning and orchestrating the Cultural Revolution thus explicitly promoted Mao's theories as the key to launching successful foreign revolutionary wars – and above all in the developing, colonial and decolonising world. By stating in the early stages of the Cultural Revolution that if 'there is great chaos under heaven, the situation is excellent', Mao proposed himself as the mastermind of world revolution. His comrades added their own sycophancy. 'Under Mao's leadership it took us just twenty-two years to liberate China,' declared Marshal Ye Jianying in 1966. 'In the next 25 years under the leadership of Mao ... we will liberate the whole world.'[38] China's was a culture of global militancy.

Mao assiduously portrayed himself in public as the friend of the suffering masses oppressed by US and Soviet imperialism: of black Americans, of the Vietcong, of struggling Communist insurgencies everywhere. The Friendship Hotel – its rooms vacated by Soviet advisers – became a hub of drifting revolutionaries, as Mao's China declared itself the global headquarters of rebellion and insurgency: anti-colonial, anti-US, anti-everything. There were melancholic Chilean bolero singers, Colombian actors, Venezuelan armchair *guerrilleros*, and the doctrinaire British Maoist Elsie Fairfax-Cholmeley who allegedly danced in jubilation around the burning ruins of the British legation when it was torched by Red Guards in 1967. (According to a compatriot in Beijing, 'her background was everything her name suggested. She was a P. G. Wodehouse aunt ... if she'd been a spider she would have had [her husband] for breakfast.') There was also a gentle, devout Muslim nationalist revolutionary, one Amadou of Niger, who drifted about the restaurant of the Friendship Hotel in billowing white robes, a silver teapot of holy water in hand, murmuring '*bonjour, bonjour*' to the seated diners. He had no particular interest in Communist doctrine; China held another sort of attraction for Amadou. After his arrival, he informed the director of the State Broadcasting Administration that the Koran permitted him to have four wives. He had already taken three in Africa but was reserving a spot for a Chinese consort and wanted to purchase one while in China. When the director explained that this would be impossible, an agitated Amadou protested that he was not asking for a handout; he was willing to pay for a woman. After managing his disappointment, he taught African languages in China for a few years before returning to Niger, where he started his own transportation business. He then tried to assassinate the king in a public procession, was caught and executed.[39]

China's domestic propaganda machine across the 1960s was glutted with references to world revolution. Films and documentaries, songs and maths textbooks, plays and board games bombarded the Chinese with images of their country leading a global community of revolutionaries. The generation coming of age in the mid-1960s were particularly receptive to this propaganda drive. It told them they did not need to miss out on the glorious military sacrifices in which their parents had participated (the Second World War, the civil war, the Korean War); they too could be revolutionaries in the global armed struggle ubiquitously conjured by the Chinese media. Chen Jian, one of the most acute archival historians of China's Cold War, has long argued that Mao's global rhetoric was simultaneously nationalist and universalist: the party exhorted the people to devote themselves to the revolution for the good of the world and the glory of China. Party propaganda domesticated the global revolution: it told the Chinese – from schoolchildren to the employees of import–export corporations – that it was as close and relevant to them as their own revolution. The higher-ups in one railway logistics department in central China hectored their workers that upping freight production would 'help the world revolution'.[40]

Reminders of this message, of the immediate relevance of the world revolution to everyday life in China, were everywhere in urban China: on wall newspapers and banners, in lectures, sports competitions and primary-school military camps. Schoolchildren trilled songs of Sino-Vietnamese solidarity: 'Oppose the American Imperialists Invading Vietnam', 'Advance Shoulder to Shoulder'.[41] Maths teachers tested students with revolutionary sums: 'Following Chairman Mao's statement in support of the African-American struggle against tyranny, 17 platoons of eternally red, revolutionary elementary school students and teachers immediately engaged in protest demonstrations and resolutely endorsed Chairman Mao's mighty statement. On average, each platoon had 45 people. Altogether, how many people participated in protest?'[42] In leisure hours, these same children amused themselves with a board game based on the principles of Vietnamese guerrilla warfare, the aim being to move unscathed through subterranean tunnels while ambushing GIs with booby traps.[43]

Every sector of society was drawn in – regardless of their professional aptitude for war. 'Chinese and Vietnamese Electric Cable

Workers Fight Shoulder-to-Shoulder!' exhorted one factory poster.[44] References to revolutionary struggle in places remote from, even unknown previously to, Chinese audiences abounded: the Congo, the Dominican Republic, Panama. Audiences were told again and again that poverty and backwardness did not matter: in the 'revolutionary war ... pushing history forward', the key element was 'human will'.[45] The ritual year filled up with celebrations commemorating foreign revolts and revolutions. The government pointedly invited, for its national days, delegations from across the developing world, so that audiences could feel that their own revolution was respected by the international community. 'All the Chinese people are with you,' Mao reassured guerrilla insurgents in the Congo in 1964, following American and Belgian intervention in that conflict.[46] Almost every announcement of US foreign policy occasioned a rally – each millions strong, each bellowing the support of the 650 million Chinese people for the victims of American imperialism – in Chinese cities the length and breadth of the country. Newspaper supplements and propaganda posters proclaimed that 'we have friends all over the world'; the radio broadcast live singalongs of 'The Peoples of Asia, Africa and Latin America Want Liberation'.[47] But this was always a parochial flavour of internationalism, driven by a narcissistic interest in how the world prized China, rather than by a disinterested solidarity. China styled itself as the patriarch of the global revolutionary family. The CCP acquired a habit of speaking for the world, and especially for the developing world, the key battleground for American and Soviet influence: China's nuclear bomb was the 'Afro-Asian bomb'; China's veto at the UN, after it regained its seat there, was 'the third World veto'.[48]

After the rallies dispersed, documentaries and plays kept up the noise about the world revolution, and China's centrality to it. *Collective Enemy of the World's People* – a mass-distributed film of 1964 – informed viewers that '[f]rom the Indochina peninsula to the Congolese jungle, from the Caribbean Sea to Cyprus, from Japan in the Pacific Ocean to Zanzibar at the edge of the Indian Ocean, the anti-American struggle of all the world's people is right now rolling like a furious billow rushing toward US imperialism causing it to sink down lower and lower until it is surrounded on all sides'.[49] Images of adoring crowds in Africa receiving the diplomatic whirlwind Zhou Enlai in 1963–64 – broadcast across every major city in China – advertised the love and respect that the Chinese revolution enjoyed on that continent. Some viewers were moved enough to sign pledges of support in their own blood, or to rush into battle in Vietnam themselves.⁵⁰ The theatre of Chinese internationalism was unabashedly ambitious, caring little for the unities of time, place and action: one musical's plot swivelled between Asia, the Middle East, Africa, Latin America and the White House, before ending in Tiananmen Square with a mass rally declaring that 'Mao's statements … *bring together* the revolutionary will of the world's people, and *encourage* the revolutionary struggle of the world's people'.⁵¹

This culture of insurgency aimed to bring the revolution into the lives of ordinary people, and also to convince them of Mao's global leadership. Chinese plays about Vietnam claimed Vietnamese characters as disciples by putting Mao's catchphrases into their mouths. Chinese performers 'blacked up' to act, sing and dance their solidarity with, but also implicit leadership of, anti-Belgian guerrillas in the Congolese civil war. 'The East wind beats on the war drum,' one song from the show chanted, as guerrilla characters took up Mao's theories of protracted war to battle American and Belgian oppression, and read Mao's *Collected Works* onstage.⁵² 'Do you think our struggle today is black men against white men?' asked black-face Chinese performers. 'You're wrong. All the oppressed people in the world, regardless of race and color, are brothers … The sun has already risen in the east. The people of Africa know how to greet the future.'⁵³

In 1966, Mao's national and international war on 'revisionism' enabled him to use the Cultural Revolution to turn on his domestic enemies, above all on Liu Shaoqi and Deng Xiaoping, who in 1962 had pulled back from the radical visions of the Great Leap Forward. Mao believed – or at least argued – that the cohort of Chinese functionaries trained in or influenced by the Soviet Union posed an internal ideological risk to both the Chinese and world revolutions. If the revisionists at home – in cahoots with those abroad – gained the upper hand, swathes of the Chinese government could be turned against the Chinese people and the revolution outside China. This was the so-called 'two-line struggle' theory beloved of Mao and his many global disciples: between Mao's continuous, proletarian revolution, and the 'bourgeois reactionary line' of the revisionists. Mao expressly launched the Cultural Revolution to eradicate Soviet influence in

China – this fear was used to justify violence against anyone suspected of foreign (Soviet or Western) connections, and to militarise Chinese society. 'What would we do if Khrushchev existed in China?' Mao speculated. 'Party committees in each province must resist [Chinese Khrushchevs] ... They will need guns.'[54] And here lies the key contradiction of the Cultural Revolution: it was a set of events with aspirations to global solidarity and liberation, which generated brute xenophobia and authoritarianism. Between 1966 and 1969, in the name of continuous revolution against bourgeois, imperialist influence, Mao's Red Guards – school and university students – declared war on anything that could be labelled 'old' or 'Western'. By 1969, the year of the 9th Party Congress which codified the power of those who had won the Cultural Revolution's early factional struggles, the PRC tottered on the brink of civil war then calcified into a military dictatorship. At least three million had been purged from the party bureaucracy; many more had been persecuted, some of them (an estimated half a million) to death. Schools and universities had been shut down and four million students rusticated for rural re-education. The Cultural Revolution's obsession with 'purist egalitarianism' persisted in public life, albeit in a less intense form, all the way to Mao's death in 1976.[55]

The campaign to push global insurgency reaped dividends for Mao during the Cultural Revolution. The idea of an approving foreign gaze – that events in China were inspiring revolutionaries all over the world – was intensely important to those propelling the revolution. The Chinese press generated articles and photographs depicting foreign adulation for Mao and his Cultural Revolution: Maophiles devouring the Little Red Book in Tanzania, Guinea, Albania, Ecuador and Algeria; international political pilgrims trekking to the 'sacred soil' of Mao's birthplace and to Yan'an; sing-offs between international delegations competing to honour Mao while on flights around China.[56] 'Mao Zedong! The sun of the East!' rhapsodised one Palestinian poet in Chinese print. 'It is you who gives hope to the entire world. / It is you who gives direction to our forward progress. / We follow closely as Mao Zedong makes revolution / Simultaneously and in unison we sweep away the vermin!'[57] A favoured trope of this propaganda was the foreign Buddhist, Muslim or Christian who abandoned their religion to convert to Maoism. 'I once believed I already worshipped the true god,' an elderly Muslim told the PRC embassy in Pakistan. 'Now I am old. I want to go to China, for I know, the true god is not anywhere else, he is in China, in Beijing. I want to represent my city's people and go worship Chairman Mao.'[58] Those who knew far better – such as Liao Chengzhi, the cosmopolitan polyglot responsible for the PRC's relations with far-flung Chinese diasporas – proclaimed that 'Africans memorise more of Mao's works than I do – Mao Zedong Thought is the red sun of the world's people'.[59] Chinese foreign aid once more rocketed: between 1970 and 1977, $1.882 billion went to Africa, compared with $428 million between 1954 and 1966.[60]

This propaganda of internationalism helps explain in part the inquisitorial fanaticism of the Red Guards and other Cultural Revolutionaries after 1966. Red Guard publications were full of references to, and images of, the global impact of Mao and the Red Guards. But they were also obsessed with stories of Mao's detractors: their sacred world revolution, although applauded by the oppressed masses, was simultaneously under attack from jealous revisionists and imperialists everywhere – precisely because of its global scope. It was the nickname 'China's Khrushchev' that condemned the most senior victim of the Cultural Revolution, Liu Shaoqi, to death by persecution in 1969 as an international traitor. The Red Guards simultaneously reserved some of their goriest vitriol for the Soviets: 'we will scrape your skin off, pull out your veins, burn your corpses and spread the ashes in the wind!' declared a 'big character' (denunciation) poster outside the Soviet embassy in 1966.[61]

As part of this upsurge of international paranoia, China's long-term foreign residents – many of whom had cut off links with their home countries to cheer China's revolution – were arrested and imprisoned: Elsie Fairfax-Cholmeley, her husband, Israel Epstein, and Gladys Yang, an Oxford graduate who had toiled since 1949 to enhance China's international image by translating into English the remnants of the high literary canon deemed politically correct by the CCP. Sidney Rittenberg, a passionate American Maophile and middle-aged Red Guard, spent nine years in a Cultural Revolution jail before leaving the country to become a successful China–US business consultant. The PRC's diplomatic representation imploded globally. In Mongolia, Cambodia, Burma and Nepal, Chinese officials waved Little Red Books in the faces of local populations; even local plasterers employed in the

Mongolian embassy were corralled into five-hour study sessions of Mao's works. In Hong Kong, the CCP supported underground Maoists who orchestrated mass rallies against British imperialism and burned alive a radio presenter who disagreed with their tactics. In 1967, Red Guards were allowed to burn Britain's legation in Beijing to the ground, and physically and sexually assault its diplomatic residents. Just one ambassador was left in post; all others were recalled for political re-education in deep rural China.

China's twisted internationalism in the 1960s transformed the country physically as well as mentally. In 1964, Mao began to argue that a multilateral attack from China's global enemies was imminent. Factories in China's industrial heartlands along the east coast were told to pack up and reassemble in the impoverished west, ready to fight a People's War. Unless steel plants were developed in the west, Mao complained, 'I cannot go to sleep at night ... I will have to ride on a donkey to get to meetings. If we do not have enough money, use the royalty payments on my writings.'[62] Mao's 'Third Front' pushed factories, mines and steel mills behind the cordon of mountains running from Beijing in the north down to Hainan in the south, which demarcates the heavily populated eastern flank of China from its more isolated west. Remote locations were deliberately chosen, to safeguard factories and workshops from enemy bombing. The amounts of capital committed to the project were staggering: between 1966 and 1975, the Third Front swallowed up almost half of national investment.[63] About 5.5 million men and women were mobilised to build 8,000 kilometres of new railways between 1954 and 1980; many, after walking for days across hundreds of kilometres just to reach the building sites, collapsed from exhaustion before they had lifted a tool or a brick.[64] If a hill presented itself at an inconvenient location, militia teams were sent to move it. Two workers died for every kilometre of the railroad laid between the cities of Chengdu and Kunming. Workers were underfed, overworked, and often suffered from dysentery, due to the lack of reliable water sources.[65] The difficulties of working in such remote, mountainous terrain, meanwhile, added exponentially to the expense: the Chengdu–Kunming line swallowed five to six times more than building the railways had cost in the 1950s, and tens of millions of yuan had to be spent deep into the 1980s to fix glitches.[66] By then, unknown numbers of half-finished or abandoned projects – factories, power stations, dormitory buildings – rusted or mouldered amid the wet green mountains of western China. It seems probable that China's economy would have emerged into the 1980s in a rather different shape had the Third Front not intervened. One economic historian estimated in 1988 that China's industrial output was some 10–15 per cent below what it would have been had investment been redirected elsewhere.[67]

In February 1969, Mao's foreign policy of international provocation approached the brink, in one of the most inhospitable spots of the People's Republic. That month, the Chinese Army launched an ambush on Soviet soldiers stationed on Damansky/Zhenbao Island, a scrap of disputed territory in the middle of the frozen Ussuri River marking the north-eastern border between China and the Soviet Union. Thirty-one Soviets and perhaps hundreds of Chinese lost their lives. Negotiations proved problematic. When Kosygin tried to telephone Mao, the Chinese operator cursed him for a 'revisionist element' and cut him off.[68] That year, Moscow actually contemplated wiping 'out the Chinese threat [to] get rid of this modern adventurer' with a nuclear attack, until allies refused to endorse the plan.[69] 'We are now isolated,' Mao observed, a little plaintively. 'No-one wants to make friends with us.'[70]

At least one other citizen of the PRC reached his own nadir not long after. In 1970, a sixteen-year-old from Changsha called Han Shaogong was sent into rural Hunan as an 'educated youth', to be re-educated by peasants there. Everything was a struggle: the constant hunger, the villagers' topsy-turvy dialect (which translated Mandarin meanings into their antonyms), their disgust for revolutionary operas, their sexual libertarianism, their impious habit of sticking portraits of Chairman Mao on toilet buckets.

Perhaps the worst of it was the back-breaking toil of peasant life. By 1970, Mao's volatile foreign policy added to its arduousness: in response to the crisis with the Soviets, everyone had to dig air-raid shelters, or 'war-preparation caves', as they were called. 'The Soviet Union', Han remembered learning, 'was going to fight down from the north, America was going to fight up from the south, and Taiwan was going to fight over from the east, so all the war-preparation caves had to be dug before the full moon was up. It was also said a very large bomb had already been launched from the Soviet Union and in a day or two it would fall on us here ... We needed to get our cave dug a step ahead of all the bombs of the imperialists, revisionists and counterrevolutionaries ... I must have hacked five or six pickaxes to pieces.' Conditions were terrifying: the cavern was only wide enough for two people lying down and was lit only by a tiny oil lamp. 'The flickering, dusky light illuminated the mud wall your nose was rammed up against, illuminated the eternal, inescapable fate that lay before you ... It made me think of how our forefathers had described hell ... [I lay] there like a dog ... sometimes kneeling, sometimes on my side, my whole body bathed in mud and sweat, struggling, panting underground in a darkness utterly bereft of daylight, with only the eyes in my head to prove I was human.' Years later, long after he returned to the city and became a famous writer, Han revisited the cave. 'The world war had never been fought in the end. The shelter we'd dug had been converted into a storage cellar for seed potatoes. Because it was damp, the walls had grown green moss and the smell of mouldering sweet potatoes wafted from the mouth of the cave.'[71]

The sectarian pettiness of China's conflict with the Soviets notwithstanding, the quarrel meant much to many. It carried meaning for generations of Chinese reared on the wolf's milk of Maoism, to those indoctrinated in the inevitability of violent revolution at home and abroad. It meant violence, and even death, for the millions of Chinese persecuted for their imputed crimes against the domestic–international revolution. And it meant something to the Soviet diplomats who, in February 1967, were imprisoned in a Beijing embassy, while on the streets of the city effigies of the Soviet premier crackled into flames.[72] When Soviet politicians tried to negotiate their release with the Chinese chargé d'affaires in Moscow, he responded only with quotations read from the Little Red Book.[73] In September 1963, Khrushchev had told the Soviet Presidium – one of the most important governing bodies – that responding to Chinese rhetorical aggression was 'task number one'.[74] In Asia, Africa and Latin America, a Soviet intelligence report found, China 'spare[d] neither funds nor time, [nor shunned] the most unworthy methods – blackmail, flattery, bribery, using the services of splitters and renegades': $60,000 to the Queen of Burundi here, tons of propaganda leaflets in Algiers there.[75] Mao-era China banged a militant drum, arguing for anti-imperialist revolution and denouncing the Soviet Union for selling out the Third World to white, developed interests.

While they attacked the Soviets, the Chinese launched a charm offensive throughout the 1960s to win over developing countries. They welcomed a continuing stream of 'Third World' visitors; they deluged Asia, Africa and Latin America with broadcast and print propaganda in local languages; they pledged generous aid packages even while at the peak of a government-manufactured famine. In so doing, they successfully presented themselves as the champion of small nations, against hegemonic superpowers. 'You are still white,' Africans told the Soviets, 'but [the Chinese] are yellow, closer to us.'[76] They reached out to Western Maoists, too, who busied themselves setting up pro-Chinese 'Marxist-Leninist' parties in the 1960s and '70s. In return for support of the Cultural Revolution, China's International Liaison Department pledged generous help for these political grouplets: tens of thousands of journal subscriptions; hundreds of thousands of dollars via Albania.[77] It became so easy to win China's confidence by proclaiming oneself a Maoist that the Dutch secret services set up one such party, led by a maths teacher, as a front for gathering intelligence about China. The ploy remained undiscovered all the way up to the Dutch government dismantling it after 1989.[78]

The Soviets' riposte was robust. They printed 3.2 million copies, in thirty-five different languages distributed to eighty-five countries, of just one of several open letters to the CCP refuting the latter's 'slanderous attacks'.[79] They poured energy and money into sponsoring local activists all over the world to write anti-Chinese copy, to show anti-Chinese films, and give anti-Chinese lectures. As relations became deeply hostile in late 1962, the New York Times speculated that Khrushchev now wished for a 'Soviet-American alliance against China'.[80] Although the Soviet Union would not collapse for another three decades, the fracture lines in Communist unity caused by the row with China initiated the slow death of the Soviet bloc.

At the same time, China's sabre-rattling abroad edged the Soviets to compete through a serious, hard-power foreign policy adjustment. The USSR stepped up aid to Algeria and Egypt; it dispatched weapons to the Congo and to Palestine. By 1976, the Soviet Union had established itself as the sponsor-in-chief of the developing world, pledging to liquidate 'all remnants of the system of colonial oppression'.[81] It lavished North Vietnam with rhetorical and material support, to woo it away from its Chinese neighbour. Between the 1960s and the 1970s, therefore, hot conflicts of the Cold War – in Vietnam, Africa and the Middle East – were driven not only by tension between the Soviets and the Americans, but also by Chinese-Soviet rivalry for influence. Soviet and Chinese leaders elbowed childishly past each other on tours of Africa. In 1963–64, Zhou Enlai visited ten African countries in less than two months. Four months later, Khrushchev pointedly made his first trip to Africa to inaugurate the first phase of the Soviet-funded Aswan High Dam. In comparison with the reception lavished upon Khrushchev, exulted *Isvestiya*, the party newspaper, the Chinese leaders were just 'pathetic'.[82] In 1969, when Soviet and Chinese leaders shared a podium in North Vietnam, at the funeral of Ho Chi Minh, one story has it that the Chinese delegation was under strict orders to send the Soviets to Coventry, and ostentatiously looked in the opposite direction if any Russian tried to speak to them.

By the late 1960s, the USSR was rhetorically and financially over-committed to making revolution in the developing world, especially in Africa and Latin America. When, after the death of Mao in 1976, China pragmatically withdrew from the contest and focused instead on domestic economic reconstruction, the Soviet Union was left the dominant Communist power in the Third World. It was a pyrrhic victory, however. Superficially, the second half of the 1970s resembled the high point of the USSR's foreign policy in the Cold War, with the accession to power of Soviet-supported regimes in Angola, Ethiopia and Afghanistan. In reality, the USSR was materially over-stretched, while its belligerent rhetoric and the expectations that this created among militant allies such as the PLO jeopardised détente with Western countries. In 1979, the USSR began its disastrous invasion of Afghanistan – a ten-year Soviet Vietnam that would end in ignominious withdrawal in 1989. Throughout the 1980s, the USSR's military expenditure – a third of the national budget – critically overburdened the state. 'Food was stolen out of the mouths of Soviet people to rescue yours,' Radio Moscow's man in Cairo had told his Egyptian fellow broadcasters in 1965, when the Soviets were wooing Nasser.[83] While the citizens of Moscow had to queue to buy everyday necessities, Afghanistan became a public relations disaster for the regime, an emblem of miscalculation and futility. In 1981, the chairman of Soviet state planning responded to an East German request for fuel: 'Should I cut back on oil to Poland? Vietnam is starving ... should we just give away Southeast Asia? Angola, Mozambique, Ethiopia, Yemen ... we carry them all. And our standard of living is extraordinarily low.'[84]

China's global militancy, and its clash with the Soviet Union, also transformed the landscapes of conflict around the world. Without Soviet encouragement of United Arab Republic (Egyptian) and Palestinian interests – dictated by the USSR's turn towards anti-imperialism resulting from competition for influence with China – it becomes hard to imagine that Nasser would have been confident enough to join the build-up to the Six Day War in June 1967.[85] Forced to fight a war on global Maoism, the Soviets abandoned a line of more pragmatic economic development and were pushed towards ideological battles. That same year, the Soviet bloc founded a new working group focused on countering the 'China problem' – InterKit (the International on China).[86] Without the Sino-Soviet Split and competitive Chinese and Soviet aid packages, the intensification of the Vietnam War also becomes hard to imagine. This duel turned the Vietnam War into the hottest conflict of the global Cold War. While it was Chinese support that first encouraged North Vietnam to confront the US, the Soviets were then trapped within their rhetoric of anti-imperialism and, despite private misgivings, publicly committed themselves to supporting the Vietnamese Communists in a way that militated directly against rapprochement with the US. It was, moreover, US perception of global Soviet intervention that helped push the 'Reagan doctrine' in Latin America, Africa and Afghanistan in the 1980s: the bankrolling of almost any Third World ally (including Afghan jihadis, the mujahideen) who pledged to fight Soviet influence. The repercussions of this strategy still haunt us today.

But the consequences of the Sino-Soviet Split and the Cultural Revolution went far beyond China's own domestic ructions, or the Soviet Union's defensive responses. Even as China's foreign policy apparatus behaved in such a bizarre and alienating way between 1966 and 1968, picking fights with governments all over the globe, it attracted millions of renegades and rebels. It seemed that no country behaving in such a self-destructive way at home and abroad could possibly have ulterior, nationalist motives; it must genuinely support the world revolution that its propaganda incessantly celebrated.

In 1968, Mao began to backtrack from the rhetorical excesses of the Cultural Revolution: he prohibited the distribution of Mao badges abroad ('give me back my aeroplanes', as he legendarily put it) and banned the phrase 'Mao Zedong Thought' from foreign affairs documents.[87] By September 1976, Mao was dead; the puppet masters of his Cultural Revolution, the Gang of Four – his formidable wife Jiang Qing, two dourly ruthless theoreticians, Yao Wenyuan and Zhang Chunqiao, and a handsome-but-dim factory worker called Wang Hongwen – were under arrest; domestic economic pragmatism was already ousting abstract dreams of world revolution. The Maoism of the 1960s would have faded into a historical hallucination but for its global afterlives: brutal civil war in Indonesia; the struggles for decolonisation and development in Africa; the shredding of Vietnam and Cambodia; the shocks and aftershocks of 1968 in Western Europe and the US (where, extraordinarily, PRC foreign-language propaganda such as *Peking Review* became reputable sources of international news); guerrilla wars in India, Latin America and Nepal. Some of these transmissions – especially to South Asia and to Peru – have continued for decades after Mao's own death. Like a dormant virus, Maoism has demonstrated a tenacious, global talent for latency. It is this history, this aptitude that we will now track across the world.

5

YEARS OF LIVING DANGEROUSLY –
THE INDONESIAN CONNECTION

In 2012 in Aceh, northern Sumatra, a local optician called Adi made a home visit to a community leader. Inong was a tall, lean, angular man in his early seventies, wearing a khaki crocheted Muslim prayer cap; he wanted reading glasses. The consultation began conventionally enough, in the yard outside Inong's house. Adi carefully placed a pair of scarlet-rimmed test lenses over his patient's drawn face. 'Is it sharper? Is this more clear?'

But as the consultation progressed, Adi turned the conversation towards less prosaic matters. He had some questions about history. In the mass violence against real and alleged Communists in 1965–66, Inong had been the head of a village death squad: he had taken a leading role in thousands of murders. Nationally, the death toll was at least half a million. The Indonesian Communist Party – until this point, the third largest in the world – was destroyed, its leaders summarily executed. Across two days, Inong had – in full view of the community – brutalised and killed Adi's older brother Ramli. This meeting, some forty-five years after the murders, had been orchestrated by the American film-maker Joshua Oppenheimer, engaged on a decade-long project – chronicled across two documentaries – to excavate Indonesian memories of these traumatic events. Inong's actions had destroyed Adi's family – his father's mind and health had collapsed; his mother was left permanently heartbroken. Despite this conspicuous trauma, Adi's tone was calm, measured throughout the interview. For this was Indonesia. Fourteen years had passed since a surge of protest – 1998's Reformasi – had brought

down the corrupt dictatorship of Suharto, architect of the 1965 genocide. Yet millions of nationally and locally powerful Indonesians –
from People's Representatives to village headmen like Inong – still
owed their political and economic clout to their participation (or at
least collusion) in the 1965–66 massacres, which annihilated or terrorised into silence most political rivals to Suharto and the army. To this
day, the perpetrators and beneficiaries of these events still present
themselves as heroes, who purified Indonesia of Communist treachery.
Victims and their families still face discrimination and the government's refusal to revise this official version; they are even threatened
with the possibility of renewed violence, should they attempt to
question the army's narrative of these events. Adi therefore had to
be careful.

'Are your neighbours afraid of you?' he asked, in a natural pause in
the prescription process. 'Yes,' answered Inong. 'They know they're
powerless against me.' His advanced age notwithstanding, there was
a wiry ferocity to him. The confidence of his answer spoke deeply of
the sense of impunity enjoyed by the perpetrators of 1965. He was
unabashed about evoking his participation in mass murder. After all,
he had allowed himself to be filmed extensively when Oppenheimer
was preparing his first film on the massacres, *The Act of Killing*, revisiting
the main site of the massacres in North Sumatra, the creeper-lined
banks of the Snake River, with an old comrade. Together they
re-enacted in painstaking detail the process of dragging victims
(stripped, except for their underwear) from army escort trucks down
to the riverbank, where some were decapitated, some were disembowelled, some were stabbed and had their genitals cut off, before being
kicked into the river; Adi's brother was subjected to all but the first of
these acts.

In front of Adi in 2012, Inong freely shared his memories.
The following is practically a monologue, uninterrupted by
questions:

If we didn't drink human blood, we'd go crazy ... Some killed so many
people they went crazy. One man climbed a palm tree each morning
to do the call to prayer. He killed too many people. There's only one
way to avoid it: drink your victims' blood or go crazy. But if you drink
blood you can do anything! Both salty and sweet. Human blood. I

know from experience. If you cut off a woman's breast, it looks like a coconut milk filter. Full of holes. There was a communist woman. She lived with her brother but he wasn't communist. He didn't want to kill his own sister, so he sent her to me ... If they're bad people, you can hack them up ... The Communist Party of Indonesia ... had no religion. They had sex with each other's wives. So people say ... They said it themselves. When we interrogated them ... Muhammed never killed anyone. He was against killing. But you're allowed to kill your enemies.

The camera focused throughout on Inong's eyes and mouth. There was an occasional twitch, accompanied by an irregular flickering of the tongue to the edge of his lips – the cinematography (accentuated by the translucence of the skin stretched over Inong's skull) slightly recalled a lean, bellicose jungle frog. When Adi posed a couple of questions, calmly pointing out only the most obvious inconsistencies in the narrative, Inong snarled: 'Are you trying to make me angry? ... I don't like deep questions! ... I'm going to the mosque ... the past is past. Luckily I drank blood.'

In the course of the filming, Adi met a number of perpetrators implicated in his brother's death. All these encounters were similarly taut with menace. The most explicit threat was made by the head of the Regional Legislature, one M. Y. Basrun. After denying that his continual re-election since 1971 was based even slightly on intimidation, he asked Adi: 'Do the victims' families want the killings to happen again? No? Then change! If you keep making an issue of the past, it will definitely happen again.' 'The confrontations were tense,' remembered Oppenheimer. 'Again and again, Adi says the unsayable, leaving the audience to feel what it is like to live as a survivor, and to perceive the contours of an oppressive silence borne of fear.' Without remembering these events, Oppenheimer and others have argued, it is impossible to understand local and national power structures in Indonesia today: the culture of impunity that exists around political violence; the collusion of the US, Australia and the UK in suppressing any social or political force that could undermine the Indonesian Army's creation of an exploitative kleptocracy open for business with multinational companies. As one of Adi's interlocutors urges him:

'Forget the past. Let's all get along like the military dictatorship taught us.'[1]

For decades, attempts to unpick the events of 1965 – which transformed the course of post-colonial Indonesia – have focused on Anglo-American involvement, or on domestic power struggles within Indonesia (most notably within the army). There were good historical reasons for this. The US and UK in particular played a nefarious part: handing over to the Indonesian Army lists of alleged Communist sympathisers; funding paramilitary death squads; beaming propaganda broadcasts from Singapore into Indonesia to spread fear and loathing of Indonesian Communism. Anglophone media in Australia, the US and the UK either buried reports of the massacres or misrepresented the violence as acts of spontaneous self-defence against bloodthirsty Communists. The army managed the crisis with calculated brutality, orchestrating mob violence spiked with religious intolerance and local vendettas.

But I argue here that Mao and his ideas also had a role in this tragedy. Indonesia was the test case in China's post-Soviet foreign policy: a key strategic target for exporting the wisdom and superiority of the Maoist model. Leading Indonesian Communists were intoxicated by the militant rhetoric of Mao's revolution in the early 1960s. It encouraged and inspired them to confront the Indonesian military; this decision in turn gave the army a pretext to trigger the horrors of 1965. Without Maoism, Indonesia's catastrophe in 1965 is hard to imagine.

Independent Indonesia was born in August 1945 of violent contradictions. Dutch colonialism bequeathed a sense of political unity to these disparate islands, but also a racist economic model devoted to siphoning off the territory's natural resources to enrich a remote European power. Anti-Dutch Indonesian nationalism, which had begun to flourish in the early years of the twentieth century, was encouraged by Japanese occupation during the Second World War – an occupation built on military authoritarianism and terror. Its figurehead, and the hero of early Indonesian independence from 1945 to 1965, was Sukarno: a charismatic, womanising orator who blended nationalism, socialism, Islam and indigenous spirituality (many believed that he survived seven assassination attempts thanks to his possession of a magic swagger stick) to create his vision of a modern Indonesia.[2] In his restlessness, volatility and promiscuity, there was more than an echo of Mao. It was the Japanese occupation – despite its grotesque oppressions – that gave men like Sukarno a platform. Under the Japanese, he could roam around rural Indonesia, delivering the kinds of nationalist sermons that had caused the Dutch to send him into internal exile for most of the 1930s. A speech Sukarno gave in 1943 explains the logic of his collaboration and gives a flavour of his oratory:

> Fifteen years ago we reiterated the fact that our Indonesian nation-alism needed to be oriented broadly, like a nationalism that was part of an international Asianism. At that time we held that when the Chinese dragon works together with the white elephant of Siam, with the sacred cow of India, with the sphinx of Egypt, with the wild buffalo of Indonesia, and when such orientation is further armed by the sun of Japan, then imperialism will be destroyed in all of Asia. So through the will of Allah and the wisdom of Japan, the cooperation of all Asian forces has indeed become a fact. The Japanese defence chain stretching from Manchukuo in the north, to Indonesia in the south, to Burma in the west, to the Philippines in the east, has indeed become one great bulwark. So, my dear brothers, do not forget that we Indonesians form a link in that chain.[3]

Indonesian militias that would later fight for independence against the Dutch were originally trained by the Japanese to resist invasion by Allied forces. Sukarno survived the war relatively unscathed by his endorsement of Japanese imperialism. As Japan's military effort failed in the summer of 1945, he shook off Japanese sponsorship and, under pressure from more radical nationalists, proclaimed a free, independent Indonesian state on 17 August 1945, two days after Japanese surrender. Other Indonesians were less fortunate: untold multitudes perished as *romushas*, labourers enslaved to boost production for the Japanese war machine.[4] Perhaps 2.4 million died in Java alone – the central island of the archipelago – of starvation due to inadequate and corrupt food distribution, the exigencies of the Japanese war economy and the collapse of trade.[5]

The independent Indonesia that emerged from this traumatic history was one habituated to violence. The anti-Dutch War of Independence of 1945–49 killed between 45,000 and 100,000 Indonesians and displaced millions more, while strengthening the power and reach of the army.[6] By the time the Dutch relinquished their claim on Indonesia in 1949, almost ten years of occupation and war had weakened the country economically, destroying lives and infrastructure. Split between advocates of Communist, Islamist, liberal and nationalist government, the new Indonesian state also lacked a clear political blueprint. (Sukarno excused this vagueness in June 1945, saying that if one were 'to make plans to the smallest detail, he himself … would never see the day of a Free Indonesia'.)[7] Sukarno wanted a one-party state but one of his influential contemporaries, Sutan Syahrir, insisted that 'top priority must be given … to democracy', and that military leaders should be kept out of the political leadership.[8] While there was a strong commitment to democracy between 1949 and 1957, the turbulent history of Indonesia's struggle for independence made Syahrir's proposals hard to realise. Expectations were high; political and administrative competence was low; and the country contended with harassment from foreign powers, especially the US, which interfered in elections and supported anti-government rebels. Moreover, the violent struggles of 1965 were foreshadowed in 1948, when a Communist attempt to establish authority in Madiun, East Java, was brutally suppressed by the Indonesian military; some 24,000 perished, including many of the senior leadership.[9]

With multiple parties competing for power, Indonesian democracy was characterised by a regular turnover of coalitions; between 1950 and 1957, cabinets lasted on average little more than a year. Politics and the bureaucracy were deeply factionalised, and founded on patron-client relations rich in corruption and nepotism. With political paralysis came economic stagnation and spiralling inflation, particularly after the price of rubber sank in 1953 and bad weather struck.[10] One of the most evocative novels of the early Indonesian Republic, *Twilight in Djakarta* by Mochtar Lubis, depicts the city's grotesque contrasts: the 'garbage coolies' living and working in unbelievable filth, unable to afford a helping of rice and broth; the kleptocrats swaggering about town in their imported luxury cars, fat on corrupt business deals.[11]

In 1956, after several years of figurehead presidency, Sukarno returned to centre stage, attacking the parliamentary system of political parties. 'Let us bury them, bury them, bury them!' The establishment the following year of martial law, in response to regional revolts, gave Sukarno an opportunity to ally with one faction of the army, divest the party system of executive power, and reinvest it in himself, as president. Sukarno now instated his version of strong-man rule, or the euphemistically named 'Guided Democracy', which banned two of the most important political parties for supporting rebellions against the government.[12] Between 1957 and 1965, it was principally the talismanic Sukarno who held the fractious country together under Guided Democracy. *Bung* (brother) Sukarno did his best to unite and inspire his nation through speeches delivered on tireless travels across the archipelago. But progress, especially economic progress, still proved elusive. Living standards fell between 1955 and 1965; the most catastrophic decline took place in the two years prior to 1965.[13]

At the end of the 1950s, two institutions emerged as antagonistic power centres in this unstable polity. Sukarno needed, and made use of, both – one to mobilise, the other to govern Indonesia, and each to keep the other in check. The first was the Communist Party (Partai Komunis Indonesia, PKI). The party had been founded in 1920 with the help of the Comintern; as the first Communist party in Asia outside the old Russian empire, it predated the Chinese Communist Party by a year. Pushed underground in 1927 after a disastrous rebellion against the Dutch, and having lost its top leaders in the suppression of the Madiun uprising in 1948, the PKI had resurged after 1950 thanks to its skill at United Front work: creating and acting with partner organisations, such as trade unions, women's and students' groups, farmers' associations, drama or singing troupes, to spread its influence. The second was the army. Friction surrounding the actual physical extent of Indonesia – Sukarno aspired to take back West New Guinea from Dutch control, and even to create a 'Greater Indonesia' to include Borneo – and regional rebellions across the archipelago nation had bolstered the military and eroded parliamentary democracy, by creating an ongoing national emergency under martial law. Military officers as a result gained experience in local and national government, as well as money, power and a stake in maintaining the socio-economic status quo. The CIA, meanwhile, also had a soft spot for the army as a bulwark against Sukarno, who regularly made passionate, if some-what vague, noises about socialism, and was too ostentatiously anti-colonial for their liking. The Americans were constantly watchful for a chance to usher in a right-wing militaristic government.[14]

Sukarno supported the PKI as the only brake on the army's power, although tension between the two was frequently destabilising. The military's loathing of the PKI went back to the Communist insurrection at Madiun in 1948, which the army viewed as a 'stab in the back' during the war against the Dutch.[15] The army saw itself as defending the republic against fractious and self-interested political parties. It reviled the PKI not only for its alleged attempt in 1948 to split the nascent Indonesian nation, but also for its imputed atheism, for its subscription to a foreign ideology and purported sponsorship by foreign powers (the Soviet Union and China), and for the challenge that it posed to elites in power since the revolution. Above all, the PKI was a hated competitor because, in its organisation and discipline, it threateningly rivalled the army itself. While martial law remained in force and Sukarno regarded the PKI only as a tool to keep the army in place, there could be little certainty for Indonesian Communists. The PKI dominated public discourse, agitating with revolutionary slogans against 'village devils' and 'capitalist bureaucrats'. But the party was weak within the state, lacking ministerial control and an armed force (until the early 1960s it paid little heed to Mao's emphasis on the 'power of the gun', instead advocating non-violent, parliamentary struggle). Especially during the period of Guided Democracy, the army seized on any suspicion of insubordination by the PKI to haul Communist Party functionaries in for interrogation. Sukarno, the PKI knew, 'held [their] death sentence in his pocket'.[16]

As Sukarno and his fellow Indonesian nationalists sought a successful path to self-determination and modernisation, one country in particular attracted them – the People's Republic of China. The parallels were too obvious to be missed: Indonesia, like China, had beaten off the depredations of colonial powers. Between 1950 (when the two states opened diplomatic relations) and 1965, an improbable variety of Indonesians from across its political and social spectrums – politicians (including and especially Sukarno), writers, artists, Communists and soldiers – enthused about China. (The invaluable Hu Yuzhi, orchestrator of *Red Star Over*

China into Chinese, had once more prepared the ground well, spending time in Indonesia during the Second World War.)

The zeal began at the top. The Chinese embassy in Jakarta assiduously courted Sukarno's mind and stomach: it regularly couriered to the presidential palace copies of Mao's works and exquisite dim sum (supposedly Sukarno's favourite) crafted by the ambassador's personal chef. Beijing published Sukarno's vanity project, his six-volume *Paintings from the Collection of Dr Sukarno* – although his interest in erotic art made this a publishing choice some way out of the comfort zone of the puritanical Chinese Communists.[17]

The government organised a magnificent reception for Sukarno's first visit to China in 1956. An airport welcoming party included almost the entire Chinese government, and 300,000 cheering, Indonesian-flag-waving spectators lined the road as a vast, flower-drenched cavalcade took Sukarno into Beijing. 'It was a throbbing red human carpet that engulfed Sukarno upon arrival,' recalled his aide, 'led personally by Chairman Mao Tse-tung. This human carpet shouted and cheered "Hidup Bung Karno" (Long Live Brother Karno).' Sukarno wept with emotion; he and Mao hugged each other like old friends. (They had never met before.) Mao serenaded the Indonesian leader: 'What are the ideals of the Indonesian people? Independence, peace and a new world. These are precisely the same ideals of the Chinese people.' The Chinese, Sukarno responded, were 'brothers ... comrades-in-arms ... The victory of China is the victory of Indonesia. And the victory of Indonesia is the victory of China.'[18] Chinese hosts thus laid it on thick, but not too thick for an enchanted Sukarno. On his brief visit to Shanghai in 1964, they lined the road between the airport and city with thousands of children, all trained to croon a popular Indonesian love song, in which Sukarno's name had been substituted for the lyrics' original addressee.[19] While Sukarno called Mao 'brother', the Indonesian leader was a little less keen on Khrushchev. A German correspondent recalled him introducing the Soviet – in Javanese – to a mass rally in Bandung as 'this unseemly little fat man' after Khrushchev had apparently insulted traditional Indonesian crafts.[20]

Sukarno was impressed by China's disciplined political leadership and mass displays of enthusiasm, and respectfully asked for Chinese guidance on key aspects of state-building, such as economic development and the appropriate relationship between politics and the army.

Chen Yi, one of Mao's marshals and foreign minister, instructed him: 'Chairman Mao Tse-tung has formulated the best leadership methods.'[21] After his visit to China in October 1956, Sukarno declared on his return that 'we made a very great mistake in 1945 when we urged the establishment of parties, parties and parties'.[22] He exhorted Indonesians to 'take China's approach' for he had returned from the PRC, he proclaimed, 'with a tremendous sense of amazement … I propose that the leaders of the people confer and decide to bury all parties.'[23] The following year, he moved Indonesia's governing system closer to China's with the switch to Guided Democracy, which gave him powers of supreme leadership. Sukarno's dictatorial decision created an administrative vacuum and strengthened the army – it put democracy on hold for four decades.[24] There was much pre-existing common ground between Mao-era China and Sukarno's Indonesia: a similar preoccupation with social discipline (hygiene, simplicity, self-criticism) and fondness for sending 'mental workers' down to the countryside to work alongside farmers.[25] As an emblem of his trust, Sukarno even allowed the PRC into his bedroom. Beginning in 1964, his health periodically became critical with heart and kidney problems. After a group of Viennese doctors prescribed surgery and leaked their diagnosis to the press, Sukarno substituted them for a team of PRC doctors both more discreet and more accurate in their diagnoses.[26] Sukarno himself justified his affection for China in rational benefit terms: 'The Chinese always praise Sukarno. They don't embarrass me around the world or treat me like a spoiled child in public by refusing any more candy unless I'm a good boy … who can blame me for saying, "Thank you, people from the East, for always showing me friendship, for not trying to hurt me".'[27]

Indonesian opinion-makers below Sukarno also revered Mao as a dignified, benevolent, timeless 'pater familias' of the revolution. He was, analogised the prime minister, Ali Sastroamidjojo, in 1955, 'like the head of a large Chinese family such as I had often met in the Chinese quarters of Indonesian towns and cities, who was respected and looked upon as an old man of great wisdom and intelligence not only by his children and his grandchildren, but also by all the local Chinese'. 'There stood Mao, large, silent, benign; he was like a god,' gushed Arnold Mononutu, Sukarno's information minister, of his first meeting with the chairman.[28] China's keynote works of external propaganda – *China Pictorial* and *China Reconstructs* – were made available for free in bookshops, libraries and schools across Indonesia. By 1954, Radio Peking was broadcasting in Indonesian for 116 hours a week.[29] Dutifully impressed by these glorious technicolour accounts of Mao's China, Indonesian admirers of the PRC between the 1950s and '60s saw a mirror image of what Indonesia could and should be. Those with Communist sympathies were obviously vulnerable to such yearnings. 'Look at the PRC,' raved a leftist character in *Twilight in Djakarta*, 'how tremendous the progress which has been initiated by Mao Tse-tung in all fields ... If it can be done there, why not here?'[30] 'Within just fifteen years, new human beings have been born in China,' declared the left-leaning writer Amarzan Hamid, 'new human beings with new creativity, new initiatives, new thinking and new feelings.'[31]

But Mao's guerrilla strategies were also applauded by inveterate anti-Communists, who cherished China for its lack of strikes and labour unrest. 'Our leaders', recalled General Abdul Haris Nasution (whom pro-PKI elements tried to kidnap and eliminate in the events that led to the massacres of autumn 1965) in his own handbook on guerrilla tactics, 'always compare the guerrillas to fish and the people to the water, using the example from Mao Zedong's teaching. The Chinese leader has explained that the "water" must be nourished in its natural political and socio-economic climate to ensure the proper development of the guerrilla fighter who "swims" in it. Therefore it is very important for the guerrilla soldier ... to maintain that favorable "climate" with the people.'[32] Indonesian parliamentarians admired the Chinese people's apparent unity and positivity. 'The whole of China is just like a spider web,' raved Jakarta's vice mayor in 1956, 'everyone talks about actions, everyone is working ... they are racing with time – everyone is united.'[33] This perception of happy diligence contrasted with the disillusion fast setting in over Indonesia. 'When we look around,' commented Mohammad Natsir, Indonesia's briefly incumbent prime minister, on Independence Day in 1951, 'we see very few joyful expressions. It is as if the independence we have obtained had brought but few benefits. It would seem that expectations have not been fulfilled. The gain is like a loss ... There is a disappointment, ideals have been lost sight of. Everywhere there prevails a feeling of dissatisfaction, a feeling of frustration, a feeling of hopelessness.'[34]

*

Mao made his way into independent Indonesia along another enor-
mously influential route: through the country's Communist Party,
the PKI.

After tens of thousands of its members were left dead or imprisoned
following the collapse of the 1948 Madiun uprising, Dipa Nusantara
Aidit, the party's young, soon-to-be leader – for almost everyone more
senior was dead – probably went into hiding in China.[35] (On this point,
though, as on many other aspects of this politically clouded history,
the evidence is not incontrovertible.) He was there when Liu Shaoqi
proclaimed in 1949 the Chinese revolution's leadership role in Asia,
with Indonesia included in its sphere of influence. Yet in the 1950s,
the PKI trod a careful course between Russian and Chinese
Communisms.

In 1951, at the age of twenty-eight and just four years after he
had joined the PKI, Aidit became secretary general. He used a
Dutch term to describe the process of his election: kinderspel (child's
play). As a career politician since his youth, he had few interests
beyond politics. His ideological leanings took him out of the upper-
class, merchant-bureaucrat milieu into which he was born, and
though he clearly felt an instinctive sympathy with ordinary working
people, he could seem 'tense and unfriendly' in company. He once
frankly informed his youngest brother (Aidit was the eldest of six)
that the only connection between them 'was the same parents,
nothing more'.[36] The party's new programme formulated by Aidit
in the early 1950s, after the wreckage of Madiun, in some ways
tilted towards Mao's revolution in the 1950s, though only with the
approval and guidance of Stalin, who thoroughly notated the draft
document and toned down its imitation of the Chinese model.[37]
According to a Soviet source, Stalin paired Aidit wth Liu Shaoqi at
a top-secret nocturnal meeting in Moscow in January 1953, deputing
the CCP to 'take over' the PKI; Aidit supposedly celebrated the
adoption agreement with a midnight snowball fight.[38] After Stalin's
revisions of the PKI programme, Indonesia was defined Mao-style
as a 'semi-colonial, semi-feudal' society. In some of his own political tracts, Aidit adapted Mao's essays in Indonesian translation
(and flattered Mao that his works needed no editing or revision).[39]
But Aidit's tactics through that decade often pulled in a different
direction from Mao's: he favoured working within the existing state,

rather than overthrowing it through armed uprising; he was publicly reserved about the extent of overlap between the Indonesian and Chinese revolutions.[40]

The 1950s were a time of dramatic growth for the PKI; Mao-style strategies helped. In ways that chimed with a Maoist approach, it paid attention to grass-roots education: to 'mass work' constructing a 'united front' of supportive organisations directly and indirectly connected with the PKI to build legitimacy and support. In tune with Mao's emphasis on the peasantry, Aidit focused party work on farmers and the countryside – the 1954 Party Congress identified the Indonesian revolution first and foremost as agrarian.[41] By the early 1950s, the party controlled not only the largest national federation of trade unions, but also Indonesia's largest national farmers' association, the Barisan Tani Indonesia (Indonesian Peasant Front): the PKI organised rural workers to demand rent reductions and to resist bandits; it distributed seeds, tools, fertiliser and fish eggs; it built wells and schools; it killed hundreds of thousands of field mice. Culture had an important role to play in PKI election campaigns: political messages would be slipped into 'People's Festivals', before the singing, dancing and boxing began. The party ran schools, seminars, conferences and vast rallies throughout the nation. Thanks to all this work, the PKI won 16 per cent of votes in the 1955 national elections, then increased its share of the vote by another million in local elections in 1957.[42] In 1958, the Central Committee began organising 'go-down' campaigns, rusticating high-ranking cadres for up to six months at a time among farmers.[43] Indonesian society was saturated with PKI messages. At a time when average newspaper circulation was less than 10,000, the PKI paper (the *People's Daily*) sold 60,000 copies. In 1956 alone, 700,000 copies of party publications rolled off the presses. By 1965, PKI membership stood at around 3.5 million, while the combined membership of its 'united front' organisations was perhaps 20 million – a fifth of Indonesia's population.[44]

These activities, as well as the salaries of perhaps as many as 5,000 full-time party officials, all needed funding; by the early 1960s, the PKI was the richest political party in Indonesia.[45] Some of the revenue came from party dues but the PKI was also ingenious at scraping together – literally – grass-roots revenue: at least two election campaigns in the 1950s were funded through dispatching PKI groups to catch green frogs and harvest banana leaves, with the profits of this hunter-gathering generating useful party revenue.[46] Chinese gold may also have helped: rumour had it that the Bank of China would lend to Chinese Indonesians if they first 'donated' to the PKI.[47]

By the 1960s the PKI had undergone an extraordinary expansion under Aidit's leadership. Donald Hindley, a long-term observer of the party, assessed it thus on the eve of the 1965 bloodletting:

> Most of the members entered the Party as illiterates or semi-literates, with little political consciousness. Almost all have been given basic political education ... it is by far the largest, the most disciplined, and the most efficient of Indonesian parties ... Meanwhile, the leaders of the other parties have, in general, been unconcerned with the masses, except to use traditional civil and religious authorities to mobilise mass support when regrettably necessary for occasions such as elections ... their parties are hollow shells.[48]

It was Aidit's success at mobilising tens of millions of Indonesians that led to the alliance with Sukarno, the 'national shadow puppet-master' of Indonesia politics up to 1965.[49] 'Can we create unity while bunging twenty per cent, sixteen millions, the Communists, down a mouse-hole?' Sukarno earthily rebuked those who opposed the inclusion of Communists in coalition cabinets.[50] 'They want me to ride a horse,' he argued, 'but insist that they must first chop off one foot of the horse. I cannot and will not ride a three-footed horse.'[51] The PKI, especially from the late 1950s, drew strength from Sukarno's public support; Aidit's programmes and manifestos were wisely studded with Sukarno's quotations.

In 1955, however, an American writer called Doak Barnett – author of *China on the Eve of Communist Takeover*, an important work of reportage polling the hopes and fears of the Chinese in 1949 – had noted a curious inconsistency at the heart of the PKI while on a visit to the party's Jakarta offices. The only reading materials on display, he noted, were 'a slick Indonesian language version of a Chinese Communist pictorial'. To Barnett, Aidit seemed young, temperate – although, he wrote, 'I had a feeling that his mild manner concealed a toughness underneath'. Aidit outlined his political project: radical land reform, nationalisation of businesses, rapid industrialisation financed by an agrarian revolution (that involved, preferably, collectivisation). 'This sounded very familiar to me,' mused Barnett.

> In broad outline it corresponds to the general ideological line pursued by Mao Tse-tung and the Chinese Communists: the idea of a two-stage revolution, the emphasis on appeals to nationalist, anti-imperialist sentiment and agrarian discontent, the proposal of a four-class coalition, the description of the peasants as the 'main force' of the revolution under the leadership of the proletariat, the desire for ultimate collectivization and industrialization, all correspond to the ideological line followed by Chinese Communists. One cannot help but think that if the PKI were formulating its own program, without benefit of the Chinese experience which Peking has itself proclaimed as the 'model' for the rest of Asia, the formulation might be somewhat different.

Aidit confirmed that 'what the Communist Party in China has done is the model for what the PKI wants to do in Indonesia'. As Barnett concluded the interview, he soberly pointed out the most significant difference between the PKI and the CCP in 1949: the latter had an army.[52] Over the next ten years, the PKI's combination of Mao-style politics without the military backup that Mao had insisted on since 1927 would prove fatal.

As the Sino-Soviet Split opened out, Aidit became more conspicuously pro-China. For the CCP now promoted itself as the global headquarters of anti-imperialism, a theme dear to both right- and left-wing nationalists in Indonesia, who since the 1920s had been predicting a global war 'between the colored races and the whites'. It was not hard to understand Sukarno's loathing for Western European and Anglo-American influence in Indonesia. He had spent years in Dutch prisons and internal exile before the Japanese invasion of 1942. In 1945, British troops facilitated the return of the Dutch, beginning a brutal war for independence against the former colonial power. During the 1950s, Western powers – above all the US –

interfered in democratic elections and supported regional rebellions that threatened to dismember independent Indonesia. Sukarno felt in turn mocked and undermined by what he called 'the already established forces of the world ... all the trouble around the globe in places like Vietnam, Korea and Guatemala was started by America's invisible government'.[53]

Especially after 1962, Sukarno, the PKI and the PRC chorused their opposition to 'neo-colonialism and imperialism' – *nekolim*, in Sukarno's parlance, a baggy term that took in both the ongoing Dutch occupation of West New Guinea and the effronteries of US foreign policy. 'Colonialism and imperialism are living realities in our world,' he told a South East Asian audience in 1963. They 'manipulate conditions in order that our nations can be kept eternally subservient to their selfish interests.'[54] To the surprise of India's prime minister, Nehru (who had been convinced that Indonesian toilets would not pass muster), Sukarno had made a great global success of hosting the 1955 Bandung Conference, and by extension of burnishing his credentials as a leader of the decolonising world. On his energetic global tours of 'revolutionary diplomacy', Sukarno called for Indonesia to become the centre of Afro-Asian solidarity against colonialism-imperialism – to him, the 'main problem in international relations'.[55] He had a particular fondness for abbreviated slogans that were definable and comprehensible in varying degrees: Nasakom stood for a blended nationalism, religion and Communism; MaPhilIndo, a strategic alliance between Malaysia, the Philippines and Indonesia; OLDEFO – the 'old established forces'; NEFO – the 'new emerging forces'. In 1962, agreeing with Sukarno, Aidit identified the enemy of NEFO – Sukarno's term for vigorous new decolonised, non-aligned nations, and exemplified by Indonesia – as 'all imperialist states, all forms of colonialism and neo-colonialism, and all the reactionary forces in the world'.[56] These pronouncements harmonised with the militant noises coming out of Beijing about the inevitability of armed conflict with imperialism.

Mao and Sukarno both had a fondness for manufacturing conflicts with neighbouring states to create a national state of emergency to push through political goals. Sukarno was, he admitted himself, 'infatuated by the rhythm of revolution'. Spirit, energy and audacity were required to solve Indonesia's institutional and material problems, he believed, echoing Mao's voluntarism; not institutional or material solutions. Military confrontation – *Konfrontasi* – with Malaysia between 1963 and 1966 was the high point of Sukarno's militancy and shared high Maoism's spirit of provocative defiance. The triggers for *Konfrontasi* were the quarrel over the proposed affiliation of Brunei to the new British-designed state of Malaysia (which Sukarno denounced as neo-colonial), the intervention of British troops in suppressing a rebellion on the island, and fundamental objections that the new state of Malaysia was a British neo-colony. Sukarno rapidly ramped up military tension with Malaysia (expressed through clashes on Borneo, between Indonesian and British-Malaysian forces), as a springboard for intensified struggle with the forces of *nekolim*: 'Crush Malaysia!' he declaimed.

Konfrontasi pushed a mobilisation and militarisation of the population, as well as resonating with the anti-imperialist, anti-Western rhetoric of 1960s Maoism. In early 1965, Sukarno pulled out of the United Nations and told Lyndon Johnson to 'go to hell with your aid'. China was delighted. 'Should US imperialism dare to launch aggression against Indonesia,' blustered Beijing's *People's Daily*, 'the Chinese people will back the Indonesian people with all their might.'[57] Unlike the USSR, the PRC had nothing to lose in denouncing the UN, for the Republic of China on Taiwan held the China seat until 1971.

The PKI, following Mao's line of militant confrontation, moved simultaneously towards urging armed struggle (despite having no army) with their enemies. 'There must be confrontation in all fields ... [keep] one hand on the gun and one hand on the plough ... the imperialists only understand strength ... The people should be armed.'[58] Aidit seemed to grow emotionally closer to Mao's China. In 1959 and 1961, at the height of the Great Leap Forward and its subsequent famine, respectively, Aidit visited the same model commune in China, where he was given the full propaganda treatment: that the Great Leap Forward and the communes had achieved an economic miracle. Aidit's Chinese minders deftly concealed the true nature of the commune system – terror, starvation, cannibalism – and reinforced the Indonesian's enthusiasm for the Maoist experiment. The internal Chinese report on his visit in 1961 commented that 'Aidit was very satisfied. He said: "You can see that the changes here [over the past two years] are huge ... I am delighted ... I wish you ever greater success in the future."' The hosting reaped dividends, for Aidit enthusiastically defended the achievements of the Great Leap Forward in the PKI newspaper in 1963.[59] Writing verse was one of Aidit's few extracurricular interests, which he took up allegedly to emulate Mao. The resulting poetry was apparently so bad that even the official PKI newspaper (which Aidit controlled) rejected it. He also took up swimming in Jakarta's rivers, to emulate Mao's dip in the Yangtze in 1956. An accomplished backflipper as a child, Aidit was probably a better diver than the lumbering Mao.[60] In likely imitation of Mao's 1927 survey of the peasant uprising in Hunan, he embarked on a tour around Javanese peasants, denouncing 'despotic landlords, bureaucratic capitalists, corrupt local officials', and told young Indonesians to go 'down to the villages and up the mountains'. Mao returned the approbation, acclaiming the PKI as a 'glorious page ... in the annals of revolution in the East'.[61]

In the voluntarist style of the Great Leap Forward, Aidit began to eschew the kind of careful, patient mobilisation that had taken place through the 1950s, in favour of statements that emphasised high Maoism's 'spirit, resolve and enthusiasm': 'The Eight-Year Plan must be replaced by a realistic "Plan of Drastic New Action".'[62] In 1963, Beijing published his tract with the self-explanatory title *Dare, Dare and Dare Again!*[63] Nationalism and audacity became the answer to any problem – geopolitical, economic, social. The Chinese turn also strengthened the PKI's focus on mobilising Indonesia's farmers through class-struggle-driven land reform: the PKI threw itself into a campaign for 'land to the tillers'.[64] Returning from a three-week visit to China in 1963, Aidit proposed a profoundly Maoist view of the world situation: 'Once daring has been aroused and has become the possession of the people, it will certainly sweep aside all barriers and obstacles.' Revolutionaries who fail to be daring 'cease to be revolutionaries'. 'Our Party and our mass organisations have got into their stride with great gusto, have swung their arms and aimed their fists against the enemies of the people with ever greater freedom ... *a rifle in one hand and a hoe in the other.*' Aidit confidently prophesied a 'political situation ... moving more and more to the left ... *not to have the courage to implement radical land reform ... is pure nonsense ... and deception of the people'*. Aidit's manifesto of revolution rejected any kind of compromise with the US – 'the centre of world reaction, the backbone of imperialism ... the most criminal and most dangerous common enemy of the people of the world' – and denounced Soviet spinelessness in its dealings with the Americans.[65]

Aidit even played a role in forging 'high Maoism'. It was the Indonesian who first globalised Mao's ideology of the 'countryside surrounding the cities' (and hence implicitly condemned the Soviet Union for failing to promote armed revolution). In 'Asia, Africa and Latin America,' Aidit declared, 'there is a revolutionary situation that is continually surging forward and ripening ... Asia, Africa and Latin America are the village of the world, whilst Europe and North America are the town of the world.' Mao and Lin Biao borrowed Aidit's admiring formulation for their own global call to arms, 'Long Live the Victory of People's War!', which in turn became the foundational text of asymmetric warfare across the world.[66]

The CCP pushed Aidit to see things thus. In September 1963, Aidit was invited on a special training course for future leaders of the South East Asian revolution, where Zhou Enlai instructed him and comrades from across South East Asia to 'go deep into the countryside, prepare for armed struggle, and establish base camps ... China has the responsibility to fully support anti-imperialist struggles in the region.'[67] Mao and his closest comrades flattered Aidit by calling him 'a brilliant Marxist-Leninist theoretician'; the 'great success and rich experience' of the PKI, they told him, exercised 'ever increasing attraction for the Communists and revolutionary people of the capitalist world, particularly of the Asian, African and Latin American countries'.[68]

Mao left a deepening imprint also on Sukarno's rhetoric. 'The armed Forces of the Republic of Indonesia will form an invincible power if they unite with the people like fish in water,' Sukarno declaimed in his 1965 Independence Day address. 'Remember – water can exist without fish, but fish cannot exist without water.'[69] As an indication of China's warmth towards Sukarno, in March 1964 it actually offered to transfer the assets of the Indonesia branch of the Bank of China – a crucial backer of the PKI – to Sukarno and his administration. In February 1965, as American involvement in South East Asia intensified, a Chinese government source enveloped Indonesia into the same strategic alliance that Beijing had already extended to Vietnam: 'solemnly' declaring 'that should the British and US imperialists dare to impose a war on the Indonesian people, the Chinese people would absolutely not sit idly by'.[70]

By this point, the Indonesian economy was under serious strain. Sukarno's nationalisation of British and Dutch investments had frightened foreign finance into flight, while national budgets were being stretched by increased defence spending. But during the manufactured national emergencies of the 1960s – which saturated everyday life with military values – the army relatively prospered. Martial law and foreign aid bolstered its political power and technical capability. At the same time, the military was put in charge of many nationalised foreign properties. Organisationally, the army command tightened its control over central and regional strike units in the early 1960s, which would enable it to mobilise quickly for the nationwide purge in 1965.[71]

During the febrile days of *Konfrontasi*, Sukarno claimed that Zhou Enlai had told him to create a 'Fifth Force': a trained, armed popular militia 21 million strong that would effectively militarise the archipelago (ostensibly for conflict with Malaysia, but in reality to challenge the army's monopoly on violence). The CCP was certainly strongly in favour of the idea, seeing it as a replication of Mao's own guerrilla tactics. 'Militarised masses are invincible,' enthused Zhou. 'I am sharing with you our own experience.' All this indicated a major U-turn in Chinese policy towards Indonesia, explicable only through the chest-thumping competition with the Soviet Union then ongoing. Between 1960 and 1963, China's Ministry of Foreign Affairs admitted that it had 'refused most of Indonesia's requests for aid'. In 1965, by contrast, Mao and comrades were open-handed in their promises of military largesse. 'If you are in need of small weapons, we can help. If your navy or air force needs any spare parts, please feel free to send your staff over to China to have a look.'[72] In total, China pledged 100,000 small arms for free; and Sukarno seems to have conspired to keep those weapons out of the hands of the army.[73]

In 1964, the ever-eclectic Sukarno borrowed for the title of his annual Independence Day speech a phrase from Mussolini – live dangerously. Sharing Mao's rhetoric, his speech placed South East Asia at the 'very center of world contradictions'.[74] Little more than a year later, this call to recklessness would take on a tragically prophetic flavour. Encouraged by their confrontational synergy with Sukarno and Mao, the PKI became more politically radical, planning the Fifth Force, with Sukarno's full blessing.[75] If successful, this projected militia of workers and peasants would finally give the PKI an army comparable to that which brought the CCP to power. 'Ignite the spirit of the wild buffalo!' Aidit commanded his Central Committee in the spring of 1965.[76] At the same time, Sukarno and the PKI became ever more careless in their rhetoric against the army, referring to it collectively as 'the moron in a general's uniform'.[77]

By the summer of 1965, all three sides of the Indonesian power triangle eyed each other suspiciously, amid an atmosphere of acute, bewildering polarisation. First there was Sukarno: both romantic and self-serving in using personal prestige and anti-Western emotion to move Indonesia away from the US and towards China; and anxious that a right-wing military junta – a shadowy 'Council of Generals' – would unseat him. Then, there was the army: substantially trained by both the United States and the Soviet Union, superior to Sukarno in brute strength but not in prestige and legitimacy, and antagonistic towards the PKI. A British officer in the embassy in Jakarta later likened Sukarno and the army to 'two Japanese wrestlers locked in a clinch. Sukarno [keeps] trying to make a throw but the Generals [will] not give way.' Should we throw one of them biscuits? queried London, running with the analogy. 'The spectators can only watch while eating the biscuits themselves,' came the reply.[78]

Last, there was the PKI itself: ambitious, after the successes of the 1950s, to advance ever closer to taking power, and emotionally drawn to Chinese strategies of 'People's War' to mobilise its civilian power base against the army. In the countryside, the PKI deployed militant land reform to redistribute some 700,000 hectares of land to 850,000 farmers. The Communists also deployed political violence. One student who fell foul of the Communists remembered that he 'felt the terrorism in the campus directed at me, and even to my younger brother. I felt as if I was in a situation where I'd be killed, or kill.'[79] In Jembrana, west Bali, for example, one PKI militiaman was notorious for swaggering about, a hibiscus flower behind his ear and a sword in his belt, intimidating opposition party assemblies by throwing snakes into the crowds and starting fights, or sinking his sword into the soft, palm-woven walls of village homes to terrify residents into attending PKI meetings.[80] High-level divisions thus translated down to the grass roots. Indonesian society on the eve of September 1965 was fiercely divided between local elites, landowners and religious Muslim leaders, on the one side, and those either tightly or loosely linked with PKI organisation, on the other. Polarisation in power between the army and the PKI led many civilians to seek one or the other as patrons – the rift, or at least the perceived rift, that this generated helped intensify much of the violence of 1965–66. 'The nation is at boiling point,' Aidit told his party. 'Therefore intensify the revolutionary struggle at all points.'[81]

In May 1965, the Indonesian foreign minister, Subandrio, obtained a draft telegram supposedly written by the British ambassador, Andrew Gilchrist, supposedly discovered in a bungalow belonging to an American movie booking agent called Bill Palmer in the rain-sodden city of Bogor, West Java. In the message, Gilchrist – a former Special Operations Executive veteran who made no secret of his antipathy towards Sukarno and his anti-British, anti-American stance (before the British embassy was stoned by Indonesian demonstrators in autumn 1963, he had allegedly authorised the kilted assistant attaché to march around the compound playing the bagpipes) – alluded to a planned British and American attack on Indonesia assisted by 'our local army friends'. British and American officials declared the telegram a forgery, but it was nonetheless cited in Sukarno's and Aidit's circles as evidence of a shadowy 'council of Generals' plotting a coup against the president and planning to take over the reins of government. On 26 May 1965, Subandrio addressed a mass rally for the forty-fifth anniversary of the founding of the PKI, and claimed that there were 'documentary proofs' of an imminent counter-revolution plotted against Sukarno.[82]

Then on 5 August 1965, Sukarno – the human lynchpin of Indonesian politics – passed out three times, vomiting profusely in between.[83] Aidit, in Beijing at the time, plausibly feared that his protector – the one man standing between him and likely annihilation by the Indonesian Army – was on the point of death, or at least incapacity. Something had to be done.

On 1 October 1965, Indonesians woke up to an unnerving ten-minute broadcast. It told, in the third person, of a sudden action by the

'September 30th Movement'. This mysterious organisation had arrested 'a number of generals' plotting a CIA-sponsored 'counter-revolutionary coup' for the upcoming Armed Forces Day on 5 October. As part of this preventative action, the government of Indonesia would be radically remade, through national and local 'Revolution Councils', to which all 'political parties, mass organisations, newspapers and periodicals' must swear allegiance.[84] Those on the streets of Jakarta that morning noticed some particularly unusual manoeuvres at Merdeka (Independence) Square, site of the presidential palace, the army headquarters and the Ministry of Defence. Here some thousand troops gathered around Sukarno's unfinished last big gesture: the National Monument – a 137-metre obelisk – in the centre of the square's 75-hectare expanse. (Even after its nominal completion in the 1970s, the building sprang leaks.)

But the most significant events of that day had already taken place in its early hours, when seven teams of soldiers had been dispatched to kidnap seven generals from their beds and bring them back to Lubang Buaya (Crocodile Hole), a copse of rubber trees around a disused well, set in a stretch of cracked ground eleven kilometres south of the National Monument. Six teams completed their missions; the seventh mistakenly grabbed an adjutant instead of General Nasution, the minister of defence. Other officers taking part in the conspiracy tried but failed to track down Sukarno – he had several wives at the time, and no one knew where he was spending the night. On learning of the night's dramatic events, Sukarno eventually made his way to Halim Air Force Base, not far from Crocodile Hole, where those apparently responsible for the attempted abductions gathered. By this point, all seven kidnapped officers had been shot or bayoneted to death, thrown down the deep well at Crocodile Hole and concealed under earth, stones and vegetation. Army propaganda later mendaciously embroidered the murders by claiming that the officers had been mutilated, and that naked PKI women had danced around the corpses.[85]

At Halim base, three groups of protagonists now congregated, in a triangle of whitewashed bungalows, a few hundred metres from each other: the officers directing the coup; Sukarno and his entourage; and Aidit and his aides. At 10 a.m., Sukarno finally met the leaders of the mysterious September 30th Movement and told them firmly to shut the coup down. He expressed little regret for the deaths of the generals, though: 'this kind of thing will happen in a revolution', he remarked.[86] By this point, however, events had already taken another turn.

Three hours earlier, General Suharto – one of the most senior surviving army commanders – had made his way to the Army Strategic Reserve Command (Kostrad) in Jakarta. Cutting decisively through the confusion and curious lack of planning and communications displayed by the conspirators, Suharto quickly took control of the situation and appointed himself army commander, sidelining Sukarno. Within twelve hours, he had cleared Merdeka Square of the movement's forces, before removing the remainder of the conspirators from Halim base. By the early hours of 2 October, the coup's leaders and their troops, some 4,000 in total, had scattered in many directions.[87] Suharto ordered loyal troops to track them down, but also to capitalise on the failed coup to purge anyone suspected of 'Communist' sympathies. The PKI was to be 'smashed', 'crushed', 'buried', 'annihilated', 'wiped out', 'exterminated' and 'destroyed down to the very roots'.[88]

Within a year, at least half a million were dead, through a combination of army and militia violence. Some were shot down with army guns (6,000 in Bali in the course of three days, for example) but many were killed by civilians with more primitive weapons – machetes, spears and swords. The army mobilised the PKI's local enemies: youth organisations of anti-Communist political parties or religious groups. With army consent and orchestration, hundreds of thousands of their members detained those associated with the PKI, burned their houses and murdered them.[89] The US media exulted at the destruction of the PKI: it was 'the West's best news for years', 'a gleam of light in Asia'.[90]

The bloodshed was driven by a variety of causes: party political hatreds and rivalries; economic disputes; feuds at all levels of society between Muslim leaders and the PKI. But it was the impunity the army gave the death squads that made it all possible. There was a clear pattern and method to the violence. Mass arrests by the army filled detention centres with suspects. By night these prisoners would be loaded into trucks and transported to remote spots in the countryside. Here they were delivered into the hands of death squads, who would stab, shoot or strangle their victims, then dispatch them into mass graves or rivers. 'No-one round here would eat fish' after the killings, cackled one former death-squad member to Joshua Oppenheimer in the 2000s, 'because they'd fed on human bodies!'[91] There were other forms of brutality too – beatings, torture and lifelong discrimination. About a million spent some time in detention camps. At least 10,000 prisoners were condemned to slave labour for a decade: bringing lands into cultivation with nothing more effective than (Chinese-made) machetes. After political prisoners were released, their families (including their unborn children) were stigmatised as 'unclean'.[92]

These confused, enigmatic events have long resisted clear interpretation. For the main characters in the drama are dead, or have refused to speak, or went on record only during interrogations and trials run by the Indonesian Army – an organisation unscrupulous about the use of torture. In November 1965, Aidit was summarily executed by soldiers who discovered him hiding in a kind of priest's hole between the walls of a bungalow in central Java. The major general in charge of Aidit's arrest stood him in front of a well and instructed him to 'say some parting words'. When Aidit embarked upon 'a fiery speech', the disconcerted officer quickly silenced him with gunshot. Sukarno, whom Suharto first isolated then placed under house arrest, died of kidney failure in 1970, in part the result of medical neglect; in his final years he complained that he was 'silent in a thousand tongues' (comprehensively muted).[93] Suharto, the political and military beneficiary of these events, merely attributed the mass violence that followed to people acting 'on their own, and because of nasty prejudices between social groups that had been nurtured for years by very narrow political practices'.[94]

The army had silenced most newspapers at the start of the post-coup crackdown, and filled the news vacuum with its own reports of PKI-sponsored violence. Suharto's absolute political control after October 1965 enabled him to blame the violence entirely on the PKI or mob instincts – rather than on the army command's careful orchestration. A propaganda film brimming with PKI-inflicted gore, *Treachery of G30S/PKI*, was shown annually on 30 September between 1984 and

Suharto's fall from power in 1998. In 1990, this version of history was physically enshrined in the Museum of PKI Treason, a low-rise building erected near Crocodile Hole, stuffed with dioramas of PKI blood-thirstiness positioned at schoolchildren's eye level.[95] The victors of 1965 achieved an Orwellian control over public memory: for decades, many remembered only that the PKI had 'made themselves so hated in the years before 1965 that their rivals jumped at the chance to slaughter them ... without any one particular person or institution's being responsible'.[96] The elated US media lent a helping hand. In an NBC broadcast from the late 1960s, a brazen local functionary told an American journalist that, the day before the violence began, members of the PKI voluntarily gave themselves up, declared their guilt and literally 'asked to be killed'.[97] Those foreign correspondents who refused to cheer at Cold War euphoria about Indonesia's defeat of Communism struggled to gain access to grass-roots Indonesia until spring 1966. Patronising orientalism was deployed in the West to explain away the killings. They were down to 'witchcraft', 'mass hysteria', 'Asian violence' or, as one *New York Times* editorial argued, a 'strange Malay streak, that inner frenzied blood-lust which has given to other languages one of their few Malay words: amok'.[98] The central, orchestrating role played by the army has only been clarified in the last decade, thanks to dedicated historians working in archives and oral histories, and to the boastful indiscretions of some of the murderers.

In order to further legitimise the harshness of the crackdown, the Indonesian Army and the US State Department claimed that the September 30th Movement was a Chinese conspiracy. 'Aidit and PKI were under heavy pressure from Chicoms [Chinese Communists] to produce abrupt and prompt victory for Chicom interests in Asia,' concluded Secretary of State Dean Rusk. Marshall Green, US ambassador to Indonesia at the time, argued hard, though spuriously, that the timing of the coup revealed Chinese influence: 30 September had been chosen so as not to clash with 1 October, National Day in the PRC (even though the events themselves took place on 1 October in Indonesia). Green also stated as fact rumours – subsequently denied – that groups affiliated with the PKI had been armed with '2,000 Chinese weapons'. Green's less than disinterested motives in drawing such conclusions shone through a memo he sent back to

Washington on 19 October: 'We have bonanza chance to nail chicoms on disastrous events in Indonesia ... spreading idea of chicom complicity [through] covert propaganda.'[99] Decades later, he still publicly claimed that 'the fourth largest nation in the world ... was about to go communist, and almost did'.[100] (Recently declassified National Security Council documents suggest that US intelligence thought it unlikely the PRC was directly involved in the coup, but seized the opportunity nonetheless to demonise the PKI as puppets of a Chinese plot.) Green and his fellow countrymen in the CIA's Indonesia station left nothing to chance: they threw money, mobile radio equipment and lists of suspected leftists at the army's death squads.[101]

The PKI's Indonesian enemies also seized on the theory of a Chinese plot. On 5 October in Medan, home to a large ethnic Chinese population, one of Sumatra's top army commanders publicly described the September 30th Movement as a 'tool of a foreign nation' – namely, China; the provincial government claimed the movement was 'in the service of Foreign Subversives'.[102] By 7 October, inflammatory posters appeared in North Sumatra demonising the PKI for its Chinese connection. 'PKI is ... attempting to change 17 August 1965 [Indonesian Independence Day] with a Peking proclamation. Aidit is the puppet master: Kidnapping is to be responded to with kidnapping, chopping up is to be responded to with chopping up. Destroy the PKI, Allahu Akbar.'[103] A dubious confession apparently authored by Aidit before his summary execution following capture (the original of which was promptly burned by a local military commander) incriminated China in the coup: the action was planned, Aidit said, after a discussion in Beijing with CCP leaders about Sukarno's health; if successful, Indonesia would have followed China's economic model. Rumours even circulated that Aidit was not in fact dead but had escaped in a Chinese submarine.[104]

In the propaganda film that Suharto's 'New Order' government made to indoctrinate generations of schoolchildren, much was made of the sinister intentions of Sukarno's team of Chinese doctors and acupuncturists, who allegedly doubled as spies and agents provocateurs while, Fu Manchu–style, administering acupuncture with electric shocks. On screen, they informed Aidit that Sukarno's demise was imminent, to panic him into launching a coup to serve China's interests. In reality, the frustrated Chinese medics flew back to China in August 1965 when Sukarno refused to take the drugs they prescribed, or to reduce his workload or sexual activity.[105]

Western academics horrified by the bloodletting of Indonesia in 1965 (and by US collusion in it) went to the other extreme in their explanation of the events. A book-length, confidential report completed in 1966 by two of the most renowned Indonesianists of their generation, Benedict Anderson and Ruth McVey, argued that the coup and its aftermath were exclusively the responsibility of the army, without any input from the PKI, much less Communist China.[106] So what was the truth behind the September 30th Movement – the most decisive moment in the history of the PKI, and one of the turning points of the Cold War?

In his 2006 book *Pretext for Mass Murder*, the American Indonesianist John Roosa provided the most convincing account to date of the events of 1965. He argued that the September 30th Movement itself could not justify the bloodshed of the retaliation that followed: it was a convenient pretext for mass murder, not a condonable cause, exploited to deadly effect by army officers who had long yearned to destroy the PKI. Yet despite his instinctive sympathy for the victims of this mass murder, Roosa traced some responsibility for the movement back to a small, secretive group of Communist leaders running high Maoist fevers: principally Aidit and a shadowy figure called Sjam, head of the PKI's so-called Special Bureau, an organisation set up to infiltrate the army.[107]

Full disclosure of one key exchange, between Mao and Aidit on 5 August 1965, might settle the matter of Chinese involvement. We may never know exactly what they discussed, for this remains a topic of intense sensitivity to the Chinese Communist Party, as it touches directly on the CCP's Cold War interference in other states. Only snippets of the transcript of the conversation are in the public domain: a Singaporean newspaper published extracts from an unreliable Indonesian military source; an academic gained access to parts of the official Chinese transcript. In both, Aidit received a frank account of the poor outlook for Sukarno's health. The Indonesian Army source reported Mao's advice as explicitly ruthless:

Mao: You should act quickly.
Aidit: I am afraid the Army is going to be the obstacle.

Mao: Well, do as I advise you and eliminate all the reactionary Generals and officers in one blow. The Army will be a headless dragon and follow you.

Aidit: That would mean killing some hundreds of officers.

Mao: In Northern Shensi I killed 20,000 cadres in one stroke.[108]

The fragments of the Chinese version are more enigmatic:

Mao: I think the Indonesian right wing is determined to seize power. Are you determined, too?

Aidit (nodding): If Sukarno dies, it would be a question of who gains the upper hand.

Mao: I suggest that you should not go abroad so often.[109]

On the actual night of 30 September, hundreds of Indonesians were at a banquet hosted by the CCP in Beijing on the eve of the PRC's 26th National Day. According to one delegate, Zhou Enlai announced that 'Indonesia will bring us a great present on our national day'.[110]

This evidence is suggestive but not a smoking gun, and political sensitivities and biases (above all, the Suharto regime's propaganda drive to incriminate the PKI and CCP in a joint diabolical conspiracy) have left the documentary record concerning direct Chinese involvement problematically fragmented and compromised. But perhaps the clearest Maoist imprint on the movement came in its methods – or lack of them. The high Maoism of the late 1950s and '60s that held such an appeal for Aidit and Sukarno drew much of its global appeal from its romantic revolutionary elan: in Aidit's paraphrase, 'Dare, Dare and Dare Again!' Believe you can win, Mao declared, be it in economic construction or revolutionary wars, and success will drop into your lap. By 1965, parts of the PKI leadership had internalised this hopeful dictum as they planned to strike against their enemies in the Indonesian Army. Consequently, even the most basic standards of operational efficiency were flouted. Sukarno put it sharply in 1967, reflecting on the abrupt end of his political life in his final parliamentary speech as presidential figurehead: the PKI leadership of 1965 had been *keblinger* – dizzy – a phrase that evokes the hysterical can-do spirit of high 1960s Maoism.[111]

In the summer of 1965, probably after Sukarno's physical breakdown in early August, it seems likely that Aidit decided upon a pre-emptive strike against a group of pro-American, anti-PKI army generals. The hit was to be managed by a 'Revolution Council' and Aidit placed in charge of preparations a 41-year-old friend of his called Sjam. 'After August,' this Sjam recalled in 1967, 'we received information from Comrade Aidit that the situation was coming to a head … all the signs pointed to the Council of Generals as having already begun its final preparations for a final seizure of state power … I explained [in meetings with the senior pro-PKI officers in the army] that … it is a matter of hit or be hit.'[112]

Sjam was a man who had not properly seen anything through in his life. The Japanese invasion of Java in 1942 – when he was eighteen – shut down the agronomy school at which he was studying. He then switched to business school but joined the revolution before finishing his studies. He claimed to have joined the party in 1949, but seems not to have made his way up the ranks – through careful, disciplined work – but rather to have leapfrogged to the top thanks to his personal friendship with Aidit, who in August 1965 placed him in charge of this most sensitive of military missions despite (by Sjam's own admission) his possessing only 'a little' military experience, and none since 1945.[113] In 1964, Sjam was appointed head of the Special Bureau, dedicated to making secret connections on behalf of the PKI within the army. His was a strongly personalised model of organisation and authority: in his interrogation testimony of July 1967, four months after being captured by the army, he declared that he was responsible only 'to the head of the party … Comrade D. N. Aidit'. His behaviour under arrest highlighted his spirit of self-preservation rather than of party discipline: he dangled revelation upon revelation in front of his inter-rogators, expressly to keep himself alive. (In a further muddying of this history, it is quite widely thought within Indonesia that Sjam fell in league with the army in the run-up to 30 September 1965.) 'As a person who has been given a death sentence,' he reasoned, 'I want to postpone it and, if possible, get it cancelled. If I sense that the sentence is about to be carried out, that I'm about to be executed, I raise another big issue so that, for the sake of another interrogation, the sentence against me won't be implemented.' (The strategy succeeded: his execution was delayed until 1986.) As instructed by

Aidit, Sjam told the handful of pro-PKI army officers he had cultivated that the generals were planning a coup against Sukarno, that there were vast reserves of support for the PKI and the president, that all they had to do was 'light a fuse' – a phrase reminiscent of Mao's 'single spark' – and the rest would follow easily.[114]

For decades, historians were puzzled as to why a movement entitled 'September 30th' was launched on 1 October. The simple explanation is that poor preparation led to the postponement. The plan for the coup, Sjam later revealed, was drawn up only ten days before it was due to be carried out and finalised just twenty-four hours before the appointed date. The plotters bandied about Maoist slogans on youthful rebellion: 'We're revolutionary while we're young, what's the point if we're already old?' Merely to mention the need for contingency plans raised suspicions of stagefright: 'Enough, don't think about backing off!'[115] While all this may have been due to Sjam's military inexperience and his proven inability to see things through, it was also a reflection of the hopeful Maoist voluntarism that PKI leaders had come to revere – with much Chinese encouragement – in the early 1960s.

Indonesia's admiration for China in the 1950s and early 1960s accounted at least in part for the participation of Supardjo, probably the most capable military officer whom Sjam involved in the coup. Like many of his peers, Supardjo had visited China during these years: he had been deeply impressed by the regime's successful wars against US-funded opponents and by its passionate anti-imperialist rhetoric. After the movement, and the PKI, were in ruins, he recalled: 'the slogan of the leadership was always: "Enough, we just have to begin and everything else will just fall into place." We ourselves believed that because it was proven in the operations led by a fellow Communist Party, such as Comrade Mao Zedong, who began with just one regiment and then destroyed the power of Chiang Kai-sek [sic] whose troops numbered in the hundreds of thousands ... The strategy was ... "light the fuse." It was enough for the fuse to be lit in Jakarta and then hope that the firecrackers would go off by themselves in the regions.'[116]

As a result, the most basic logistical issues were ignored. There were no radio communications between different commands; Sjam insisted on using couriers to activate other parts of the rebellion. As the plan for 30 September was only set a day in advance, the couriers sent out across Indonesia's sprawling archipelago were stuck on buses, trains and ferries while the movement fell apart and PKI provincial branches were left with no idea what was happening, or how to respond. There were no arrangements in place even to feed the soldiers detailed to guard the presidential palace. After going hungry for a day and a night, many deserted.

The last-minute planning meeting on the night of the kidnappings was frenzied. There was, Supardjo recalled, 'an extremely packed agenda. It was already late into the night, and the codes related to the execution of the action had not yet been determined.' The coup's military commander, a Colonel Untung, was exhausted after multiple consecutive night shifts in the palace guard. The action that would 'light the fuse' – the kidnapping of the generals – had not been rehearsed; neither was there a clear chain of command for its organisation. The plan was to seize the generals alive then bring them before Sukarno and make them beg for forgiveness (for their alleged conspiracy against the president). But the kidnapping teams – two of which, detailed to secure the most important generals, were led by military novices who had barely learned how to hold guns – received no clear instructions for how to secure them. 'Grab them,' was all they were told. 'And make sure not one of them gets away.'

Everything promptly went wrong. The generals were killed before they could be compelled to repent before Sukarno. Sukarno himself could not be found at one of his multiple wives' residences, and when he learned of the coup refused to back the movement. There was no contingency plan. The deaths of the generals – and the excavation of their bloodied corpses from Crocodile Hole – fuelled the army's demonisation and destruction of the PKI. Physically, the site remains the cornerstone of the justification of Indonesian military rule today: a monument over the well features seven heroic, looming statues of the murdered generals, and friezes portraying PKI men murdering and dumping the corpses down the hole while scantily clad PKI women cavort ecstatically; a neighbouring frieze depicts a calm, authoritative Suharto commanding the restoration of peace and order (including women resubmitting to their domestic role as gentle child-rearers). Aidit fled to the provinces as the

military counter-coup gained ground, but nothing had been organised there; the need for escape had not been foreseen. Supardjo later
remembered that doubts had been raised on the night of
30 September, but were 'suppressed with the slogan "Whatever
happens, we can't turn back" ... Suggestions and questions were
responded to by pointing out the irresolution of the questioner.'[117]

On hearing of Aidit's death, Mao penned a pragmatic little poem:

Sparse branches stood in front of my windows in winter, smiling before
    hundreds of flowers
Regretfully those smiles withered when spring came
There is no need to grieve over the withered
To each flower there is a season to wither, as well a season to blossom
There will be more flowers in the coming year.[118]

Undaunted by the setback, in August 1966 the Chinese media underlined: 'To achieve complete victory, the Indonesian revolution must
take the road of the Chinese revolution, i.e. adopt as its main form
of struggle the armed agrarian revolution of the peasants.'[119] The PRC
told the remaining would-be revolutionaries still in Indonesia to refuse
to be 'pushed around at the whim of the Indonesian reactionary forces
... To survive one must carry out struggle ... inspired by the invincible
thought of Mao Tse-tung and fearless of violence and even of being
beheaded.'[120]

The sights, sounds and smells of this ghastly time in Indonesian
history were particular. Military commanders in dark glasses, bearing
swagger sticks, threatening strikers with summary execution, declaring
the existence of piles of documents stuffed with Communist plots to
murder religious groups. The cries of the tortured floating out over
fields of sweet potatoes.[121] The scent of coffee plundered from a
Chinese merchant, scattered over the roads.[122] The smarting smell of
burning houses. The rumbling of a truck with a malfunctioning
exhaust pipe come to pick up shackled prisoners with nowhere to
run to.[123] Red paint swabbed – on army orders – over the doors of
ethnic Chinese suspected of sympathy for the PRC: an invitation to
army-sponsored student militias to storm them.[124] A child watching –
from the fragrant refuge of a frangipani tree – a neighbour being
stoned. Headless bodies scattered amid rubber trees.[125]

The statistics are appalling. The Australian embassy tallied, two days before Christmas 1965, an average of '1,500 assassinations per day since September 30th'.[126] In the following six months, perhaps 80,000 were killed in Bali alone, where mass graves lie next to tourist beaches.[127] Sarwo Edhie, the commander of the army's Para-Commando Regiment, claimed shortly before his death in 1989 that 'three million were killed. Most of them on my orders.'[128] This is likely to be an exaggeration – best estimates of the dead range from 500,000 to 1 million – but it evokes this military insider's perception of the scale of the massacre.

The violence also ended any resistance in Indonesia to big-business capital. The PKI had been a key organising force behind Indonesia's trade union movement, for example. As an Australian diplomat observed on 19 November 1965: 'it has apparently become the practice in factories and other workplaces for the army to assemble the labour force and ask them whether they wish to continue work as usual or not. Those who decline are asked again, and, unless they change their mind, summarily shot.'[129] With the army's 'pacification' of the population, and the downfall of the United States' antagonists Sukarno and Aidit, Western and Japanese capital began to flow into the country. The coincidence of army, Cold War and global economic interests was made clear by an American NBC broadcast about the aftermath of the massacres, with shots of an American rubber processing factory looming out over a becalmed Indonesian landscape, as 'Communist' prisoners marched to and from the plant.[130] The massacres of 1965–66, in Joshua Oppenheimer's analysis, created Suharto's Indonesia: a quelled nation of factories and sweatshops, in which the army and paramilitaries could act with impunity. As he collected the footage for his films, Oppenheimer felt as if he had 'wandered into Germany 40 years after the holocaust, only to find the Nazis still in power'.[131]

6

INTO AFRICA

One story, two eras.

In 1965, John Cooley, Africa correspondent for the *Christian Science Monitor* – at the time, one of only two national US papers, and correspondingly influential – published a tract called *East Wind Over Africa*. Its title was a reference to Mao's incendiary 1957 speech in Moscow and its pages sketched Communist China's sweep across the continent, 'from Cairo to Capetown, and from the Islands of the Indian Ocean across the mountains and bushlands to the Gulf of Guinea'.

Somewhere in the African Bush a tribesman smeared with red camwood paint, wearing animal skins, bends over a transistor radio. A Radio Peking speaker exhorts him in his own language to throw out the white colonialists who are robbing his country. In a nearby town an African schoolteacher listens to a Peking broadcast in French, English, Swahili or Lingala on political economy, telling him how Africans must shake loose the domination of the monopolists and imperialists, 'with the United States at their head.' In his classroom, because no other materials are available, he uses books and magazines from Peking for teaching English. One of his students has just received an airplane ticket for Peking from the Chinese Embassy: he is going on a grant for a year's study in China. In another farming community a village policeman is startled to find a manual on guerrilla warfare tactics sandwiched between innocent-looking textbooks on how to repair tractors. All over Africa, from Casablanca to Capetown, such scenes take place daily. Peking is engaged in a propaganda effort on the African continent that is probably unprecedented anywhere, unless perhaps by the Soviet propaganda in Eastern Europe after the Second World War.[1]

Cooley embellished his thesis with a deliberately imperialist colour. 'By expelling the United States entirely from Africa, Mao Tse-tung's planners could advance far toward their declared objective of isolating the United States on the world scene … In Africa nothing is settled. Few final boundaries, ideologies or national loyalties are clearly drawn. To Peking's planners, Africa is the flux of a new world Afro-Asian society, the stuff of a major revolutionary outpost in a Sinocentric world.'[2]

Now fast-forward to February 2014. Half a century after John Cooley's panicky assessment, Jane Goodall – a veteran animal rights campaigner and long-time resident of Africa – condemned Chinese involvement in Africa under the headline 'China Is Africa's New Colonial Overlord'. In Africa, she wrote, 'China is merely doing what the colonialists did. They want raw materials for their economic growth, just as the colonialists were going into Africa and taking the natural resources, leaving people poorer.'[3] In 2007 two correspondents for the New York Times, Howard French and Lydia Polgreen, reported a similar story from Lusaka, the capital of Zambia. 'We are back where we started,' they were told by a Chamber of Commerce leader, at the site of a now quiet factory that once clattered out millions of metres of colourful cottons. 'Sending raw materials out, bringing cheap manufactured goods in. This isn't progress. It is colonialism.' Since coming under Chinese ownership, it had only dispatched unprocessed cotton to China's own textile factories. 'Who is winning?' a local politician asked rhetorically. 'The Chinese are, for sure. Their interest is exploiting us, just like everyone who came before. They have simply come to take the place of the West as the new colonizers of Africa.'[4]

This anxious narrative about China in Africa has held steady for fifty years. For decades, it proclaims, the PRC – preaching political and economic revolution while Mao was alive, promising no-strings-attached development since the 1980s – has set its cap at Africa. It has built an empire through investment and aid; cheap manufactures; medical, military and political education; and plentiful gifts or sales of weapons. Chinese government officials unsurprisingly portray China's presence in Africa in far more benign, win–win terms: as 'promoting peace and development'.[5] According to the Ministry of Foreign Affairs, the 2017 completion of a Chinese-constructed railway linking Mombasa and Nairobi demonstrated 'China speed, China quality, China contribution and China spirit, translating the principle of sincerity, practical results, affinity and good faith, as well as the value of justice, friendship and shared interests into concrete actions'.[6]

It is undeniable that China since the late 1950s has deployed hard and soft power in its determination to exert influence over Africa. In the Mao era this translated into enormous aid budgets. By 1971, China was throwing 'more than' – in Zhou Enlai's revealingly hazy formulation – 5 per cent of its national budget into foreign aid; in fact, two years later it had reached 6.92 per cent. Compare this proportion with the 0.7 per cent of national income that the much wealthier UK annually reserves for international aid (a figure which is regularly threatened with cuts). It is estimated that the PRC paid out more than $24 billion in international aid between 1950 and 1978 (multiply that figure by about 4.5 to translate into contemporary dollars); 13–15 per cent went to Africa. The real figure is likely to be much higher – Mao-era China was notably vague in distinguishing between outright gifts and interest-free loans, and in stipulating timetables for repayment.[7] It thus seems certain that Mao-era China spent a greater proportion of income on foreign aid – including in Africa – than did either the US (around 1.5 per cent of the federal budget in 1977) or the USSR (0.9 per cent of GNP in 1976).[8] In Africa this is a story of ambitious outreach across a vast, disparate continent in which China did not have an immediate geopolitical compulsion to involve itself. Through this undertaking, which came at huge cost to the Chinese people – stunning amounts of aid were provided at moments when the country could least afford them – the PRC changed from being a recipient of international aid, to becoming a donor. It is hard to understand China's current self-projection as a global political and economic power without keeping in mind its self-reinvention as an international benefactor under Mao.

The story of China in Africa – both in Mao's lifetime and since – is far more complex and interesting than Western cynics or Chinese Panglossians suggest. In addition to its other drawbacks, the oversimplification of this story by some commentators has troubling overtones of racism. It construes Africans as passive, simple minds, susceptible to every one of China's 'machinations'.

Again, Cooley's analysis is emblematic: 'Africa, especially Black Africa, is vulnerable to subtle personal diplomacy like that of the Chinese.'[9]

The reception of Maoism in Africa tells us about the appeal of China's message of anti-colonial, anti-Western rebellion, in the era of decolonisation – a time when a host of new states were searching pragmatically for political and economic models to fast-track them into becoming modernised nations. But Mao-era China's outreach to Africa is also a story of conspicuous failures, mistranslations and miscalculations – of diplomacy and intrigues both careful and reckless. The story takes in Algeria, Ghana, Cameroon, Zambia and many other African states, but this chapter will zoom in on Tanzania and Zimbabwe (Southern Rhodesia, until 1980), two countries where different aspects of the Maoist repertoire were applied with particular vigour through the late 1960s and 1970s. The outcome of these experiments – famine in Tanzania; one-party thuggery and economic calamity in Zimbabwe – contrasts the charismatic appeal of Mao's ideas and models of rebellion and self-reliance, with their manifest failure to create stable, responsive institutions for governance.

Communist China exerted a symbolic influence on Africa from the very beginning of the continent's decolonisation. The veteran Kenyan political scientist Ali Mazrui wondered if the homophony between Mao and Mau-Mau – the revolt that pushed the British to grant independence to Kenya – was more than a coincidence: if 'the designation of Kenya's "peasant revolt" [was] a corruption of "Mao Mao" in honour of Mao Tse-tung'. The name seems to have achieved currency in 1948, the year that Communist victory in China's civil war began to look credible. Was it purely happenstance that one of its leaders, Waruhiu Itote, called himself 'General China'?[10] Walter Sisulu, the secretary general of the African National Congress, visited China in 1953, charged with a mission from Nelson Mandela (who had acquired the complete works of Mao around 1950) to 'talk to the Chinese about revolution'. 'Listen chaps,' the CCP apparently responded, 'revolution is a very serious affair. Don't play with it. Don't take a chance unless you are really ready for it.' The discouragement notwithstanding, Sisulu was impressed by China – except 'I never liked Chinese food ... I would say I want English food.' (For unclear reasons, Chinese hosts at one

point served him camel.)[11] The trip, he remembered, made him a
Communist.[12] He returned 'with encouragement, but no guns'.[13]

China's actual intervention in Africa intensified during the Great
Leap Forward – when Mao and his lieutenants volunteered for leadership of Africa, Asia and Latin America. ('We are the Third World,'
Mao once presumptuously told a group of foreign visitors.)[14] In spring
1961, following the worst year of the famine, Marshal Ye Jianying
insisted that 'No country in this world has had more experience than
we ... [This experience is] for the benefit of other countries and
nations which are still not yet liberated. They are very much in need
of the kind of experience which will enable them to crush imperialism
and feudalism and to gain independence and democracy ... Mao
Zedong's ideology [is] the compass.' A secret People's Liberation
Army policy document from the early 1960s noted that Africa was
mired in the experiences of China's past, and needed a helping hand
to catch up:

> Africa itself looks like the seven powers of [China's] Warring States
> [*c*.500 BC] ... [It is] a huge political exhibition, where a hundred flowers
> are truly blooming, waiting there for anybody to pick ... Africa is now
> both the centre of the anticolonialist struggle and the centre for East
> and West to fight for the control of an intermediary zone ... We must
> tell them, in order to help them, about ... the revolutionary experience
> of the Communists in this generation ... In Africa we do no harm to
> anyone, we introduce no illusions, for all we say is true.[15]

The PRC began with a diplomatic offensive: inviting African leaders
to China, and hosting and banqueting them lavishly. Chinese hospitality
melted hearts – especially of those who were discriminated against
in racist regimes in Africa, such as ANC delegates. Chinese warmth
overwhelmed visitors with 'a rush of feeling that the world was on
[their] side'.[16] There were flowers, confetti, gongs, cymbals, firecrackers, cheering multitudes, limousine cavalcades, and tête-à-têtes
with the heroes of the Chinese revolution. While in the early 1950s
hardly any Africans travelled to China, between 1957 and 1959 there
were eighty-four delegations from the Belgian Congo alone.[17] In the
first half of 1960, Mao met 111 African representatives (having met
only 163 in the entire decade preceding).[18] At the same time, the

chairman's vocal support for the black liberation movement in the US won him the love of prominent pan-Africanists building bridges between the US and Africa. The celebrated American pan-Africanist William Du Bois spoke passionately for Sino-African solidarity: 'China is flesh of your flesh and blood of your blood.' China and Africa, Mao told a banqueting hall of trainee guerrillas, were 'one and the same'. 'You're more or less like us,' one of the Chinese instructors told his pupils. 'We're not really yellow nor [are] you really black.'[19]

As so often, the Chinese Communists chose their guests well. One visitor in particular paid rich dividends. Secretary general of the Zanzibar Nationalist Party Abdulrahman Mohammed Babu was an exuberant, omnitalented organiser, anti-colonialist and Marxist who became the first East African to be invited officially to the PRC. An admirer called Babu a 'sociable socialist'; a British acquaintance acidly described him as 'a veteran of Chelsea cocktail parties and [the Labour Party's] Movement for Colonial Freedom in London'; and the CIA in Africa badly wanted him assassinated.[20] Babu had long revered Mao's China and his visit in 1959 intensified his veneration. As he later recalled:

> In the 1950s, it was almost obligatory for young radicals to read as much as possible about the Chinese revolution and its success in 1949 ... I studied ... China as a development model in contrast to the western model. China, in short, was a symbol of a poor humiliated country emerging, through their own effort and against all odds, into a contender for world leadership. It evoked all the emotions of joy and hope for the oppressed who were still struggling under very difficult circumstances ... The meetings with the Chinese leadership and the late night discussions with them on all questions of anti-imperialist struggle were most inspiring and helped to mould my world outlook ... the leaders I met included, of course, Chairman Mao, Chou en Lai ... Deng Tsiao-Ping, and others. These were people of very strong character, well known for their resilience, perseverance and self-discipline who had liberated a quarter of the human race from repression and warlordism.[21]

Appointed East and Central Africa correspondent of the Chinese government news agency, Xinhua, Babu went on to become a very effective mouthpiece for Mao's model of armed revolution, introducing it to a younger generation of Zanzibari sympathisers, such as a good-time revolutionary called Ali Sultan Issa. On visiting China himself in 1960 (when the famine was reaching its peak), Issa was taken on a trip to retrace the route of the Long March. He accepted everything he saw as unvarnished reality.

> The tour opened my outlook and broadened my horizons, to see how the communists had made huge sacrifices and how, wherever they went, they confiscated lands and gave them to the peasants ... They took me to many cities. Poverty was not so visible there as in India; everyone had food and something to wear ... I had not been as impressed by the greatness of the Russians as I was with the Chinese ... I was free to develop and put all ideologies to the test, to see which was most viable and most suitable to our own conditions in Zanzibar. In China, I was deeply impressed by their vast and formidable country, by the people's sacrifice and their achievements, so that when I returned to Zanzibar I was in complete agreement with Babu about China, that this was the ideological line to follow.[22]

China followed up these invitations with scholarships – distributed through men like Issa – to Zanzibari students. '[S]ome students did not last very long in China,' Issa remarked. 'Our boys wanted their freedom to drink and have sex, but in China, everyone's eyes were ... asking "Why do you want to fornicate?" ... [But] most of them returned to Zanzibar and that was how we managed to politicize the whole island.'[23] In January 1964, insurgents violently ousted Zanzibar's Arab rulers (much of the island's Arab population were killed or fled). A loose coalition of moderate and radical socialists took over government through a 'Revolutionary Council' – including Babu, who became minister of foreign affairs, under the presidency of Abeid Karume, subsequent architect of a repressive dictatorship. In an interview that year with the PRC's international news outlet, the New China News Agency, Babu slotted Zanzibar neatly into the Chinese schema of global insurgency. 'The victory of the Zanzibar revolution was only a step in the revolution in Africa, Asia and Latin America. The Zanzibar people send greetings to Chairman Mao because they learned a lot from his works.'[24] (Aspects of the Zanzibari revolution were strikingly similar to the Chinese: former political elites reduced to street-sweepers; independent newspapers banned; private shops turned into malfunctioning cooperatives; security forces with arbitrary powers to imprison and kill.) When, in spring 1964, Zanzibar entered a political union with Tanganyika, the nearest state on mainland Africa, to form independent Tanzania, Babu persuaded its first president, Julius Nyerere, to visit China in 1965. Babu travelled to China ahead, to ensure the visit was flawlessly choreographed. It all worked out beautifully. 'If it were possible,' sighed Nyerere in wonder, 'for me to lift all the ten million Tanzanians and bring them to China to see what you have done since the liberation, I would do so.'[25] Across the next ten years, Nyerere would become a key African Maophile.

The PRC reserved some of its most experienced diplomats for postings in Africa. It is no coincidence that, while China's Ministry of Foreign Affairs imploded during the early years of the Cultural Revoluion, while Chinese diplomats all over the world were recalled to China for re-education by the peasants, the only ambassador who remained in station was Huang Hua – Edgar Snow's old translator – in Cairo. China's best diplomatic weapon, however, was Zhou Enlai, who, on a 1964–65 tour around Africa, described 'an exceedingly favourable situation for revolution ... a mighty torrent pounding with great momentum on the foundations of the rule of imperialism, colonialism and neo-colonialism'.[26] Zhou recited Mao's poetry, advised local Marxist-Leninist parties about le moment juste for seizing power, scooped up diplomatic recognition for the PRC by Tunisia, and chatted in French with the king of Morocco while an orchestra played the overture from Swan Lake. Even cynical Western reporters admitted that Zhou was able to 'hug babies without looking like a politician and pump hands without a trace of humbug'.[27]

One of the least risky – though rather costly – ways of promoting Maoism to Africa was to inundate the continent with 'external propaganda', as evoked by John Cooley at the start of this chapter. By 1960, China was exceeding the Soviets in broadcasting to Africa for fifteen hours every week (the USSR managed only thirteen and a half).[28] News agencies were bombarded with images of Sino-African cooperation: Chinese officials and engineers grinning toothily while shaking hands with African co-workers, or labouring on African roads, or blasting holes into African cliffsides. And, of course, pictures of black Africans diligently reading Mao's works. In Mali, an estimated four million copies of the Little Red Book were distributed – one for every inhabitant.[29]

Chinese aid and investment – credits, loans, outright gifts – were a big part of the charm offensive. Tanzania alone received US $45.5 million in 1964, although Ghana, Algeria, Kenya, Mali and other nations also benefited.[30] But all previous acts of generosity were dwarfed by China's offer to finance the Tan-Zam Railway in 1965. The railway, running from Zambia's copper mines to the capital of Tanzania, Dar es Salaam, was far more than a massive infrastructure project; it was also an integral part of the struggle for decolonisation. Once completed, it would liberate Zambia from reliance on Portugal's port in Mozambique. The whole enterprise was covered by an interest-free loan from the Chinese of some $415 million.[31] The Western international community was so stunned by the Chinese offer that rumours began to circulate that the railway would be made of bamboo.[32] When newly independent Guinea desperately needed help in 1959, China delivered over the following year at least 10,000 tons of rice gratis. (Doubtless to Chinese delight, the Soviets made a hash of their own aid package, unloading onto the dock of the capital Conakry misaddressed piles of snowploughs.)[33] Throughout the 1960s, Chinese agricultural technicians also scattered over the continent, growing tea, rice, vegetables, tobacco and sugar, and drilling for water. Arguably the most successful form of Chinese outreach was its medical teams, who travelled deep into the most isolated parts of Africa to treat fevers and rheumatism, and to disinfect wounds. One man renamed his son Chinois after a Chinese doctor saved the boy's life. Acupuncture became so trusted as a remedy that Zanzibaris suggested bad-tempered neighbours should visit Chinese medics to be cured.[34]

The very creation of a Chinese aid programme to accompany its overtures to Africa (and compete with the Soviets) marked the PRC's determination to rebrand itself as a global power. On his diplomatic tour to Africa of 1963–64, Zhou Enlai announced 'Eight Principles' that would govern Chinese aid to the continent. 'Thanks to this assistance, friendly and newly independent countries can progressively develop their national economies, free themselves from colonial control, and consolidate world anti-imperialist forces.' The Chinese government 'never asks for any privilege and never poses conditions', Zhou declared; it seeks 'to aid [recipients] to move forward, step by step, on the pathway of self-sufficiency'. Furthermore, 'the experts that the Chinese government sent ... have the same standard of living as the experts of these countries. Chinese experts are forbidden to formulate any special demands or to benefit from special advantages.'[35] This last principle had a particular appeal for African audiences used to Western or Soviet technical advisers as sweating white men in pale suits, insulated (by porters and five-star hotels) from any hardship, ordering locals around from the comfort of a shooting stick.

A diplomat based in Guinea in the early 1960s noted that unlike Soviet or European Communist aid missions, Chinese teams 'stress manual labour and do not hesitate to perform the humblest tasks, as in road-building, along with the Guineans. Their rice experts and their engineers live like the Guineans, in native villages ... earning no more and eating no better than the Guineans they work with. They create an impression of frugality and austerity.'[36] The Chinese approach boiled down to two simple prescriptions: 'One, don't beat; two, don't scold' (*yi bu da, er bu ma*).[37] The Zanzibari revolutionary Ali Sultan Issa later remembered how he experienced the difference between the Chinese and the Soviets: 'the Chinese were backward ... but still they helped ... the Russians were advanced with Sputnik and everything, and yet they were ... very mean and arrogant ... it was through our experience and contact with the Chinese that we looked for our solutions through the Chinese way'.[38] Admiring Tanzanians asked their Chinese military instructors: 'How come you are so hardworking, so positive, so practical and competent?'[39] (The Chinese seized the opportunity to stress the importance of their political education.) Zambians who shared a training camp with a handful of Chinese instructors marvelled even at the quality of food that the army cook provided, repeatedly acclaiming it as a 'miracle'.[40] Back home, China opened its universities to African students, offering generous scholarships – their stipends equalled senior engineers' salaries.[41]

China also donated a harder form of currency to Africa: military training both in China and in Africa – across the PRC's foreign aid programme as a whole, this form of assistance took up 20 per cent of the budget (we lack the precise proportion for Africa) at the end of the Mao era.[42] It came in two forms: instruction to standing armies (for example, in Tanzania and Zambia); and training 'freedom fighters' – guerrillas pledging to liberate their countries from colonial or neo-colonial rule (such insurgents charged that some post-independence governments, for example that of Cameroon, had allowed colonial interests to return by the back door). Many African independence movements at some point passed out of PRC schools of guerrilla training at Changping, north-west of Beijing, or the Nanjing Military Academy. Between 1964 and 1985, the PRC spent between $170 and $220 million training some 20,000 fighters from at least nineteen African countries.[43]

We know almost nothing from internal Chinese records about the training of these foreign revolutionaries, for it remains an issue of immense political sensitivity within the PRC. But African accounts are less secretive. At the time, the journey to China was clandestine. Two recruits – one from Mozambique, the other from Southern Rhodesia – bumped into each other en route. Determined to keep up the cloak of secrecy, both lied about their final destination until they washed up together in Hong Kong and found themselves getting on the same train to China. Students at Nanjing were not uncomfortable: they did not even have to make their own beds. Recruits from anglophone African countries ate English food, the francophone ate French cuisine. The official name of the course – offering training in the use of bazookas and sub-machine guns – was 'economic development'. 'Special engineering' was code for sabotage, using pineapple-shaped anti-personnel mines. There were lessons on strategy and tactics, and long hours of films, plays and operas enacting conflict between landlords and peasants. Instructors made an effort to link Chinese ideas to African reality: Zulu campaigns during which enemy forces had been surrounded were equated with Mao's strategy of 'surrounding the cities from the countryside'. Students were told to create 'liberated zones', or base areas, as Mao had done in the 1930s.[44]

From at least 1960, Nelson Mandela engaged closely with Mao's military strategies, discussing them with comrades over dishes of *umvubo* (mashed brown bread with sour milk). ('It could be that he did not know how to cook or was lazy to cook,' speculated a forbearing comrade.) That year, as the ANC moved from non-violent to violent resistance of South Africa's apartheid government, at least six ANC members travelled to China to study Mao's guerrilla war: how to make weapons, how to carry out hit-and-run raids. It was, remembered Raymond Mhlaba, an ANC leader later sentenced to life imprisonment at the same trial as Nelson Mandela, 'extremely interesting and useful'. The Chinese even carried out cosmetic surgery on Mhlaba, removing a growth from his forehead that had made him too recognisable to South African police. Well pleased with the result, he left China (in his own words) 'a trained and handsome soldier'.[45] As Mandela prepared for the ANC's shift to armed struggle, he carefully read Mao on guerrilla warfare, matching South African analogues to Mao's milestones in the Chinese revolution and making dozens of pages of notes.[46] The ANC's blueprints for action held close to his reading. Shortly before Mandela was arrested and imprisoned in 1962, the ANC planned to have their armed wing funded substantially by China, alongside the Soviet Union.[47]

African guerrillas recited Mao's 'Three Main Rules of Discipline and Eight Points for Attention' and reminded each other that 'the popular masses are like water and the army is like a fish'.[48] A founder of the South West African People's Organisation (SWAPO) admitted: 'We all read Mao, as a practical manual of guerrilla warfare.'[49] A member of the Mozambique Revolutionary Committee felt that 'The methods of the [Chinese] Army ... are right for Africa. The Russian methods are wrong – they were partly afraid of the peasants and crushed and collectivised them. The Chinese had to build a National Liberation Army on solid peasant support; they taught us we had to utilise 30 million Africans in southern Africa.'[50] Mao's championing of revolutionary audacity gave marginalised rebel groups confidence: those who 'dared to struggle' would triumph in the end.[51] Africans retooled Mao's defiant catchphrases for their own purposes. In African translations, enemies were no longer 'paper tigers', but 'emasculated paper tigers ... which shall not escape being crushed to pulp'.[52]

In 1961 a team of Cameroonian guerrillas smuggled into China learned the 101 of insurgency: how to blow up bridges, houses, railways, tanks, trucks, power plants and broadcasting stations; how to sabotage airfields and telecommunications; how to conduct ambushes and psychological warfare. A large tranche of the training was dedicated to political education: there were lectures on Communism, its applicability to rural areas, and its inevitable global victory over imperialism. Planning to join the Armée de Libération Nationale Camerounaise, the graduates returned to Africa with bags containing Chinese lecture notes, a detailed political programme, binoculars, cameras, transistor radios and a spruce uniform (consisting of black denim trousers, black leather windcheaters, Chinese-style leather caps and green belts). 'It appears to be the intention', noted with trepidation the British diplomat who had the chance to rummage through their bags after they were apprehended en route to Cameroon, 'to hold other courses at intervals with the aim of producing a regular supply of African guerrilla leaders to return to their own countries in the dual role of rebels against their legal governments and militant agents of China, with the purpose of carrying the Cold War into Africa.'

These Cameroonian recruits were a mixed bunch of drifters: out-of-work taxi drivers, bakers, travelling salesmen. The 24-year-old François Faleu received 'consistently bad reports' from his school, yet 'took a great interest in the Chinese course and made comprehensive notes, showing a far greater enthusiasm for his lessons in sabotage than he appears to have shown in school'. The tactics taught were ruthlessly Maoist. 'Terrorist activities must be carried on,' one student scribbled in his notebook during a conversation with Shanghai's 'Peace Committee', 'killing off all the puppet agents and traitors and carrying the struggle into the country. The country can do without the towns but the towns cannot do without the country.' 'The assistance given', the British diplomat concluded, 'by the Chinese authorities, amounting to nothing less than the organisation and training of a rebel army to destroy the democratically constituted government of Cameroun, can now have no objection [sic] other than that of establishing Chinese Communist domination in that part of Africa.'[53] The curricula of training camps set up in Ghana and Tanzania were heavily flavoured with Mao too: they dwelt on People's War, building base areas, ideology, guerrilla strategy. This emphasis on political education – it occupied up to a quarter of course time – replicated practice in the PLA, and was of course an ideal opportunity to proselytise Mao's thought.[54]

If British diplomatic reports were to be believed, 1960s Africa was crowded with China-trained rebels, from Cameroon, Guinea and Mozambique, to Angola and South Africa. Chinese diplomats in the Central African Republic stockpiled illustrated leaflets 'designed to popularise guerrilla tactics'. Leopoldville Radio reported in March 1966 that 2,000 'Rwandan Watutsi exiles, trained by Chinese instructors, were concentrating on the Rwanda-Burundi border, preparing to attack Rwanda, overthrow the government and establish an operational base for subversion ... Mozambique security forces recently captured from terrorists ten automatic pistols, four automatic rifles, thirty-two anti-personnel mines and a quantity of hand grenades – all of Chinese make.'[55] Tanzania, which had become the self-styled centre of the African liberation movement, hosted training camps for guerrillas; many of the instructors were Chinese. Ghana's first president, Kwame Nkrumah (a passionate advocate of African unity and opponent of colonialism both old and new), hired Chinese military instructors after bad experiences with Russian advisers, who had got roaring drunk and tried to seduce the wife of an orderly. Whereas the Russians had demanded a car and unlimited drink, the Chinese requested only secrecy, food, furniture and a cook, and got straight down to work. Mr Li, the explosives expert, demonstrated with chemicals from Shanghai; Mr Zhang commando-crawled over the palm-fringed drill ground, teaching his students the art of laying anti-personnel mines. Nkrumah went on to publish his own guerrilla warfare manual, but its 'stilted English' – according to one reader – came directly from the Chinese instructors; the manuscript 'was based on Mao's Selected Military Writings [with] countless quotations from Mao'[56]. Kenneth Kaunda of Zambia frankly admitted in 1968 that 'the only people who will teach young Africans to handle dangerous weapons are in the eastern camp. How can we expect that they will learn to use these weapons without learning the ideology as well? When they come back, we can expect not only a racial war in Africa, but an ideological one as well.'[57]

There was quite simply a lot of affection for China in 1960s and '70s Africa. 'Ninety per cent of the population are peasants,' commented one Guinean. 'They all call Chairman Mao their father. Even though many have never seen even a photograph of Chairman Mao, they all know who he is.' 'Chairman Mao is a great man,' acclaimed a Kenyan, 'a great Marxist-Leninist, the second Lenin, he is not only the leader of the Chinese people, but also of the African people.'⁵⁸ A Cameroonian trade unionist chose to put his admiration into song:

> The boat of hope is forging ahead in the foam
> At its helm standing erect is a giant
> Mao Tse-tung, successor to Marx, Lenin, Stalin
> Helmsman of the new era
> Who guides the revolution of the peoples
> ... As your students we will
> Forever be loyal to your teachings.
> And like the sunflower follow
> The sun which is your thought.
> Once again, let's wish Mao Tse-tung a long life.⁵⁹

The man who 'opened the gates' of Africa to China was Julius Nyerere.⁶⁰ Nyerere was an ardent anti-colonialist and advocate of African liberation, who saw in Mao's China a model of anti-imperialist, self-sufficient, agrarian development suitable for a poor, rural country such as Tanzania. Tanganyika's own decolonisation had been peaceful – a process eased by Nyerere's own skill as a mediator and orator. He was a highly educated teacher of biology and English, who had studied economics, history and (in an extracurricular fashion) socialism at the University of Edinburgh. But having witnessed in 1964 Zanzibar's revolution and the mutiny of Tanganyika's newly decolonised army, Nyerere was no stranger to political violence. The latter crisis was only resolved with the help of a British garrison and aircraft carrier from Yemen. Nyerere was thus not averse to the imposition of military and authoritarian solutions: in 1962, he declared his own organisation, the Tanganyika African National Union (TANU), the only legal party in the newly independent state; unsurprisingly, Nyerere was re-elected unopposed every five years until he handed on to his chosen successor in 1985.

Like China under Mao, Tanzania under Julius Nyerere always thought beyond its borders, despite – or because of – severe economic problems at home. 'Tanzania is not yet wholly free,' Nyerere declared, 'because Africa is not wholly free.'⁶¹ When Tanganyika won independence in 1961, colonialism was still very alive in much of Africa.⁶² Zhou Enlai, in a speech addressed to the prime minister of the Republic of the Congo in 1967, echoed Nyerere's sentiment. 'Why do the Chinese people cherish such a profound friendship for our Congolese and other African friends? This is not only because the Chinese people shared in the past the same experience with the African people of being subjected to colonialist aggression and oppression and are both now confronted with the common task of struggle against imperialism, but also because the Chinese people who are armed with the great thought of Mao Tse-tung are fully aware of the fact that without the liberation of all oppressed people and oppressed nations of the world, the Chinese people cannot win complete independence.'[63]

Common interest – the quest for egalitarian development and anti-colonial liberation – and carefully orchestrated Chinese charm led to Nyerere importing Maoist China's models. He referenced the symbols of the Chinese revolution whenever possible, the Long March being a particular favourite. Nyerere's anti-colonialism blurred into socialism via a somewhat idealised view of pre-colonial economic relations on the continent. 'Our Africa was a poor country before it was invaded and ruled by foreigners. There were no rich people in Africa. There was no person or group of persons who had exclusive claim to the ownership of the land. Land was the property of all the people ... Life was easy ... Wealth belonged to the family as a whole; and every member of a family had the right to the use of family property. No one used wealth for the purpose of dominating others. This is how we want to live as a nation. We want the whole nation to live as one family. This is the basis of socialism.'[64]

Nyerere also fell in love with China's Great Leap Forward rhetoric of 'self-reliance' – an idea that had its roots in the stories of Communist self-sufficiency spun so effectively to Edgar Snow.[65] (In reality the Communist Party of China could not have survived the 1930s and '40s without regular handouts from the Soviet Union; by the 1950s, it was a client state.) Self-reliance appealed particularly to a Tanzania anxious not to be swept up into the superpower conflicts of the Cold War. 'When elephants fight,' Nyerere quoted a Swahili proverb, 'it is the grass which gets crushed.'[66] From 1960, the political implosion of the neighbouring Congo – the overthrow and murder of Patrice Lumumba by his army chief-of-staff Mobutu Sese Seko and associated thugs, with covert backing from Belgium and the US – haunted Nyerere. 'The events in the Congo have demonstrated', he concluded, 'that it is possible for a colonial power to leave by the front door, and the same or different external forces to come in by the back ... [we are entering] the Second Scramble for Africa.'[67] Nyerere studded his essays with calls to 'self-reliance' and after a six-week tour of Tanzania in the winter of 1966, which the Tanzanian press described as his own 'Long March', he launched a social and economic revolution entitled 'ujamaa': a socialist war on poverty, fuelled by autochthonous hard work.[68] Nyerere's ambition for Africa was galvanised by his perception of China's own trajectory:

> Africa will be free ... we shall not surrender the goal because we cannot see it clearly, any more than you [the CCP] surrendered because you could not see the China of today from the caves of [Yan'an] ... you sympathise with us in our struggle, just as we sympathise with the Chinese people's determination to defend their own country and build it according to their own desires ... faith can move mountains ... You believe in the creative power of the people; you believe in your great leader, Chairman Mao Tse Tung; you believe in the spirit of self-reliance and self-criticism; and you believe in the oneness of the oppressed peoples of the world.[69]

As Tanzania's National Central Library stockpiled copies of the Little Red Book, Mao's book of quotations began to generate imitations in Tanzania and elsewhere in Africa: there were little green books of Nyerere's sayings; in 1965, The Little Blue Book collected those of Abeid Karume, Nyerere's brutal vice president; and in Ghana, the Axioms of Kwame Nkrumah were also published in book form.[70] In the 1970s, the Libyan dictator Mu'ammar al-Gaddafi, fascinated by Mao's ideas – 'All methods of education prevailing in the world should be destroyed through a universal cultural revolution' – based his Green Book of political, social and cultural theories on Mao's Little Red Book.[71] Tanzanians set off on their own 'Long Marches' imitating Nyerere imitating Mao.[72] Schoolchildren coveted Mao pins and laboured in the fields instead of studying algebra and Shakespeare, while teenagers imitated the Cultural Revolution's attacks on Western culture and consumerism, denouncing 'Playboy and the Beatles, tight trousers and miniskirts, cosmetics and beauty contests'. 'You are our Green Guards,' Nyerere exulted, sending them out on marches around the country, wearing green shirts and badges emblazoned with images of himself and Mao.[73]

Nyerere rolled out his *ujamaa* dream of Tanzanian socialism in February 1967: nationalising banks, industries and natural resources; collectivising rural Tanzania into socialist villages; and dispatching Tanzanian youth to labour camps in the countryside where they were lectured on the need for 'dedicated exertion, the suspicion of ... consumption ... the virtues of frugality and self-denial'.[74] The campaign was pervaded by the spirit of Chinese collectivisation, in its fixation on 'self-reliance', its slippery shift in the early 1970s from voluntary to compulsory participation and its hope that collective spirit and industriousness would magically guarantee success. Again, like its Chinese precedent, *ujamaa* failed, generating starvation and poverty. (At almost the same moment – in spring 1972 – the Sinophile Babu also experienced firsthand Nyerere's toughness when he was thrown, without due process, into solitary confinement in Tanzania and sentenced to death for allegedly planning Karume's assassination that April. Only an intense campaign by Amnesty International secured his release.)

Although not as rigidly implemented as Stalin's or Mao's collectivisation, Nyerere's 'villagisation' also relied on coercion. His ambitious, forced mobilisation of the population led to an escalation of violence reminiscent of government brutality against farmers in China's Great Leap. Youth Leaguers – Nyerere's young vigilantes – burned the houses of those who resisted moving. 'Anti-*ujamaa*' behaviour became a punishable crime. 'When Tanzania Youth League Members come to anyone,' complained one letter to a national newspaper in 1973, 'he is sure of being beaten severely, forced to run long distances and pay a large sum of money.' As in China, *ujamaa* preached the mobilisation of women, which in reality meant a double burden: women were expected to dedicate themselves to both farming and family work. 'Destroyed, where we were living, there!' one woman said of Nyerere's *ujamaa* enforcers. 'If you had stayed and they met you, they burned with fire.' Tanzanians were only weakly committed to collective farming, and preferred to concentrate on their private plots; they were underequipped, slashing at wasteland armed with only hoes and machetes. A 1976 report soberly observed *ujamaa*'s results: 'There is not enough food for many children, and even adults often pass the whole day without eating any food of substance.'[75]

★

What did Mao and the CCP hope to achieve in Africa? 'Chinese policy', declared the British Foreign Office, 'is undoubtedly to use Dar es Salaam at one end, and Brazzaville at the other, for subversion across the waist of Africa.'[76] In reality, the story was a little more confused. Mao, his lieutenants and the exporters of the Chinese model – military instructors, aid workers, railway engineers and builders, doctors – saw an opportunity both to liberate Africa from centuries of colonial exploitation and to disseminate the greatness of Mao. The two aims were so closely intertwined that few, if any, acknowledged the existence of contradiction between internationalist idealism and national gain. Through the 1960s and early 1970s, Mao and his closest subordinates, Zhou Enlai and Lin Biao, publicly declared that Africa was 'in revolutionary upsurge', following the model of Mao's 'People's War'. Everything about Mao-era China's campaign to aid Africa was politicised: the work schedules for the Tan-Zam Railway; the introduction of rice cultures in Guinea; the curricula of visiting students in China; the handing out of medicine – every material act had to advertise the superiority of the Maoist world view. Africans – be they patients, students or railway workers – were the 'seeds of revolution'.[77] To qualify as a doctor to Africa, candidates had to possess (in this order of priority) 'good political thought, clear personal history, no complicated social or overseas relations, good professional skills, good health'.[78] The Chinese medical teams were arguably the most effective means of propagating Maoism, because of the sheer number and range of people they saw in their clinics, the walls of which were thoroughly pasted with images of the chairman. If these medics studied a local language, the first sentence they would master was: 'Chairman Mao sent me here.'[79] Opticians tested eyesight using passages from the Little Red Book. When a doctor had cured a Zanzibari man's cerebral embolism, the Chinese medics told him that his recovery was due to Chairman Mao. The man recorded his recovery for posterity by posing for a photo with his son and the doctors, the Africans waving pictures of Mao above their heads.[80]

There was at least some genuine idealism to this project. China was ingenuously hopeful about the prospects of the African revolution. 'Among the independent countries in Africa,' speculated one policy document from the early 1960s, 'if only one or two of them complete a real national revolution ... the revolutionary wave will be able to swallow the whole African continent, and the 200 million or more Africans will advance to the forefront of the world.'[81] As Khrushchev did with the Cuban revolution, Mao felt an emotional connection with the Algerian war of independence. 'Chinese aid is granted you unconditionally,' he promised a National Liberation Front (FLN) diplomat; it arrived (in the form of uniforms, small arms and ammunition) through Morocco, Tunisia and Albania.[82] Mao personally gave classes in revolution to the FLN at Zhongnanhai during a 1959 visit.[83] Naive idealism shines through the (many) poems that Chinese soldiers, builders, medics and agronomists composed while toiling on Africa's alien soil. 'I'm not far from my homeland – only 30,000 kilometres,' lyricised one particularly prolific agricultural surveyor. 'The temperature is scorching: over 43 degrees. / I am seeking the happiness of the human race. / However many hardships I experience, it will still be sweet.'[84]

Yet this idealism smoothly combined with nationalist, even imperialist goals. Mao's own rhetoric confused world revolution and Chinese glory: 'If we can take the Congo, we can have all of Africa.'[85] Africa thus became a passive territory to be scrambled for. When in the 1950s Mao gave a Cameroonian visitor a copy of his (1938) *Problems of Strategy in the Guerrilla War against Japan*, he scrawled in the frontispiece: 'In this book you can read everything which is now going to happen in the Cameroons.'[86] Chinese military instructors 'hammered' the theory of People's War into Palestinian guerrillas who, on their return to the Middle East, lectured an irritated Nasser about the virtues of Mao's strategies. Nasser bluntly pointed out that the population of the Middle East was nowhere dense enough for a guerrilla to move Maoist-style 'like a fish through the water' (of the people); neither was there anywhere for the Palestinians to build a base area, safely out of the reach of Israel. The Chinese were 'annoyed' at Nasser's heretical common sense.[87]

There was a clear logic of self-interest to China's Africa game: the continent was strategically all-important in the chess game of winning entrance to the United Nations. Every year a debate took place in the UN as to which of the 'two Chinas' should take the seat at the UN: the mainland PRC or the ROC on Taiwan. Eventually, it was the small but numerous African nations that tipped the balance in the mainland's favour. In 1971, after six African states dropped their opposition to the PRC, Beijing won the UN seat from the ROC. More than a third of

the supporting votes mainland China received came from African delegates who, 'arms swooping above their heads, jumped up and down in
their seats as wild applause engulfed the circular chamber'.[88] Mao personally reserved aid packages for those African nations that recognised the
PRC, and his passion for guerrilla struggle was always tempered by
national concerns. If a regime did not recognise the Communist government diplomatically, the latter would support guerrilla rebels on its
fringes. If diplomatic recognition was in the offing, as happened in
Cameroon in 1965, support for anti-government guerrillas might fade
away.[89] African leaders played the same game, threatening to switch
sides to either the PRC or ROC; the imminent loser would have to
produce enough aid to guarantee continuing recognition.[90]

One evening in March 1962, a rumpus erupted at the Peace Hotel in
Beijing. A Zanzibari student, known as Ali, visited the hotel's kiosk
and asked to buy some cigarettes. An argument ensued when the shop
assistant either refused to sell them, or to sell them in the quantity Ali
desired. Several other hotel employees appeared and dragged Ali off
to the yard outside the hotel, where they beat him senseless, as well
as striking a heavily pregnant Zanzibari woman – a presenter at Radio
Peking who tried to intervene – with long-handled spittoon covers.[91]
    The incident infuriated a young Ghanaian medical student in Beijing
called John Hevi. He organised a hunger strike among Africans in
China in protest at the incident before breaking off his studies
and returning home. He then penned a book-length denunciation of
the hypocrisies of China's doctrine of 'Sino-African Friendship'. The
resulting 1963 publication, *An African Student in China*, failed to find
anything laudable about life in China. The accommodation was
squalid, the social life 'spleen-burstingly' dull.[92] Above all, though, it
was the insincerity that Hevi objected to: his hosts' endless rhetoric
about liberation and racial equality, he argued, glossed over Chinese
expansionism and the worst type of colonial racism. 'China can only
be compared with Nazi Germany; like the Nazis, the Chinese
Communists are searching their borders and adjacent territories with
hungry eyes, looking for more and more *Lebensraum*.'[93]
    While the heavily choreographed and monitored Chinese hospi-
tality machine was expertly geared for short-term visits – and worked
wonderfully on susceptible egotists like Sukarno and well-wishers like

Nyerere – it could not maintain the same level of intensity for guests who stayed several years. African students like Hevi were turned off by political regimentation (in language classes, mastering 'the people's communes like a newly risen sun, light up the path of progress for the Chinese people' took priority over 'a cup of water'), and by paucity of food, consumer goods (though their access was far better than local Chinese) and sexual opportunities.[94] 'God knows there is a lot we've got to do to make Africa free,' concluded Hevi. 'But what sort of freedom can Africans expect from the hands of those who keep their own people in such subjection?'[95]

There were a number of obstacles to the exporting of Maoism to Africa, beginning with language and culture. In May 1967, a sharp-eyed American diplomat in Dar es Salaam noticed that one of Mao's quotations, emblazoned across 'a big-character banner draped on the front of the Chinese Communist Embassy', had become somewhat mangled in translation. 'Since there are no tigers in East Africa, and thus no word for "tiger" in Swahili, the translation appearing below the Chinese ideographs solemnly declares that "Imperialism and all enemies of progress are paper leopards."'[96] A Chinese embassy reception in Freetown, Sierra Leone, in 1972 went badly when the African audience kept on bursting into laughter at speeches meant to be serious, then left early.[97] Film showings at Chinese embassies in Africa were in general not very successful, due mainly to the lack of alcoholic drinks served. (American embassy showings, by contrast, were careful to provide better refreshments – and usually more entertaining films.)[98]

Suffering from Cold War nerves, the Western media hyped China's influence in Africa. What were the 'Aims Behind the Acrobats', wondered *The Economist* in a report on a travelling Chinese troupe. American newspapers shuddered at the announcement in 1965 that China would build the Tan-Zam Railway. 'Red Guard Line Chugging into Africa', ran the headline in the *Wall Street Journal*. 'The prospect of hundreds and perhaps thousands of Red Guards descending upon an already troubled Africa is a chilling one for the West.'[99] 'CHINESE USE TANZANIA AS ARMS CENTRE,' shrieked the *Sunday Telegraph*.[100] British embassies in Nairobi and other African cities spun anxious reports about Chinese activities. Why were Chinese embassy officials in Khartoum so 'remarkably' out and about, given how few Chinese there were in Sudan? How had one Mohammed Magin Bagalalliwo, a Ugandan setting off for a holiday in the Sudan, ended up at the Peking Hotel, Moscow, apparently 'on his way to China'?[101] Diplomats insisted on using phrases like Chinese 'infiltration of Sierra Leone', when 'relations with' would have been more appropriate.[102] After the PRC was accused of directly aiding revolution in Zanzibar in 1964, it turned out that the 'Chinese Communist troops' identified as assisting the revolutionaries were ethnic Chinese harvesters of sea slugs who had worked on the island for decades.[103]

Julius Nyerere was frequently irritated by accusations of slavish loyalty to China from the British and Americans. On a visit to London in 1965, he expressed annoyance at the Cold War conspiracy theories over his relationship with China. Yes, he admitted, 'Tanzania invited seven Chinese technicians to train our reorganized army in the use of the weapons we were getting from that country ... China has given us a grant of £1 million, and made credits available to us totaling more than £10 million.'[104] But Nyerere added that there were '246 Chinese in Tanzania – and 16,000 British'.[105] The Western diplomatic panic about seven Chinese military instructors was so great, Nyerere observed, one might think that he had 'employed 70,000 of them'. 'When it comes to actual facts this country is completely Western, in government, in business, in the schools, in everything.'[106] The year after Nyerere became president of an independent Tanganyika, he had published his first of two translations of Shakespeare's plays (*Julius Caesar*, followed by *The Merchant of Venice* in 1969) into Swahili.

Chinese workers in Africa impressed through their frugal work ethic but their political regimentation inhibited their easy mixing with locals. The Chinese, remembered one Zanzibari civil servant, 'always moved around in groups. You never found a Chinese person alone ... mostly we didn't bother ourselves about them because they kept to themselves. I heard about the wonderful Chairman Mao Tse Tung with his Red Book, which I never read. My image of China in those days was a country ... that sent us commodities that were of poor quality.'[107] In 1967, a Chinese agrarian adviser in Tanzania suffered severe bee stings, but his comrades would not allow him to be treated by a non-Chinese doctor. By the time a compatriot medic had been found, the man had died.[108] In the early 1970s, the Chinese chargé d'affaires and his translator in Zambia were killed in a traffic accident while visiting a Chinese construction project. The disposal of their bodies posed serious political problems. On making enquiries, the Chinese railway workers discovered that the only crematoria in Lusaka were run by ethnic Indians. 'In order to show our resistance to the reactionary Indian faction [China had fought a sour border war with India in the early 1960s], we carried out a home-made cremation': throwing petrol over the bodies in the military camp until they were consumed by flames.[109] The Chinese were at times antagonistic to other aid workers: they refused to allow a group of Americans building a road parallel with the Tan-Zam Railway to enter the land alongside the route, and besieged them for five hours, chanting slogans and brandishing steel-tipped rods all the while.[110] Chinese political education alienated some. President Houphouet-Boigny, leader of the Ivory Coast, had his own suspicions about Chinese ambitions. 'At Nanjing, in China, Africans are being taught to assassinate those whose eyes are open to the Chinese danger, in order to replace them with servile men who will open the gates of Africa to China ... We should be blind if we failed to realise that China, which is overpopulated and would soon have a thousand million mouths to feed, looks enviously at our huge continent populated by only 300 million. If we are not careful we shall be served up as Chinese soup.'[111] One angry resident of Dar es Salaam alleged that Chinese doctors 'inject the sick people' then 'present them with the gift of small red books'.[112] (On the plus side, local workers on Chinese-run projects found it easy to take a break if they sat under a tree apparently reading a copy of the Little Red Book.)

Chinese evangelism dramatically increased during the Cultural Revolution. In March 1967, Kenyan newspapers published parts of a pamphlet supposedly issued by the New China News Agency, provocatively entitled 'New Diplomats Will Bring the Great Proletarian Cultural Revolution to Africa'. China had just pulled all but one of its diplomats back to Beijing; according to this pamphlet, they were poised to 'return to Chinese embassies in Africa' as 'new revolutionary diplomats' ready to 'form militant local Red Guard units to purify the revolutions in Africa'.[113] Chinese officials exasperated African participants in the international merry-go-round of Afro-Asian solidarity meetings with their demands for ideological endorsements. 'I am tired of being asked what I think of the Soviet position when I am eating a sandwich,' fulminated a Kenyan delegate, 'and what I think of the

Chinese position when I am drinking my tea. I would like to be able to eat in peace.'[114] At a Chinese diplomatic reception in Dar es Salaam in 1967, a Chinese diplomat asked a Tanzanian his opinion of Mao. On receiving the response that 'Mao was the great leader of the Chinese people just as Nyerere was the great leader of the Tanzanian people', the diplomat immediately offered a correction: Nyerere was 'the leader of Tanzania, but Chairman Mao was the leader of the whole world. There was to be no misunderstanding.'[115]

But political promiscuity was too deeply established in East Africa for such monotheism to succeed. Take the example of Issa, the Zanzibari revolutionary and disciple of Babu with simultaneous weaknesses for jiving, Mao and narrow-legged Italian tailoring; we heard him complain earlier about the absence of good times for African students in China. There was undoubtedly a Maoist steel to him. Recalling the Zanzibari revolution of 1964 (in which the island's prisons were thrown open and common criminals freely given weapons), he observed that 'thousands of people died, generally Arabs. I cannot say how many. A revolution is not a tea party ... [Mao's] sacrifice of lives was justified ... I would have done the same things, yes.'[116]

Yet Issa never fitted the self-sacrificing, disciplined model of the Mao-style Communist. Aged thirteen, he began secretly tippling on coconut wine and absconding from his boarding school at night to 'have as many girls as possible ... my number one pastime was dancing and seducing'. He left secondary school early, frankly telling the headmaster that 'I want to work, so I can drink and fornicate'.[117] The flaky Issa regularly let his political comrade and friend Babu down. Once he stood him up for a meeting when a girl dragged him back to her parents' house for drink and sex; and when in 1951 Babu arranged to meet him two months hence in London, it took Issa a whole two years to reach Britain. During that time he had married, impregnated then divorced (by letter) a South African prostitute, learned the jitterbug, developed a passable Frank Sinatra impression and almost enlisted in the US Army to fight in Korea.

Issa's first four children were named Raissa (after a Bolshoi ballerina), Fidela (after Castro), Maotushi (after Mao) and – self-explanatorily – Stalin. Amid countless other infidelities, while his wife was teaching Swahili in China he conducted liaisons with two Englishwomen *on the same plane* between Uganda and Sudan.[118] As a minister in President

Karume's Zanzibari dictatorship of the 1960s, he sent Tanzania's youth down to starvation conditions in rural camps to cure their 'declining respect' (according to Issa, the idea came 'from the Chinese'), while he regularly smoked marijuana and abandoned his wife (and mother of his four children) for a London party girl (with whom he had another four children, before abandoning her to a council house in Retford).[119] In the meantime, his ministerial colleagues imprisoned the husbands of any woman with whom they wanted to sleep. In the 1980s, as Zanzibar battled economic decline, Issa persuaded an Italian financier to back his opening of the island's first beach-resort hotel. One visitor observed him singing 'revolutionary songs in Spanish, Russian, and Chinese to his slightly disoriented Italian hotel staff'.[120]

On 17 December 1971, Ma Faxian – chief of staff for the Nanjing-Shanghai military zone – was given a full eight days' notice that he was to undertake a new mission: to travel to Zambia and train, under conditions of great secrecy, the country's army for two years. His commander told him flatly: 'This is a task that will help the world revolution, it is the concrete application of Chairman Mao's revolutionary diplomacy. In sending you to fulfil this tough but glorious assignment, the organisation hopes that you will be modest and circumspect, strengthen internal unity, overcome every difficulty and strive to complete this task.' His piece said, Ma's superior made the somewhat unconvincing request: 'Feel free to give your own views.'[121]

Unusually for a military agent of Mao's world revolution, Ma decided to put his life on the record. Deep into retirement, he relayed the story of his African mission to Li Danhui, one of China's best historians of the Cold War. His account is revealing of the motivations of the foot soldiers of Mao's world revolution – and of the successes and failures of their missions.

When John Cooley wrote of central 'control operations' for China's Africa offensive, he implied a tightly organised operation by revolutionary automatons dedicated to brainwashing an entire continent.[122] Reality was different. Ma was doubtless an impressively competent and committed individual. Without any background in African affairs or any foreign-language skills, he travelled out to Zambia – a country rich in political and economic uncertainty – and constructed a military school and curriculum from scratch. The pressures and hazards he encountered were enormous. Classified as top secret by the Zambians, the training had to take place far from any established settlement, in an isolated, uninhabited stretch of mountainous woodland. The instructors and students lived in tents, cooking their meals around campfires. The fastidious Ma observed that water was so tightly rationed that 'we couldn't even wash our feet every day'.[123] The Chinese had to bring everything with them: bowls, chopsticks, scissors. Telling his story more than three decades later, Ma remained every bit the disciplined (if long-winded) Communist Party soldier. 'Our great ideal was to liberate mankind. We came to Zambia … to carry out the task of proletarian internationalism … under the guidance of Chairman Mao's path of revolutionary diplomacy, we wanted to unite with the Zambian Army, develop friendship, and … accelerate the death of imperialism and colonialism. Our concrete task was … to positively propagandise Mao Zedong's military thought.'[124] Ma piously based the training programme on Mao's military strategy and on the idea of 'people's war'. His curriculum featured five days of Mao-dominated political education in every twenty in order to 'expand the influence of our party, our army and our country in the Zambian military'.[125] As Ma worked thus on 'developing friendship', his students were not just military men; the minister of defence and President's Kaunda's own son also attended classes.[126]

In practice, the mission had its share of human imperfections. The team picked to carry out the assignment – eleven military experts, five translators and one cook – were a disparate group, previously unknown to each other. One of the instructors was a liability from the beginning: he was melancholy with family problems – someone at home was clearly displeased that he had been dispatched some 11,000 kilometres away for the foreseeable future.[127] When the group of Chinese first encountered Zambians (an advance party sent to Beijing), the two sides could only smile at each other, for none of the translators had yet arrived – a significant obstacle in Mr Ma's mission to 'support the world revolution [through] propaganda about Mao's military philosophy'. Ma knew almost nothing of Zambia when he was served with his short-notice appointment. His sole source of information for days afterwards was a two-hour briefing from military intelligence, which focused on doctrinaire Marxist political analysis of the country. Only in the Q&A session afterwards had Ma and comrades been able to ask more practical questions: What is the weather like in Zambia? What do Zambians eat? Should the Chinese instructors bring their own toothpaste, tea and underpants? (Yes.)[128]

Given the top-secret nature of this military mission, Mr Ma and company were intriguingly slapdash about security on their departure and journey. Several family members came to send him off at the airport in Beijing; another fifteen or so swung by to say hello during a five-hour stopover in Shanghai. During another stopover in Karachi, the group had no idea what to do in an international airport or where to spend the night while waiting for their flight on to Africa; no one had given them any instructions. They decided to take refuge in the waiting room and see what happened. Fortunately, someone from the Chinese embassy turned up and asked them – again with a disarming lack of discretion – if they had just come in from Beijing.[129]

Once in Lusaka (where they lived while not teaching military recruits in the bush-camp), Ma's team became more vigilant. Indeed, security arrangements now severely limited the group's opportunities for mixing with Zambians. Ma and his comrades were permitted no unauthorised contact with non-Chinese, including their immediate neighbours; neither were they allowed to walk more than two hundred metres beyond the house they occupied in Lusaka, and that only in daylight. Every night spent in the capital, one of the party would be on sentry watch, looking out for suspicious activity. 'We were to keep ourselves extremely secret,' Ma recalled. 'Everyone was always to carry a box of matches, to burn their personal papers and possessions at a moment's notice.'[130]

Ma was consistently disappointed by lackadaisical Zambian approaches to hospitality. At the welcome ceremony held for the instructors at the training camp, the Zambians had prepared no tea, cigarettes or food. Instead, they trooped expectantly into the kitchen of the Chinese team. 'We'd prepared nothing!' Ma told his interviewer, his consternation still palpable thirty-six years on. The Zambians had contravened the most fundamental laws of hospitality. 'We were the guests, they were the hosts!' Ma and company had to grit their teeth and tell themselves: 'It's all for friendship … [But] they tricked us.'[131]

Time and again through Ma's stay in Zambia, this experience was repeated, when he felt that Zambians were taking advantage of Chinese generosity: guzzling Chinese fizzy drinks meant only for special occasions, inviting themselves over for meals, cadging sun hats. (This was not how Chinese people behaved, remarked the culture-shocked Ma. 'They were like silly children.')[132] Far from being masterful puppeteers of the Zambians, Ma and his comrades were frequently wrong-footed by their hosts' demands. A simple example concerned seating facilities in the camp. When the Chinese instructors arrived, they brought with them nothing but tents and tools to create an inhabitable area. They then fashioned neat little stools out of foraged wood to sit on during classes. But, Ma recalled, the Zambians had a habit of asking for anything they took a liking to: soon enough, they requested one of the home-made stools. 'For the sake of friendship' the Chinese advisers gave it up; as a result one of the instructors always had to stand, musical-chairs-style, during classes.[133]

One of Ma's compatriots, an engineer on the Tan-Zam Railway, was baffled by his African co-workers' addiction to spending their wages on dancing and drinking.[134] Ma too was disappointed by the Zambian students' lack of grit. Enthused for the first three weeks, the students promptly lost interest. Three months, they said, was too much for a training course: they longed to return home. 'They liked being praised, but were less keen on criticism,' Ma complained. They did not look after their equipment, or want to practise what they had learned. Within weeks of the course beginning, some were arriving late, or not at all, for class.[135] Ma recounted an anecdote in which a Chinese foreman on a construction project found an African worker taking an unauthorised nap under a tree. When the Chinese man challenged him about it, the African replied without embarrassment: 'God has told me to rest.'[136]

Still, Ma and his mission certainly made gains for Maoism. 'Before, our leaders didn't allow us to read Chairman Mao's works,' reported one of Ma's Zambian students. 'Now we can ... Because our army equipment is all from China, we need to study ... Mao's works.'[137] Ma observed that students were far more interested in Mao's political and military theories than they were in the practical classes: he was surprised by how quickly they began to apply them to Zambia's own situation.[138] Students adored Maoist military films, with their message that the strength of the people was more important than advanced weaponry. When a film had finished, amid claps and cheers, the audience would stay in their seats and demand a repeat showing. 'These are the best films in the world,' one viewer commented, extrapolating: 'the Chinese army is the best in the world'.[139] A visiting Chinese magician was also a great success, though with counterproductive consequences. One fine spring day, the Chinese embassy in Zambia received a visitor: a childless Zambian so impressed with the performer's display of supernatural powers (pulling fish, flowers, ducks, sweets out of thin air) that the African now requested the conjuror conjure him his heart's desire: a son. An awkward scene ensued, with Chinese diplomats explaining that the show was all trickery and sleight of hand, and the Zambian refusing to believe it, or to leave. Finally, a Chinese attaché had to ask the Zambian Foreign Affairs Department to send a representative to extract the petitioner.[140]

Mao's Africa adventure cost China. As Ma Faxian's memoir shows, African countries were often skilled at extracting maximum value from their sponsors – and the rivalries between the PRC and the USSR, and between mainland China and the Republic of China on Taiwan, made it possible for the unscrupulous to play one side off against the other. Public pledges of reverence for Mao from developing countries or struggling guerrilla movements should not, therefore, be taken at face value. Political pilgrims to China often had transparently ulterior motives in acclaiming Mao as the global guru of revolution. A PLO delegation in 1965 began its audience with a paean to the chairman: 'We are inspired, inspired by your military works ... Your swimming is as glorious as the Yangtze ... You are the symbol of great liberation and freedom in Asia, Africa, and Latin America.' After about ten minutes of this, the speaker finally got to the point: 'The aim of my visit is to ask for support.'[141] And it seems that the Palestinians received it. In the 1970s, the PLO leadership boasted that 'the Chinese give us everything we ask for'.[142]

China will never be able to produce a precise figure for the cost of its aid to Africa during Mao's lifetime: there were too many bad loans, too many projects that ran over budget, too many technicians and advisers who ended up staying on years after their mission was meant to have finished. By 1972, for example, China's investment in the Tan-Zam Railway was already double what had originally been projected.[143] A British resident in China during the 1970s remembers the official explanation for pinched railway schedules: 'the trains have gone to the Tan-Zam'.[144] And some paid for China's African revolution with more than goods or currency: 145 Chinese aid workers died in Africa during the Mao era.[145] Africans too lost their lives in Chinese projects. Just as Mao argued that 'millets and rifles' were more important than high-tech weaponry, he insisted that ideologically motivated, low-skilled masses were more effective than industrialisation: they achieved 'more, faster, better, cheaper'. But speed led to carelessness and lack of quality control. Tunnels leaked, trains derailed, accidents proliferated. In 1971, 870 people died or were injured in at least 1,000 accidents in Chinese projects in Africa; the following year, there were 1,806 accidents, resulting in 1,703 injuries and 67 deaths. Chinese technicians found it hard to pass on management of the projects to their African counterparts before they left.[146] One project in Sierra Leone was grassed over within two years of the Chinese experts' departure.[147]

And for all that expenditure of effort in the interest of 'world revolution' and 'friendship', the recipients of this aid could be carelessly ungrateful. When Ma Faxian's comrades, after more than two and a half years of instructing and gifting seats, fizzy drinks, cigarettes and Chinese dinners to their Zambian students, returned to China, no one saw them off. Much less did all this effort lead to Zambia following China's path. In 1974, President Kaunda decided to resolve border issues with South Africa and Southern Rhodesia through peaceful negotiations rather than armed struggle. Anti-Chinese messages now began to appear in the Zambian media. For Ma, there had never been any real meeting of minds between the Chinese instructors and their Zambian pupils. The problem with people in the capitalist system, he bitterly concluded, is that 'all they can do is take from other people, but they won't give you back even a hair from their bodies'.[148]

Most of Mao's 'freedom fighters' were disappointingly unsuccessful, as Mao himself admitted in an extraordinarily frank conversation with the notorious military tyrant President Mobutu of Zaire, who visited China in January 1973 to secure diplomatic and economic cooperation. 'Lumumba never made it here,' Mao began. 'Indeed he never did,' agreed Mobutu (omitting to recall that in 1961 he had sent Lumumba to his death, handing him over to thugs who tortured then murdered the first post-colonial, democratic leader to take over the Congo after almost a century of appalling Belgian rule). 'We supported him, and a few others, such as [Antoine] Gizenga and [Pierre] Mulele. But not you!' reminisced Mao, chuckling at the memory. '[We] gave them money and

weapons, but they didn't know how to fight and couldn't defeat you ...
I don't think they are up to much.' 'They were confronting Mobutu: I
was resolute,' the African replied. 'That hat of yours frightened them,'
Mao laughed, referring to Mobutu's trademark leopard-skin hat.
Mobutu – ever the sinister dictator – swatted away Mao's lame attempt
at a joke. 'No. It's my air of authority.' Mobutu himself remembered
a different opening gambit from Mao, which is close enough to Mao's
unpredictable conversational style to be plausible: 'Is that really you,
Mobutu? I've spent a lot of money trying to have you ... killed.'[149]

If there were few Chinese success stories in Africa, the guerrillas of
Zimbabwe were the exception.

On 28 April 1966, seven members of the Zimbabwean African
National Liberation Army, the armed wing of the Zimbabwe
African National Union, pushed deep down into what is now north
Zimbabwe (formerly Southern Rhodesia), searching for an electricity
pylon to bomb. Though they were quickly gunned down by Rhodesian
helicopters before they could do much damage, the military fiasco was
soon mythologised as a 'heroic sacrifice' and as the start of the
Chimurenga war of liberation against Ian Smith's white Rhodesian
government. In a sense, Mao had sent them. The seven guerrillas had
been trained in China and when the Rhodesian intelligence service
searched the dead bodies after the massacre, they found a notebook
recording one soldier's experiences at Nanjing Military College in 1965.[150]
Joseph Khumalo, himself a Nanjing graduate and one of the ZANU
commanders who decided to throw the seven guerrillas into Southern
Rhodesia, later explained the strategy: 'Mao Tse-tung said "where there
is war there is sacrifice ... fight, fail, fight, fail until you succeed."'[151]

At least three groups of ZANU guerrillas travelled to China for
training in the 1960s. In 1970, Chinese instructors – men like Ma
Faxian – were sent to Itumbi in south Tanzania to teach ZANU trainees
for two years in an abandoned farm and gold mine before the organisation's own Nanjing graduates took over the work. These graduates
included Josiah Tongogara, the military leader with greatest responsibility for ZANU's success in the war against white-ruled Southern
Rhodesia. (He seems to have learned also from the split personality of Mao's sexual politics: Tongogara was both attentive to the
welfare of post-partum women under his command *and* pressed female

guerrillas into sexual servitude while refusing them access to contraception or abortions.) They spent most of the first month teaching recruits – through use of Mao's essays – to 'speak bitterness': to analyse and confront the ways in which government and society were keeping them down. From there, they moved onto reconnaissance, sabotage, the use of bazookas. The path to protracted war did not always run smooth. To begin with, going off to train as a guerrilla 'was a sort of adventure', remembered John Mawema, later chief of security for ZANU. 'What we saw in the films. People shooting each other. You know, wanting to become cowboys of some sort. But as you go for training you are given the political line of the party, the ideology and the objectives of the armed struggle. Then you realised that all you were thinking was wrong ... I did nine months' training and the party was more concerned about political education than military training ... [in] the basic teachings of Mao on guerrilla warfare. We dealt more with the party line than military training because the Chinese, who had twenty instructors at the camp, believed that you have got to be matured politically in your head before you go and shoot ... You know the Chinese are very particular about such behaviour.'[152]

Until 1968, ZANU interpreted Mao's dictum that 'power comes out of the barrel of a gun' perhaps too literally. The organisation and its Soviet-funded rival ZAPU (Zimbabwe African People's Union) went on repeating the error of April 1966, hurling guerrillas over the border from Zambia into Zimbabwe and into doomed encounters with the white Rhodesian forces. In 1968 alone 160 fighters were killed.[153] 'We thought that it was easy to just go and get a gun and go and fight in Zimbabwe,' Mayor Urimbo, ZANU's political commissar, explained, 'but it was very difficult for that group in 1966. That was why they failed ... It was realized that the people had to be mobilized if we were to conduct a successful struggle. Tongogara in particular had learned [that] in China.'[154] Fay Chung, an ethnically Chinese educationalist and critical member of ZANU, describes the deep impact of Maoist military strategies on Tongogara: he 'entered the liberation struggle as a lowly soldier. He received his military training in the [Nanjing] military academy in China and forever held the Chinese as his mentors in morality as well as in military skills and strategies. It was from the thoughts and practices of Mao Tse Tung that he learnt that the guerrilla must merge with the people. He taught his soldiers that they were never to mistreat the peasantry ... It was probably also from the Chinese that he learnt that it was essential to eliminate his enemies. He saw issues in black and white, and believed that those who opposed or betrayed the liberation struggle for Zimbabwe deserved to be executed, and he did not flinch from playing the role of executioner.'[155] He would have been a plausible challenger to Robert Mugabe had he not been killed four months after Zimbabwe's independence in 1979 when the car he was travelling in was struck by a wayward trailer.

The official media in Zimbabwe acclaim Mao's ideas as the key to the success of ZANU against Ian Smith's white minority state of Southern Rhodesia. Articles on ZANU's history are studded with Mao's strategies and sayings: 'the guerrilla must move amongst the people as a fish swims in the sea'; 'if you want to know the taste of a pear, you must change the pear by eating it yourself'. 'Without mass mobilisation,' wrote the government's official newspaper the *Herald*, 'the war of liberation would have been difficult to execute because the people's support was critical.'[156] Chinese training continued until 1979 – up to the very eve of peace talks.[157] The Maoist strategy gave ZANU's guerrillas a sense of audacious possibility, as well as techniques for reaching the Zimbabwean grass roots. 'In the Soviet Union,' recalled Rex Nhongo, a ZANLA commander, 'they had told us that the decisive factor of the war is weapons. When I got to Itumbi, where there were Chinese instructors, I was told that the decisive factor was the people.'[158]

Like African Maoists all over the continent, the Zimbabweans were political omnivores. Every guerrilla took a *nom de guerre*: these ranged from the heroic-sounding Jekanyika (the one whose campaign affects every corner of the country) and the cunning One O'Clock Muhondo (surprise the enemy while he is having lunch) to the unexpected Margaret Thatcher (woman guerrilla with a strong and determined willpower). Many also took Mao or Zhou Enlai as aliases.[159] One Zimbabwean Mao served as political commissar to a commander who went by the name James Bond: 'the two made a sensational team', their comrades recalled after the pair were killed in 1974.[160] Spirit mediums were also used liberally, advising combatants to avoid a path if a snake crossed their way, and to desist from eating particular relishes. This diversity of influences notwithstanding, the ZANU curriculum was conspicuously Maoist. Songs set Mao's code of conduct and messages to music, ending with: 'These are the words of wisdom /

Handed down to us by Mao Tse-tung / The revolutionary sage.'
Liberation will come with the 'barrel of the gun': 'Only the gun, the
gun is the answer.'[161]

Tongogara's Maoist approach transformed ZANU's prospects
during the 1970s. Following Mao's strategy of mass mobilisation and
political education, ZANU educated the black rural majority about
their grievances against white rule, persuaded them that the struggle
was necessary, and established political and supply networks in remote
parts of Southern Rhodesia.[162] As the British Army had done during
the Maoist-infused Malayan Emergency after 1948, Rhodesian counter-
insurgency forces responded by creating 'protected villages' to 'drain
Mao's "sea" away from the guerrilla "fishes"'.[163] These camps were
desperate places, rife with poor hygiene, disease and abuses by government workers. Moreover, Smith's government was not in any hurry
to win hearts and minds by widening democracy to the black African
population.

In contrast to the simplistic but intense political education meted
out in ZANU, the Rhodesian Army was staunchly non-political and
non-philosophical. 'The Rhodesians' vague conservatism [and] hole-
in-the-corner racism', recalled Paul Moorcroft, a journalist who
reported the war on the ground, could not compete with ZANU's
'sense of mission' for which Mao's works were 'the bible'.[164] ZANU
needed every ounce of Maoist discipline to survive the insurgency,
for it was a conflict scarred by routine brutality against civilians, and
by biological and chemical warfare. The Rhodesian Army's special
forces unit – the Selous Scouts – hired agents to distribute uniforms
to ZANLA guerrillas painted with a toxin called parathion; corned
beef and jam were injected with thallium; cigarette boxes were soaked
in poison. Those affected died in solitary agony in the Rhodesian bush,
abandoned by their comrades.[165] These gruesome methods did little
to change the outcome of the struggle. By the time Ian Smith's
government agreed to negotiate in 1979, ZANU was in control of
two-thirds of rural Southern Rhodesia – the countryside surrounding
the cities, in Maoist terminology. It was the rural vote in the 1980
elections that brought Robert Mugabe to power, where he stayed until
2017. His successor, Emmerson Mnangagwa, also trained in China in
the 1960s; after he ousted Mugabe in late 2017, Mnangagwa was accurately acclaimed an 'old friend of China' by President Xi Jinping.

There are several explanations for the political, economic and social horror of Robert Mugabe's Zimbabwe. The inequality and racism of Southern Rhodesia's colonial past – in which whites commonly referred to blacks as *houtie* (wooden heads) and 'oxygen-wasters' – have left their mark. 'The use of violence as a political tool was well entrenched,' observed Fay Chung, witness to decades of Southern Rhodesian/Zimbabwean history, 'especially among the poor, for whom violence against the rich was a way of expressing their frustrations. Violence had been used during the war when "sell-outs" who supported the settler-colonial regime suffered beatings, or were even executed by freedom fighters.'[166]

Robert Mugabe's own personality is another factor: his ruthless obsession with power turned him into the oldest-serving head of state in the world at the point of his fall; and his country counted the cost. But the imprint of Maoism has not helped Zimbabwe. In the Cultural Revolution–era strategy that dominated their politics and army through the 1970s, ZANU inherited a deeply flawed political model. As we will see again in its export to Peru, India and Nepal, 'high Maoism' offers an effective set of military strategies for challenging a state. Its record in power, however, is extremely problematic. The Maoism that men like Tongogara studied in the 1960s helped bequeath ZANU a conspiratorial, totalitarian political template, in which the party – and the man at the top of the party – are always right; in which those defined as 'enemies of the People' (as defined by the party) can be annihilated; and in which military interests rule supreme.

Facing penury in the late 1970s – to no small degree due to its ruinously generous aid programme – China's post-Mao rulers changed their approach to Africa: selling arms rather than supplying them for free, offering commercial loans not politically determined grants. In so doing, China successfully buried memories of its role fostering guerrilla insurgencies through the 1960s and '70s – except in the case of Zimbabwe, it seems. 'No country [has] helped ZANU more,' Robert Mugabe gratefully told Zhao Ziyang, the rising star of the CCP during the 1980s.[167] On a 2015 visit to Zimbabwe, Xi Jinping embraced this shared past: 'China and Zimbabwe, in spite of the vast distance between them, have maintained a traditional friendship that is deep and firm. During the national liberation struggle in Zimbabwe, the Chinese people steadfastly stood behind the Zimbabwean people as comrades-in-arms. I was touched to learn that many Zimbabwean freedom fighters who received training from the Chinese side both in China and at Nachingwea camp in Tanzania can still sing [Mao's] songs such as the "Three Rules of Discipline and the Eight Points for Attention."'[168] At a reunion in 2016, veterans began chorusing it. The *Herald* – the government and party mouthpiece – reported that 'some of the comrades seemed transfixed, perhaps remembering the days when these were the maxims by which they lived'.[169]

Moved by this relic of 1960s Maoism – Mugabe sang China's praises, while blaming all Zimbabwe's economic problems on Western sanctions – China's government built a National Sports Stadium and a military academy in Harare, to create national spectacle, and to police its audiences. In military, political and psychological support offered by China to Mugabe's regime – in which life expectancy halved between 1980 and 2017 – the legacy of global Maoism lived on.

Xi's willingness to acknowledge this shared history suggests one of the ways in which he is attempting to rehabilitate the Mao era – including its foreign policy – into China's contemporary self-image. Certainly, it is hard to make sense of the closeness of the contemporary Sino-Zimbabwean relationship without keeping in mind the links stretching back to the 1960s insurgency. This is a curious diplomatic sleight of hand. China's presence in Africa today is focused on safe economic returns – including for its huge stake in Zimbabwe's diamond fields – and therefore on political stability, rather than on the kind of 'revolutionary upsurge' that Mao cherished while sponsoring ZANLA in the 1960s and '70s. And yet Xi presumably feels that the 1970s are distant enough to blur into the feel-good factor of the 'all-weather' friendship between Zimbabwe and the PRC.

In the autumn of 1976, President Marien Ngouabi of the People's Republic of the Congo organised a memorial ceremony for Mao – his 'elder brother' – in the forests of Owando, his home town in the centre of the country. As China's own functionaries at home and in Africa pulled free of Mao's cult, those Chinese diplomats –

indifferent to, or loathing, Mao for the chaos of the Cultural Revolution, since it had condemned most of the foreign service to re-education in rural China – who attended the ceremony were unnerved, even sickened by the encomia: 'Here, lingering in the African forest, was the cult of [the] former leader.'[170] After 1976, Mao's successors tried within China to return the genie of high, revolutionary Maoism to the bottle – and keep it there. But in Peru, India and Nepal, his spirit has continued to float free in the decades since his death.

7

MAO'S DOMINOES?
VIETNAM AND CAMBODIA

In 1964, the US Department of Defense released a short educational film, *Red Chinese Battle Plan*, to show their servicemen. Such productions are not usually renowned for their subtlety of analytical vision, and this one was no exception. 'Red China's battle plan,' the narrator intoned, to a sinister cymbal beat. 'It is a blueprint for world revolution ... divide and encircle, conquer and enslave.' The graphics showed huge arrows extending from China to Asia, Africa, Europe, South and North America. On reaching their targets, the arrows became a snarling dragon stretched across the entire world. 'Mao's blueprint for conquest is succeeding just as planned ... today, Communist China seeks to spread its own brand of global revolution ... the ideological centre of a world enslaved.' The film portrayed Mao's ambitions as global, but focused this fear on one territory above all. Vietnam, the film asserted, was the beachhead for global Maoist revolution: there, the Vietnamese Communists were deliberately replicating Mao Zedong's guerrilla war of the 1940s.[1] If Vietnam fell, so might the rest of the world. Lyndon Johnson, who after the assassination of John F. Kennedy escalated US involvement in the war throughout the 1960s, reiterated the point in another 'public information' broadcast in 1965: 'Why Vietnam?'

> The declared doctrine and purpose of the Chinese communists remain clear: the domination of all southeast Asia ... the domination of the great world beyond ... half a world away has become our front door. If freedom is to survive in any American home town, it must be

preserved in such places as south Vietnam ... it is up to us ... we must have the courage to resist. [Visuals feature a picture of a laughing Mao.] We did not choose to be the guardians at the gate. But there is no one else. Nor would surrender in Vietnam bring peace. Because we learnt from Hitler at Munich that success only feeds the appetite of aggression.[2]

This was the 1960s incarnation of the 'domino theory' beloved of American politicians from the 1950s to the 1970s: the belief that China was responsible for turning Vietnam Communist, and that once Vietnam had been turned, a 'chain-reaction' would follow 'throughout the Far East and Southeast Asia'.[3] American obsession with Chinese-Maoist expansionism thus helped create the greatest foreign policy and military disaster in US history: the decade-long intervention into Vietnam. The insignia of the American Military Assistance Command in Vietnam – to be found on the upper arms of US soldiers serving in that theatre – was a sword cleaving in half (or perhaps stopping forces flowing out of a breach in) the Great Wall of China.

Note especially Johnson's comparison between Mao and Vietnam, and Hitler and Munich. This analogy for the failure to act in Vietnam was political orthodoxy in 1960s America. To underestimate China's ambitions, said Dean Rusk, Secretary of State during the 1960s, would recapitulate 'the catastrophic miscalculation that so many people made about the ambition of Hitler'.[4] To America's leadership, Lin Biao's global application of Maoist revolution – 'Long Live the Victory of People's War!' – was a Maoist *Mein Kampf*, committing Beijing to undermine vulnerable colonial and newly independent nations'. 'The Johnson administration – including me – interpreted the speech as bellicose and aggressive,' remembered the defence secretary Robert McNamara, 'signalling an expansionist China's readiness to nourish "local" forces across the world ... Lin's remarks seemed to us a clear expression of the basis for the domino theory.'[5]

Long after the fact, the American architects of the war effort admitted that China's militant rhetoric had blinded them to the actuality of Chinese capacity to menace US interests. 'In retrospect,' McNamara considered thirty years later, 'one can see the events of autumn 1965 as clear setbacks for China.* ... But, blinded by our assumptions and preoccupied with a rapidly growing war, we – like most other Western leaders – continued to view China as a serious threat in Southeast Asia and the rest of the world.' Qiang Zhai, a pathbreaking historian of Mao-era China's intervention in South East Asia, argues that the American debacle in Vietnam might have been avoided had the Americans not feared Chinese influence there so much. 'Chinese behaviour [convinced] leaders in Washington that Beijing was a dangerous gambler in international politics and that American intervention in Vietnam was necessary to undermine a Chinese plot of global subversion by proxy.' By this reckoning, one of the hottest conflicts of the Cold War was motivated by the desire to 'contain and isolate Communist China'.[6] It was Maoist China's threatening potential that helped create world-changing events: the Vietnam War, and its many consequences (the global protest movements of 1968, Watergate, the US's unconscionable decision to prop up the exiled Khmer Rouge insurgency through the 1980s). Together, they significantly undermined US power and prestige in the world.

As the dragon in *Red Chinese Battle Plan* sprawled across the continents, US policymakers assumed that Communist parties in old Indochina – divided after the Second World War into Vietnam, Cambodia and Laos – would exult at the dragon's advance. Instead, China, Vietnam and Cambodia each harboured their own, differing interpretations of the domino theory. China's leaders did view Vietnam and other parts of Indochina as dominoes in the 'world revolution', often speaking high-handedly of these territories as a natural extension of China's own interests. The Vietnamese feared that Indochina would become China's domino, while the Cambodians and the Chinese were suspicious of Vietnamese ambitions to dominate the region. Through the critical decade of the 1960s, at least, Western policymakers played down or ignored the fact that for centuries if not millennia the Vietnamese had perceived – and resented – the Chinese empire as an expansionist power.

---

* That year, the Indonesian anti-Communist coup and the defeat of two Beijing allies, the overthrow of Ben Bella in Algeria, and India's defeat of China's ally Pakistan in Kashmir, all boded ill for Beijing's aspirations for international heft.

In spring 1975, the 'dominoes' of Indochina all fell to Communism. But this was no unified 'tide of opposition' to the 'free world'; instead the historical enmity of Vietnam towards China, and of Cambodia towards Vietnam, drove two more wars in the region and destroyed alliances that Cold Warriors had once thought unbreakable. For ten years up to 1972, the US committed hundreds of thousands of American lives and billions of dollars to a war built on the assumption of Chinese control of Vietnamese Communism. In the years that followed, an extraordinary game of musical alliances ensued. Kissinger and Nixon fell for the decaying charms of Mao and Zhou Enlai; Vietnamese Communism – until this point, founded on the teachings of Mao Zedong, 'the dazzling mirror' (Làm gu'o'ng sáng) – de-Maoified at speed. Both Vietnam and China scrambled to make up with their former bitter adversary the United States (which, following the amoral creed of 'my enemy's enemy is my friend', kept the Khmer Rouge in the United Nations until 1989). Through the 1980s, China and Vietnam fought each other while the US and Chinese together facilitated and funded war by the Khmer Rouge – easily the most extreme offshoot of global Maoism – against Vietnam. Global Maoism played a role in these tragic events.

I will not provide here a straightforward chronological history of the Vietnam War or the Khmer Rouge; this can be found elsewhere.[7] Neither do I intend to point the finger solely at Chinese Communist intrigues in creating the vast human tragedy of Indochina from the 1960s to the 1980s: nationalists in Cambodia and Vietnam, politicians in the USSR and USA, the earlier iniquities of French colonialism – all helped lay waste to this region. It is in part the fact that the conflict reflects so badly on all political players which explains the confusion of much of the historical record, for no side is interested in shining a light on these events. In China's case, the collapse of the Soviet Union, the Reagan Doctrine's triumphal assault on global Communism and China's own retreat from global revolution in the 1980s have all helped obscure memories of the PRC's central part in these conflicts. But Mao-era China's role needs to be written back into this history. In a contemporary context in which the PRC is once more asserting the relevance of its model to developing countries and looking to expand its power in South East Asia in particular, it is an especially timely moment at which to explore China's historical repertoire of involvement in the region.

We have seen how Mao's militant rivalry with the Soviet Union drove insurgency in Indonesia and parts of Africa. Events in Indochina showcased another consequence of Mao's competition with the USSR, namely his championing of nationalism within the Communist movement. Mao's trashing of the Soviets as 'great-power chauvinists' and his insistence on the national uniqueness of China's contribution to Marxism set a daring example to other Communist parties.[8] In China, Vietnam and Cambodia, Mao and Maoism encouraged toxic and competitive nationalisms. Indochina – according to American fears of the 1950s–70s, the hotbed of Maoist insurrection – disintegrated into nationalist wars. On Mao's watch, ideology was replaced by national interest.

'You have a row of dominoes set up, you knock over the first one, and what will happen to the last one is the certainty that it will go over very quickly,' President Eisenhower analogised in 1954. 'So you could have a beginning of a disintegration that would have the most profound influences.'[9] Though discredited today, the domino theory gave a fairly accurate account of Chinese Communist ambitions in Indochina. Confidential conversations between Chinese and Vietnamese leaders from the 1950s to the 1970s turned regularly to an overarching project of world revolution. The horror of the Vietnam War was explicitly justified because, in Zhou Enlai's words, it was fought 'for the world revolution' as well as for Vietnam. It was, in China's view, a key domino whose fall would have ramifications for the rest of Asia.[10] For this reason, China threw some $20 billion in aid at North Vietnam, trained thousands of its students and cadres in China, and supplied myriads of useful items: roads and bullets, uniforms and scented soap, soy sauce and lard, ping-pong balls and mouth organs.[11]

In strategy discussions with Vietnamese leaders, Mao casually projected his sense of ownership across South East Asia. While discussing a road-building programme in Laos, for example, he airily remarked: 'Because we will fight large-scale battles in the future, it will be good if we also build roads to Thailand.'[12] In the early 1970s, Vietnamese Communist leaders like Le Duan – later the sworn enemy of Chinese influence, a man who in private called Mao 'that bastard' – were similarly gung-ho about spreading the revolution across South East Asia, announcing that 'We want to smash the US–Japan alliance as well as the alliance between the US, Japan, and the regional bourgeois class. We have to establish a world front that will be built first by some core countries and later enlarged to include African and Latin American countries.'[13]

China had for centuries served as a political, cultural, linguistic model for Vietnam. Indeed, for large stretches of its history, parts of Vietnam had been directly ruled by China; the rest of the country, lying beyond direct Chinese sovereignty, Chinese emperors traditionally regarded as 'ours'. As a logical extension of Chinese domination, Vietnamese Communism from its very beginnings was entangled with that of its northern big brother. After graduating in 1924 from the Comintern's University of the Toilers of the East in Moscow, Ho Chi Minh went to Canton (Guangzhou), in south China, which at that point was the centre of the Chinese Communist revolution. While in China, Ho set up cells of a Vietnamese revolutionary party fighting French colonial rule, a precursor to his later Vietnamese Workers' Party (VWP). The CCP freely helped Ho with his political ambitions, partly bankrolling a Special Political Institute for the Vietnamese revolution (complete with hidden escape trapdoor), not far from the CCP's own headquarters in Canton. Ho shared with Mao from the very start an intellectual and ideological faith in the vanguard role to be played by the peasantry in a future revolution. In autumn 1938, Ho made a pilgrimage to the headquarters of the Chinese revolution in Yan'an and hailed the CCP as 'the elder brother of the Vietnamese people'.[14]

Successfully feigning Chineseness – he spoke and wrote Chinese well enough to pen classical poems – saved Ho's life at least once. In January 1933, Ho spent an uncomfortable few weeks in a Shanghai that, six years after Chiang Kai-shek's brutal purge of Communists, was crawling with French Sûreté agents eager to arrest the Vietnamese revolutionary. With the help of underground CCP members, he finally managed to set sail for Moscow, via Vladivostok, from Shanghai's bustling international dock on the Yangtze, boarding his ship disguised as a wealthy Chinese businessman. In Vietnam in 1940, as he plotted the insurgency that would eventually end French colonial rule in 1954, he passed himself off as a Chinese journalist, with the Chinese name that would later win him global celebrity: Ho Chi Minh (Hu Zhiming in Mandarin pronunciation – Hu Who Enlightens).[15]

Ho's friendship with the post-1949 Chinese leadership stretched back to the 1920s, when both he and his later Chinese comrades were finding their way in the revolution. He first met Zhou Enlai in Paris in the early 1920s, then renewed that friendship in Canton in the mid-1920s, and again during the Second World War. Whenever Ho visited China after 1949, he inevitably received red-carpet treatment: Zhu De, founder of the People's Liberation Army, took him to the cinema; Mao told anyone listening that he and Ho 'were kinsmen'.[16]

Ho Chi Minh was not the only Vietnamese Communist to venerate Mao and his revolution before the declaration of his Democratic Republic of Vietnam (DRV) in 1945. Vo Nguyen Giap, one of the chief architects of the military strategy that so demoralised first the French and then the US armies that battled Vietnamese Communist forces between the 1950s and '70s, also read the works of Mao in the late 1930s, with a view to making use of Chinese strategies for guerrilla and protracted war.[17] Dang Xuan Khu, general secretary of the Indochinese Communist Party from 1941, expressed his admiration for the CCP through changing his name, sometime after 1936, to Truong Chinh: Vietnamese for Long March (a switch that the Chinese found 'deeply gratifying').[18] Most of the Vietnamese leadership, remarked one insider, were plagiaristic 'disciples of Mao'.[19]

Once Chinese Communist armies gained breathing space in their own civil war with the Nationalists, they helped train Ho's officers and intelligence agents in Ho's pro-independence force, the Viet Minh, for the war with the colonial French Army that began in 1946. Truong Chinh explicitly modelled Viet Minh tactics on Mao's military writings. 'Helping the people of Vietnam with their struggle is our unshirkable international duty,' Liu Shaoqi told Luo Guibo, his special envoy to Vietnam, in 1950.[20] Luo's posting was not a cushy one. During a two-week meeting in the jungle with the Vietnamese politburo, he was accommodated in a hut made of bamboo and sunflower leaves. 'The tropical miasma was overwhelming,' he recalled thirty years later. 'The rats came out to enjoy themselves, the centipedes danced, poisonous snakes had fun with us by squeezing into my boxes of documents and my cotton quilt, while enormous moths and mosquitoes circled the mosquito nets at night, the latter taking large bites out of me whenever they got the chance.' Liu had personally briefed Luo to offer the Vietnamese a crash course in Maoist warfare, while Chinese military advisers provided essential training at regimental and battalion levels.[21]

Without Chinese assistance, the demoralisation of French armies in the first Indochinese war would have been unthinkable. In 1950,

China also dispatched to North Vietnam the Chinese commander of Ho's choice: Chen Geng, a bookish-looking general with a robust Communist pedigree – he had survived the purges of the 1920s, the Long March, Rectification and the civil war. Chen, like other Chinese advisers in Vietnam, vigorously promoted Mao's 'People's War', telling the Viet Minh they should 'concentrate [their] forces and destroy the enemy troops by separating them' – just as the Chinese Communists had done in their war against the Guomindang.[22] He taught the Vietnamese to observe Maoist military discipline: publicly praising role models, commemorating victories and martyrs, 'rectifying' – zhengfeng in Chinese, chinh huan in Vietnamese – party and army.[23] 'Mao's military thought', Giap agreed, was 'very applicable to Vietnam'.[24] At moments of military crisis, China bolstered Vietnam's frontier with its own soldiers. Every decision that Chinese military advisers made on the ground was immediately fed back to the CCP leadership; little happened, it seemed, without Beijing knowing of it. In 1950, during a military campaign to secure Viet Minh bases on the border with China, Mao himself directed the closing stages of the campaign. 'If you can properly solve these ... problems,' he told the advisers in a bossy telegram, 'victory will be yours.'[25]

In 1990, Bui Tin – a loquacious Vietnamese colonel turned journalist who had travelled in the tank that smashed through the gates of Saigon's presidential palace in April 1975 as the city fell to Communist armies – defected to France, disillusioned by the corrupt authoritarianism of Vietnamese Communism in power. Five years later, he published a memoir which was, among many things, an acidic account of Chinese influence on the Vietnamese Communist movement. 'Maoism after 1951 began to stultify our consciences and has caused lasting harm right up till now ... Repression was mistaken for enlightenment and progress.'[26] Coming from a well-heeled, Franco-Sinophile background, Bui Tin had studied at an elite francophone school. Writing in exile, he recalled the cosmopolitan routine of his childhood Sundays: 'All day ... we would eat only French food with knives and forks on a table set with napkins. Bowls and chopsticks were forbidden. So too were Vietnamese clothes. My brother and I had to wear European-style shirts and shorts. My father would also read French poems to us.'[27] He entered the anti-colonial, Communist resistance as a young patriot with a personal tragedy: his mother had been shot dead through the chest, in her own kitchen, by French troops in 1948. Bui saw the Indochina war as an anti-colonial conflict until 1950, when North Vietnam fastened itself to the new People's Republic of China, Mao suits became de rigueur and curly hair a bourgeois, imperialist abomination.

> The ever-increasing amount of military and civilian aid from China enabled the Viet Minh to strengthen its position. But ... tension grew ... large numbers of Chinese advisers arrived ... The friendly, even cosy atmosphere which had previously existed disappeared with talk of orthodox class warfare. Marxism had come to Vietnam via Maoism ... What is the Communist Party? It plays the leading role in every aspect of society. It is constant, correct and absolute ... The individual is as worthless as a grain of sand, and to be crushed underfoot ... Chinese books, films and songs were everywhere ... Mao Tse-tung's song 'The East is Red' assumed the status of an official anthem ... Only after that came a song in honour of Ho Chi Minh and the *Internationale*. At the same time, a campaign got underway to encourage the reading and speaking of Chinese while a constant stream of cadres was sent north to study in Peking, Shanghai, Nanking, Nanning and Canton ... Having just escaped from the long night of being slaves to the French, we were dazzled by the new light of the Chinese Revolution which was acclaimed as our role model. We accepted everything impetuously and haphazardly without any thought, let alone criticism.[28]

At the 2nd Party Congress, held in northern Vietnam in early 1951, Marxism-Leninism, Stalinism and Mao Zedong Thought were sworn in as 'the basic theory of the party'.[29] 'The thinking of Ho Chi Minh and the rest of the leadership in those days was to regard Mao Tsetung thought as the only way to follow,' remembered Bui Tin. 'A French journalist asked Ho Chi Minh why he had written so little about politics. The reply came back "What is there for me to write about? All the theory that is needed has been worked out and written by Mao Tsetung."'[30]

One fine day in May 1953, an audience of 5,000 gathered at the foot of the pine-tree-lined Mount Voi, about a third of the way to the Chinese border heading north from Hanoi. The congregation was partly camouflaged with tree branches: as shade from the sun, and as concealment against French bombers. No such cover for the accused, a slim woman dressed in brown, kneeling beneath a scarlet banner that read 'Overthrow the despotic landlord Nguyen Thi Nam, take back the land for the peasants!' For eight and a half hours, members of the audience rushed up to Nguyen to snarl, scream, slap and spit their loathing of her. 'Down with the evil landlord! Down, down, down!' roared the cadres orchestrating the trial. The audience chorused the refrain back. The list of her crimes included collaboration with the French and Japanese, betraying the resistance and the Viet Minh, exploiting and starving people, and murdering 259 individuals. 'Execute the reactionary wicked landowner Nguyen Thi Nam!' the judge shrieked in conclusion. 'Execute her!' answered the crowd. Six weeks later, she was stood against a tree trunk and shot by a five-soldier firing squad. On inspecting the body, the squad's captain found only four bullet holes. Muttering that 'one shot missed the target', he blew her brains out with his own pistol.[31]

This was the overture of North Vietnam's land reform. Ushered in by the 2nd Party Congress, it was closely modelled on its Chinese-Maoist predecessor, for the leaders of the PRC had made its ongoing support for the anti-French war effort contingent on the campaign.[32] China thus gifted Communist Vietnam not only countless tons of material aid but also a means of organising Vietnamese society in its own image. The revving engines of Chinese jeeps – carrying to villages Mao-suited leaders of land reform brigades, who held absolute power over life and death – formed part of this period's soundscape of terror.[33]

On that hot day in May 1953, the audience gave a flawless performance of this Chinese script and choreography. An uninformed observer of this scene would not have guessed that the case against Nguyen Thi Nam was intensely controversial. Her socio-economic profile fitted the bill: she was a wealthy trader and plantation owner. But she also happened to be an ardent patriot who had given the Viet Minh leadership sanctuary during the Second World War, provided generous famine relief in her community, and through donations saved Ho Chi Minh's new regime from financial collapse in 1945. She could have protected her two sons from having to fight against the French; instead, she encouraged them to join the revolution. Yet Luo Guibo insisted that the Vietnamese Communists made an example of her. Ho Chi Minh had blanched and quoted a French saying: 'A woman should not be touched, not even with a rose petal ... [We] cannot open the campaign by shooting a woman, especially one that has nourished communist soldiers and [is] a mother of an officer in the People's Army.' But Ho could never say no to Luo. 'Uncle Ho knew it was not right,' recalled one of his closest liaisons with the Chinese, 'but even he did not dare to tell [the Chinese advisers] ... They were the sons of God, Mao's special envoy.'[34] Ho's acquiescence and the execution of Nguyen gave the North Vietnamese Communists impunity to annihilate those deemed to be enemies of the state.

As hoped, the campaign did reap political and military benefits for the party. During the battle of Dien Bien Phu in 1954, which destroyed French resolve to hold on to Vietnam, some 200,000 peasants won over by land reform helped the Communist armies by hauling military supplies across the country. The meetings, the propaganda, the political education mobilised thousands to fight and die on the mountain slopes of Dien Bien Phu.[35] Yet the campaign has also gone down in popular memory as one of the party's greatest mistakes: for its excessive harshness and fanatical violence, for polarising society between the have-nots and the have-littles. Even a government institution like the Vietnam Institute of Economics stated in 2002 that almost 80 per cent of 'cruel and bullying landowners' had been wrongly categorised. In Vietnam today, land reform remains a volatile topic. A brand-new exhibit on the subject was unveiled in the National Museum of History one Monday in September 2014. By the Friday of that week, it had been shut down because the public discussions that resulted refuted government orthodoxy that the campaign had made life better for millions of poor peasants.[36]

'We did not realise what a mistake it was going to be,' observed Bui Tin forty years later. 'Land Reform occurred after we had heard hundreds of Chinese advisers introduce the process on the basis of experience in their own country ... Everything was cut and dried. He is a landlord even though he owns only 10 square metres. Therefore he is bad, greedy, cruel and the evil hand of imperialism ... even though the system of land tenure in northern Vietnam was different from that in China and few people owned more than a few hectares.'[37] The death toll of land reform – somewhere between 10,000 and 30,000

Vietnamese – was 'the result of the mechanistic application of Chinese experience imposed by their advisers ... Ho Chi Minh was to blame ... [but] it was Mao Tsetung who really forced his hand.'[38] Land reform set a precedent of blind imitation of Chinese campaigns. 'What the Soviet Union and China are today, Vietnam will be tomorrow,' went the slogan.[39] The makers of propaganda films were sent to China to study the principles of heroic socialist realism. The Vietnamese state's crackdown on two periodicals calling for freedom of speech echoed China's Anti-Rightist Campaign of 1957; Ho and his party carefully matched their own responses to Khrushchev's Secret Speech and to de-Stalinisation with those of Mao. The Great Leap Forward's preoccupation with backyard furnaces, and inflating targets and achievements, became 'almost a way of life', Bui Tin recalled. '[T]he press reported production of over 100 tons of rice per hectare and then 200 tons, which was in excess of what China had claimed to achieve. Of course these statistics were totally unrealistic and unrealisable in both countries, but in the case of Vietnam it was all part of the ... competitive emulation of Mao Tse-tung thought.'[40]

The Chinese influence was decisive in turning the first Indochinese war in favour of the North Vietnamese. In May 1953, the French expressed a new determination to resecure Vietnam as a colonial possession: they appointed an intellectually brilliant new commander, General Henri Navarre, evocatively dubbed 'the air-conditioned general' for his coolly calculating persona.[41] As in the past, the leadership of the CCP assumed a dominant role in plotting out the approaching campaign, dictating a precise order to attacks. The Chinese plan forced a confrontation with the French in the north-west of the country, near the border with Laos. On hearing where the Viet Minh troops were headed, Navarre decided to stage a showdown in the region, parachuting his battalions into the valley village of Dien Bien Phu. If the French held the village, he theorised, they could prevent the Vietnamese Communists from taking over the north-west and moving on to assault Laos. Chinese advisers applied Maoist strategy, telling the Vietnamese to concentrate on 'separating and encircling the enemy, [to] annihilate them bit by bit'.[42] After six months of gruelling siege, the French garrison was overrun by the Viet Minh; around 10,000 French soldiers became prisoners.[43]

The Geneva Conference that followed the surrender of the French garrison at Dien Bien Phu was, in many respects, the PRC's diplomatic 'coming out party', as Zhou Enlai shuttled between French and Vietnamese negotiators to produce the outcome that the PRC wanted. The following year, the Chinese delegation would again shine at the Bandung Conference for Afro-Asian Unity, but Geneva was an opportunity to dazzle old and new imperial powers in the West. Behind the scenes, the brilliant and faithful Huang Hua (Edgar Snow's old friend) was working away at international PR, in his respectable flannel jacket, waistcoat and Oxford bags: running press conferences and ensuring that Zhou Enlai's speeches got into all the right hands. Under Huang's direction, the spacious house in Geneva that the PRC delegation rented was carefully furnished with Chinese antiques, reassuring visitors that the Communists were upholding China's glorious cultural traditions. In these sedate, cultured surroundings, Huang screened to a full house a new Chinese movie, a soupy opera that his diplomatic master Zhou Enlai pointedly described as China's *Romeo and Juliet*: *The Love Story of Liang Shanbo and Zhu Yingtai*. The Chinese Communists, ran the subtext, are not brainwashed automatons; they have emotional lives too. It was, Huang later remembered, 'a full house; those who came late had to stand. Even US journalists, who had not been invited, came.' Hearing of the screening, Charlie Chaplin (living in nearby Lausanne) was filled with a desire to see 'New China'.[44]

The North Vietnamese, meanwhile, were bullish: they wanted to capitalise on crushing the French at Dien Bien Phu to unify 'the entire Indochina'. It would take only two to three years, Giap argued, as long as the US kept out of the conflict.[45] But in the end, as usual, the Chinese laid out a course of action; the Vietnamese followed it. In this instance, the Chinese emphasised the need for a peaceful, negotiated solution to avoid galvanising the US and the old European colonial powers into a united front. Chinese interests heavily shaped the Geneva settlement: after four years of military hostilities with Western nations (principally, the US and France), China was apprehensive of drawing the US into direct military intervention in Indochina. If the Vietnamese were to go on fighting openly, the Chinese would unavoidably be drawn into helping them. Mao and his lieutenants therefore told the Vietnamese Communists to postpone their ambitions for military unification. In July 1954, the Vietnamese delegation at Geneva agreed to the division of the country between north and south at the 17th parallel: through the rumpled terrain of the Annamite mountains.

Without Chinese assistance, the North Vietnamese would have had no bargaining power at all. Compare and contrast Vietnamese success in defying and ousting the French from North Vietnam, with the Malayan Communist Party's inability to best the British in their own anti-colonial struggle between 1947 and 1957. Chinese material aid was the crucial differentiating factor. But the help had been self-interested. The Chinese were the real winners from Geneva: Zhou Enlai had established himself as a suave international diplomat and the settlement had created a buffer zone in South East Asia between Communist China and Western spheres of influence. Although the DRV was eager to export Communist-led insurgency to Laos and Cambodia, to create an 'Indochina Federation', Zhou Enlai and his fellow Chinese diplomats were wary of a Vietnamese-dominated military alliance between the three countries, and had done their best to shut the idea down.[46] The Vietnamese Communists would always resent the Chinese for pressuring them to accept a suboptimal outcome – a divided Vietnam – at a time when they were confident that reunification by force was within reach.

Regardless of the Geneva settlement, the DRV soon resumed its offensive to unify Vietnam under Communist rule. Aid from the PRC kept flowing, the Chinese making immense sacrifices on behalf of their Vietnamese 'brothers'. In January 1959, and in addition to existing long-term economic and technical help, China gave North Vietnam a new loan of 300 million yuan, for which repayment was not required until 1967. Another 100 million yuan was given outright, following on from an 800-million-yuan gift in 1955.[47] 'All my equipment from top to bottom,' recalled Bui Tin of that time, 'from my solar topee to my rubber sandals, and even my underpants ... was made in China.'[48] Vietnamese leaders repaid Mao's largesse by genuflecting to his 'theory of revolutionary war ... his stress on the peasants, his idea of rural areas encircling the cities, and his concept of protracted armed struggle as a "model strategy for many Communists in Asia, Africa and Latin America"'.[49] Ho Chi Minh fondly described relations between North Vietnam and China as being 'as close as lips and teeth' and recounted 'the special significance of the Communist victory in China for the Vietnamese people'.[50]

Behind this affectionate facade, the relationship was breaking down by the mid-1960s. The tensions had origins deep in history: in Vietnam's millennia-old position as the smaller neighbour of successive Chinese empires. Even in the post-1949 era of progressive, supposedly egalitarian world revolution, China's leaders still spoke from high to low when addressing their Vietnamese counterparts. China flattered the USSR with the nickname 'elder brother' but expected similar deference from the Vietnamese. The Vietnamese, meanwhile, continued to resent the Geneva settlement. The compromise led to the Vietnamese Workers' Party in the south of the country losing 90 per cent of its members: 70,000 were killed and almost one million jailed under South Vietnam's autocratic ruler Ngo Dinh Diem. (It is estimated that 200,000 of these prisoners were permanently injured by torture.) Without Geneva, leaders of the VWP believed, the millions of Vietnamese deaths from the reunification war of 1959–75 could have been avoided.[51] Mao's rows with the Soviets were also puzzling and frustrating to the Vietnamese. Ho Chi Minh, who wrote loving letters to Stalin in French and to Mao in Chinese, was genuinely upset that the two biggest socialist states had fallen out and strove, unsuccessfully, to serve as marriage counsellor between the two. His colleagues were upset for more practical reasons: if the socialist world was busy feuding, it would not be able to pool its energies and resources to help Vietnam against the mighty US. By the mid-1960s, after the American war effort intensified, the North Vietnamese were growing quietly irritated over the Chinese decision to block the transport of Soviet military aid across Chinese rail lines and airspace. The Vietnamese started to suspect that the Chinese wanted a protracted war in Vietnam for their own strategic purposes: to let the Vietnamese go on dying just to keep the US tied up.

But what really shook Vietnamese enthusiasm for the PRC was the creeping perception that Mao, and his policies, were flawed. Already in 1959, the North Vietnamese press was dubious about the virtues of Mao's Great Leap Forward, while the sons and daughters of political cadres studying in China during the late 1950s wrote letters home about how hard it was to get hold of anything, asking their families to send them grain, vegetables and soap.[52] Vietnamese enthusiasm for the Maoist model in practice decreased yet further with the Cultural Revolution: the prospect of emulating China by pulling apart a disciplined, functioning party structure during a bitter war for survival with the most powerful country in the world was sheer insanity. As they continued to depend on Chinese aid, the Vietnamese Communists could not freely express their views, but their non-committal replies in conversation with Chinese leaders were expressive. In 1967, Prime Minister Pham van Dong and General Giap responded to a forty-minute presentation from Zhou on the Cultural Revolution with only one brief question.[53] Duong Danh Dy, a veteran Vietnamese diplomat to China, remembered that 'almost every Vietnamese ... immediately saw the flaws of the Cultural Revolution ... Uncle Ho asked everyone [at a party meeting], "Is there anyone in this room who understands China better than I do?" Of course no one said anything, and then he said, "And yet even I cannot understand what this 'Cultural Revolution' actually is."'[54]

Revulsion across the cities of the United States and Western Europe at the American war in Vietnam played a big part in selling the virtues of Mao's China to students and other discontented radicals. Many Western rebels saw the Vietnamese as simply inheriting and propagating the theory and practice of Mao's revolution – People's War, both in protracted and guerrilla form – expounded in Lin Biao's 'Long Live the Victory of People's War!' This assumption massively burnished their image of Mao and the PRC. Yet by the mid-1960s, the Vietnamese Communists were self-confident enough to see the flaws in the increasingly idealised visions of Maoist military strategy emanating from Lin Biao. Where was the mention of outside – Soviet and US – aid in helping Chinese armies fight the Second World War?[55] How on earth were the Vietnamese to win any kind of decisive victory against the Americans and the US-supported South Vietnamese Army without the kind of big guns that the Soviet Union could provide? From the Tet Offensive onwards, the Vietnamese began to favour attacks on cities, a tactic that Zhou Enlai denounced as Soviet, and as an affront to the Maoist strategy of protracted war, of encircling the cities from the countryside. As one of the major shifts of the Cold War began in the late 1960s – China and North Vietnam moving towards talks with the US – both suspected each other of selling out to the Americans, and scolded the other accordingly. Above all, the North

Vietnamese felt that Chinese rapprochement with the US would remove a crucial deterrent to escalation of the American war effort – the threat of Chinese intervention. 'The Chinese government told the US that if it did not threaten or touch China, then China would do nothing to prevent the attacks [on North Vietnam],' General Giap remembered. 'It was like telling the US that it could bomb Vietnam at will, as long as there was no threat to the Chinese border ... We felt that we had been stabbed in the back.'[56]

But by the time the friendship between China and Vietnam was breaking down, China had acquired another best friend and (it hoped) loyal disciple in the region: the Cambodian Khmer Rouge.

By the summer of 1975, Mao was manifestly ailing. Thanks to his height, he maintained a facade of bulk, but close scrutiny of the drape of his suits – the fabric arms hanging, barely filled, from the shoulder seams – exposed how age had wasted his once robust frame. The advance of Lou Gehrig's disease – amyotrophic lateral sclerosis, a form of motor neurone disease – had seized his throat muscles. Increasingly, only the coterie of trusted young women he kept around him – Zhang Yufeng, his former personal train stewardess turned lover turned nursemaid; Tang Wensheng, his favourite Chinese-English translator during the Cultural Revolution – were able to interpret to the wider world the gasps and grunts that emerged from his larynx. By April 1976, in one of Mao's final audiences, with the New Zealand prime minister, Robert Muldoon, Mao was little more than a vegetable. Once he had been lifted from his armchair to shake hands, he 'slumped back in it in a state of seeming collapse', remembered Muldoon. 'What emerged from Mao's mouth were occasional grunts and groans as he struggled to get out the necessary word. The interpreter/nurse, intelligent and gentle, would decipher these noises – sometimes seeming to peer into his larynx – [presumably in Mandarin] to a male interpreter who put them into polished, often colloquial, English.'[57]

And yet an hour-long meeting on 21 June 1975 provided an extraordinary tonic for the fading helmsman. It was with Pol Pot and Ieng Sary – the secretary general and foreign affairs supremo respectively of the Communist Party of Kampuchea (CPK, known colloquially as the Khmer Rouge). It was their first foreign visit after the fall of

Phnom Penh and the takeover of Cambodia two months previously. During that time the Khmer Rouge command had ordered the evacuation of all cities and towns to the countryside (an estimated 20,000 people died of snap executions, hunger and disease in the emptying of Phnom Penh alone); the liquidation of anyone who had served the pre-revolutionary government; the abolition of money and markets; and rapid, forced collectivisation.

One photograph captures the animation of the encounter. All three men are in Mao suits. Ieng Sary, with his round, jowly face, is to the right grinning broadly, grasping Mao's spindly right wrist with both hands. Pol Pot – appropriately enough, given his obsession with clandestinity – appears out of focus, standing a few steps back from Mao and Ieng. (It was only in 1977, on another visit to China and due to pressure exerted by his hosts, that Pol Pot revealed to international audiences that the CPK, under his leadership, was ruling Cambodia; till then, the faceless 'Angkar' – Organisation – had been officially in charge.) But the real energy in the photograph emanates from Mao. An intent look on his face, he is gesturing forcefully. Two of his fingers are splayed, suggesting he is making a point with them. (In his figures of speech across several decades, Mao was fond of deploying digits: referring to Stalin's 'three rotten fingers' – to express his thesis that Stalin was 70 per cent correct, 30 per cent incorrect – or metaphorically nibbling, biting or breaking the fingers of his military enemies, to stand for the strategy of guerrilla war engagements.)

What was Mao saying? Only fragments of the conversation have escaped into the public domain: even within the profoundly sensitive realm of Maoist China's relations with foreign political parties, those with the Khmer Rouge remain unusually embargoed. This has led in recent years to Orwellian denials by the Chinese Ministry of Foreign Affairs of any involvement with the Democratic Republic of Kampuchea (DRK) – the state that Pol Pot founded in spring 1975. This despite the fact that, in the words of Andrew Mertha, one of the leading analysts of PRC–Khmer Rouge relations, 'Without China's assistance, the Khmer Rouge regime would not have lasted a week.'[58] Yet Chinese historians devoted to preserving the political record have leaked parts of the conversation from June 1975. Here are some of the highlights of what we have.

> Pol Pot (exceptionally excited): We are extremely happy to be able to meet the great leader Chairman Mao today!
>
> Mao: We approve of you! Many of your experiences are better than ours. China does not have the right to criticize you ... You are fundamentally correct ... Right now [in China], we have ... a capitalist country without capitalists ...
>
> Pol Pot: ... In future, we will be sure to act according to your words. Since I was young, I have studied many of Chairman Mao's works, in particular those concerning people's war. The works of Chairman Mao have led our entire party.[59]

Pol Pot brought two of his own translators to China. One of these was killed in a 1978 purge, and took to his grave his memory of what was discussed, but the other interpreter survived to flee to France in the 1980s. (He was one of the fortunate: while the Khmer Rouge chaotically deserted Phnom Penh as Vietnamese-Soviet tanks rolled towards it in early January 1979, one of their last acts was to kill any Chinese-language interpreter they could lay their hands on – presumably because they were party to top-secret discussions of a potentially damaging nature.) In an interview with French media in 1994, the surviving interpreter revealed some more of what Mao had said. Apparently, the chairman had complained about the 'obstruction of evil rightist forces' in China. Consequently, he was 'unable to give full play to his ambitions, and to accelerate communism. Fortunately, his ideal could flower in Cambodia. He was confident that the Khmer Rouge were the future standard-bearers of world revolution.' 'What we wanted to do but did not manage, you are achieving,' he told his visitors.[60] Imagine Mao's excitement: after almost two decades of rhetorical fireworks and burdensome overseas aid budgets, his revolution had finally succeeded outside China.

Eight months later, Pol Pot received his own memento of this meeting. Zhang Chunqiao, a member of the 'Gang of Four' – Mao's Cultural Revolution steering committee – paid a visit to Cambodia. Pol Pot decided to emerge from the shadows to meet Zhang off the plane. A film of the meeting has survived. The two men hug each other with stiff joy, then walk – clapping, faces arranged into rictus grins – the standard ceremonial walk between two files of cadres, soldiers and masses. They converse companionably on a sofa.

They clink glasses, smiling sleekly. Then Zhang presents to Pol Pot a great trophy: a gleaming metal-framed landscape print – big and heavy enough to require two lesser comrades to support it while Zhang and Pol Pot admire the picture. It is the snapshot of Pol Pot's peculiarly animated meeting with Mao, the previous summer.[61]

Again, we do not have a complete record of what Zhang and Pol Pot discussed, though we do know that Zhang helped author a slim constitution for Democratic Kampuchea, which in practice guaranteed Cambodians only one freedom: to work.[62] But at least one well-connected Chinese historian has argued that Zhang was there to hand-deliver a Chinese-authored blueprint for Cambodia's own Great Leap Forward and Cultural Revolution – a programme of purges and collectivisation. A speech that Pol gave a few months later fluently spoke the language of the Cultural Revolution: 'There is a continuous, non-stop struggle between revolution and counter-revolution. We must keep to the standpoint that there will be enemies 10 years, 20 years, 30 years into the future ... [But i]f we constantly take absolute measures, they will be scattered and smashed to bits.'[63]

Only half a year later, shortly after the death of his patron Mao, Zhang Chunqiao himself would be purged; in 1980 he was put on trial as chief architect of the Cultural Revolution and sentenced to life imprisonment. With a few exceptions, the trademarks of Zhang and his close comrades' politics – the public violence, the mass campaigns, the deafening slogans, the continual purges and hunts for 'enemies of the revolution', the obsession with communal farming – began to fade from China. 'But if the Gang of Four had not been purged after Mao's death,' the same well-informed Chinese historian pondered, 'if they had taken power as they expected to, China might have walked the same path as Cambodia.' He paused. 'I've visited the Killing Fields. As a Chinese person, I feel responsible.'

On Christmas Day, 1978, in response to three years of rhetorical and military aggression from Democratic Kampuchea, the Democratic Republic of Vietnam hurled 150,000 soldiers across the border into Cambodia. In less than two weeks, the Vietnamese Army had captured Phnom Penh, forcing the Khmer Rouge leadership to retreat to

Thailand. Across the first half of 1979, Cambodia's new Vietnamese rulers put the leaders of the Khmer Rouge on trial *in absentia*. The legal process became a high-profile part of Vietnam's spiralling anti-China campaign. The genocide, the trial documented, was 'a manifestation of the reactionary nature of both the Peking expansionists and the Pol Pot–Ieng Sary genocidal criminals'.[64] Testimonies related a thorough-going Chinese conspiracy to murder the Cambodian people and implement a 'dream of world hegemony' through exporting Mao's revolution via its Khmer Rouge puppets. Pol Pot and Ieng Sary had planned 'to carry out genocide ... to close the country to all relations with foreign ones, except China ... They wanted to impose on the Cambodian people the "cultural revolution" imported from China.'

In every village, there were talks about a secret decision of Pol Pot: 'They are going to replace the Kampuchean population with millions of Chinese.' ... those ditches dug everywhere began to be filled up with corpses ... Pol Pot stated ... that the most valuable Chinese aid was Mao Zedong Thought ... In a word, the Pol Pot–Ieng Sary clique [turned] our whole country into a hell of blood and tears ... furthering the reactionary Peking rules scheme of expansionism and hegemonism ... the mode of diabolical society which Pol Pot and Ieng Sary established in Cambodia is a product of Maoism.[65]

These statements portray the Chinese in Democratic Kampuchea as the power behind the throne. But the copious documents collected for the trial need to be treated with caution, for their aim was to legitimise the Vietnamese occupation of Cambodia as a defence against Chinese imperialist schemes. Do less polemical parts of the historical record bear this interpretation out?

Saloth Sar – Pol Pot's real name – first encountered Mao in the early 1950s, while failing (three years in a row) a course in radio electricity in Paris. He became radicalised by Communist texts alongside his future Khmer Rouge comrades: practically the entire future politburo travelled to France during this decade on government scholarships. Like Mao in the 1930s, Sar fell headlong for Stalin's *Short Course* – in particular, for its exhortations of constant struggle against enemies in the party. Sar and his classmates were also fascinated by tales of the French Revolution: by the glorification of intellectual revolutionaries as liberators of humanity and its repudiation of half-measures. Mao's appeal lay in his strategies for revolution in colonial or semi-colonial territories, and for his demand of unbending loyalty to the Communist organisation. 'The moment you oppose the Communist Party, you become a traitor ... Whoever wants to oppose the Communist Party must be prepared to be ground into dust. If you are not keen on being ground into dust, you had certainly better drop your opposition.'[66]

After 1953, Sar returned to Phnom Penh, to take a job as a high school teacher; a dozen years passed. He was, in the memory of at least one of his pupils, an inspired and inspiring teacher, in the habit of reciting French poetry to his students. Within the Communist Party – in the 1950s known as the Khmer People's Revolutionary Party, after 1960 as the Workers' Party of Kampuchea, becoming the Communist Party of Kampuchea in 1971 – he was known best for his smile and accommodating manner. He took the unmilitant alias Pouk (mattress), to evoke the softening role that he played in the party.[67]

His outward manner notwithstanding, Sar was a hard nationalist (as a student writer in Paris in the early 1950s, he took the pen name 'original Khmer'), paranoid in particular about Vietnamese influence on Cambodian Communism.[68] While the Vietnamese saw themselves as historical victims of Chinese expansionism, many Cambodians viewed Vietnam as a comparable threat. In 1953, Sar spent time in Vietnamese Communist camps on the border with Cambodia, afterwards complaining that the Vietnamese commanders 'didn't trust me ... They didn't give me any kind of work to do. All I was allowed to do was cultivate cassava.'[69] There were multiple reasons for Cambodian resentment towards the Vietnamese Workers' Party through this decade. The latter had failed to negotiate for a Communist Cambodian state in the Geneva settlement of 1954. Instead, it had urged the Cambodian Communists to abandon armed struggle and accommodate themselves with the head of state, the mercurial, ruthless Prince Sihanouk, whose own approach to the Cambodian Communist movement veered between the contemptuous (he authored the dismissive sobriquet 'Khmer Rouge') and the brutal (in 1962 he tortured and murdered the party leader Tou Samouth, whose demise gave Sar the chance to step up as full party secretary). Under

Indonesia's President Sukarno with Mao, during the former's first visit to China in 1956. Sukarno was delighted by the warmth of his reception.

Mao warmly greets D. N. Aidit, the leader of the Communist Party of Indonesia (PKI), in August 1965. The exact content of their conversation, which took place less than two months before the alleged PKI coup against the Indonesian Army on 1 October 1965 (the September 30th Movement), remains a subject of historical speculation.

Following the military seizure of power, a group of Indonesian anti-Communist youths search for Aidit in central Java, November 1965. Aidit was captured later that month and summarily executed. An estimated 500,000 suspected Communists were massacred by the army and their supporters between 1965 and 1966.

Mao thronged by enthusiastic visitors from Africa and the Middle East. As part of a charm offensive to win allies away from the Soviet Union, from the late 1950s the PRC welcomed a stream of guests from the developing world.

Julius Nyerere, first president of independent Tanzania and the man who 'opened the gates' of Africa to China, with Zhou Enlai in 1965.

A scene from *War Drums on the Equator*, a 1965 play staged in Beijing, expressing PRC solidarity with Congolese guerrillas fighting the American- and Belgian-backed forces of Mobutu. Chinese actors have 'blacked up' to represent the Congolese.

Chinese army instructors in Ghana demonstrate how to lay anti-personnel mines in the early 1960s. Similar instructors travelled to other African countries in the 1960s and 1970s; many taught both the military and political strategies of Mao Zedong. This knowledge transfer had the greatest impact on Southern Rhodesia, where ZANU guerrillas successfully deployed Maoist strategies in a civil war that brought white-majority rule to an end.

Explosive chemicals from Shanghai apparently used in Chinese military training in Ghana in the early 1960s.

Josiah Tongogora, the military leader who masterminded ZANU's success in the war against Ian Smith's regime in Southern Rhodesia. Fay Chung, a participant in ZANU's war effort, recalled that he 'received his military training …in China and forever held the Chinese as his mentors in morality as well as in military skills and strategies'.

Ho Chi Minh, president of North Vietnam, embraces Zhou Enlai in 1960. Ho's friendship with the CCP leadership went back to the 1920s. He first met Zhou in Paris during that decade.

A late 1960s board game for Chinese children depicting the anti-American war in Vietnam. The winner 'destroys the American imperialists first' by reaching circle 41. Box 23, for example, reads: 'You relentlessly beat the American imperialists, proceed to number 26.' During these years, expressions of solidarity for the Vietnamese Communists saturated PRC youth culture.

Sitting on armchairs, facing the photographer, from left to right: Zhou Enlai, Sukarno, Prince Norodom Sihanouk, Chen Yi (PRC Minister of Foreign Affairs). The occasion is the tenth anniversary of the Bandung Conference, in April 1965. Zhou seems to be commanding the room's attention.

Zhou Enlai welcomes Sihanouk back to Beijing after the latter's carefully choreographed tour of the Khmer Rouge 'liberated zone' in Cambodia in spring 1973. Zhou played a key role in arranging the alliance between the Khmer Rouge and Sihanouk. This alliance encouraged many rural Cambodians, who revered Sihanouk, to join the Khmer Rouge.

Mao meets Khmer Rouge leaders Pol Pot (centre) and Ieng Sary (right) in Beijing in June 1975, two months after the Khmer Rouge takeover of Cambodia. Although physically ailing, Mao looks exceptionally animated.

Jubilant Khmer Rouge guerrillas pose for the cameras after the fall of Phnom Penh on 17 April 1975. After their takeover of Cambodia, the leadership immediately ordered the evacuation of all cities and towns to the countryside. An estimated 20,000 people died in the emptying of Phnom Penh alone.

A girl carries her sister in Phnom Penh in 1979 after the Khmer Rouge flee Vietnamese invasion.

A Vietnamese militiawoman leads an injured Chinese soldier captured during the Sino-Vietnamese War of February–March 1979.

The governor of Heilongjiang, Li Fanwu, has his hair shaved and torn by Red Guards in autumn 1966 in front of an audience in a public square; he was accused of bearing a resemblance to Mao. The image gives a flavour of the violence meted out by the Cultural Revolution's 'mass democracy'.

La révolution n'est pas un dîner de gala

One grotesque example of Western misreadings of Maoism: an excerpt from *Lui* magazine's special China supplement from 1967, entitled 'The Little Pink Book' and illustrated by Mao quotations and snaps of young women dressed – if at all – in Mao jackets. The caption here is the ubiquitous 'revolution is not a dinner party'.

Robert F. Williams asks Mao to
sign his copy of the Little Red
Book, on the viewing platform
overlooking Tiananmen
Square, around 1966. Williams
was a highly influential
advocate for Mao's ideas within
the American black liberation
movement of the 1960s.

A portrait of Mao
hung by student
protestors outside the
Sorbonne in Paris in 1968.
The banner next to
the portrait quotes a
favourite Maoist dictum:
'Serve the People'.

these conditions of domestic repression, Saloth Sar and most of the future leaders of Communist Cambodia went underground in 1963, to wage war from Cambodia's jungles.

In 1965, Sar went to North Vietnam and then on to China. The contrast in reception was stark. In Vietnam, he felt fobbed off by the exhortations of the party general secretary, Le Duan (who, as Ho Chi Minh's health failed, was becoming the most powerful man in Vietnamese Communism), to engage in political, not military, struggle, threatened by Le's consistent assertions that the Cambodian struggle was identical to the Vietnamese, and infuriated by VWP documents that portayed the Cambodian Communists as a subsidiary of the Vietnamese organisation. The Vietnamese, he complained, were planning to create 'one integrated party to represent a single integrated territory'.[70] In China, by contrast, he was thrilled to witness the overtures to the Cultural Revolution, including the publication of Lin Biao's 'Long Live the Victory of People's War!' We do not know whether Sar met Mao. But two of Mao's future Cultural Revolution allies, Chen Boda and Zhang Chunqiao, certainly gave him private tutorials in Maoist fundamentals ('political power comes from the barrel of a gun', the 'dictatorship of the proletariat') and offered him material aid too. Flattery ('nauseating but effective', one observer commented) was also applied. The mayor of Beijing called the Cambodian a 'true Marxist-Leninist'; Sar returned the compliment by acclaiming Maoism as 'the Marxism-Leninism of our day'.[71] Getting close to Beijing made perfect strategic sense to Sar. 'If we want to keep our distance from Vietnam, we will have to rely on China ... friends in China ... give us spiritual, political and strategic support ... we need have no more doubts about the correctness of what we are doing.'[72] In 1966, Sar even renamed his party along Chinese lines: as the Communist Party of Kampuchea, rather than the Vietnamese-style Workers' Party of Kampuchea.

The following year, Sar declared a nationwide insurgency, which he announced in a worshipful letter to the Central Committee of the CCP. (As the letter went via Vietnam, it was no doubt read in Hanoi before it made its way to the Chinese embassy in the city.) 'Our past experiences', Sar wrote, 'in using political violence and, in part, armed violence, from the end of 1966 to the middle of 1967 have convinced us that organizationally and ideologically our people are ready ... to launch a true people's war ... we have studied, are studying and are determined to go on studying continuously and without let-up the extremely precious experiences of the Cultural Revolution ... [Mao Zedong is] the great, guiding star who brings unceasing victories.'[73] The uprising began in the north-east of the country on 18 January 1968, perhaps facilitated by weapons that the CCP sent down the Ho Chi Minh Trail.[74] By the end of the year, the civil war had spread to twelve of Cambodia's nineteen provinces.[75]

The enthusiasm of Saloth Sar/Pol Pot – and many other members of Cambodia's left-wing intelligentsia – for China did not come out of nowhere. After diplomatic relations between an independent Cambodia and the PRC began in 1958, the Chinese embassy in Phnom Penh wove an intricate and effective intelligence and influence network: a mesh of friendship associations, above-ground diplomatic links and below-ground Communist Party liaisons (the chief representative on the ground of the CCP's International Liaison Department was euphemistically known around Phnom Penh as 'Consultant Number One' of the Chinese embassy). There was a careful division of labour: one organisation was responsible for fomenting anti-American feeling in Phnom Penh; another for indoctrinating young Cambodians in the virtues of Maoist theory; yet another coordinated feel-good lion dances.[76] In the universities, the job of selling the PRC was entrusted to visiting Chinese students, who did excellent work on – among others – a brilliant Chinese Khmer mathematics major (the second highest-scoring student in the country) called Kang Kewk Iew.[77] Kang joined Pol Pot's maquis in 1970 (the year that Saloth Sar took on this alias); between 1975 and 1979, under the party name Deuch, he ran the Khmer Rouge's security headquarters, Tuol Sleng. After he hastily abandoned the ghastly premises in January 1979 – having killed most of the remaining prisoners – Vietnamese soldiers found it stocked with Little Red Books in Khmer and the copious biographies and self-criticisms that detainees had been forced to write and rewrite, before being bludgeoned to death; thousands of green flies hovered over the blood-streaked floor.[78]

Thanks to Chinese government influence in Phnom Penh during the 1950s and '60s, Maoism was in the air and on the curriculum in many of the Chinese-medium schools in the capital: here, students

Maoism infected Cambodia

devoured the Little Red Book, and sang revolutionary songs. A Cambodian Chinese who, aged eight, followed his parents back to the mainland not long after 1949 witnessed the execution of his uncle as a landlord and starved during the late 1950s. When, in the summer of 1961, just past the apex of the famine, he returned to Cambodia 'saddened and disappointed ... my younger brothers and sisters [who had stayed in Cambodia] refused to believe what I said had happened in the mainland ... almost every Chinese school in Phnom Penh was secretly controlled by the CCP. They encouraged Chinese students to join the Vietnamese and Cambodian communist parties.'[79] The CCP in Cambodia was, in the words of one of its most devoted operatives from the 1950s to the 1970s, practically a 'state within a state'.[80]

At the peak of the Cultural Revolution, Phnom Penh's Chinese schools fluttered with red flags and its students bristled with Mao pins. They chorused Mao quotation songs; they marched down the streets shouting slogans and calling upon the Cambodians to struggle against their government, scratching out the face of the country's ruler, Sihanouk, on posters, then trampling and burning the paper. When Sihanouk asked Zhou Enlai to put a stop to it, Zhou – unusually obtusely – requested merely that Sihanouk permit 'Cambodian Chinese their right to love Chairman Mao, the CCP's socialism and the PRC'.[81] But such clumsy attempts to manhandle Cambodia into Maoism were the exception. The real work was done behind the scenes. When Sar's 'People's War' began for good in 1967, the PRC's networks distributed automatic rifles, grenade launchers and mortars to the Communist rebels through its embassy, intelligence agents in schools and Chinese aid workers scattered across the country.[82]

Between the early 1950s and the late 1970s, one of the Chinese embassy's most gifted and energetic agents in Cambodia was Zhou Degao, an ethnic Chinese journalist who cadged and toiled his way through a low-level education, before becoming a writer on one of Phnom Penh's main Chinese-language papers. His articles popularised Mao in Cambodia and, using his cover as a journalist, he made surveys of the countryside for his CCP contacts. Through insiders, he gained access to secret government documents, which he passed on to the Chinese embassy. His patriotism and loyalty towards China was emotional and instinctive. His memoir does not feel the need to explain it, merely narrating how Zhou gravitated towards his local CCP cell, where he read Mao and became a loyal servant of the party, and a trusted agent of the Chinese embassy. On only one occasion did the embassy pay him for his efforts; at no point did he receive any kind of diplomatic or personal protection for working in the perilous political context of post-independence Cambodia. He even drew his family into this work: both his wife and daughter were couriers between the Khmer Rouge and the Chinese embassy.[83]

It is an indication of Cambodia's importance to Beijing that by 1969 Mao's chief of intelligence, Kang Sheng, had taken personal responsibility for work in the country. Kang's information was always ahead of the game. That year, he learned of secret plans by members of Sihanouk's government, led by Lon Nol, the prime minister, to launch a coup against the Cambodian ruler in 1970. Kang summoned Zhou Degao to Beijing for a briefing about how to handle the approaching coup, including establishing secret lines of communication with the CPK in the jungle. Zhou's journey was an intriguing combination of the clandestine and the incompetent. The Beijing authorities had failed to inform the border officials in Guangdong that an important Cambodian operative would be passing through. Consequently, Zhou was searched so thoroughly that a top-secret note embedded in his shoe sole was discovered and he was detained for two days until Beijing verified his identity. When he eventually arrived in the capital, Zhou wept with emotion (and perhaps exhaustion) as his car passed Mao's residence on the way to Zhongnanhai.[84]

But neither the CPK nor patriotic Overseas Chinese were Mao's most effective tools in Cambodia before 1975. This accolade belonged to Prince Norodom Sihanouk, first Cambodia's king and then head of state from 1941 to 1970.

Norodom Sihanouk ascended to the throne in the twilight years of the French empire in Indochina. The French governor – who had selected him as monarch – had low expectations of him: Sihanouk's job was to serve as a French puppet in the gilded cage of the royal palace (*'Qu'il est mignon, ce petit!'* the wife of the Vichy-era French governor of Indochina had exclaimed while beholding a teenage Sihanouk).[85] The young king displayed early promise as a playboy: by the age of twenty-four, he was the father of six publicly acknowledged children, and probably yet more that went unacknowledged. But historical accident made Sihanouk a different kind of ruler. When, in 1945, the Japanese Army – having tolerated French Vichy rule over Indochina for five years – brusquely ended white European dominion over Cambodia, Vietnam and Laos, Sihanouk gained a taste for independence and never lost it. Although the post-war French government attempted to reinstate their colonial authority in Cambodia as in Vietnam, the credibility of their colonial enterprise was gone. In 1954, on the back of the decolonisation agreements for Vietnam at Geneva, Cambodia also won independence and Sihanouk became head of state. The following year, however, Sihanouk abdicated the throne (his father took his place) and reinvented himself as a campaigning politician in the country's post-independence elections. It was a move of political genius: free of rules that the monarch should not participate in the business of government, Sihanouk could now campaign vigorously for himself while still basking in the deifying adoration that many Cambodians – especially the less educated majority – had for him as the godlike 'Monseigneur-Papa'.

In Sihanouk, there was something of King Julian, the ludicrous King of the Lemurs from the children's animation *Madagascar*: his manic self-esteem, his tendency to high-pitched giggles, his paternalistic condescension to his subjects ('the little people'). But in his repression of opposition, there was nothing remotely absurd. Sihanouk's self-indulgence contrasted grotesquely with his capacity for brutality: as domestic dissent grew in the last few years of the 1960s, especially on the left, he allowed his armed forces to suppress it with impunity. Trucks loaded with the decapitated heads of those who had fallen foul of the army would tour Phnom Penh to terrify other would-be insurgents. He ordered forty teachers accused of subversion to be thrown off a cliff.[86] When rumour whispered (untruly, as it happened) that Sihanouk had disposed of two leftist critics by rolling over their heads with a bulldozer, and of a third by dissolving him in sulphuric acid, the story was easily accepted.[87]

But decolonisation complicated Sihanouk's politics. His instinct that North Vietnam would – and should – prevail over both the French and over US-backed South Vietnam led him to support the Vietnamese Communists, principally through allowing Chinese aid to move down the stretches of the Ho Chi Minh Trail that veered into Cambodia and by tolerating Vietnamese Communist camps deep into Cambodian territory. It was this permissiveness that triggered the US carpet bombing of Cambodia in the early 1970s, which destabilised the country and facilitated the rise of the Khmer Rouge. Sihanouk, then, was a curious political animal: a man who at home cut off the heads of suspected Communists by the truckful, but who abroad considered Ho Chi Minh, Kim Il-sung, Mao Zedong and especially Zhou Enlai among his very best friends.

China's wooing of Sihanouk began in 1955, when Zhou Enlai – the undisputed star of the Bandung Conference – invited him to a sumptuous Chinese lunch at Zhou's hotel in Indonesia. A photograph from the tenth anniversary of the conference depicted Sukarno, Prince Sihanouk and Chen Yi (PRC Foreign UN minister) lounging in armchairs around a dark varnished coffee table. All three pairs of eyes were on one person: Zhou, the heavy-eyebrowed charmer of Chinese diplomacy.[88] The Bandung encounter was the beginning of an extraordinary relationship between the god-king Sihanouk and Communist Zhou.

In 1970, Zhou Enlai was swiftly there for Sihanouk at a moment of crisis. That spring, Sihanouk left Cambodia in the midst of a mounting emergency. Nixon's saturation bombardment was destroying the country. Perhaps 150,000 Cambodians died during the campaign; Phnom Penh was flooded with starving, desperate refugees. Sihanouk was to travel first to France (for his annual 'cure'), and then to Moscow and Beijing to plead with those last two governments to persuade the Vietnamese Communists to retreat from Cambodia and thereby remove the pretext for the bombing. During Sihanouk's absence, his cousin Sirik Matak and Prime Minister Lon Nol not only overthrew him in a coup, but sponsored Sihanouk's vilification in Cambodian public life; he was condemned to death *in absentia*. When, still following his original itinerary, Sihanouk arrived in Beijing in March 1970, Zhou was there at the airport to embrace the prince as he stepped off the plane. Zhou had also convened Beijing's entire diplomatic corps to form an airport reception party and made sure that Sihanouk's rapturous welcome was reported in every Chinese news service. 'You remain the Head of State,' Zhou told Sihanouk. 'The only one. We will never recognise another.' Both Mao and the Vietnamese Communists acclaimed Sihanouk as a 'comrade-in-arms', and pledged to support his struggle to return to power.[89]

Sihanouk would always protest that China's support was uncondi-tional and disinterested, motivated only by personal friendship, not by national interest. But a glance at the geopolitics of South East Asia and at Zhou's behind-the-scenes activities puts the lie to that claim. For someone else was in Beijing when Sihanouk arrived, someone Zhou Enlai was careful to keep concealed from Sihanouk: Pol Pot, the *nom de guerre* that Saloth Sar had taken that year. As we have seen, Zhou Degao alleged that Beijing had advance warning of the Lon Nol coup, and Zhou made sure that Pol Pot not only knew exactly what was going to happen but also invited him to Beijing to exploit the fallout.[90] Zhou and Mao's primary interest lay in using Sihanouk's crisis to nurture the CPK. As Zhou played the concerned friend to Sihanouk, as Mao lavished him with praise – even congratulating him for establishing a casino in Phnom Penh – Pol and Zhou brokered a 'united front' between Sihanouk and the prince's former nemesis, the Khmer Rouge.[91] By May 1970, the Khmer Rouge had announced they would join hands with their former mortal enemy Sihanouk in a move roughly equivalent to Lenin allying himself with Tsar Nicholas in 1914.

In practice, this required China to fund and host lavishly a Cambodian government in exile which had pledged to conduct armed struggle to the end with Lon Nol: the Gouvernement Royal d'Union Nationale du Kampuchea, a coalition between the Khmer Rouge and Sihanouk. (The acronym of this organisation, GRUNK, reads in English as the only – unwittingly – absurd element of this appalling political entanglement.) Sihanouk's highly emotional state – he did not sleep for four days after receiving the news of the coup – seems to have prevented him from giving any serious thought to the viability of the agreement. Instead, he burst onto the Chinese airwaves on 4 April, instructing his subjects – the 'little people' – to 'go into the jungle and join the resistance forces already there'.[92] Tens of thousands obeyed him, their recruitment transforming the fighting strength of the Khmer Rouge. Sihanouk's reassuringly 'royal' government thus became a Trojan Horse for the most extreme Communist experiment in history.

Until Phnom Penh fell to Khmer Rouge troops in 1975, Chinese officials worked to keep these antagonistic collaborators – Sihanouk and the CPK – together. They wooed Sihanouk above all with hospi-tality. While the puritanism of the Cultural Revolution raged around him, he existed exquisitely in the old French legation building, east of Tiananmen Square. There were chefs to provide him with Chinese, Khmer or French cooking, depending on his mood; there was a swimming pool, a tennis court, a cinema and a terrific wine cellar. His North Korean friend Kim Il-sung kept his table supplied with foie gras. Sihanouk's GRUNK was comfortably accommodated in the north-west wing of the Friendship Hotel, while the princelings of the Cambodian royal family lounged about the complex's pool. Zhou invited a representative of the Khmer Rouge to devise a budget. When he asked for $5 million, Zhou shook his head and doubled the sum – half was to fund the Beijing show, the other half for the Communist operation in Cambodia.[93]

On 16 May 1970, Sihanouk appeared alongside Mao on the rostrum overlooking Tiananmen Square, in front of a mass rally. Both men wound each other up with enthusiasm, Mao shouting 'Long Live Cambodia! Long Live Prince Sihanouk!', and Sihanouk echoing the sentiment in Chinese and presumably in his trademark, high-pitched tones: 'Mao zhuxi wansui! Long Live Chairman Mao!'[94] Later in the summer, to welcome Sihanouk back from a visit to Pyongyang, Zhou and Mao mobilised a million-strong crowd to dance and sing around pyramids of flowers displayed across Tiananmen Square. That same evening, Zhou hosted a state banquet with hundreds of guests in the Hall of the People. It was, Sihanouk recalled, a 'euphoric' occasion. Zhou hummed 'loudly enough to be heard by the diplomats, my musical composition "Nostalgia for China" ... when the Orchestra of the Chinese People's Army played the piece ... Zhou led the (prolonged) applause and then rose, followed by all the guests ... to drink a glass of the national spirits, Mao-t'ai, to my health.'[95] The contrast with Sihanouk's treatment by the US – which had pulverised Cambodia with its B-52s – and by the USSR – which had maintained state-to-state relations with the Lon Nol government – was striking.

In early 1973, Sihanouk left the freezing streets of Beijing for a choreographed tour around a Khmer Rouge guerrilla base area in north Cambodia. Nothing was left to chance. Sihanouk and his wife Monique travelled down the Ho Chi Minh Trail in a caravan of jeeps, accompanied by a hundred bodyguards, servants and medics, and a Chinese film crew to ensure that every moment of the Sihanouk–Khmer Rouge friendship was recorded for propaganda value. Wooden cottages had been constructed along the route, with running water and plumbing; freshly baked baguettes were served at every meal. Eventually, the royal couple reached a base area in the dense jungle at Mount Kulen. There, amid hillsides gushing with waterfalls, Sihanouk and Monique settled into a chocolate-box Khmer-style stilt house, with veranda and eaves carved into undulations reminiscent of an Alpine chalet, ceramic pot plants to either side: 'our White House in the liberated zone!' Monique exclaimed into her diary.[96] The Chinese photographers compiled a special issue of *China Pictorial* – its flagship magazine of 'external propaganda', translated into multiple languages – on the visit, testifying to the legitimacy of the united front. Here was Sihanouk hugging members of the Khmer Rouge, there was Princess Monique relaxing on her hammock. In another symbolic set of vistas, the Khmer Rouge took Sihanouk to visit Angkor Wat, the emblem of Cambodian historical greatness and patriotism, to demonstrate the Khmer Rouge's supposed religious tolerance and respect for the past. Throughout the visit, Sihanouk was prevented from having any unmediated contact with ordinary Cambodians. Pol Pot was an ambient presence, but was never introduced to Sihanouk as the actual power within the party.

On Sihanouk's return to China, Zhou Enlai ensured the usual triumphant reception. At the landing strip in Beijing, amid the blasted arid plains of east Beijing, 5,000 Chinese people dressed in ethnic minority costumes danced, sang, cheered and waved flags. Above the crowd two vast pictures loomed: one, the standard Tiananmen portrait of Mao; the other, a statesmanlike image of Sihanouk in Western suit and tie. In between stretched a large red banner with white characters proclaiming '10,000 years to the Sino-Cambodian People's Great Friendship!' Sihanouk paraded at the head of the returning party, regally waving, smiling broadly. One pace behind, a look of determination on his face, was Zhou Enlai.[97]

Behind the hospitality, Mao and Zhou were engaged in hard-nosed strategising. Just six days before Mao and Sihanouk were exchanging 'Long Lives' on the rostrum of Tiananmen Square, Mao had received the Vietnamese Communist supremo, Le Duan. Mao had agreed with Le Duan's view that the expulsion of Sihanouk from Cambodia was a sign that the Cambodians had 'stood up'. 'Sihanouk is a difficult character,' Mao added. 'If you rub him up the wrong way, he'll curse you out. But ... [i]f he leaves [us] now, he's lost.'[98] In his realistic moments, Sihanouk understood the role he played. 'They will spit me out like a cherry pit the moment they have won,' he told the *New York Times*.[99] And indeed, among themselves, the Khmer Rouge described Sihanouk as a 'scab that will drop off by itself'.[100] But Zhou's charm offensive had worked its magic; Sihanouk stood by the alliance and allowed the Khmer Rouge to use him to recruit tens of thousands of Cambodians. 'I must sacrifice myself, for the honour of China,' he declared, 'and his excellency Zhou Enlai who helped so much Cambodia and myself.'[101]

While Sihanouk lived the high life in late–Cultural Revolution China, his dour CPK minder Ieng Sary had other things on his mind. Spending almost four years in China up to spring 1975, he dedicated himself to intense political study. He was granted more audiences with Mao than Sihanouk, and carried everywhere with him well-thumbed copies of Mao's works – in French, of course, for he was a Paris-educated intellectual. He seems to have toured the country, visiting military installations, communes, 'May 7 Cadre Schools' (established to reform intellectuals through hard labour and study of Mao), the village of Dazhai (acclaimed as a model of self-sufficiency, later revealed to have been propped up by army labour and state subvention) and *laogai* – 'reform through labour' camps. He marvelled at the miracles achieved with Mao's thought: for example, at the schools where study of Mao's works had cured deaf-mutes. On Ieng Sary's return to Cambodia in 1975, the experiences of the Cultural Revolution were a constant reference point for him as the Khmer Rouge set out to reshape the country.[102]

When Pol Pot and Ieng Sary visited China in June 1975, two months after Phnom Penh had fallen to the Khmer Rouge, they were euphoric with success. Within twenty-four hours of their victory they had forced at gunpoint the population out of Cambodia's cities and into an unprepared countryside: the first stage in realising their vision of radical egalitarianism. Mao and Zhou, meantime, could congratulate themselves on the completion of their mission: Maoism, exported.

In spring 1976, half a year before his death, Mao would be informed of Sihanouk's 'retirement' as head of state, the dissolution of the monarchy and the takeover of all state functions by the Khmer Rouge. That April, on the first anniversary of the founding of Democratic Kampuchea, Mao dispatched a telegram of congratulations: 'The Chinese people are extremely happy to see the vast and deep changes occurring in Kampuchea. We are confident that under the correct leadership of the Kampuchean revolutionary organisation, the Cambodian people will achieve even greater victories.'[103] Thus, as one of his last political acts, Mao gave his blessing to a Cambodian Cultural Revolution that was more radical still than its Chinese predecessor.

There was much in the Khmer Rouge ideology and practice that was clearly Maoist. The borrowings were first linguistic. Slogans like 'the super great leap forward', 'the wind from the East always vanquishes the wind from the West', 'everyone has to rely solely on his own strength', 'if you have a revolutionary position, you can do anything' and 'revolution is not a banquet' were light-touch plagiarism of Mao's words.[104] Then came the Khmer Rouge's applications: the imposition of slave labour, the ambition to 'turn the Khmers into rice-producing machines who consume no fuel and not too much rice', and the abolition of all currency and salary distinctions (an idea that Mao toyed with in the last two years of his life).[105] The evacuation of the cities was an extreme version of Cultural Revolution–era rustification. The creation of mess halls and the abolition of family dining replicated the collectivisation of the Great Leap Forward.[106] The Khmer Rouge took to an extreme Mao's preference for political correctness over expertise, promoting indoctrinated youngsters (some of whom adopted the name Mao) while murdering educated professionals.[107] At Kampong Son, a crucial petrol refinery, most of the management and workforce were between eight and eighteen years old – they called Chinese advisers in their thirties and forties 'grandfather'. This veneration of juvenility made the Chinese technicians nervous: one engineer refused a chance to visit Angkor Wat because the pilot detailed to him was only seventeen.[108] 'We have creatively and successfully applied Mao Zedong's thought to the realities of Kampuchea,' boasted Pol Pot. 'For Kampuchea, the most precious Chinese aid has been Mao Zedong thought.'[109] Pol Pot was, according to a Vietnamese diplomat in 1977, '100 per cent pro-Mao'.[110] (Though like North Korea and North

Vietnam, the Khmer Rouge had no use for the anarchic mobilisation of the Cultural Revolution.)

Material as well as ideological aid for the Khmer Rouge came from China – guns and food, salaries for the leadership, the black cloth from which their pyjama-like uniform was cut, the imitation leather belts that kept them up, the portraits of Pol Pot that attempted to create a personality cult for the Khmer Rouge leader. The ubiquitous red-and-white-checked *krom* – the multi-purpose scarves that provided the only splash of colour in the Khmer Rouge costume, that served as protection from the sun, as bags, and as manacles and blindfolds for those about to be executed – were also made in China.[111] In 1975, after the Khmer Rouge victory, the Chinese government immediately made perhaps the largest single grant of aid in its history: $20 million as an outright gift; $980 million as an interest-free loan. China even printed a currency for the Khmer Rouge, although the latter refused to use it. Huge Chinese ships began docking shortly after the fall of Phnom Penh, bringing rice and weapons, oil and farming equipment, medicine and sewing machines, cloth and anti-malarials, bicycles and hoes; they often returned empty.[112] The Khmer Rouge suspicion of modernity and foreign influence did not extend to military technology: in that area, at least, they wanted the best that their staunchest ally could provide. On 5 October 1977, the PRC Ministry of Defence pledged a full armoury to the Democratic Republic of Kampuchea, ranging 'from walkie-talkies to jet fighters'.[113] DRK pilots and navy personnel travelled to China, while five hundred Chinese Army instructors arrived in Cambodia. Fifteen thousand Chinese advisers and technicians bustled around DRK building projects between 1975 and 1978.[114] (Mao's representatives in Cambodia took advantage of their sojourns to poach tens of thousands of geckoes: their dried heads were a prized aphrodisiac in China, and perhaps a commodity still of interest to the sex addict Mao.) Propaganda film-makers were trained in China, to ensure that the DRK was captured cinematically 'dans le style Mao Tse-toung', as Sihanouk put it.[115] The photographer who took thousands of mugshots of doomed prisoners on arriving at Deuch's Tuol Sleng prison – the processing headquarters of the Khmer Rouge terror machine – learned his trade in China.

Only seven of the almost 20,000 individuals sent to Tuol Sleng survived. Most of these were artists, preserved on the personal orders of Pol Pot, who in 1978 began looking for draughtsmen and sculptors to illustrate his personality cult. That year, three carvers were set to work to construct a seven-metre-high statue of Pol Pot, made of gold and silver stored in the prison. According to one survivor, the plan – never realised – was to destroy the Wat Phnom temple complex in the capital 'to make room for [a] statue which would resemble the statue of Mao Tse tung in China'.[116]

The go-it-alone nationalism of Mao's revolution combined with the Khmer Rouge's innate jingoism to produce the murderous self-confidence of Pol Pot's regime, a state unanswerable to any external authority. (The Khmer Rouge deliberately isolated themselves, permitting only nine states to maintain embassies in Phnom Penh.) The Khmer Rouge embraced Mao's creed of national Communist exceptionalism (oblivious to the irony that it represented a foreign model). Already during the final battles for Phnom Penh in April 1975, Pol Pot declared his revolution to be self-sufficient. He had won a 'clean victory', he declared, 'without any foreign connection or involvement'. This was spectacularly untrue. There was artillery, and perhaps even entire divisions from Vietnam; there was a flow of weapons that had travelled down the Ho Chi Minh Trail from China.[117] In their rivalry with Vietnam the Khmer Rouge paraphrased Mao's boasting competitions with Khrushchev from the late 1950s: 'What takes us ten years takes Vietnam thirty years. So Vietnam cannot catch up with us ... We can harvest ten bunches [of rice] to Vietnam's only two ... they walk at a one-year speed; we walk at a three-year speed.' Once in power, the Khmer Rouge leadership disdained even their political progenitor: 'The Organization', it proclaimed in political meetings in 1975, 'is outstripping Mao.'[118] 'We can surpass even our Chinese brothers,' assured Pol Pot's sister-in-law. 'With one giant leap forward we can reach the goal of communism.' Already fanatical nationalists by temperament, the Khmer Rouge leaders spoke a derivative dialect of the alpha-male Communist competition begun by Mao: 'the name of our country will be written in golden letters in world history as the first country that succeeded in communisation without useless steps'.[119]

Chinese largesse towards the Khmer Rouge might in theory have bought them boundless influence over the new Democratic Kampuchea. Did Mao think, perhaps, that with their $1 billion in loans, they were buying themselves a political laboratory in South East Asia?

Chinese responses were, outwardly, glowing. At the end of 1976, Chinese journalists travelled around the country, and left with the promise of publicity for 'the excellent impressions we have gained ... A radiant democratic Cambodia is emerging in the east like a glowing red sun rising.'[120] (The parallels with Mao's own iconography were blatant.) On a visit to Cambodia less than a year before the Khmer Rouge collapsed, Zhou Enlai's widow, Deng Yingchao, acclaimed it as 'a pine tree standing firm on a high mountaintop which cannot be destroyed by any force. Under the correct leadership of the Communist Party of Kampuchea, the Kampuchean people are certainly moving forward toward a bright and glorious future.'[121]

Yet from the very start, the Cambodian Communists proved unruly allies. In hospital for bladder cancer and with only eight months left to live, Zhou Enlai in the summer of 1975 warned Pol Pot's close comrade Khieu Samphan that 'The road to socialism is not easy. China is still walking this long, long road ... Don't follow the bad example of our Great Leap Forward. Take things slowly.' For the CCP perhaps also feared that the radical ambitions of the Khmer Rouge would jeopardise Chinese hopes to acquire a stable ally in South East Asia. Khieu produced 'an incredulous and superior smile' at the man, now on his deathbed, who had created the alliance with Sihanouk that made their rise to power possible.[122] The Khmer Rouge treated Sihanouk – with whom Mao and Zhou had a warm, if exploitative relationship – pretty much as they pleased: keeping him under house arrest, cutting off all contact with foreign visitors, including those from China; working and starving his relatives to death. Their only concession was to desist from sending Sihanouk himself to certain death in the co-operative. Chinese diplomats were sequestered from Cambodian life. 'The embassy was cool in the hot season,' remembered one. 'There was a swimming pool large enough for exercise ... food was flown in weekly from Beijing. [But] we were all nervous and bored ... The Cambodian government asked us not to go on walks but we went anyway. One or two soldiers followed us always, usually walking fifty yards behind ... In one and a half years I never saw a Cambodian taking a promenade.' 'We must beware of China,' a DRK Foreign Ministry report warned in 1976. 'She wants to make us her satellite.'[123] As the regime's paranoia reached its peak in

1978, even 'working with China' could become grounds for execution of ministers.[124]

When the Khmer Rouge leadership suddenly decided to evacuate the cities and abolish currency, the experience of the Cultural Revolution was considered too moderate. 'These Chinese really had no idea what to do,' snorted Pol Pot. 'Mao stopped his Cultural Revolution, but we have a Cultural Revolution every day.'[125] The proclamations of the Khmer Rouge were saturated with nationalist braggadocio. 'The expulsion of the population of Phnom Penh is a measure one will not find in any other country's revolution ... International revolutionaries can learn a lot from Kampuchea ... The Khmer revolution has no precedent. What we are trying to do has never been done before in history.'[126]

The ethnic Chinese in Cambodia were as vulnerable as any other group. Suspected of being capitalists or Taiwanese agents or educated or simply not Cambodian enough, hundreds of thousands perished – about half of an original population of 430,000. With many survivors fleeing the country after 1979, little more than 60,000 ethnic Chinese were left in Cambodia by the mid-1980s.[127] Relative to other parts of the Cambodian population (two million are estimated to have died in the Khmer Rouge genocide), they suffered disproportionately because so many of them were urban business people – and thus automatically classified as enemies of the regime – in April 1975.

The PRC's behaviour towards the DRK was also increasingly determined by nationalism. During his final year Mao drew comfort from the idea that his revolution had travelled to Cambodia. But by 1977, the ideological bond between China and Democratic Kampuchea had severely weakened. Mao's anointed successor, Hua Guofeng, had arrested and purged the Gang of Four only a month after Mao's death – to the initial horror of Ieng Sary ('they are good people!').[128] After 1978, the man in charge of China, Deng Xiaoping, was an individual whom Khmer Rouge leaders had in the Gang of Four's heyday denounced as a counter-revolutionary. What held the PRC–DRK alliance together into the 1980s and beyond was national interest – or rather, shared national enmity to Vietnam.

Relations between China and Vietnam, and Vietnam and Cambodia cracked even before the Americans had left Indochina. In the early

1970s, Pol Pot had purged or killed any Cambodian Communists who had trained in Vietnam. A hundred border clashes between Chinese and Vietnamese forces took place in 1974 alone. As civil wars were won in Vietnam and Cambodia in April 1975, the two countries scrambled to define their sovereignty against each other, and against China. Hanoi grabbed the Spratly Islands (one Chinese official recalled that he 'tasted ash' on hearing the news), and asserted its claim to the Paracel Islands (at that moment, under Chinese occupation). CPK forces attacked Vietnamese populations on islands in the Gulf of Thailand. As soon as Phnom Penh fell to the Khmer Rouge, Ieng Sary asked Beijing to stop sending their military aid through Vietnam, along the Ho Chi Minh Trail; now it could be delivered direct to the Cambodian port of Kompong Som. At the same time, Pol Pot declared war on Cambodia's Vietnamese minority. Soon camps in South Vietnam housed as many as 150,000 refugees from Cambodia.[129]

In spring 1975, China nervously watched the precipitate American departure from South Vietnam and dreaded a resurgence of Vietnamese and Soviet influence in the region. Chinese leaders sniped at Vietnamese victory, claiming that Mao's People's War, not sophisticated Soviet weapons, had won the south, or lecturing the Vietnamese to 'learn from the Khmer Rouge how to carry out a revolution'.[130] When Le Duan visited Beijing that September asking for an extension of Chinese aid (in which he was not above expressing humble gratitude for past Chinese assistance), Mao did something unprecedented: he refused. 'Today, you are not the poorest under heaven,' he told Le. 'We are the poorest.'[131] Just the previous month, China had promised $1 billion across five years to Communist Cambodia. The affronted Le Duan committed what was – in Chinese eyes – an act of diplomatic war: he cancelled the reciprocal banquet that was standard operating procedure for visits to Beijing. 'An extraordinary act for a fraternal party leader,' the Chinese protested.[132]

Like the Cambodians, the Vietnamese – who had been writing Chinese assistance and influence out of their own historical record for years – now exulted that *they* were leaders of the global revolution, for 'the epoch-making victory of the Vietnamese people has contributed to bringing about an important change in the world balance of forces'. To mark their victory over the Americans, the victorious Vietnamese reached for poems commemorating the expulsion of the Chinese in the fourteenth century: 'There are no more sharks in the sea / There are no more beasts on earth.'[133] Their Communist nationalism was a compound of historical grievance and Mao-style chauvinism. Although, since the 1950s, it was first French and then American military power that had laid waste to Vietnam, in the Vietnamese imagination the bogeyman was still Chinese. In the 1970s, North Vietnam was littered with shrines to military heroes and heroines who had defied Chinese invasion. Why, an offended Deng Xiaoping asked a Vietnamese visitor in 1975, did Vietnamese school textbooks take 'the threat from the north' as their 'main theme'?[134] To this day, Vietnam's National Museum of History gives far more space to conflicts with China than to the virulent war with the US. The struggle for independence against China, for more than a millennium, remains the headline story.

While the Vietnamese saw China as a greedy expansionist power, the Cambodians viewed Vietnam – whose rulers between the fifteenth and eighteenth centuries expanded their dominions from their original powerbase in the Red River Delta in north Vietnam, to the southern-most tip of the contemporary country – with similar hatred. Mutual distrust and scorn between Cambodia and Vietnam sank deep into the language: Cambodians called the Vietnamese *yuon* – literally, savages – while the Vietnamese had long referred to the Cambodians as 'highland barbarians'.[135] After 1975, therefore, China, Vietnam and Cambodia – self-confident about their cultural and political superi-ority – were vying for regional leadership. For much of the twentieth century, the theory of 'Indochinese solidarity' against French occupation had papered over these vicious divisions, but with imperialism in retreat by the early 1970s, old and new quarrels quickly emerged. By 1978, each state was publishing broadsides – translated and published all over the world – denouncing the treachery of the others.

Although Mao and his comrades were supposedly schooled in the Marxist internationalist rhetoric of equality between fraternal Communist parties, in reality they often talked from high to low. Despite the aggressively modernising facade of the Chinese Communist state, the frequent Vietnamese delegations to Beijing often had echoes of imperial tributary visits. China's attitude to Vietnam was a mess of socialist fraternalism and Confucian imperialism. Beijing's unspoken assumption was that, by waiving discussion of repayment of the vast loans provided, the Vietnamese would remunerate in a different coin:

by acknowledging Chinese political superiority and returning to China's 'sphere of influence'. This expectation shines through Mao's micromanagement of Vietnamese military strategy ('You should pay attention to your strategy,' he bossed Vietnamese leaders. 'You must not engage your main force in a head-to-head confrontation with [the Americans] and must well maintain your main force. My opinion is that so long as the green mountain is there, how can you ever lack firewood?').[136] The perceived inequalities in relations between the three states are nicely caught by the different leaders' use of the royal, collective 'we' while in conversation with each other. Mao, Zhou and Deng Xiaoping airily used it with the Vietnamese, when discussing a war on Vietnamese land, fought by Vietnamese; Vietnamese leaders did the same when telling the Cambodian Communists what to do. Mao Zedong once told a Vietnamese envoy to Beijing: 'We belong to the same family. The North [Vietnam], the South [Vietnam], Indochina, and Korea, we belong to the same family and support each other.'[137] As Vietnam shed its deference towards the PRC, Chinese officials evoked a sense of blood betrayal: Vietnam's 'ungrateful black heart' and 'swollen-headed arrogance' flouted the norms of filial piety.[138]

Relations between China, Vietnam and Cambodia went on fracturing through the second half of the 1970s. In 1975, Pol Pot presented a Vietnamese delegation with a baby crocodile. His meaning was not spelled out – was he conveying that the Vietnamese were crocodiles, or hoping that they would be eaten by crocodiles? – but the gift was, as one journalist observed, 'rich in dire symbolism'. From March 1977, the Khmer Rouge set out to purge Cambodia entirely of ethnic Vietnamese. That autumn, the Vietnamese toured foreign journalists around eerily silent villages on the Cambodian border, filled with piles of the rotting, mutilated corpses of Vietnamese Cambodians. On the last day of 1977, Democratic Kampuchea broke off relations with Vietnam.[139]

During their last twelve months in power, the Khmer Rouge's obsession with the Vietnamese threat intensified; their paranoia about external and internal enemies drove wave upon wave of purges. China's refusal to abandon or even moderate the Khmer Rouge – Cambodia was too useful a bulwark against the Vietnamese – widened its own rift with Vietnam. As frontier conflicts intensified, any Vietnamese successes fed Khmer Rouge suspicions that the border region was rife with traitors.[140] Meanwhile, internal political power games played havoc with the lives of hundreds of thousands of ethnic Chinese in Vietnam. In 1978, China called upon ethnic Chinese in Vietnam to resist 'Soviet influence', while Hanoi began clamping down on their communities in the south, where many Overseas Chinese were traders and restaurant operators. Hundreds of thousands crossed the border into south China.

For a mixture of reasons – Vietnam's lack of public gratitude, its increasingly close relations with the USSR, its harrying of the ethnic Chinese, its understandable responses to atrocities committed by China's ally the DRK – in July 1978 Deng Xiaoping decided to 'teach Vietnam a lesson [for its] ungrateful and arrogant behaviour'. As he told Lee Kuan Yew, Singapore's right-wing prime minister: 'These ungrateful people must be punished. We gave them $20 billion of aid, Chinese sweat, and blood and look what happened.'¹⁴¹ Between February and March 1979, China and Vietnam went to war, with Deng's troops hammering Vietnam's northern border. It was the last time that Chinese armies would try – at disastrous human cost – the 'human wave' style of attack deployed back in the Korean War. At the end of the conflict in mid-March, the border region – the one zone of Vietnam untouched by American bombers, nervous of provoking China; where Ho Chi Minh had once headquartered, respectfully mulling Chinese advice – had been devastated. Visiting the area five months after the war, the journalist Nayan Chanda recalled: 'With the tiled roof blown off, the iron beams of the central market stood like a skeleton against a stark sky. A twisted sterilizer, a piece of an oxygen cylinder, and the wheels of a mobile bed stuck out of concrete and rubble, suggesting where there once was a hospital. An iron bridge ... lay in the water like bended knees ... I saw a sullen, miserably poor populace trying to rebuild life in the ruins with undamaged bricks from the rubble.'¹⁴²

Two months earlier, on 7 January 1979, Vietnamese troops entered Phnom Penh, only hours after the Khmer Rouge government had evacuated the capital to escape Vietnamese invasion.¹⁴³ It was a city in which the clock of human activity seemed to have stopped. Its concrete infrastructure was just about still in place, but had been invaded by the natural world: banana, coconut and papaya trees sprouted out of the pavements, which were littered with ungathered fruit. Instead of workers, shoppers and *flâneurs*, pigs, chickens and geckoes traipsed through the grassy streets. In the empty houses, rats made their homes among abandoned tables, sofas, beds, televisions, telephones, clothes, records, musical instruments and photograph albums – the ruins of everyday life abandoned at gunpoint on 17 April 1975.[144]

Shortly before leaving the city, Pol Pot had released Sihanouk from house arrest and dispatched him to denounce Vietnamese aggression against Cambodia before the UN in New York. Sihanouk promptly tried to defect, but neither the US nor France wanted him. On 13 February 1979, then, Sihanouk returned to China, once more an exile. Zhou was three years dead but his wife, Deng Yingchao, was at the airport to meet him. 'We have been friends not just for a few years,' she shamelessly assured him, 'but for more than two decades. Please believe us when I say that Chinese people stick to their word. We always speak in good faith to our friends.' Once more, Sihanouk was powerless to say anything except: 'I completely believe you.'[145] He would rely on Chinese hospitality for the rest of his life – sometimes resisting, sometimes submitting to pressure to rekindle his alliance with the Khmer Rouge. Pol Pot also did well from PRC largesse. A billion dollars of Chinese funding kept Pol Pot's military and political ambitions alive; Chinese doctors saved him from cancer. Ensconced in a brick house, its terrace fragrant with orchids, on the Thai-Cambodia border, Pol Pot directed the insurgency against the Vietnam-supported government in Phnom Penh, while starting a family and leafing through issues of *Paris Match*. As his organisation finally collapsed around him, Pol Pot died peacefully of illness in 1998, before any historian could ask him searching questions about Democratic Kampuchea or his relationship with China.[146]

Zhou Degao, the PRC's faithful foot soldier in Cambodia, was cut utterly adrift. Marginalised, starved and almost executed by the Khmer Rouge, he made his way to China in 1977 to present a deeply critical report of the CPK. But officials in Beijing bawled him out for lacking discipline, for meddling in the affairs of the Central Committee, for criticising their best ally in Indochina. Completely disillusioned with the Chinese government and disgusted at his mistreatment by uncouth apparatchiks, Zhou fled China and renounced his CCP membership. 'I was a patriotic idiot,' he concluded. After toiling on menial jobs in Hong Kong, he eventually succeeded in emigrating to the United States. Although he served out his working life as a school cleaner, unable to put his education and experience to proper use, he ended his autobiography with a paean to the 'liberty and security' he experienced in his adopted home, this 'free country, with rule by law', whose B-52s only three decades earlier had been pulverising his native Cambodia.[147]

Contemporary China tries to be Cambodia's best international friend: its aid exceeds that provided by the US, it has built a new parliament and funds Cambodian students to take courses in China. China's ambassador to Cambodia proclaimed in 2010 that 'the Chinese government never took part in or intervened into the politics of Democratic Kampuchea'.[148] But tour guides in Tuol Sleng are strained towards Chinese tourists, and frequently dwell on the role played by the CCP in the Khmer Rouge's lethal four years in power. Their counterparts in Vietnam are similarly open about their sense of antagonism. 'Don't be fooled by appearances,' the son of Mao's foreign minister Chen Yi overheard one Vietnamese guide tell an English-speaking group, 'into thinking that we're good friends with China. Actually, China is our greatest enemy.'

8

'YOU ARE OLD, WE ARE YOUNG, MAO ZEDONG!' MAOISM IN THE UNITED STATES AND WESTERN EUROPE

In the mid-1970s, a Kerala-born Singaporean called Aravindan Balakrishnan – leader of the Workers' Institute of Marxism–Leninism–Mao Zedong Thought in London – made a bold prediction. By the close of 1977, the People's Liberation Army of China would move swiftly to free the world – they would be in London and Washington before the imperialists there had even realised they were coming. When nothing seemed to have changed by the close of that year, the prophet quickly covered himself. First, he deferred the prophecy's fulfilment to 1980. Second, he explained that the timing was immaterial anyway, for the Chinese under Mao were so advanced that they would liberate us through a different kind of warfare: by taking over our brains without us realising it.

Balakrishnan's institute was a fraction of a fraction; a splinter. In 1974, 'Comrade Bala' marched out of the minuscule Communist Party of England (Marxist–Leninist) – later expanded to the Communist Party of Britain (Marxist–Leninist), membership around 300–400 – to found his own sect.[1] The reason for the schism, according to Comrade Bala, was that their former CPE-ML comrades had turned their backs on the 'great glorious, and correct Communist Party of China', in favour of the 'International Fascist Bourgeoisie'. At the peak of his authority, he commanded the loyalty of some twenty-five individuals, living commune-style at the Mao Zedong Memorial Centre, at 140 Acre Lane, Brixton, London.[2] It was an intense existence. Every day, members of the commune attended meetings, handed out leaflets, tended the bookshop – always adorned by Mao badges, always ready to back up an argument by 'upholding the authority of the Communist party of China and Chairman Mao as the leaders of the world revolution', often under a huge banner of Mao.[3] Any income earned by members was donated to the organisation. The group's mission, when it was not awaiting liberation by the Chinese Army, was to create a 'stable revolutionary base in and around Brixton', thus selected 'because it is the worst place in the world'.[4] No cooperation was tolerated with any other part of the British left or the trade unions ('organs of fascism'). Any perceived transgressions against group-think resulted in expulsion.[5]

In 1978, the commune was raided by the police and subsequently disappeared from view. The only trace left in public perception was a folk memory that Balakrishnan's sect had inspired the late-1970s sitcom *Citizen Smith*, in which the would-be revolutionary, Afghan-coated loafer Wolfie Smith plots to steal a Scorpion tank to invade the Houses of Parliament but ends up only obliterating a suburban garden full of gnomes. The commune dwindled, first to five and then to four women (the fifth died in mysterious circumstances, following a fall from a window). Twenty-six years passed since Bala's first prophecy failed to come true; on he went, preparing for Maoist world revolution and emancipation by the PLA.

Then in October 2013, Freedom – a charity dedicated to helping women in forced marriages – received a telephone call from a woman, with a horrifying story to tell. She and two other women had been held as captives for decades by Balakrishnan and his wife; one, now aged thirty, had been born into captivity. With the help of the police, the three women were freed and guided to a safe place while Balakrishnan and his wife were out of the house. Two years later, when the Crown Prosecution Service brought charges against Balakrishnan, the full extent of decades of abuse was revealed: sixteen charges of sexual and physical assault, including rape, wrongful imprisonment and child cruelty. The intensity of psychological control that Comrade Bala had achieved – through criticising or beating the women for 'bourgeois tendencies' – was frightening. One woman testified that she had lost any 'right to question ... [He had] a sense of absolute power and control.' After demanding sex from her, Balakrishnan forced her to keep a diary of their encounters, which he then used to humiliate her in self-criticism meetings. 'It is like he takes a wire brush to your brain. That pain. There is no secret, no element of your self that he has left unexplored and that isn't open at all times to being humiliated and criticised ... He was the leader. He had the right over your mind and body. He would say he had the right to make you breathe because he could put a finger on your throat and make you die.'[6] When they went out, they walked in Khmer Rouge–style single file, so that no one needed to 'look right or left, but ... just follow the shoulder in front'.[7]

This episode encapsulates the potency, sectarian parochialism and horror of Maoism's travels in Western Europe and the United States. Admittedly, the Workers' Institute of Marxism–Leninism–Mao Zedong Thought was on the extreme millenarian fringe of this scene. Its adulation of Mao and the CCP went far beyond doctrinal respect. In the eyes of Balakrishnan and his followers, Mao's CCP had achieved a kind of scientific-occult mastery over the world. It had developed electronic weapons (called 'Jackie') to prevent its enemies' nuclear missiles from taking off; it could remotely sabotage American press conferences. Balakrishnan told his daughter that Mao had once zapped him with a death ray from a London taxi meter.[8] But this lunacy marks a difference of degree, rather than of kind, with other Maoist parties across Western Europe and North America, many of which developed a secular-religious zeal for Mao and for the policies of the CCP.

Like many admirers of Mao in Western Europe, neither Balakrishnan nor his disciples were uneducated farmers or proletarians: all had completed at least undergraduate study. The Brixton Maoists also illuminated the special attraction that Maoism had to ethnic minorities ('internal colonies', to borrow the American usage) within white-dominated societies. Over two-thirds of the group was made up of those from non-European, mostly Asian origins.[9] Balakrishnan himself had become politically radicalised after moving from India to Singapore, aged eight, in 1949 – the year of the Chinese revolution, and the high point of the Malayan Emergency and the battle between the MCP and the British colonial government.

The numbers of Maoist adherents in Western Europe and North America look insignificant to us today. In Norway – which could boast the greatest number of Maoists per capita – the Security Police (POT) counted only 20,000 Maoist sympathisers left at the end of the 1990s.[10] Until 1984 (when the Revolutionary Internationalist Movement was founded in France, on which more later), there was no international organisation – analogous to the Soviet-sponsored Comintern – for coordinating Maoist activities; China never hosted such a body. Yet the influence of Maoism in Western Europe and North America during the 1960s and beyond was greater than the numbers of its supporters suggest. The reach of its appeal was striking: it attracted students, oppressed ethnic minorities (African, Asian, Hispanic Americans), urban terrorists, cultural celebrities, philosophers – and Shirley MacLaine, who in 1975 wrote an adulatory account of a six-week visit to China during which she found her way out of a midlife crisis.

While the culture and politics of Cultural Revolution China permeated Western radicalism during the 1960s and '70s, this remains one of the significantly under-told stories of this epochal moment of cultural revolution. Mao and his ideas of continuous, peasant revolution appealed to both left-wing rebels, and civil rights campaigners. Within Europe, Mao's Cultural Revolution galvanised Dadaist student protest, nurtured feminist and gay rights activism, and legitimised urban guerrilla terrorism. In the United States, it bolstered a broad programme of anti-racist civil rights campaigns, as well as sectarian Marxist-Leninist party-building. Much of this Maoist activism was powered by enthusiasm for, not by expectation of material aid from, China. The best that most of these groups could hope for was that some organisation in Beijing would buy a few hundred copies of their magazine. 'You'd put it in a box and you'd send it over there, and I don't know they'd try to teach kids English with it or something, the poor fucks,' remembered one such activist-editor. 'And you'd get a wad of ready that you'd use to run your publication.'

The historian Frank Dikötter has argued that several of the domestic results of the Cultural Revolution were unintended, or even the reverse of what had been planned. (By the early 1970s, for instance, some rural officials – exhausted by the caprices of central party directives – allowed local farmers to distance themselves from the tyrannies of central socialist planning and carve off private plots.)[11] A similar argument can be advanced for the spread of Cultural Revolution Maoism in Western Europe and North America. Mao and his supporters envisioned the Cultural Revolution as launching a global, grass-roots movement that would destroy 'Yankee imperialism' and the governments allied with the US. Yet over the long term, enthusiasm for the Cultural Revolution splintered the radical left and assisted neo-liberals in consolidating power from the 1980s. One outcome of the instability of the late 1960s in the US and parts of Europe was the gradual shifting of consensus in favour of order and established power on the right – paving the road to Ronald Reagan and Margaret Thatcher – a trend that has not significantly reversed itself since.

It would be inaccurate, however, to argue that the legacy of the global Cultural Revolution was obliterated by, or indeed wholly responsible for, the rallying of right-wing politics. In central and eastern India the currently resurgent Maoist Naxalite movement, whose beginnings in 1967 were inspired by the Cultural Revolution, is considered by some the government's biggest security challenge – Chapter Ten will explore this manifestation. And although I have no intention of muting the tragedies, absurdities and misapprehensions of the Cultural Revolution's global travels, I also want to consider some of the positive legacies of far-left politics in Western Europe and the US, such as the encouragement of civil activism. There is perhaps a story to be told about the expansion of Maoism that also led to the dissemination of ideas such as 'serving the people', 'consciousness-raising', and 'cultural revolution' in education, which have had an impact on feminist, gay rights, racial equality, environmental and academic movements outside China. In West Germany, for example, former militants in Maoist parties migrated into the Green movement of the 1980s, significantly shaping the political landscape of a united Germany over the next decades.

Some historians of contemporary Germany argue that Maoist-infused urban terrorist groups such as the Red Army Faction (also known as the Baader-Meinhof Gang) have received attention disproportionate to their activities. (The intensity of the state's response to this organisation also made it loom larger in popular perception.) But these groups seem more significant when considered as part of a bigger picture: they shared an enthusiasm that raged across Western Europe and the US, that provided an infrastructure of solidarity across disparate countries and ethnic groups, and that – theoretically and sometimes practically – linked rebels in the West with political defiance all over the world: black liberation in Africa, war in Indochina, resistance in the Middle East, peasant struggle in India. Looked at individually today, these groups – like Comrade Bala's institute – seem like Cold War relics; in some cases, even jokes. If we put them together, however, they become a networked political phenomenon that tells us much about radical politics, the troubled history of post–Second World War democracy, and the global translations and mistranslations of China.

From the late 1960s, a surprising range of individuals across Western Europe and North America ran a Maoist fever. In 1970, the broadcaster and author Andrew Marr – at a private prep school in the Scottish Borders – decided that he wanted to start a Cultural Revolution. So he wrote to the Chinese embassy, explained his enthusiasm, and asked for some materials to distribute among his classmates. He failed to mention in his letter that he was only eleven years old. The Chinese embassy saw a serious potential propagandist and sent him a large box of Little Red Books, which he distributed to his schoolfellows. In fact, the embassy was so deluged by demand for Little Red Books from pupils at another prep school that it was forced to write them a letter – read out in assembly by the headmaster – asking that no more copies be requested.

In New York smart shoppers – including, rumour had it, Brigitte Bardot and Sammy Davis Jr – snapped up Mao suits at $130 a throw. Black Panthers sauntered down the streets of New York dressed as Chinese peasants (except for the Afro and dark glasses), declaring that they wanted to be 'black like Mao'.[12] The director Sergio Leone fronted his 1971 movie *A Fistful of Dynamite* with one of Mao's most famous quotations ('A revolution is not a dinner party, or writing an essay, or painting a picture, or doing embroidery; it cannot be so refined, so leisurely and gentle, so temperate, kind, courteous, restrained and magnanimous. A revolution is an insurrection, an act of violence by which one class overthrows another'), until anxious Hollywood censors cut it.

On returning to the US after a guided tour around China in 1972, Shirley MacLaine wrote a fulsome travel memoir entitled *You Can*

Get There From Here. 'The best proof of Mao's theories was the modern Chinese people themselves,' she wrote; they were so 'open and vital'.

> [I]n China, we saw low food prices, and streets free of crime and dope peddling. Mao Tse-tung was a leader who seemed genuinely loved, people had great hopes for the future, women had little need or even desire for such superficial things as frilly clothes and make-up, children loved work … Relationships seemed free of jealousy and infidelity because monogamy was the law of the land and hardly anyone strayed … I had a growing feeling that the Chinese way might be the way of the future.

Her book ended with a paean to Chinese authoritarianism. 'I as one who aspired to art and the supreme importance of the individual, was changing my point of view as to just how important individualism really was … I was seeing that it was possible somehow to reform human beings and here they were being educated toward a loving communal spirit through a kind of totalitarian benevolence … Maybe the individual was simply not as important as the group.' A year after returning from China, she concluded that Mao's dictum to 'serve the people' was also a personal instruction to 'serve myself' and opened a one-woman, high-kicking cabaret in Las Vegas, announcing (while draped in zircon-studded peach chiffon) to perplexed reporters on the first night that 'Mao Zedong is probably responsible for my being here'.[13]

Europeans took the whole business both a little less, and a little more, seriously than everyone else. A 1967 issue of *Lui* magazine (a home-grown French *Playboy*) included a special China supplement, entitled 'The Little Pink Book', illustrated by snaps of young women dressed – if at all – in Mao jackets and playfully assuming faux-militant Cultural Revolution, Red Guard-style poses, and by Mao quotations; one young woman, naked except for a rifle, leapt out of a vast white cake, to the inevitable caption 'Revolution is not a dinner party'. Copies of the Little Red Book flew off the shelves of left-wing bookshops: 4,000 were sold by one such Parisian establishment in January 1967 alone.[14] Scrawled big-character posters were pasted over French campuses, denouncing university governance and police blackmail. Students occupying the Sorbonne in 1968 pinned portraits of Mao on pillars and windows. University activists took lessons in radicalism from the Red Guards, satirised by Malcolm Bradbury's 1975 campus novel, *The History Man*, in which one student keeps a small dog called Mao to nip reactionary lecturers on the ankle.

In the shadowy, factional world of French Marxist politics, meanwhile, the embrace of Maoism was an altogether rougher affair. As a breakaway Maoist grouping split the French Communist Party – struggling to reconcile its rank and file to Khrushchev's 'peaceful coexistence' during the 1960s – divided Communists turned to paramilitary activity, with Maoist convention delegates taken hostage, coshed and beaten by thugs from the mainstream party.[15] Young French Maoists were prepared to make major lifestyle sacrifices for their beliefs: abandoning the natural career paths of France's educated elite (a large number came from France's pre-eminent institution of higher education, L'Ecole Normale Supérieure) for stints mortifying their intellects by toiling alongside the proletariat in factories or in the countryside as *établis*. Although length of stay varied – some lingered a few weeks or months, others persevered for six years; a very few settled for life – most managed to hang on longer than another celebrated Maoist sympathiser, Jean-Paul Sartre, whose one and only dinner at a worker's home almost finished him off, after the rabbit stew he was served induced a violent asthma attack.[16]

Violence became a regular feature of the cult of Mao. Students founding a 'counter-university' in north Italy offered courses in Mao's revolution, and two of their leaders went on to found the Red Brigades which, between 1970 and 2003, committed some 14,000 acts of violence, resulting in seventy-five deaths. A West German film-maker used Mao's Little Red Book when making in 1967 the first German Film and Television Academy short about violence. In *The Words of the Chairman*, a woman dressed in a Mao suit folded a page from the book into an arrow before throwing it at a blood-spattered Shah of Iran. 'We must cleverly transform Mao's words,' intoned a voiceover. 'In our hands they must become weapons.' The cameraman, Holger Meins, subsequently became a lynchpin of the Baader-Meinhof Gang, devising a bomb casing that could be hidden under a dress, to enable female operatives to transport explosives under cover of pregnancy. Two of the gang's founding members waved Little Red Books in the air at their first trial in Frankfurt in October 1968. Their urban terrorist organisation would cause thirty-four deaths in the 1970s alone, with heirs to the original movement still carrying out assassinations in the early 1990s.

Where did Western Mao fever come from, and what did it mean?

In autumn 1969, at his trial for inciting riots with six fellow defendants (the so-called Chicago Seven) at the Chicago Democratic Convention the previous year, Abbie Hoffman – dark, telephone-wire hair; performance protester and LSD-tripper – said and did many things. On one day alone, he fancy-dressed in judicial robes, gave the one-fingered salute while being sworn in as a witness and denounced his judge in Yiddish ('You would have served Hitler better') before offering to set him up with 'a dealer he knew in Florida'. This was a low-key performance for Hoffman. On 21 October 1967, he had sworn publicly to levitate and zap the Pentagon with 'good orange energy'.*

With greater analytical incisiveness he also opined, of himself and his fellow defendants, that 'we couldn't agree on lunch'. Even close collaborators in the protest movement, he was saying, were contrarian individualists, each pursuing their own agenda. There was some truth in what he said: 1968's key protest at Chicago almost fell apart over the centrepiece stunt – to nominate as presidential candidate for the protesting Yippees (Youth International Party) Mr Pigasus, a pig. Hoffman and his co-founder of the Yippees, Jerry Rubin, each chose a pig, one handsome and one ugly, and almost came to blows over which should receive the nomination. But although the rebellions of the late 1960s splintered between countries, factions, ideologies and wild individualisms, there was at least one unifying factor: rage at the American war in Vietnam.

In March 1965, the first anti–Vietnam War 'teach-in' took place at the University of Michigan: an all-nighter of lectures, rallies,

---

* In *Time*'s poker-faced account, the plan of Hoffman and his comrades was described as follows: '[B]y chanting ancient Aramaic exorcism rites while standing in a circle around the building, they could get it to rise into the air, turn orange and vibrate until all evil emissions had fled. The war [in Vietnam] would end forthwith.' 'Protest: The Banners of Dissent', *Time*, 27 October 1967.

discussions, which drew at least 2,000 participants. The following month, at least 15,000 marched on Washington, under the aegis of the radical student organisation Students for a Democratic Society. Thousands again came out onto Paris's Place de la Bastille in December 1966. By 1967, protest marches in the US were topping 100,000, and were spilling into Catholic cathedrals (interrupting the giving of the liturgy) and into hospitals; they were drawing in women and men, blacks and whites, Hispanics and Asian Americans, students and intellectuals, army veterans, rabbis and greetings-card makers. In February 1967, an organisation calling itself the Angry Arts spread a 'collage of indignation', touring on floats between Greenwich Village and Harlem; a ballet dancer fluttered his hands (in protest) to Massenet's 'Méditation'.[17] On 15 April, at least 125,000 – and possibly far more; the police had braced themselves for 400,000 – marched behind Martin Luther King from Central Park to the United Nations, to the chant 'Hell, no, we won't go', and 'Flower power'. Lit draft cards were passed hand to hand like torches and then cast into a flaming coffee can. Two and a half years later – a period during which two leaders of the civil rights and anti-war movements, Martin Luther King and Robert Kennedy, had been assassinated – around 250,000 took part in a carefully choreographed 'March Against Death' in Washington. A stream of protesters, each representing a death in Vietnam, processed past the White House. Solidarity marches took place in other cities: in Paris, London, Stockholm, Berlin, Tokyo and Mexico City. At an International Vietnam Congress held in February 1968 at the Freie Universität, West Berlin's hotbed of protest, 10,000 protesters from Western Europe converged. 'We will make the Vietnam Congress into an international manifestation of solidarity with the bombed and struggling people,' wrote Rudi Dutschke, the German student leader.[18] On Friday 26 April 1968, students all over the world skipped classes as an anti-war protest.[19] (The fervent radical H. Bruce Franklin – hired by Stanford University to teach US literature but probably giving his students more Mao than Melville – tended in any case to convene his classes not in lecture halls, but at demonstrations.)

Max Elbaum – participant, observer and later historian of the American New Left of the late 1960s and early 1970s – spelled out the direct connection between condemnation of American foreign policy and the growing popularity of Marxism. It was after 1968 that

Marxism spread widely among sixties activists. Washington's stubborn continuation of the war in Vietnam was a prime factor in this ideological shift. Despite massive protest at home, international isolation, growing economic difficulties and ... overwhelming evidence that victory was impossible, the US refused to withdraw. Something beyond a single misguided policy simply had to be operating. Young activists ... identified that something as the drive of an imperial system to defend its worldwide sphere of influence.[20]

'Vietnam', Susan Sontag explained, 'offered the key to a systematic criticism of America.' For some, Maoism provided a framework for that criticism. First, in a context in which rebellion was lionised in opposition to Cold War conformity, admiration for Communist China was one of the most contrarian enthusiasms imaginable – not just in the US, but also across Western Europe where newspapers predictably expressed their terror of 'Red China'. Solidarity with China followed the logic of 'my enemy's enemy is my friend'. Since the quashing of the Hungarian uprising in 1956 and with the invasion of Czechoslovakia in 1968, the Soviet Union no longer represented an emancipatory alternative to the forces of capitalist oppression. The People's Republic of China – bigger than Vietnam, more remote than Cuba, more radical than them both – looked the best option.

Ho Chi Minh was venerated as the leader of Vietnamese resistance to the United States. Yet Mao's China commanded greater political prestige, because it was seen as having originated the successful formula for 'asymmetrical' guerrilla warfare practised in Vietnam. Throughout the 1960s, the PRC had seized public opportunities to denounce the toothlessness of the Soviet response to imperialism and promoted itself, Elbaum recalled, as 'a new center for the world revolutionary movement (in a way that the Cuban and Vietnamese parties did not) ... as the shining example and prime champion of liberation movements waged by people of color all over the world'.[21]

In the US in particular, another political cause pushed radicals towards Maoist sympathies. Here, the struggle against violent white oppression of non-whites had a powerful local relevance, in the context of the civil rights movement, which politically awakened many activists before the anti–Vietnam War movement escalated. For dispossessed ethnic groups in the US in the second half of the 1960s who began to call themselves 'internal colonies', Mao's anti-imperialist stance resonated strongly. 'For blacks, Latins and Asians, and the whites who identified with the Third World, Mao was Marx and Lenin and Stalin but he wasn't white,' observed Ethan Young, the 'red diaper' baby turned student activist from Chicago.[22] For Max Stanford, co-founder of the Maoist-inspired Revolutionary Action Movement, one of the first US organisations to try to harness urban unrest among black populations for revolutionary purposes, it was Mao's focus on the peasantry that rang true. 'What we got from Mao ... was that the countryside or the peasantry of the world would move first and surround the cities of the world. Asia, Africa, Latin America – that's 90% of the world ... No compromise. No peaceful coexistence ... We saw ourselves as the peasants surrounding the cities. Seasonally employed black men.'[23]

Dennis O'Neil, a student radical in the late 1960s and after 1970 one of the founding members of the Revolutionary Union, the largest American Maoist party, perhaps typified the progression of American rebels from the civil rights movement, to anti-Vietnam War protests, and on to Maoism. Growing up in small-town New England, in a declining lower-middle-class family with memories of better things (in his words, 'a great American downward mobility story'), he won scholarships to local private schools – which made of him a Marxist. 'There I learnt about class. You can't tell me there's no ruling class in this country because I went to school with the little motherfuckers ... We the scholarship students were required to do manual labour in the afternoons where everyone could see us, to show gratitude for our scholarships ... Obviously, it didn't inculcate gratitude in anyone with an IQ above that of peat moss.'

In 1964, he studied South East Asia in his social sciences class. 'Every day, we read the *New York Times*, the *Wall Street Journal*, the *Christian Science Monitor* ... and after a while I concluded that the National Liberation Front [the Communist political and military organisation in South Vietnam] was right, that it was their country and that we had no business being there ... I didn't make it much further at that school.' By 1967, he had encountered Mao – first through the Little Red Book, then in rediscovered books from the 1930s and '40s (by Edgar Snow, Jack Belden, Agnes Smedley), and later in the forests of mimeographed radical publications springing up across US campuses.

I made the same evolution as hundreds of thousands of people in that age cohort ... At first you're against the [Vietnam] war because war's horrible ... And then you're against the war because it's a system: the system of imperialism, which has to have wars. So we need to have a revolution: the civil rights movement had won some battles but not freedom from oppression. What kind of revolution? A socialist revolution. And the Cultural Revolution is the gateway drug to that. Mao says that the masses are the makers of history. This is very important to us because we came out of movements, like civil rights, that were based on that: on ordinary, everyday people facing down horrific terror to register to vote.[24]

An accident of Cold War censorship intensified the impact of Maoist thought and practice. William Hinton – a farmer-writer, whose sister Joan left the Manhattan Project to make contact with the Chinese Communists – had lived in China between 1945 and 1953, accumulating copious notes about the agrarian revolution taking place there. When he returned to the US at the height of McCarthyism, his notes along with his passport were promptly confiscated by the Senate Committee on Internal Security. Blacklisted from any teaching jobs, he returned to farming for the next fifteen years. After a decade-long legal battle, he retrieved his papers from the US government and in 1966 published *Fanshen* (Turn Around), a vivid, vital account of the Chinese Communist revolution at the rural grass roots. It became a runaway global success, selling hundreds of thousands of copies across ten languages. The book was required reading throughout the radical movement – among feminists, Maoists and terrorists – in the US.

In West Germany, Cultural Revolution China's self-styling as the vanguard of global anti-imperialism also appealed to the 1960s New Left. Rudi Dutschke (later dubbed the 'Berlin prophet' of Mao Zedong) rather presumptuously declared in 1964 that 'In the judgement of the character of our era, an era of national liberation in Asia, Africa and Latin America, I am Chinese'.[25] Gerd Koenen – a satirical memoirist of what he terms West Germany's 'little Cultural Revolution' between 1967 and 1977, and a former leading member of a Maoist party – terms the revolutionary Third World the 'defining discovery' of the 1960s protest movement in West Germany. Dutschke, Koenen argues, equated violent protest in his country with independence wars in the

Third World – both were part of a universal project to overthrow global capitalism: he believed that the model of guerrilla warfare held for West Germany as it did in Asia, Africa and Latin America.[26] One cell of radical German students in 1969 referred admiringly to Lin Biao's theories of 'encircling the city from the countyside' in their plan to politicise the countryside around Munich by recruiting cadres in rural Bavarian discotheques.[27]

For activists in the African American liberation movement in the late 1960s, like Huey Newton and Bobby Seale, members of the West Coast branch of the Black Panthers, Mao's message as packaged into the Little Red Book seemed almost made for the turbulence of a new black militancy that gained traction after the assassinations of Malcolm X and Martin Luther King. Mao's appeal lay in his message of supporting anti-colonial armed struggles, of advocating guerrilla warfare, of building a vanguard party and of defying both Cold War superpowers. When asked why he had a poster of Mao on the wall of his apartment, the Black Panther Eldridge Cleaver replied: 'Because Mao Zedong is the baddest motherfucker on planet earth.'[28] The style and design of the Little Red Book also suited the rough and tumble of struggle. It was easy to understand (and therefore ideal for teaching low-literacy recruits), physically compact and hardily packaged in red vinyl. In early 1967, Newton and Seale famously sold copies to students to finance the purchase of their first guns. Once the shotguns had been bought, remembered Seale, '[we] used the Red Books and spread them throughout the organization ... Where the book said, "Chinese people of the Communist Party," Huey would say, "Change that to the Black Panther Party. Change the Chinese people to black people."'[29] One Bronx resident, who lived near the headquarters of the New York chapter of the Black Panthers, recalled seeing members of the organisation forced to run around the block quoting from the Little Red Book – 'Serve the people!' 'Power comes out of the barrel of a gun!' – as punishment for arriving late for meetings.

The FBI worried that almost half of black Americans under twenty-one nurtured 'a great respect' for the Black Panthers, while the white supremacist J. Edgar Hoover – who denigrated Martin Luther King and other African Americans as 'burrheads' – called the organisation 'without question ... the greatest threat to the internal security of the country[,] schooled in ... the teaching of Chinese Communist Leader Mao Tse-tung'.[30] The public, collective swagger of the group has become iconic: the images of Afroed urban warriors, leather-jacketed, black-bereted and toting guns inside the chambers in the California State Assembly. Governor Ronald Reagan, picnicking with a group of thirty schoolchildren nearby, fled to his offices at the sight of them.[31]

But it was a slightly earlier organisation – the Revolutionary Action Movement (RAM) – that was arguably the first US group to try to harness urban unrest among black populations for revolutionary purposes, and that engaged more closely with Mao and his revolution. RAM came to Mao through the mentorship of Robert F. Williams, an advocate of black militancy within the 1960s civil rights movement. Williams was born in Monroe, a town in the American South where the Ku Klux Klan gathered, thousands strong, in the town square, rallied by the local police chief. Williams joined the civil rights protest movement against segregation, and famously orchestrated a campaign on behalf of two black boys, not yet teenagers, imprisoned for kissing a white girl. Williams stood out for his insistence that oppressed black Americans had to defend themselves physically, as well as engage in verbal protest and civil disobedience. Williams felt an instinctive sympathy for the Cuban revolution and visited Cuba in 1960, where he became friends with Castro. When in 1961 Williams looked for asylum – he was fleeing a framed-up kidnap charge, for which the FBI had launched a massive manhunt – Castro offered him a place of refuge from where to campaign against the mistreatment of black Americans.

Williams was attracted by Mao's justification of violence to achieve political aims, by his emphasis on mobilising the poorest groups in society, and by his readiness to take on the US. He began a correspondence with the chairman in 1962. The following year Mao lauded the black American struggle as part of the global revolution, thereby winning credibility as champion of Afro-American rights against a racist US government. For Williams and his wife, Mabel, and other black rights campaigners, subject to often lethal harassment from their political and legal establishments, Mao's solidarity was deeply significant.[32] 'We are not alone,' concluded Malcolm X.[33]

When Williams and his wife first visited China in September 1963, they were subjected to some standard five-star flattery dished out to foreign visitors. 'The name Robert Williams is even known to Chinese children,' Guo Moruo – a romantic poet turned party hack – assured them.[34] In 1966, disillusioned by racism encountered in revolutionary Cuba, the Williamses and their two young sons moved to Beijing, convinced that China was the only part of the Communist world where they could escape anti-black prejudice. Here – the family stayed until their return to the US in 1969 – Williams enthused about Mao, the Cultural Revolution and its relevance for the African American cause.

> Chairman Mao Tse-tung is the first world leader to publicly speak out in support of the Afro-American in his struggle against racial discrimination ... On its National Day of 1966, China allowed me to speak, as a representative of Afro-American freedom fighters, to an assembly of one and one-half million people. This was unprecedented in the long arduous history of the Afro-American liberation struggle. I spoke uncensored. This is quite in contrast to the occasion of the so-called great March on Washington wherein Negro leader John Lewis of the Student Nonviolent Coordinating Committee had his speech censored and blue-pencilled by arrogant white overlords who succeeded in emasculating black manhood.[35]

Williams revelled in what felt to him like a moment of genuinely global turmoil, with guerrilla fighters from all over the world learning from a transnational repertoire of warfare. In 1968, he was in Hanoi to congratulate Giap on the Tet Offensive. Giap promply returned the compliment. 'We learned from Detroit to go into the cities,' he told Williams, referring to the 1967 African American riots in the city against segregation and police brutality.[36]

The US media was quick to accuse the Williamses of fighting China's 'racial campaign against Russia and the United States', promoting the 'policy of total revolution advocated by the Chinese Reds'.[37] The reality was somewhat less coherent. From China, Williams managed an international correspondence – with Ghanaians, Cubans, Puerto Ricans, Americans, Madagascans, Ugandans, Tanzanians, Nigerians, Japanese, French and an Israeli (who called himself Maoist

Mike) – which conveys the sprawl of militancy, ardour for Mao and his Cultural Revolution, idealism and flakiness that constituted global protest in the 1960s. Among the sheaves of letters Williams received, recipes for home-made napalm nestle alongside requests for postcards of Chinese fridges. A note from a member of a North American Progressive Workers' Movement reported hearing 'a black man say as he stepped back from a group of his brothers on a Harlem street corner: "Fuggit Man I'm for Mao!"' A fourteen-year-old 'Japanese sister' sent her best wishes on learning that Williams had been ill. 'I'm sure the great Mao Tse Tung and my yellow brothers will try as hard as they can to help you ... I too, like my Red Guard Chinese brothers, will be a good revolutionary.' A missive from one Seymour Fartz, an aspiring paramilitary in the seven-strong Socialistic Cuban-American Board, spent much longer describing his group's accoutrements – jodphurs, tunics, epaulettes, eighteen-inch boots – than their political programme.[38]

Yet it was true that Williams validated and communicated Mao and his revolution to activists and sympathisers of the black rights cause. Through the Williamses, wrote one correspondent, 'over 95% of the African Americans [would come to] know and accept China'.[39] Max Stanford, born in 1941 in Philadelphia, became one of Williams's most dedicated disciples in the US. At the time, Stanford recalled, Philadelphia was not the worst sump of white American prejudice – 'you could sit next to white people in Woolworths in Philadelphia, though you couldn't in Washington' – but entertainment was segregated: there were three 'white cinemas' and one 'black'. Eventually, one of the white cinemas opened to African Americans, but Max and his friends could only go on Saturday afternoons and were restricted to sitting in the very top tier; Stanford would rain popcorn down onto the heads of the white children. His activist father gifted his young son life membership in the National Association for the Advancement of Colored People (NAACP), one of the oldest African American civil rights organisations. After military service in the Second World War, Stanford Sr retrained as an exterminator and young Max tagged along on jobs during the summer holidays. 'In one particular house,' he remembered, 'my dad told me to go and spray a boy's room; he was about my age. The boy had a proper chemistry lab in his room, metres long. I sprayed the room. Afterwards, my dad and I had lunch in a park. He said to me: whatever that boy gets to do, you're going to have to work ten times harder to get in the door.' Max had until then been failing at school but now found a work ethic: he skipped a grade, went to a better school, got into college. There, he was educated in the strategies of the civil rights movement. He and his classmates attended sit-ins, lectures from Martin Luther King and freedom rides. They picketed a bowling alley that only allowed blacks in on Wednesdays and demonstrated outside shops that wouldn't allow black women to try on dresses. In the early 1960s, he began the Revolutionary Action Movement.

For activists like Stanford, Communist theory and practice were obvious sources of inspiration, for it was the 'world capitalist system' that had created black slavery in America in the first place. Veteran civil rights activists educated new recruits such as Stanford with three essays by Mao: 'On Art and Literature', 'On Practice', 'On Contradiction'.

In 1964, I started reading the military writings – they appealed because we believed in armed self-defence. You organize and work with the people, you work at building up with the mass line. As Mao would also say, the people are the sea and you're the fish, you've got to work with the people. Malcolm [X] was also heavily influenced by Mao ... we saw Mao as the leader of people of colour in the third world who were fighting capitalism and colonialism and imperialism.

Mao's militancy was irresistible: 'Being young, we thought we could skip the bourgeois stage of revolution – like Ho Chi Minh, like Mao.' Stanford and his comrades also loved the way that Mao was 'so down to earth. We tried to make what we did as plain as possible, so that average African Americans could understand what we were saying. Lenin was a genius but very academic.'

In 1964, RAM followed Robert Williams in breaking with non-violent strategies for confronting white racism. Adopting Williams as the organisation's honorary chairman, it made plans for a Maoist 'world black revolution'. Through the summer of 1963, RAM had built a network of secret political cells across the US. There was a Central Committee and a youth section, the Black Guards (who studied Mao and his Red Guards), which would be followed by a Black Liberation Army. RAM made extraordinary efforts to mobilise local communities: in just three days in 1963 in Philadelphia, Stanford and fourteen comrades distributed

35,000 political leaflets door to door; they shouted themselves hoarse on bullhorns in protests against union discrimination at a local construction site.[40] The project was ambitiously global: Malcolm X was charged with finding locations in Africa to train cadres, while Robert Williams 'would prepare Latin America and Asia' to support the struggle.[41] The more trigger-happy Californian chapter of the Black Panthers – which so alarmed Ronald Reagan – 'saw a revolution as one gigantic shootout', complained Stanford. RAM, he insisted, had a much deeper immersion in Mao's ideas, aspiring to re-create the organisational discipline of the CCP 'within our community ... We saw the CCP as a positive model of how to build a party.' In this black Cultural Revolution, 'the enemy was capitalist culture. We had to undergo a transformation as a people: a psychological break from capitalism.'[42]

The Black Guards were educated Chinese-style, remembered Stanford. 'The Chinese had materials, so we would give them to the Black Guards as part of their political education ... and they'd have to interpret them in their own language. At least once a week, we had political education, and they would have to explain it: they had to write at least one page, and then they had to speak it like they were teaching it. I'd developed these ideas for political education by reading Mao's materials.'

Stanford and the Black Panthers also adapted Mao quotations for their own struggles. 'To die ... for the racists ... is lighter than a feather. But to die in the service of the people is heavier than any mountain and deeper than any sea,' ran one slogan*; phoney comrades were called 'paper panthers'.[43] Sometimes, Black Power paraphrases were a little freer: 'Revolution is not a dinner party' was reworked as 'Pick up some guns and don't be bullshitting'.[44]

The protest culture of the late 1960s was, of course, politically polyglot: a mash-up of Che Guevara, Ho Chi Minh, Amilcar Cabral, Herbert Marcuse and Wilhelm Reich, the Freudian pioneer of free love and orgasms. ('Power comes out of the lips of a pussy,' the sex-obsessed Black Panther Eldridge Cleaver would sometimes say; at

---

* The original Mao quotation, from the essay 'Serve the People', runs: 'To die for the people is weightier than Mount Tai, but to work for the fascists and die for the exploiters and oppressors is lighter than a feather.'

other times it came 'out of the barrel of a dick'.) Yet amid this smorgasbord of influences, the theory and practice of Maoism exercised a particular fascination. Maoist language was so ubiquitous throughout Italy in the late 1960s that neo-fascists scrawled on Florentine walls the same Cultural Revolution slogans – 'Rebellion is justified' and 'Bombard the headquarters' – that were being shouted by left-wing students in Milanese piazzas.[45]

Across Western Europe and the US, Cultural Revolution Maoism stood not just for earnest anti-imperialism but also for youthful rebellion. In each of the countries in which Mao fever took hold, youthful protest movements had personal and local, as well as international, reasons for revolt. Students in Western Europe resented their cramped institutions of higher education, and the authoritarian methods of the university leadership. In Italy, the student population more than doubled through the sixties, without any coterminous expansion of university facilities – remote and imperious professors were referred to resentfully as 'barons'. The privations suffered by workers migrating from the south, meanwhile, turned Italy's industrial heartland in the north into a tinderbox of discontent that would come alight during the 'hot autumn' of 1969. Between 1950 and 1968, numbers of students had almost quadrupled in West Germany, where student hostility to the establishment was intensified by suspicions about its Nazi past. Even the president of the Federal Republic of Germany (FRG) from 1959 to 1969, Heinrich Lübke, stood accused of complicity in the building of concentration camps.[46] The Cultural Revolution told the discontented and the young that it was 'right to rebel'; that 'young people, full of vigor and vitality, are ... like the sun at eight or nine in the morning ... The world belongs to you.' At one anti–Social Democratic Party demonstration in West Berlin in 1969, the students chanted paraphrastically: 'You are old, we are young, Mao Tse-Tung!'[47]

The Cultural Revolution inspired many US students because it chimed with their own anti-establishment project. '1968 hit and students looked around for validating events all over the world,' remembered Dennis O'Neil. 'Before then, we hadn't paid attention to the Cultural Revolution.'[48] 'The Cultural Revolution,' Ethan Young contended, 'was seen as the student movement in power. It was a successful, world-changing version of what was going on in Paris, Berkeley, West Berlin.'[49] For those from left-wing backgrounds, China's Cultural Revolution

offered an alternative to the staid Soviet Union: continuous revolution. For the less ideologically minded, O'Neil recalled, it was all about
'putting dunce hats on your high school teachers'.[50] American and
European identification with the aims of the Cultural Revolution in
1968, therefore, tells us far more about these distant observers of Mao's
politics than about Mao's politics itself.

In West Germany, rebellious students imitated the political behaviour of the Cultural Revolution as part of a broader project of
Bürgerschreck – shocking the bourgeoisie. It was the apparent chaos
of Maoism that appealed – Soviet Communism had fallen out of
favour precisely due to its publicised repressions and ossified bureaucracy. 'To stick on a Mao button,' remembered Gerd Koenen, 'recite
the words of the Great Chairman, or pin his smiling portrait to the
wall as the Mona Lisa of the world revolution signified the most
radical and striking antithesis to the "old" bourgeois world.'[51] Students
exuberantly remade the rhetoric and political theatre of the Cultural
Revolution into an anarchic Dada-Maoism. They translated and distributed translations of Red Guard posters: revolutionaries 'use our
sorcery to turn the old world on its head, crush it into pieces, turn
it into dust, create chaos and great disorder, the bigger the better!'[52]
In 1968, another group successfully upstaged a lecture by the interior
minister with a choreographed taunt: a women ringing a cowbell,
students hurling painted eggs, two activists stomping around the stage
in Nazi uniforms, and a nine-year-old boy reading out Mao quotations.[53]

Dieter Kunzelmann, one of the most prominent Maoist sympathisers in West Germany, had links with the French Situationists and
the Dutch Provos – two artistic groups of the 1950s and '60s ambitious
to make political rebellion through cultural provocation.[54] Mao's words
played a role in many of the publicity stunts carried out by West
Germany's first political commune, Kommune 1, founded in 1967 by
Kunzelmann and Rainer Langhans. Describing the goals of the
commune, Kunzelmann quoted Mao's irreverent view on intellectual
authority: 'dogma has less value than cow dung. At least dung can be
used as fertilizer.'[55] Kommune 1 gleefully interpreted the Cultural
Revolution as a kind of playful experiment. They invoked Mao to
generate outrage, without necessarily endorsing, or even thinking very
hard about, the chairman's political programme. In one escapade,

members of Kommune 1 scrambled to the top of the ruined Kaiser-Wilhelm Memorial Church in West Berlin – before its bombing in 1941, a neat, kitsch symbol of German unity – and showered passersby with hundreds of Little Red Books. (The male members of the commune also happened to be coercively promiscuous: 'whoever sleeps twice with the same woman, already belongs to the establishment'.[56] One of their number asserted that his orgasm was 'of greater revolutionary consequence than Vietnam'.)[57]

The French Maoists enjoyed their share of stunts too – most notably, the 'liberation' of some twenty sacks' worth of caviar, foie gras, champagne and cheese from the luxury food emporium Fauchon, quickly redistributed to a *quartier* dominated by poor French Africans. Notices about the heist scattered over the pavement advertised that 'we aren't thieves; we're Maoists'.[58] Maoism became officially rock and roll when Mick Jagger interrupted a Rolling Stones concert in Paris to appeal for the release of the one raider apprehended.[59] French Maoists thought of China as the 'freest country in the world', perceiving the Cultural Revolution as one long, fantastic, libertarian fiesta to challenge the stultifications of Gaullist France.[60]

At least partly to discredit the protesters as exotic sectarians, Italian broadsheets straightforwardly identified the chief influence on rebellious students: they were *i cinesi* (the Chinese) and *Maoisti* (Maoists).[61] The mayor of West Berlin in 1967 also referred to the rebels at Freie Universität (one of the Berlin centres of student protest) by the shorthand the 'FU-Chinese'.[62] By February 1968, the State University at Milan, La Statale, had become the hub of the student protest movement. Students at both the State and nearby Catholic University locked up their rectors and put '"reactionary" lecturers on trial'.[63] Once more, the broadsheets unequivocally fingered Mao as the inspiration and model for the ferment, terming the night life that sprang up around the student occupation of university buildings, complete with impromptu rock and jazz performances, the 'Nights of Mao'.[64]

Mao was easily conscripted to alternative, countercultural lifestyles. *Lotta Continua* – 'Continuous Struggle', an Italian far-left paper with some mainstream reach – created an image of Mao that suited its own purposes: 'the more anarchic Mao, the Mao that swore ... [Our] Mao was unorthodox.'[65] Chris Milton was the son of two Americans, Nancy and David, who taught in China in the early years of the Cultural Revolution. Having taken part in the Red Guard movement in his high school, Chris returned to the US in 1968 and became a vector of the Cultural Revolution within the student movement, celebrated for his high-energy, first-hand testimonies of student rebellion in China. One of his interviewers asked him what he thought of a 'cultural revolution' coming to the US: 'groovy', he replied.[66] 'At Christmas,' remembered Dennis O'Neil – the activist who has dedicated most of his adult life to building Maoist organisations in the US – 'I'd get one of those standard Mao portraits, put it on card stock, and with a bit of construction and cotton wool, turn him into Santa with a little red hat and a puff of beard and put it on top of the tree ... you've got to be able to goof about.'[67]

In industrial action in late-1960s Italy, techniques of public humiliation gleaned from images and reports of the Cultural Revolution's Red Guards merged with much older repertoires for public shaming (*charivari*, literally 'rough music'). Unpopular bosses were represented at marches or on factory gates by dead and dismembered animals; managers' doors and offices were smeared with manure; the pockets of one strike-breaking worker were filled with human excrement. 'Revolution is not a gala lunch!' ran one Maoist paraphrase.[68] For these protests were not just about wages and material conditions; they were focused also on breaking down oppressive top-down regulations in factories, just as Italian student protests aimed to remake the authoritarian organisation of their universities. The Red Guards' violent humbling of 'class enemies' in the Cultural Revolution seemed to offer a carnivalesque repertoire of radical disruption.

In the Black Panther movement, Maoism was intertwined – sometimes manipulatively – with sexual liberation. One day, Bobby Seale at Black Panther headquarters was nonplussed to discover queues of young black men demanding copies of the Little Red Book. A little digging revealed that Black Panther women had told their suitors that 'if you want to get next to us, why don't you check out the Red Book?' 'The sisters laid the revolutionary ideology right on them,' Seale noted in admiration. 'We had tried for a long time ... to get these brothers motivated, but it took some sisters ... to bring [them] in.' Late one night, a distressed female Panther came asking Seale for some advice. 'If a brother doesn't know the ten-point platform and program, I shouldn't give him any, should I? ... We got in bed, you see, and I asked him if he knew the ten-point platform and program. He said he did, so I sat there drilling him, and he missed about ten words.' Meantime, the 'brother' had got restive: 'I'm going to find a sister in the Party I dig who doesn't know the program any better than I do, and we're going to have some real equality.' Black Panther men could throw the language of political correctness back on the women. '[E]very once in a while,' Searle wrote, 'you'd get a brother calling a sister counter-revolutionary. And the sisters were getting mad about that because it seemed to be related only to the fact that the sisters didn't want to sleep with the brother.'[69]

Many European and American Maoists were educated, even privileged individuals – a long way from the lumpenproletarians that Mao's rural revolution began to target in the late 1920s. France's leading Maoists were overwhelmingly based in Paris; some came from France's wealthiest aristocratic families. Indeed, one Count Charles-Henri de Choiseul-Praslin worked as an *établi* in the Renault factory and went to prison for selling Maoist publications. (Now in his seventies, he still has no regrets about having rejected the elite career for which he was preparing in 1968: entry to L'Ecole Nationale d'Administration.[70]) Some Italian *'figli di papa'* (daddy's boys and girls) attended Maoist party meetings and demonstrations in mink and leopard-skin coats.[71] A few visited China, on controlled, choreographed trips that celebrated the achievements of Chinese socialism – the more hippyish of their number were required to have their hair cut at the border. They showed little inclination to subject China to the same excoriating criticism applied to their own societies. During their 1967 visit to China, one group of French students burst into tears, sobbing that 'it's too beautiful to be in China during a revolution'. As Parisian protesters back home acclaimed the Cultural Revolution as the epitome of the carnivalesque, French Maoists in China were often received by Kang Sheng, Mao's brutal head of secret police; they were happily oblivious of his sinister day job and long back story as 'Mao's pistol'.[72]

This passion for Mao was in many ways independent of China itself: hardly any of these radicals studied Chinese, or in China. Consider this recollection by an Italian Maoist sympathiser during the 1960s:

[Maoist] China was a challenge to the society in which we lived: to our authoritarian education, our oppressive factories, our conciliatory and bureaucratic communism ... the European New Left movement took the Cultural Revolution as a point of reference, without worrying too much about learning what kind of thing it really was ... We had a vague, confused feeling of the anti-authoritarian and libertarian character of the initial phases of the Cultural Revolution ... we did this without noticing the violence that the Cultural Revolution had set off in the mythical China of Mao.[73]

A faction of Pisan students around 1968 had a quasi-religious take on Mao, completely divorced from his anarchist atheism: they admired in particular his Zen Buddha-like 'lack of facial hair, his big, smooth face, that half-closed stare – it made us think of a world in which patience ... represented a necessary lesson for a movement that was itself in a tearing hurry'.[74] Gerard Miller – a French Maoist turned psychoanalyst – has an almost exclusively light-hearted take on the engagement with Maoism by French youth of the late 1960s and early 1970s. 'It's impossible to understand the passionate interest in China that thousands of French teenagers of my generation felt if you imagine that we were in love with the idea of the iron fist. Quite the contrary: what dazzled us about Mao was his spirit of mischief, his insubordination ... To me, Mao's China at the end of the 1960s was much more "olé-olé" [than rival Communist faiths] ... during these years there was frankly nothing better to do in France than to be enraged; and nothing better for the enraged than to be Maoist.'[75]

In this utopian, politically promiscuous phase, many radical students in Germany, France, Italy and Norway picked up on the superficial, anarchic aspects of Maoism that appealed, and overlooked the rest. To be fair, they were not the first Westerners to exoticise China for their own purposes. Since the West began engaging in concerted outreach towards China – with the sixteenth-century launch of missionary overtures – the 'celestial empire' has been viewed by churchmen, merchants and philosopher-intellectuals as a potent dreamland of near-paradisiacal opportunity: for Christian conversion, for economic profit, for lessons in government. The embrace of Maoism by Western radicals is therefore a recent repeat of an age-old predisposition towards identifying conveniently remote, exotic China as a repository of political, social, cultural and economic virtue. The Cultural Revolution fever of the 1960s and beyond once more showcased the ability of Westerners to create an imaginary China largely divorced from empirical reality.

There was minimal acknowledgement that Mao's precepts – developed for a rural revolution – were barely applicable to the urbanised West. Although some of France's most celebrated philosophers threw themselves into the Maoist vogue, it was not an over-thought decision. French Maoism gave Sartre a revolutionary rush of blood to the head – he used its slogans to justify political violence on the part of the 'oppressed', while condemning 'bourgeois political violence' as 'repressive'. The hyper-intellectual writers associated with the avant-garde magazine *Tel Quel* saw mainly themselves reflected in Chinese politics. Mao's Cultural Revolution was the 'greatest historical event of our time' led by a poet and philosopher just like them: here 'writers and artists had a leading role to play'. In the autumn of 1971, the journal declared – in the style of one of China's terrifying mass rallies – 'Down with dogmatism, empiricism, opportunism, revisionism! ... Down with the corrupt bourgeoisie! Down with filthy revisionism! Down with the binarism of the superpowers! Long live revolutionary China! *Long live the thought of Mao Zedong.*' China partisanship led to some questionable intellectual positions. Julia Kristeva – *Tel Quel* doyenne – argued, as part of her global apologia for things Chinese, that foot-binding was an emblem of female power. The magazine's offices were redecorated in big-character posters; the editor donned a Mao suit. The autumn 1971 issue shifted 25,000 copies – more than double the magazine's usual circulation.[76]

So far, so fun – if you like that kind of thing. But after 1968, Cultural Revolution Maoism in Western Europe and the US discovered its authoritarian roots. Mao the provocative jester became Mao the tough party man. As the student movement lost momentum or disintegrated in the face of state repression, Mao and the CCP provided a blueprint for creating disciplined, militarised parties that could carry out grass-roots revolutionary work in factories – and sometimes the countryside – and orchestrate confrontational street protests. 'We realized', observed Ethan Young, that 'we lived in a country that had a lot of deep-rooted social as well as political conservatism. And the harder that we attempted to practice rebellion, the more difficult we found the process of actually changing people was ... So we looked for vehicles, formulae, means to bring about the kind of changes we wanted, and we looked for models. And China, especially China during the Cultural Revolution, represented a particular model for a particular time.'[77] Almost all such new parties pledged unswerving loyalty to the PRC's policies. They constituted an intermediate stage in the evolution of 1960s protest towards violent political extremism, and were a major factor in the steady fracturing of the left throughout the 1970s.

In West Germany, the student movement petered out with the passing in 1968 of a new state Emergency Law which – twenty years after the fall of the Nazi regime – permitted the government to suspend democratic rights in the context of internal or external emergencies. Student activists had hoped to use protest against the proposed law to build an alliance with the trade unions. After this unified protest platform disappeared following ratification, activists unable to access the trade unions' nationwide membership base to continue their agitation created their own tighter forms of organisation. Kommune 1 was replaced by a host of soundalike Marxist-Leninist cadre parties, the so-called K-Gruppen (Communist Groups), such as the Kommunistischer Bund Westdeutschland (KBW), the re-formed Kommunistische Partei Deutschlands (KPD) and the Kommunistische Partei Deutschlands/Marxisten-Leninisten (KPD/ML). Life within the K-Gruppen demanded absolute submission to party demands and exhausting self-criticism sessions. The thoughts of Mao seemed to take on a quasi-religious dimension, providing a complete, and completely superior, world view, and offering the answer to everything (including the prevention of natural disasters and the healing of life-threatening injuries). Make-up was banned, marriage became a 'revolutionary act', clothes were made out of an uncomfortable scratchy military twill, toilets had no doors. Even playtime was political: toys were collectively owned, and children were to be trained to patrol against class enemies, Red Guard–style.[78]

In Italy, one of the more fervent and surreal of such groups was the Union of Italian Communists (Marxist-Leninist), founded on 4 October 1968 and led by Aldo Brandirali, a cultish figure proclaimed by his accolytes 'the great and just comrade national secretary'. 'We absolutely belonged to the Cultural Revolution, just as the Red Guards did,' Brandirali recalled twenty-seven years later.[79] Brandirali's followers at demonstrations shifted their worship smoothly from Mao to their own party leader: 'Stalin! Mao! Bran-di-rali!' went the chant. For members of the group, Little Red Books were essential accessories, though by this point in the European leftist movement this was no longer sufficient to distinguish the seriously left-wing from those advocating alternative lifestyles more generally. The organisation's Maoist mood was clear from the party's magazine, *Serve the People* (a slogan taken from one of Mao's canonical speeches and particularly idolised during the Cultural Revolution), and from its members' addiction to the Little Red Book.

During the 1970s, Brandirali's party produced the most striking spectacles of Italian Maoism, staging militaristic parades of 'pioneers' (party youth) adorned with red neckerchiefs; vast, radiant portraits of Mao floated above the marching crowds. Alluding sharply to the religious elements of the party's Maoism (in West Germany, incidentally, the Little Red Book was known as the *Mao-Bibel*), the mainstream press called the group's pioneers '*i chierichetti di Mao*' (Mao's altar boys); or, picking up on their paramilitary pretensions, '*i balilli di Mao*' (a reference to Mussolini's Fascist youth group). 'In the name of Mao', militants had to give up all luxury goods to the party: books by 'bourgeois' authors, record players, mopeds, hair-dryers and toasters, all of which would be sold off to generate money for political campaigns. The only politically correct consumer items were plaster casts of Brandirali: one hand raised in a clenched fist, the other clutching a baby. From 1973, the group also policed its members' sex lives, decreeing that 'orgasm must be simultaneous', with masturbation, anal and oral sex all prohibited because they were 'manifestations of a petty-bourgeois mentality'. As the 1970s proceeded, discontented rumour had it that Brandirali had, with the money 'donated' by other party members, bought himself a red Alfa Romeo (the Giulia model) and a high-end villa (while forcing all party branches to display a photo of him in a green 'Mao Zedong-style' uniform). He was expelled from his party in 1976, the same year in which his idol Mao died.[80] He later converted to Catholicism ('Jesus smiled at me') and served in Silvio Berlusconi's government.[81]

In France too, thousands of young French Maoists made major lifestyle sacrifices for their beliefs after 1968. Olivier Rolin, leader of the military wing of the largest post-1968 Maoist party, Gauche Prolétarienne (GP), described *établissement* (a self-chosen stint of prole-tarian work) as a flight 'exactly like the Exodus . . . the result of a quite radical reflection on the crisis of the intellectual'.[82] There was a self-loathing, self-destructive quality to French Maoism that was particu-larly susceptible to the anti-intellectualism and anarchic politics of the early Cultural Revolution in China. Most *établis* were complete stran-gers to manual work. In the mid-1960s, Robert Linhart, the leader of the breakaway Maoist faction in the French Communist Party and the philosopher Louis Althusser's favourite pupil, was acclaimed as the brilliant 'Lenin of L'Ecole Normale Supérieure'. A decade later, he wrote a moving memoir expressing his shock, his exhaustion, his mal-coordination on the assembly line at a Citroën factory.[83] Other undercover Maoists with energy to spare earnestly lectured their fellow workers on Mao. One bemused mobiliser recorded the upshot of factory agitation in his group's publication: 'none of the workers wants to stay in our organisations'.[84]

The numbers involved in these parties were not enormous. At their largest, the K-Gruppen probably drew in somewhere between 100,000 and 150,000 individuals.[85] Some estimate a maximum of 800–1,000 members of the Revolutionary Union during the 1970s; perhaps 150 remain in its successor organisation, the Revolutionary Communist Party, today. At the peak of the movement in the 1970s, there were around 7,000 French Maoists.[86] Yet in France, for example, Maoist parties commanded disproportionate cultural capital, largely due to their ability to attract talented writers and intellectual celebrities to their cause. The militant GP gained much lustre from the support of Jean-Paul Sartre and Simone de Beauvoir. Both sold copies of the main Maoist newspaper, *La Cause de Peuple*, on the streets of Paris after de Gaulle's government had banned it in 1970. As police closed in on these two celebrity distributors, another militant snapped at the gendarmes: 'You're not going to arrest a Nobel laureate!'[87]

The quasi-religious dogmatism with which many of these Maoist parties interpreted the Chinese model led to extreme sectarianism. Indeed, in almost all of their Western European and North American guises, Maoist parties were as enthusiastic about consensus-building as the *Life of Brian*'s People's Front of Judaea. Dennis O'Neil, on being asked whether he was still a Maoist, answered in the affirmative. 'Other Maoists might not consider me one, but fuck them.'[88] As an American *établi* in the 1970s, Ethan Young witnessed the factionalism of US Maoist party-building. 'The machine shop I was working in on the South Side of Chicago was a focal point for many different, mostly Maoist, groups ... I found myself lost in the alphabet soup, and getting used to approaches from all sorts of different groups, and having people say to me, did you hear what these jerks did last week, look at this leaflet they put out.'[89] In the United States, the 1960s left wing later divided into over fifty groupings that subscribed in some degree to Maoist ideas and outlook, all competing fractiously to recruit each other, somehow failing to reach the real proletariat.[90]

The radicalism inspired by the Cultural Revolution bled into the terrorism of groups such as the Red Army Faction (RAF) in West Germany and the Red Brigades in Italy, both of which posed serious threats to the states within which they operated. Indeed, across the US and Western Europe security services viewed any form of Maoist politics as a credible menace: the French police kept extensive files on Maoist groups; and in the USA, the FBI and CIA waged war on the Maoist-influenced radical movements of the 1960s and '70s through the infamous and often illegal COINTELPRO (Counterintelligence Program) and MHCHAOS (the MH designating a campaign of global scope; six feet of files were compiled on one American Maoist alone).[91] In West Germany and Italy, in particular, the state's security apparatus would succeed in strengthening itself in the second half of the 1970s in response to political violence that drew significantly on Maoist inspiration.

The Weathermen – one of the most notorious left-wing terrorist organisations in the US – genuflected to Mao. Their revolutionary organisation, the manifesto stated, 'is akin to the Red Guard in China, based on the full participation and involvement of masses of people in the practice of making revolution; a movement with a full willingness to participate in the violent and illegal struggle'.[92] In France in June 1968, the interior minister announced a global Maoist plot on national prime-time television.[93] Police archives of the late 1960s diligently document the activities of French Maoists. Reports alleged that

a Chinese 'cultural mission' was running courses in political training
and sabotage in Albania for young 'Afro-Asians, South Americans ...
French, Italians, Germans, Belgians and English'.

> They are ... ushered onto coaches covered with portraits of Mao ...
> Every day the students attend a class on particular problems posed by
> Maoist thought, which inevitably feature virulent criticism of life in
> Western Europe and the United States. A group of French students
> has confessed ... that they were training to create maximum damage
> in guerrilla actions in their home country ... They march for hours in
> the sun, and also carry out demanding night marches in inaccessible
> and mountainous areas. This severe 'school of terror' does not neglect
> the making of grenades and time bombs, or the use of pistols and
> other small arms ... On graduating, these young people will be sent
> back to their respective countries, equipped with a subversive intel-
> lectual mission and also vast quantities of [Maoist] propaganda.

France underwent a pivotal moment of Maoist violence on 25
February 1972, when a young worker, 23-year-old Pierre Overney, was
killed in a stand-off at the Renault factory orchestrated by the confrontational tactics of Gauche Prolétarienne. Despite its fire-breathing
rhetoric – 'kidnapping bosses is justified' and the ubiquitous 'revolution
is not a dinner party' – the stomachs of the leadership turned on
witnessing the resulting bloodshed; the leader of the riot, Pierre Victor,
abandoned the Renault factory in tears.[94] This tragedy was the beginning of the end of any kind of mainstream presence for militant
French Maoism.

The 1960s Mao cult among West German radicals also rattled both
media and government, who opportunistically exaggerated the threat
posed in order to discredit protests. Responding to fears expressed in
the Bundestag in 1969 about the convergence of apparently rising
East Asian power and domestic student revolt, Chancellor Kiesinger
answered simply: 'I can say only: China, China, China.' When
members of Kommune 1 conspired, in the so-called Pudding
Assassination plot of April 1967, to cover the visiting US vice president
in yogurt and flour, the Berliner *Morgenpost* splashed sensationalist
headlines across its pages: 'FU-Students Manufactured Bombs with
Explosives from Peking'.[95]

The rhetorical militancy of Maoism and the Cultural Revolution was undoubtedly an influence on those members of the West German student movement who chose to cross over to a violent, underground revolution. The Maoist theory of 'continuous revolution' pushed parts of the student movement to seek ever more extreme positions from which to continue the revolution after the protests themselves faltered in 1968.[96] While some revelled in radical-chic *Bürgerschreck*, for others Maoism validated violent rebellion against the West German state apparatus – an apparatus that the student movement had denounced as genocidal (through its alliance with US foreign policy in Vietnam) and fascistic (due to its Nazi connections and police violence against student protesters). Several West Germans who later migrated to terrorism were steeped in the Maoist mood of the late-sixties protests – including the stunt-loving Dieter Kunzelmann. At an early stage in their thinking on urban warfare, two of the founding members of the RAF, Andreas Baader and Gudrun Ensslin (sporting Mao badges on their leather jackets), marshalled some fifty young people from a care home into a militant group and gave them lessons on the Little Red Book. One fringe of the student movement favoured a catchphrase that carried clear echoes of Mao's appraisal of the early phase of the Cultural Revolution, 'There is great chaos under heaven; the situation is excellent': 'Endless terror brings endless fun'.[97]

The RAF's first manifesto, on 'The Urban Guerrilla Concept', was larded with the usual quotations from Mao: 'imperialism and all reactionaries [are] paper tigers'; 'whoever is not afraid of being drawn and quartered, can dare to pull the emperor from his horse'. A further tract from 1972 argued that all violence committed by the RAF was to 'serve the people'. Mao's works thus created the initial frame of reference for the RAF, which in turn helped draw in other participants in the protest movement. Till Meyer, who would later join another terrorist group, the 2 June Movement, and take part in the 1975 kidnapping of Peter Lorenz (a candidate for mayor of West Berlin) which successfully bargained for the release of jailed RAF members, recalled his initial response to 'The Urban Guerrilla Concept' when a copy was thrust into his hands at a demonstration: 'At the top, I saw the Mao quotation. I greedily drank the whole pamphlet down. I was excited.'[98] In addition to the domestic menace that the RAF represented, the internationalist dimension to these groups further unnerved national security services and governments across the world. In the case of the German urban guerrilla organisations of which the RAF became the best known, they swam within a murky terrorist scene with connections to Ilich Ramirez Sanchez (better known as Carlos the Jackal) and Palestinian groups.[99]*

The Italian picture was similar. From 1970 the Red Brigades declared war on the Italian political, economic and judicial establishment, played out in acts of 'people's justice' and 'proletarian violence' against 'the bosses and their lackeys'. Renato Curcio, one of the founders of the Red Brigades, had drunk deeply of the late-sixties enthusiasm for the Cultural Revolution. Alberto Franceschini, later his close comrade in the Red Brigades, described Curcio standing outside Trento University wearing a T-shirt with a picture of Mao and handing out copies of the Little Red Book.[100] Franceschini recalled of the Brigades' first kidnapping that they decided to hang around the neck of their victim, a business executive, a notice on which was written: 'Hit and run. Nothing goes unpunished. Strike one to educate one hundred.' 'We got "hit and run" from Mao. He had written that the principle of partisan tactics is to hit and immediately run. We liked this also because it made you think of the jungle, and we were convinced that it would conjure in the enemy's mind a picture of wild animals.'[101] In the militant circles in which the Red Brigadists moved, 'phrases, slogans, whole speeches were directly or indirectly dedicated to the Great Helmsman'.[102] In March 1978, they kidnapped the former prime minister, Aldo Moro. On 10 May 1978, after the Italian government had refused for two months to release political prisoners in exchange for Moro's freedom, one of the terrorists shot him ten times and dumped his body in a car parked in the centre of Rome. The Red Brigades saw themselves expressing the mass line through violence perpetrated 'in the name of the masses', even as they translated Mao's

---

* Violence from the right wing, it should be remembered, was as great if not a greater threat. In 1968, 'Red' Rudi Dutschke was shot three times in the head and chest by a neo-Nazi house-painter who had a portrait of Hitler hanging on the wall of his flat. The protest movement also experienced appalling state violence. The brutal West German police response to protests against the Berlin visit of the Shah of Iran on 2 June 1967 was a pivotal, infamous moment in shaping protesters' opposition to the government.

injunction towards 'self-reliance' into a clandestine existence that isolated them from ordinary Italians. But the Maoist influence, it must be pointed out, existed alongside a cornucopia of other inspirations that included the heroic, John Wayne–esque myths of the Second World War partisans, Che Guevara and the Uruguayan guerrillas, the Tupamaros. Franceschini even alleged that the Red Brigades were offered state-of-the-art weapons from the Israeli secret service, who hoped that, if allowed to thrive, such terrorist organisations would keep the Italian government too distracted to offer support to the Palestinians.[103]

Subscription to the idea of a future, violent revolution was a thread that united many of the Maoist-inspired parties of the 1970s, across Western Europe and the United States, even if they did not transform this conviction into homicidal action. Preparing for the final battle was as far as some of them went. In Germany in 1977, as the KBW grew convinced that the apocalypse of global capitalism was drawing nigh, the organisation broadcast the idea that a decisive 'armed uprising was the only way to remove the capitalist system ... before it embarked on a new imperialistic world war'. Military drills were carried out in parks, so that cadres would be battle-ready. 'A housewife used to modern kitchen and cleaning appliances', they hopefully conjectured, 'would have no difficulty using a machine gun.'[104]

In the US, the militant Black Power movement was ready for a fight in 1966. That year, RAM distributed 'The World Black Revolution', an apocalyptic manifesto fronted by a picture of Mao, scattered with gobbets of Maoism and advocating all-out urban guerrilla war against the white establishment, in which substantial parts of New York and Washington would be 'blown to bits'. In the coming 'War of Armageddon ... the "devil's" forces of evil are destroyed by "God" (Allah), the forces of righteousness ... Let the cry across the planet be "burn, baby, burn".'[105] When Robert Williams showed the manifesto to Mao in Beijing, apparently even the Great Helmsman thought they 'might have taken it a bit far'.

Conservative intellectuals – particularly those who have weighed into the 'Culture Wars' of the past two decades – like to claim that, over the past half-century, young left-wing radicals of the 1960s have successfully undertaken a 'long march through the institutions' (in Rudi Dutschke's phrase), overrunning the establishment with politically correct values. It is true that the countercultural rebellion of which Maoism was a part decisively eroded social and cultural conservatism in the United States and Western Europe, and that the effects of this liberalisation are discernible in public life today.

Western Maoism fed into the women's and gay liberation movements, into educational reform, and aspirations to racial equality in public life. *Tout!*, the journal of the more liberal wing of French Maoism (the group Vive la Révolution), hosted early explorations of women's and gay rights issues. Feminists based their 'consciousness-raising' – railing at the discrimination they suffered from male classmates, teachers, boyfriends, husbands and colleagues – on the Chinese revolution's 'speak bitterness' sessions. 'There's something else that we absorbed from the Chinese revolutionary experience that's harder to put into words,' mused Carol Hanisch, backbone of the radical feminist group Redstockings and populariser of the phrase 'the personal is political'. 'Call it inspiration ... hope ... the spirit of revolution.'[106] Although there could be plenty of macho in American Maoism, too. In 1963, RAM called a 'Black Vanguard Conference': 'a secret, all-black, all-male conference to draft strategy'.[107]

Mao-style criticism/self-criticism later blurred into the confessional habits of therapy and self-help. The Cultural Revolution–inspired dissent of the 1960s and '70s contributed to reforms of secondary and higher education, to make teaching methods and curricula more participatory, more representative, more accountable to diverse communities. African or Chinese American activists (such as John Bracey, at the University of Massachusetts from 1972), who stayed in the educational system rather than joining radical parties, contributed to the struggle for black and ethnic studies in universities.

Another connection can be drawn between Cultural Revolution–inspired rebellion and the sceptical enquiries of post-structuralism – Michel Foucault went through a Maoist phase in the early 1970s, which led, among other things, to necessary and searing indictments of the French prison system.[108] Paradoxically, the idealised vision that French intellectuals had of the Cultural Revolution – the totalitarian apogee of Mao's own power projection – as a moment of rebellious mass democracy segued into a concern with 'human rights' and support for humanitarian organisations such as Amnesty International.[109] Maoism had a role to play too in the emergence of post-colonial and subaltern studies. India's Naxalite Maoism led to South Asian intellectuals engaging with 'subaltern' experiences and consciousness; this perspective has reshaped approaches to writing history and culture in the West.[110]

Some former French Maoists have become cultural and political celebrities. Alain Geismar, former leader of the militant Gauche Prolétarienne, served through the 1990s in a succession of Socialist Party governments. Between 1973 and 2006, Serge July – another former GP leader – founded and edited *Libération*, a newspaper that originated from the organised Maoist left but evolved into an influential mainstream broadsheet. Olivier Rolin became a novelist – his seventh novel, *Paper Tiger*, stars a burnt-out '68-er, trying to explain the death of a comrade to the latter's grown-up daughter. Numerous West German ex-Maoists have enjoyed successful careers in mainstream politics, for the most part in the Green movement.[111] It would be impossible, remembered Mario Capanna (who later served in the Italian Chamber of Deputies), 'to deny the fascination that the Great Helmsman exercised over me ... [One] element of the fascination sprang from his great dialectical ability and the simplicity of his language. All the success that I achieved speaking in the assemblies or, later, on the electoral platform, I owe to him.'[112] Shirley MacLaine's film career continued unabated after her Maoist interlude. By 1980, she was starring in *A Change of Seasons*, a *ménage-à-quatre* scenario set in a Vermont ski chalet, and never looked back. Approaching the end of the millennium, she predicted that, in the twenty-first century, 'we are going to deal more and more on a realistic basis about sightings of our space brothers and sisters'.

But the success stories of Western Maoism perhaps feature disproportionately in public perception, obscuring its personal tragedies and political casualties. The tragic story of Robert Linhart is a case in point. In the throes of the May 1968 demonstrations, he suffered a nervous breakdown that confined him to hospital for months. In 1981, he attempted suicide with a massive overdose, but eventually regained consciousness after weeks in a deep coma. He has barely spoken since.[113] Max Elbaum blames Cultural Revolution fever for the marginalisation of the contemporary American left, writing that 'the most damage was done by Maoism': by a dogmatic loyalty to the theory of the Cultural Revolution and to the twists and turns of Chinese domestic and foreign policy. 'Maoism's problems were crystallized in Mao's Cultural Revolution slogan that "the correctness or incorrectness of the ideological and political line decides everything." This dictum was cited endlessly by the main Maoist groups, despite the fact that it completely ignored material conditions and the balance of political forces ... it not only fostered ultra-left analyses and tactics, but a theoretical purism that led directly to bitter confrontations over even minor points of doctrine and constant interorganizational competition.'[114] After years of sectarian struggles, according to Elbaum, America's left wing was too exhausted to resist the conservative resurgence of the Reagan years: its assault on the trade unions and its tough line against socialist and Communist governments in the Third World. Ethan Young recalls the psychology prevailing among those who emerged from the American Maoist parties of the 1970s: 'The sectarianism leaves the scar. People who've lived through the sectarian wars react violently against suggestions of forming new parties ... They have memories of being lost in interminable debates and struggles that led nowhere. Some people's lives were torn apart; they were cast out of their groups. There were some suicides. And definitely a deep, deep demoralisation, disillusionment and despair.'[115] Italian Maoist groups of the 1970s, observed Aldo Brandirali, 'were the product of an explosion of communism that fractured into a thousand splinters ... it was a crisis ... or only the fragment of a crisis ... It was the end.'[116]

The type of political activism practised in these parties was not, in any case, practically sustainable over the long term. It was divisive and time-consuming. There wasn't much money in it. By the late 1970s this first generation of would-be revolutionaries were hitting thirty and were starting to think about families, careers and pensions. And much of this activism ran out of steam when governments in countries badly affected by left-wing terrorism cracked down hard on these groups, and anyone deemed to be a sympathiser.

The first nine months of 1977 witnessed eight RAF murders and one kidnapping (of the industrialist Hanns Martin Schleyer). West Germany's predicament became an international concern when on 13 October four members of the Popular Front for the Liberation of Palestine hijacked a Lufthansa plane carrying eighty-six passengers, and included in their ransom demands the release of ten RAF members held in the Stammheim prison in Stuttgart. The West German government brought the hostage crisis to an end through a surgical strike on the plane at Mogadishu airport carried out by its new anti-terrorism squad; on learning of the failure of the hijacking on 18 October, three imprisoned RAF leaders (including Baader and Ensslin) committed suicide. That same day, the RAF terrorists holding Schleyer executed him and abandoned his body in the back of a car.

These events – the crescendo of terrorist violence, together with the resolve of the West German state to mobilise security forces that had previously been shunned by a government nervous of raising the ghost of Nazi authoritarianism – caused the German left to abandon its widely held view of the state as a totalitarian enemy to which guerrilla violence was an acceptable response. They re-engaged with mainstream, peaceful politics (often environmental issues), while the state's resolution of the Mogadishu crisis won it a wave of patriotic affection. This was also a pivotal moment in the West German state's competition for credibility with East Germany – in which the fall of the Berlin Wall in 1989 confirmed the West's absolute victory.[117]

For Cultural Revolution enthusiasts in organisations identified as genuine threats to the state, their commitment cost them dear. COINTELPRO'S original justification – on its establishment in 1956 – sprang from the Cold War clash of ideologies: namely, to systematise surveillance of the American Communist Party, accused of pro-Soviet espionage. In 1965, as anti-Vietnam War and Black Liberation protests gathered pace, J. Edgar Hoover expanded it to encompass a 'hard-hitting and imaginative program ... to expose, disrupt, misdirect, discredit or otherwise neutralize the activities of [civil rights and black liberation organizations], their leadership, spokesmen, membership and supporters'. RAM, among others, was a target. Illegality and ruthlessness predominated. 'You don't measure success in this area by apprehensions,' one operative observed in 1974, 'but in terms of neutralization.'[118] The FBI's tactics were various: blackmail, buggings, mail intercepts, drenching a Black Panther printing press with a chemical compound that smelled of 'the foulest ... feces imaginable', bombings – or, in the case of the talented Chicago non-violent organiser Fred Hampton, emptying fifty rounds of gunfire into the sleeping body of their target.[119]

A former RAM activist was pursued for years by the US security services – on charges of rioting and assassination plots. The fact that he had a poster of Mao pasted on his bedroom wall when the police burst into his apartment to arrest him on the first assassination charge in 1967 was almost incriminating enough evidence. He reflected on the toll that political activism had taken on his life: 'After '68, it took me 10 years to get out of legal entrapment ... I was attacked and beaten unconscious in California ... I couldn't get a job ... Half of my family is crazy, totally estranged. My oldest son is in penitentiary ... My children feel they grew up in a situation where I could not provide in the way that other fathers could ... My wife thought Mao was ugly.' Nonetheless, he feels that Mao still has lessons for the African American struggle today. 'As we grew older, we really understood the nature of protracted struggles. It's been going on all our lives. Your strategy and tactics differ when you understand it's a protracted struggle. You learn retreat. All of that is in the philosophical principles of Mao ... if your mass line is working with the people, with the masses of African-American people and what they are concerned with ... then it will lead to a leap of their consciousness; the movement will continue to grow.' In 2015, Max Stanford too was still calling for 'a new cultural, political, historical re-education process' to defeat the US establishment: 'Black Lives Matter! We Will Win!'[120]

The Cultural Revolution's rhetoric of anti-authoritarian rebellion inspired revolts outside China that took aim at a broad range of political, cultural and social custom: at domestic and foreign policy; colonial rule; electoral representation; relations between the sexes; education, film and literature. The impact of the Cultural Revolution (upper case) is part of a much more diffuse (and often liberalising) process of cultural revolution (lower case) that has transformed society, culture and politics since the 1960s, especially in the developed West. In countries riven by deep historical, ethnic or socio-economic fault lines (post-fascist Germany and Italy; post-segregation America; post-independence India), the Cultural Revolution's legitimisation of political violence served as the spark that lit a prairie fire – a fire that in some instances is still burning today. The United States is regularly jolted by revelations of racist police brutality: for veterans of the

African American liberation struggle inspired by Cultural Revolution Maoism, some of the political ideas suggested by their readings of Maoist theory and practice remain relevant. The US government acknowledged the potency of these ideas and techniques with its virulent pushback of repression through COINTELPRO. But the rhetorical and actual violence of Cultural Revolution politics, in combination with the often dogmatic, sectarian way in which events were interpreted by radicals outside China, also generated setbacks: for the individuals who devoted so much time and energy to these ideas, and for the left-wing causes in which they militated.

As for Comrade Bala's stronghold: the former Mao Zedong Memorial Centre is now occupied by an Algerian restaurant offering home-style cooking at £15 a head and exquisite North African pastries. Whether out of respect for the building's former use, or for some other reason, the shopfront windows are draped with heavy velvet curtains as red as the shroud over Mao's body in Tiananmen Square.

9

RED SUN OVER PERU –
THE SHINING PATH

A photograph taken on Boxing Day morning 1980 – what would have been Mao's eighty-seventh birthday – shows a Lima policeman in aviator shades shimmying up a lamp post. To his right, a bemused bystander in a check suit and heeled cowboy boots looks on. Two metres up the lamp post a small dog hangs from a wire: fur matted with rain, jaws open, stiff with death. Its head has been pushed through a poster emblazoned, in capitals, with 'Deng Xiaoping'.[1]

That day, this macabre exhibition was replicated at seven other locations throughout the city. Police initially feared that explosives had been stuffed inside the animals but once this possibility had been discounted, their job was merely to remove these grisly pendants. The event made a shallow splash in the local press but was quickly forgotten by Lima's inhabitants, who went back to business as usual.

A decade later, these strange events returned to haunt Limeños. The ritualistic killing of strays to denounce Deng Xiaoping – the man who broke with many of Mao's keynote Cultural Revolution policies (collectivisation, mass mobilisation, class apartheid) – was the symbolic beginning of the Maoist insurgency of the Communist Party of Peru – Shining Path, led by a portly philosophy professor called Abimael Guzmán. Across the 1980s, this war became the most destructive conflict in the history of independent Peru, as rural populations were devastated by revolutionary violence and by savage state retaliation. At the start of the 1990s, the horror closed in on the capital, and by 1992, Lima was paralysed by Shining Path's random terrorist attacks. In February, an Afro-Peruvian welfare activist called Maria Elena Moyano, who had publicly criticised Shining Path's violence, was first shot and then, still alive, dynamited in front of her two sons at a fundraising barbecue in a shantytown in south-east Lima. A car parked in Lima's business district – packed with 400 kilograms of explosives – detonated in July, killing twenty-five and wounding 155 people.

The Shining Path began its activities in 1969 with a few dozen followers in an impoverished corner of the Andean highlands; two decades later, it had brought the capital to its knees. By the early 1990s, the magical realism evoked in the Latin American literary boom had become a black reality for the country. Peru was in the grip of cholera epidemics, inflation running at more than 12,000 per cent, and a millenarian left-wing cult of Mao in which a provincial philosophy prof was deified as Peru's 'Chairman Gonzalo' and the 'greatest living Marxist-Leninist'. Between 1980 and 1999, the civil war killed 69,000 people, annihilated the possibility of political moderation, gave gangster-oligarchs an excuse to bulldoze democracy, and distended the country's cities with at least 600,000 refugees from Maoist and state violence.

Witnesses and victims of the conflict struggled to explain its ferocity. Some blamed Peru's economic and social conditions, in particular the centuries-old neglect and exploitation of indigenous peoples who made up a third of the population. Yet one long-term resident of Peru, a Belgian priest, disagreed: 'what such terrible conditions generated, usually and spontaneously, in the people that suffered them was not rebelliousness, but rather fatalism, passivity, or religious resignation ... the explosions of violence could only be understood if given social conditions came together with an ideology that deliberately and consciously proposed exercising violence as a response'.[2]

That ideology was Maoism. The grisly dead-dog stunt on Mao's birthday had been a passionate declaration of loyalty to Mao. To Mao's global disciples, Deng was a traitor – responsible for a palace coup against the Cultural Revolution and, after Mao's death, the architect of China's capitalist revival. To label him a dog was a direct reference back to invective deployed by Mao himself, who denounced his enemies as 'running dogs' (of capitalism, imperialism, feudalism and so on). Throughout the 1980s, the followers of the Shining Path – or *senderistas*, as they were known – would organise, sing, fight, torture and kill in the name of a Peruvian Maoist revolution, waging protracted guerrilla warfare, 'two-line struggle' against revisionism, and liquidating markets, inequality, religion and political dissent.

Viewed from one historical angle – the emergence of neo-liberalism under Reagan, and China's own shunning of the Cultural Revolution in the early 1980s – Shining Path's project was bizarrely out of its time. It was also ill-suited to Peru. Few of the preconditions for Mao's own revolution in the 'semi-colonial, semi-feudal' China of the 1940s seemed to be present: Peru in 1980 was a democracy; it was largely urban and literate; and there was no colonial invader to fight, no militant social rebellion to capitalise upon, no massive inequality of land ownership.

Yet if we consider these events in the context of the historical, political logic of the 1960s and '70s, when the Shining Path came to life, the movement's doctrines become less surprising. For at that point, dreams and plots of Maoist insurgency ran in the bloodstream of the global radical left. However cultish the group would later come to seem, in the 1960s and '70s many of its ideological under- pinnings were fairly standard. Mao's ideas of continuous revolution and political militancy had permeated deeply enough to be satirised in mainstream Western pop culture, in Monty Python's *The Life of Brian* or the Beatles' 'Revolution'. In Peru, meanwhile, big-talking Maoist militants were ten a penny: 'nothing special', as two Dutch agronomists there in the 1970s remarked.[3] As the Shining Path terror- ised Peru throughout the 1980s, a journalist upbraided General Morales Bermúdez – president between 1975 and 1980 – for failing to prevent the insurgency. 'We were getting intelligence reports that Guzmán was proposing armed struggle,' he admitted. 'But at that point, more than 70 political groups were saying the same thing. We couldn't foresee that [Shining Path] would actually act on it.'[4] In many parts of the world, confidence in Maoism was fading with China's own denunciation of the Cultural Revolution. But in the Peruvian context – in a country scarred by gross socio-economic and political inequities – and in the hands of particular, schematic personalities, these ideas could incubate, then resurge with the same sectarian passion that they had provoked in the 1960s.

Abimael Guzmán was one of thousands of Latin Americans – presi- dents, painters, poets, philosophers, agronomists, labour activists –

who travelled to Mao's China and returned full of admiration for its achievements. Within this group, Guzmán belonged to a subset (about a thousand strong) that had received military training, as well as flattering hospitality, there. They pored lovingly over China's 'external propaganda' and spread the Maoist word across the continent in travel books, pamphlets and lectures; in reading groups, classrooms, and at rallies. Like many parts of the developing world, Latin America after the Second World War was looking for political and economic models on both sides of the Cold War – oscillating between reform and revolution, democracy and dictatorship, while the US intensified its meddling in the continent by backing right-wing dictators to contain the spread of socialist ideas. After the Sino-Soviet Split, Communist parties in Latin America – as in the rest of the world – began fracturing into pro-Chinese and pro-Soviet factions. Unlike the rest of the world, however, in several Latin American countries – Peru, Brazil, Colombia, Bolivia and Paraguay – the Chinese factions were about the same size as the pro-Soviet groupings, indicating the strong attraction that the Chinese revolution exercised through the continent.

Some had personal reasons for admiring Mao's China. The PRC's ardent hosting machine melted the hearts of many visitors – one Mexican labour activist was delighted by the hundreds of Chinese (including schoolchildren, who resembled 'porcelain dolls') who turned out to greet him at a railway station in a snowstorm.[5] Across the Latin American left as a whole, Mao's analysis of pre-revolutionary China resonated in a continent marked by inequality and US economic domination. Mao's China was lionised as a state that had broken with Western dependence and bid for self-sufficiency through the economic miracle of the Great Leap Forward.[6] Some Latin American visitors fell for Mao himself: they were mesmerised by his 'high and shining forehead', by 'a man so great and at the same time so modest, so sure of the victory of all the people of the world over their oppressors and of the necessity of recognising that obstacles exist and that it is necessary to destroy them'.[7] One Bolivian wrote ill-advised love poems to Stakhanovite Chinese women, including to one who 'On that enjoyable night in Wuhan / Danced so much with me / And sliding between my arms / Was like a handful of lilies'.[8]

Across the continent, radicals and leftists absorbed Mao's military maxims; Guzmán was far from the only Latin American dreaming of a Maoist 'People's War' in the 1960s. The Mexican guerrilla Florencio Medrano Mederos – a veteran Communist and agitator for land reform who always kept Mao's works within reach – planned protracted war in south-east Mexico.[9] In 1959, the CCP laid on a five-month training course for delegations from twelve Latin American Communist parties, openly proselytising Mao's revolutionary doctrines: on organising the peasantry, the mass line and armed struggle. The curriculum was monopolised by Mao's works: Marx, Engels, Lenin and Stalin were nowhere in sight. The lessons were accompanied by instructive tours around the country. 'Most returned', one Peruvian participant recalled, 'certain that ... the road travelled by the Chinese Revolution would have to be repeated in the countries of Latin America.'[10]

There were thus plenty of China-inspired, and often China-trained, radicals in Latin America of the 1960s and '70s. For the most part, though, this phenomenon had no tangible impact on the political stability of their home countries. Take the case of one aspiring revolutionary, whom I will call Juan (not his real name). Born into a good family in the 1930s, he hung on at university – deep into his thirties – as the leader of a band of student militants. The early 1960s were, generally speaking, a fine time to be a globetrotting, armchair *guerrillero*. At the merry-go-round of international Communist conferences, there was not only lively entertainment (in the form of Chinese and Soviet delegates hurling insults at each other – Revisionist! Adventurist!) but also no shortage of liaison officers eager to gain disciples by handing out free trips to a smorgasbord of Communist utopias. Thanks to such junkets, Juan visited Budapest, Prague, Helsinki, Moscow and Hanoi (where he met Ho Chi Minh). It was not a livelihood – his wife and mother-in-law supported Juan's four children with their day jobs – but it was the revolution. And it was a free round-the-world ticket in an era before cheap flights.

In 1964, at a Youth Festival in Europe, Juan was invited – all expenses paid – to visit China (where he was received by Chairman Mao). On a second visit two years later, he attended a guerrilla-training course for a few months. He spent a holding week in a comfortable Beijing hotel, before being escorted to the suburbs of Nanjing, where he lived for two and a half months with a Chinese minder and interpreter in a house in the country. There, he ate, slept and took classes on Mao for six hours a day – alone apart from his

Chinese interpreter – given by a team of eight pleasant, serious, patient Chinese teachers. The Chinese had a plan for him: 'they thought that I could create a guerrilla "foco" back home, to rival the many guerrilla groups financed by Cuba, an ally of Moscow ... They fed me two main ideas: first, that I should merge with the poorest masses, second, that I should dare to fight.' His practical training, however, was limited: he fired a rifle only a few times and threw just a handful of grenades. His hosts ensured that he had no opportunities to network with other revolutionaries; the closest he got to other Latin Americans was overhearing snatches of Spanish spoken in neighbouring farmhouses. Nonetheless, the experience made him a lifelong devotee of Mao and the CCP. Although Juan never learned Chinese, or studied any other aspect of China, he became 'a priest for the Maoist religion', as his son recalled. 'He wanted to become the president back home, using Mao Zedong thought and military strategy.'

On Juan's return home, he joined a guerrilla band, communicating what he had learned in China, such as Mao's strategy of surrounding the cities from the countryside. He later admitted that this adherence to the Chinese model was a 'fundamental error', for 'the situation in my own country was very different from the Chinese. Since the discovery of oil the peasants abandoned agricultural activities and migrated to the places where oil companies operated as they received better salaries and living conditions there.' Moreover, he and the other guerrillas did not get on – followers of Castro, the Fidelists, would not tolerate a Maoist in their midst and gave him a week to get out, if he wanted to live. After only three months in the maquis, Juan returned to his earlier career of campus revolutionary.

In the mid-1960s, security forces raided the university and arrested Juan as a Communist. Taking advantage of a personal connection with a minister, his family got him released – on condition that he went into exile. Juan and his family settled first in London, where his older sons – approaching their teens – thoroughly enjoyed themselves, growing their hair long and wandering Carnaby Street. But Juan was unhappy: instead of doing politics, he was having to make a living by writing an occasional society column for a couple of glossies back home. Using his connections with China, he won an invitation to work in the People's Republic and the family relocated again. Almost fifty years later, one of his children still remembered how remote China felt. On a multi-stage flight that stopped in Paris, Rome, Cairo, Karachi, Dakha and finally Shanghai, their aircrafts became steadily less populated. As they crossed the Himalayas, the siblings raced up and down the aeroplane's empty aisles – the plane was theirs except for a Swiss diplomat and a woman of mixed Chinese European heritage. So as not to brand their passports with evidence of a visit to China, the authorities merely slipped them their visas stamped on loose pieces of paper. (A South African flying to London from secret radio training in China in the early 1960s failed to destroy the sheet before his plane took off, and had no choice but to eat it while on board, to the bemusement of the passenger sitting next to him.)[11]

In China, Juan and his wife worked for the government – polishing Spanish-language texts for 'external propaganda' six days a week – from 1968 to 1970, through some of the most tumultuous phases of the Cultural Revolution. But the revolution kept them at arm's length. They were not allowed to know anything of their co-workers, not even basic personal details. From time to time they were taken on tours around model factories and communes. Their children had a mostly grand time in the palatial ghetto for 'foreign experts': the Friendship Hotel, still three-quarters empty since the departure of the Soviets back in 1960. By day, they learned Chinese through Mao's quotations. Outside lessons, they lounged around the pool, bounced on trampolines and raced around Beijing on their bicycles; they kissed their first girlfriends in the bomb shelters built underneath Beijing against Soviet nuclear attack.

But Juan once more grew restless. Booze became the breaking point, recalled one of his children. 'In our country, revolutionaries like to talk revolution over good wine and whisky. My father would not touch rum, our native liquor. But he couldn't find Scotch or wine here. The only place that you could get it was the diplomatic club. And we weren't allowed there. Or we were only allowed there through diplomats' invitation. There weren't many diplomats, and we didn't get on with the ones that were here. The one time we did get invited, we bought a huge pack of caviar – half a kilo. I was so sick of it by the end that I was feeding it to the cat. Dad got his Scotch, too. But it didn't last long.'

Fortunately, by 1970 there was a new president back home – in fact, one of Juan's old professors – who declared an amnesty for guerrillas and political exiles. The family was able to return. 'The revolution is done in China,' Juan explained to them. 'We now need to make revolution in our own country.' There, Juan threw himself into insurrection by founding a bookstore, plastered with images of Mao, peddling Chinese political propaganda. Since the Chinese government sent the materials for free, he could break even, selling enough to pay the rent on the shop. When the line changed after the fall of the Gang of Four, and the Chinese government no longer wanted these materials distributed because they did not fit with their newly non-interventionist, non-revolutionary foreign policy, Juan's Chinese sponsors had an ingeniously simple way of shutting him down: they sent Juan a bill for all the materials that for six years they had been providing gratis. Still today, Juan keeps a plaster bust of Mao on his desk.

This Maoist encounter ended very differently from that of Abimael Guzmán's – mainly for reasons of personality. But in its beginning and middle, the story is very similar, suggesting the scope and intensity of infatuation with Maoist methods among the Latin American hard left in the 1960s. Both Juan and Guzmán turned into zealous Maoists through visits to China at the high point of the Sino-Soviet Split; both developed a doctrinal devotion to the teachings of Chinese Communism and Mao's theories of guerrilla warfare. Thanks to a greater capacity for abstraction and hard work, Guzmán lived out his infatuation in practice. Today, Guzmán seems a political freak; in Latin America in the 1960s, he was part of the mainstream.

Abimael Guzmán is not an easy character to sketch. The quintessential doctrinaire Communist, he has tried hard to write personal feelings out of his life story. When Peru's Commission for Truth and Reconciliation – set up after the collapse of both Shining Path and the regime that had destroyed Peruvian human rights while fighting the insurgency – interviewed him in 2002, he summarised his childhood thus: 'I did not have political concerns then.'[12] Yet his early life had not been straightforward. He was born out of wedlock in 1934 in Tambo, near Peru's southern coast, to a philandering lottery winner by the same name and to an affectionate, educated, self-effacing woman called Berenice Reynoso. Between the ages of ten and twelve, he was passed from one household to another – from his mother to an uncle, and then to his father and stepmother. This instability notwithstanding, the boy was well cared for: each guardian ensured that the bookish Abimael received an excellent education; his step-mother doted on him. He read 'everything that fell into his hands' at every available moment (including during games of hide-and-seek).[13] Unusually for a bookworm, however, he developed a youthful interest in joining the army.[14]

As an undergraduate at the University of San Agustin in the city of Arequipa, a former national capital, he became the disciple of an authoritarian, disciplinarian philosophy lecturer called Miguel Angel Rodríguez Rivas. 'He was very intelligent,' recalled one colleague of Rivas, 'but he was crazy ... if his thinking suffered a deviation it could take him anywhere in the world, and he would follow it, thinking that he was dutifully following sacred Reason.'[15] Guzmán's other great undergraduate influence was a painter called Carlos de la Riva, a passionate (his nickname was 'Carlos de la rabia', 'enraged Carlos') Mao-phile who after a trip to the People's Republic in 1959 wrote an influential book on Mao's China with the self-explanatory title *Where the Dawn Is Born*. Through his studies, Guzmán was also thoroughly schooled in European high culture: he read Kant, Marx, Dostoevsky, Voltaire and Rousseau; he listened to Bach, Mozart, Wagner and Brahms. (In the 1980s, Guzmán would justify his personality cult by likening himself to the bass solo in the final movement of Beethoven's choral symphony, who bellows 'Joy! Joy!' above the full orchestra.) By 1960 – shortly before the Sino-Soviet Split – he had joined the Communist Party of Peru. That year, he had his first glimpse of rural poverty when he carried out a grass-roots investigation of the life of the Arequipa poor. Among many horrors, he saw 'two families who were so poor that not only had they been living in the same room, but whose space was demarcated by a stream which carried the foul-smelling waste from a leather curer next door ... it was one thing to read about poverty and another thing to see it.'[16]

In 1961, demonstrating his ability to move between the worlds of abject desperation and intellectual abstraction, he completed two graduating dissertations: 'On the Kantian Theory of Space' and 'The Bourgeois Democratic State'. The first rejected Kantian idealism in favour of Marxist materialism; the second denounced elections and bourgeois support for liberty and equality as 'useless to the trapped and downtrodden masses'.[17] In the second dissertation in particular, it is easy to see the preoccupations and fixations that would lead him to Mao: an equation between the horrors of slavery and modern capitalism, 'semi-feudalism' and colonialism; and an assertion of the 'inalienable right to rebellion' of oppressed societies.[18] A millenarian, Maoist voluntarism – which would later become a keynote of Shining Path ideology – glimmered through. 'The destiny of peoples resides in the people themselves ... Fresh winds are blowing and stiffening the unbribable soul of all the peoples. Humanity shakes before our very eyes and, in its inextinguishable and undefeatable ascending march towards better times, gives birth to new societies.'[19] A member of the committee for his dissertation viva recollected that the event went on for over four hours: although no one on the panel agreed with his views on Kant, they passed him unanimously due to his 'knowledge and exploration of the subject'. The ideologue-in-training had talked them into submission.[20]

As a young man, according to fellow students, Guzmán stood out for his intelligence, reserve, intellectual self-confidence and charisma. 'Sometimes he would interrupt a class to start a long philosophical discussion,' one of them recalled. '[H]e immediately won the admiration of those he was meeting for the first time. I remember that he knew the [Marxist and Leninist classics], and many times he ridiculed those who thought they knew more than him ... He was not a fan of jokes ... sometimes, he did not understand them.'[21] The owner of a bookshop that Guzmán frequented as a very young man remembered: 'Sometimes he would spend hours reading books before choosing which one to buy. He favoured works of philosophy and politics ... I don't think that he had many friends because he always walked behind his books.'[22]

In 1962, Guzmán was hired as a professor of philosophy by the Universidad Nacional de San Cristóbal de Huamanga in Ayacucho, the provincial capital of the eponymous southern central region of Peru that would become the epicentre of the Shining Path insurrection. This was one of the most isolated and impoverished parts of Peru, a country that in the 1960s was the second poorest in Latin America. The name of the city commemorated desperate violence: in the local

Quechua language, Ayacucho means Corner of the Dead – here, an Inca ruler had made a last stand against Spanish conquest. While churches studded its hispanophone capital, life expectancy in the Andean sierra surrounding the city stood in 1979 at fifty-one – the lowest in Peru; roads and transportation barely existed.[23] Anyone who could get out left – songs described the migrating natives of Ayacucho as 'orphan birds'.[24]

Until the military government imposed land reform in the late 1960s – and still for some time after – inequality and exploitation openly thrived. The region was rank with racism: of whites and mestizos (those of mixed European and indigenous background) towards those of darker-skinned indigenous heritage. Local grandees – the *gamonales* – denounced 'the Indian' as 'lazy, miserable and gluttonous', 'like savages': 'we Spaniards should have killed the Indians', they declared.[25] One notorious grandee swindled countless Indians out of their land, persuaded a woman to marry him by threatening to kill her if she refused, then mortally wounded the officiating priest when the latter complained that the administrative documents weren't complete – all without judicial punishment. 'All the hard and dirty work was done by [the Indian],' recalled a white memoir of the 1950s, 'it suited his nature. To be Indian was to be trampled on, brutalised – an Indian could do anything: sleep at people's feet ... die of cold. An Indian wasn't allowed to be hungry: he was used to hunger and therefore could go without food for a day or two, it didn't matter because it suited his nature. He was less than human; he wasn't human.'[26] The harsh inaccessibility of the Andean sierra weakened the presence of the state – and where it was present, its representatives were often abusive and corrupt. Ayacucho's concentration of marginalised ethnic groups thus presented a large potential support base for an ideology preaching Mao's message of radical egalitarianism and rough social justice.

There was, in theory, a way out of poverty and exploitation. Social inferiority was tied not only to skin pigmentation, but also to a lack of education – to be educated denoted high class. Literacy was the key to social and economic opportunities: a literate Indian could become a *gamonal*. When in 1969 an ethnographer interviewed 499 peasants in the area, 91 per cent believed that 'with an education, a man can be whatever he wants'.[27] When Ayacucho's university reopened in 1959 after a century of closure, it is easy to see how influential and potentially disruptive the institution could become: it represented the only hope of social mobility in a desert of deprivation. In order to make the university a success story, its administration headhunted some of Peru's most brilliant intellectuals: two leading anthropologists, Eduardo Valcárcel and Efraín Morote Best (all three of Morote's children would join Shining Path; his son Osmán would rise to deputy leadership); José María Arguedas, one of twentieth-century Peru's most celebrated novelists – his wife would also later join Shining Path. The classes on offer, the types of assembly and recreation that a university makes possible, challenged long-established habits of thought and behaviour. And when young provincials educated in Ayacucho's capital returned to their homes, they questioned old hierarchies and habits. The reopening of the university thus opened an inch of social mobility, and generated miles of expectation. As the novelist and long-term admirer of China Oswaldo Reynoso recalled: 'In an area of deep economic divisions, for the first time the children of landowners and professionals shared classrooms with peasants; they drank beer together, they got to know each other. This drove a revolutionary fervor in Ayacucho.'[28] Between the 1960s and '70s, the university helped turn the region into a political hothouse.

After Guzmán joined the university staff, he quickly made an intellectual impact. Schooling first-year students in Marxist materialism, he soon acquired a committed band of disciples – just as Rivas had done in Arequipa. They nicknamed their teacher 'Shampoo'. 'He washed your brains,' remembered one student, 'he cleaned your thoughts when confused; he clarified problems, he had an answer for everything.' 'He cultivated uncertainty and mystery around him,' recalled another. 'For his supporters, whatever he said was the last word on any subject. He made them so optimistic, so self-confident. That self-confidence is what I remember most about a friend who was later killed in the jungle by the army.' Intolerant of dissent, Guzmán was 'a fanatic who had the power to fanaticize others'.[29] Anyone who dallied with other political views was ostracised from the group. One of his disciples deliberately crossed the road to spit in the face of another university professor who had been spotted associating with two of Guzmán's political rivals.[30]

Young Peruvians – especially first-generation, provincial-university students – were vulnerable to dogmatism in the 1960s and '70s: they were avid for theories but not for thinking critically about them. Uneasy in their new modern, urban surroundings, these undergraduates sought clear answers, and found them in an abundance of textbooks – originally published in Stalinist Russia and circulating widely in Peruvian universities – that taught them the Marxist-Leninist world view. They learned about the authoritarian transformation of society through revolution and the wisdom of the single-party system. These books, recalled one lecturer, became 'a sort of shortcut toward modernity ... the key for the substantial and positive transformation of the world'. 'Can you imagine what that means to a twenty-five-year-old kid?' asked one anthropology graduate looking back at that time. 'It was to learn to handle a secret language, an abracadabra that let me open all the sesames.' China's hispanophone publicity apparatus also reached a receptive audience. Beijing's key generator of 'external propaganda', the Foreign Languages Press, scattered across Peru the *Works of Mao* and colourful magazines, their glazed pages advertising 'a peasant-centred version of revolution for semifeudal countries'.[31] Radio Peking broadcast the wonders of Mao's revolution not only in Spanish, but also in two indigenous languages, Quechua and Aymara.[32]

Luis Kawata Makabe, teaching natural sciences at the university in Ayacucho in the 1970s and for a time Guzmán's closest lieutenant (he declared that as long as a student knew the Four Principles of Mao, they would pass), had perfected a two-hour pitch to potential new recruits to Guzmán's clique. Entitled 'Matter and Movement', it ranged from the creation of the universe to contemporary Peruvian society. He was also the group's resident guitarist, who – as a member of a band called the Red Angels – provided the music that announced Guzmán's imminent arrival at parties: 'He is coming, he is coming ...' Deeper into these soirées, the group would perform soupier romantic classics: 'Kiss me, kiss me hard, as if tonight is the last time'.[33]

What distinguished Guzmán from the average cultish professor, and what gave him his uncompromising ideology and method, was his encounter with Maoism in the early 1960s. He began with the make-it-happen Mao – 'A Single Spark Can Start a Prairie Fire' was one of the first pieces he read – but it was the arid doctrinal arguments of the Sino-Soviet Split that fully won him over. From his earlier reading of Stalin, Guzmán had already learned to appreciate 'the transforming capacity of war'.[34] Now, devouring the militant polemics that the CCP hurled at the Soviet Communist Party, he became convinced of the global need for revolutionary violence. 'The seizure of power by armed force,' Guzmán underlined, 'the settlement of the issue by war, is the central task and the highest form of revolution.'[35] Guzmán shared with his fellow Latin American revolutionary Che Guevara a worship of armed struggle; but unlike Che – whom he dismissed as a 'chorus girl'[36] – he also venerated (in increasingly abstract terms) 'the masses' and the prospect of grass-roots organisational work.[37] In 1964, when the Peruvian Communist Party (PCP) split into pro-Soviet and pro-Chinese camps, Guzmán went with the latter, which renamed itself PCP-Bandera Roja (Red Flag).

In 1965, Guzmán travelled to China to see the 'seat of Chairman Mao ... the centre of world proletarian revolution' for himself. In comparison with the treatment received by Juan – the two men may have crossed paths or narrowly missed each other, as both trained in Nanjing – Guzmán's reception was only three-star. There was no meeting with Mao, only opportunities to glimpse him from afar at a reception or rally. Still, the impact was huge. Almost fifty years later, writing from the most secure cell in the most secure prison in Peru, Guzmán remembered the visit in almost romantic language: 'it was one of the most transcendental and unforgettable experiences of my life'.[38] Amid the doctrinaire prose of Guzmán's autobiography, his account of China stands out for its emotional intoxication:

> factories, people's communes, barracks, shopping centres, universities, schools, hospitals and clinics, art studios and shows; squares and streets, boiling tumults of energy overflowing with optimism ... politics in command ... building the new society, socialism, laying the founda- tions for future communism ... Beijing, historic and legendary Tiananmen Square: the monumental gate of heavy, dark red and Chairman Mao's imposing portrait, the Museum of the Revolution, the Great Hall of the People ... the Great Helmsman's own calligraphy in golden letters ... the immense sea of masses, Marx, Engels, Lenin, Stalin and President Mao guiding the fight; forests of red flags with hammers and sickles, banners, slogans; workers, peasants, soldiers, women, young people, the Chinese people, a million-strong rally

roaring 'Down with Yankee imperialism!' ... the East is Red, songs
and dances reviving the long, massive struggle of the revolution ...
Thirty years have passed, what can I say: only that I owe so much ...
to President Mao Zedong and to Maoism ... I can never repay this
debt. It served me in what I came to do later.[39]

China taught him 'masterful lessons ... in the highest school of
Marxism the world has ever seen': in underground party work, and
the intimate relationship between politics and violence. 'When we
were handling delicate chemicals they urged us to always keep our
ideology first and foremost, because that would enable us to do
anything.' He graduated from this explosives course with a sense of
superhuman power: 'they told us that anything can explode ... we
picked up a pen and it blew up, and when we took a seat it blew up,
too ... anything could be blown up if you figured out how to do
it ... That school contributed greatly to my ... appreciation for
Chairman Mao Tse-tung.'[40]

The debt was more than ideological. Until 1967, Mao's China
funnelled money and perhaps weapons to Bandera Roja for training
in different parts of Peru. The Chinese Communists funded a ragtag
of Latin American leftists – sometimes with extraordinary casualness.
A Chinese diplomat standing outside the Peruvian embassy once
accosted a member of another militant left-wing group – an Indian
from north Peru – when he was passing by the embassy. Mistaking
him for a Peruvian Chinese, the diplomat immediately offered to
support his cause, training dozens of militants for months at a time;
the group launched a guerrilla insurgency against the state in 1965.[41]

In 1967, Guzmán paid a second visit to China (he may have also
returned in 1975, in which case he could have encountered Pol Pot –
the Peruvian later dismissed the Cambodian as a 'pseudo-Marxist').
Although he was not successful in his primary mission – to persuade
the Chinese to reinstate their financial aid to Bandera Roja, which
had been recently cut off – he would return speaking ever more
fluent Maoism: 'whoever has not carried out investigation does not
have the right to speak'; 'he who does not fear being torn into pieces
can pull the emperor from his horse'; 'power comes from the barrel
of a gun'; 'the correctness or incorrectness of the political line
decides all'. He emphasised the need to apply Mao's idea of

'two-line struggle' to conquer revisionism within the revolution, and the status of Latin America as a 'zone of revolutionary storm'.[42] Above all, he had experienced the Cultural Revolution as 'the greatest mass movement in history ... the highest summit of the world proletarian revolution ... crushing the capitalist roaders in the Party'. Schooled by China, his world view became increasingly Manichaean: on the one side were the 'brave masses'; on the other 'sinister imperialists' and 'sewer rat revisionists'.[43] He witnessed large-scale purges of erroneous books and people; he began to idolise Mao as 'the third stage' of Marxism. In China, he further concluded, 'the main form of struggle is war; the main form of organization, the army ... Without a people's army, the people have nothing.'[44]

Those who specialise in the analysis of Shining Path – Sendero Luminoso in Spanish – have founded their own discipline: senderology. One such senderologist observed that Guzmán 'flash-froze' constituent elements of the Cultural Revolution for his own insurgency: in particular, the veneration of permanent revolutionary violence against political enemies and the destruction of all political rivals (including non-state welfare organisations, or community collective farms).[45] He yearned to create for himself 'a disciplined party of young radicals, armed with the words contained in the Little Red Book – simple ideas destined to rock society'.[46] Guzmán and his future followers would also learn to live and breathe Mao's simplistic theory of contradiction: the idea that history is driven forward by conflict between binary forces. They would combine materialist Marxism with pseudo-Christian religious zeal; glorification of the masses with sanguinary sacrifice of the masses; the cult of Professor Abimael Guzmán with the extirpation of rank-and-file individualism.

Guzmán's encounters with China gave him tremendous prestige within his China-oriented faction, and galvanised his political militancy back in Peru. In 1970, he founded a new groupuscule – the Communist Party of Peru – Shining Path. The reference to a *sendero luminoso* was taken from the writings of José Carlos Mariátegui, the founder of the PCP, but reflected as well imagery popular during China's Cultural Revolution. Guzmán took a new *nom de guerre*: Gonzalo. At the new party's inception, Shining Path had fifty-one members, twelve of them in Ayacucho.[47]

If Guzmán-Gonzalo had been the only Mao-phile in his intellectual community, the impact of these ideas would have been limited. But by the start of the 1970s, Mao fever had set in among his peers. A quarter of the professors at Guzmán's university in Ayacucho had travelled to China, including Antonio Díaz Martínez, who published in 1977 a book about China's agrarian revolution – based on a 1974 visit – that idealised the commune system and the Cultural Revolution's rhetoric of leadership by the masses. His courses had only one text-book: the Little Red Book.[48] This hagiography of the Maoist agrarian model – published as China abandoned it – helped convince Shining Path activists that they were fighting a just war for a peasant-run paradise on earth: 'countryside as centre, city as complement'.[49] The book's authoritative academic veneer sowed sympathy for the Maoist model in wider intellectual circles. Guzmán, his colleagues and his disciples liberally distributed *Peking Review* for free and blasted audiences with film reels of model operas and Red Guard rallies at Tiananmen Square.[50] Two bemused Dutch agronomists in Ayacucho in the late 1970s recalled the aura of quaint normality that enveloped the burgeoning Shining Path. Non-party classmates and professors would josh followers of Sendero: what were they doing at the university when their ideology prescribed People's War in the countryside?[51]

For ten years, Guzmán planned and prepared for the Armed Struggle, around the nucleus of his university. (The terms '*terroristas*' and '*universitarios*' would later be used interchangeably to refer to senderistas – Shining Path militants.)[52] A neglectful, even absent state presence in rural areas of the *departamento* made it possible, and Guzmán was well placed to indoctrinate at multiple levels of the educational system. In the 1960s, he was in charge of the under-graduate Core Curriculum – which was presumably how the Little Red Book ended up as a set text for anthropology and philosophy courses.[53] In 1963, he set up a high school for training rural teachers through the region. Later, he became director of university personnel, which enabled him to fill vacancies with his supporters, as well as control the disbursement of student aid and scholarships. Pro–Shining Path professors turned their undergraduate teaching groups into Maoist think tanks, guiding students to research theses about the socio-political power structures of rural communities in the area, which always seemed to end with Maoist analyses of 'rural bourgeoisie, rich peasants, middle income and poor peasants'.[54] The easy, militant solutions to Peruvian ills preached by Guzmán appealed to young provincials frustrated by the lack of career opportunities for the newly educated. While the reopening of the university had widened access to higher education, it had not been accompanied by an expansion of graduate employment opportunities. A young provincial would typically undergo great financial hardship and intellectual effort to receive a degree, then discover on graduation that teaching back in the villages they had worked so hard to escape was the best professional option open to them. On graduating, Guzmán's disciples therefore scattered in a proselytising network across the sierra, plotting to use their remote communities as springboards for the revolution. 'They were young, thin, serious, introverted,' observed Gustavo Gorriti, the Peruvian journalist who tailed the Shining Path story between the 1980s and '90s, 'in general from poor families ... obedient children and siblings, neat, quiet, hard-working ... To see them wrapped in an aura of explosions and inexplicable ferocity was only the beginning of a much bigger surprise for many families.'[55] Guzmán's first wife, Augusta la Torre, was a tremendous asset: beautiful, ardent – skilled at talking poor sierrans into the organisation.[56] In 1988, she would die in mysterious circumstances – it seems most likely that she developed doubts about the revolution she had helped start and committed suicide to protect her husband's cause from her own wavering.

Senderista high school teachers would first organise other teachers, who in turn would organise students. 'Viva Peking!' one young teacher – only a high school graduate – scrawled over walls in his sierra village in scarlet letters in 1976.[57] This network also fed back crucial data to the party centre in Ayacucho city: on topography, community power structures, peasant aspirations, the names and profiles of local bigwigs whom the armed struggle would eliminate. It was through the exploration of local geography and society by his former student disciples that Guzmán was able to select Chuschi – an area where traditional patterns of deference were already weak – for the first action of the armed struggle.

The Shining Path was notable for its ability to attract some of the brightest and the best. A notable early recruit was Elena Iparraguirre. Born in 1948 into a comfortable, loving, middle-class family a little south of Lima, she received a fine education, studying for two

master's – one in Lima, the other in Paris. By the 1970s, she was happily
married to a chemical engineer, with whom she had two daughters.
But there was also an extremist side to her character, which she traced
back to the religiosity instilled in her during her convent-school girl-
hood. 'I remembered that the Christian martyrs were eaten by lions
in the circus without denying their faith,' she reminisced in 2012. 'In
some way my own story was inspired by these images. I learned from
the martyrs to tolerate everything to preserve purity.' After joining the
Shining Path in the early 1970s, Iparraguirre first encountered Guzmán
in 1973 in a class on Communist Party history at a cadre school. He
won her over, she recalled, because he made her 'feel chosen' as part of
a special elite. 'It didn't matter to him that we were a small group of
young people – mainly young women. He could have been in the
Sorbonne. He spoke for hours, explaining everything in detail.'
Iparraguirre was seduced both politically and physically by Guzmán
(at some point in the 1980s, she became his consort); in the late 1970s,
she deserted her husband and children and disappeared underground.
Her talent for organisation and analysis enabled her to rise quickly to
a position of leadership.[58]

Another recruit was one Eduardo Mata Mendoza, a former
hospital director who abandoned his post to disappear into the
countryside, dressed in poncho, sandals and hat. He and his wife
gave away their child, just a few months old, to devote themselves
to the revolution. The social standing of such early recruits not only
won the movement prestige, but also facilitated its survival: when
Mata was arrested shortly after going underground, a team of his
medical peers successfully campaigned for his release.[59] Other recruits
were far more politically naive: impressionable young men and
women from the countryside. Guzmán 'fanaticised all those students',
recalled one resident of rural eastern Ayacucho.[60] 'Sendero selected
the smartest students to indoctrinate,' recalled a headteacher at
Vilcashuaman, an ancient Incan settlement in the region, 'the leaders
who could best influence their classmates.' They were then dispatched
to the countryside, where they took over the curriculum, teaching
children and teenagers to chant 'Mao, Mao'.[61] 'They said,' remembered one militant, 'that Ayacucho was going to be a liberated zone
by 1985 ... an independent republic ... It was a way of getting the
young people's hopes up, no?'[62] The prospect of weapons could be

a big draw, another young man recollected: Shining Path militants recruited '[a]dolescents who were desperate to learn about weapons, for example a machine gun. For them to use dynamite was a big deal ... They blew [things up] just for the sake of blowing [them] up. Nothing more.'[63]

The life story of 'Nicario' suggests the casualness of some young recruits' motives for joining up. After leaving his rural secondary school in Ayacucho, he drifted into casual labour processing coca leaves. A handful of Shining Path cadres – students, all of them – arrived in his community in 1981. One of them invited him to a meeting. 'I accepted easily ... because at the time ... Shining Path was quite active, with assaults ... So us young people started to talk about that. We already wanted to attend ... [The] military commander directing the assembly ... came with his machine gun ... He introduced himself in a deep voice: "Yes, *compañero* [comrade]." Just like that, with his boots and everything ... He told [us] to come to a certain place – "we'll be waiting for you there."' For Nicario, that was all it took: a machine gun, boots and a deep voice. Once he had joined, it was his duty to bring along to subsequent meetings 'one or two trusted friends, so that the group grew'. And so Nicario became a full-timer in operations that destroyed experimental farms and executed those 'who had been talking bad'.[64]

On 9 September 1976, Mao died in Beijing. Later that month, Guzmán dispatched a worshipful message of condolence to the Chinese embassy in Lima ('Eternal glory to Chairman Mao Zedong!') and honoured his hero at a memorial meeting.[65] It was his last public appearance for sixteen years. Far from discouraging him, Mao's death convinced him that the time had come to unleash a People's War in Peru – to keep flying the flag of Maoism. 'It was now the moment to defend the revolution,' Guzmán would later observe. 'We began [our armed struggle] to defend the revolution.'[66]

At 2 a.m. on 17 May 1980, five hooded men – four students and their leader, a teacher – broke into the voter registration office in the market town of Chuschi, tied up the registrar, and burned the local tools of democracy: the voter registry and ballot boxes. It was the first salvo in the Shining Path's war on Peru, the Beginning of the Armed Struggle (BAS; Iniciación de la Lucha Armada, ILA).[67]

In the preceding three months the Shining Path had prepared for military struggle through an intensive series of meetings to establish the 'correct' political line within an iron framework of quotations by Mao, and to 'rectify' (that is, purge) those who opposed Guzmán. Admittedly, Mao was not the sole influence on Guzmán's bookishly violent revolution. An obsessive reader, he declaimed passages from *Julius Caesar* and *Macbeth* to his disciples to teach them the finer points of conspiracy and treason. Probably for its account of the power of ideology, he distributed excerpts from Washington Irving's justly neglected *The Life of Mahomet*: it likened Muslims to 'the tempests which sweep the earth and sea, wrecking tall ships and rending lofty towers'. Aeschylus' *Prometheus Bound* provided an instructive 'example of the capacity of unyielding rebellion'. There were less literary texts too: Stalin's scorched-earth speech to the Soviet people in the days following the Nazi invasion in 1941 offered a premonition of what Shining Path, and the state's brutal response, would do to Peru. Guzmán would directly import this uncompromising model of warfare, in which any human cost was justified in pursuit of the cause. But the strategy came from Mao: protracted warfare, surrounding the cities from the countryside and, most important of all, revolutionary voluntarism – through sheer force of will, the masses under the leadership of a disciplined Maoist party could defeat the state.

Guzmán's blood-soaked Maoism shines through this excerpt of his oratory, worth quoting at length for its queasy, millenarian combination of the abstract and the visceral.

> Let us open the future, actions are the key, power the objective ... history demands it, class exhorts it, the people have prepared for it and want it; we must do our duty and we shall. We are the initiators ... we begin the strategic offensive for world revolution, the next fifty years will see imperialism's dominions swept away along with all exploiters ... the people's war will grow every day until the old order is pulled down ... President Mao stated: 'the storm approaches, the wind roars in the tower' ... revolution's invincible flames will grow until they turn to lead, to steel, and, from the din of battle and its unquenchable fire will come the light, from darkness will come radiance and there will be a new world ... The people rear up, arm themselves, and rise in revolution to put the noose around the neck of

imperialism and the reactionaries, seizing them by the throat and garroting them ... The flesh of the reactionaries will rot away, converted into ragged threads, and this black filth will sink into the mud; that which remains will be burned and the ashes scattered by the earth's winds ... We will convert the black fire into red and the red into light ... Comrades, we are reborn! We have learned to manipulate history, law, contradictions ... The progress of the world, the country, and the party are pages in the same book ... Marxist–Leninist–Mao Tse-tung thought, the international proletariat, and the peoples of the world, the working class, and the people of the nation, the party with its committees, cells and leaders: all of the great actions of the centuries have culminated here at this moment in history. The promise unfolds, the future unfurls: BAS 80.

The audience intoned in response: 'Glory to Marxist–Leninist–Mao Tse-tung Thought! ... Led by Comrade Gonzalo, we begin armed struggle!'[68]

On Christmas Eve 1980, the first blood was shed in an attack led by Dr Mata: a sixty-year-old farmer and his nineteen-year-old hired help were assassinated by a guerrilla squad at their ranch in Ayacucho. More than propaganda or organisational work, guerrilla terror now became the cornerstone of Shining Path strategy. It intensified the glorification of violence: the killing swiftly became industrial, based on the principle of a 'quota' needing to die before the revolutionary utopia could be created. Guzmán claimed that Mao had inspired this call for bloodshed: 'Marx, Lenin, and principally Mao Zedong have armed us. They have taught us about the quota and what it means to annihilate in order to preserve.'[69]

The aim – to provoke the state into indiscriminate retaliation and for the people in turn to rebel against government brutality – was crude but, as it turned out, cruelly effective. The more excessive the state response, the more discredited Peru's democracy, and the more disillusioned the populace, would become. Guzmán was prepared to sustain horrendous losses. He told his cadres frankly that they would have to 'cross the river of blood': that 'many party militants would die ... and they would die in the worst possible ways. Their families would be destroyed ... there was very little in Peru's history that prepared it to confront the level of violence that would eventually be unleashed. Dozens, hundreds of thousands of dead.'[70] The revolution envisioned by Shining Path resembled ever more closely a compact of death. Shining Path melded Mao's optimistic 'a single spark can light a prairie fire' with a much darker, quasi-religious concept of purification in rivers of blood. It fostered a spirit of reckless confrontation.[71]

By spring 1983, Shining Path had overrun the *departamento* of Ayacucho: teenagers proselytised in schools; students sang senderista anthems rather than the national one; farmers had to gain exit visas from guerrilla leaders to leave their villages. The party executed anyone they deemed collaborators with the state: this could even include serving the police food in a restaurant.[72] The victims were often ordinary: post office workers, mine guards, cooks, farmers, and members of their families – any individual who did not share Shining Path's worship of violence.[73] Party discipline was similarly brutal. Petty misdemeanours – theft of a can of tuna fish and three crackers, falling asleep on sentry duty – were punished by strangulation. 'If I touch you on the shoulder,' one cadre told his division, 'you are the one who can no longer exist within the Party.' 'Forgiveness did not exist,' recalled one of the foot soldiers. 'Loyalty or death.'[74]

Yet it is impossible to understand the success of Shining Path without considering the ineptitude of the Peruvian state's response during the first half of the 1980s, when the insurgency was taking root. Although the Shining Path fighters were military novices when they started, they were assisted by the incompetence and grotesque malpractices (human rights abuses, corruption) of the police. (According to one critic, officers were too pot-bellied to climb hills in pursuit of *guerrilleros*.)[75] At the start of the war, Peru's government should have been riding high on popular support. In 1980, democracy was returning peacefully after twelve years of military dictatorship. In reality, however, it was hampered by basic political and administrative failings. For example, when the military dictatorship handed over to the new democratic administration, the previous government's mountain of information on subversive groups – including Shining Path – mysteriously disappeared. Thus Peruvian democracy entered the new decade blind to subversion from within, with its intelligence service severely under-resourced (even its fleet of official cars had been smashed up by the son of its director – an aspiring but untalented racing driver). Army intelligence knew of, but had been careless about, Shining Path preparations for at least three years before the Beginning of the Armed Struggle in 1980. In one of the most popular beach resorts north of the capital, one group had openly carried out firearms practice in the dunes.[76]

When the state eventually woke up to the threat, it responded with indiscriminate viciousness, fuelled by racism and misogyny rife through the police and army. Democracy soon faltered. In 1982, the Peruvian government placed Ayacucho in a state of emergency, and authorised the army to unleash scorched-earth tactics to eliminate the insurgency.[77] The minister of defence, Luis Cisneros Vizquerra, lifted his strategy from Argentina's Dirty War (nine years of 'state terrorism' between 1974 and 1983, in which the government destroyed political opposition through tens of thousands of murders and disappearances). 'If we kill a hundred people and there is one subversive among them, then it will have been worthwhile.'[78] As they route-marched across the sierra, soldiers sang: 'Shitty terrorists, we will come into your little houses, we will eat your little guts, we will drink your little blood, we will cut off your little heads, we will stab your little eyes, we will crush your little ankles.'[79] This filthy war generated an Andean Vietnam. One army educational video shows a muscular, bare-chested soldier in camouflage trousers at the 'Training Camp of the Dagger'. Roaring like a beast, he charges towards a trough in front of the camera. There, after stabbing a machete into the ground, still roaring, he kneels and douses himself in the dark red, viscous liquid in the trough. Officers were initiated by washing in the blood of dogs they had stabbed to death, or by dining on oatmeal mixed with gunpowder.[80]

One sergeant casually tortured an Indian truck driver, then decided to silence him by tying him to a tree and breaking his neck. 'He didn't die,' recalled one of his comrades. '[A] couple of shots finished the *cholo* [a derogatory term for darker-skinned people from the countryside]. Well, and where were we going to stash him? Any place is fine, so what, the puna [high-altitude desert] is so huge.' Rape was a ubiquitous weapon of war. 'One day, they gave us a *chola* to waste,' a naval sergeant reminisced. 'Great, so where can we do it? We ... found a

deserted house. It had all the conveniences, furniture, a television . . .
one by one we gave it to the poor *chola* . . . Here one learns to be a
shit . . . the boys played her like a yo-yo. Then we wasted her.'[81]
Practically anyone speaking Quechua was suspected of terrorism. In
one massacre alone, at Accomarca in Ayacucho, seventy-one civilians
died, including twenty-three children. Between 1988 and 1991, Peru
had the highest number of 'disappeared' of any state in the world.[82]

Shining Path conducted its campaign with greater care, though
with comparable brutality. Despite the unhinged millenarianism of
Guzmán's rhetoric, in down-to-earth military terms the beginning of
the insurrection was marked by diligent creation of organisational
structures in north, south and central Peru. A good student of Mao,
Guzmán was devoted to the practicalities of guerrilla warfare and to
the strict discipline set down in the Chinese People's Liberation Army's
'Three Rules' and 'Eight Points of Attention'.[83] 'His undoubtedly superior schematic intellect', analysed Gorriti, who closely followed
Guzmán's thinking throughout the 1980s, 'defined the intermediate
objectives along the way and then marked out a detailed route to each
one – segment by segment, step by step. In the history of guerrilla
rebellions, in few if any did sheer resolve, backed by exhaustive planning, play such a preponderant role.'[84] Shining Path meticulously
constructed its military machine. At the bottom were local guerrillas
and party committees who could provide information and control
communities. Above this operated a regional force, roaming across
several provinces. The best fighters from this middle force formed the
national insurgent army, capable of set-piece military operations.[85]
The organisation armed its militants through extensive raids on mines,
which yielded case after case of dynamite, kilometres of fuses, myriads
of blasting caps. The whole process was unspectacular: simply slow,
persistent and incessant. Shining Path began their insurgency with
little more than sticks of dynamite on slingshots. But their combination of sparse, primitive firepower and fierce Maoist self-belief was
remarkably effective against the Peruvian state, whose presence
was scant or non-existent around Ayacucho (police had been withdrawing since the late 1970s, in the face of a string of muscular
youth protests about educational issues). In the early days of the
insurgency, while Ronald Reagan dreamed of a Star Wars programme
of nuclear armament, Mao's dictum that people were more important

than weapons was borne out – senderistas were simply more determined and organised than their better-armed state counterparts.

The storming of a police station at Tambo in south-west Peru – Guzmán's home town – in October 1981 showcased Shining Path field strategy. The group took advantage of the vulnerability of the station: it was understaffed, and its doors were open to the local population. Almost thirty guerrillas, armed with four machine guns, a few revolvers and a bottle of acid, killed three of the policemen and civilians (including a one-year-old boy) in the station, and wounded another four, before melting away into the dusk. Only one member of the raiding party was slightly injured. The guerrillas were inexperienced and not heavily armed – but unsqueamish about collateral damage.[86]

The state fell into the trap that Guzmán had set for it. Shining Path calculated that by provoking murderous retaliation, it would gain legitimacy, sympathy and recruits. That calculation initially proved correct. While tens of thousands died or fled the violence, significant numbers were driven to join Shining Path. From her own prison cell in 2010, Elena Iparraguirre admitted that the leadership had decided in June 1986 to sacrifice its prisoners in Lima jails by telling them to start a riot that could only end in a massacre. The strategy was to 'induce genocide', and to have Alan García – the popular, left-leaning young president – 'stain his hands with blood'.[87] The gamble worked out. After negotiations between the rioting prisoners and the government failed, García – dragged into emergency cabinet meetings while Lima was hosting a congress of the Socialist International – authorised the military to retake the prisons by force. Terrible violence ensued: at least 226 inmates lost their lives, of whom about 100 were Shining Path prisoners murdered in cold-blooded, extrajudicial executions. The insurgency now attracted a flood of recruits – many of them friends and relatives of the dead.

Despite the caring rhetoric of individuals like Iparraguirre and Guzmán towards the suffering 'masses', the ideologues of Shining Path held a confused, condescending set of attitudes to the peasantry. They identified them as victims of the white-dominated state, as communities in need of rescuing from the 'mechanistic and utilitarian Western culture that colonises them'; but farmers were also guilty of a backwardness that needed to be eradicated. Shining Path was marked, moreover, by a sense of elite intellectual infallibility. Its leaders confidently saw themselves as 'intellectuals who possessed a proletarian class consciousness' and therefore the right to command Peru's rural proletariat.[88] (The Shining Path leadership itself was devoid of proletarians.)[89] If peasants rejected Shining Path authority – as they did in 1983 in Uchuraccay, central Ayacucho, where they killed seven senderistas in retaliation for the murder of locals – the response was swift and brutal. 'We have swept out those *chutos* [pricks] made of shit,' declared one cadre after a massacre in the village killed 135 out of 470 inhabitants.[90] Looking back on another massacre at Lucanamarca, also in central Ayacucho, in which eighty peasants were hacked, burned or shot to death, Guzmán coolly mused in 1988: 'Excesses can be committed ... the principal thing was to make them understand that we were a hard bone to chew, and that we were ready to do anything, anything.'[91]

Shining Path was never an egalitarian peasant war, therefore, but rather the schema of educated urban intellectuals, who reproduced in their own structures of command and position the racial, class-based hierarchies that they pledged to overthrow: pale-skinned, hispanophone, educated elites on top; darker-skinned, impoverished Quechuaspeakers at the bottom. This carelessness towards 'the masses' is clear from the ways that Shining Path incriminated civilian populations in their violence. As they 'merged' with local communities, they exposed them to punitive violence from the army. They would regularly oblige villagers to witness and sometimes carry out torture and execution of 'bad elements', to implicate them in the bloodshed. Maoist tactics dictated that 'when the enemy advances, we retreat'; if the army approached, senderistas fled, leaving local populations to suffer the consequences. Villagers recalled that they felt like 'clothes hung out to dry, flopping helplessly in the wind. They had no protection from the authorities in the town or the police ... if the senderistas wanted to get you, you were buggered.'[92]

This ruthless violence established Shining Path in, but then alienated it from, communities. 'Sendero started out giving dreams, but ended up delivering a nightmare,' commented one witness.[93] Children were forced to become guerrillas: 'against their will, whether they wanted to or not, they showed them arms, knives, spears; if you don't accept it, you'll die'.[94] They understood little of Mao: a few pre-breakfast readings from philosophy essays, nothing more. The party at first tried to ban fiestas, but then realised that the booze made villagers indiscreet in identifying informers: 'drink made them reveal what they had told the military. Right there we would take them away, and kill them later that night. No one witnessed this, only the dark canyons.'[95] Girls aged twelve or thirteen were turned, effectively, into comfort-women or child-bearing slaves – they were conscripted to bases, from where they returned pregnant. Shining Path 'have deceived us', cried anguished mothers.[96] In some base areas, voluntary recruits coexisted with conscripts whose families had been annihilated in senderista attacks.[97] Deserters and dissenters suffered cruel public execution; in a massacre of Amazonian tribal captives in November 1989, one of the prisoners was crucified.[98] Meanwhile, Shining Path's definition of political crimes broadened, until even looking sad could be punishable by death. The old and the sick were vulnerable to liquidation, condemned as a 'parasitic burden' (recalling the Khmer Rouge saying 'to spare you, no gain; to kill you, no loss'). The army would later discover mass graves of Shining Path victims – more than a thousand in one pit alone.[99] By the mid-1980s, terrified locals on the Andean sierra began to dub senderistas ñaqa, Quechua for a species of malevolent, flesh-eating spirit.[100]

In the early 1990s, some 3,500 villages across the areas of Peru most affected by Shining Path activity had organised self-defence patrols (rondas campesinas) against the guerrillas. The state and army now signalled that they no longer regarded peasants as enemy collaborators with the Shining Path, but rather as valued allies. In 1991, the army handed out to Andean farmers inhabiting the conflict zone 10,000 Winchester Model 1300 shotguns – 'blessed by a priest as if for a Holy War'.[101] The Peruvian state had broken a major taboo, in place since the Spanish Conquest, against permitting Indians to possess military hardware comparable with that possessed by their post-Incan rulers. In an attempt to win hearts and minds, army marching songs evolved from 'terrorist / if I find you / I will eat your head' to 'Good day / The soldiers of Peru salute you'.[102] The rifles distributed to farmers replaced more primitive weaponry: machetes, spears, and hand grenades fashioned out of evaporated-milk tins and nails. In 1990, militant local peasants in central Peru stoned thirteen suspected guerrillas to death, then delivered a sack full of their severed heads to the local army HQ.[103]

★

When trying to account for the appeal of Sendero, it is worth pausing briefly to consider the apparent attraction of the movement to women – for women played a greater, more senior role in the Shining Path than in any other Communist insurgency in the world. From 1990, two out of the five on the politburo, and eight out of the nineteen-strong Central Committee were women. Lower down the ranks, 40 per cent of militants were thought to be women. This high level of female participation was conspicuous in the context of Latin American left-wing guerrilla groups, which had previously tended hard towards Machismo-Leninismo. One police training manual was openly terrified of these women, who were often given the job of delivering the *coup de grâce* to police and soldiers in armed engagements: 'They are more determined and dangerous than the men, they behave in an absolutist way, and they consider themselves capable of carrying out any mission ... they are extremely severe ... they exploit and manipulate ... they are impulsive and risk-taking.'[104] Enraptured foreign visitors in the 1960s and '70s often acclaimed Mao's China – where 'women can hold up half the sky' – as a starry example of socialist feminism at work. Was there a feminist promise in Peruvian Maoism that drew so many women into Shining Path?

If it was the social inequities of the sierra that helped attract recruits to Shining Path, women constituted one of the most underprivileged groups in the region, and were the lowest of the low when it came to access to education and opportunities. 'My sheep and my cow are worth more than you!' an Ayacuchan woman told her granddaughter in the 1950s.[105] Some women – especially those from more humble, racially marginalised backgrounds – clearly joined up because they could advance more quickly than in conventional Peruvian society. Flor, aged nineteen, had one wish: to find a job as a bilingual secretary at an American oil company. When she was rejected because of her dark skin, she joined Shining Path and within a year had been promoted to a leadership position.[106] In her recollections from prison, Elena Iparraguirre claimed that the guerrilla units were havens of gender equality – including in sexual promiscuity. 'The women were commanders, and did the same as the men.'[107]

But in practice Shining Path's was a deeply limited version of feminism: unthinking submission to party diktat was always more important than female empowerment. And the ultimate authority of the party rested of course with a man: Abimael Guzmán, who surrounded himself with a nurturing, protective *cúpula* (dome) of female minders. In 1990, in the greatest intelligence coup that the security services had so far enjoyed, a video of Guzmán with his closest subordinates was discovered in a raided safe house. It showed 'President Gonzalo' at ease with his female retainers – dancing Zorba the Greek style, taking photographs, arms touching – while the other men nervously kept a greater distance. One historian who interviewed many of the high-ranking women in Shining Path from their prison cells described them as 'very strong and determined' but observed 'a devotion and respect for Guzmán that came close to mystic passion'. Even after twenty years in prison, senderista women would be sure to cook Guzmán's favourite dishes before the visit of their legal counsel, then charge the lawyer with delivering the treats to their 'red god'.[108]

There was a religiosity to Shining Path Maoism that was arguably not present to the same degree in China, except at the most febrile heights of the Mao cult. The Shining Path appropriated for Guzmán elements of the Cultural Revolution's visual deification of Mao. In posters, Guzmán was a handsome, professorial superhero (in glasses and a dark suit) outlined in golden effulgence, one muscular arm waving a red flag, the other clutching a Red Book, standing over throngs of dark-skinned Andean masses.[109] (The intelligence services were less deferential to Guzmán's physique, nicknaming him *el Cachetón* – cherry-cheeks – for the pouchiness that his face developed while in hiding.) Senderistas had to sign away control over their lives with a 'letter of submission' to 'President Gonzalo': 'I express my greeting and full and unconditional submission to the greatest Marxist– Leninist–Maoist on Earth, our beloved and respected President Gonzalo, chief and guide of the Peruvian revolution and of the world proletarian revolution ... I give you my greeting and full and uncon- ditional submission to the scientific ideology of the proletariat: Marxism–Leninism–Maoist and Gonzalo Thought, especially Gonzalo Thought, all-powerful and infallible ideology that illuminates our path and arms our minds.'[110] The party organisation deliberately kept the core of card-carrying militants small – it never expanded beyond about

2,700 – in an attempt to maintain the solidarity of a close-knit religious community of the chosen few; recall Elena Iparraguirre's identification with the persecuted early Christians.[111]

Although Guzmán claimed never to have had an interest in religion, his rhetoric borrowed from the Bible as well as from Mao. Guzmán's vision of Shining Path's place in history was Genesis Mao-style: 'Our people were enlightened by a more intense light, Marxism–Leninism–Mao Zedong Thought; at first we were blinded at that first breaking of endless light, light and nothing more … The communists arose and the earth shook, and as the earth shook the comrades advanced … And so, the shadows began to roll back for good, the walls trembled and were breached; with their fists dawn opened, darkness became light … Their souls were joyful and their eyes shone with the light.' He had a fondness for pseudo-scientific Communist prophecy: 'A chapter will say: great effort was required, we shed our share of blood, and in difficult moments we buried our dead, dried our tears and continued battling … Such will be history: in this sense we are on the inevitable path toward communism, to arrive at full and absolute light. The blood of those who fell cries out: light, light, to communism we arrive! This will be written, this is what history will say … Nothing can stop the revolution, that is the law, that is destiny.'[112] Christian ideas of sin joined with Maoist self-criticism: no one – except Guzmán – was above suspicion of political impurity, or immune to public humiliation.[113] And like global Maoists the world over, the leaders of the Shining Path ignored in-depth analysis of and lived experience in the world's only Maoist state, China, between 1949 and 1976. No ranking member of Shining Path learned Chinese or had knowledge of China independent of Maoist propaganda.

The religious intensity of senderistas' beliefs helps make sense not only of the passionate commitment that made the insurgency such a formidable force, but also of the egregious errors of the movement. The correctness of Mao's and Guzmán's analyses could not be questioned – even though they bore little resemblance to contemporary Peru. In Shining Path writ, Peru was a semi-feudal, semi-colonial country, just as Mao had defined China in the 1940s. This ideological reading of Peruvian reality ('as Chairman Mao says') dictated one response alone: revolutionary violence. 'Since feudal oppression, not democracy, exists in our country, we have no Parliament or legality to use,' Guzmán declared; 'armed struggle and the creation of revolutionary support bases to feed it' were thus the only solution.[114]

Educated senderistas therefore liked to tell themselves that nothing had changed on the sierra for hundreds of years: that it remained a zone of passive slaves, under the imperious rule of gringo or mestizo hacienda-owners, awaiting liberation by the revolution. In reality, by the 1970s it already diverged from this stereotype. When the military government took power in 1968 – bundling the president, still in his pyjamas, into a plane and flying him out of the country at 2 a.m. – 2 per cent of Peru's 14 million inhabitants owned 90 per cent of its land. But the government's land reform programme enacted that year redistributed more than 8.6 million hectares of land to more than 370,000 families. Although the reform ultimately faltered through disorganisation and mismanagement, it transformed the realities of rural land ownership and serfdom: sharecropping was largely abolished after 1968 (by contrast, 30 per cent of China's land was owned by absentee landlords before 1949).[115] To use a Maoist turn of phrase, Peru's land reform – for all its failures – had dampened the prairie, so that it could no longer be lit by 'a single spark'.

In the sierra of the 1980s, there were peasants who now had something – a smallholding – to defend. Although there was much poverty and discontent at state neglect and corruption, this was not a situation of imminent revolution. Still, senderistas would arrive in communities and tell *campesinos* (farmers) to invade private estates, even though the big haciendas had already been broken up by the previous decade's land reform – Shining Path's first victim owned only sixty acres.[116] 'Does Shining Path want us to invade our neighbour's garden?' one puzzled woman asked.[117] Mao's semi-colonial diagnosis did not really fit either: despite ongoing US economic domination, since the late nineteenth century Peru had not suffered foreign invasion. In other important ways, too, Peru at the start of the 1980s was very different from China in the 1930s. Peru was democratic, two-thirds of its population lived in cities, and three-quarters of Peruvians were literate (compared with one-tenth for both those last two categories in China in 1950).[118] Electrical engineers, agronomists, anthropologists, foreign NGOs, civil society welfare activists were at work, striving to improve life in Peru. Maoist scripture said that the poorest peasants would be the backbone of the revolution, but in Peru these were Indians who had their own structures of authority, and some violently resisted the imposition of white or mestizo senderista rule over them.

In the pursuit of self-sufficiency, Shining Path tried to close communities' access to weekly markets. 'Where would we get our salt and matches?' one local asked matter-of-factly.[119] Shining Path, from the start, was no mass line, but rather a centralised, top-down model, in which local communities were both idealised and dictated to. In other words, Guzmán yearned for the 'blank page' so beloved of Mao, on which he could write beautiful, new things.* It was Guzmán's frustrated encounter with a Peruvian society that was far from blank that generated the atrocities of Shining Path. The objective was to destroy any alternatives to the party: thus they killed mayors and champions of slum welfare; they demolished rural development projects; they beheaded rival left-wing organisations. 'The key is to raze,' explained a party document. 'And to raze means to leave nothing behind.'[120]

The year 1992 was, in the words of Carlos Degregori, a former university colleague of Guzmán's who later became one of Peru's most informed senderologists, 'the worst year in the contemporary history of Peru'. The country was a cataclysmic state. Half the country's population and a third of its territory were under army control. Tens of thousands had already lost their lives and at the start of the decade, Shining Path had declared that 'the triumph of the revolution would cost a million deaths'. Lima was the Beirut of Latin America, shaken by car bombs, blinded by blackouts, petrified by the public assassinations of community leaders.[121]

The government looked to be on the run. One of the first acts of Alberto Fujimori – surprise winner of the 1990 presidential contest against Mario Vargas Llosa, the elite establishment candidate – was to summon the army commanders and tell them that Shining Path were on the point of taking Lima in a major offensive.[122] In and around the capital, the state began to resemble the losing side. Before and after the prison massacres of 1986, Sendero prisoner communities had

---

*   The Chinese, Mao believed, were 'poor and blank. A clean sheet of paper has no blotches and so the newest and most beautiful words can be written on it.'

created practically autonomous colonies within the city's jails. They ran spotlessly clean and well-ordered 'senderista wings', where they cooked their own food, held meetings and clinics, sang political songs (in Spanish and Chinese), performed plays (which included instructions on how to build car bombs) and Cultural Revolution–style dances, and freely shouted 'imperialism and reactionaries are paper tigers'.

They covered the walls with collectively painted technicolour murals of Guzmán. One group of inmates painted a quotation by Mao six metres off the ground. A visiting journalist asked them: 'If you can paint that high, why don't you escape?' 'We don't want to escape,' came the answer. 'We want to show our captors that they are dwarves. It drives them mad trying to work out how we did it.'[123]

In 1992, the Shining Path colony in a women's prison staged a performance for some visiting film-makers from Britain. Dozens of identically dressed – slim black trousers, khaki shirts, red kerchiefs – women marched and sang, in perfect unison, hymns to Chairman Gonzalo and to 'the great pilot who led the Great March and the Cultural Revolution, the shining light of Maoism in the East, built after a millennium of oppression and exploitation'. Such performances had a huge propaganda impact, within and without the prisons. Inside, they helped radicalise other inmates. Ironically, students who had been imprisoned by the state on unproven suspicion of supporting the insurrection only came under the Shining Path spell on encountering their indoctrination in jail. The outside world was impressed, too. 'They're very disciplined in the prisons,' mused some Limeño woodworkers. 'Maybe they're the people who could lead us to a better life.'[124] As in other parts of the Sendero organisation, political discipline in the prisons was watertight: anyone suspected of treachery was assaulted mentally and physically. A former leader who had fallen out with Guzmán was humiliated and isolated; on his release, he was a broken man.[125]

The root cause of the state's loss of sovereignty inside and outside the prisons was the general economic calamity driven by the exigencies of civil war. When, in the late 1980s, Sendero prisoners smashed the padlocks to individual cells, the state simply could not afford to replace them and prison authorities lost control over their captives. For inflation stood at 2,775 per cent in 1989; by 1990 it had risen to 7,650 per cent.[126] When Robin Kirk, an American journalist and human rights activist, visited a women's wing in 1992, the prison's chief of security left her at the entrance to the wing. 'You enter at your own risk,' he told her with a pleasant smile. 'I won't send a guard in there with you, or to bring you out again.'[127]

On the evening of 16 July 1992, a Datsun – cherry-red, no number plate – cruised down a residential side street round the corner from one of the largest banks in Tarata, Lima's business district. Its driver and passengers bailed out of the moving car as it drifted towards an apartment block; they jumped into a Toyota parked nearby and fled the scene. Shortly after, the explosives inside the car generated a blast 300 metres in diameter. The bombing claimed twenty-five lives and wounded 155, leaving some 300 families homeless and causing millions of dollars of damage. Footage from that night shows bodies white with dust and red with blood; a man in his shirtsleeves, crazed by trauma, shouts a name into the bonfire raging in the shell left of his apartment block. Andean villagers had been dying for years, but the Tarata bombing was so shocking to Limeños because, for the first time, the carnage took place in a wealthy white neighbourhood.

Shining Path's strategy remained staunchly Maoist. The underground Guzmán took to emphasising Mao's three-stage military plan for state capture from the 1940s: after strategic defence, the insurgency had moved on to 'strategic equilibrium'. This second stage preceded imminent victory: strategic offence. (This three-point plan would become holy writ to the Nepali Maoists in their own civil war after 1996.) By closing in on Lima, Guzmán was enacting Mao's injunction to 'surround the cities from the countryside', although by this point rural militias had chased most senderistas out of their original Ayacucho heartland.

Guzmán's elusiveness made the insurgency all the more frightening. He was 'everywhere and nowhere'. At the time, recalled one Limeño policeman, 'people thought Guzmán was like the rain: you can't see where it comes from. He was like the serpent that slithers by unseen. The *campesinos* said: "Ah, he must be a god."'[128] But in 1990, the Peruvian government started approaching the insurgency more methodically. It established a 'Special Intelligence Group' (GEIN), a counterterrorism unit within the police that would actually collect and analyse intelligence, rather than kill, rape and burn. Under the directorship of a meticulous, old-fashioned policeman called Benedicto Jiménez, agents tailed likely senderistas; they went undercover as ice-cream vendors; and they finally read Mao. GEIN quickly came to one conclusion: Guzmán had to be in Lima. Jiménez and his team eventually honed in on a yellowish, box-like house in Surquillo, a lower-middle-class part of the capital. (It later transpired that Guzmán had favoured middle-class areas, within a stone's throw of army headquarters, for his refuges.) The residence was rented by a 28-year-old ballet dancer called Maritza Garrido Lecca, who came from a comfortable, urbane Limeño family with links to the Peruvian cultural aristocracy – her musician uncle was on chatting terms with Mario Vargas Llosa. But the police had begun to investigate Maritza after arresting her aunt, a former nun turned Shining Path treasurer called Nelly Evans, in January 1991. Several clues suggested this was Guzmán's hiding place: Garrido Lecca was in the habit of buying far more bread, meat and liquor than she and her husband could possibly need; the house was far too big for two people alone; and empty packets of medicine for treating psoriasis (Guzmán's long-term skin affliction) and stubs of Winston cigarettes (Guzmán's favourite brand) were turning up in the trash. The final giveaway was Garrido Lecca's purchasing of extra-large men's underpants – unlikely to fit her slim husband.

On 12 September 1992, the police stormed the house. The raiding party found Guzmán – bearded, rotund, wearing thick glasses – and Elena Iparraguirre in a party planning meeting (the Lima press claimed they were watching television, like an old married couple). When one of the officers rushed at Guzmán, Iparraguirre struck the policeman. Guzmán did not stir but said forcefully: 'Calm yourselves. Who are you?' Both leaders surrendered without a shot being fired. When Guzmán was searched, police found on him a Mao badge which he claimed, probably falsely, had been personally given to him by the chairman in China. 'Pleased to meet you,' Guzmán greeted the chief of counterterrorism, before adding unnecessarily: 'I am Abimael Guzmán Reynoso.'

Following his capture, Guzmán was no longer the terrifying Scarlet Pimpernel of global Maoism, but rather – in the New York Times's scornful formulation – a 'former philosophy professor with a bad case of psoriasis ... last seen by the public in a videotaped drunken "Zorba the Greek" dance [who] does not cut the dashing revolutionary image of Che Guevara or the young Fidel Castro'.[129] The first photos taken after his capture dismantled his deification: they showed him stripped to the waist, podgy, bespectacled. In a badly planned defence, Maritza Garrido Lecca claimed she did not know Elena Iparraguirre except as a tenant, then shouted Shining Path slogans.[130]

With Guzmán's capture, Shining Path collapsed like a paper tiger. By the end of 1992, nineteen out of the Central Committee's twenty-two members were in jail and Guzmán had been sentenced to life imprisonment. The following year, he turned his back on armed struggle and told his remaining disciples to negotiate with the government. Amazed at their war god's volte-face, his followers accused the state of torture and of brainwashing, until a visibly well Guzmán repeated the message a second and then a third time on national television. In 1986, Guzmán had instructed senderista prisoners to sacrifice themselves in order to force the state into a brutal response that would win sympathy and recruits. Now with his own safety at stake, he dissolved the entire movement. Other former militants also succumbed to pragmatism: some became police informers; others started small businesses. Others again returned to their old communities, raking up bad memories. Bus drivers with a black sense of humour entertained their passengers by announcing ersatz stops on their routes: 'Arequipa, Cuba, Perestroika, Estalinismo, Maoismo, Pensamiento Gonzalo'.[131]

A political wing of Shining Path survives in Peru today under the name of MOVADEF (Movement for Amnesty and Fundamental Rights) and some form of the military struggle straggles on as Sendero Luminoso Proseguir (Continues). This second group has changed with the times, however. While in the 1980s, indiscriminate violence was dealt out to anyone suspected of disloyalty to the cause, now – for a cut of the profits – they offer protection to cocaine mules passing through the stretch of jungle they control, feed them bananas and invite them to play football. Sometimes, these new-wave senderistas wake their guests at two in the morning for an hour of political lectures, but that's as far as their doctrinal zeal goes.[132]

The clearest legacy of Shining Path is desolation: of human life and of political process. Maoist insurgency and counter-insurgency combined to hijack Peruvian democracy and the state apparatus during the 1980s and far beyond. In April 1992, two years into his presidency, Fujimori dissolved institutional checks and balances – Congress, the judiciary, the constitution – which, in his words, 'were delivering the country to terrorism'.[133] Gathering full legislative powers to himself, he imposed a permanent state of emergency that disabled the judiciary's already limited independence – even though the intelligence coup that later in the year succeeded in decapitating Sendero had nothing to do with emergency powers, and everything to do with old-style police work. By the time Fujimori fled the country in 2000, following a disputed election 'victory', he was wanted for corruption – up to $4 billion had 'disappeared' from the public coffers – and human rights violations committed by the army thanks to the impunity that emergency legislation had granted them.

Although Guzmán and Iparraguirre remain unrepentant Maoists in jail (when they are not reading popular science books or listening to classical music), their ideology represents mainly trauma to the rest of the populace – and especially to the poorest parts of that society, the 'masses' whom Shining Path pledged to cherish. In other parts of Latin America, the urban, educated middle class absorbed the worst of political violence. In Peru, by contrast, impoverished rural communities suffered disproportionately. Seventy-five per cent of those killed in the war spoke Quechua as their mother tongue (even though those native speakers made up only 16 per cent of the population in 1993). Seventy-nine per cent of the dead lived outside urban areas (relative to 29 per cent in the population as a whole). If the rest of the country had suffered from the violence as badly as Ayacucho, the war would have exacted 1.2 million casualties – 340,000 from Lima.[134] Up until the publication of the Truth and Reconciliation Commission's report in 2003, there had been estimates that 25,000–30,000 had been killed during the conflict. The report calculated that more than double that number – almost 70,000 – had died.

The Shining Path war and its aftermath exposed the deep fissures in Peruvian society: between urban and rural ('We did not know, we did not want to know,' runs the middle-class refrain); white, mestizo and Indian; Quechua- and Spanish-speaking – after all, the most shocking aspect of the Truth and Reconciliation Commission's report was that it discovered 40,000 deaths in the sierras and jungles that the Peruvian governing classes *had not even noticed*. Without these splits, rural communities could not have been forgotten by comfortable city-dwellers, or obliterated pitilessly by the army and police, or still be awaiting reparations today. Small wonder that *campesinos* call the war a time of *chaqwa*, Quechua for 'chaos and disorder'. 'Life wasn't worth anything,' remembered one survivor. 'We lived like rabbits in holes ... They hunted us like animals. And, to this day, we live forgotten.'[135]

In 2007, Lurgio Gavilán – senderista turned soldier turned priest – travelled back into the Ayacucho countryside. It was here 'where I once walked, my head filled with such utopian thoughts about how the country might change ... Twenty years had passed and I went back to look for myself along the trail.' Gavilán recounts his extraordinary life story in a sad, understated memoir, *When Rains Became Floods*, scattered with images that quietly foreshadow his own life. He begins by tracing out a journey he took in the early 1980s along a serpentine path, lined with sweet-sour orchid berries, between the 'mountains, forest and deep gorges' of his native Ayacucho. Shining Path emerged, he remembers, at that time: 'when the first mangoes, oranges and tangerines begin to ripen, and appear yellow as glints of light through the thick green forest of the Apurimac River'. The insurgents resembled 'the dark clouds of the south. Clouds don't always come filled with good rain. They often flood the fields or destroy the crops. That's how Shining Path came to my community, disguised as good rain. The first drops gave us hope for life, for social justice. But the rains lasted longer and longer. And fear appeared, because the water began to destroy and clean away "all that was old".' Gavilán communicates the daily texture of the insurgency, its ambivalent mix of promise and terror. 'Everywhere you went, they were talking about social justice. On the radio we heard young people and professors talking about a people's war. Our parents and others said: "The organization is already here" or "They say they have killed over there".'[136]

Gavilán's reasons for joining the insurgency aged twelve were as apolitical as those of many other teenagers. His older brother, Ruben, had already joined. He was a classic Shining Path recruit, an earnest student who used to chat to Lurgio about Che Guevara as they fished in the local river, and Lurgio wanted to be by his side. Looking back on his and his peers' motivations, Gavilán asks:

'[We] were the people the state forgot. Something had to be done. But what could a child, in the depths of the Andes, nourished by yucca, dried potato and toasted corn, know of the leaders' politics? ... What could a child know about communist policy or Gonzalo's thought? Nothing. All we wanted was a more just and egalitarian society. Did we children know anything about the consequences of the war we fought?'[137]

In June 1983, Ruben Gavilán paid his share of the quota. At a brief meeting that month, he had given his younger brother a copy of Mao's *Five Essays on Philosophy* (Lurgio was practically illiterate). A few days later, Ruben's skull was shattered by a Peruvian Army grenade and his body buried in an unmarked grave. Lurgio kept on in the movement, marching and singing songs that 'made us feel as if we were made of steel': 'We are the initiators of the peoples' war, / forming detachments, carrying out actions. / Gonzalo brought the light, / taking from Marx, Lenin and Mao, / he forged the purest steel. / ... Tearing down old walls, dawn breaks optimistic.' On the brink of starvation, Lurgio was captured and conscripted into the army (he escaped execution only because the Spanish-speaking soldiers who caught him could not understand village militiamen's pleas in Quechua to kill him). In 1995, he left the military to become a Franciscan priest. 'This was yet another sort of life: the struggle for egalitarian communism through peaceful means,' he writes.[138]

Leaving Ayacucho city by bus early one morning in 2007, Gavilán recalls that his fellow passengers began 'reading from the book of memory: "this is where my brother died! My uncle died here!"' Now and then, the bus conductor would jump out to place flowers amid rocks. 'I felt as if memory was feeding on my blood, like fleas or white lice did when I lived clandestinely and walked with my rifle in hand, reading the bible of Mao Tse-tung.'[139] Once open and hospitable, the locals were now menacingly suspicious of strangers. 'They look you up and down as if you are an enemy ... They are as poor as they were then ... If the [Shining Path's] promises had come true – that everyone would be equal, that no one would be rich or poor ... or if the state was interested in the peasants ... as they always say in the presidential campaigns – surely these men would no longer be scraping through these fields just to survive, as I have scraped through my life in order to tell this story.' An old man approaches: hair grey, eyes watery. Gavilán hallucinates it is his dead brother. When the vision clears, Lurgio thinks to himself: 'Surely this man must have given us food back then; he must have belonged to Shining Path's support base.' Lurgio asks if he had witnessed the horrors of war. 'I saw,' the old man answers simply.[140]

CHINA'S CHAIRMAN
IS OUR CHAIRMAN –
MAOISM IN INDIA

In July 2011, I visited India for the first time, to discuss a book I had written on the Opium Wars and modern China's traumatic clash with British imperialism. I had spent much of the preceding four years steeped in accounts of China's victimisation by the international system and was fully expecting to engage with memories of colonial suffering shared between India and China – for the British rulers of Bengal had forced Indian farmers to grow and process the opium whose sale in China generated vast riches for the British empire. But most of my Indian interviewers did not see China as an injured party. To them, China was a threat. I was blindsided by a stream of questions about contemporary Sino-Indian relations, rather than about India's ordeals in the nineteenth century. What did I think of the way China threatened India's border? How exactly was China aiding Pakistani terrorist attacks?

This fear of China springs most immediately from an uneasy sense of competition. Cover features comparing the Chinese dragon to the Indian elephant ('the two perennial rivals vying for leadership in Asia') are a staple of the international media.[1] In India in 2011, there was a palpable sense that the country was falling behind in this contest: that given the choice, the country would willingly trade its large reserves of soft power – from Bollywood and its cosmopolitan anglophone high culture – for the hard economic power that China's manufacturing boom and buying up of US debt had won the country.

But there is a deeper history to Indian suspicion of China, rooted in conflicts of the Cold War. The temperature of Sino-Indian relations plummeted after the flight of the Dalai Lama to India in 1959, then froze over with the 1962 border war. Chinese and Indian troops still periodically face off over perceived infringements of military space in Jammu and Kashmir. But arguably it is Maoism that casts one of the longest shadows over Sino-Indian relations. South Asia's Maoist insurgency began in 1967, as one of the major regional explosions of the Cultural Revolution's 'spiritual atom bomb'. Whereas the Western European and US versions of this conflagration sputtered out in the 1980s, in India and Nepal its legacy continues to this day. Since 2005, Indian politicians have identified the Maoist insurgency across central India as 'the biggest internal security challenge facing our country'.[2] In Nepal, the Maoist Communist Party waged a decade-long civil war, which culminated in a political revolution in 2006, and the leaders of the Maoist Party – Prachanda, Baburam Bhattarai – have played a dominant role in Nepali national politics since. The Indian and Nepali insurgencies are linked strategically: in 2001, a joint congress attended by Maoist insurgents from both groups projected a 'Compact Revolutionary Zone', a Maoist empire sprawling from Nepal down through India's Bihar, Chhattisgarh, Jharkhand, Orissa and Madhya Pradesh, ending in the southern central state of Andhra Pradesh. The two movements have assuredly influenced and encouraged each other. In intelligence analyses, South Asia's Maoist insurgency shifts in and out of terrorist status: the US only removed the Nepali Maoist Party from its global terrorist list in autumn 2012. P. Chidambaram, India's interior minister in 2010, seemed to judge the Maoists more significant than the country's greatest external menace, from Pakistan. 'Jihadi terrorism can be countered, usually successfully, if you are able to share information and act in real time. But Maoism is an even graver threat.'[3]

In two significant ways, the phenomenon of Maoism in South Asia consolidates our picture of global Maoism. It reminds us of the remarkable ability of these ideas to travel, to translate across borders, ethnicities, languages and societies. In South Asia, the theory and practice of the Cultural Revolution continue to transform states and societies. And in the social composition of its leadership, the Indian and Nepali Maoist insurgencies follow a now familiar pattern.

As in Peru, Cambodia, Western Europe and the US, the leadership of South Asian Maoism sprang from an educated elite. But Indian (and subsequently Nepali) Maoism also tells us something about the chameleon attributes of this political programme. In South Asia, Maoism has had to adapt to the caste system and ethnic fractiousness of Indian society, whose complexity, as Pankaj Mishra observes, 'makes textbook Marxists despair'.[4] As in West Germany, Maoist politics have merged with environmental protest. Yet despite the apparent success of Indian Maoists in building in the post–Cold War era a political movement sustained by a Cold War ideology, they have also demonstrated the weakness of this doctrine: their orthodox Maoist fixation on armed struggle has contributed to escalating the violence suffered by the impoverished rural communities for which India's Maoists claim to fight.

The Maoist insurgency in central eastern India today would not have been possible without the intersection of three elements in the 1960s: the existence of an impatient, militant wing of the Communist Party of India (CPI), a deep socio-economic and political crisis in India two decades after independence, and the eagerness of the Chinese Communist Party to support rhetorically (and in limited ways materially) an Indian revolution inspired by Maoist revolutionary strategies.

The CPI's radical turn – towards a violent, rural revolt against India's rulers – sprang out of dissatisfaction at its pre-independence alliance with the politically dominant Congress Party. In June 1947, two months before Congress took power from the British, the CPI's Central Committee pledged to 'fully cooperate with the national leadership in the proud task of building the Indian Republic on democratic foundations'. This meant discouraging workers and farmers from launching mass protests, urging them instead to wait for the government to fulfil 'its promise through legal channels'. For a radical faction of the party, memory of this abandonment of militancy was a lasting source of shame. As Charu Mazumdar, the violence-obsessed founding father of Indian Maoism, reminded his disciples: 'Learn to hate our past; only then you will be good revolutionaries.'[5]

Within a few months of independence, the CPI's general secretary made the doctrinal judgement that would subsequently justify Maoist insurrection against the new state, declaring that 'Britain's domination has not ended, but the form of domination has changed'. Now the bourgeoisie had been 'granted a share of State power in order to disrupt and drown the national democratic revolution in blood'.[6] In short, India's independence and democracy were a sham; this reasoning made it possible for some to argue that armed struggle, à la Chinoise, was necessary to install the genuine proletarian rule of Mao's 'New Democratic Revolution'.

An attempt at an agrarian Maoist revolution followed close on the heels of this analysis – for like Burma and Malaysia, parts of India were also swept up with enthusiasm for Communist success in the Chinese civil war of the late 1940s. It is hard to underestimate the glow of prestige that surrounded the CCP after its military victories against the Nationalists. One veteran Bengali CPI activist put it bluntly: 'Indian communists were unable to create a path to revolution, while Mao achieved this in 1949. So Mao was greater than our communists.' In April 1948, a dissident wing of the CPI – an organisation that, until that point, had been a stalwart supporter of the Soviet Union – proclaimed: 'Our revolution ... differs with the classical Russian Revolution; but [is] to a great extent similar to that of Chinese Revolution. The perspective is likely not that of general strike and armed uprising, leading to the liberation of the rural side; but the dogged resistance and prolonged civil war in the form of agrarian revolution, culminating in the capture of political power ... The path is that of Chinese liberation struggle under the leadership of Comrade Mao Tse-Tung, the practical, political and theoretical leader of the mighty colonial and semi-colonial revolution.'[7] This faction applied its theories to Telengana, a state in central India with high levels of inequality between landowners and landless sharecroppers.

Many of the features of the later Indian Maoist movement were present in this first uprising, in which members of the CPI organised revolts against landlords, massive redistributions of land and village self-government, in the face of violent retaliation by the army and police of Hyderabad State (under whose jurisdiction Telengana fell). Mao's ideas spoke to India's rural dispossessed: one foreign observer remarked that, as in the Maoist model, Communist guerrillas in Telengana were swimming like fish in the sea of the rural population, which included members of low-ranking castes and of India's 'scheduled tribes' – ethnic minorities below even the untouchables.[8] In late 1948, the national army of India invaded, to prevent the secession of Hyderabad State from the centre (Hyderabad's hereditary ruler, the Nizam, had refused to join the Indian Union the previous year). After absorbing Hyderabad, the central Indian state heavily repressed the Telengana rebellion, arresting some 10,000 suspected Communists and killing 4,000.[9] As in the Malayan Emergency, the civilian population was herded into camps, to prevent them from helping insurgents; all too often, these camps became hell-pits of disease – another hallmark of the Indian state's response to domestic Maoism some sixty years later. Torture and execution were common: one grim army interrogation technique was 'peeling the skin in the design of the hammer and sickle'.[10]

After the state's repressive response to Telengana, a more conservative line held sway in the CPI. By 1956, the leadership declared that it was determined to bring socialism to India by 'peaceful means'.[11] But the radicals in the party never put to rest their ambitions and the Sino-Soviet rift gave traction to those who yearned for more extreme action. Geography further encouraged a radical tendency to favour the Chinese model. 'We read Marx, Engels, Lenin, Stalin and Mao,' recalled one veteran Indian Maoist. 'Mao was obviously the most attractive because India was so similar to China. It was the peasant orientation. I analysed: there are two types of revolution, the Soviet and the Chinese type. The Soviet type was for more developed, European countries. We tried to find our way from Mao.'

Radical Maoism in India began properly in 1962, the year of the Sino-Indian border war, when the two countries clashed over long-contested boundary lines to the west and east of their shared frontier. Tensions had intensified over Indian aid to the Tibetan revolt of 1959 and aggressive patrolling manoeuvres by the Indian Army, and in October 1962 Chinese forces defeated Indian troops on both stretches of the disputed border. That year, fearful of insurrection from within, the Indian government imprisoned some 150 members of the Communist Party of India, convinced that they were seditious pro-Beijingers. The policy was counterproductive. Many of the CPI's pro-China group were Bengalis and were therefore locked up in Kolkata's Dum Dum jail. There, they turned the prison into a Maoist debating society. 'With so many leaders lodged under the same roof,' remembered Kanu Sanyal, a leading Maoist activist between 1967 and his death by suicide in 2010, 'Dum Dum Central Jail became the de facto headquarters for the party's West Bengal Provincial committee.'[12] Among those imprisoned, a thin Darjeeling Communist called Charu Mazumdar stood out for the fervour of his Sinophilia. He proposed that 'the Provincial Committee [of the CPI] should observe 1 October as the Chinese Revolution Day inside the jail premise itself'.[13] While his comrades pleaded for a little circumspection – given that India was presently at war with China – Mazumdar defiantly 'declared himself a member of the Chinese Communist Party'. Even those who sympathised with the Chinese world view 'found the announcement a little too excess [sic]'.[14] Two years later, in 1964, the pro-China CPI (Marxist) split from the CPI. It fractured again in 1967, and in 1969 the CPI (Marxist-Leninist) was born – the precursor to all the Indian Maoist subgroups that would multiply through the 1970s and beyond.

Communist Party narratives all too often shun the personal, and instead focus on doctrinal debates, or collective causes and effects. (All truth is 'class truth', insisted Marx.) But it is impossible to understand the turbulent course of Indian Maoism without taking a careful look at its most influential leader and theoretician, Charu Mazumdar, whom both his admirers and detractors have dubbed the 'Mao of India'.

By his background and his physique, Mazumdar was a poor fit for the rough and tumble of Communist insurrection. He was born in 1918 into a landowning family. He grew into a diminutive man of books; not a tall, robust army man like Mao. One story went that he permanently undermined his health as a student when he became addicted in turn to wine, opium and marijuana.[15] After dropping out of full-time education at about the age of twenty, he found a new drug in Communism and spent the next two and a half decades organising rural resistance to the Indian state. By the 1960s he was a committed, full-time revolutionary, careless of the material poverty and physical hardship that this brought him and his family. 'My father never had a job,' recalled his son, Abhijit. 'He didn't earn anything. My mother [an insurance agent] did everything. She took care of the huge household of a decaying landlord family ... she looked after the three children and the non-earning adults of the family, her sister-in-law and father-in-law ... She did political work too, she'd leave us and go to the mountains in Darjeeling, to organise the women workers of the tea gardens.'[16]

During the 1960s, Mazumdar was already frail with cardiac asthma that required medication with oxygen tanks – Mazumdar's nemesis, the Bengali police chief who oversaw his final arrest, sneeringly described him as 'this gasping old rebel'.[17] Mazumdar had to be carried on the backs of comrades when travelling about the countryside; by the late 1960s, he had suffered two heart attacks. In a picture taken in 1967, the ankle-length lungi tightly swathed around him draws attention to his stick-like, almost two-dimensional slightness. Nevertheless, one early convert characterised him as an 'overwhelming personality'; Kanu Sanyal – who later expressed deep dissent with Mazumdar's violent militancy – described him as a high-pitched, enthralling orator.[18] Another comrade described him as 'remarkable ... In conversation, he can sweep you off your feet. But his moods are unpredictable.'[19] Some attributed Mazumdar's political extremism to a keen sense of his own mortality. 'He knows he can die any day,' commented a senior Kolkata policeman in 1969. 'Possibly he thought, knowing his time was short, "Let me be the Chairman, let me be the Mao of India." He is a megalomaniac. Anyone who seems to him to threaten his supremacy, he expels ... when he gets excited, the way he looks, the way he starts to shiver all over, the expression on his face – then he does not look like a normal human being, he looks like a madman.'[20]

Mazumdar was a cosmopolitan sectarian. Abhijit remembered that Mao was everywhere in his upbringing. 'My [older] sister used to read Mao aloud, as if she were lecturing us ... as if she were under a spell.' At the same time, 'my father was very well-read. He was an avid reader of English and world literature, of pulp fiction, as well as economy and politics. He was very fond of Agatha Christie, and used to read it while travelling. He also loved English and Hollywood movies ... from *Ben-Hur* to Sophia Loren. He was very open-minded ... My father was not a violent man.'[21] Others disagree. For Dilip Simeon, a student Maoist turned writer and academic, Mazumdar 'was a homicidal maniac'.[22] 'He's a worshiper of Kali, you know, the goddess of death,' remarked Kolkata's police commissioner at the height of India's 1960s Maoist fever.[23]

Self-marginalising, educated, physically and mentally unstable, Mazumdar was the ideal receptor for the anti-establishment chutzpah of the Cultural Revolution's high Maoism. Between 1965 and 1966, Mazumdar composed his 'Eight Historic Documents' advocating the application of Mao's line to India. (In yet another sign of the curious laxness of the Indian police vis-à-vis Communist ideas during this period, these were smuggled into Dum Dum jail, where they were avidly read by Communist leaders still detained there by the Indian state.) 'We should remember the teaching of Comrade Mao,' he insisted. 'The tactic which was adopted by China's Great leader Comrade Mao Tsetung ... should be adopted by the Indian Marxists ... Chairman Mao has said ... Chairman Mao has said ... Chairman Mao has said ... Freedom comes out only from the barrel of a gun.' Mazumdar called for the formation of 'combat units', which would 'always keep in mind Mao Tsetung's teaching: "Attacks are not for the sake of attacking merely, attacks are for annihilating only."' He proposed a radical Communist organisation based on the principles of conspiratorial armed insurrection, directed by disciplined party cadre groups: 'To think of seizing power without arms, is nothing but an idle dream.' His strategising was thick with Maoist voluntarism, and with a quasi-religious devotion to Mao as messiah of the revolution.

> Apparently the government might look powerful, because it has in its hands food and arms. The people do not have food; they are unarmed. But it is the unity and firm spirit of these unarmed masses that smash all the arrogance of reaction and make the revolution successful. So Chairman Mao has said: 'The reactionary force is actually a paper tiger.' ... However terrible the appearance of imperialism, however ugly the snare laid by revisionism, the days of the reactionary forces are numbered, and the bright sunrays of Marxism–Leninism–Mao Tsetung thought shall wipe off all darkness.[24]

It took another two years for what Marxists call 'objective conditions' seemingly to validate Mazumdar's prescriptions. In Europe and the United States, the cultural and political crises of 1968, and the dalliance with Maoism were pushed substantially by one of the most materially privileged generations to be born in those countries – the baby boomers. In India, the rebellions of the late 1960s – which were dominated by Charu Mazumdar's Maoist insurrection – sprang out of an intense political, economic and generational crisis. Twenty years on from independence, India seemed far from realising the high-flown ambitions expressed in 1947. The sense of failure existed on many levels. Crucially, India was starving: 1967 was a year of severe famine, in which the government was forced to import grain from the US. Prime Minister Indira Gandhi called it 'scarcity conditions', but the farmers of Bengal felt it less euphemistically.[25] Newspaper offices in Kolkata were flooded with reports of rural horror: of farmers unable to feed their families (much less pay their debts to landlords) killing their wives and children then committing suicide. (One veteran of the Maoist insurgency of the late 1960s was born in Bengal in 1943, the year of another horrendous famine. 'Growing up, I was always hungry, and that's why I was always angry.')

The post-1947 government's toothless attempts at land reform had not only failed, but in some areas had resulted in greater concentration of land among the wealthy. Poor farmers were enmeshed in webs of indebtedness, first mortgaging then losing their land to pay for access to agrarian necessities, such as fertilisers and irrigation. The discrimination of the Indian caste system against Dalits (untouchables), ethnic minorities and women made the misery of the poorest even more entrenched. The landless in Bihar, in the words of one contemporary account, 'lived like animals in hovels less than a man's length, subsisting on 3 to 5 rupees per day and the master's *kesari* – an animal feed made of husk which produced painful skin disorders and arthritis ... the *banihar* [labourer] worked often for nothing. Wearing a clean dhoti, remaining seated in the presence of the master even on a cot outside his own hut, walking erect, were taboo.' Rape of lower-caste women by upper-caste men was 'an accepted social evil'.[26]

In late May 1967, a spark – to use Mao's phrase – lit a prairie fire. Two months earlier, in the village of Naxalbari (at the northern extreme of West Bengal), a collective of impoverished farmers in the local peasants' association had risen up against landowners who had exploited legal loopholes to accumulate vast holdings: 'armed rallies and public meetings became a daily routine', remembered Kanu Sanyal, Charu Mazumdar's lieutenant at the grass roots.[27] When the largest local tea plantation laid off some forty workers in retaliation, workers seized the harvest and, armed with bows and arrows, put to flight a police force sent to quell the rebellion. For two months, the old structures of power, wealth and authority were in chaotic retreat. Landlords fled. Criminals were tried in kangaroo courts, overseen by senior Communist organisers. At least two condemned as thieves were executed the day they were tried.[28] When on 24 May 1967 local police attempted to arrest Sanyal, they were surrounded by farmers armed with bows; one policeman, with the Tibetan name of Sonam Wangdi, died after being struck by an arrow. The following day, the police returned in force to open fire on an activists' camp: eight women, two children and one man were gunned down – the insurgency had eleven martyrs.[29]

While Communist organisers went underground and spread out to the states of Bihar and Andhra Pradesh, from his sickbed in rural Bengal Charu Mazumdar fanned the flames with Maoist slogans. One in particular, 'China's Chairman is Our Chairman, China's Path is Our Path', began to appear on walls all over Bengal. The rebellion in Naxalbari struck a chord with burgeoning discontent in the cities, especially among the students of Kolkata's Presidency College and Delhi University. Thousands of students, representatives of India's most educated, abandoned their studies and took the 'revolution highway' (title of Dilip Simeon's wryly sad autobiographical novel of radical India in the 1960s and '70s), scattering through the countryside to proselytise Mao's revolution. This combination of rural and urban rebels came to be known as the 'Naxalites'. 'We were ready to storm heaven,' Simeon remembered.

> [T]here was something electric about being young in the late 1960s ... Students the world over were affected by a radicalism that came not from the campuses, but from factories and fields in every continent, from Vietnam, Cuba, South Africa and Palestine ... it coincided with explosive discontents in India, where anti-Congress state governments were elected for the first time in numbers in 1967, and the Communist movement was riven with demands for a more 'revolutionary' approach ... Somehow it felt as if we had no option [but to become revolutionaries], that this was like the freedom movement all over again, that if young and committed Indians did not do what was necessary to change the dreadful conditions in which most of our fellow-countrymen and women lived, we would be betraying the most precious values of life.[30]

It helped that Mazumdar's Cultural Revolution rhetoric encouraged youthful rebellion against teachers, exams and books. 'Down with the bourgeois education system!' Mazumdar shouted, encouraging students in March 1969 to drop out of school and skip exams (although Indian state radio delighted in informing listeners several times a day that Mazumdar's wife went on sending their three children to school).[31] A documentary film-maker born in the 1950s self-mockingly recalled spending his teenage years 'painting stencils of Mao onto the walls of College Street in Kolkata, shouting "China's Chairman is Our Chairman". We had no idea what we meant, what we wanted. At the time, we thought we'd just open the door and revolution would step through.'

Mazumdar and Sanyal claimed leadership of the chaotic actions unfolding across India, and in 1969 established a party nominally coordinating this Maoist insurgency: the Communist Party of India (Marxist-Leninist). Its journal, *Liberation*, announced the programme in 1970: 'Our revolution is a part of the ... Cultural Revolution ... The emergence of our party ... is the victory of the revolutionary people of India and also the victory of the all-powerful thought of Chairman Mao on the soil of India ... Long live Chairman Mao! A long, long life to Chairman Mao!'[32] Violent, Mao/Lin Biao–infused rhetoric of guerrilla warfare and the Cultural Revolution's exhortation to 'annihilate class enemies' merged with youthful iconoclasm to produce terror in the cities and the countryside. Walls were vulnerable to Maoist slogans; figures 'in authority' – politicians, judges, teachers, police officers – were at risk of assassination. One off-duty policeman was killed coming out of a Kolkata cinema because, when buying the ticket on the black market, he had revealed his occupation.[33] A day in the city's suburbs with fewer than twelve bomb explosions was defined by the police as 'peaceful'.[34]

In 1970, Mazumdar penned a widely circulated essay on guerrilla warfare that the authorities quickly dubbed a 'murder manual':

The method of forming a guerrilla unit has to be wholly conspiratorial. No inkling ... should be given out even in the meetings of the political units of the Party. This conspiracy should be between individuals on a person-to-person basis. The petty-bourgeois intellectual comrade must take the initiative in this respect ... He should approach the poor peasant who, in his opinion, has the most revolutionary potentiality, and whisper in his ears: 'Don't you think it is a good thing to finish off such and such a jotedar [landlord]?' ... We should not use any kind of firearms at this stage. The guerrilla unit must rely wholly on choppers, spears, javelins and sickles ... The guerrillas should come from different directions pretending ... to be innocent persons and gather at a previously appointed place, wait for the enemy, and, when the opportune moment comes, spring at the enemy and kill him ... a time will come when the battle cry will be: 'He who has not dipped his hand in the blood of class enemies can hardly be called a communist.'[35]

'I've seen our activist comrades at work,' reported one urban Naxalite in 1970. 'They enter a village and pull out the landlord. Then they convene a people's court in the village. When the people vote to execute the oppressor, our comrades hand him over to them, with his entire family. The peasant comrades hack them all to pieces. Then, with the bleeding chunks of meat, our comrades inscribe the thoughts of Chairman Mao on the village walls. The first time I ever saw this I felt a little queasy. It was due to my petty bourgeois upbringing. The activist comrades are workers and peasants themselves, and don't have these sentimental scruples.'[36]

By 1970, Mazumdar had plans for the revolutionary conquest of India, issuing an 'instruction booklet' to all Naxalites. 'The aims of the movement are to create a liberated zone in the rural areas through annihilation of the class enemy ... [It] will spread and increase until it encloses the cities. In 1974, we will be ready to undertake our Long March, as our Chinese comrades did ... through the whole of India. Nobody will be able to stop us ... we will liberate everyone.'[37]

Lu Xun – one of the defining literary voices of early-twentieth-century China – was a witness to China's earliest phase of revolution, in the first decade of the twentieth century, and to the execution of many failed insurrectionists. One of the most flamboyant was Qiu Jin, a cross-dressing rebel who fled an arranged marriage for a career plotting revolution in Japan, returned to China to throw bombs at a Qing official, and was arrested and executed in 1907. Deeply saddened by her death, Lu Xun condemned the irresponsible encouragement of others. Qiu Jin had been, he famously observed, 'clapped to death' by her revolutionary fellows. The same could be said of the first wave of Indian Maoists. The feverish applause of the Chinese press, thousands of miles away, helped convince thousands of urbanites that the events at Naxalbari were the beginning of a nationwide revolution that would conquer India in a handful of years.

In the run-up to the Cultural Revolution, Beijing had done its best to encourage Indian adulation by dispatching political propaganda to rebels in the Indian Communist Party via Kathmandu and Delhi: copies of the Little Red Book and *Peking Review*. (By 1967, the stilted propaganda of the latter had become the preferred news outlet of Indian radicals.) The CCP also dispatched helicopters to the border between Tibet and India to drop pamphlets in Hindi, English, Bengali and Nepali.[38] China could appeal in multiple, unexpected ways. Abhijit Mazumdar – whose childhood home was stacked with Maoist paraphernalia – remembered with especial fondness the records of Chinese songs that reached their household via Kathmandu. 'They were pinkish and very soft; we could play with them without damaging them. Indian records were always very hard, but the Chinese ones were flexible. We'd use them as a toy, and we'd also listen to them.' Deep into his fifties, he could still perform 'The East is Red': '"China has produced a new sun, that is Mao Zedong." My sisters and I used to sing that with pride and shining eyes ... We were influenced by the whole alchemy of the Cultural Revolution ... We didn't know about its specific policies. Rather, it was the image of it from the posters, the red flag, the confident look in people's eyes, the boldness, the idea of rebellion against authority.'[39]

The Chinese Ministry of Foreign Affairs today denies any connection with India's Maoist insurgency, past or present. Indeed, it constitutes such a red-line issue that if you search for it on the ministry's website, a cartoon of a square green bureaucrat springs up on your screen holding a 'NOTICE!' that tells you: 'Mistaken search, your search terms contain illegal words!'[40] But in publicly available English and Bengali sources, and in some highly restricted Chinese materials, there are clear records of direct connections. Charu Mazumdar's first emissary to China was a short, stocky, hardy Communist farmer called Krishna Bhakta Pourel from the India-Nepal border. It was March 1967, and Mazumdar wanted to send to China a copy of his hymn to the Maoist revolution, his 'Eight Historic Documents'. 'At the time,' Abhijit recalled, 'neither my father nor any of the other leaders in his group had a clear idea of how to get from Siliguri [their home town, in north West Bengal] to Beijing. So he asked Krishna to try out the route on foot – he was strong, and he knew the mountain paths.' Krishna duly sold his second-hand bike in Naxalbari market for 75 rupees, bought as much polished rice as he could with the proceeds, placed the 'Eight Documents' at the bottom of a large sack, poured over the rice to conceal them and set off. His journey was unproblematic until he was captured by bandits near the border between Nepal and Tibet, who held him captive and tortured him for several weeks. On being released by them, he resumed his travels until he was arrested by People's Liberation Army soldiers on the Tibetan border. They were about to shoot him as a spy – he was unable to communicate in either Tibetan or Chinese – when he burst into tears and produced a small picture of Mao. He was then flown to Beijing from Lhasa and granted audiences with CCP leaders. He handed Mazumdar's documents over to Mao's international security stalwart Kang Sheng, received a few months of training in Mao Zedong Thought and started back for India in late autumn.

Without this assurance of Charu Mazumdar's dedication to Maoist principles, it is hard to imagine that Beijing would have so quickly acclaimed the May 1967 clashes at Naxalbari as a triumph of the global Maoist revolution. Within five weeks of their occurrence, the *People's Daily* hailed the Naxalbari uprising as 'Spring Thunder Over India'; Radio Peking dubbed it 'the front paw of the revolution' and proof positive of the correctness of applying Maoist strategy to the Indian revolution.[41] In early July 1967, the *People's Daily* published a hymn to the Naxalites that was a (doubtless deliberate) plagiarism of Mao's 1927 'Report from Hunan'. 'In the past few months, the peasant masses in this area, led by the revolutionary group of the Indian Communist Party, have thrown off the shackles of modern revisionism and smashed the trammels that bound them ... All imperialists, revisionists, corrupt officials, local tyrants and wicked gentry, and reactionary army and police are nothing in the eyes of the revolutionary peasants who are determined to strike them down to the dust.' Again borrowing from the lexicon of Maoist jargon, India was diagnosed as suffering under four 'big mountains on the backs of the Indian people ... imperialism, Soviet revisionism, feudalism and bureaucrat-comprador capitalism'.

Revolutionary peasants in the Darjeeling area have now risen in rebellion, in violent revolution. This is the prelude to a violent revolution by the hundreds of millions of people throughout India. The Indian people will certainly cast away these big mountains off their backs and win complete emancipation. This is the general trend of Indian history which no force on earth can check or hinder ... This is Mao Tse-tung's road, the road that has led the Chinese revolution to victory, and the only road to victory for the revolutions of all oppressed nations and people ... Such trash as 'Gandhiism', 'the parliamentary road' and the like are opium used by the Indian ruling classes to dope the Indian people.[42]

In the autumn of 1967, Kanu Sanyal and three comrades retraced Pourel's pilgrimage to China, travelling also through Nepal. In Kathmandu, the Chinese ambassador received them warmly, offering them tea, snacks, money and – most importantly of all – escorted passage to China. The journey had none of the comforts of the Soviet travel agency Intourist's treatment of foreign visitors – seats on Aeroflot and rough Russian champagne. To cross over from Nepal into Chinese-controlled Tibet, the four revolutionaries from Bengal had to crawl for an hour and a half across a dilapidated kilometre-long wooden bridge, contemplating as they did so – through gaps left by missing slats – a torrential river far below. After gruelling ascents of three mountains, the party finally encountered a People's Liberation Army escort who would take them on to Lhasa. There, while reeling from altitude sickness, they were joyfully reunited with Pourel on his way back from China, then flown on to Beijing. The journey was shrouded in secrecy: before entering Lhasa, Sanyal and his three comrades were disguised in PLA uniforms.

In Beijing they received the usual hospitality meted out to foreign visitors – a tour around the city, an invitation to the VIP gallery on the rostrum at Tiananmen Square, visits to model communes. The four Indians were also invited to spend a year in China studying the theory and practice of Mao's revolution. Anxious to return to India, they agreed to stay just three months. A special course was quickly designed for them at a camp on a mountain some distance from Beijing. Twenty days in each month were devoted to military training; the rest to political education. The former consisted of eight hours of instruction a day in using rifles, revolvers, machine guns and grenades; free time was dedicated to revolutionary tourism or film-watching. The course was physically challenging: their instructors began by ordering them to run across a large field; Kanu Sanyal collapsed unconscious only halfway across. But they made progress: breaking their journey home in Tibet, they test-blasted the home-made explosives they had made in China (which the Chinese authorities had allowed the Indians to take onto the civilian plane that took them from Beijing to Lhasa); the bombs worked just fine.[43]

The highlight of their visit was an audience with Mao. One evening, late in 1967, shortly before their return to India, the Indian comrades were shown into a long corridor at the Great Hall of the People, on the western edge of Tiananmen Square. At the other end of the corridor stood Mao Zedong and Zhou Enlai. Overcome with excitement, the Indians began shouting down the corridor 'Mao Zedong zindabad, Zhou Enlai zindabad' (Long live Mao Zedong, long live Zhou Enlai). As they approached their idols, they realised that Zhou was echoing their slogans, wishing Mao and himself long life in Bengali. As soon as Zhou had introduced them to the chairman as the Naxalite revolutionaries, Sanyal recalled, 'Mao instantly clasped me to his chest … I got completely lost in his hug. It was such an overwhelming experience that I was robbed of words.'[44] However, even Mao – not renowned for his modesty – seems to have been uneasy at the cloying devotion of the Indian revolutionaries, telling them that their slogan 'China's Chairman is Our Chairman' was immature. At the end of the audience, though, he gifted them each a consolation cigar and told them that once their revolution was successful, he would resolve the border dispute – the most toxic issue in Sino-Indian relations – by handing over 90,000 square kilometres of disputed territory. (He was repeating an offer he had made in 1959 to some earlier travelling Indian Communists.)[45]

On their way home, via Tibet, the PLA escort discussed with the Indian comrades a plan to build a network of military training camps between India and China, along the Nepalese and Bhutanese borders. These camps, run at Chinese expense, would offer military training but also serve as staging posts to enable China to pass arms to the

Indian revolutionaries.* As a parting gift, the PLA told the Indian party to pick up an advance of 10,000 rupees from the Chinese embassy at Kathmandu for 'establishing secret transit camps to China [as decided with] PLA officers at Lhasa'.[46]

The staged tours around China made a deep impression on the Indian revolutionaries and they seem to have accepted everything they saw at face value. Through Chinese interpreters, the visitors were fed, and swallowed, a garbled propaganda history of the Chinese revolution, in which Mao personally cooked for his soldiers.

We learned that any obsolete things could be changed ... We therefore spontaneously felt the urge to accept the teachings of the Cultural Revolution, we were so amazed at their results ... We saw peasants' and workers' communes where everyone worked collectively and children went to schools, paid for by the Chinese government. The parents didn't have to feed them, the government subsidised everything. It was so encouraging. We decided: if our country is free one day, we'll have this system in our country ... doctors and nurses were always ready to serve children ... there was no sign of gender inequality, no caste ... When Indian peasants listened to our accounts of experiences of China, they used to say these initiatives (communes and so on) should be started in our country too.

Mao's willingness to meet Indian revolutionaries turned the latter into lifelong, emotional admirers. 'Mao was our mother, a romantic poet,' remembered one. 'I met him in Beijing. He could not have been a brute, though he's depicted as one. In reality, he was sensitive, romantic to the core.'

China's generous, carefully managed hospitality towards wisely chosen foreign guests paid dividends. The CCP courted Joan Robinson, professor of economics at the University of Cambridge, who, on her way back to the UK after a visit to China in 1967, gave a widely reported

---

* Although I have not found anyone who would admit to attending them, one veteran Naxalite revolutionary told me with a grin on his face and laughter in his voice that 'officially I didn't go to China, and officially I didn't do military training there', before proudly informing me he had met Mao (who left China only twice in his life, to visit the Soviet Union in 1949 and 1957).

lecture in Delhi on the virtues of the Cultural Revolution. Dilip Simeon recalled the power of her testimony:

> A professor at Cambridge. A world-famous economist. She goes to China and comes back wearing a Mao cap. She goes to the Delhi School of Economics, waving a Little Red Book and preaching about the virtues of the Cultural Revolution, talking about what a wonderful thing was going on in China. She was asked: 'But what about all the dogmatic things that are going on in the Cultural Revolution?' And she reads from the Little Red Book and says: Chairman Mao says dogma is worse than cow dung.[47]

The sermon lent Robinson's authority to the Cultural Revolution. 'That's where we were getting our doctrines from,' explained Simeon. China's propaganda also worked wonders on the majority of Naxalite rebels who were unable to visit China. 'We brought a radio-set down to the countryside,' remembered one Kolkata revolutionary, 'and played Radio Peking, which was available in Hindi, Urdu, Bengali, Telugu. The peasants took decisions guided by it.'

Halfway through Dilip Simeon's *Revolution Highway*, the novel's student protagonists make the decision to go from undergraduate to underground. Following an ultra-brief training course by the party (which consists largely of receiving a copy of the Little Red Book), these new Red Guards are let loose across rural Bengal proselytising Mao's revolution to a series of bemused farmers. Success eludes them. One student is told to leave as soon as he takes out his Little Red Book; another is diagnosed by the local wise man as mentally ill, for his ramblings about China. A third student 'had barely begun reading from the Red Book to a peasant tending a patch of rice paddy when he got stuck in a marsh. The news travelled quickly and a small crowd of villagers gathered to watch him sink into the mud and slime. The peasant who had been the target of his world-historic propaganda wore the expression of someone accosted by a talking parrot.' One farmer finally passes the student 'the long end of a bamboo which he clutched desperately, bruising his hands as he emerged from the morass. The *Thoughts of Chairman Mao* disappeared into Mother India.'[48]

★

By 1972, the first phase of Indian Maoism was showing cracks. Mazumdar's shrill but disorganised authoritarianism was one cause. Sanyal, who later revealed himself as a bitter enemy of Mazumdar's annihilation strategy, carped that the party leader, despite his Communist faith, remained an individualist by conviction, 'desperate to leave his ... mark on the pages of his times'.[49] One of the last political conversations that Sanyal had with Mazumdar before both men were arrested in 1972 focused on the latter's desire to be called 'the great leader' in party discussions.[50] By then, the CPI (Marxist-Leninist) had begun sniping at itself verbally and physically: two members of a rival faction were assassinated by Charu Mazumdar loyalists in late 1971.[51] For too long, Mazumdar had focused his strategy on terroristic conspiracy, denouncing the path of legal political activities (mass organisations, public meetings, trade unions and so on). This resulted in a chaotic, even non-existent party structure. Dilip Simeon recalled his experience of going underground: 'It was very haphazard, very chaotic ... And the line of the party was pure conspiracy, any open activity was forbidden ... So the traditional Maoist techniques of consciousness-raising were not on the menu. Then how the hell are you going to recruit people unless you undertake some kind of public activity?'[52]

The CPI (Marxist-Leninist)'s stance on the Bangladesh war of 1971, moreover, robbed the party of moral credibility. In the spring of 1971, Pakistan sent troops in to suppress Bangladesh's rebellion against Pakistani rule. Although the revolt seemed to fit perfectly Lin Biao and Mao's definition of a 'struggle for national liberation', geopolitical self-interest led China to support Pakistan's invasion and oppose the Indian Army's assistance to the Bangladeshi independence movement. As the crackdown became increasingly bloody, as Bangladeshi refugees flooded into West Bengal, the CPI (Marxist-Leninist)'s defence of Pakistan and attack on Indian military aid to the Bangladeshis (following China's line on the conflict) became ever more grotesque. Dilip Simeon was one of many who left the movement as a result. 'We were utterly disgusted ... Our narrow doctrinal explanations gave us no handle on this gigantic event, on the atrocities committed by the Pakistani army ... we were the only people in India supporting the Pakistani army, calling it a plot to dismember Pakistan ... I just couldn't bear it. There were 10 million refugees, we saw them with our own eyes, rotting in the streets of Kolkata and all over Bengal ... all that commitment to world revolution and the suffering masses disappeared into thin air. The Chinese were supplying the Pakistani army with guns and bombs.'[53]

Then, on 16 July 1972, the movement was decapitated with the arrest of Charu Mazumdar, who died twelve days later in custody. A police intelligence officer who interrogated him recalled their meeting: 'he was such a lean and thin man, with a very fragile structure ... nothing impressive about his physique. But what impressed me was that there was so much fire inside such a small frame. The way he would speak against the government and about his philosophy. He was a man so convinced of his cause, every sentence spoke of his commitment, his hatred of the system and the need to overhaul it. Where did the anger come from?' But the revolution had exhausted him. The police officer denied the conspiracy theories that have circulated since the day he died, that Mazumdar was killed by the police. 'He had to have all sorts of injections just to sustain him. He died a natural death in custody. His whole body was weak. No one should have any doubts about that.'

The second phase of Indian Maoism was coming to an end. By 1973, almost 32,000 individuals accused of Naxalism were in India's jails; some had been held for almost five years without trial.[54] One such prison, Amnesty reported, possessed a single tap for seven hundred prisoners.[55] Police brutality was ferocious: torture, solitary confinement and chains were the norm.* Between 1970 and 1972, eighty-eight prisoners were killed in 'jail incidents'.[56] Stories of torture and extrajudicial killings – supposed 'encounters' between the police and Naxalites in which the police were forced to defend themselves, to cover up cold-blooded murder of prisoners – were rife. For the Delhi-based sinologist Sreemati Chakrabarti – who called the first wave of Naxalism an 'overdose of China' – the movement had two legacies: 'police atrocities' and 'hooliganism in politics'.[57] They remain with India today.

*

---

* One Bengali revolutionary was left partly paralysed by a beating; at one point during our meeting, he glanced down at his fingers: 'The police broke all of them, because I was a writer.'

As the 1970s wore on, Charu Mazumdar's organisation splintered into at least fifteen pieces, all laying claim to the mantle of the CPI (Marxist-Leninist), including: Central Team, Red Star, New Democracy and the (un-ironically named) CPI (Marxist-Leninist) Party Unity. In Bihar during the 1990s, some of the worst Naxalite violence took place between Maoist factions, as well as between Naxalites and state-backed high-caste militias.[58]

At the same time, some Naxalite groups switched strategies. State capture through Mao-style armed struggle was still the ultimate goal and all factions traced their heritage back to the Naxalbari uprising and Charu Mazumdar. But other Maoist tactics were now heeded, such as the need for legal, front organisations with greater popular reach; above all, the survivors of the first phase of the insurrection yearned for a base area, under party control, in which cadres could take refuge from the Indian state. For Maoism not only promised the instant gratification of class warfare ('annihilating class enemies'), but also – as succour to the defeated – preached the necessity of protracted guerrilla warfare, of slow building of base areas. In the aftermath of Naxalbari's original rebellion in 1967, activists had striven to create similar insurgencies: in Uttar Pradesh, Punjab, Orissa and Assam, but most successfully in Bihar and in Andhra Pradesh. In July 1969, two cadres who had been trained in China, Kanu Sanyal and Sourin Bose, explored a potential new base area for the revolution in Srikakulam, in Andhra Pradesh. There, Maoist leaders encountered Dalits and members of the most vulnerable and exploited group in Indian society: the so-called 'tribals' or Adivasis. While India's new government after 1947 had vowed to make up for millennia of oppression suffered by Dalits and Adivasis, in reality little had been done to lessen the worst of caste violence or the exploitation of tribal people. In the three weeks they spent with these marginalised groups, the two revolutionaries strove to pass on a toolkit of revolution: lessons in arms operation and explosives manufacture, and classes in Marxist–Leninist–Maoist thought.

Some of the splinter groups, like CPI (Marxist-Leninist) Liberation, opted to participate in elections while simultaneously preparing themselves 'for winning the ultimate decisive victory in an armed revolution'.[59] The People's War Group (PWG), originally active in Andhra Pradesh, declared by contrast that 'People's War based on Armed Agrarian Revolution is the only path for achieving people's democracy ... in our country'.[60] In Bihar, the Maoist Communist Centre (MCC) backed the 'Protracted People's War' advocated by Mao. 'The concrete economic and political condition of India leads to the very conclusion that the path shown by the great leader and teacher, Mao Tse Tung, the path of the Chinese Revolution ... is the only path of liberation of the people of India.'[61] In October 2004, India's Maoist factions demonstrated the wisdom of the opening sentence of one of Mao's favourite books, *The Romance of the Three Kingdoms*: 'what has long been divided must unite'. Encouraged by the Nepali Maoists, PWG and two other factions united into the Communist Party of India (Maoist) (CPI [Maoist]). With each of these groups active in different parts of the country, the new coalition had, in theory at least, a wide, dispersed presence throughout India. Today, the government – perhaps to justify ballooning defence and security budgets – claims that 225 of India's 626 districts (covering 40 per cent of the country, an area populated by 400 million people) are drawn into the Maoist insurgency. On paper, it is one of the largest-scale and oldest continuous insurrections in the world.[62]

The cadres and policies of the People's War Group in Andhra Pradesh have driven the millennial resurgence of Indian Maoism. One of the earliest PWG leaders, Kondapalli Seetharamiah (also known as KS), established legal front organisations, the most effective of which was the Radical Students' Union (RSU) that channelled talented, idealistic graduates towards the movement, some of them from India's best families.[63] One of the most famous examples is Khobad Ghandy, son of a senior executive at Glaxo, who grew up between a seafront apartment in Mumbai and a vast bungalow in the hills south of Pune, whose brother owned Mumbai's first ice-cream brand to contain real fruit (Kentucky's). Khobad Ghandy was educated at India's Eton (the Doon School), where he was in the same class as Sanjiv Gandhi, and studied chartered accountancy in London (coincidentally, the same subject for which the Zanzibari revolutionary Babu originally came to the city; both men segued into radical politics while qualifying). After his return to India in the late 1970s, Ghandy passed through the Radical Students' Union before joining the PWG underground in the 1990s, with responsibility for carrying out propaganda in urban areas. His arrest in Delhi in 2009 generated shock among the urban middle classes. 'Suddenly,' recalled

Rahul Pandita, a journalist who for years has studied the contemporary Maoist movement at its jungle roots, 'my friends, ordinary urbanites, began talking about it. "Who is this man? He doesn't look like a terrorist, like we imagine Maoists to be. He used to live in a lovely sea-facing house, his parents used to play bridge ... He's a man who could have gone anywhere, he could have had the cushiest of jobs, but he chose to live in the jungle."'[64] Until recently, the leadership of the movement came mostly from the 1970s–80s Andhra Pradesh regrouping: many (including Ganapathi, the supreme leader, and Kishenji, the head of the guerrilla army until he was killed by Indian police in 2011) graduated from Andhra Pradesh colleges, where they first encountered radical politics.

After 1980 the militant People's War Group began the migration that continues to define the Maoist movement in India today. Perceiving the need for a true 'Yan'an of India', namely a base area far enough from state authority to be secure and impoverished enough for a radical socio-economic agenda to gain traction, KS spotted in Bastar, south-east Chhattisgarh, two useful characteristics: forest so dense that the state apparatus had virtually no physical presence; and a tribal population that was ruthlessly exploited by external contractors and government officials, who siphoned off the region's natural resources. 'You can get lost in fifty feet,' Rahul Pandita remembered. 'There's nothing there. You won't encounter another person for miles after miles.'[65] Economic relations in the area were brutal: an Adivasi would be paid, according to rates dictated by these outsiders, five paise, or 0.06 pence, for a day's hard work – at constant risk of snake bites – collecting tendu leaves, to wrap bidi (cheap Indian cigarettes) for the multi-billion-dollar domestic industry. The state's agents took advantage of the Adivasis' intense lack of worldliness: one writer travelling around the area in 2001 noted that their basic units of counting didn't extend beyond twenty.[66] The tribal peoples were starving and the women were exposed to random sexual violence from government officials.[67] The exploitation they suffered, Pandita analysed, was 'something beyond racism. They're not even considered humans. It's like you can rape someone, and it's nothing.'[68]

KS sent squads to set up a new base in Bastar. The venture began badly: one five-man squad from Andhra Pradesh almost died of starvation en route, for the few locals they encountered in the jungle ran away, terrified of the strangers. But the Maoists slowly established a foothold by focusing on the grievances most central to Adivasis' lives: economic exploitation and randomised violence. They organised locals into 'mass struggles' against those who took advantage of them. A tax collector 'who was exploiting schoolgirls was caught by the Naxal guerrillas, beaten up and then tied to a tree. Then the women of that area were asked to assemble and instructed to spit at his face.' One by one, they did.[69] Tarakka, an Adivasi woman from west Chhattisgarh, joined the Maoist movement in her late teens out of sheer disgust with forest officers stealing her father's food and raping her friends with impunity. By 2010, she was a commander, proud of her skill with a gun as well as at making chutney. 'The police doesn't come here,' she told a journalist. 'They know they will be slaughtered.'[70] In 1985 alone, and in just one small area on the western border of Chhattisgarh, the Maoists seized from government control 20,000 acres of land.[71]

Taking another leaf from the book of Mao, the surviving Naxalites in Andhra Pradesh and Chhattisgarh were careful to package their message culturally as they regrouped during the 1980s and beyond. One star of their show was a singer of 'untouchable' background called Gaddar ('Revolution'), who went underground to join PWG in 1985, collected Telugu folk songs and remade them with Maoist messages and slogans ('Long Live Naxalbari ... the ultimate win for agrarian revolution ... Who is this landlord? ... What right does he have to exercise power over us? ... Red Salute!').[72] He reached out to groups particularly victimised by mainstream Indian culture – Dalits and women – adapting and communicating the message of Maoism to India's caste-riven society. Onstage, he was a dynamic presence, with his booming voice, flowing curly hair and beard, bright eyes and vivid facial expressions. Identifying with the poorest in society, he performed wearing shapeless trousers and a rough blanket. While singing in the jungles, there would be a drum hanging over his left shoulder, a loaded rifle over his right.[73] It's uncertain, though, how Gaddar would have fared under Mao's own puritanical cultural tsars: a visitor to his house in 1995 spotted cassettes of Phil Collins and British dance club hits next to Mao's works. In 1995, PWG suspended him for six months for taking a break to write songs for a movie.[74] In April 2017, he broke with the Maoists and applied for a vote in India's elections.

India's Maoist insurgency redux took a more militarised turn in the late 1980s, when a splinter from the Tamil Tigers trained Maoist cadres in using explosives – especially landmines, which they grew proficient at triggering with the most miscellaneous, even primitive objects (including Y-shaped twigs). This emboldened them to attack any symbol or representative of the Indian state. One surrendered Maoist guerrilla could compare the training that he received in the movement with that received in the Indian Army in the country's troubled north-east and north-west: the latter 'was nothing in comparison. [The Naxals] have a lot of motivation ... But look at the central forces. You just need to burst a cracker and they will all roll over.'[75]

Both the guerrillas and the government use the term 'Maoists' (Maobadi) for the insurrection (although this name is often used interchangeably with 'Naxalite'). Does the movement continue to live up to this label? The constitution of the CPI (Maoist) certainly remains overtly Maoist. It subscribes to the analysis of India as 'semi-colonial and semi-feudal': a country at the mercy of imperialism and its Indian collaborators (the 'comprador big bourgeoisie') and feudalism. This assertion of India's political bankruptcy logically dictates all-out hostilities: state capture through protracted war, Mao-style. 'The Protracted People's War will be carried out by encircling the cities from the countryside and thereby finally capturing them ... the [Cultural Revolution] initiated and led by Mao Tse-tung was a great political revolution carried out under the conditions of socialism by the proletariat against the bourgeoisie and all other exploiting classes to consolidate the dictatorship of the proletariat and there by [sic] fighting against the danger of capitalist restoration.'[76] '[O]ur revolution', declares the Party Programme, 'will follow the path of the Chinese Revolution.'[77] The leaders draw on Chinese revolutionary mythology to motivate their rank and file and incite them to violence, telling stories of class struggle that they claim come from the Chinese revolution. 'A bonded labourer who is ill-treated by his landlord feels that the latter has no heart. So, when the peasants attack the landlord's house, the labourer says that he would like to kill his master himself and check whether he has a heart underneath his ribcage.'[78]

For the rank and file, however, Rahul Pandita identifies only one meaningful slogan: *datt kar khao, datt kar chalo* (eat as much as you can, walk as much as you can). Having investigated the movement for more than a decade, he writes that 'It is difficult to get the younger guerrillas to open up ... It is futile to ask them why they joined just as it is futile to ask Adivasis in the villages what they would want in terms of a better life ... Only when one spends time with them does one understand that it is mostly because the uniform offers them a sense of who they are, makes them one large group, gives them some purpose in life.' Others drift in and out, periodically abandoning village life for small-scale grievances. A sixteen-year-old called Kohli ran away to the Maoists because his father slapped him for spilling a small cupful of milk. For some, joining the Naxalites is an adolescent rebellion, a way of escaping the control of their families, and experiencing the world beyond their village.[79] Supriya Sharma, who for several years was the *Times of India* correspondent in Chhattisgarh, never encountered a grass-roots cadre who knew Mao or the history of Maoism.[80]

Participants and supporters of the Maoist movement in India today argue, quite simply, that the Maoists are representing, mobilising and giving voice to those forgotten or victimised by the Indian state and by sources of power and authority (local elites, national and multinational corporations eager to extract the mineral wealth of the jungles of central India). In 2008, four years after the unification under the CPI (Maoist), the Indian government commissioned a group of experts on poverty and conflict in rural India (including the sociologist Bela Bhatia, who has been visiting and writing about Maoist-affected areas for decades) to investigate support for the political solutions of the Maoist movement. The group acknowledged the geographic and socio-economic complexity of the areas concerned. But the conclusion drawn was clear-cut: 'The intensity of unrest resulting in extremist methods and effort to resolve issues through violent means as a challenge to state authority is in response to the gathering of unresolved social and economic issues for long durations.'[81]

These conflicts have sharpened since the beginning of the twenty-first century due to sweeping changes to the Indian economy. In the 1990s, the Indian government set out on a path towards economic liberalisation: exit the 'licence raj', enter deregulated opportunities for entrepreneurs. There have been benefits: India has lifted itself out of the national bankruptcy that it faced in 1991. But the rise of big business – in particular, the mining industry – has transformed attitudes to the mineral-rich jungles in which Maoist guerrillas took refuge in the 1980s. Many believe that the state was prepared to turn a blind eye to the Maoist insurgency in areas like Chhattisgarh during the 1980s and '90s, in effect ceding these areas to Maoist domination through its non-presence; Maoist cadres took to running their own local governments there. But when the government began granting lucrative mining contracts to corporations in the early 2000s, Maoist-organised resistance threatened to obstruct the state raking in rich levies from industrial development. Since the start of the new millennium, the Indian government has been ambitious to turn Chhattisgarh into a busy network of pipelines, railways and roads, devoted to sucking valuable iron ore and minerals such as bauxite, platinum and corundum out of the land. According to this blueprint, power is to be provided by mega-dams, flooding many villages and displacing their inhabitants. Although private businesses carry out the day-to-day work for implementing this programme, a large share of the riches generated falls into state hands through levies, sale of contracts and so on (in 2010–11, this income generated almost 20 per cent of state revenue).[82] In addition, local representatives of the state all get their cut from private extractors and traders anxious for their business plans to advance as smoothly as possible.

In the time-honoured fashion, the long-term residents of this land, the poorest Adivasis, have been swindled out of the profits. For centuries, outsiders – traders in teak, tamarind and now in minerals – have 'persuaded' these tribal peoples to part with the valuable natural resources of their environment for a fraction of their international market value. In south Chhattisgarh in 2001, government enforcers – charging with lathis (thin truncheons) if locals resisted – forced residents to sell up for 11,000 rupees an acre; fourteen years later, as industrial development advanced, this land was valued at three million an acre. In 2007, rapes and arrests orchestrated by the state helped push through land acquisition in an adjoining district by one of India's biggest multinational corporations.[83] There are vast environmental, as well as socio-economic, downsides to this mining revolution: virgin forest destroyed by coal mines, once-flowing rivers static with red sludge, a heavy pall of black smoke hanging over the forest from iron-ore plants. The plan for one series of mining waste dumps in the same part of Chhattisgarh, an environmental impact assessment report observed, would 'destroy the drainage of the entire valley ... the entire culture of the people would likely become extinct'.[84]

This shift in the state's priorities has escalated the conflict with Maoist guerrillas in states like Chhattisgarh and Jharkhand since 2005. That year, the Federation of Indian Chambers of Commerce and Industry made the following revealing comment: 'The growing Maoist insurgency over large swathes of the mineral-rich country-side could soon hurt some industrial investment plans. Just when India needs to ramp up its industrial machine to lock in growth and when foreign companies are joining the party – Naxalites are clashing with mining and steel companies essential to India's long-term success.' Violent confrontation escalated. Big business acquired 'Consent' for acquiring iron-ore mines by local thugs placing pistols to the temples of villagers while they signed No Objection letters.[85] The CPI (Maoist) and its armed wing, the People's Liberation Guerrilla Army – with its subscription to Maoist military and political strategies – offered the most muscular form of resistance to such strong-arming. In 2006, Manmohan Singh, who as finance minister from 1991 was the architect of India's liberal market economy, identified the Maoists (to general surprise) as the 'biggest internal security threat to the Indian state', three years coincidentally after the government had liberalised mining contracts, thereby turning the Maoist base area of Bastar into 'the most valuable piece of real estate in the country'.[86]

The state has mobilised its own special forces to oust the Maoists in operations code-named Green Hunt, Greyhound and Cobra – labels that deliberately dehumanise their targets. Yet the most toxic mobil-isation against the Maoists was the creation in Chhattisgarh of Salwa Judum, a local vigilante army, in 2005. Although the Indian state insists on translating the name as 'Peace March', specialists in the local language, Gondi, agree that 'Purification Hunt' is in fact a closer equivalent in English. It was initially portrayed by the media as a popular, civil self-defence movement of long-suffering tribals against Maoists, which the government and police subsequently supported in recognition of its 'popular' legitimacy. The reality was different. In the early 2000s, the police and government organised groups waging local vendettas into patrols confronting local Maoist governments. By 2005, these patrols – now formally named Salwa Judum – began holding almost daily rallies bolstered by state security forces; villagers were intimidated by fines and violence into attending. The organisation received 860 million rupees of government funding, plus government-issued weapons.[87]

In stark contravention of international laws against scorched-earth policies, Salwa Judum plundered and destroyed villages accused of helping or harbouring Maoists. Villagers would be beaten, raped, mutilated and murdered on the pretext of finding members of Maoist village governments. Survivors were herded into 'relief' camps (described by one academic witness as 'open-air prisons'), or went into impoverished exile. In early 2006, the Maoists began their retaliation, with dozens dying (sometimes ordinary villagers caught in the crossfire) in single encounters between the two sides. While Salwa Judum left burnt bodies in their wake resembling 'broiled fish' and countless cases of collateral damage (the young, the elderly, the sick – anyone unable to flee the pillage fast enough), villagers wrote desperate letters to activists beyond the forest: 'If the Salwa Judum catches people it kills them, tears apart their body, slits their tongue and heart etc ... We want to say and write much more but our pen fails us here.'[88] The only winner from this human tragedy was industrial development, which could unfold on the back of Salwa Judum's 'emptying' of villages. State security forces and their allies claimed that they were only killing Maoists, but journalists and other eyewitnesses testified to police officers shooting ordinary civilians, dressing them up in brand-new fatigues and photographing them to substantiate claims that they were Maoists killed in 'encounters'.

Salwa Judum, recalled Rahul Pandita, an eyewitness to many of its horrors,

> ensured that the Maoist movement travelled from one part of Chhattisgarh to another, to areas totally untouched by Maoists, due to atrocities committed by Salwa Judum militia. People were so angry at being victimised. There was a village without Maoist presence, which had rejected Maoist presence in the past, which hadn't been interested in what the Maoists had to tell them, or in revolutionary theories. But one day these paramilitary forces landed, they raped,

killed, plundered then went away. The same evening, Maoist guerrillas came to the village and they said, 'Look we've been telling you about this all along. Do you want to live a life of dignity even if it lasts a couple of years, or a dog's life for ten years?' Ten to fifteen youngsters from the village joined the movement on the same day. That's how the arc spread from south to north Chhattisgarh. Those were terrible times.[89]

In early 2010, a typewritten note slid under the door of the prize-winning novelist Arundhati Roy's hotel room confirmed a meet-up with (in her sarcastic turn of phrase) 'India's Gravest Internal Security Threat'. 'Writer should have camera, tika and coconut,' the note prescribed. 'Meeter will have cap, Hindi Outlook magazine and bananas.' Roy arrived punctually for the rendezvous, dutifully bringing the objects specified.

> Within minutes a young boy approached me. He had a cap and a backpack schoolbag. Chipped red nail-polish on his fingernails. No Hindi Outlook, no bananas. 'Are you the one who's going in?' he asked me ... I did not know what to say. He took out a soggy note from his pocket and handed it to me. It said, 'Outlook nahin mila (couldn't find Outlook).'
>   'And the bananas?'
>   'I ate them,' he said, 'I got hungry.'
>   He really was a security threat.[90]

With this preamble, Roy begins her extended essay, 'Walking with the Comrades', about the ten days she spent with the CPI (Maoist). In passionate prose, she champions India's poorest and most voiceless – the Adivasi communities assaulted in turn by big-corporation development, environmental degradation and Operation Green Hunt. Roy paints the Maoists – some minor reservations notwithstanding – as a credible alternative to the repressive, mendacious, greedy machinery of the neo-liberal Indian state.[91]

Other civil rights campaigners also hold sympathetic views, despite heavy-handed state repression of such opinions. (Successive Indian governments have demonised and even criminalised any connection with or whiff of sympathy for the Maoist cause. Between June and

August 2018, at least ten left-wing activists – most of them defenders of civil society from state attacks – were arrested on charges of 'Maoist links'.) For one such seasoned campaigner (anonymised here), Maoism represents a particular form of resistance in contemporary India: 'The Maoists are advancing Adivasi movements for rights over forest areas, to achieve their own revolution: social transformation of power in India.' Commentators such as Roy and Gautam Navlakha – another activist who was permitted a visit around Maoist areas, and who was arrested in August 2018 – have both condemned what they see as the egregious levels of structural violence and hypocrisy within India's power structures. 'People lament violence,' complains Navlakha. 'But we are the most violent society on earth.' India's republic is 'broken', argues Roy; violence is both epidemic in, and the only solution to, Indian state repression. 'How else are you going to fight the Indian state?' Navlakha asks. 'Unless you believe all is hunky-dory here. Conditions drive people to take to violence.' (Though he has also denounced the Maoists' use of kangaroo-court brutality against their enemies.)

Sympathy for those downtrodden for decades and centuries is eminently understandable. Moreover, such is the intensity of government propaganda against the Maoists (and currently against civil rights activists) that it is easy to comprehend why a public intellectual like Arundhati Roy would seek to counter-attack with exposure of the state's own abuses in Chhattisgarh. (Between 2009 and 2012, 91 per cent of the sources used by Indian English-language newspapers were from the government or the police.)[92] The empirical detail of her reportage communicates the remarkable way in which India's jungle Maoists have adapted the vague image and prestige of Mao as a rebel 'leader' with 'vision', to give coherence to their anti-state, anti-corporate struggles on behalf of the poor and their degraded environment.[93] They invoke the classic, uncompromising rhetoric of Maoist militancy to argue that only violent uprising can battle the depredations of the Indian state, a sham democracy allied with multinational business. 'The question is whether to live a life of slavery and indignity and die of hunger by remaining docile or engage in peaceful protests … or take up arms to completely eradicate the grounds that give birth to all kinds of suppression and oppression,' says Ganapathi, the current leader of CPI (Maoist).[94]

When the Maoists arrived in Chhattisgarh, there was no script for the local Adivasi language, Gondi; the Maoists have worked to formalise it in writing – and to produce a Gondi edition of the Little Red Book. New recruits became literate within a year of joining up. In a region where Adivasis routinely die of basic ailments such as diarrhoea, the Maoists have provided medical services through mobile units staffed by Mao-style 'barefoot doctors' (a term for medics with rudimentary training, popularised during the Cultural Revolution). Even those critical of the Maoists have noted their impact on education and health care. The Maoists in Bastar have also raised consciousness (*tifa juexing* is the original Chinese phrase). Once-scorned tribals confidently meet the gaze of others, while the controversy provoked by the Maoist insurgency has at least brought the sufferings of Adivasis to national attention.

Roy rightly notes the historical irony by which China has shifted from being a Mecca for anti-state rebels, to becoming an economic icon to the would-be neo-liberal Indian state, as well as a voracious consumer of Chhattisgarh's minerals. But her reportage somewhat sidelines the ideological rigidities of the Maoists, and the enormities of the Communist heritage from which they draw inspiration. (In some left-wing Indian intellectual circles, Mao retains a political respectability he has long lost in the West. Insufficient attention to Maoism as history and lived experience can result. Within Indian publishing, the memoirs of Mao's persecutions or the sensational exposé of Mao by his doctor as a cynical, megalomaniac sex addict, which had such an impact on Western anglophone readers, have not reached general audiences.) Roy's travelogue around jungle Maoism, moreover, bears a resemblance to an earlier vector of global Maoism: Edgar Snow's *Red Star Over China*. There is the same disarming humour, the *Boys'/Girls' Own* zing of adventure, the gleeful deflation of any suspicion of danger or threat from the Maoists, their depiction as good-hearted, idealistic rebels with beautiful smiles, who laugh and love poetry; who are just like any other type of anti-state resistance in India today. Rahul Pandita, who in 2009 scored a massive journalistic coup in securing the first interview with Ganapathi, the reclusive, mysterious Maoist commander-in-chief, in time became unsettled by the parallels between his own relationship to the Bastar Maoist leader and Snow's with Mao.

I'd read *Red Star Over China* around 2006: about Snow's meetings, about how Mao would suddenly appear then disappear, then reappear, smoking a cigarette. Ganapathi was like that – he struck me as a Mao-type figure ... [Our conversation] seemed to me a scene from *Red Star*, as if the dynamic were influencing us both, as if I were meeting Mao: it was Ganapathi's mannerisms, the way he spoke about ushering in this revolution ... I had to pull myself out of that situation ... Any sensible guy will know what happened in China or in Stalinist Russia ... or in any authoritarian regime.[95]

There is, for sure, welcome critical ambivalence in Roy's account. She reports one conversation with a guerrilla that reveals how closely they monitor what she writes about them. She also remarks that, were the Maoists to come to power, she would be the first person they would hang.[96] But her portrayal of rebels with a cause also tends to mute the uncomfortable truth that the Maoist leadership subscribes to an intolerant, totalitarian ideology that insists that India today closely resembles China of the 1930s and that decrees an inflexible trajectory both for its enemies and for the marginalised groups it professes to champion. She represents the insurgency as poor tribals versus a predatory, polluting state, simplifying the complex social and political make-up of the movement. She barely acknowledges that her travels and access were managed, mediated or orchestrated by the party. While she denounces lies and manipulations by Indian politicians, she casts little doubt on the verisimilitude of the image the group presents of itself in the jungle, writing earnestly of foot soldiers' 'faith, and hope – and love – for the Party', and concluding that 'it surely is a People's Army'.[97]

The anthropologist Alpa Shah has spent more than a decade studying the Maoist movement and its context in central India; this includes eighteen months living in Adivasi communities in Maoist-controlled zones as a participant-observer. She describes it as an 'intimate insurgency'. The Maoists have lived and worked in some areas for twenty or thirty years, and for locals have far more credibility than the exploitative state. Like Arundhati Roy, Shah is very supportive of the interests and rights of Adivasi populations, and has also 'walked with the comrades' in the jungles. She writes sympathetically of the egalitarian

ideals of the Maoist movement – in particular, the willingness of
high-caste Maoists to erase caste hierarchies in day-to-day life, by
sharing food with untouchables, for example. But her work in
Jharkhand up to 2010 complicates Roy's portrayal of freedom fighters
defending those at the bottom of caste and ethnic hierarchies. Shah
has observed high-caste and male domination of Maoist hierarchies;
despite its attempts to dissolve caste and ethnic divides, the movement
replicates the inequalities baked into Indian society. It is dismissive of
the positive attributes of Adivasi society – its relative gender egalitarianism, its biodegradable way of life – assuming that these patterns
of existence must and will be erased by modernisation.[98] Their stated
idealism notwithstanding, the Maoists' political dogmas glorify
violence and help contribute to a vicious circle of repression and
retaliation by an Indian state arguably too powerful to be challenged
by a guerrilla insurgency. Aditya Nigam, a Delhi-based professor of
development, is unsparing of the Maoists and their upper-class
bias. 'The adivasis cannot represent themselves; they must be represented ... They must be represented either by agents of the state ...
or by the revolutionaries [and] the voice of the revolutionary is almost
always that of a Brahman/upper caste ... So we have a Maoist-aligned
intelligentsia vicariously playing out their revolutionary fantasies
through the lives of adivasis, while the people actually dying in battle
are almost all adivasis.'[99] Perhaps symptomatically, Ganapathi is
referred to rather archaically as 'GP sir' by the rank and file.[100]

Accusations of corruption and extortion (both small- and large-
scale) by Maoist cadres are also rife. Between 2000 and 2010, some
mining companies doubled their productivity in Chhattisgarh and
Jharkhand after negotiating with the Maoists. One mine operator
estimated in 2010 that Maoist groups in Jharkhand could be making
an incredible $500 million a year in protection money paid by indus-
trialists. 'It works like a tax,' the man explained, 'just another business expense and now everything runs smoothly.'[101] Wikileaks have
revealed that Essar, which runs a massive iron-ore extraction operation in Bastar, has paid the Maoists 'a significant amount'.[102] 'Extortion
money is part of a huge system,' explains Rahul Pandita, 'being used
to fund war ... You have the People's Liberation Guerrilla Army –
about 12,000 strong. You're running these networks, you need money
for ammunition, for explosives, some of it might be going into

personal coffers as well, but it's not improving lives of Adivasis. Not infrastructure, education, water, nothing. Nothing.'[103] There is authoritarianism in the Maoists, too: villagers in Maoist-controlled areas in Bastar have to ask permission before they are allowed to leave their villages; women in Jharkhand are forced to attend Communist festivals even when they feel disaffected or have more pressing tasks; violence is meted out to those who disobey.

In the 1960s and '70s, Dilip Simeon was in the vanguard of the student Naxalite movement, until his beliefs were crushed by witnessing the refugee fallout of the Bangladesh war and China's self-interested aid to Pakistan, which assisted the Pakistanis in killing perhaps as many as three million Bangladeshis (perhaps 400,000 Bangladeshi women were raped). Simeon returned to academia, where he directed his left-wing sympathies into labour history. At the same time, he became a passionate critic of political violence, for he had experienced it from both ends of the spectrum. In the 1980s, he was beaten brutally by six young men from a right-wing vigilante group, due to his involvement in an employment dispute at his university: his left leg was broken in two places, he lost five teeth and his jaw was permanently damaged – it took nine weeks of rehabilitation before he could walk again.[104] To him, the Maoist ideology that, rhetorically at least, continues to fuel the insurrection in central India is 'ludicrous, along with the ideas that underpin it: the idea that India is like China was in the 1930s; that in India democracy is a complete fraud and a conspiracy that means nothing to millions of people; that an armed struggle along the lines of the Chinese revolution is possible; that the state can be seized by violent revolution from the countryside – all this is a chimera'.[105]

He acknowledges the existence of appalling violence in India, but condemns the Manichaean view of politics with which the Maoists have responded. 'The sheer violence of the situation in India gives stamina to an ideology which says there's nothing but violence ... if you then say that all these inadequacies of democracy can be redeemed only by an [armed] overthrow of democracy, then you ultimately end up helping this process of degeneration ... you don't need a violent revolution to overthrow the constitution. You need a non-violent mass movement to defend the constitution.' Simeon draws a direct line between political terrorism of the late-colonial period, Mazumdar's 'murder manual' and the 'historical murder' ('killing in the name of the future') perpetrated by the Maoist movement in India today.[106]

Because it is so difficult and dangerous to carry out long-term ethnographic work that reflects the complexities of the terrain, it is hard to piece together the Maoists' exact plan for government, should their insurgency succeed. In the style of global Maoists everywhere, they are strong on emotional appeals to rebellion, but weak on envisioning structures that will tackle the worst ills of the state: improved transparency, checks and balances to corporate and government power, economic plans for reducing the inequalities that have persisted and indeed increased since 1947. One senior policeman spoke of frustration during peace talks with the Maoists, when the latter failed to submit any substantive demands to advance negotiations. 'The blueprint for creating a state is very vague,' agrees Rahul Pandita. 'Yes, land will be equally distributed, all will work for the benefit of society ... But in terms of how this country would run, they have absolutely no idea. I asked a senior Maoist ideologue this question. He said: many poor people don't have enough saris to wear, so when we take over we'll make factories to create saris, production will increase, the saris will go to these women, that's how we'll start this whole production exercise and become a Maoist state.'[107]

Like Dilip Simeon, Alpa Shah and Nandini Sundar believe there is only one long-term solution to this horror: the proper exercise of India's constitutional democracy – 'a predicament and promise that no citizen can escape from'.[108] Yet Sundar herself knows from bitter experience the limits of India's democratic institutions, having spent years bringing a Public Interest Litigation against Salwa Judum and the state of Chhattisgarh. In July 2011, a judge found for Sundar and her activist allies, and in an impassioned speech compared the enormities committed by instruments of the state in Chhattisgarh to the colonial horrors evoked in Joseph Conrad's *Heart of Darkness*. Nonetheless, since then few Salwa Judum perpetrators of rape, murder or plunder in Chhattisgarh have been brought to justice – not to speak of the architects of this vigilante force. None of their victims has been compensated for their losses; 'Maoists' are still killed in 'encounters' with the police or security services.[109] And meanwhile,

Rahul Pandita angrily observes, 'the life of an Adivasi is not getting better in any sense'.[110]

'The activists insist on talking of the "root causes" of Maoism,' Sundar says, summing up the dilemma. 'The security experts brush aside any reference to "root causes" and insist we talk of "Maoist violence". The academic debate what violence means, the journalists worry about their next big newsbreak. And so it goes on, this endless parlour game of seminars and working lunches and papers on the conflict. I can no longer see the child in the forest.'[111]

II

NEPAL –

MAOISM IN POWER?

On the afternoon of 3 August 2016, Pushpa Kamal Dahal sat in the Nepali parliament, calmly listening to the speaker announce his appointment as prime minister. The declaration complete, Pushpa Kamal was thronged by colleagues offering their congratulations. Mostly men of middle age or older, dressed in Western-style suits and open-necked shirts, they draped their new prime minister with red, orange, yellow and lime-green scarves and necklaces of fat marigolds until he was garlanded from his shoulders to his ears with silk and flowers. An extravagant splotch of tika – the vermilion powder traditionally used to mark celebrations and bring good fortune to major life ventures – occupied the central third of his forehead.

This was a decorous kind of accession – taking place in a space not always renowned for such harmony. Only eighteen months before, the parliamentary chamber had witnessed angry brawls, during which MPs had tossed chairs about, knocked over tables and hurled microphones at the speaker; serious bruising had resulted.[1] But the sedate conventionality of the occasion camouflaged how outlandish this political outcome was. For Pushpa Kamal Dahal is better known as Prachanda – the Fierce One – the *nom de guerre* he adopted while leading a Maoist insurgency against the Nepali monarchy and state between 1996 and 2006. For more than a decade, Prachanda had devoted his considerable energies and abilities to waging war on the parliamentary system, which he had denounced – in high Maoist style – as a 'sham' to be swept away by armed revolution.

Prachanda's elevation as prime minister (his second stint as premier since 2008) seems to represent an extraordinary triumph for global

Maoism, for the Nepali Maoists are the only such group outside China to have attained state power through espousing the strategies of Mao Zedong. Yet the reality is far more complex. Prachanda has had to grapple with an unstable political legacy and uncertain future. Nepal is still coming to terms with ten years of divisive violence, and Maoist politicians have to accommodate the radical visions that once defined their programme within the inherent conservatism of a dysfunctional, high-caste-dominated parliamentary system. To some observers, Nepal's Maoism has challenged social injustices and reformed national politics along more inclusive lines; to others, it illuminates the hypocrisies and failings of Maoist theory and practice. Either way, the trajectory of Nepali Maoism is one of the most interesting and perplexing political experiments in contemporary history. How can an ideology that apparently belongs to a different country and era not only take root, but achieve such dazzling success? For the story of Nepali Maoism is, in the words of one of its most lucid chroniclers, Aditya Adhikari, that of 'an exotic, anachronistic rebellion', occurring in a mountain kingdom associated with clichés of spirituality, fuelled by a Marxist variant that neo-liberalism was supposed to have crushed in 1989.[2] How adaptable has Nepali Maoism proved, and did those adaptations transform it into something fundamentally non-Maoist? What role will it play in Nepal's future?

The Maoist insurrection began at 10 p.m. on 12 February 1996, when thirty-six members of the newly formed Communist Party of Nepal (Maoist) (CPNM) rushed a police station in Rolpa, north-west Nepal. They were hardly a crack squad. Apart from a motley assortment of home-made firearms, they possessed only one rusty rifle, dating from the late 1980s. The attack was supposed to take place at 8 p.m., but the group lost their way while crossing dense forest in the dark. Instead of surrendering as the guerrillas had hoped, the policemen launched a spirited defence, returning the Maoists' fire for hours. On capturing a few explosives, the Maoists melted back into the night.[3]

A decade later, the Maoists had fought their way to a position of decisive political influence. Pushing back against the firepower of the Nepali police and army, their People's Liberation Army was 10,000 strong and had wrested 80 per cent of Nepal's territory from state control. Their armed rebellion was the principal reason for the collapse of the monarchy and the establishment of a federal republic in Nepal after 2006. Between 2006 and 2016, two leaders of the CPNM served between them three terms as prime minister of Nepal and many other senior party figures held government positions. Although the CPNM did not realise their original ambition – state capture resulting in unchallenged control of the country, as achieved by the Chinese Communist Party – Nepal is now the only country in the world where you can encounter self-avowed Maoists in power.

As with so many stories in this book, the militant visions of Nepali Maoism arose from two twentieth-century contingencies: the radical turn of the 1940s into the 1950s (which brought decolonisation to South Asia, Communist revolution in China and the end of Rana rule in Nepal); and the expansive zeal of the Cultural Revolution and its after-shocks throughout the late 1960s. Without understanding the long-range impact of these events, it is impossible to make sense of the apparently paradoxical eruption of a Maoist insurgency in 1996 – seven long years after Francis Fukuyama had declared that humans had reached 'the end of history' with capitalism's definitive victory over Communism.

In 1951, a coalition of rural discontents in Nepal and dispossessed Nepali exiles in India launched a military assault that removed from power the Rana dynasty, an oligarchic clan that for a century had run the country as a self-serving, exploitative, caste-ridden regime. Nine years of party-based rule and partial democracy ensued until the resurgent Shah monarchy banned all political parties in 1960 and instated three decades of rule by *panchayat* – elected local councils. In reality, however, ultimate authority lay with the king. Nepal remained a royal autocracy until popular demonstrations forced the reintroduction of parliamentary democracy in 1991. Economic change also stalled. Despite various attempts at land reform, in 1990, 5 per cent of Nepalis owned 40 per cent of the land.[4] Where poorer farmers did own their own land, it was often divided up into parcels too small to support a family all year round. As a result, labour emigration grew (above all to India): from around 328,000 in 1961 to almost 660,000 in 1991 (in addition to very substantial internal labour migrancy).[5] Numbers have skyrocketed since, to an estimated 14 per cent of the population – 3.2 million migrants in 2000, for example.[6]

Education was arguably the biggest success story of the Nepali state between 1951 and 1991. In order to limit the ability of Nepalis to question the status quo, the Ranas – like the colonial French in Indochina – had stringently limited access to education. In 1950, the country had fewer than 330 schools and literacy was no higher than 5 per cent. By 1991, three million children were in primary school and literacy had risen to 40 per cent.[7] But, as in Peru between the 1960s and 1980s, frustrated political, social and economic expectations, combined with burgeoning education rates, made the perfect recipe for left-wing unrest in Nepal.

The Nepali Communist movement was, on the one hand, weakened by even higher than normal tendencies to fracture: in the thirty years that followed the founding of the Communist Party of Nepal (CPN) in 1949, it split at least seven times, each fragment loudly claiming to be the only true heir to the original party. On the other hand, its political goals – equality, land reform, bridging the divide between urban and rural areas – enjoyed a high level of popular legitimacy, even if very few politicians or private individuals had much idea how such objectives might be institutionalised. Communist factions were welcomed at the rural grass roots, especially in the impoverished west of the country. 'In Nepal,' explained one of the country's pre-eminent political scientists, Krishna Hachhethu, 'Communism as a label has a great appeal. More than 50 per cent of voters vote for parties with a Communist tag. Surveys show that people consistently vote for economic equality over freedom.'[8] Sympathy for such goals dominated even the centre ground of Nepali politics: between the 1950s and the 1980s, the Nepali Congress Party also advocated 'a socialism in which the whole country would be "like one family"'.[9]

Into this receptive environment entered China's glossy foreign propaganda. Communist victory in 1949 spoke eloquently of the success of the Maoist model. Comrade Rohit – born in 1939 and a hard-left politician since the 1950s – described how as a child 'I visited a library in Bhaktapur [his home town] and told the librarian that I was interested in tales of bravery. They gave me a small book entitled *The Life of Mao*, through which I learned about Mao's love of serving the people, his patriotism, the way he brought China forward.'[10] Nepali readers identified with Mao's diagnosis of 1930s China as semi-colonial and semi-feudal: for them, caste-based agrarian society provided the semi-feudalism; India was the colonial threat. Pushpa Lal Shrestha, the founder of the CPN in 1949, adopted and endorsed this analysis.

In a nascent publishing market, Chinese propaganda could make a big impact. C. K. Lal – one of the most astute journalistic commentators on Nepali society and politics – remembered the widespread naivety of his schooldays in the 1960s. 'The new literates read and believed anything. And the Chinese and the Soviets liberally distributed free material – *China Pictorial*, for example, was handed out at school. When I was at school in the Terai [along Nepal's southern edge] I started a children's library and wrote to several embassies in Kathmandu asking for materials. Only the Chinese and the Soviet embassies responded, by sending us *China Pictorial* and *Soviet Union Illustrated Monthly*, or some such. In our library the only brand-new volumes, usually bound in red, were Chinese and Soviet. We kept them in the nicest place, even though we couldn't read them because they were in English.'[11] The multilingual propaganda of the Cultural Revolution radicalised the future leaders of the CPNM as they passed through schools in the 1960s. Two senior veterans of the Maoist civil war, husband and wife team Baburam Bhattarai and Hisila Yami, recalled that many Maoist treatises arrived in Hindi first, via India.[12] Logistical and intellectual links between Nepali and Indian Communists were close: the CPN was founded in Kolkata in 1949, and the Nepali Communists were schooled ideologically by their Indian comrades.

As China's quarrel with the Soviets intensified, young left-wing Nepalis insinctively sided with Mao. Prachanda would later remember a friend commenting on a portrait of Mao in the late 1960s: 'This is the supreme leader of China, where there is no disparity between the rich and the poor, or the weak and the powerful. There, everyone is equal.'[13] For decades, Khagendra Sangroula, a prolific translator from English into Nepali, kept an avid domestic market supplied with Mao's writings. By 1965, he recalled, Mao was 'everywhere in Kathmandu: wide and loud. Most of my friends were China-tilted.'[14] The best-stocked pro-China bookshop was Pragati Prakashan (run by a notorious skinflint called Niranjan Baidya, who underpaid those he commissioned to translate political texts into Nepali).[15] Its shelves held Mao's essays, poems, the Little Red Book, and a variety of Chinese propaganda such as *Peking Review*. In a smart soft-power move, the PRC also distributed both the cream of pre-1949 left-leaning literature – for example, the fiction and essays of Lu Xun, an acclaimed writer and on-off fellow traveller to Chinese Communism – and a selection of socialist realism from the post-1949 pantheon. The latter included Yang Mo's *Song of Youth* and Li Xintian's novella *Bright Red Star*, both of which sold an appealing vision of Maoist activism and idealism to Nepal's literate bright young things. 'The shop was a propaganda machine,' Sangroula described. 'The Little Red Book, "Serve the People", "The Foolish Old Man Who Moved the Mountain", "Where Do Correct Ideas Come From" and "Report from Hunan" were the most widely read and discussed ... Mao was the only person who wrote about very complex things in a very simple way that even ordinary peasants could understand.'[16] For these readers, 'Mao was like a god. Khrushchev was like a demon. Everything published from China was like a bible, a Quran. Everything published from Russia was bad.'[17]

The Nepalese government played a peculiarly tolerant, positively encouraging role in the country's Mao fever. In 1960, King Mahendra suspended parliament, outlawed political parties and seized political power on the grounds that the multi-party system had led to corruption and political anarchy. Under these circumstances, public discussion of and open participation in party politics became practically impossible (several leaders of the previously above-ground political parties were incarcerated). Yet Mao's works remained curiously available, for Mahendra wanted to cultivate Nepal's Communists as a counterweight to Congress, the largest political party before 1960. 'You could publish anything so long as it didn't directly criticise the king or the Panchayat,' observed Sangroula. 'Mao's writings were all available.'[18] And because of the clamp on domestic political discussion, the generation growing up in the 1960s and '70s were often better informed about foreign affairs. Through the 1950s and '60s, King Mahendra – viewing good relations with China as a bulwark against Indian influence – was surprisingly friendly with the PRC. China returned the compliment, instructing its media to label him a 'progressive king' and turning a blind eye to his imprisonment of Communists. Almost $10 million went into building a road between Kathmandu and Tibet in the early 1960s, and on the eve of the Cultural Revolution, 16.8 per cent of China's foreign aid went to Nepal.[19] When India – permanently nervous about Chinese influence in the region, but particularly so in the aftermath of the 1962 border war – protested that such aid made Nepal, and therefore India, more vulnerable to Maoist Communism,

Mahendra confidently replied that 'communism does not travel by taxi'. In 1967, Chinese technicians and engineers working in Nepal began handing out Mao badges and Little Red Books to their co-workers, who had to 'salute Mao's portrait and chant slogans praising him' before getting paid.[20]

Despite the ructions caused by the Cultural Revolution and the Maoist inspiration for the Naxalite movement just over the border in India (which Nepali radicals tried to replicate in 1971–72 in Jhapa, a district a little west of Naxalbari), the monarchy almost simultaneously launched the Back to the Villages programme for Nepal's educated youth, a campaign directly modelled on the Cultural Revolution project of rusticating intellectuals to be re-educated by the rural masses. Its architect, Khamal Raj Regmi, was a voracious reader of Mao; the programme's chairman, Vishwa Bandhu Thapa, had been toured and banqueted in China by Zhu De and Zhou Enlai, to extensive coverage in *Peking Review*.[21] University students were compelled to spend at least a year working – most likely teaching – in a Nepali village before they could graduate. The theory was simple: the programme would integrate the nation, reduce the divide between urban and rural areas, and enable Nepal's most educated to contribute to village development.[22]

It did not quite work out like that. In 1968, Sangroula, a student of English literature, grew convinced that there would be a revolution in the next ten years, by which point his bourgeois education would be useless. He and about a dozen comrades therefore decided to join the Back to the Village Campaign to spread the word. Heading west, Sangroula recalled,

> I had a hundred Red Books in my bag, and a head full of dreams. In the evenings and early mornings, I taught young boys the Red Book, Mao's works about women, children, revolution, guerrilla and protracted warfare. 'Revolution is not a dinner party, power comes out of the barrel of a gun', and so on. Most of the boys had bad houses and bad land, they led a poor and difficult life ... I didn't have concrete ideas about what they would do. I was a romantic revolutionary. I hoped they would be impressed by my propaganda and take the path of the revolution ... The Cultural Revolution was

very much the inspiration. It represented the idea that teachers and professors should go to the countryside, and that there shouldn't be a gap between theory and practice. That teachers and professors should be remoulded. The boys were so shy: they said, whatever the teacher says, goes.[23]

Despite the conspicuously subversive uses to which Sangroula and others tried to put the Back to the Villages programme – for which Sangroula was repeatedly arrested and interrogated – it took the government until 1979 to cancel it.

Discouraged by government repression, and now married and with a child, Sangroula returned to Kathmandu where he was commissioned by Niranjan Baidya to translate the second, third and fourth volumes of Mao's works and some Chinese fiction, including Yang Mo's *Song of Youth*, into Nepali. Baidya had been given money from China to arrange the translation, but he seems to have pocketed much of it, as Sangroula was only paid 6,000 rupees.[24] These translations would become the educational nucleus of the Maoist civil war between 1996 and 2006. *Song of Youth*, meanwhile, was one of a core group of texts that Maoist cadres claimed inspired them to join the party. 'We grew up reading your work,' Prachanda repeatedly told Sangroula; still today, the Maoist leader defers to the translator as a cultural guru.[25] Nepali Maoism was a heavily literary phenomenon, steeped in texts; once more, it was revolution by the book.[26] Fiction and Mao's essays, especially, welcomed young readers into an imagined world of political commitment.[27] And although many young, illiterate Nepalis joined the revolution in its western stronghold due to its promise of social change, educated, literate elites formed its nucleus. The then Maoist minister of information, a veteran guerrilla commander from the east of Nepal called Surendra Kumar Karki, remembered in 2016 how he acquired his Maoism through English texts. 'I learned about the Cultural Revolution through Westerners writing about China: Agnes Smedley, Edgar Snow, William Hinton, Han Suyin. I went through all the books on China by Westerners.'[28] Hisila Yami – one of the most senior female leaders in the movement – traced her period of true political awakening to her time in Newcastle in the early 1990s, when her master's course enabled her to read voraciously – including *Red*

Star Over China, of which she procured copies for the young Maoist party back in Nepal.²⁹

Most of the top Maoist leaders were members of high castes. One of the best educated of them all was Baburam Bhattarai, the brains of the movement. Born in 1954 in rural Gorkha, central Nepal, Bhattarai was a beneficiary of the reforms that made education possible for Nepalis. In Nepal, as in many other places in the world, the 1960s were a time of possibility and questioning. At school and university, many encountered tales of democracy and revolution elsewhere in the world and wondered why Nepal still lived under an autocratic monarchy. Bhattarai finished school in 1970, making headlines by passing out top of his national cohort in the School Leaving Certificate; this academic success opened doors to further study in Kathmandu, then in India. Education transformed the life possibilities of a boy who had had to travel miles to reach primary school and help in the fields after class. The final phase of this education – writing a PhD thesis entitled 'The Nature of Underdevelopment and Regional Structure of Nepal – A Marxist Analysis' – enabled Bhattarai to develop the ideological justification of the Maoist war.

Yet despite the sense of regional, ideological and literary closeness with China, Nepali Maoists had little interest in establishing unmediated channels of information about life in China. The influential translations of Chinese writing into Nepali (Mao's works, Lu Xun's, Yang Mo's *Song of Youth* and so on) were all from English versions. Until recently, opportunities to study Chinese were rare. In the 1960s and '70s, only two individuals in the foreign ministry had expertise in Chinese affairs and spoke Chinese. As in India, there was a head-over-heels infatuation with Chinese ideology, but little interest in exploring the actualities of Maoism in China. 'I've never been to China,' declared Khagendra Sangroula, 'or even to the Chinese embassy myself. I like Mao, China and the Chinese revolution, but I wasn't interested in going there.'³⁰

This intense literary, rather than empirical, relationship with Maoism has left a very particular imprint on Nepali Maoism. In the West, the passion of young radicals for Maoism faded as China publicly lost confidence in the Maoist experiment after Mao's death, and as memoirs relating the horrors of the Cultural Revolution and Mao's own ruthlessness began to circulate widely during the 1980s. In Nepal, by contrast, the intensity of Maoists' ardour for literary and ideological texts has created a relationship with Maoism that fixates on abstractions and ideals, rather than on lived experience under Mao's policies – despite the fact that evidence of the effects of Mao's rule, in the form of Tibetan refugee camps in the Kathmandu Valley, was under the noses of Mao's Nepali admirers.

In Nepal, the chilly abstractions of the Sino-Soviet quarrel still matter, and the ideologies of the Cold War remain live issues. Mohan Bikram Singh joined the CPN in 1953 at the age of eighteen, then left to build an independent Communist party and organisation in western Nepal which became the training ground for the future leaders of the Maoist 'People's War'. Like most of the Nepali left wing of his and later generations, he favoured Mao's model of revolution: mass organisation in rural areas, preparation for armed struggle and ultimate state capture. He envisioned his stronghold in Pyuthan, western Nepal, as Nepal's Yan'an. His problem (or perhaps it was his genius) is that he has never felt Nepal was ready for armed revolution. Despite this lifetime of deferral, he retains a zeal for the correctness of the ideological prescriptions that he has subscribed to for so many decades. Still an ardent Maoist in his eighties, when asked when he first encountered Mao, he immediately zooms in on the Sino-Soviet dispute of the 1960s. 'The Great Debate', he calls it, his eyes shining.[31]

In 1984, remnant Maoist parties around the world which had straggled on past the fractures of the 1970s and China's own repudiation of the Cultural Revolution came together in the Revolutionary Internationalist Movement (RIM). It united groups from Turkey, Bangladesh and Haiti, Peru's Shining Path, and from the UK the Nottingham and Stockport Communist groups. The organisational drive came from the Revolutionary Communist Party of the US, under the leadership of Bob Avakian. A reclusive figure, given to speaking in dogma through his official spokesperson and inclined to purges of his 150-strong membership, Avakian had created his own Mao-style personality cult – his most charismatic act has been to put together, in imitation of the Little Red Book, his own little grey book of sayings, *Bullets*. Avakian and the members of RIM had an evangelical zeal towards Maoism, returning to the utopian imaginings of the 1960s and the absolute certainties expressed in *Peking Review*. Mohan Bikram

Singh was a founding member of RIM's first congress. 'The rise of Deng Xiaoping,' he remembered, 'made Communists all over the world anxious. We in RIM believed that Mao needed saving.'[32]

From its beginnings, RIM engaged in heartfelt but turgid debates about revolutionary ideology – light years from the consumerist, Reaganite visions taking hold during the 1980s. In the West, Avakian and his nucleus of devoted disciples could easily be dismissed – as one former, expelled comrade called them – as 'nothing-burgers'. But would-be revolutionaries in Nepal, who harboured an intense, textual relationship with Maoism, were galvanised towards civil war by the organisation; it represented international validation for armed revolution. RIM's line under Avakian was, Singh recalled disapprovingly, 'more anarchic than Marxist-Leninist. They felt there was no need to analyse any particular situation, that you could start armed struggle at any time. So they were always saying: it's the right moment to start armed revolution in Nepal. Armed struggle will then create its own conditions.' To RIM, the Shining Path was a glowing example to be emulated.

The ever-patient Singh was sceptical and later broke with RIM, but his less phlegmatic subordinates in west Nepal took RIM's bait. 'RIM was the main instigator behind the armed movement,' Singh claimed.[33] Mohan Baidya alias Comrade Kiran, son of a Communist schoolteacher, formed his own faction of the CPN in 1985 (the official pretext being that Singh had committed 'bourgeois' adultery and therefore no longer belonged to the revolutionary vanguard).[34] After his attempts to launch armed insurrection failed in the late 1980s, Kiran conceded the leadership to Prachanda, another former disciple of Mohan Bikram Singh. In 1991, as Nepal began a new experiment with multi-party democracy and public political activism became possible once more, this faction (calling itself Unity Centre) resolved to launch a 'people's war to bring about a new democratic revolution in Nepal'. In 1994, it went underground, to prepare for war; the following year, it became the CPN (Maoist).[35] 'RIM gave us no material support,' Kiran recalled. 'Its support was theoretical.'[36] In Nepal's context, that was enough – it was the single spark to light a prairie fire.

Before C. K. Lal became a full-time political commentator, he was a civil engineer. 'I was said to be a very good engineer,' he told me with a self-ironising smile. 'Though I was considered one of the Maoists' fiercest critics during the war, there was no open enmity between us, because I had helped build the Karnali Bridge, which linked far-west Nepal, and one of the Maoists' strongholds, to the rest of the country. That bridge opened the area to the outside world.' As an executive committee member of the Nepal Engineers' Association, in 1986 Lal co-organised the World Congress of Engineering Education, to be held that year in Kathmandu. He later recalled anodyne planning meetings sometimes taking an odd direction during chitchat over tea and biscuits. '"The police stations in rural areas are above cowsheds," my colleagues would muse. "It would be so easy to disarm and rout the police there. And do you know – the guards in banks are armed only with a gun that takes fifteen minutes to load, and even then is not guaranteed to fire. A clever person can loot a bank with a stick." I didn't think anything of it at the time.'

But Lal had clearly often thought back over that exchange, and what it meant for Nepali Maoism.

> Many of those colleagues later became activists or leaders of the Maoist movement. Almost everyone initially with the Maoist movement in the mid-1990s was a middle-class, educated professional with college degrees: Prachanda, who trained as an agricultural scientist and teacher, who worked for a while as consultant to a USA-funded project. Baburam Bhattarai, a trained urban planner and political economist with a PhD. Badal, who headed their military wing, started out studying agricultural engineering in Russia. Kiran, a literary critic with a high Sanskrit education. Many others were teachers: mostly middle class, professional, with college degrees, who thought that [Nepali] plebeians needed to be led by the vanguard. In other words, the classic Marxist set-up.

'Perhaps,' he mused sceptically, 'it was [always] a completely educated middle-class exercise, a short cut to power, rather than a real revolution ... these are very clever political entrepreneurs, who have pasted on the grand name Maoist.'[37] The Maoist leaders were for the most part Brahmins – 'gods on earth' according to certain Hindu scriptures – and consciously strove to style themselves as 'Maoist Brahmin Warrior-Kings'.[38] Members of lower castes, meanwhile, became rank-and-file activists and soldiers. They were the ones in the firing line, while leaders like Prachanda, Bhattarai and Yami saw out much of the war as non-combatants, hiding among Nepali communities in India. 'Prachanda was careerist,' recalled Mohan Bikram Singh, his political mentor through the 1970s. 'With him, it was about personal ambition rather than ideas and ideologies.'[39]

But elite opportunism is not enough to explain the success of the Maoist movement after it began its armed struggle in 1996. At that time its rhetoric of radical transformation fell on fertile ground. Although NGO foreign aid flooded into newly democratic Nepal after 1990, its distribution was unequal and corrupt, with local bigwigs successfully diverting it into projects that directly benefited them. While the advent of democracy had raised expectations, economic growth after 1990 was disappointing. Many farmers could only produce enough food to feed themselves and their families for a few months of each year; this shortfall in sustenance exposed them to exploitative working conditions and forced them to rely on exorbitant loan rates to buy food and other essentials. These inequalities were aggravated by hierarchies of power within Nepali society resulting in the exploitation of female labour, the economic and social oppression of low castes and untouchables by higher castes, and the marginalisation of ethnic minorities. Statistics had a depressing story to tell: in 2001, life expectancy in Nepal was fifty-nine on average, but stood at only forty-two in the far west.[40] Many Nepalis voted with their feet. In 1997, over 10 per cent of the working population migrated to India, the Gulf States, Malaysia and other parts of Asia; the remittances they sent back constituted perhaps as much as a quarter of Nepal's GDP. These proportions would only increase over the next two decades.[41]

The Nepali state was neglectful at best, exploitative and aggressive at worst. Those who clung on to power in Kathmandu hardly represented the socio-economic and ethnic diversity of the population in general; taxes were used to develop urban, rather than rural areas. The dysfunctionality of Nepal's democracy, meanwhile, prevented (indeed still prevents) most administrations from pursuing the kind of coherent socio-economic reform programmes the country needed. The democratically elected governments formed after the restoration of multi-party politics in 1990 were mostly unstable coalitions. Between 1994 and 1999 alone, Nepal had at least (depending on how you count them) three different governments, rising and falling amid corruption scandals, cynical factionalism and votes of no-confidence. Prachanda, Bhattarai and other radicals argued convincingly that the stooges of the old *panchayat* regime, who had kept Nepal impoverished and inequitable since the 1960s, had slipped smoothly into positions of power in the new 'democracy' – in other words, the old inequities were being reproduced under the guise of an inclusive, liberal political system. Further attempts at land reform between 1995 and 2001, for example, were steadily defanged, redistributing only 0.425 per cent of Nepali land.[42]

Meanwhile, the police and judiciary were failing ordinary Nepalis. What happened in Dullu, western Nepal, in 2000 is illustrative of this failure. That year, it was reported that a policeman from the local station had seduced and eloped with a local woman, then abandoned her in a nearby town. Outraged villagers burned down the police station and the police abandoned Dullu. The resulting power vacuum was quickly filled by the Maoists.[43]

The nucleus of the insurgency lay in the chronically neglected districts of Rolpa and Rukum, in mid-western Nepal. Here the population was ethnically dominated by the Kham Magar, one of the janajati ('tribal') groups in the country. They carved out a precarious existence: only 10 per cent of the land was farmable, and this fed its occupants for barely six months of the year.[44] Nepali Communists – people like Mohan Bikram Singh – had taught and worked in these communities since the 1950s. These early activists seem to have practised the Maoist ethos of 'serving the people': travelling from village to village, striking up relationships with locals whatever their caste or politics, and helping with domestic and agricultural chores. Some activists adopted the more aggressive parts of the Maoist repertoire against local elites, forcing them into humiliating rituals, in which their faces were smeared with soot or their necks garlanded with shoes.[45]

Prachanda's Unity Centre proclaimed in 1991 that they would 'follow the path of People's War with the strategy of encircling the city from the countryside', as 'developed by Comrade Mao'.[46] After the vanguard section of Unity Centre had become the Communist Party of Nepal (Maoist) in 1995, Bhattarai and Prachanda mobilised for 'People's War'. 'The class struggle launched by [politically] conscious peasants in the western hill districts, particularly in Rolpa and Rukum, represents a high level of anti-feudal and anti-imperialist revolutionary struggle,' a Central Committee meeting pronounced, which 'has given birth to a new element in the Nepali communist movement and inspired us to become increasingly serious about undertaking armed struggle'. The new party pushed forward on two distinctly Maoist fronts: training in guerrilla warfare on the one hand, and on the other political education promulgated through mass meetings, songs and dances, which taught cadres and sympathisers to 'violently confront "reactionary" state power'.[47]

In November 1995, the state launched Operation Romeo against the Maoists. Some 2,200 policemen were unleashed upon Rolpa and Rukum, where they looted, raped and tortured. More than 6,000 people fled their homes.[48] Local communities became increasingly polarised between Maoist radicalism and the brutal state response, with many feeling that the state was waging war on the most vulnerable parts of society. In 1998, when the 'People's War' was fully under way, the Nepali Congress government unleashed Operation Kilo Sierra Two (also identified as 'Search and Kill'). 'If [the Maoists] don't respect the Constitution,' ran its maxim, 'we don't have to stick to the Constitution.' Widespread, indiscriminate police brutality drove many over to the Maoists.[49] When the Royal Nepalese Army joined the fight in 2001, they behaved with even greater impunity.[50]

On 4 February 1996, the Maoists presented an ultimatum to the Nepali prime minister: if the government did not agree within two weeks to forty demands – ranging from the effective abolition of the monarchy and of the caste system, to the end of discrimination against women and ethnic minorities, the establishment of a Constituent Assembly and radical land reform – the CPNM would initiate Protracted War. When the government failed to respond – and after waiting only nine days – the CPNM embarked on their 'People's War'. Guerrilla groups attacked police posts in Rukum and Rolpa, ransacked banks, made bonfires of loan contracts and verbosely lectured locals on the Maoist New Democratic Revolution before disappearing back into the forest and hills.[51]

★

On a clear bright December morning in 2016, at a tea shack on a dusty Kathmandu roadside, I met Comrade Kamala, a Maoist commander during the civil war and a minister in the post-war Constituent Assembly. In her late thirties, robustly built and wearing her gleaming long hair loose, she was a strong presence. She spoke in a powerful voice, accompanied by expressive gestures, her frequent laughter revealing brilliant white teeth. When I asked to take her photograph (just as an aide-memoire, to be archived with my notes), she arranged herself with care then confidently stared into the camera. She had an extraordinary story to tell.

Kamala was born to a Magar family, in a village in a remote part of Rukum, the district that became the original homeland for the Maoist insurgency. Although her family had enough to eat, her own childhood was blighted by her parents' (especially her mother's) devotion to social traditions that regarded girls as inferior. While her older brother progressed through school, she had to look after the animals, which meant spending days away from home in the hills, walking with the herd. In 1990, the same year that her brother passed out of school and went to university, she turned eleven and her family decided that she was to be married. 'The night before the engagement was due to take place, I ran away from home and hid by a huge boulder,' she recalled. 'I cried there all night. Eventually, my mother brought me home and agreed to postpone the marriage. "If you ever marry me off, I'll kill myself," I told her. It was my first rebellion.'

That year, a group of young radical Communists that in 1995 would become part of the CPNM arrived in the village. The current system of government, they told locals, was 'a multi-party democratic sham. When our revolution triumphs, women will be empowered and go to school.' Kamala was impressed and inspired. She had always wanted to attend school but could barely sign her name. With the support of a newly formed women's committee, she taught herself to read and write in just two months, staying up all night while she was out with the cattle. Her first ever letter – sent to her brother studying in town – got straight to the point: 'Why is life so unfair? Why do you go to school but I don't? Aren't we born of the same mother?' Kamala then secretly took on odd jobs – hard labour like hauling stones – to pay for her school enrolment, books and uniform.

When her mother discovered what was going on she thrashed Kamala so hard she broke three sticks in the process. 'I didn't cry once. I was so desperate to go to school,' Kamala told me. In 1994, when her mother died of a stroke at the age of forty, her father resigned himself to his daughter's ambitions. Kamala quickly became the top student in her class, and an active member of 'the fighters' group', the youth wing of the Maoist party, which provided ideological, physical and firearms training. The organisation also helped her to resist the prospect of an arranged marriage, which her family tried to force on her again in her mid-teens.

On 13 February 1996, Kamala entered history, as one of three women guerrillas participating in the CPNM's first attacks of the 'People's War'. 'It was freezing cold up in the mountains; heavy snow,' she remembered. 'We walked for two days and two nights in three teams.' These physical challenges notwithstanding, Kamala's attack went like clockwork. 'Our team attacked a police station in Rukum. When we arrived at midnight, we found about a dozen policemen there, fast asleep, on the second storey of the building – the ground floor was full of goats and cows. They were completely unarmed: the one policeman with a gun was away, at the district headquarters. They were scared to death and surrendered straight away.'

Kamala is a striking advertisement for the Maoists' achievements in Nepal – a country where the burden of work inside and outside the home has traditionally fallen on rural women and where, at the time of the civil war, violence against women was accepted as normal. One late-twentieth-century study showed that 57 per cent of judges believed that a husband could hit his wife to 'correct her attitude'.[52] To this day in far west Nepal, menstruating girls and women are thought 'impure' and routinely banished to freezing and insanitary outdoor sheds, where an unknown number die each year. As an individual disadvantaged by gender, ethnicity and social class, from one of the most underdeveloped parts of the country, Kamala drew from the Maoist movement organisational, ideological, physical and moral support in her fight for self-realisation. In 2005, she was promoted to brigade commander and after the peace agreement of 2006, she was invited to Kathmandu to form part of the interim legislature. In the first Constituent Assembly (the government that reinstated Nepal's political process between 2008 and 2012), she was voted in as a member of parliament through the electoral amendment that selected around half of MPs through a quota requirement within proportional representation. During 2011–13, she served as a minister.

The Maoist insurgency made these achievements possible. 'I'm happy,' she told me. 'Things are better now. People have learned to rebel. Thirty per cent of the movement were women. That we have a female president and speaker, that far more women in my village now go to school, this is all down to the movement.' The 'People's War' even brought her romance. At fifteen or sixteen, she fell for one of the activists who had first awoken her politically in the early 1990s. 'He gave me education when I most needed it. He gave me a new life. I thought of him as my saviour. He was also impressed by my rebellion.' They married in 1997, in a party political ceremony: 'we swore always to put the interests of the party above our own personal interests; that we would never betray the party.'

Listening to her, I got the feeling that she would probably have found other ways of rebelling, even if the Maoists had not come to her village. She emanated mental and physical toughness. 'The idea of impossibility doesn't exist in the diary that I keep,' she told me. In 2002, she was in the military front line when eight and a half months pregnant with her first child, responsible for preparing a major offensive. After leading injured comrades to safety at the border with India, she went into labour. Eighteen hours later, the baby was born but the placenta was retained and she was rushed to India for surgery. The day after the operation, 'I crossed back into Nepal with the baby and walked day and night for a week to return to Rolpa.' She named the boy Azaad – Freedom. (She laughed a lot while telling that story.) In 2006, after the peace accord, she went back to her old school to complete her School Leaving Certificate, the essential qualification that marks graduation from high school. Her comrades in the party were opposed to it: during the civil war, the CPNM had lectured young people that 'bourgeois education' was useless, in order to persuade them to join up. But Kamala ignored them. 'Ten years had passed, and I had killed a lot of enemies, but I passed the exam. It was all over the news, a feel-good story. I still have all the cuttings. I'm now doing my BA.'

The CPNM had given her a role, a career and above all a clear ideology by which to understand the revolution and her part in it. Mao was ubiquitous through her training: 'He was quoted all the time.' She studied a biography of Mao – most likely the excerpt from *Red Star Over China* that was circulated as an educational text within the CPNM. The movement at the grass roots was steeped in Mao, and in the culture and strategy of Mao's CCP. Still today, former recruits recite quotations from their training attributed to Mao. 'The correctness or incorrectness of the political and ideological line decides everything,' recalled one young Dalit woman. 'Power comes out of the barrel of a gun,' remembered a member of a song-and-dance troupe. 'Politics is war without blood, war is politics with blood. This was repeated so many times, to validate the armed struggle ... We performed model operas from China. The cadres would give us an outline of the plot, the context, then we'd adapt them with our own favourite tunes.'[53]

Despite his scepticism about the movement's leadership, C. K. Lal speaks admiringly of the effect that the Maoists had on rural conscious-ness. 'Once the Maoist war started, people stopped fearing the police because guns levelled the ground. Think of it from the point of view of a Dalit, who has never held a real gun in his hand. Or someone even more marginalised than him: a Dalit woman. She doesn't have to fire it. She goes to the village where she had to walk with her head bowed. Suddenly, so-called upper-caste people, if they don't bow, they change their path, when they see her. Imagine that confidence, that power.'[54]

In the course of the civil war, the Maoists designed their own 'cultural revolution': a puritanical campaign against alcohol and 'old' beliefs, ranging from religion to caste discrimination. This included dismantling the horrendous discrimination and prejudice that for centuries had persecuted Dalits. Maoist seizure of power in the coun-tryside depended on mobilising untouchables and ethnic minorities into violent rebellion against local elites. When the Maoists arrived, remembered one Dalit, they asked:

> What do you want? And our heart went out to them ... because they'll put an end to untouchability ... And so, I was attracted to Maoism ... My frame of mind became warlike ... I did not give in because someone had oppressed me ... I went to the rich to take them down a peg or two, and I took away some of their wealth, I 'grilled them three times', I 'ground them three times'.[55]

Women often made easy recruits. They were told in one part of western Nepal that, if they joined the Maoists, 'they would be allowed to choose their own husband. They would be free ... to dance and sing whenever they wished ... to travel around the country and they would be given soap to wash themselves ... above all, they would be given a gun and would be able to eat anywhere free of charge.'[56] Reality was less rosy. Inevitably, there were chasms between the theory and practice of gender equality. Some girls were forcibly recruited, or abducted; and in many places they continued to shoulder the burden of most domestic tasks. According to one (male) Maoist official, one 'could expect complete gender equality only after the class struggle was successful'.[57]

On 6 June 2005, six members of Nama Ghimire's family – his son, daughter, son-in-law, sister-in-law and two grandchildren – boarded a bus from the village of Madi, in a forested valley some two hundred kilometres south of Kathmandu, to market in Bharatpur. It was a popular journey: about a hundred people piled into the vehicle, and several had to travel on the roof (alongside two goats). At 8 a.m., as the bus progressed along a yellow rubble road, it suddenly leapt about twelve metres into the air, splitting into two sections. A group of Maoist commandos had detonated five kilograms of explosives on the highway exactly as the bus passed through. All six of Ghimire's relatives perished in the blast, along with at least thirty-two others (including four other children; state media put the casualty list at fifty-three). When the bus crashed back to the ground – its metal sides in tangled shreds – the goats had remained somehow unharmed, still tethered to the roof, amid the appalling carnage. The survivors of the Ghimire family were left emotionally shattered: 'my wife still can't come home because it breaks her heart', mourned Nama Ghimire ten years on.[58]

The Maoists' target had been a handful of Royal Nepalese Army (RNA) soldiers on the bus, but the casualties were overwhelmingly civilian. Prachanda quickly apologised for the attack, calling it a 'mistake'. Nonetheless, the bombing has subsequently been seen as emblematic of the Nepali Maoists' reckless worship of violence and military means. For although the CPNM did manage to persuade some members of Nepali society of the righteousness of their cause, coercion played an equally, if not more, important part in their success. The victory of the Chinese Communist Party in 1949 was above all an armed conquest, rather than a triumph of mass persuasion through moral mandate; by 2006 the power of the CPNM in much of the Nepali countryside followed a similar pattern.

Although the leadership did lift a number of tricks from Mao's political toolkit – the careful use of cultural troupes to 'sugar-coat' political messages, the circulation of Mao's essays with civilian messages ('Serve the People', 'The Foolish Old Man') – Mao's deepest imprint on the 'People's War' in Nepal was military. The country, the Nepali Maoists argued, remained 'semi-feudal, semi-colonial' behind the facade of a phoney multi-party democracy, and armed struggle was necessary to bring 'real' democracy to Nepal. On the basis of this analysis, the party's military strategy adopted Mao's concept of protracted warfare. Prachanda and his comrades-in-arms reverently cited Mao's prescriptions on moving from 'strategic defence, to strategic equilibrium, to strategic offence'.[59] CPNM documents openly proclaimed Maoist slogans glorifying the army and war as the ideological foundation of their new state: 'The people without army have nothing of their own', 'The main instrument of the state is the army', 'In New Democratic revolution the main form of organisation is the army and the main form of struggle is the war.'[60]

The 'People's War' began modestly enough. In 1996, Prachanda travelled north-east from Rolpa up to the border with Tibet, where he obtained his first two rifles.[61] One didn't work; both were (like Prachanda's own Maoism) relics of the Cold War, part of an arsenal that the CIA had air-dropped in 1961 to aid Tibetan rebels plotting rebellion against Chinese occupation. Another ghost of Cold War conflict offered military training: Naxalite guerrillas from Bihar and Andhra Pradesh helped their Nepali comrades to get battle-ready. As it progressed, the Maoist movement in Nepal became steeped in gun worship: 'comrades showed how much they loved [captured] weapons that were won with the blood of their comrades', recounted one battle report.[62] 'What a beautiful procession of warriors!' rhapsodised a member of a 4,000-strong marching column. 'Is this sight any different from the Long March of the Chinese revolution led by Comrade Mao?'[63]

Aravindan Balakrishnan, a Kerala-born Singaporean who became leader of the Workers' Institute of Marxism-Leninism-Mao Zedong Thought in London. In 2015, he was convicted of sixteen charges of sexual and physical assault, including rape, child cruelty and false imprisonment of the small, all-female collective that made up his institute.

Idalgo Macchiarini, the first kidnap victim (in March 1972) of the Maoist-influenced Italian urban terrorists, the Red Brigades. The notice around his neck reads: 'Hit and run. Nothing goes unpunished. Strike one to educate one hundred.' One of the group's leaders, Alberto Franceschini, later recalled: 'We got "hit and run" from Mao. He had written that the principle of partisan tactics is to hit and immediately run.'

The symbolic beginning of the Maoist insurgency of the Communist Party of Peru – Shining Path. On 26 December 1980 – Mao's birthday – Shining Path operatives hung dead dogs from eight lampposts in Lima. The dogs' heads had been pushed through a notice emblazoned with the words of Deng Xiaoping, Mao's successor who broke with many of the Chairman's keynote Cultural Revolution policies.

Abimael Guzmán, leader of the Shining Path insurgency. He originally built his following out of student and academic disciples at the Universidad Nacional de San Cristóbal de Huamanga in Ayacucho, the provincial capital of the region of Peru that would become the epicentre of the Shining Path insurrection.

Female Shining Path prisoners in Lima in the early 1990s sing and march towards a huge, idealised mural of their leader, Abimael Guzmán. 'Nothing is impossible' has been painted high on the wall above their heads – Shining Path's paraphrasing of Maoist voluntarism.

A grieving Peruvian Quechua mother searches for the body of her son. Between 1980 and 1999, the Peruvian civil war killed 69,000 people; both sides – government and Shining Path forces – committed countless atrocities. Impoverished rural, indigenous communities suffered disproportionately from the violence.

The 'Mao of India', Charu Mazumdar (fourth from left) and comrades in front of Mazumdar's residence in Siliguri, north-east India. Mazumdar's zeal for Mao's revolutionary strategies galvanised the Maoist-Naxalite rebellion that began in north India in 1967. The ongoing Maoist insurgency in India today traces its heritage back to this first rebellion.

An Indian-Chinese pantheon of Maoist leaders in the village of Naxalbari, near the site of a police massacre that took place during the Naxalite insurgency in 1967.

People's Liberation Guerrilla Army fighters attend a Communist Party of India (Maoist) congress in the jungles of Bihar in 2007. The previous year, the Indian government named the Maoist insurgency the 'biggest internal security threat to the Indian state'.

A local woman looks out over toxic effluents resulting from big-corporation mining of bauxite deposits in Orissa. The Indian government's determination to generate revenue from mining contracts in the mineral-rich states of east India has dispossessed – often in brutal ways – many locals of their land. The CPI (Maoist) has offered the most muscular form of resistance to such strong-arming.

The Nepali Maoist leadership in the 1990s: second from left, Baburam Bhattarai; third from left, Hisila Yami (married to Bhattarai); first from right, Prachanda, 'the fierce one'.

A family photograph of Hisila Yami and Baburam Bhattarai with their daughter Manushi (an extremely talented and able political activist in her own right), also from the 1990s. Note the image of the captured Abimael Guzmán in prison uniform in the background. The Shining Path – as a post-Mao Maoist insurgency – were a significant ideological inspiration to the Communist Party of Nepal (Maoist).

A victim of a CPN (Maoist) bus bombing south of Kathmandu in 2005.

The Nepali Maoist leader Comrade Kiran in 2016, pictured between a gold statue of Mao and a vase inscribed with Mao's calligraphy; both items were carried back from his first visit to China in 2009. In 2012, Kiran broke from the CPN (Maoist) to form a faction that vowed to return to armed struggle to capture the state.

Bo Xilai at his sentencing to life imprisonment for corruption in 2013. During his rule as party secretary of Chongqing between 2007 and 2012, Bo made Mao a conspicuous part of the political mainstream once more.

Gu Kailai, disgraced wife of Bo Xilai, testifying at her husband's trial. In 2012, she was given a suspended death sentence for the murder of the British businessman Neil Heywood. The scandal destroyed Bo's ambitions for national leadership.

Side-by-side trinkets of Xi Jinping, current president of China, and Mao. Building on Bo's Maoist revival, Xi has re-normalised aspects of Maoist political culture: criticism, self-criticism, the mass line, the personality cult.

An irreverent depiction of Mao from Zhang Hongtu's 'Mao Series'. Other portraits from the series show Mao with tiger stripes and ogling a statue of the Goddess of Democracy.

A 37-metre-high golden statue of Mao built in the countryside in Henan, central China. For unclear reasons, it was demolished a few days after it was unveiled in early January 2016.

Without coercion, Maoist expansion would have been unthinkable. In Deurali, north-west of Kathmandu, villagers remembered the first Maoists arriving in the second half of the 1990s as aggressive foreigners. 'We were very scared,' recalled a local seamstress. 'Ten or twelve arrived here and I fed them. Not willingly, I was forced to.' Villagers were compelled to attend their meetings. 'If you didn't, they'd break your legs: at night they'd beat you without being seen.' 'Some days,' another villager added, 'we had to offer them food in our own home. Some days we ourselves couldn't even eat. Who would join them willingly?'[64] In Jumla, in the north-west, an old woman was badly beaten after telling local Maoists – who always asked for the best food, such as meat, rice and dairy – 'the police always paid for anything they took and you always ask for free'.[65] In some cases, civilians were hacked to pieces with primitive, brutal weapons like kukhuris (a machete-style knife, with a curved blade) and hammers. One tea-shop proprietor was blindfolded and regularly beaten for months just for having served policemen.[66] 'They did not leave us to find out about things from other parties,' remembered one individual from central Nepal. 'The Maoists said that other parties could not call any meetings ... we said: any party should have the right to call meetings ... It can't be only you who dance.' Behind all participation lay the threat of force. 'They used to say, "if you don't go, we'll fix you, we'll kill you" ... by doing so, they rose higher and higher ... And we went with them.'[67]

The Maoists exacted levies, in cash and in forced labour. Villagers had to construct the so-called Martyrs' Road, a 91-kilometre route connecting villages in west Nepal, and a key propaganda weapon in the Maoists' campaign to portray themselves as builders of the new as well as destroyers of the old. Stints of punishing corvée labour ran for ten days, at eight hours a day; workers slept in tents alongside the road. 'A mother suffers while giving birth to a child,' one Maoist overseer rationalised the scheme. 'How can she know in advance the joy she will feel after the child is born?'[68] As the CPNM moved into the end game of the civil war between 2004 and 2006, it aimed to 'militarise the entire population and create a mentality of resistance' in the cause of a 'popular armed uprising' against the government. Local people – men, women and children – and pack animals were conscripted into winding convoys to convey supplies to the army.[69]

The 'every person a soldier' spirit of the Great Leap Forward was present here in kind, if not in degree.

Teenagers were forcefully drafted. In 2003 the Maoists launched a massive conscription campaign, with the slogan 'One house, one Maoist'.[70] One girl's story ended happily enough, when she became an artist in the army and made a love match with a Nepali People's Liberation Army soldier. But she was originally abducted, after the Maoists had ferociously beaten her father, leaving him half deaf.[71] If teenagers deserted, their families would suffer the consequences. 'My daughter ran away, and what didn't they do to us!' one villager remembered. 'They said: "Bring her today or we'll lock up your house and kill your daughter on the spot as soon as we see her."' There were punishments for any infractions of Maoist authority. Adulterers had their legs crushed.[72] A bomb was set off near the house of an old man who broke a ban on alcohol during a holiday celebration.[73] Children had to be slapped into silence, for fear of them committing an indiscretion. 'I was terrified. We only have fear; we are terrified! That's all we have ... fear! I am frightened all the time!' admitted one village woman.[74]

Conscripted child soldiers were deeply scarred by the conflict. One girl – named Trisha by the ethnographer who spoke with her – began as a terrorised forced recruit, but ended, almost a decade later, habituated to violence. First abducted by the Maoists in the late 1990s at the age of seven, she was held in a cave alongside 250 other people, with little food and water. In between sentry duties, she was forced to train with weapons. 'When I was unable to carry out orders, they slapped me sometimes,' she remembered. 'The commandants used to bring in the criminals and punished them Muslim style: by cutting their throats and using other great torture methods ... by cutting the bodies with kukhuris and spreading salt and chilies on the wounds ... These things happened in front of my eyes, actually the commander forced me to watch it all in order to make me stronger.' Every time she wept she was punished, and even tortured. But after her parents managed to extricate her, she found it hard to return to normal family life, having been brutalised by her experiences. She eventually slipped away to rejoin the Maoists, financing her journey by selling jewellery she had stolen from home. She learned how to handle sub-machine guns and other weapons.

Although failures were again punished by beatings, 'At that time, I was very excited to think that in the future, I would be able to beat up a lot of people'. Even after she left the movement, she remained infatuated with guns, wearing a bullet around her neck as an ornament. She nostalgically recalled learning to make grenades (which she referred to as 'apples'). 'I can still smell the gelatine on my fingers.'[75]

Given this widespread experience of terror tactics, then, how are we to understand the victory of the Maoists in apparently free national elections in 2008, following the king's relinquishing of power in 2006? In some places at least, it seems that villagers did whatever it took to enjoy a quiet life. In the run-up to the election, one woman from Deurali remembered, 'they came every day: "You'll be punished like this, you'll be punished like that, give us your vote," so we had to vote for them.' She and her neighbours were convinced that the Maoists would have massacred the villagers if they had not won at the ballot box. She felt relief at the Maoist victory, rather than ideological euphoria. 'This was a very good thing. They got what they were looking for. They got it easily, and ... we've got peace and quiet.'[76] Despite the Maoist emphasis on mass mobilisation, then, it was terror that generated political compliance. 'Nobody became a Maoist from their own will,' claimed a village government official in 2005.[77]

The civil war generated countless acts of horrifying violence on both sides. Before the RNA joined the civil war in 2001, it enjoyed an international reputation for restraint; within weeks of beginning counter-insurgency operations, this reputation was squandered. Sometimes, the military acted as agents provocateurs, waving Maoist flags and carolling Maoist hymns: any local who – either enthusiastically or for fear of Maoist reprisals – responded positively was shot on the spot. Rape became a weapon of war, to terrorise civilians or extract information from suspected female Maoists.[78] Like conventional armies the world over when faced with a guerrilla insurgency, the RNA tended to see almost any civilian they encountered as a potential aggressor. The army once threatened to bury an entire village alive if they helped Maoists.[79] As one clear indication of the lack of trust and communications between the military and civilians, in March 2004 a 4,000-strong Maoist force camped within hours of RNA and government headquarters in Beni, central Nepal, and planned and trained for a massive assault, while the RNA command remained entirely ignorant of their presence.[80]

Despite the army's involvement in the conflict, from 2002 Nepal's government became ever more ineffectual and confined to Kathmandu. King Gyanendra had succeeded his more popular brother Birendra in 2001, after the Crown Prince Dipendra – apparently delirious with whisky and hashish – had shot his father and eight other members of the royal family. The new king's response to the Maoist crisis had been to hijack the parliamentary system to enhance his own powers: he installed as prime minister a political dependent, Sher Bahadur Deuba, who sent in the Royal Nepalese Army and declared a state of emergency, which drastically limited constitutional rights. Then, on 1 February 2005, the king sacked his prime minister and formally asserted executive power over the government. Party leaders and civil rights activists were arrested; RNA soldiers took control of the country's media. The Internet was shut down for a week. Habeas corpus was dead.

But fifteen years of democracy since 1990 had left urban Nepal – and Kathmandu in particular – intolerant of this kind of repression. Anti-monarchy sentiment welled in the capital through 2005 and on 6 April 2006 it erupted into a general strike – the so-called second 'People's Movement'. After the regime enforced a curfew, armed forces clashed with growing numbers of protesters; police violence only increased the militancy of ordinary people. Eighteen days after the strike began, the king was forced to reinstate parliament. This marked the beginning of the peace process.

The crisis gave the CPNM the opportunity to write a new chapter in the history of global Maoism. From the early 2000s, leading Maoists had started to realise that they would not be able to achieve their ultimate goal – seizure of state power – by military means alone (although the party's most radical wing never accepted this). While the pragmatic Prachanda favoured bargaining with the king (the quintessence of feudalism), his top ideologue, Baburam Bhattarai, advocated using the crisis of the monarchy to negotiate with other parties to form an alliance against the monarchy. Most Maoists around the world have fixated on Mao's ideas in isolation from their historical application in China (or swallow a Mao-era propaganda account of these experiences). They believe that Mao's writings constitute a perfection of theory and practice that have to be rigorously adhered to. Bhattarai, very unusually, considered the history as well as ideology of Maoism. For him, the degeneration of one-party states into oppressive dictatorships was a crucial lesson of twentieth-century Communism. Marxists of the new millennium, he thought, had to learn from the past and embrace democracy. Bhattarai was in favour of a new democratically elected Constituent Assembly that would limit or abolish the king's powers and place the army under civilian control.[81]

Bhattarai's insight was deeply controversial. Plenty of other party leaders remained attached to violent overthrow of the state and believed in the infallibility of the Maoist model even while it became clear that victory on the battlefield would be impossible. In the early 2000s not only was there a military stalemate, but also an international environment deeply unfavourable to the Maoists. After 9/11 the US pumped $22 million into Nepal to help the army fight the Maoists. 'You have a Maoist insurgency that's trying to overthrow the government,' Colin Powell declared on a visit to RNA headquarters in January 2002, 'and this really is the kind of thing that we are fighting against throughout the world.'[82] Between 2003 and 2012, the US government kept the Nepali Maoists on their list of global terror groups. For years, India had turned a blind eye while senior Maoists – Bhattarai, Yami, Kiran – hid among Nepali migrant communities in India. In early 2004, it changed its hands-off policy and began arresting CPNM leaders on Indian soil. Dealing with its own rebooted Maoist insurgency, the Indian government could not allow the Maoists to succeed. As one official put it: 'We could have lived with a Maoist dictatorship if it was 5,000 miles away but, across an open border, we cannot risk it.'[83]

Prachanda bristled at Bhattarai's criticism of strong-man leadership à la Stalin, and by the time they trekked back to Nepal from north India in mid-2004, they were hardly speaking to each other. In January 2005, at a week-long politburo meeting, Prachanda denounced Bhattarai for a number of crimes against the party: power-seeking, having a bourgeois class perspective, conspiring with Indian expansionism. Bhattarai and his wife Hisila Yami were removed from the leadership and kept under virtual house arrest for months.[84] Bhattarai now faced the real possibility that the armed revolution he had supported with all his intellectual energies would consume him in a

Stalinist purge. 'Prachanda could have [had me] killed,' he later recalled matter-of-factly. 'We were prepared for that ... He told me later, there were some people who wanted to bury me alive.'

With Bhattarai sidelined, Prachanda made one last desperate attempt at military victory but a large-scale attack on Khara, an army base deep in west Nepal, was badly miscalculated. '[C]arnage is probably the most appropriate word to describe what took place,' concluded Sam Cowan, a professional soldier turned military analyst, 'wave after wave of attackers were mowed down by machine-gun fire.'[85] A chastened Prachanda now publicly acknowledged that armed victory for the CPNM was unfeasible. Bhattarai was discreetly released from house arrest and dispatched to India, to engineer negotiations between the CPNM and the other Nepali parliamentary parties. On 22 November 2005, a 12-point agreement was reached in Delhi, establishing the Maoists' commitment to democratic rule, and agreeing to a cross-party collaboration to combat the autocracy of the king, who stepped down six months later. When a new Constituent Assembly convened in 2008, it brought to an end 240 years of dynastic rule.

In the 2008 elections, the Maoists secured 221 out of a possible total of 575 seats. Both the civil war and the democratic gamble, it seemed, had paid off: the CPNM had 'surrounded the cities from the countryside'.

But the trajectory of the Maoists in and out of power since then has not been a steady one; it has stumbled over issues of representation, federalism, transparency, the role of the military and political consistency. Has the movement remained Maoist after coming to power? If so, how has this form of Maoism changed Nepali politics and what does it tell us about the potential of global Maoism today?

Even passionate critics of the Maoists – of whom there are many in Kathmandu, across the political spectrum – concede that the Maoists accelerated, and placed centre stage, a more inclusive identity politics, one that sought to give political representation to the people of Nepal in all their diversity. After 1998, the CPNM organised political fronts among different ethnic groups. It awakened consciousness of rights; whether it will ever succeed in following through by helping disadvantaged groups attain those rights is a different question. The Maoist insurgency also accelerated the collapse of the Hindu monarchy – the ultimate political support of the caste system, a key source of exclusion. In the peace negotiations that followed the People's Movement of April 2006, the Maoists successfully pushed hard to institute a quota requirement within proportional representation in the 2008 elections. This meant that almost half the Constituent Assembly's seats (204) would be reserved for the representation of particular groups previously marginalised in national politics – for example, women, Madhesis (ethnic Indians living along the border with India), Dalits, Janajatis, residents of specified underdeveloped regions; this quota brought people like Kamala into government. The results, though symbolically significant, were a little patchy. (Smooth implementation was not helped by the fact that when the PR schema was drawn up, the total percentage of different proportions added up to 116.2 per cent.)[86] Dalits won 8 per cent of Constituent Assembly seats in 2008 (having had no representation at all after the 1994 and 1999 elections); yet this figure lies below the proportion of Dalits in the Nepali population (around 13 per cent).[87] Although the greatly increased presence of Dalits in national politics should be recognised and celebrated, under-representation of oppressed castes and ethnicities in government remained the norm after 2008.

In Nepal today, many feel that Prachanda and his comrades have betrayed their former pro-minority stance, in the course of protracted negotiations for a new constitution that have brought several governments down. The constitution that was finally completed in September 2015 (discussions began in 2008) has been hugely controversial: in the six weeks up to September 2015 alone about forty-five Nepalis were killed in violent protests.[88] In 2013, the parties of traditional power-holding – Nepali Congress and the nationalist Communist Party of Nepal (Unified Marxist–Leninist) – again won the majority of votes, and the Maoists were pushed back to eighty seats. Consequently, between 2013 and 2015 the key decisions about the new constitution were monopolised by the usual high-caste, principally male politicians (who also happen to dominate the leadership of the Maoist party). The geographical boundaries between the seven new regions proposed in the 2015 constitution were fiercely disputed: underprivileged groups feared that the divisions, which split areas of high concentration of poorer minorities, would fracture them as a collective and prevent them from challenging the political influence of higher-caste groups. The constitution also discriminated against women's rights to citizenship and self-determination within the family: Nepali women with a foreign or absent Nepali husband (a substantial number, as so many men go abroad to work) cannot pass on their Nepali citizenship to their children unless the husband becomes Nepali or returns – this limitation did not hold for Nepali men. Prachanda proclaimed it 'a victory of the dreams of the thousands of martyrs and disappeared fighters'.[89] Others veered between calling it 'suboptimal' and 'a conservative backlash'.[90]

Prachanda and his CPNM comrades have been blamed for the constitution's failures to deliver on the promises of the 'People's War'. This is not always fair. In the years after 1990, Nepal's political culture was already clearly sick, as politicians expended their energies on power-preservation rather than on resolving the country's severe socio-economic deprivation. 'Nepal's house is on fire and the politicians are arguing about who gets to sleep in the master bedroom,' sniped the American ambassador in 2002.[91] Nepali politics has arguably returned to business as usual since 2008 – the Maoists have been sucked into, but are not to blame for, the habitual horse-trading of Kathmandu politicking. Geopolitical constraints have been another huge problem for the Maoists in power. India has consistently fought Maoification of the Nepali state, and has been an insistent, interfering presence throughout the peace process, offering patronage to Kathmandu politicians who support Indian interests. Prachanda's first premiership ended prematurely in 2009 after India manoeuvred Nepal's other political parties into blocking his attempt to replace the veteran chief of the Nepalese Army, General Katawal – the Maoists' old battlefield foe – with someone more pliant. China has also tried to apply a brake on federalism and championing ethnic minority rights, due to tensions surrounding their rule in Tibet.[92]

But because their insistence on the necessity of armed struggle cost the lives of some 17,000 Nepali people, the Maoists have not unreasonably been held sternly to account over the realisation of the vision for which they fought with such violence. Ten years on from the completion of the peace process, with the Maoist programme of political diversity severely compromised and more Nepalis than ever before fleeing economic stagnation or destitution to face discrimination and exploitation in dead-end jobs in Asia and the Gulf, many have been compelled to ask: 'did we fight a war for ten years, for this?'[93]

★

On 1 September 2011, at Prachanda's private residence in Naya Bazaar, central Kathmandu, the Maoist leader instructed his highest-ranking military commanders to hand over to an independent monitoring committee the most important set of keys in Nepal. They fitted the grey concrete, UN-audited containers that since 2007 had held within them some 3,500 firearms belonging to the Nepali People's Liberation Army (NPLA). Prachanda was thereby disarming the force that had led him from a career as an obscure village school science teacher to a holder of state power. This action was the outcome of five fraught years of negotiations about the combined fates of the two most controversial institutions of the civil war: the NPLA and the RNA, renamed the Nepalese Army (NA) after the abolition of the monarchy. While both sides argued about relinquishing their military autonomy, the NPLA's rank and file (authors of the military victories that had helped the Maoist leadership to such traction in national politics) put their lives on hold, confined to cantonments that had been established after the peace agreement of 2006. Eventually, in 2011 it was agreed that the NPLA would be dissolved and a limited number of soldiers (fewer than 1,500 as it turned out, of a total force of 19,602) integrated into the NA. The process has pulled apart a party that – remarkably for a Maoist grouping – had held together for some twenty years.

While Prachanda and Baburam Bhattarai negotiated with Nepal's parliamentary parties, many Nepali Maoists – among the leadership and the rank and file – wanted to fight on. One brigade commander recalled a growing sense of militancy between 2005 and 2006: 'just before peace, that was the most heated time. We hated the enemy so much. We spoke of standing on his back and shooting him in the head ... We were still on full recruitment mode when the 12-point agreement began. We were really confident ... I didn't understand why we retreated militarily. We were told later: this is a suspension and not a stopping of hostilities. We were thinking strategically about expanding in the cities.' During the anti-monarchy protests in Kathmandu of April 2006, protesters furiously refuted the home minister's claim that the demonstrations had been infiltrated and orchestrated by Maoists. In reality, however, with the Maoist army stationed around the capital, the CPNM had sent thousands of cadres into the city to provoke confrontation; to escalate conflict. 'If protest was weak, we'd make it stronger,' recalled an operative close to Prachanda.

'And we'd turn the protest violent if necessary. We were well coordinated. There were 200–300 people in one group. The party's instructions were to build up to the takeover of Kathmandu. There was a major military force just outside Kathmandu. There were at least 500–1000 Party members scattered among crowds with small arms.' After the king's promise to reinstate parliament at the end of the month, the protests dissipated, much to the disappointment of the CPNM, which seemed to have come within a whisker of state capture. 'If we'd seized power in Kathmandu, the rest would have been history,' rued the same cadre. 'The overriding feeling was of mass rebellion, people were desperate for change. Had we sustained it, even international powers wouldn't have been able to stop us ... I don't think it would have been all that bloody.'

Kathmandu's residents were not so sure. As Maoist forces moved closer to the capital, some kept a packed bag close to hand, ready to flee the city for fear of Khmer Rouge–style destruction. (In 2016, a high-ranking Maoist speculated that Pol Pot was 'honest and sincere', and implied that the skeletons in the killing fields of Cambodia were the invention of the Western media to discredit Communism.)[94] By that time, many urban residents had felt the pinch of Maoist menace. Anyone with steady employment – business people, teachers – was used to receiving a call from the Maoists, asking for payment of 'a loan' (never repaid), consisting of a quarter of their salary, usually between $50 and $500. 'If you don't pay up,' the caller would say, 'you'll be annihilated.'

The CPNM leadership was also split over the question of peace versus war. When Prachanda agreed to Bhattarai's plan to negotiate, one of the strongest proponents of ongoing armed struggle, Comrade Kiran, was in an Indian jail. When he was released following the peace agreement and returned to Nepal, he griped that the Maoists would lose their 'revolutionary edge' in parliamentary politics.[95] Prachanda vigorously played all sides: making small talk with American officials, lunching with the Indian establishment, and assuring the party's hard line that he still meant revolution through state capture.

In 2007, Prachanda agreed to confine the NPLA to cantonments, while the process for integrating them into the NA was designed. By the time the cantonments were finally disbanded, in 2012, the party for which they had fought had pulled itself to pieces. As if tempting fate, Prachanda had renamed his party (after a merger with a smaller group) the Unified Communist Party of Nepal (Maoist) in 2009. In 2012, a faction that still upheld the need for armed struggle – led by the senior ideologue Kiran – split away to form the Nepal Communist Party (Maoist); another group, the Communist Party of Nepal – Maoist, splintered off in 2014 under the leadership of another 'People's War' veteran, Comrade Biplab. Both these fractions are united by the conviction that state capture was possible in 2005, and that a return to armed struggle is inevitable (even if the war-making – between the dash Maoists and the cash Maoists, as the joke has it – has so far been limited to battles over hyphens versus brackets). This would all be little more than a faintly ridiculous echo of a Monty Python sketch, were it not for the fact that when the Maoist weapons were buried in UN-monitored concrete back in 2007, Biplab secretly stashed away a third of the NPLA's arsenal, to keep his options open. 'He doesn't believe Maoism failed,' remarked the Kathmandu-based writer Sudheer Sharma. 'He just thinks it needs to be completed. Like the revolution in Russia failed in 1905, then succeeded in 1917.'[96]

The attachment of the CPNM and its successor factions to armed struggle is not just a threat to Nepal's domestic stability. The fixation on the military during the years of the civil war has come at the expense of political attentiveness: a lack of focus on the careful institutional change needed to facilitate the transformation of Nepali society and economy. This carelessness reflects the Maoists' failure to engage critically with China and with Mao's legacies. The cadre close to Prachanda who mobilised hundreds of Maoists in April 2006 through volatile urban protest and potentially lethal encounters with the Royal Nepalese Army, who was so determined to capture the state, had a very rudimentary understanding of the ruling record of the CCP, of what a Maoist state in Nepal would have looked like, or of the complexities of democratic checks and balances. 'Afterwards, Nepal would have looked like Mao's China. As we were true Maoists, therefore the state built would have been that of Mao's China, probably around or after the Cultural Revolution ... We would have let other parties compete, as long as they were pro-people.' I asked who would define what counts as a 'pro-people party'. 'The Maoist party ... We could have avoided the bad things of the Cultural Revolution and have done good things.' As he explained this to me, I noticed on his shelf a handful of Nepali Maoist memoirs, a volume about Chinese Marxism and a self-help book: *The Power of Positive Thinking*, by Norman Vincent Peale.

But perhaps we should not overstate the importance of Maoist ideas on the movement's leaders. The most influential Nepali Maoists – for good and for ill – are above all pragmatists. As of 2016, Baburam Bhattarai no longer calls himself a Maoist, and has founded a new political party proposing to pair post-Mao-style economic reforms with democracy. Observers have noted Prachanda's flip-flops and concluded (mainly with a sigh of relief) that he is a non-ideological pragmatist. 'From 2001, I was meeting regularly with the Maoists,' observed Krishna Hachhethu. 'I knew what sort of people they were. I knew I didn't need to be afraid of them. Prachanda loses more ideological baggage at every meeting.'[97] No economic puritan, the erratic Prachanda (leader of the 'cash Maoists') has been associated with numerous scandals of extravagance, embezzlement and crony capitalism. He has reportedly spent the vast sum of 100,000 rupees on a Chinese-made bed, and there are allegations that his son siphoned off government funds to finance an ascent of Everest. The lack of institutional accountability means we will probably never know the half of it. Prachanda – or the party leadership – also seems to have creamed off, for mysterious purposes, part of the salaries paid to NPLA soldiers during the five years that they were confined to cantonments.

Maybe these men were only ever superficially Maoists – and this takes us back to C. K. Lal's scornful appraisal of them as high-caste 'political entrepreneurs' interested in ideology as a means to political power, rather than implementing it as an abstract ideal. 'They saw an opportunity and they seized it. So if they come to power, they behave like any politician. There was never any risk of them repeating what the Khmer Rouge did. They're not ideologues ... They're very calculating: it's always cost-benefit.'[98] In 2017, the parliamentary Maoist group (now named CPN–Maoist Centre) merged with Nepal's centre-right, nationalist, anti-India Communist Party of Nepal – Unified Marxist–Leninist. 'The Maoists', Aditya Adhikari predicted, 'will most likely have to abandon all support for identity-based movements, local autonomy and decentralisation.' An election victory for this new merger, he continued, would centralise 'power in the hands of the party and a monopoly over all sections of society. They will try to ensure that there is no civil society, only groups directly affiliated to the ruling parties. All encroachments on democracy will be justified on the basis of anti-Indian nationalism. These tendencies will then become the defining characteristics of "communism" in Nepal.'[99]

In Nepal today, there is a combination of disappointment, disillusionment and anger at the Maoists in power. For every Kamala, there are hundreds of Maoist cadres and soldiers left behind. NPLA fighters wasted five years of their lives sitting in cantonments, waiting for the state to decide their fate while their commanders embezzled their pay. Others, acting on the party's orders, dropped out of school, repudiating the 'bourgeois education' that would be useless after the revolution. 'My generation is paralysed,' sighed a former Maoist cultural worker in his late thirties. 'They didn't get education. They don't have political connections or money to make something of themselves. They picked up guns and risked everything, and then discovered that society hadn't changed. Many have left Nepal, and gone to the Gulf or Malaysia to labour. We feel sad that in ordinary people's kitchens, nothing has changed. There are so many frustrations. This generation is too weary to pick up guns again. Maybe the next generation will.'

The clearest institutional winner of the Maoist civil war was – as with the Cultural Revolution in China – the army. C. K. Lal's own attitude to violence has shifted over the course of the past twenty years. 'At the beginning, I was against violence [and for] non-violent change. Then, after 2002, when the emergency was declared and the army mobilised, I thought, maybe in Nepal no change has ever occurred without taking up guns ... Dictatorships aren't voted out ... But then it took a year or two for me to realise that guns aren't such a great equaliser because in the end bigger guns always win. And those more powerful in society can always have more and larger guns, and more people to operate them. We're now back to the status quo in Nepal ... The state's guns are getting bigger and more plentiful.'[100] Between 1996 and 2016, the army and police force doubled. 'Our army is growing,' agreed a veteran democracy campaigner. 'It can threaten the leaders if they don't satisfy the army, if they don't cooperate. The army benefits from political misrule. If democracy is mismanaged, I don't think our leaders will be able to keep the army within limits.'

In December 2016, I had an audience with Comrade Kiran, one of Nepal's staunchest remnant Maoists. We sat in a meeting room furnished in the style of Chinese officialdom: walls lined with armchairs and sofas, interspersed with lacquered coffee tables. The most Chinese touch of all was the golden statue of Mao, placed next to a gaudy red glass vase engraved with one of Mao's poems in faded gold print. The vase was a little dusty at its base and filled with plastic pink roses. These two pieces of memorabilia Kiran had lovingly carried back from his first pilgrimage to China, in 2009. It must have been a strange, unsatisfactory visit. For the comrades in the CCP had spent most of the 'People's War' denouncing Mao's Nepali imitators as aberrant, as besmirching Mao's good name. China's party state backed the Nepali monarchy until almost the end, while embracing at home the deep inequalities of a market economy. When communications finally opened up after the CPNM formed the government, one of the CCP's earliest, privately delivered pieces of advice was to abandon the name 'Maoist'. ('They said Prachanda Path was fine, but not Maoism,' Hisila Yami remembered. 'They were embarrassed.')[101] 'Of course, we had different views,' recalled Kiran tactfully.

Kiran lives and breathes the Communist ideology that has determined his life choices. He came over as eager to eliminate the expression of individual human impulse, and to attribute all decisions, all events to the scientific wisdom of Communism. Talking to him in his reception room thus felt like entering a foreign country, where dry abstractions of party doctrine rule. When I asked how he himself had practised Maoism in his daily life before and during the civil war, he replied: 'We decided to carry out Mao's line, to develop an ideological and political stance ... The guiding principle was Marxism-Leninism-Maoism and New Democracy.' I tried to ask him about his family: 'They're all in the movement,' he answered. Did he feel bitter at Prachanda's choice to abandon the armed struggle? 'I don't feel it personally,' he said evenly. 'But he and his group betrayed the revolution.' I wondered what his Maoist state would have looked like. 'There would have been land reform. We would have ended bureaucratic capitalism. Everyone would have been empowered ... We could have taken a stand against expansionist, colonial, feudal interests. There would have been a scientific culture ... a powerful party, but with no bad ideas in it.' State capture was within reach in 2005, he believes, and the armed struggle will resume in the future. 'The parliamentary system failed, revolution is inevitable.' I asked if he ever went into battle himself. 'I was trained to use a gun. But I never fought.'[102]

Kiran has dedicated his life to moulding Nepalis into good, scientific Communists. But as I drove from his office, the only suggestion of radical change visible on the streets of Kathmandu manifested in the name of a dressmaker's shop along the way – 'New Man: Shirting, Suiting, Tailoring'. Somehow, I didn't think that was the kind of transformation that Kiran had striven for over the past four decades.

MAO-ISH CHINA

In the spring of 2000, a Singaporean friend invited me to watch a new musical in Beijing – *Qie Gewala* (Che Guevara). Alternating between episodes evoking the life of the Argentinian revolutionary, and scenes located in noughties Beijing, the show resonated with a Cultural Revolution aesthetic of Manichaean struggle, in which Mao-era revolutionary morals were contrasted with the spiritual vacuum of contemporary China. Its cast was divided into two groups: goodies (all played by men) versus baddies (all played by women). When a good character tried to do something good – for example, rescue a drowning child – a baddy would stop him (by arguing that the child lacked economic value and was therefore dispensable). 'Mao Zedong, Mao Zedong, we will follow you in a hail of bullets and shells,' pledged one song. The audience roared approval.[1] At a Q&A with the cast afterwards, the thirty-something director berated himself and his fellow modernised urbanites for 'spending too little time, *too little time* in contact with the labouring people'.

This glimpse of a neo-Maoist revival – all shouted songs and slogans, and Cultural Revolution–esque choreography – made an impression but at the time my mind was on other things. I was in Beijing for four months to research a dissertation on China's obsession with winning a Nobel Prize in Literature – an emblematic part of the country's post-Mao craving for international 'face' bequeathed by Western institutions. China's Nobel complex appeared to signal a clean break with the value systems of the Maoist past. To me, *Qie Gewala* was interesting but niche: a hangover from the recurring guilt of metropolitan Chinese literati across the past century towards the uneducated, impoverished Chinese 'masses'. Cycling back to my university accommodation in the west of the city through the streets of Beijing that night, I passed the flagship Western designer stores of Beijing's busiest shopping street, Wangfujing, and countless small businesses – *xiaomaibu* – trying to make their way through China's privatising economy. They – not relic Maoism – seemed to be China's inexorable direction.

I was wrong. Eighteen years later, China is ruled by the strongest, most Maoist leader the country has had since Mao. Xi Jinping – son of one of Mao's own revolutionary comrades – has renormalised aspects of Maoist political culture: criticism/self-criticism sessions, Mao's strategy of the 'mass line', the personality cult. In early 2018, he and his Central Committee abolished the 1982 constitutional restriction that limited the president to only two consecutive terms: like Mao, Xi could be ruler for life. In a clear break with post-Mao China's reserved approach to foreign affairs, Xi and his closest advisers have reasserted the PRC's global ambitions and relevance with an energy and confidence unseen since Mao's CCP proclaimed China the centre of the world revolution.

Xi's China is of course different (almost beyond recognition) from Mao's: tied into global finance, its political equilibrium and legitimacy bound to economic performance rather than ideological purity, its media too diversified for a single official message to convince its increasingly well-travelled, ambitious (and tax-paying) citizens. Xi's revival of the Maoist political repertoire, moreover, is opportunistically partial. An authoritarian party-builder, Xi is happy to invoke Mao's historical prestige – as founder of the CCP-in-power and of the PRC – to enhance his own prestige and push forward his own objectives (disciplining the party, removing opposition to his rule, recentralising power). But he has buried memory of the Cultural Revolution's mass mobilisations of society. How will Xi's selective revival of the Maoist political repertoire sit within a China that is so transformed from the Mao era?

The Great Helmsman's influence manifests itself in strange, unstable ways in contemporary China – just as it has done throughout its global travels. Recall the massive golden statue of Mao from the early days of 2016, towering out of the blasted Henan countryside, mysteriously funded by some pious local, mysteriously hacked to pieces after a public outcry over its expense. Or consider Bo Xilai's noisy neo-Maoist revival in the summer of 2011, launched in the interests of propelling him into the politburo; only nine months later, Bo was arrested on accusations of accepting $3.6 million in bribes. (His wife was also detained for, and subsequently found guilty of, murdering the British businessman Neil Heywood; she had allegedly laundered $1.2 billion abroad.) Then there is Han Deqiang, one of the founders of a webzine called Utopia, a defining bastion of chauvinist online Maoism. In 2013 he retreated from this militant organisation to found an organic commune in rural Hebei that venerated both Mao and a Thai Buddhist movement (the 'Pure Earth Village'), while still reminiscing proudly about punching an old man who bad-mouthed Mao on the edges of an anti-Japan march in 2012.

The confusing diversity of this Maoist resurgence begins to suggest the complexity and potency of Mao's legacy in China, where it shores up apparently unassailable state authority *and* inspires attacks (both implicit and explicit) on that authority. In the PRC – to adapt a turn of phrase from Che Guevara – there are two, three, many Maos.

In the late 1950s, Mao occupied the northern half of Tiananmen Square: his six-metre-long portrait, suspended from the viewing plat-form on which he surveyed admiring crowds, gazed down at his own words (inscribed in his own calligraphy) on the Monument to the Heroes of the Revolution.[2] After his death, Mao annexed the rest – the south – of the square when in 1977 his orange, embalmed body was set inside a large mausoleum in order, party planners explained, 'to underline further the political meaning of Tiananmen Square'.[3]

But in other respects, things were not going Mao's way. Less than a month after his demise in September 1976, the executors of his Cultural Revolution, the so-called Gang of Four – his wife Jiang Qing and her three collaborators, Yao Wenyuan, Zhang Chunqiao and Wang Hongwen – were arrested. Although one of Mao's protégés, the faithful Hunanese party secretary, Hua Guofeng, directly succeeded Mao, he reigned on borrowed time. For Deng Xiaoping – arguably the toughest of Mao's surviving first-generation revolutionary peers – was busy manoeuvring himself into the paramount leadership. By 1980, Deng had mobilised enough support among the party elite to push Hua out of any meaningful position of power.

In culture, economics and foreign policy, the headline story of the 1980s was de-Maoification. The first sign of unravelling came in the economy. Already by the early seventies, some rural Communist cadres – perhaps exhausted by the caprices of central party directives – had allowed local farmers to escape some of the tyrannies of central socialist planning. Free-wheelers carved off individual plots from communes, sowed non-staple crops that were extremely profitable in a growing black market, and returned to sideline occupations such as animal rearing and handicrafts that had been condemned as 'capitalist' since the mid-1950s. In south China, goods supposedly controlled by government monopoly were openly sold privately; gangs of entrepreneurs roamed the coastline trading in contraband.[4] Deng Xiaoping and his lieutenants (such as Zhao Ziyang) formalised and accelerated this process; by 1982, the communes – the foundation of Mao's economic and political strategy – had been dissolved.

During the Cultural Revolution, books by and pictures of Mao had been the safest choice of ceremonial gift. In one (perhaps apocryphal) story, a couple received 102 copies of Mao's works as wedding presents. Enough portraits of Mao had been manufactured for each Chinese person to own three.[5] More than a billion Little Red Books had been printed.[6] Now billions of volumes of Mao's works were mouldering in warehouses: not only were they taking up space needed for post–Cultural Revolution manuals on modernisation – Deng Xiaoping was agitated about how far behind China had fallen in science and technology during the late Mao era – they were also responsible for 85 million yuan in bad loans, and required round-the-clock guarding by a specialist army division. (Despite their best efforts, about 20 per cent of Mao's books succumbed to cracking and mildew, thanks to unsteady temperatures.) The CCP resorted to radical solutions. On 12 February 1979, the Propaganda Department banned the sale of the Little Red Book and – barring a few copies to be held in reserve – ordered all extant volumes to be pulped within seven months. Up to 90 per cent of remaindered Mao-era political books were turned into mulch – including the entire run of the fifth volume of Mao's *Selected Works*.[7]

The former propagandists of global Maoism no longer believed in the message they had been trained to communicate. In 1978, some of the writers and editors of the Foreign Languages Press (FLP), which had churned out *Peking Review* and the other works of 'external propaganda', were sent to study abroad and finally had an opportunity to view for themselves the Western world, which for decades they had been so certain that China was about to liberate. One FLP editor and veteran of the Cultural Revolution's exhausting political and social upheavals was shocked by everyday life in small-town Australia.

> Before I left China, all the propaganda was about how people in cap-italist countries were suffering, oppressed – that anything to do with capitalism was bad, and anything to do with socialism was good. But when we actually went abroad, we found it was nothing like that. The culture shock was very strong. Everything was so different from China – including at the everyday levels of civilisation, of civility. Every morning, the parents took their children to school, and picked them up at the end of the day. I thought: how lucky these children are. I wept to see it. I'd spent all these years doing external propaganda in China, but I had no idea how people were living abroad.

The distribution warehouses and bookshelves freshly emptied of musty Maoist volumes were now refilled with texts that depicted the Mao era with horror, despair and contempt. The cultural thaw produced a smorgasbord of styles and genres – from semi-abstract poetry, to magical-realist fiction and absurdist drama – but most converged on their opposition to life under Mao. They depicted the crushing of the individual, the inhumanities of the Mao cult, the corruption and life-wasting absurdities of socialism, the excesses of the Cultural Revolution and the horrors of the *laogai* prison camps. By the late 1980s, de-Maoification had entered the fine arts too. Zhang Hongtu, in his 'Material Mao' series, featured the helmsman in a series of undignified postures, disguises and colorations: Mao with tiger stripes, Mao with a false (Stalinist) moustache, Mao with pigtails, Mao the lecher ogling a statue representing the Goddess of Democracy. Irreverence hit the big screen, with the so-called Fifth Generation of film-makers demolishing stereotypes about CCP heroes. In 1988, the message reached the small screen also, when the documentary *Heshang* (Death of the [Yellow] River), a wildly popular polemical series attacking the PRC's backwardness and lack of openness to Western democratic culture, lampooned Mao worship as the epitome of back-ward cultishness.[8] Although party hacks dutifully penned paeans to Deng's 'Four Modernisations', there was no cultural capital to be had from such work. Reaction against the CCP's orthodoxies was the most prominent cultural theme of the 1980s.

A boiler serviceman turned writer called Zhu Wen personified this new scorn for the Mao years. He was a Cultural Revolution baby, born in 1967 in the mountains of Fujian as his teacher-parents travelled into exile in the rural south-east. Zhu Wen went to college in Nanjing in the 1980s, during the final gasps of a Mao-style education system when students still had to preface every essay with a quotation by Mao.[9] His protagonists – in stories that lampoon the political, social and cultural disfigurements of post-Mao China – are almost all swaggering, amoral young males, in turn pitying and mocking their parents' submission to 'politics in command', and either tormented by or fleeing the servitude of the planned economy: its collective dorms, its stultifying bureaucracy, its life sentences of tedious toil.

Chen Xiaolu, son of Chen Yi, Mao's direct contemporary and one of the founding marshals of the PRC, witnessed at first hand China's post-Mao transition. In 1966, Chen Yi had the misfortune to be minister of foreign affairs, and as such was attacked by Red Guards in the ministry for his supposed bourgeois capitulations on the global stage. Although Mao and Zhou protected him from the worst extremes of Cultural Revolution violence, he was demoted, sickened and died in 1972. Chen Xiaolu, meanwhile, joined the Red Guards himself, terrorising his teachers. Some forty years later, his conscience was sufficiently troubled by the memory to offer a public apology – a rare act for the Red Guard generation. After joining the Ministry of Foreign Affairs, he participated in the de-Maoification of the early Deng era, when he was posted to London in 1981. 'After we arrived in the UK, we realised that we were the ones who were suffering. The British standard of living was much higher than ours. It was a real shock that things weren't as we'd been told ... It made us reflect coolly on our own society and values ... We couldn't go on as before.'

Still, speaking in 2016, he did not believe that the decades of high Maoism had been wasted:

People inevitably make mistakes. Countries inevitably make mistakes ... But without the Cultural Revolution, we wouldn't have the reforms. We have this saying: things turn into their opposite when they reach the extreme. Without the Cultural Revolution, China would have been like the USSR. Without reforms, we wouldn't have China now. How else could we have caught up with the most advanced parts of the world? ... Without the disaster of the Cultural Revolution, without all those empty things that people said back then, we wouldn't have a unified understanding that it was wrong.

At the same time, Mao's revolutionary foreign policy was shaken off like an old skin; only national interest, and the scars of war, were left behind. The shift towards diplomatic pragmatism had begun in the early 1970s, as Mao sanctioned his subordinates to pursue cautious rapprochement with the US and to patch up antipathies with right-wing states in the developing world. The extraordinary spectacle of Nixon's 1972 visit to China – in which the notorious 'red-baiter' was serenaded by a People's Liberation Army band rendition of 'Home, Home on the Range' – resulted. After the chairman's death, Deng – an admirer of the modernising Singapore model – made friendly with Lee Kuan Yew and, to please the Singaporean prime minister, told the CCP's old client Chin Peng that there would be no more funds for his protracted revolutionary war in Malaysia.[10] Out of funds and international allies, the veterans of one of South East Asia's first anti-colonial insurgencies finally signed a peace accord with the Malaysian government. The octogenarian Ah Cheng emerged from the jungles of the Malaysia-Thai border to settle in a designated 'peace village' where, with undaunted revolutionary spirit, he remained devoted to the Maoist spirit of 'self-reliance' – milking rubber trees, raising pigs, growing vegetables.[11] By the time Chin Peng died in Bangkok in 2013, the Malaysian government had twice refused his request to return to Malaysia. After his death, they prohibited the repatriation of his ashes. In Burma in the early 1980s, the indefatigable Huang Hua brokered a ceasefire between the Burmese Communist Party and Burma's military dictatorship. China took in as political refugees the generation of BCP leaders they had nurtured; younger elements had already discarded their elders for being politically dogmatic and for funding themselves through opium cultivation. By the end of the decade, these veterans were marginal, impoverished figures, who could occasionally be glimpsed in the cities of south and west China, their Mao jackets tattered, their toes poking through their old cloth shoes.[12]

The 'revolutionary diplomacy' of the Mao era had mostly become an embarrassing memory, to be expunged in Orwellian style from the official record: recall the Ministry of Foreign Affairs denial of assistance to the Khmer Rouge, or blocking of reports on Indian Maoism. As with economic de-Maoification, the transition out of Cultural Revolution militancy and back to a more decorous statecraft began before Mao's death. In August 1967, members of the Chinese legation in Portland Place, London, charged out of the building and battled police with axes and baseball bats in order to demonstrate their own loyalty to the Cultural Revolution's violent attacks on 'capitalism' and 'imperialism'. (One diplomat jumped on, and then clubbed into submission, an abandoned policeman's helmet.) By the early 1970s, relations had reharmonised and Chinese government representatives in London were rambling companionably around Aberdeenshire with their Foreign Office counterparts.[13] Deng's ongoing support for the Khmer Rouge after their expulsion from Phnom Penh by the Vietnamese Army superficially evoked a continuation of ideological alliances with the ultra-Maoist CPK. In reality, it was a self-interested way of tying down an enemy nation – Vietnam – in military conflict. Deng's relations with Vietnam epitomised his ousting of ideology by nationalism – for almost as soon as the existential menace to China's southern border vanished, with US forces retreating from the country in 1973, Vietnam was no longer perceived as a revolutionary comrade but rather as a regional competitor. By funding the Khmer Rouge's war with Vietnam, China could delay Vietnam's economic reconstruction after decades of war. It was also a way of draining the coffers of Vietnam's main backer, the Soviet Union, whom the PRC had long since identified as an even greater menace to its national interests than the US. By funding and training Afghan mujahideen on its western borders, the PRC again aimed to bleed its old rival.

But Mao was never purged from PRC politics. The Soviet Union could discard Stalin and still have Lenin as revolutionary founder; the CCP only had Mao.

The struggle over disposing of Mao – literally and symbolically – began hours after his death. Back in 1956, Mao had specified that he wanted to be cremated. Instead, the politburo under the leadership of Mao's acolyte Hua Guofeng – who was parodied as adopting the

'Two Whatevers', namely to follow whatever policies and instructions Mao had; some snarked that he walked, waved and wore his hair like Mao – told the late chairman's shocked doctor on the morning of 9 September 1976 that Mao's body was to be indefinitely preserved.[14] In economic policy, Hua's successor and ouster Deng Xiaoping conspicuously diverged from Mao's: Deng venerated foreign science, technology and investment without fearing that they brought with them corrupting bourgeois influence. But – for reasons of tactics and conviction – Deng's political, institutional framework remained deeply Maoist.

'It isn't only [Mao's] portrait which remains in Tiananmen Square: It is the memory of a man who guided us to victory and built a country ... We shall not do to Mao Zedong what Khrushchev did to Stalin at the 20th Soviet Communist Party Congress,' Deng told the Italian journalist, Oriana Fallaci, who served as one of his principal conduits to Western audiences, in 1980.[15] As the CCP's reception rooms underwent a political spring-clean after Deng's rise, party elders insisted that at least some of Mao's portraits had to stay, for 'we were there too ... if Mao goes, our actions will also be questioned'.

In autumn 1979, Deng commissioned a document that would define party orthodoxy on Mao's contribution to the revolution and the PRC. The editing process was long and tetchy. Deng dragged the document through nine drafts: earlier versions were, in turn, too critical, too boring and too anti-Mao.[16] A year on, Deng convened a meeting of 5,600 cadres – many of whom had only recently been rehabilitated and returned to office after the Cultural Revolution – to receive feedback on a draft. The reunion quickly erupted into a Speak Bitterness meeting, with Mao as the target of struggle.[17] But Deng never intended the occasion to be much more than a venting exercise, for he had already determined that Mao should be treated gently. 'When we write about [Mao's] mistakes, we should not exaggerate, for otherwise we shall be discrediting Comrade Mao Zedong, and this would mean discrediting our Party and state.'[18]

The final draft was completed and promulgated in 1981 as the 'Resolution on Certain Questions in the History of Our Party Since the Founding of the People's Republic of China'. Within its pages, the adjective 'great' was never far from Mao Zedong's name (as in 'the Chinese people's respected and beloved great leader and teacher').

The 1959–61 famine that killed tens of millions was described euphem-istically as causing 'serious losses', while the Cultural Revolution was excused away as merely an error of judgement by a 'great proletarian revolutionary'. The ills of that movement were down to the plotting of the Gang of Four, which Mao had supposedly worked to thwart. The document ended by calling 'upon the whole Party, the whole army and the people of all nationalities to act under the great banner of Marxism-Leninism and Mao Zedong Thought, closely rally around the Central Committee of the Party, preserve the spirit of the legendary Foolish Old Man who removed mountains and ... turn China step by step into a powerful modern socialist country ... Our goal must be attained!'[19] In 1993, Deng himself admitted that plenty of this was 'not true', and that those older cadres who had wanted a tougher line on Mao had been historically justified.[20] But historical justice was not the business of the resolution. Instead, it built on a strictly Maoist model of a single supreme leader (Deng, this time) consolidating power, discrediting his rivals (principally Hua Guofeng) and overriding institutional challenges, despite the existence of wide-spread dissent elsewhere in the party and the country. Already in 1979, Deng had established the 'Four Cardinal Principles' of China's future trajectory: 'We must keep to the socialist road; we must uphold the dictatorship of the proletariat; we must uphold the leadership of the Communist Party; we must uphold Marxism-Leninism and Mao Zedong Thought.'[21] In comparison with these iron precepts – what the oppositional journalist Liu Binyan called the 'four sticks' with which the party beat any dissenters through the 1980s – cultural de-Maoification and Deng cavorting at a Texan rodeo in a ten-gallon hat were just so much flim-flam.[22] A Soviet briefing on the post-Mao Chinese government had it about right: 'the foam has gone down but the beer remains'.[23]

'Not to engage in debates – this was an invention of mine,' Deng once proudly asserted.[24] In fact, this was a technique long fomented by Mao: even as he superficially incited debate, the overall vision always remained his. Although Deng had officially repudiated Mao's mass political movements, they returned regularly through the 1980s: the 1983 Anti-Spiritual Pollution Campaign – in which wearers of long hair and flared trousers were harassed, and petty thieves often summarily executed – and the campaigns against bourgeois liberalisation of 1985 and 1987. In 1983, Deng's second in command, Zhao Ziyang, feared that 'another Cultural Revolution almost seemed to be on the horizon'.[25]

Mao remained at the heart of CCP celebrations. The ninetieth anniversary of his birth, 1983, was marked by books, films and postage stamps, while 1,200 dancers were deployed in a commemorative extravaganza entitled 'The Song of the Chinese Revolution'.[26] Although Deng wavered between reformists and conservatives in his quest to build a stronger China, ultimately he would always come down on the side of the latter, returning to the 'Four Cardinal Principles' of political control. Visiting China in the late 1980s, the veteran China-watcher Orville Schell observed that it was a country still 'deeply anchored in the era of Chairman Mao. Like those species of arctic animals whose mottled summer coats become white in the wintertime, China, too, had a notable capacity for sudden changes in political appearance that left the creature beneath far less altered than one might imagine.'[27]

The grisliest proof of this would come in June 1989, when Deng snapped after countrywide protests challenged the CCP, and his own rule. Zhao Ziyang, a key protagonist in the party's handling of the 1989 protests, directly blamed the Maoist heritage for Deng's draconian decision to send the army in against students and other protesters. 'Deng tended to think in a certain way that was formed during the years when class struggle was the primary objective.'[28] Mao's inviolable status beyond the politburo was exposed by an incident during the Tiananmen protests on 23 May. That day, three young men from Henan travelled to the square, unfurled a banner reading 'Time to End 5,000 Years of Autocracy' and hurled paint-filled eggs at Mao's portrait. Within minutes they were apprehended by members of the student union founded a month earlier to coordinate anti-government protests, hauled before a press conference where they were obliged to disassociate their actions from the student protests, and handed over to the Public Security Bureau. Their prison sentences ranged from sixteen years to life imprisonment. All three were tortured, kept in solitary confinement and starved; at least one of them lost his mind.

In the immediate aftermath of the brutal repression of the protests on 4 June, intellectual heterodoxy was ousted by a resurgence of political orthodoxy. As the questioning spirit of the 1980s was excoriated as ideologically degenerate, the party's apostles of political correctness called for 'cultural works that reflect socialism, give expression to communist ideals and the spirit of the socialist age ... and that can fill people with enthusiasm and create unity amongst the masses'. Party stooges churned out invective against prominent liberals, while urging upon the literary rank and file the urtext of cultural Maoism, Mao's 1942 'Talks on Art and Literature at the Yan'an Forum'.[29] In 1989, 370,000 copies of Mao's portrait were printed. By 1991, the figure had surged to 50 million.[30]

Then, in early 1992, Deng Xiaoping offered the Chinese people a way out of this dawning ice age. Convinced that the survival of the CCP depended on the spread of material prosperity, he called for an end to ideological hang-ups about the capitalist nature of economic liberalisation, and for an unleashing of market forces to achieve 'faster, better, deeper' economic growth. To Deng, it was irrelevant whether the economic means were capitalist or socialist, provided that the political end of preserving party rule was achieved. The meanings of Mao changed also. Until the early 1990s, memory of Mao had remained an elite concern: a topic of high-level internal party wrangling and the subject of contradictory *People's Daily* editorials. After that point, Mao began to percolate into popular religion and mass consumerism – and often a combination of the two. Taxi drivers hung pendants bearing his image from their rear-view mirrors, while stories circulated that those who did so escaped injury and death in traffic accidents. By 1994 a village in Hunan had installed him as a god in his own personal temple (a sculptor skilled in creating Buddhist carvings had been commissioned to create his icon); the temple welcomed 40,000–50,000 worshippers every day before it was shut down by the party in summer 1995 for 'encouraging superstition'.[31] Devotees dizzy with zeal began to spot Mao's likeness in China's mountains.[32] Already in the consumer-starved 1960s and '70s, the Mao cult had expressed itself in 'transitional objects' of varying eccentricity: Little Red Books, Mao badges, wax replicas of mangoes that Mao had presented to thirsty Red Guards. As China became the factory of the world after Mao's death, these material possibilities multiplied: Mao was emblazoned on charms, pendants, the plastic covers of pagers – the must-have status symbol in the newly market-oriented China of the 1990s.

Towards the end of this decade, the first Mao-nostalgic restaurants in cities like Beijing sprang up with titles like Serve the People, or

Eating Bitterness. When I started visiting China in 1997, I was shallowly amused by the twin set of musical cigarette lighters you could buy at urban street stalls: one depicting Mao, playing 'The East Is Red'; the other depicting Deng, playing 'Für Elise'. Tourists in David Tang's chichi store Shanghai Tang snapped up contemporary remakes of Cultural Revolution-era alarm clocks in which the minute hand was a Red Guard waving a Little Red Book. A business-savvy distant relative of Mao's, Tang Ruiren, had the nous to open a Mao Family Restaurant on a hill by the old Mao homestead in Shaoshan. The dining experience included having a Mao badge pinned on you as soon as you arrived, and undergoing pressure to order 'Chairman Mao's favorites' – coincidentally, the priciest dishes on the menu. Mao was becoming big business.[33]

For educated urbanites adapting to the retrenched market reforms after 1992, the Mao cult could be explained as comfort kitsch. But there were many millions who could not take such a relaxed, recreational approach. After becoming state premier in 1998, Zhu Rongji allowed thousands of unprofitable State Owned Enterprises – the former 'iron ricebowl' of hundreds of millions of Chinese workers – to be sold off or wound up. Workers feeling intense economic pain in the late 1990s and early 2000s denounced their treatment at the hands of state 'streamliners' by looking back to the more egalitarian days of Mao. In spring 2002, on the still-frozen streets of Liaoyang – once the north-east heartland of the Maoist economic model – tens of thousands of retired, laid-off or unpaid steel workers marched in protest, demanding money to feed their families and heat their homes (several had already frozen to death), and accusing corrupt managers of siphoning off factory funds into private companies. Bobbing along the human sea were portraits of Mao. As they marched, one woman wept: 'Chairman Mao should not have died so soon!'[34] Zhang Hongliang – born in 1955, a Beijing professor also known as the 'attack-dog' or 'red tank driver' of contemporary China's neo-Maoists, who before migrating into academia worked in the government's nuclear weapons department – remembered a hymn of optimism popular from his university days in the late 1970s: 'In Twenty Years, We Will Meet Again' (in a beautiful motherland transformed for the better by the post-Mao reforms). 'Well, more than twenty years have passed, and it's not as the song promised. Our mountains have dried out. Our water is poisoned. Our resources are exhausted. Our society is full of contradictions and robbers. When I was small, we never locked our house.'[35]

The Liaoyang marches in 2002 ushered in a new era of Mao-tinged protest. In 2002, as Deng Xiaoping's successor, Jiang Zemin, controversially allowed business people to join the party, he also shut down two print journals that were the last bastion for far-left, Maoist debates about politics and society.[36] The action had two consequences. First, it intensified leftists' angry sense of being marginalised and under attack from the forces of market-oriented reform. Second, the silencing of real-world platforms for the far left coincided with the eruption of Internet access and use in China. Many Maoists outside the state now embraced this new form of informational guerrilla warfare – including Han Deqiang, a soft-spoken economics professor at Beijing University of Aeronautics and Astronautics, and co-founder of Utopia.

These Internet Maoists were notable for their angry, anti-Western nationalism. From the start, the CCP was at best ambivalent about them – since the conflagrations of 1989, the party has been wary of any cause that generates popular outrage or protest. One of the earliest focal points for neo-Maoist mobilisation was the furore surrounding the criticism of school textbooks by a philosophy professor called Yuan Weishi in the liberal weekly *Freezing Point* in 2006. Yuan challenged textbook doctrine on the Boxer Rebellion (1899–1901), an event of great patriotic sensitivity in China as it triggered a brutal Western and Japanese reprisal against assaults on foreigners by a popular religious sect (the 'Boxers'). Instead of focusing on foreign atrocities, Yuan instead accused the Boxer rebels of mindless jingoism, of attacking 'civilization and humanity' – they, and not imperialist aggression, 'brought greatest tragedy to the country and the people'.[37] Cyber-leftists assailed Yuan and his apparent exculpation of Western aggression against China. The government's response was to shut down both *Freezing Point* and three of the most popular and vocal leftist websites.[38] It could neither condone the liberalisation of history nor tolerate free-wheeling denunciations from the left.[39]

By 2007, Utopia had become the best-known neo-Maoist organisation in China. It began in 2003 as a website attached to a bookshop, a small establishment near the west gate of Beijing University, the country's most prestigious place of learning and the home of Chinese cosmopolitanism. Utopia's importance in the political scene sprang from its reach: it drew in academic leftists (some with close party-state connections), state officials, full-time netizens, artists, writers and cultural critics based at the university. The bookshop sold 'pan-Leftist books' not easy to find in China's commercial bookstores, which were by now studded with self-help manuals teaching ambitious parents how to get their children into Harvard. Utopia's aim was to create, in the words of its mission statement, 'a small platform through which social progress can be facilitated by pursuing a fairness-first society ... and an open, idealized and responsible public spiritual homeland'.[40] The website gave space to blogs, articles and online discussions by pro-Mao voices. In 2005, for example, it mobilised public opinion – through an online petition – in support of a migrant worker from far north-west China who had killed his employers after they refused to pay him his wages, which he needed for his father's medical emergency.[41]

The groups and individuals clustered around sites like Utopia have called themselves *Mao Zedong zuopai* (Mao Zedong leftists, sometimes shortened to *Mao zuopai*). Because their 'base area' has always been the Internet, it has been hard to quantify them accurately: a 2012 survey suggested that 38.1 per cent of a sample were politically 'left'; Zhang Hongliang estimated in 2014 that 'most people at the bottom of society were Mao-leftists'. Back in the early 2000s, they took to reviling online the post-Mao reforms that brought the market back to China, describing them as an 'evil' usurpation of power by 'revisionists and capitalists' (many of them in the CCP) over the past forty years.[42] Revering the high Maoism of the Cultural Revolution, they believed that these 'revisionists' were in league with foreign imperialists and 'traitors to the Chinese'. All the problems currently experienced by Chinese society – income inequality, corruption, environmental degradation – validated the wisdom of Mao's analyses, and bore out the need for his continuous revolution to purify the Communist Party by inciting the masses to struggle against it. Some took these ideas very seriously indeed, declaring that China needed another Cultural Revolution and championing its ideal of 'mass democracy'. 'We raise high the banner of Mao Zedong Thought,' Zhang Hongliang wrote in 2012, 'in particular the two cores of Mao Zedong Thought – serve the people, and to rebel is justified. Serve the people – that means

prosperity for all. To rebel is justified – that means "mass democracy".'
In contemporary neo-Maoist speak, 'mass democracy' can be realised
through the 'four big freedoms' of Mao's Cultural Revolution: 'great
contention, great relaxation, great debate, big-character posters'. This
approach to 'freedom of expression' would, they believe, lead naturally
to the masses controlling public opinion.[43]

But there were preconditions to freedom of expression under mass
democracy: it had to be 'socialist' and 'patriotic'. The Utopians' rhetoric was almost inevitably nationalistic. Mao was idealised as an alpha-
male patriot, uncompromising on international questions. The Internet
Maoists took a militant attitude to foreign affairs, regarding every
problem arising on China's frontiers – Taiwan, Xinjiang, Tibet, the
South China Seas, the Diaoyu Islands – as a result of American interference. Since they believed that the US was dedicated to containing
China, some advocated that China should support any Middle Eastern
resistance to the US.[44] For similar reasons, many neo-Maoists have
admired North Korea for its brinksmanship with America. At the same
time, the dictatorship of the proletariat and of the patriotic masses
should be exercised over the 'right-wing liberals' selling the country
out. Once more related to their veneration for Mao, the new leftists
(many of whom have at least an undergraduate education) were deeply
suspicious of intellectuals as a category. They viewed 'knowledge
workers' inside and outside government as 'comprador traitors and
the running dogs of imperialism': 'the more knowledge they have, the
more reactionary they are'.[45] In economic policy, the neo-Maoists
wanted a return to collective, commune farming, and opposed dissolution of State Owned Enterprises (the backbone of the Mao-era
economy), privatisation and globalisation, all of which (they argued)
had enabled foreign and corrupt nationals to suck wealth out of the
country.[46]

These neo-Maoists also repudiated any ambivalence about Mao's
historical record as revisionist conspiracy theories. They defended the
1957 Anti-Rightist Campaign as 'far more humane than Stalin's purges',
and furiously refuted any suggestion that tens of millions died as a
result of human error in the Great Leap Forward. The persecution
of 'class enemies' during the Cultural Revolution was 'completely
necessary'.[47] 'You can't trust books written about the Cultural
Revolution,' a neo-Maoist graduate of Beijing University (who later

went on to study at one of the UK's best universities) told me, 'because they're all by intellectuals, who were brought down by it. [In reality] the Cultural Revolution was very gentle towards its enemies; it didn't kill anyone. All that happened was a few intellectuals killed themselves, maybe because a few youngsters had denounced them.' He admitted that he had read only a few memoirs about the Cultural Revolution, and no archival materials or history books (because they would all contain the same biased viewpoint). The neo-Maoists accused the post-Mao order of deploying Nazi propaganda techniques to blacken the Mao era: 'a lie repeated a thousand times becomes a truth'.[48] In the end, their arguments and readings of the past and present, of history, economic, society and culture, almost always came back to nationalism: anyone who attacked Mao and his policies was accused of plotting to destroy the Chinese people's self-esteem. The greatest significance of the global economic crisis, contended Zhang Hongliang in 2008, was to return the 'Chinese race' to its traditional place as the 'centre of the world'.[49]

This nationalism blurred easily into violent jingoism. In high Maoist style, leftist websites periodically launched large-scale vilification campaigns against their political opponents – often human rights, civil society and democracy activists – whom they denounced as 'traitors to the Chinese'. In late 2010, a leftist site called Progressive Society featured mugshots of eight 'slaves of the west', which included the late dissident and Nobel Peace Prize winner Liu Xiaobo, the civil rights lawyers Teng Biao and Xu Zhiyong, and the prominent critic of the CCP Yu Jie. Hangman's nooses had been photoshopped around their faces.[50]

In late 2007, I found myself in China for another four months. Beijing had changed. In 2001, the year after I watched the musical about Che Guevara, the capital had won its bid to host the 2008 Olympics. By 2007, pre-Olympic preparations were demolishing much of the city to accommodate vast cavalcades and venues. The flow of rural migrant labour into the city had turned into a flood. Every day I encountered a dusty, marginalised underclass making possible Beijing's glittering reinvention but finding themselves shut out of its benefits. As I worked in a nineteenth-floor apartment, a worker abseiled – with minimal safety equipment – down a half-finished roof on the block opposite.

A tradesman from south-east China told me that he hardly saw his son because he was not allowed to bring him to school in the capital. At the same time, the environmental impact of China's economic miracle was clear. I did a lot of cycling that winter – the apartment I rented was in the south-east, and my university in the north-west – but none of it did me any good. I used to return home to news broadcasts instructing Beijingers to avoid going out because of perilous pollution levels.

As the costs and divisions of China's economic reforms increased, the voices of its critics grew louder. In the winter of 2007, I had my second encounter with China's angry neo-Maoists. My entrée to this world was a meeting at the Beijing headquarters of Utopia, where a group had gathered to denounce Ang Lee's film *Lust, Caution* – a sex-stuffed tale of Japanese-occupied Second World War Shanghai, in which a patriotic female resistance worker ends up sacrificing herself for the political collaborator she is supposed to help assassinate. The film, the meeting agreed, was 'an insult to the Chinese people', a 'Chinese traitor movie', 'a sexually transmitted skin disease' and, in the language of the Cultural Revolution, 'a big poisonous weed'. After these predictably nationalist denunciations, however, the discussion took a slightly surprising turn. What the speakers were really bothered about was the utter spinelessness of the Chinese government's response to the film. China's true problems were the traitors within, not the enemy without: the 'comprador power group' at the heart of the party state, who identified with the West and Japan, who thought China would be better off if it had been a colony for the last two centuries. Economy, culture and politics were rife with the 'running dogs of capitalism', who were turning China into the imperialist West's 'concubine' – this was an existential threat.

By 2007, Beijing's leftists viewed themselves as an oppositional force, persecuted by the contemporary party establishment. Nationalistic neo-Maoists had become a headache for the ruling CCP. Although the party still made liberal use of Mao's image to shore up its historical legitimacy, the Great Helmsman's actual policies were a long way from the doctrine of prosperity and stability that the CCP had adopted since the rise of Deng. But the neo-Maoists could not be easily silenced by political crackdowns, for they had appointed themselves the watch-dogs of both Mao's legacy and the CCP, sniffing out 'anti-CCP propaganda'.[51] An out-and-out attack on the neo-Maoists risked provoking claims that the present CCP had betrayed Mao. 'Anyone who opposes the CCP and Chairman Mao Zedong is our enemy', read the blood-red banners at meetings held by neo-Maoist groups. The following position statement – made at a 2011 meeting in north-west China to denounce liberal intellectual critics of Mao – demonstrated how neo-Maoists skated adroitly between allegiance to Mao and the CCP: 'Chairman Mao Zedong is the leader of the Party and the people, the creator of the People's Republic of China and the People's Liberation Army, and as such we cannot condone the wanton distortion and slander of his magnificent image ... attacking leaders of the Party and the people in the interests of traitors and collaborators is not permitted by the Party. It is not permitted by the people. Even less is it permitted by human history.'[52] Jude Blanchette, an observer of China's extreme leftists, summarised the CCP's dilemma: 'crush the neo-Maoists and risk laying bare the Party's abandonment of its socialist sympathies; allow them to operate untethered and risk a populist revolt'.[53]

In 2008, the neo-Maoists began acting with greater impunity. That summer, their own pro-Mao nationalism connected with widespread anger at perceived anti-China bias in the Western media's reporting of pro-Tibet protests during the Beijing Olympics torch relay in Australia, Europe and the US. Between 2008 and 2009, from little more than a hundred, the Utopia website's articles spiked to 84,214; the group organised marches and red tourist trips to revolutionary sites.[54] As they became more skilled at using the Internet to spread their views and organise their followers, they increased in daring too. A major confrontation erupted in spring 2011, when one of their bêtes noires, an elderly liberal economist called Mao Yushi (no relation to the chairman), published an unusually open criticism of Mao Zedong, accusing the latter of being responsible for more than 30 million deaths by starvation and of crippling China through his fixation on class struggle.[55] Mao Yushi had personal experience of Mao's destructive politics. In the Anti-Rightist Campaign of the late 1950s, he almost died of starvation after being sent into internal exile to the north-east during the great famine – he survived only by eating insects. During the Cultural Revolution, he was whipped and threatened with execution by roving bands of Red Guards.

Nonetheless, in the summer of 2011 Maoist websites submitted a petition – with 10,000 signatures – demanding that the government arrest Mao Yushi for 'slandering Mao Zedong and attempting to overthrow the Communist Party'. 'The whole nation is waiting for ... the dawn of a day when Mao Yu-Shit [*sic*] and other anti-Mao reactionaries who vilify Mao are annihilated.'[56] Phone harassment forced Mao Yushi to switch off his mobile. Banner-holding, chanting leftists occupied the courtyard outside his house, while Public Security officers looked on. The neo-Maoists were, in the common lament of liberal intellectuals, *changjue* – rampant.

In the early hours of 6 February 2012, an implausible old woman drove three hundred kilometres through the emerald-green rice paddies of western China that line the road between Chongqing and Chengdu. At 2.31 that afternoon, she reached her destination: the American consulate in Chengdu. She was implausible because she was in fact a 52-year-old man called Wang Lijun, one of the more notorious police chiefs in China. Until that moment, he had been the enforcer of party rule in the sprawling, smoggy city state of Chongqing: a flamboyantly grisly individual who carried out his own autopsies and claimed to have developed an innovative technique for harvesting organs from death-row prisoners while they were still alive.

But now he was on the run, having fallen out with Bo Xilai, the party secretary of Chongqing – hence his disguised flight to the American consulate. He had several interesting stories to tell the US diplomats about his boss. Revelations about money laundering on a global scale and political malfeasance such as phone taps were just the warm-up. Then came the bombshell. Bo's wife, a lawyer called Gu Kailai, had three months earlier poisoned a middle-aged British businessman called Neil Heywood. At the time, Wang had covered it up by signing off on an autopsy that claimed death by alcohol poisoning and hastily cremating the body; he now promised his interlocutors a blood sample from Heywood's heart that would prove the presence of fatal toxins.

Although the consulate promptly forwarded their unexpected visitor to State Security in Beijing, the scandal of Wang's attempted defection transformed Chinese politics. It caused the downfall of Bo, a man who – up to this point – had shown himself to be the most audacious and ruthless politician in China. On the point of selection to the inner circle of the politburo – the Standing Committee – he was sacked and sentenced to life imprisonment for corruption; his wife received a suspended death sentence; and his former police chief was imprisoned for fifteen years. The fall of Bo and Wang shone a spotlight on staggering levels of iniquity in Chongqing: the two men had created a personal fiefdom in which they arrested, tortured and executed at will to extract assets both for Bo's personal use and to fund extravagant local development schemes to win him popularity. The whole affair brought to light an orgy of power-crazy malfeasance: it was an example of the deep corruption of second-generation revolutionaries, who had moved smoothly from the political purges of the Cultural Revolution to tangles of embezzlement, police brutality and murder – the one constant being their sense of privilege and entitlement.

But to remember Bo just as a failed gangster and a source of PR heartache for the CCP obscures his singular contribution to Chinese politics. This contribution is not massive, international corruption, abuse of judicial powers, multiple infidelities or even murder – for such actions have been part of countless officials' portfolios over the past twenty-five years. His major innovation was rather to have made Mao a conspicuous part of the political mainstream once more. At the start of Bo's time in Chongqing, in late 2007, the Mao era had almost been written out of the public narrative. Chinese officialdom was in a futuristic building frenzy: to prepare for the 2008 Olympics, Beijing had welcomed every star achitect it could find to demolish the old city and push up outlandish new structures, as the government did its level best to create the image of a First World metropolis. When the Olympics started on 8 August 2008, it escaped no one that, in an opening ceremony veering between Confucius' Analects and acrobats in fluorescent pea-green spandex, Mao and his era were absent.

Behind this dazzling facade, however, socio-economic anomie flourished among the many who had lost out in post-1992 China's scramble to make money – hence the success of Bo's Mao revival. In his four years in Chongqing, Bo created a political model radically different from the rest of reform-era China. In his famed 'Sing Red, Strike Black' campaign, his regime cracked down hard on corruption (his own excluded) and rich businessmen, and diverted at least some of the confiscated wealth into lessening urban-rural inequality, building social housing and infrastructure, and raising salaries. Bo led a resurgence of Mao-ish culture – choirs tens of thousands strong bellowing revolutionary hymns, television schedules saturated with Mao-era classics, government servants sent down to the countryside.[57] Chongqing's university quarter was overshadowed by a brand-new, twenty-metre-high, stainless-steel statue of Mao.[58] After almost a decade of consensus, managerial rule by the then party leader, Hu Jintao, Bo Xilai resurrected a very Mao-style leadership: personalised, flamboyant, built around a revival of populist Maoist political values. Seasoned observers of Bo in his domineering prime saw it straight away. 'He's trying to mobilise society like Mao did during the Cultural Revolution, and to do that you usually have to brainwash people first,' commented the publisher of *Caijing*, at the time China's hardest-hitting investigative news magazine.[59] 'I have seen Bo Xilai characterized as a Western-style politician, which I find amusing,' wrote one Chongqing native in early 2012. 'Bo is a product of China's political system, pure and simple. His education was Mao worship and he has not transcended it; his ideas are all out of old playbooks.'[60]

It was in some ways a surprising journey for Bo to have made. During the Cultural Revolution, his father, Bo Yibo – Mao's revolutionary peer – was paraded with his head in an iron rack in front of tens of thousands at Beijing's premier sports stadium, imprisoned, tortured and starved. Bo Xilai's mother died in mysterious circumstances while under Red Guard captivity. The adolescent Bo and his two brothers were themselves publicly humiliated and sent to a thought-reform camp north of Beijing. Bo's strange voyage out of the 1960s and into his experiment in Chongqing told the CCP that, almost forty years after Mao's demise, the Mao era offered a repository of symbols commanding popular appeal and emotional support (such as 'red songs'), which they could deploy while keeping the actual historical traumas of Maoism locked in a box called the past.

By the spring of 2011 leftists young and old were intoxicated with Bo. Utopia provided a virtual loudspeaker for his experiment in Chongqing (the 'Chongqing Model'). 'These red songs, soaked with the bright red blood of revolutionary martyrs, are the spiritual medicine people need to free themselves of the poison of western class society and spiritual opium,' opined one contributor to the site.[61] It seemed that one of their own was finally heading for the politburo. Han Deqiang exulted: 'The river runs to the east for thirty years, the river runs to the west for thirty years, now it will run east for another thirty years ... Only Bo can save communism and save China.'[62]

But on 15 March 2012, as part of the fallout from Wang Lijun's defection, Bo Xilai was placed under arrest. His rise and fall have left a heavy mark on China. His detention led to foreign-media probes into corruption in China, which discovered that $126 million had been accumulated by Gu Kailai's relatives, and $2.7 billion had made it into the hands of the family of then-premier Wen Jiabao.[63] In the immediate aftermath of the Bo debacle, the party state shut down online centres of popular leftism, such as Utopia, which had so excitably supported Bo's 'Chongqing model'. (Many were allowed to reopen, in toned-down versions, a few months later.) But Bo also created a space for publicly celebrating Maoist values that Xi Jinping – member of the same second generation of CCP leaders – directly occupied after Bo was purged and Xi ascended in his place to the secretary generalship of the CCP, in November 2012. (Foreign investigations of the Bo scandal had also revealed that Xi Jinping's siblings had siphoned off more than $1 billion.)

On 17 November 2017, the seven o'clock news on China Central Television (CCTV) – the country's largest state television station – made a revealing editorial decision. On announcing the lead story – Xi Jinping attending a prize-giving ceremony for those who had made special contributions to building a 'Spiritual Civilisation' (a key objective for the CCP's 'socialism with Chinese characteristics') – the programme-makers simply beamed into households all over China four minutes and sixteen seconds of the spiritually civilised assembly applauding Xi Jinping as he processed along the front row of delegates, shaking hands and acknowledging their gratitude.[64]

Four minutes and sixteen seconds. The echoes of Mao – for example, the 1966 documentaries showing the chairman receiving millions of adoring Red Guards in Tiananmen Square – were too loud to be missed.

Just a month earlier, the official media's adulation of Xi had notice-ably intensified at the 19th CCP Congress in Beijing. This five-yearly event sets policy direction and confirms the party leadership for the next half-decade. On the first day of the congress, in a speech lasting three and a half hours, Xi had set out his vision for China. The press venerated him as the 'core leader' (a term associated with Mao and Deng), the 'great leader', 'the pathfinder for the new era', 'the helmsman' (a phrase previously reserved for Mao).[65] In an arguably deliberate ambiguity, Xinhua – the official Chinese international news agency – acclaimed him as 'world leader': perhaps a leader of world stature, perhaps leader of the world.[66] 'Xi Jinping Thought' was written into the constitution as the road map to national rejuvenation under the leadership of the Chinese Communist Party, the first time such an accolade had been granted to a party leader since Mao and Deng.

In theory, the 19th Party Congress marked the halfway point of Xi's leadership stint. Since Deng Xiaoping somewhat regularised the succession procedure in the 1980s, CCP etiquette has held that a new party secretary has ten years – two terms – in power before handing on. This was legislated in 1982 by inserting into the constitution a two-term limit on the honorific title of state president, which leaders since Deng have held in parallel with the party secretaryship (even though the latter is the far more meaningful position). Since the early 2000s, moreover, an informal rule has encouraged party leaders to retire at the age of sixty-eight. For some time, however, many had speculated that Xi Jinping would try to extend that gentleman's (and those at the top are all men) agreement and like Mao and Deng try to extend his term to twenty years, perhaps even life. A party secretary's midpoint congress is usually the moment at which a likely successor is indicated. Conspicuously, Xi's new seven-strong Standing Committee contained no individual who, in five years' time, would be younger than the unofficial retirement age. Only four months later, these suspicions were confirmed, when Xi – through the rubber-stamping National People's Congress – abolished the two-term limit on the presidency. The change gave Xi the go-ahead for lifetime rule.

This was the culmination of the Xi cult that has been growing since he took power in November 2012. A quasi-religious aura has built around the leader that has not been seen since the days of Mao.

The Chinese Internet hums with rock ballads and raps hymning him: 'China has produced a Big Daddy Xi / He'll fight any tiger, no matter how big / He's not afraid of anything on heaven or earth / We all dream of meeting him.'[67] Discussing Xi 'incorrectly' can have serious consequences – intimidation, expulsion from the party, prison and worse. Members of groups targeted by Xi – academics, writers, lawyers – are nervous even of speaking his name, for fear of charges of subversion. In 2016, when I asked a well-known and usually plain-speaking public intellectual a question about Western media portrayals of Xi's image, he blanched. 'I cannot talk about him. If you ask these questions, you'll get me into trouble, and you'll get yourself into trouble too.'

Analysts have worked to draw out the particulars of Xi's vision for China, especially his emphasis on national revival and on 'socialism with Chinese characteristics'. There is much detail in Xi's plans to chew over: the government's relationship with private business and foreign investment; the approach to environmental degradation; how to revitalise the rural economy. But few of Xi's headline approaches are particularly new: the CCP has been openly promoting nationalism since the 1990s; in 2007 a high-profile CCTV series and exhibition at the Military Affairs Museum were entitled *The Road to Rejuvenation*. 'Socialism with Chinese characteristics' has, again, been in the mainstream of political discussion since the 1990s, when even hairdressers would advertise 'hair-cutting with Chinese characteristics'. Yet Xi does have one stand-out innovation. Emulating Bo Xilai's invocation of Maoist themes, Xi has, for the first time since the chairman's death in 1976, reinserted into the mainstream of Chinese national life some of the symbols and practices of Maoist politics. After some forty years of post-Mao reforms China remains socially, economically and culturally hybrid, but Xi's repertoire for political control is resurgently Maoist.

Xi has saturated the media with references to himself and monopolised state powers. Through the creation of new, centralising posts occupied by his allies, he directs work on all aspects of economic, political, cultural, social and military reform, as well as national, Internet and information security.[68] In early Maoist fashion, Xi has intensified party control alongside cultivating personal power. He has reinstated the party as the disciplined, monolithic, solely legitimate representative of China, its people and national interest.* This has been a mammoth task, for Xi inherited a CCP mired in a crisis of shameless oligarchic corruption. To achieve his goal, Xi has invoked distinctly Maoist language and techniques. Just five months into his tenure, he launched the Mass Line Campaign – a very conscious throwback to Mao's original, pre-1949 concept – through which the public were invited to criticise officials, who, pending investigation, would be 'rectified': a favourite word for Xi, and one with strong echoes of Mao and his first ideological suppression in 1942. Hand in hand with the mass line has come a crackdown on corruption at almost all levels of the party. A 2016 CCTV propaganda documentary about the fight against corruption, entitled *Always on the Road*, invoked Mao's Yan'an as a reference point for political purity and hard work.[69] Xi has walked the Maoist walk, as well as talked the talk. He celebrated the 120th anniversary of Mao's birth by pledging to 'hold high the banner of Mao Zedong Thought forever', and by bowing three times to the statue of the helmsman on a visit to the Tiananmen Maosoleum.[70]

The ultimate aim of the campaign is not necessarily justice or economic probity: it is to shore up party authority. The documentary *Always on the Road* interviewed several purged party leaders convicted for corruption. Each made two key points. First, that the error they committed was their own personal mistake: it was nothing to do with the political system lacking proper checks and balances on party power. And second, that their primary crime was not one against the tax-paying Chinese people whom they had defrauded: it was against the party, which they had let down through their indiscipline.

---

* Although the party has long dominated – in theory and practice – the government of China (a dominance enshrined in the seventh paragraph of the preamble to the current constitution), in practice the intensity of its control has oscillated at different moments in the seventy-year history of the PRC. The party under Mao, and especially after he took to meddling in the day-to-day running of the economy after 1957, *was* the PRC government. Even after Mao destroyed much of the CCP apparatus and personnel in the early years of the Cultural Revolution, his personalised control was assured through local governance by Revolutionary Committees, the institutions that replaced the old party bureaucracy. The 1980s saw a serious attempt to separate party and government powers, spearheaded by the reforming premier Zhao Ziyang, but the political crackdown of spring 1989 strengthened Mao-style party control over the state.

While Xi's anti-corruption campaign has dressed itself in the cloak of responsiveness to 'The People', it has in reality prioritised party power. Before Xi's anti-corruption campaign began in 2013, China possessed a dynamic civil society, thanks to the social networking possibilities of the Internet, and to the energies and courage of new generations of lawyers and activists. But Xi's government has cracked down hard on such extra-party forms of monitoring and scrutiny. The imprisonment of Xu Zhiyong – a lawyer who led a grass-roots campaign for greater financial transparency in officialdom – is just one of the most high-profile examples. The anti-corruption campaign has empowered above all the Central Commission for Discipline and Inspection, the party's own investigation agency which, under conditions of complete opacity, and above the national legal system, has absolute power to arrest, judge and punish any individual deemed to have offended party discipline. Directing it, of course, is Xi. This is a clear throwback to the party's monopoly on political and legal power under Mao as paramount leader.

At the same time, Xi has tightened the party's control of history. In a move unprecedented for a Communist state, the archives of Mao-era China had opened up in the first decade of the new millennium. Both Chinese and non-Chinese researchers could access vast quantities of government documents from municipal, provincial and county archives, and also read and photograph – on presentation of only a passport or identity card – declassified material from the Ministry of Foreign Affairs (the first, and so far only, PRC ministry to open its archive). Even if access stopped at the close of 1965 – the eve of the Cultural Revolution, the most sensitive foreign policy period for Mao's China – the foreign affairs declassifications opened the lid on many formerly closed areas, such as the PRC's relations with North Korea and Vietnam. For the first time, researchers could access copies of documents dispatched to the Ministry of Foreign Affairs by the International Liaison Department, the super-secretive institution responsible for relations with foreign Communist and revolutionary parties.

Under Hu Jintao, although it was dangerous to criticise Mao openly (on Hu's watch the 'stability maintenance budget' went up to an annual $111 billion, $5 billion more than the PRC spent on national defence), it was possible tacitly to marginalise Maoist history.[71] In the early 2000s, a furore erupted in Shanghai when news broke that Mao had been quietly removed from some school textbooks. A government official told me that it would have gone unchallenged if foreign media had not drawn attention to it, triggering the protest of some older cadres. 'If you want to liberalise anything in China,' he advised, 'don't publicise it.' Within weeks of becoming leader, however, Xi denounced any public ambivalence about the Mao era as 'historical nihilism'. In Xi's schema, the Mao era and post-Mao China are an indivisible whole, providing a unified historical, symbolic source of legitimacy – the Reform period cannot be used to criticise the Mao era, and vice versa.[72] This ruling has effectively meant a clampdown on serious, informed public debate about post-1949 history. By 2013, only 10 per cent of materials formerly available at the Ministry of Foreign Affairs archive were still open to researchers. Even anodyne documents in local archives were pulled from the shelves by administrators hypersensitive to possible indiscretions.

Compared with the Mao craze, the cult of Xi is – it must be said – pale and unconvincing. Stacks of his *Collected Works* gather dust in bookshops; for almost twenty years, the propaganda outlets for Xi worship – *People's Daily* and CCTV – have been losing audiences. Transmogrified from the Mao era, China is now a country where everything has a price, even in left-leaning media – across one Maoist website I visited, my attempt to read articles about ideology was slowed by a roving pop-up trying to sell me plush towels in the design of the banknote that carries Mao's image. In September 2014, I spent an hour browsing stalls at a National Red Collectors' Convention south of Tiananmen, where flotsam and jetsam from the Mao era were for sale – one stall was devoted solely to Little Red Books. There were also manifestations of the new Xi Jinping cult in the form of large porcelain plates emblazoned with his portrait next to versions depicting Mao. 'History has proved that only Mao's way was correct,' one vendor told me. 'He turned a rotten old China into new China. And now we can make money out of it.' Apart from his unquestioning veneration for the party, Xi has little personally in common with Mao. An engineer and apparatchik by training, he lacks Mao's self-taught, folksy literary range and philosophical pretensions; he keeps regular hours and has only been married twice. The party under Xi, as under all its leaders since Mao, is terrified by the prospect of a Cultural Revolution–style bottom-up mobilisation of society.

These large discrepancies between Mao's and Xi's China notwith-standing, Xi has calculated (correctly, it seems) – like Bo Xilai – that there is now enough temporal distance between the present and the memories of bad times under Mao for it to be safe to deploy the helmsman's fuzzy, father-of-the-nation symbolism. Xi's big project is the 'Chinese Dream' – in English you might call it 'Make China Great Again': the restoration of China to its old, pre-nineteenth-century glory.[73] Like Mao, and unlike Xi's immediate predecessors, Xi and his people have reached for an emotional political message to bolster the CCP's legitimacy. They have striven to create a smooth unity between his administration and the Mao era, between a fantasy of China's past imperial greatness and a promise of the country's future magnificence under CCP rule.

When, another seven years after my 2007 encounters with Utopia, I resumed my travels around neo-Maoist circles in 2014, I could perceive a newly contented assurance replacing their previous edgy dissidence. Those working in academia seemed to be flourishing: now, they were busy, important people, for these were fat times for Marxism-Leninism Institutes. Among the urban neo-Maoists I met, there was a near-universal approval of Xi Jinping, who had become a Mao-style figure to be unquestioningly venerated; their anti-state dissent had practically vanished. 'There are now people in the government who support our viewpoints,' one told me. 'That's because we're right. We do it for faith, for belief, for the country. Not for Western bribes. Red Culture is in our genes. We're bringing it back.' Xi Jinping's talk of national rejuvenation has stoked the neo-Maoists' patriotism. Zhang Hongliang saw Mao's thought as a holy writ currently spreading across the world: to the US legal system and the Western Europe welfare states. He believed the moment was ripe for China to take on the mantle of global domination from the West, currently reeling from a combined cultural, financial and political crisis.

> In the West, happiness is exclusively material. In the East, happiness is spiritual. The sense that everyone is growing at the same time. Chinese society's dependence on [Western-style] competition over the past thirty years has turned the Chinese into tigers and wolves ... Now people are looking eastwards. They are realising that Western philosophy is wrong ... After 500 years Western civilisation has reached the end of

the road. And Eastern culture must replace it … China, not India, is the carrier for Eastern culture … The revival of the Chinese nation depends on the revival of socialism because only socialism can realise common prosperity, and only this can knit the Chinese nation into a strong, integrated whole … So the revival of socialism in the twenty-first century is an irreversible trend. This is the fundamental belief of China's left wing. We represent the hope of the nation.

In helping engineer this process of spiritual socialist revival, Zhang somewhat incongruously described his role in corporate, establishment terms: 'I'll advise – like a company consultant', mediating between ordinary people and the CCP.

In 2007 the Utopian Han Deqiang had joined in the struggle session of *Lust, Caution* with a nationalist jeremiad: 'The West is the culture of animals, it turns everyone into animals. The West is a wild culture. China is a civilisation. The West is a savage civilisation. The West is about to annihilate the rest of the world. All Western philosophy is childish.' Like most other Utopians, he applauded Bo Xilai's campaigns in Chongqing, and protested Bo's innocence after his dramatic fall in March 2012. During the forced shutdown of leftist websites through the summer and autumn of 2012, Han declined to stay quiet. He achieved his greatest notoriety on 18 September 2012 when – at a demonstration protesting Japanese claims to the Diaoyu Islands – he slapped an eighty-year-old man who, on seeing a placard which read 'We Miss You Chairman Mao', retorted: 'Miss him, my arse.'

The following year, Han made a dramatic lifestyle choice. Concerned by China's burgeoning spiritual and physical crisis (since the 2000s, the country has been repeatedly rocked by food safety scandals), and reassured by the helmsmanship of Xi Jinping ('he is carrying out Mao's policies … he is leading a struggle between good and evil … I can now leave the leaders to get on with the job, while I do my own thing'), he decided to withdraw from the pugnacity of wired leftism to found his own utopia on a collective, organic farm in Hebei Province, south of Beijing. The influences were a befuddling mix of Thai Buddhism and veneration for Mao, though Han did not see any contradiction. 'Mao is a Buddha. The Buddha wants to deliver all living creatures from torment, and Mao wanted to liberate mankind.' I queried his Buddhist definition of Mao, given the chairman's veneration of political violence. A nationalist answer came back at me. 'There are two legs to Maoist thought,' he explained, 'violent class struggle, and serving the people ... Class struggle comes from the West. Serve the people comes from Chinese tradition.' Bad Western influences therefore corrupted Mao's Buddha-like instincts and caused the brutality of the Cultural Revolution. For all his own combativeness, Han remained a passionate devotee of the party state, and frowned upon the mass mobilisations of the 1960s. 'Intellectuals, editors and journalists who oppose government and party,' he observed disapprovingly, 'are heirs to the Cultural Revolution's rebel spirit.'

The farm, and Han Deqiang, seemed more Maoist than Buddhist. His periodic assaults on (Western) materialism notwithstanding, he displayed on his desk some impulse-bought plastic Mao memorabilia. In another Maoist nod, Han wanted the farm to be self-reliant, though he admitted that the home-made toothpaste had so far been a runny failure. In his vision, the farm was a school as well as an enterprise, populated mostly by students and twenty-somethings tired of the rat race. The model was Mao's work-study, and the chairman's conviction that thoughts can be moulded through labour. 'We hope to labour on three types of "field",' announced Han's manifesto: 'on the farm ... on Chinese medicine, and also on the mind, to educate a new, righteous human.'[74] In this setting, Han seemed to be playing out a helmsman-like persona. As he strolled around the farm, hands lightly clasped behind his back, anyone we encountered addressed him as 'Teacher'. 'Chairman Mao may be gone,' one young woman told me, 'but Teacher makes us feel closer to him.' While we walked, a photographer trailed behind. Han – presumably accustomed to his every action being recorded for posterity – was entirely unfazed. He gave the workers lectures on classical literature but his own take on intellectuals was straight out of Mao. 'I don't like writers. I'm completely opposed to any kind of specialisation, or professionalisation.' The photographer tailing us told me that in his previous urban life he had been a lawyer. 'But I don't have much opportunity to use that here.' 'We don't need law,' Han chimed in. One consequence of Han's suspicion of experts, I presumed, was the surfeit of squashes around the farm; the whole place seemed to be tangled with vines and their gourds. Han admitted there was such a glut that they were making an experimental shampoo out of them. He seemed unduly impressed by my ability to identify carrot plants from their feathery leaves.

I imagined Yan'an in the 1940s might have looked like this: here was a unified community of knowledge, practice and understanding, self-strengthening against the turbid outside world. 'This is a new kind of society,' one farm worker told me. 'We're transforming our value system. On the outside, everyone is focused on their own feelings, or on poisoning the earth to earn money. Here, our thoughts and ideals work together. We do things collectively.' Mao was a constant, almost divine inspiration. 'We all have Chairman Mao buttons. I use the spirit of the chairman. When I'm tired, or having problems, I'll think about how Chairman Mao came onto this earth. It gives me strength. So does singing songs. For example, "The Sun is Reddest, Chairman Mao is Dearest".' Despite Han's attempt to remake himself as a spiritual man of the soil, plenty of his muscular nationalism remained. He was critical of North Korea: 'They treat their leaders there like gods.' I suggested that he did the same with Mao. 'That's different. He was a god. Mao was in heaven. North Korea's leaders are' – he gestured at some lean-tos nearby – 'at the level of these sheds.' I asked him what he felt now, a few years on, about having hit the elderly man at the demonstration. He answered without hesitation: 'I'm glad! I did the right thing!'

There is a frightening simplicity to these neo-Maoists' analyses and analogies. However well educated or well read they claim to be – both Han Deqiang and Zhang Hongliang boast about their own wide reading: Dickens, Hugo, Balzac, Zola, Cervantes, Goethe, Heine, the Western philosophical canon – they suffer from a failure of imagination about the effects of political violence and untrammelled power in the hands of a party or individual. 'The process of any revolution is bloody, chaotic,' observed Zhang Hongliang philosophically. 'But we can't judge revolutions on that attribute . . . For example, an operation will be very painful, with lots of blood loss. But the result is worth it. You're healthier afterwards. Likewise, a baby will be filthy with all sorts of muck when born, but no mother would abandon her baby because of that.' The Utopian Maoists paradoxically combine an affection for revolutionary insurrection with a reverence for the state, and an obsession with serving it. But Zhang's plan for government under 'mass democracy' was sketchy, to say the least. 'Members of a Maoist government will serve as technical personnel to implement the ideas of the masses. They'll be like a doctor that sees sick people. They won't be high above us; they'll specialise in bringing together people's viewpoints. Like actors, musicians, doctors, teachers and football players who specialise in different things, they'll just be another sort of profession.'

Even if intemperate Utopians have become more docile since Xi took power, the CCP leadership has not lost its unease towards popular Maoism. For there are still unaffiliated Maoists in China today, who take at face value Mao's directives to revolt. Yuan Yuhua, a native of Henan born in 1946, was an outspoken rebel during the Cultural Revolution. Interviewed for a Japanese documentary a few years ago, his eyes still shone at the memory of it: 'for years, Party officials had punished us for speaking out, and suddenly we had freedom to complain, to protest'. In 1976, as the Cultural Revolution shut down after Mao's death, he was sentenced to fifteen years' imprisonment, spending some of it in solitary confinement. He was released just in time to participate in the protests of spring 1989. In the 1990s, he set up one of China's most remarkable political organisations: a 'thought salon' in his native city of Zhengzhou, in which for twenty years debaters from across the political spectrum gathered to discuss Mao and his legacy. Here a middle-aged migrant labourer earning 200 yuan from his fourteen-hour working day would call for a return to Maoist class violence; and a sixty-something eyewitness of the Cultural Revolution would recall watching, as a thirteen-year-old, two young men being beaten to death.[75] 'If Mao were alive today,' Yuan acknowledged, 'he wouldn't appreciate my style of rebellion.'[76] A self-avowed Maoist dissident called Li Tie was sentenced to ten years' imprisonment in 2012 for 'subverting state power': he had argued that Mao was a democrat and had bolstered his defence of human rights with Mao's own words.[77]

Arguably the most curious Maoist in China today is a septuagenarian writer called Zhang Chengzhi. He was born in 1948 in Beijing to a poor Hui Muslim family who had to suppress their own religious identity amid Mao's crackdown on faith. As a student Zhang embraced the Cultural Revolution: he even credits himself with inventing the term Red Guard in 1966. He threw himself into the violence of 1966–68 and volunteered to be rusticated to Inner Mongolia, one of China's toughest environments, where he almost died of starvation. He returned to Beijing in time to play a starring role in the post-Mao literary thaw, penning tales of life on the Mongolian steppe that were both romanticising and stylistically experimental. In 1987, he began to rediscover his Muslim roots and converted to the Jahriyya, a sect of Chinese Islam characterised by an ascetic, uncompromising attitude to faith. Two years later, he renounced all institutional ties to Chinese state and party, resigning from the CCP's main literary organisation, the Writers' Association. Since then, Zhang has evolved into a polemical essayist, his subjects ranging from literature and architecture to the War on Terror, from the Chinese revolution to the break-up of Yugoslavia. He remains a passionate defender of Cultural Revolution Maoism, a fervent Muslim, and a critic of both Han Chinese culture and the United States. He still venerates Mao's rhetorical zest for disobedience. 'The rebel spirit is the quintessence of Mao's thought [and] of the revolution.' It was Mao and his Cultural Revolution that enabled Zhang to travel and experience the complexity of China. He witnessed the poverty of life on China's rural margins and the loathing of its minorities for the Han Chinese government. 'I became an intellectual who could see the world from the perspective of the lowest stratum of society,' he has written. 'Young people like me lost our faith in state-sponsored theory ... The Red Guards' rebellious, iconoclastic spirit joined with ordinary people's struggles for freedom of the spirit and mind.'[78]

He has also drawn from his 1960s Maoism a lifelong hatred of 'imperialism'. For Zhang, imperialism is the keyword that unlocks contemporary geopolitics and that has led him to embrace a particular kind of pan-Islamism. The Iraq War is just like the Vietnam War; Iraqi resistance to the United States is identical to the Chinese Communist army fighting Japan in the Second World War; global Muslim opposition to America and Israel is the contemporary incarnation of the anti-imperialist 'Red Guard Spirit'. And like a true child of China's 1960s, Zhang invokes the name of Mao Zedong as 'a symbol of rebellion' against the current American-dominated world order: 'for Chinese like me who continue to oppose neo-colonialism, the international balance of power makes it necessary for us to look to him as a bastion of human dignity'.[79] The China that Mao built, in Zhang's view, shares a political and cultural Third World identity with global Islam. Therefore, 'Muslims must strive to unite with Chinese civilization.'[80]

Zhang lavishes praise on rebels of the 1960s who demonstrated a clear pro-Muslim tilt in their opposition to US domestic and foreign policy, such as Malcolm X and Muhammad Ali. He is also obsessed with the Arab-Japanese Red Army (AJRA), an organisation founded in 1971 by a splinter from the Japanese pro-Maoist urban guerrilla group, the Red Army Faction.[81] Members of the AJRA fled to Lebanon, where they embraced the Palestinian cause, relying on the Popular Front for the Liberation of Palestine for money and training. In 1972, the AJRA took part in an attack on Lod airport that killed twenty-six (including seventeen Puerto Rican pilgrims) and injured eighty; this and other terrorist actions won the organisation notoriety in the West, Israel and Japan.[82] But to Zhang, the AJRA exemplifies the border-crossing ideals of the Cultural Revolution: global solidarity with the suffering people of the Third World. His essays on the AJRA resonate with passionate admiration for its militants and with guilt that he himself did not go to the Middle East to join the Palestinian resistance during the Cultural Revolution.

There are inconsistent and troubling aspects to Zhang's politics. Although his books laud the virtues of collectivism, his writing is in fact curiously individualistic. Zhang, the lone, reflective, persecuted rebel, is the solitary hero of many of his essays; a thinly veiled autobiographical version of this same Zhang appears in much of his fiction. 'I am a child of the great 1960s, and carry on my shoulders its emotions and its seriousness,' he writes melodramatically, 'my feet and heart are pricked all over by thorns.'[83] Despite his much-vaunted championing of those at the bottom of Chinese society, he has little to say about the plight of historically one of the most oppressed groups in China: women. In his fiction, female characters often seem to exist solely in order to be abandoned or snubbed by a strong male protagonist.[84] While Zhang emphasises the importance of education, and argues hard for the need to build a modern Muslim education system in China, he seems untroubled by low access to education for Muslim Chinese women, writing that for them 'a good husband is more important'.[85] And as the self-nominated author of the term 'Red Guard', he is not averse to the use of political violence – as long as it is meted out for the right reasons. 'You shouldn't make an excessive fuss about the principle of beating people up.'[86]

Nonetheless, in a China that permits little intellectual dissidence, Zhang does maintain a genuinely disputatious stance. In a provocative move, for example, Zhang called a 2007 Chinese-language collection of essays *Five Colours of Heresy*. The book is divided into five sections, each named after the colours that represent the different passions that sustain Zhang: green for Islam, yellow for Mongolia, blue for Xinjiang, red for Mao's Chinese Communism; the significance of the final colour, black, is not clarified, though it seems to stand for the intended incendiary nature of his work. 'My writings are black bombs, thrown out into this shameless world,' he declares. The mere fact of identifying himself with these causes places him on the intellectual margins of contemporary China. Yet Zhang goes further, calling himself 'a heretic within each color ... Although these colors are part of me, I don't pursue the system attached to any of them ... Most party secretaries would find my Redness objectionable; orthodox Muslims would find my Greenness too heterodox.'[87] Unsurprisingly, a figure like Zhang Chengzhi has few admirers in the Chinese mainstream. His is a controversial, minority stance. Officialdom is discomfited by his extolling of Red Guard rebellion; nationalists dislike his defence of Muslim rights and identity; liberals (and many former Red Guards) reject his unapologetic admiration for Mao Zedong. Zhang is a Maoist in the Groucho Marx sense – outside any powerful club or system. His Maoism has shaped him into one of the most perplexingly contradictory individuals I have ever encountered. His serial self-reinventions represent another legacy of the Cultural Revolution, which forced people to live with multiple personalities in order to survive.

Repenting his failure to interpret Mao's exhortations to 'liberate the world' by leaving China to join the global revolution in the 1960s, Zhang in 2011 designed an unconventional publishing project. He decided to produce a revised twentieth-anniversary edition of one of his most famous books – a fictionalised history of Chinese Islam – in a limited, private print run of fewer than a thousand copies, to be sold at 1,500 yuan (almost $230) apiece.* Zhang pledged all the profits of this venture directly to Palestinian refugees, in order 'to live up to the original aspiration of the Red Guard era'.[88] (The very idea of such a venture verges on the eccentric in the context of contemporary Chinese literature, where many authors are arguably even more

---

* It seems that no public publisher dared take on the project, due to the book's radical religious message.

preoccupied with advances, royalties and media fame than they are in the West.) Once the funds had been gathered, Zhang made contact with a Palestinian NGO, which arranged for him to visit a Palestinian refugee camp and present envelopes containing $200 each to hundreds of Palestinian families. Zhang was anxious that this philanthropic transaction should be 'hand-to-hand' (*shou di shou*): in other words, 'people-to-people' (*minjian*), rather than handled and sanctioned by government bodies, in either China or Jordan. His actions communicated a vision for global justice that was simultaneously radical, cosmopolitan, outside the state, and consciously modelled on Mao's Cultural Revolution rhetoric of Third World solidarity.[89]

Despite their differences, one feature unifies the disparate voices of contemporary neo-Maoism: the CCP's relative tolerance for their existence, in the context of an absolute intolerance of non-party political organisation or activism on any other part of the political spectrum. Han Deqiang's farm experiment was forced to shut down at the end of 2016, but mainly under legal pressure from the parents of Han's student labourers, who were horrified that their offspring had chosen to throw away their education and earning capacity on manual labour. Zhang Chengzhi complains that he cannot express himself in China on issues ranging from literature to revolution, religious freedom to foreign affairs; he often publishes his most sensitive work in Hong Kong or translated into Japanese. His platforms for public expression – such as lectures and media coverage – are assuredly constrained: journalists refer to him as 'a sensitive topic'. But since Zhang's political dissidence is leftist in orientation, it does not so far seem to have brought down crushing state censure; consequently, he does not suffer the heavy-handed repression meted out to advocates of liberal democracy, such as the late Nobel Peace laureate Liu Xiaobo. (The imprisonment of the self-avowed Maoist Li Tie was also doubtless driven by his overt championing of democracy and human rights during the Arab Spring.) It is much easier for the government to crack down on criticisms of Mao and Mao-era history than it is to suppress neo-Maoists who portray themselves as defenders of the faith. And certainly, anyone who has attempted to dispute official readings of Mao and the Mao era, or to pose any kind of challenge to CCP authority, is vulnerable in Xi's China. In January 2017, Mao Yushi became only the latest liberal to have his social media platform shut down, and civil society activists and lawyers have suffered much worse – extrajudicial 'disappearances' have risen precipitately under Xi.[90] What use the neo-Maoist left will make of this slightly enhanced latitude for organisation and contention outside the CCP is one of the most intriguing questions for political participation in China today.

Strange events were afoot in 2016, the fiftieth anniversary year of the Cultural Revolution. Public discussion that went beyond the official state media's definitive condemnation (issued on 17 May) was banned, for 'history has shown that the Cultural Revolution was utterly wrong … Completely denying the values of the Cultural Revolution is not only an understanding throughout the party, but also a stable consensus of the whole of Chinese society.'[91] The half-centenary generated conferences, articles and books outside mainland China; within China, academics were fearful even of mentioning it in class. Xi's hostility to the topic was not surprising, for he and his family had suffered greatly during this period in history. His half-sister lost her life amid political persecution; his father was imprisoned; Xi himself was roughly ejected from a gilded life amid the Beijing Communist aristocracy and banished to manual labour in the impoverished north-west.

That same spring, unknown parties booked the Great Hall of the People, the go-to venue for massive state functions and funerals, for a Mao-era song extravaganza on 2 May – almost fifty years to the day after Mao issued the directive (exposing 'counter-revolutionary revisionists' at all levels of the CCP) that launched the Cultural Revolution. It was an open celebration of Maoist culture, and an affirmation of its relevance to China today. Across the stage's backdrop glowed portraits of Mao and China's current chairman, Xi Jinping. The girl group 56 Flowers – a number chosen to stand for the national unity of China's fifty-six official ethnic groups – alternated classics of Mao worship ('Sailing the seas depends on the helmsman … Making revolution depends on Mao Zedong Thought') with reverent ditties portraying Xi as the kindly uncle of the suffering poor.[92]

As soon as the concert was over, however, the controversy began. Voices on social media – including the relatives of those purged during the 1960s – censured the event's celebration of Cultural Revolution messages. The extreme political orthodoxy of the venue indicated that the concert must on some level have had official backing; 56 Flowers claimed that members of the party, government and army were in the audience.[93] Yet the organisers of the concert remained a mystery. On investigation, state media declared that the organisation that had booked the hall – the 'Office for Promotion and Education of Socialist Core Values' – was a fake. Some observers, bemusedly trying to read the tea leaves of this incident, wondered if it had been arranged as a caricaturing criticism of Xi's Mao-ishness. Culturally, the whole show was – like most things in China today – messily hybrid. 56 Flowers, founded in 2015 to sing the praises of the CCP and PRC, modelled themselves on the hyper-commercialised, giant youth bands manufactured in South Korea and Japan – Exo, AKB48 and so on.[94] The tickets, costing between $58 and $320, were priced at market economy levels – a decision unlikely to have impressed Mao, who would have liked to abolish money. We will probably never know the truth behind this curious evening: in the days after the concert, most of the publicity photos, videos and media articles about the event faded from the Internet. But its confused denouement tells us plenty about the contested status of Mao's legacy – caught between official opportunism and ambivalence, commercial kitschification and inchoate grass-roots sentiment – in China today.

CONCLUSION

On 11 March 2018, China's annual parliament – the National People's Congress – voted overwhelmingly in favour of abolishing the constitution's restriction limiting any one president to two terms in office. 'The 64-year-old Mr Xi essentially became a president for life,' concluded the *Washington Post*, 'in a return to personal dictatorship that China has not seen since Mao Zedong. Forgetting the lessons of Mao's often disastrous reign, Mr Xi is attempting to construct a 21st-century model of totalitarianism and offer it as an example to the rest of the world.'[1] The news dismayed but did not surprise many China-watchers, for credible rumours had been circulating for months and years that Xi Jinping would want to stay on beyond the ten years that his two predecessors had spent in office. Yet non-specialist commentators seemed wrong-footed. 'Remember how American engagement with China was going to make that communist backwater more like the democratic, capitalist West?' asked another *Washington Post* opinion piece.

> For years, both Republican and Democratic administrations argued that the gravitational pull of US-dominated international institutions, trade flows, even pop culture, would gradually [result] in a moderate new China with which the United States and its Asian allies could comfortably coexist ... All we had to do was stay patient, maintain our influence and let China evolve ... Well, Chinese President Xi Jinping has just engineered his potential elevation to president for life ... the powers-that-be in Beijing have their own agenda, impervious to US influence.[2]

Many, it seems, had assumed that, as China turned commercial and capitalist after the death of Mao, the country would become 'more like us': that Mao and Chinese Communism were history.[3] The opposite has happened. Mao, his strategies and political model remain central to the legitimacy and functioning of China's Communist government. For decades, Western analysts have been too quick to overlook or dismiss the persistent influence of the Maoist heritage in contemporary China. In this book, I have argued that Maoism has been underestimated not just as a Chinese but also as a global phenomenon. I have sought to re-centre its ideas and experiences as major forces of the recent past, present and future that have shaped – and are shaping – the world, as well as China. What themes have emerged from observing Maoism's global travels?

We have seen that Mao's revolution of 1949 – coinciding with the onset of decolonisation – exercised a particular and enduring appeal within the polarised context of the Cold War. As dozens of new countries (often underdeveloped, and predominantly rural) broke out of European and Japanese empires and searched for workable state-building models, many were suspicious of American intentions and unwilling to embrace the Europeanised blueprints of Soviet Russia. Mao's revolution, by contrast, represented an alternative apparently suited to poor, agrarian states that had suffered at the hands of colonialism. Mao's talent for pithy sound bites made his vision more easily communicable to low-literacy recruits. His attacks on China's 'semi-feudal, semi-colonial' society, together with the reputation accruing from his own revolutionary success, won him tremendous moral prestige in the decolonising and post-colonial world – and also among educated Westerners uncomprehending of, and disgusted by, the European imperial project.

Maoism has also had an emotional and practical attraction for insurgencies against existing states that were colonial, repressive or neglectful (or a combination of the three). In Peru, Nepal and parts of India, the organised militancy and hopeful voluntarism (the belief that material conditions can be transcended by willpower) of Maoist doctrine enabled the determined and the desperate to mount redoubtable challenges to dysfunctional, exploitative governments.

While crossing the globe, Mao's ideas and practices have been implemented in both rigid and adaptable ways. Indian and Peruvian Maoists tried to superimpose onto (more or less) functioning democracies an intractable vision of 1960s Maoism that preached piti-less class struggle directed by a conspiratorial, authoritarian Communist Party. Maoism's trajectory in Western Europe and the US has been far more wayward. Here, rebels took Maoism as a toolkit for protest. Their engagement with the Cultural Revolution – which in China played out with chaotic repressiveness – scattered into diverse anti-establishment projects (some with their own authoritarian tendencies).

Some of the translations of Mao's ideas have been outright distor-tions. One bewildering example is the way in which Maoist sympa-thisers in the West and in Nepal read or implemented Mao's ideas as championing the rights of underprivileged minorities. Maoism in China was in fact violently intolerant of minority rights: consider, as just one example, the tremendous suffering of the Tibetan people during Mao's Great Leap Forward and Cultural Revolution.

Maoism's global journeys have generated other incongruities. Mao is rightly seen as the first major Communist thinker to champion the revolutionary potential of an impoverished rural majority. And yet – both in China and beyond – the rural poor have suffered most at the hands of Mao's theories and practices. In the PRC, farmers starved in their tens of millions after the Great Leap Forward; in India, Nepal and Peru, it was inhabitants of the countryside that constituted the majority of victims in Maoist insurgencies. Their leaders, paradoxically, have come from the educated classes of which Mao himself was so suspicious.

Mao's key idea about the need for violent rebellion to sweep away social injustice and his practical strategies to achieve this aim – party-building, mass work, protracted guerrilla warfare – have attracted the discontented across decades and territories. Educated persuaders have used these emotional ideas to galvanise insurgencies, sometimes with enormous bloodshed. But except in China, Maoist insurgencies have failed to translate into stable political power. (And even in China, the Maoist fondness for mass mobilisation has threatened to topple the regime at least twice, amid the catastrophic aftermath of the Great Leap Forward and in the first two years of the Cultural Revolution.) Mao's promise of 'mass democracy' has never delivered: in practice, it has usually resulted in the triumph of those who shout the loudest, or fight and plot the hardest. A Beijing taxi driver once summed up for me, during a five-minute conversation, Maoism's eighty-year political appeal and its limitations. 'The good thing about China under Mao is that everyone was equal. Not like now, when people will do you over for money, and even beggars won't leave you alone until you give them 100 yuan.' I asked if he would therefore like to turn the clock back to Mao's era. 'No,' he quickly replied. 'I'd rather get myself some education.' To this member of an over-worked, underprivileged economic class in China today, equality of opportunity is more attractive than forcible equalising of outcome.

The story of Maoism's international travels reveals also the PRC's repertoire of global interventions. It undermines the historical orthodoxy – propagated by China but widely accepted in the West – that Mao-era China had no engagement with the world beyond its borders. Through the research for this book, I began to grasp the enormous amounts of time, energy and money that the PRC under Mao put into projecting its image and influence abroad. This task was vast and various. Chinese hosts provided Simone de Beauvoir's hotel room with a brass double bed and pink silk sheets; she was enraptured. On the occasion of a ceremonial visit by a key ally, Prince Sihanouk of Cambodia, public security emptied the streets of an entire city and repopulated them with plain-clothes police disguised as ordinary urbanites. The CCP threw billions of dollars at African railways and health care, and financed guerrilla insurgencies across the globe. Although Mao's China often did not play by international rules, it did play.

Maoism's global engagements have had unpredictable results, reflecting the unstable history and political objectives of China between 1949 and 1976. In South East Asia, they brought bitter nationalist warfare; in West Germany, they produced Maoist hippies keen on both the Little Red Book and free love; in Africa, China's vast aid budgets were happily received by pragmatic state-builders with little interest in implementing Maoist politics. Large investments – in Vietnam, Cambodia and Zambia, for example – bought little or no political traction. In Peru and Nepal, by contrast, the mere dispersal of propaganda and inviting of a handful of hard-line left-wingers on tours of China, won Mao devotees willing to sacrifice tens of thousands of their countrymen to implement a Maoist revolution. The consequences of Maoist foreign policy interventions still haunt global politics today: in India, Nepal and Cambodia (where Hun Sen, a former

Khmer Rouge commander with an appalling record of political violence, is currently one of the world's longest-serving prime ministers). Last but not least, Maoist history and ideology – the memory of Chinese sacrifice in the Korean War and the two states' shared ideological origins – have preserved the PRC's support for North Korea; without that assistance, we would not be confronted by the current threat of potential nuclear destabilisation and by harrowing human rights abuses in North Korea.

And what of the future? What does China's Maoist past and current partial Maoist revival tell us about the PRC and its likely behaviour as a global actor in years to come? I will re-emphasise: despite certain marked continuities between Mao's and Xi's China, contemporary China is not replaying *in toto* the Mao era. Even if this were possible in an economically transformed PRC, there is much about the Mao era that Xi would like to bury – above all the chaotic mass mobilisation of the Cultural Revolution in which his family suffered badly. Nonetheless, as a dedicated man of the party who has devoted much of his first five years in power to disciplining and strengthening the CCP, Xi is steeped in the Maoist heritage: in its symbolism and iconography; in its secretive, opaque party structure dependent on control of the military; in its aversion to political heterogeneity; and in its ambition to establish China as a global leader. Today's PRC is a party state determined to exceed in 2024 the life span of the Soviet Union, to become the longest-lived Communist regime in world history, and to go down in history as having achieved the 'rejuvenation of the Chinese nation' by the time of its centenary in 2049. In the attempt to realise these objectives, the memory of Mao – as the founder of a Communist and reunified China in 1949 – will always loom large. Mao was a skilled storyteller, who wove together a narrative of modern Chinese history and China's place in the world to create an emotional political appeal. In a similar vein, Xi Jinping has used the Great Helmsman's techniques to create both myth and mystique of leadership, and to burnish the CCP's image four decades after Mao disappeared physically from the scene.

Xi Jinping has pushed harder on foreign policy than any of his predecessors since Mao. He travels a great deal, to massive domestic media fanfare. He and his close advisers are the first leaders since Mao to talk confidently of the international relevance of the Chinese/CCP model.[4] And they are doing more than talking. China's surging economic, political and military power means that the projects of Xi and the CCP – inflected as they are by their Maoist heritage – will have a growing impact on global politics and global institutions. China under Xi is a place increasingly intolerant of diversity. At present, this intolerance is directed at individuals and groups with an alternative vision for organising China, from civil rights lawyers to the Uighur inhabitants of Xinjiang. But the Chinese party state is also moving to undermine certain international norms, including those of holding states to account for human rights abuses.[5]

In the context of a global great-power vacuum created by the inward turn of the United States under Donald Trump, China under Xi has an unprecedented opportunity and ambition to shape the contemporary world. Early evidence suggests that the CCP is deploying strategies developed under Mao – the so-called United Front – to increase its influence abroad, especially in Australia and New Zealand. Beginning in the 1930s, the United Front Department successfully courted international favour for the CCP through individuals or organisations disguised as politically neutral. Hu Yuzhi – the transmitter of *Red Star Over China* across the sinophone world – was one of the department's most effective operatives. Australian and New Zealand analysts are disquieted by evidence of CCP surveillance and control of student organisations, and by the links and funding between the CCP and candidates for political office. Xi's Belt and Road Initiative (BARI), meanwhile, plans to invest $900 billion over the next decade on infrastructure across Asia, Africa, the Mediterranean – with rail links running as far as Belgium. We can hear echoes of Mao's own approach to international engagement in Xi's rhetoric. Mao merged appeals to international solidarity with an unfaltering sense of his and China's right to world leadership, and refused to acknowledge any conflict between the two. Xi's regular invocations of 'win–win' for both China and countries hosting BARI projects similarly reject anxieties that this mega-venture might also serve as a vehicle for asserting China's national interests – for exerting an economic or political imperialism in the territories concerned.

To inject a note of realism, however, China's soft-power influence lags far behind its hard power. Under Mao, the CCP's attempts to export Chinese ideas about revolution and governance across the world produced patchy results: failures were multiple, successes unpredictable. This experience helps illuminate the challenges that the contemporary project of establishing a global 'CCP model' may face. The PRC today remains anxious to gain broader international understanding and acknowledgement of China's political, economic and cultural achievements. But to what extent can a power such as China, with both a strong sense of identity and a strong impulse to control this identity domestically and internationally, export its ideas to global audiences? Despite massive promotion, six months after the second volume of political writings by Xi Jinping was published in November 2017, fewer than one hundred copies had been sold in the UK.

How will the PRC weather the contrast between the CCP's Maoist heritage and the hybrid, globalised nature of contemporary China? How will it reconcile its expansive, internationalist rhetoric and intolerant nationalism? Perhaps China's current ability to tolerate paradoxes is the most notable legacy of Mao – that dedicated admirer of contradictions. For two decades, the CCP has skilfully adapted technologies once seen as inimical to authoritarian Communist regimes – the Internet, video games – to bolster its own legitimacy. And although Mao's own ideas and rule became increasingly dogmatised in the last decade of his life, his revolution – born out of war – bequeathed to China an adaptive, 'guerrilla-style' mode of policymaking. Maybe that is why China, for the time being, can be ruled by a party that continues to emphasise its Marxist-Leninist-Maoist heritage, while proclaiming the necessity of market forces; that proclaims its possession of a 'comprehensive plan' at a time when China is more complicatedly diverse than at any point in its history. Maybe this explains also why it has a leader who has revived Maoist strategies fifty years after his family were torn apart by Mao's policies.

Perhaps we should get used to the contradictions of Maoism. It looks like they will be with us for some time yet.

CHRONOLOGY

Date	Mao and Maoism in China/ History of the PRC	Global Maoism
1893	Birth of Mao Zedong in Hunan, south China.	
1918–20	Mao experiences the New Culture Movement in Beijing and begins to write radical essays. In Shanghai, he meets and is influenced by the first leader of the Chinese Communist Party (CCP), Chen Duxiu.	
1921	Mao is one of thirteen delegates attending the founding Congress of the CCP.	
1923–27	Mao takes an active part in the 'United Front' brokered by the Comintern between the Nationalist Party (Guomindang, GMD) and the CCP, in the propaganda bureau and organising peasant associations. He writes 'Investigation of the Peasant Movement in Hunan' in March 1927.	
1928		Edgar Snow arrives in China.

Date	Mao and Maoism in China/ History of the PRC	Global Maoism
1928–34	Following Chiang Kai-shek's purge of Communists, Mao takes refuge with a small force in Jiangxi, and with the military commander Zhu De establishes a Soviet government. He takes up with a new consort, He Zizhen, shortly before his wife, Yang Kaihui, is shot in 1930 by a GMD commander in Changsha, for refusing to denounce Mao. Chiang Kai-shek attempts to annihilate Communist forces in Jiangxi. Mao develops guerrilla tactics to resist the GMD's superior military force. Following an internal mutiny, Mao and his supporters launch a purge of the 'Anti-Bolshevik League'.	
1932		Snow meets Song Qingling.
1933		Snow marries Helen Foster (aka Nym Wales) and moves from Shanghai to Beijing.
1934	Mao joins the Long March, breaking out of Nationalist encirclement of Jiangxi. In Zunyi, Guizhou, Mao successfully bids for military leadership of the CCP.	

Date	Mao and Maoism in China/ History of the PRC	Global Maoism
1935	The survivors of the Long March reach Shaanxi, in north-west China. Mao contends with other rivals for political leadership of the CCP.	
1936		Snow visits the Communist state in north-west China.
1937	Chiang Kai-shek agrees to a second 'United Front' with the CCP, against Japan. Chiang declares war on Japan. North, east and central China quickly fall to the Japanese Army.	Snow completes *Red Star Over China*. A Chinese translation quickly follows. The book becomes a global bestseller. One of Snow's interpreters while researching the book, Huang Hua, becomes a prominent translator for foreign visitors to Yan'an.
1938		The teenage Chin Peng, future leader of the Malayan Communist Party (MCP), becomes an avid reader of Mao, after encountering a Chinese edition of *Red Star*. Ho Chi Minh visits Yan'an.
1938–41	Mao successfully defeats rivals to win political control of the CCP. Inspired by the portrait in Edgar Snow's *Red Star Over China*, young urbanites travel to Yan'an to join the Communist state. CCP membership increases from 40,000 in 1937 to around 800,000 in 1940.	

Date	Mao and Maoism in China/ History of the PRC	Global Maoism
1940		Hu Yuzhi, editor and co-translator of *Red Star* into Chinese, travels to Singapore, where as an undercover member of the CCP he advertises the virtues of the Communist cause to rich and influential Chinese Malayans.
1942–43	Mao launches the Rectification Campaign.	
1943		As a war correspondent in the Soviet Union, Snow learns from three young female partisans that their group has studied how to fight the Nazis through reading *Red Star*.
1945	Japan surrenders. Peace negotiations between the CCP and GMD collapse. Civil war resumes.	
1948		The British government declares an "emergency" in Malaya, the term given to the strikes and assassinations organised by the MCP under Chin Peng. The MCP wages its guerrilla war against the British colonial state from Malaya's jungles. MCP leader Ah Cheng travels to China. A faction of the Communist Party of India (CPI) leads an uprising inspired by Maoist strategies in Telengana, which is suppressed bloodily by the new Indian state.

Date	Mao and Maoism in China/ History of the PRC	Global Maoism
1949	Communist victory in the civil war. The Nationalist government flees to Taiwan. Mao Zedong proclaims the People's Republic of China and agrees to an alliance with the USSR.	After the Communist takeover of China, a debate about 'Who Lost China?' begins in the US. Following Joseph McCarthy's accusations of Communist sympathies, wartime China specialists are denounced and marginalised. Mao and his lieutenants open the Marxism-Leninism Academy in Beijing, offering political and military training to international Communists (the majority from Asia). Pol Pot travels to Paris (to study radio electricity), where he encounters the works of Mao.
1950	Mao decides to intervene in the Korean War. Two flagship campaigns of the early PRC, Thought Reform and Land Reform, are launched.	50,000 Korean officers and soldiers who have fought in the Chinese Communist revolution return to North Korea. Some 7,000 GIs are captured by Chinese–North Korean forces in the Korean War. The CCP sets up the International Liaison Department, responsible for relations with foreign Communist parties and left-wing insurgencies. Liu Shaoqi dispatches army advisers to North Vietnam to assist Communist forces under Ho Chi Minh.

Date	Mao and Maoism in China/ History of the PRC	Global Maoism
1951		Edward Hunter publishes *Brainwashing in Red China: The Calculated Destruction of Men's Minds*. Internal MCP propaganda documents begin to emphasise the importance of Maoist strategy. Under the leadership of Ho Chi Minh, North Vietnam begins a PRC-style land reform.
1953	Armistice brings about cessation of hostilities on the Korean peninsula.	Thousands of US POWs are released from imprisonment in Korea. Twenty-one choose to go to China, instead of being repatriated. Project MK-Ultra, the CIA's mind control programme, is authorised. Walter Sisulu, secretary general of the ANC, visits China on Nelson Mandela's instructions to ask for material assistance for revolution in South Africa.
1954		The French Army suffers a military defeat against the North Vietnamese Communist Army at Dien Bien Phu. The PRC delegation at the Geneva Conference, led by Zhou Enlai, negotiates successfully for a divided Vietnam. An independent, neutral Cambodia emerges from the conference, ruled by King, later Prince, Norodom Sihanouk. At a press conference, President Eisenhower expounds upon the 'domino theory' in South East Asia.

Date	Mao and Maoism in China/ History of the PRC	Global Maoism
1955		Zhou Enlai popularly advocates the 'Five Principles of Peaceful Coexistence' at the Bandung Conference. Sihanouk abdicates from the Cambodian throne, and successfully runs for election as prime minister.
1956	Brief period of political openness in the PRC during the Hundred Flowers campaign. Khrushchev's Secret Speech and advocacy of 'peaceful coexistence' with the West open a rift between the Soviet and Chinese Communist parties. Mao terms de-Stalinisation 'revisionism'.	The CCP encourages the MCP to negotiate with the British colonial government, at Baling. Land reform in North Vietnam comes to an end; Ho Chi Minh's government apologises for errors and excesses committed.
1957	The Anti-Rightist Campaign cracks down on criticism of the government.	
1957–58	The Great Leap Forward, a utopian plan for China to catch up with the industrial West within a few years and achieve Communism. Mao orders bombardment of Taiwan.	
1958		Kim Il-sung launches the Ch'ollima movement, closely following China's Great Leap Forward.
1959		North Vietnamese students in China complain in letters home about the privations caused by the Great Leap Forward.

Date	Mao and Maoism in China/ History of the PRC	Global Maoism
1959–61	Famine, resulting in large part from the policies of the Great Leap Forward, causes the death of at least 30 million Chinese.	
1960		Mao commissions a committee to write 'Long Live Leninism', a manifesto asserting China's leadership of the world revolution. The Zanzibari revolutionary Ali Sultan Issa visits China on a political tour.
1961		Chin Peng travels to China, where Deng Xiaoping instructs him to resume armed struggle. In the worst year of the famine, PRC foreign aid is 50 per cent higher than the annual average of the previous decade. A team of Cameroonian guerrillas is trained in China.
1962	At the '7,000 Cadres Conference', Liu Shaoqi criticises the Great Leap Forward and backtracks from collectivisation.	Pol Pot is elected party secretary of the Cambodian Communists (at the time, the Kampuchean Workers' Party). Max Stanford co-founds the Revolutionary Action Movement in the USA. During the Sino-Indian border war, members of the CPI are imprisoned; while in jail, they diligently study and discuss Mao's works.

Date	Mao and Maoism in China/ History of the PRC	Global Maoism
1963		D. N. Aidit – leader of the Indonesian Communist Party (PKI) – visits China and authors political tracts heavily influenced by Mao's voluntaristic rhetoric of global revolution. Robert F. and Mabel Williams visit China. Mao declares the American black liberation movement part of the global struggle against imperialism.
1964	Mao launches the Third Front, to shift factories from east China to the far west.	The Zanzibar revolution takes place, partly driven by students returning from courses in China. On a tour around Africa, Zhou declares 'an exceedingly favourable situation for revolution'. Zimbabwean insurgents visit China for military training. The US government escalates involvement in the war between North and South Vietnam by putting American troops on the ground. Max Stanford starts reading Mao's military essays.

Date	Mao and Maoism in China/ History of the PRC	Global Maoism
1965	Mao's minister of defence, Lin Biao, publishes 'Long Live the Victory of People's War!', declaring the global strategic relevance of Mao Zedong Thought to revolutions and insurgencies.	An attack on the Indonesian Army leadership apparently coordinated by Aidit, a faction in the PKI and sympathetic army officers fails. The army establishment, under the control of General Suharto, takes control of the country and orchestrates a nationwide massacre of suspected leftists. Julius Nyerere, first president of independent Tanzania, visits China; the PRC offers to fund the construction of the Tan-Zam Railway linking Tanzania with Zambia. Pol Pot travels to China, where he is warmly received and witnesses the build-up to the Cultural Revolution. As a member of the newly formed pro-Chinese faction of the Peruvian Communist Party, Abimael Guzmán visits China. In Bengal, Charu Mazumdar writes the 'Eight Historic Documents', a revolutionary manifesto heavily influenced by Mao.

Date	Mao and Maoism in China/ History of the PRC	Global Maoism
1966	The Cultural Revolution begins. Mao receives millions of Red Guards at Tiananmen Square. Destruction of the 'four olds' commences. Schools and universities are closed. Liu Shaoqi and Deng Xiaoping are purged from the leadership.	Clarence Adams, one of the twenty-one GIs who 'chose China' at the end of the Korean War, decides to return to the US. Nyerere undertakes his own 'Long March' around Tanzania. Seven China-trained fighters of ZANLA – the Zimbabwean African National Liberation Army, the armed wing of ZANU, the Zimbabwe African National Union – carry out the guerrilla raid that is later identified as the start of the Chimurenga war of liberation against Ian Smith's white Southern Rhodesian government. Robert F. Williams moves to China.

Date	Mao and Maoism in China/ History of the PRC	Global Maoism
1967	Red Guards begin to seize power in organisations across China. The 'Shanghai People's Commune' is declared in February. Struggles between Red Guard factions, Party organisations and the army increase in violence. Liu Shaoqi, 'China's Khrushchev', is placed under house arrest. Civil war looms.	The USSR establishes InterKit, a pan-Soviet-bloc organisation to counter Chinese influence in the world. Nyerere launches *ujamaa*, a programme of collectivisation, nationalisation and villagisation modelled on Mao's policies. Pol Pot declares a nationwide Communist insurgency in Cambodia. In Paris, *Lui* magazine features a soft-porn supplement entitled 'The Little Pink Book' and quoting Mao. Abimael Guzmán visits China a second time, to witness the purges of the Cultural Revolution. Police shootings of civilian protesters at Naxalbari spark the Naxalite Rebellion. Kanu Sanyal and three other Indian comrades visit China, where they meet Mao and attend a training course. Nepal's government launches a 'Back to the Villages' campaign, influenced by Mao's ideas on rusticating youth. The CCP sends Burmese Communist Party leaders who have studied and worked in China for many years back to Burma, to fight an insurgency against the Burmese state.
1968	The People's Liberation Army cracks down on radical rebellion. The Red Guards are demobilised and begin to be sent to the countryside for 're-education'.	Student protests take place around the world. Many in Europe and the US borrow from the rhetoric and practice of the Cultural Revolution. Rudi Dutschke is shot by a neo-Nazi.

Date	Mao and Maoism in China/ History of the PRC	Global Maoism
1969	The 9th Party Congress confirms a new Cultural Revolution leadership, with Lin Biao as Mao's successor. Liu Shaoqi is denounced as a traitor and dies in prison.	With Mao's personal approval, the CCP builds a broadcast complex for the MCP in Hunan, south China: 'Voice of the Revolution'. Hundreds of Chinese soldiers die in a border clash with the Soviet Army on Damansky/Zhenbao Island. Nixon orders the bombing of Cambodia, as punishment for the country tolerating Vietnamese Communist camps. Charu Mazumdar and Kanu Sanyal found the Communist Party of India (Marxist-Leninist). Urban terrorism, carried out by supporters of the Naxalite Rebellion, grows in Kolkata.
1970		Mao informs Edgar Snow that he would welcome a visit to China by Richard Nixon. Sihanouk is deposed by Lon Nol and is offered refuge by Mao and Zhou Enlai in China. The CCP brokers an alliance between Sihanouk and the Cambodian Communists under Pol Pot. In West Germany, Andreas Baader, Ulrike Meinhof and others found a guerrilla group, the Revolutionary Army Faction (RAF). In Italy, Mara Cagol, Renato Curcio and Alberto Franceschini found the Red Brigades. In Peru, Abimael Guzmán founds the Communist Party of Peru – Shining Path. All borrow from Mao's language and strategies.

Date	Mao and Maoism in China/ History of the PRC	Global Maoism
1971	Lin Biao apparently plans a coup against Mao. When the plot fails, Lin dies in an airplane crash, trying to flee China.	Sergio Leone opens the film *A Fistful of Dynamite* with a quotation from Mao: 'A revolution is not a dinner party.' With Chinese support, Pakistan sends troops to Bangladesh to suppress rebellion. Young Nepali radicals try to replicate the Naxalite Rebellion at Jhapa.
1972	Mao hosts visit by President Richard Nixon to China, formalising Sino-US rapprochement.	Edgar Snow dies of pancreatic cancer in Geneva, attended by a team of PRC doctors. Ma Faxian arrives in Zambia to train the national army for 'the world revolution'. Shirley MacLaine undertakes a six-week guided tour around China. Charu Mazumdar is arrested and dies shortly after in captivity.
1973	Zhou Enlai reveals Lin's attempt to assassinate Mao at the CCP 10th Congress.	China under Mao establishes diplomatic relations with Mobutu's Zaire; Mao admits to Mobutu in conversation that he has been funding guerrilla insurgents in Zaire for years. US and North Vietnam sign Paris Peace Accords. Final US troops withdraw from Vietnam. Through CCP orchestration, Sihanouk makes a highly publicised visit to the Khmer Rouge guerrilla base area in north Cambodia.

Date	Mao and Maoism in China/ History of the PRC	Global Maoism
1974	Zhou Enlai is diagnosed with bladder cancer. Deng Xiaoping returns to central power.	Border clashes between Communist Vietnam and China begin. Aravindan Balakrishnan founds the Workers' Institute of Marxism–Leninism–Mao Zedong Thought.
1975	Zhou Enlai estimates that China is spending 'more than' 5 per cent of its national budget on foreign aid.	Death of Chiang Kai-shek in Taiwan. Phnom Penh falls to the Khmer Rouge, who abruptly abolish money and evacuate urban populations to the countryside. Saigon and South Vietnam fall to Vietnamese Communist armies. The Communist Pathet Lao, with military assistance from North Vietnam, take over Laos. Receiving Pol Pot and Ieng Sary in Beijing, Mao enthuses about the Khmer Rouge revolution. The CCP makes available $1 billion in aid to the new Democratic Republic of Kampuchea, while refusing further aid to the Vietnamese Communists. Sihanouk returns to Cambodia and is almost immediately placed under house arrest. Pol Pot presents to a visiting Vietnamese delegation a baby crocodile.
1976	Zhou Enlai dies in January. Mao's death in September brings Cultural Revolution policies to a formal end. The 'Gang of Four', Mao's key allies in launching the Cultural Revolution, are arrested by Mao's designated successor, Hua Guofeng.	Zhang Chunqiao, one of the architects of the Cultural Revolution, helps co-author the constitution of Khmer Rouge Cambodia.

Date	Mao and Maoism in China/ History of the PRC	Global Maoism
1977		While on a visit to China, Pol Pot announces publicly for the first time that the new government of Cambodia is the Communist Party of Kampuchea, and that he is its leader. In the 'German Autumn', the RAF in West Germany carry out a kidnapping and a spate of murders; a Palestinian group hijacks a plane at Mogadishu airport, demanding the release of RAF prisoners. When the hijacking is foiled, RAF leaders commit suicide in prison.
1978	Ousting Hua Guofeng, Deng Xiaoping takes power. Deng calls for the rapid development of the economy.	Deng Xiaoping meets Lee Kuan Yew in Singapore and agrees to stop supporting the MCP.
1979	The CCP Propaganda Department bans the sale of the Little Red Book and orders all extant copies to be pulped within seven months. Building on unofficial changes from the early 1970s, the communes are dismantled.	A Vietnamese invasion of Cambodia expels the Khmer Rouge leadership to guerrilla bases in Thailand and tries the Khmer Rouge *in absentia*. A Vietnamese White Paper denounces Chinese treachery against Vietnam. China under Deng Xiaoping 'teaches Vietnam a lesson' in a border war. Sihanouk returns to exile in China.

Date	Mao and Maoism in China/ History of the PRC	Global Maoism
1980	The Gang of Four are put on trial in Beijing. All are found guilty.	ZANU under Robert Mugabe take power in Zimbabwe. The Communist Party of Peru – Shining Path declares war on the Peruvian state and Deng Xiaoping. India's People's War Group begins to build a base area in Chhattisgarh. The CCP brokers a peace agreement between Burmese Communist insurgents and the Burmese state.
1981	The CCP publishes its official evaluation of the Cultural Revolution and of Mao, the 'Resolution on Certain Questions in the History of Our Party Since the Founding of the People's Republic of China'. Deng upholds the 'Four Cardinal Principles', including Mao Zedong Thought.	
1983	The Anti-Spiritual Pollution Campaign targets corrupting influences from the West.	
1984		The Revolutionary Internationalist Movement is founded in France, to 'save' and continue global Maoism.
1986		The Shining Path leadership coordinates an uprising of prisoners inside Lima jails. Massive bloodshed results.

Date	Mao and Maoism in China/ History of the PRC	Global Maoism
1989	Pro-democracy demonstrations are violently suppressed by the People's Liberation Army. Jiang Zemin takes over presidency of the People's Republic of China but Deng Xiaoping continues to hold supreme power.	The MCP and BCP sign peace accords with Malaysian and Burmese governments respectively.
1991		After a thirty-year suspension, democracy resumes in Nepal. A radical, Maoist faction of the Nepali Communist Party resolves to launch a 'People's War'.
1992	Deng Xiaoping calls for faster market reforms in the Chinese economy.	Shining Path violence in Lima escalates. In September, Guzmán is arrested in a police raid. The leadership and the movement quickly collapse.
1994	China's first Internet network is set up. Villagers in Hunan install Mao as a god in his personal temple.	
1995		The Maoist faction in Nepal renames itself the Communist Party of Nepal (Maoist) (CPNM) and begins training in guerrilla warfare in western Nepal. The state polarises local communities by unleashing police brutality against suspected Maoists and civilians accused of supporting them.

Date	Mao and Maoism in China/ History of the PRC	Global Maoism
1996		The CPNM issues forty demands for radical reform to the government. Before the deadline for state response has expired, small groups belonging to the CPNM carry out the first guerrilla raids of their 'People's War'.
1997	Deng Xiaoping dies and Jiang Zemin succeeds to position of supreme power. Hong Kong returns to mainland China.	
1999	Major anti-American protests follow the NATO bombing of the Chinese embassy in Belgrade. The Chinese government bans Falun Gong.	
2001		Nepal's Crown Prince Dipendra shoots nine members of the royal family and himself. The deceased king's brother, Gyanendra, takes the throne and declares a state of emergency due to the Maoist insurgency.
2002	Jiang Zemin begins power handover to his successor, Hu Jintao, and shuts down two far-left print journals. Thousands of laid-off workers in Shenyang protest economic privations and corruption, marching with portraits of Mao.	
2003	Han Deqiang and others found the neo-Maoist Utopia website.	The Indian government liberalises the system granting mining contracts.

Date	Mao and Maoism in China/ History of the PRC	Global Maoism
2005	Utopia mobilises public opinion – through an online petition – in support of a migrant worker from far north-west China who killed his employers after they refused to pay him his wages.	The Indian state helps mobilise a local vigilante army, Salwa Judum, against Maoist influence in Chhattisgarh. Horrendous human rights abuses result. At least thirty-eight die when Maoist commandos blow up a bus carrying a handful of Royal Nepalese Army soldiers. King Gyanendra declares emergency and asserts absolutist power. The CPNM and opposition parties agree to collaborate to combat the king's autocracy; the Maoists make a commitment to democratic rule.
2006		India's prime minister, Manmohan Singh, calls Indian Maoist groups the 'biggest internal security threat to the Indian state'. After weeks of violent protest, King Gyanendra agrees to restore the Nepali parliament. The Nepali government signs the 'Comprehensive Peace Agreement' with the Maoists.
2007	Bo Xilai is appointed chief of the CCP in Chongqing.	The Nepali parliament abolishes the monarchy.

Date	Mao and Maoism in China/ History of the PRC	Global Maoism
2008	Violent protests erupt in Tibet. The Olympic torch relay is disrupted by pro-Tibetan independence demonstrators; urban Chinese respond angrily to perceived Western bias in reports of the Tibetan unrest and the torch relay. Far-left cyber-nationalists add their voices to the protest. Around 12,000 people die in the Sichuan earthquake. Beijing hosts the Olympic Games.	The Nepali Maoists sweep to victory in the elections for the first Constituent Assembly. CPNM leader Prachanda becomes prime minister.
2009	Violent protests break out in Xinjiang. The Chinese government condemns the dissident Liu Xiaobo to thirteen years in prison, for co-authoring the pro-democracy Charter 08.	Prachanda's premiership ends after a clash over control of the army.
2010	Liu Xiaobo is awarded the Nobel Peace Prize. China overtakes Japan to become the world's second largest economy, after the US. China's Gini Coefficient reaches 0.61 (any coefficient above 0.40 denotes extreme income inequality), representing an increase in inequality of more than 100 per cent since the 1980s.	
2011	Bo Xilai's revival of Maoist culture peaks, with 100,000 gathering in a Chongqing stadium to sing 'red songs'. The British businessman Neil Heywood is found dead in a Chongqing hotel room.	Prachanda agrees to the integration of the Nepali People's Liberation Army within the state's National Army. Baburam Bhattarai, senior CPNM ideologue, becomes prime minister.

Date	Mao and Maoism in China/ History of the PRC	Global Maoism
2012	Bo Xilai's police chief, Wang Lijun, tries to defect to the US consulate. He reveals large-scale political malfeasance and money laundering, and alleges that Bo's wife Gu Kailai poisoned Neil Heywood. Bo and Gu are arrested and subsequently condemned to life imprisonment. Xi Jinping is appointed general secretary of the CCP. Utopia is shut down. Han Deqiang slaps an elderly man who disparages Mao at an anti-Japan demonstration.	A faction advocating armed struggle breaks from Prachanda's Maoist party.
2013	Xi Jinping launches a Mao-style 'mass-line' website and swingeing anti-corruption campaign. He visits Mao's mausoleum in Beijing on the 120th anniversary of Mao's birth. Han Deqiang founds an organic farm collective.	Freedom Charity assists three women to escape from abusive, slave-like existences to which Aravindan Balakrishnan has subjected them. Chin Peng dies in Bangkok. The Malaysian government refuses a request to repatriate his ashes.
2014	Xi Jinping intensifies a crackdown on civil society: lawyers, freedom of media expression, academia.	
2015		Nepal's parliament passes a constitution.
2016	China's media pass over largely in silence fiftieth anniversary of Mao's launching of the Cultural Revolution. The girl band 56 Flowers perform pop hymns to Mao and Xi Jinping at a concert in the Great Hall of the People.	Prachanda begins his second stint as prime minister of Nepal.

Date	Mao and Maoism in China/ History of the PRC	Global Maoism
2017	Xi Jinping Thought is written into the constitution of the PRC after the 19th CCP Congress in Beijing.	The mainland Chinese media begins to emphasise the global relevance of the CCP as a political model.
2018	Xi Jinping and his supporters remove the restriction limiting the president to two terms (ten years) in office.	

ACKNOWLEDGEMENTS

Many individuals helped me while writing this book. I would first like to mention two very important people who, to my tremendous sadness, did not live to see it completed. The first is my father, William (Bill) Lovell, who encouraged me unconditionally in everything I attempted, and who passed onto me his passion for languages, histories and literatures. The second is my agent, Toby Eady, who supported me through many ideas, conversations and missteps – without his belief in the concept of the book, it would not have found a publisher. Both my father and Toby lived through a good deal of the history covered in the book; I would have so loved to have their opinion on what I ended up writing.

I have been exceptionally fortunate to have such sympathetic, expert publishers. Stuart Williams, director of The Bodley Head, took the time to discuss the book when it existed only as an unwieldy book proposal. Big thanks are due to Stuart and to my long-suffering editor, Jörg Hensgen, both of whom meticulously guided the book through publication. I'm also very grateful to Jessica Woollard, who with great warmth and professionalism took over as my agent after Toby passed away; and to Jamie Coleman, who offered invaluable ideas and enthusiasm to the book at the proposal stage. Katherine Fry was an acute, constructive copy-editor.

The list of those who advised me on sources and interpretations is a long one. I apologise to anyone I inadvertently leave out. I will begin with those who generously read all or parts of the book before publication. Odd Arne Westad, the doyen of global Cold War history, took time to review the manuscript. The following individuals read individual chapters: Aditya Adhikari, Tom Bell, Jude Blanchett, Tania Branigan, Kerry Brown, Timothy Cheek, John Ciorciari, Robert Cribb, Ilaria Favretto, Sebastian Gehrig, David Gellner, Karl Hack, Alec Holcombe, Marcie Holmes, Stephen Lovell, Rana Mitter, Sergey Radchenko, Geoffrey Robinson, George Roberts, Matthew Rothwell, Hilary Sapire, Alpa Shah, Steve Smith, Orin Starn, Blessing-Miles Tendi, Hans van de Ven, Alex-Thai Vo, Jeffrey Wasserstrom, Robert Winstanley-Chesters, Yafeng Xia and Taomo Zhou. Many thanks to Chan Koonchung, who permitted me to use his term 'Mao-ish', and for amazing hospitality in Beijing.

Parts of the research would not have been possible without the expert help of research assistants: Christine Chan, Stephan Grueber, Lucy Ha, Thelma Lovell (on whom more later), Jean Mittelstaedt, Sherzod Muminov, Quoc-Thanh Nguyen, Aiko Otsuka, Nikolaos Papadogiannis, Onon Perenlei, Nayan Pokhrel, Michael Stack and Victoria Young. Patrick French opened his address book to me and unlocked the possibilities of oral-history research in South Asia. Huge thanks to the Baggaleys for hospitality in Paris, and to Donald and Lucy Peck for giving me essential guidance in India – I needed every bit of it.

In addition to those already mentioned, the following gave invaluable help and advice: Jennifer Altehenger, Sunil Amrith, Andrew Arsan, Susan Bayly, Jasper Becker, Anne-Marie Brady, Benoît Cailmail, Adam Cathcart, Jung Chang, Chen Jian, Chen Yung-fa, Cheng Yinghong, Alexander Cook, Frank Dikötter, Max Elbaum, John Foot, Paul French, Jeremy Friedman, John Garnaut, Karl Gerth, Robert Gildea, Jeremy Goldkorn, Christopher Goscha, Jon Halliday, Tim Harper, Henrietta Harrison, Julio Jeldres, Prashant Jha, Ben Kiernan, Monica Kim, Andreas Kühn, Barak Kushner, Marie Lecomte-Tilouine, Daniel Leese, Rachel Leow, Lorenz Lüthi, Elidor Mehili, Andrew Mertha, James Miles, Pankaj Mishra, Bill Mullen, Lien-Hang Nguyen, Antonio and Victor Ochoa, Natasha Pairaudeau, Daniel Pick, Sunil Purushotham, Jessica Reinisch, Lucy Riall, Sidney Rittenberg, Jon Rognlien, Orville Schell, Michael Schoenhals, Zachary Scarlett, David Scott Palmer, Mark Selden, Philip Short, Thula Simpson, Quinn Slobodian, Christopher Tang, Patricia Thornton, Frank Trentman, Cagdas Ungor, Richard Vinen, Stephen Wertheim, Frances Wood, Judy Wu, Marilyn Young, Zheng Yangwen and Qiang Zhai. I am more grateful than I can say to everyone who agreed to be interviewed by me. I quoted many of these individuals directly in my book; for obvious reasons, I prefer not to mention some of them by name. I benefited hugely from contact with mainland Chinese scholars of the Cold War. Naturally, none of these individuals is responsible for my interpretations, conclusions or errors.

Two organisations made work for the book possible, by generously funding extended periods of leave from teaching, and research expenses. A Philip Leverhulme Prize gave me invaluable time to read and explore, enabling me to think beyond my limited initial framework for the project. A British Academy Mid-Career Fellowship in 2016–17 gave me time and money to make two crucial final research trips and turn my research into a book. I am deeply grateful to these two institutions, which play such an important role in UK research.

I have the privilege of working in a wonderfully supportive institution, Birkbeck College, surrounded by brilliant, generous colleagues, some of whom I have thanked individually above. I would like to give especial thanks to a succession of heads of department who have allowed me leave and supported me in many ways since I began work on the book in 2011: Catharine Edwards, John Arnold, Fred Anscombe and Jan Rüger. I am grateful also to my very understanding and encouraging Executive Deans, Miriam Zukas and Matthew Davies. Thanks are due to the editors of the *China Quarterly*, who have allowed me to use sections of my article 'The Cultural Revolution and Its Legacies in International Perspective', published in its September 2016 issue and also in *Red Shadows: Memories and Legacies of the Chinese Cultural Revolution* (Cambridge University Press, 2016); and to the editors of the *Journal of Asian Studies*, who have allowed me to quote from my article 'From Beijing to Palestine: Zhang Chengzhi's Journeys from Red Guard Radicalism to Global Islam' which appeared in its November 2016 issue.

My wonderful husband has constantly listened to and advised on my anxieties and frustrations, solved countless impasses and valiantly held the fort at home while I travelled for research. My mother has offered exceptionally warm encouragement, and fantastic reading assistance in German and Italian. Throughout the project, she has been a great source of insight on conceptual frameworks. Both read the first draft of the manuscript quickly, and at an inconvenient time; both improved it immeasurably with their wise comments and interventions. My siblings and their spouses unfailingly support with their solicitude. My children magnanimously tolerate their mother's distractedness (even the five-year-old has learned to ask on returning from school, 'How was the book today?'), though sometimes wonder why she surrounds herself with such depressing reading matter. My parents-in-law are always solicitous and along with my mother have gifted me guilt-free work time by brilliantly entertaining my children. It is my family who have made the book a possibility, and a pleasure to write; they make everything seem worthwhile.

NOTES

Abbreviations used in Notes

AMFA   Archive of the Ministry of Foreign Affairs, PRC
BMA   Beijing Municipal Archives
SMA   Shanghai Municipal Archives
UKNA   UK National Archives

Introduction

1. S. Bernard Thomas, *Season of High Adventure: Edgar Snow in China* (Berkeley: University of California Press, 1996), 147.
2. David Halberstam, *The Coldest Winter: America and the Korean War* (London: Pan Macmillan, 2009), 385.
3. Cagdas Ungor, 'Reaching the Distant Comrade: Chinese Communist Propaganda Abroad (1949–1976)', unpublished PhD dissertation, Binghamton University, 2009, 250–1.
4. Abimael Guzmán, 'Interview with Chairman Gonzalo', by Luis Arce Borja and Janet Talavera, *A World to Win* 18 (1992): 79, at http://bannedthought .net/International/RIM/AWTW/1992-18/GonzaloInterview-1988.pdf (accessed on 15 January 2018).
5. David Scott Palmer, 'The Influence of Maoism in Peru', in Alexander C. Cook, ed., *Mao's Little Red Book: A Global History* (Cambridge: Cambridge University Press, 2014), 140.
6. Carlos Iván Degregori, *How Difficult It Is to Be God: Shining Path's Politics of War in Peru, 1980–1999*, ed. Steve J. Stern, trans. Nancy Appelbaum (Madison: University of Wisconsin Press, 2012), 25.
7. Fay Chung, *Re-living the Second Chimurenga: Memories from the Liberation Struggle in Zimbabwe* (Stockholm: Nordic Africa Institute, 2006), 124.
8. 'Murozvi: Rare Breed of Cadre', *Herald* (Zimbabwe), 11 April 2017.
9. Simbi Mubako, 'Heroes Special – General Tongogara: The Legend and Role-model', *Sunday Mail* (Zimbabwe), 10 August 2014. This article contains 'fish' reference from higher in the paragraph.

10. Nandini Sundar, *The Burning Forest: India's War in Bastar* (Delhi: Juggernaut, 2016), 13.

11. Republished as *Broken Republic: Three Essays* (London: Hamish Hamilton, 2011).

12. See James Miles, *China: Rising Power, Anxious State* (London: Penguin, 2012); Michael Sheridan, 'China Struck by Flood of Red Culture', *The Times* (London), 1 May 2011; Koichi Furuya, 'Mao-era Songs Make Comeback in China', *Asahi Shimbun*, 1 July 2011; 'Princelings and the Goon State', *The Economist*, 14 April 2011.

13. Sheridan, 'China Struck by Flood of Red Culture', and 'Red Culture Finds Its Way into Chinese Prisons' at http://chinascope.org/archives/5727/109 (accessed on 19 January 2018).

14. Tania Branigan, 'Red Songs Ring Out in Chinese City's New Cultural Revolution', *Guardian*, 22 April 2011; 'Chinese City of 30m Ordered to Sing "Red Songs"', *Sydney Morning Herald*, 20 April 2011.

15. 'Princelings and the Goon State', *The Economist*, 14 April 2011 (translation slightly adapted).

16. 'A Maoist Utopia Emerges Online', *South China Morning Post*, 26 June 2011.

17. Guobin Yang, 'Mao Quotations in Factional Battles and Their Afterlives: Episodes from Chongqing', in Cook, ed., *Mao's Little Red Book*, 73.

18. Jonathan Spence, *The Search for Modern China* (New York: Norton, 2013), 430.

19. Sebastian Heilmann and Elizabeth Perry, eds, *Mao's Invisible Hand: The Political Foundations of Adaptive Governance in China* (Cambridge, MA: Harvard University Press, 2011).

20. For a very thought-provoking collection of essays in Chinese on the global impact of Mao's ideas, see Cheng Yinghong, *Mao zhuyi geming: Ershi shiji de Zhongguo yu shijie* (Maoist Revolution: China and the World in the 20th Century), manuscript received by courtesy of the author. The global travels of Maoism in general, and of the Cultural Revolution in particular, have become the focus of increasing academic attention in recent years. We currently possess accounts of the impact of Cultural Revolution Maoism on some individual national territories – for example: on France, Richard Wolin, *The Wind from the East: French Intellectuals, the Cultural Revolution and the Legacy of the 1960s* (Princeton, NJ: Princeton University Press, 2010); on Italy, Roberto Niccolai, *Cuando la Cina era Vicina* (Pisa: Associazione centro de documentazione de Pistoia, 1998). (There is, incidentally, no English-language monograph on the influence of Maoism within the majority of West European states, for example, within Italy, West Germany or Norway.) In 2014–15 alone, two volumes of essays on global Maoism were published: Alexander C. Cook, ed., *Mao's Little Red Book: A Global History* (Cambridge: Cambridge University Press, 2014) and *Comparative Literature Studies* 52.1 (2015). Since 2000, China historians and political

scientists such as Zheng Yangwen, Anne-Marie Brady, Alexander Cook, Cagdas Ungor and Matthew Johnson have pioneered a more transnational perspective on China's approach to cultural diplomacy in the Cold War. *The Cold War in Asia: The Battle for Hearts and Minds* (Zheng Yangwen, Liu Hong and Michael Szonyi, eds, Leiden, NL: Brill, 2010) argued for the importance of the Asian theatre in general, and of the impact of Mao-era China in particular, to Cold War culture and diplomacy. But the topic of global Maoism has not yet received the comparative, synthetic treatment that this geographically complex topic requires. The existing literature for the most part deals with national case studies as individual entities: for example, Maoism in France (see Wolin's *The Wind from the East*), India, West Germany, Italy and so on. Occasionally, two case studies are considered alongside each other, for example the USA and France by Belden Fields in *Trotskyism and Maoism: Theory and Practice in France and the United States* (New York: Praeger, 1988). However, atomised national case studies are more often the norm. The two books that aim at more comprehensive coverage of global Maoism, Robert J. Alexander's *International Maoism in the Developing World* (New York: Praeger, 1999) and *Maoism in the Developed World* (New York: Praeger, 2001) are reference books of discrete national case studies, each a few pages long. Although containing useful information, the books' form does not lend itself to careful, transnational analysis.

21. Ren Xiaosi, *The Chinese Dream: What It Means for China and the Rest of the World*, 'Foreword' (no page number) (Beijing: New World Press, 2013).

22. Private communication.

23. Odd Arne Westad, *The Global Cold War: Third World Interventions and the Making of Our Times* (Cambridge: Cambridge University Press, 2005) and *The Cold War: A World History* (London: Allen Lane, 2017); the works of the other historians mentioned are too numerous to list in full, but those available in English include Chen Jian, *Mao's China and the Cold War* (Chapel Hill: University of North Carolina Press, 2001); Lorenz Lüthi, *The Sino-Soviet Split: Cold War in the Communist World* (Princeton, NJ: Princeton University Press, 2010); Sergey Radchenko, *Two Suns in the Heavens: The Sino-Soviet Struggle for Supremacy, 1962–1967* (Washington, DC: Woodrow Wilson Center, 2009); Zhihua Shen and Yafeng Xia, *A Misunderstood Friendship: Mao Zedong, Kim Il-sung and Sino-North Korean Relations, 1949–1976* (New York: Columbia University Press, 2018); Danhui Li and Yafeng Xia, *Mao and the Sino-Soviet Split* (forthcoming). Regrettably few of Yang Kuisong's excellent and prolific works have so far been translated into English; see, for example, 'Mao Zedong and the Indochina Wars', in Priscilla Roberts, ed., *Behind the Bamboo Curtain: China, Vietnam, and the World Beyond Asia* (Stanford, CA: Stanford University Press, 2006), 55–96. See also the bibliography for more of his writing in Chinese.

24. David Scott, *China Stands Up: The PRC and the International World* (London: Routledge, 2007), 53, 54, 56.

25. See, for example, *Peking Review*, 24 June 1966, 11–12.

26. Scott, *China Stands Up*, 58.

27. *Peking Review*, 6 September 1963, 10.

28. See Jeremy Friedman, *Shadow Cold War: The Sino-Soviet Competition for the Third World* (Chapel Hill: University of North Carolina Press, 2015); Gregg Brazinsky, *Winning the Third World: Sino-American Rivalry During the Cold War* (Chapel Hill: University of North Carolina Press, 2017).

29. See discussion in Zhihua Shen and Julia Lovell, 'Undesired Outcomes: China's Approach to Border Disputes During the Early Cold War', *Cold War History* 15.1 (2015): 89–111.

30. See the book-length exposition of this idea in Chen Jian, *Mao's China and the Cold War*.

31. James R. Holmes, 'In Iraq, ISIS Channels Mao', *The Diplomat*, 24 June 2014; Lillian Craig Harris, 'China's Relations with the PLO', *Journal of Palestine Studies* 7.1 (Autumn 1977): 137. See also Manfred Sing, 'From Maoism to Jihadism: Some Fatah Militants' Trajectory from the Mid 1970s to the Mid 1980s', in Rüdiger Lohlker and Tamara Abu-Hamdeh, eds, *Jihadi Thought and Ideology* (Berlin: Logos Verlag, 2014), 55–82.

32. *Profile*, BBC Radio 4, 19 November 2016; Victor Sebestyen, 'Bannon Says He's a Leninist: That Could Explain the White House's New Tactics', *Guardian*, 6 February 2017.

33. Geremie R. Barmé, 'A Monkey King's Journey to the East', *China Heritage*, 1 January 2017, at http://chinaheritage.net/journal/a-monkey-kings-journey-to-the-east/ (accessed on 19 January 2018).

34. David Smith, 'How Trump's Paranoid White House Sees "Deep State" Enemies on All Sides', *Guardian*, 13 August 2017.

35. See, for example, Dan Berger, 'Rescuing Civil Rights from Black Power: Collective Memory and Saving the State in Twenty-First-Century Prosecutions of 1960s-Era Cases', *Journal for the Study of Radicalism* 3.1 (2009): 1–27.

36. Odd Arne Westad, ed., *Brothers in Arms: The Rise and Fall of the Sino-Soviet Alliance, 1945–1963* (Stanford, CA: Stanford University Press, 2000), 2.

37. 'The Brilliance of Mao Tse-tung's Thought Illuminates the Whole World', *Peking Review*, 24 June 1966, 11.

38. Philip Short, *Pol Pot: The History of a Nightmare* (London: John Murray, 2004), 299–300.

1 What Is Maoism?

1. Didi Kirsten Tatlow, 'Golden Mao Statue in China, Nearly Finished, Is Brought Down by Criticism', *New York Times*, 8 January 2016.

2. See, for example, http://www.weibo.com/1618051664/DbADXazPf?type=comment#_rnd1506690880942; http://www.weibo.com/1699540307/Db

AMMsFI5?type=comment#_rnd1506690915924; http://pinglun.sohu.com/s9000706448.html.

3. 'Henan nongcun jinse Mao Zhuxi diaosu yi bei chaichu' (Golden Chairman Mao Statue in the Henan Countryside Demolished), at http://society.people.com.cn/n1/2016/0108/c1008-28030829.html (accessed on 21 January 2018).

4. Jasper Becker, *Hungry Ghosts: China's Secret Famine* (London: John Murray, 1996), 272.

5. See B. Raman, 'India & China: As Seen by Maoists', at http://www.orfonline.org/research/india-china-as-seen-by-maoists-part-ii/ (accessed on 2 January 2017).

6. Lucien Bianco, *La Récidive: Révolution Russe, Révolution Chinoise* (Paris: Gallimard, 2014), provides a book-length treatment of this issue. See S. A. Smith's thoughtful review in *Cahiers du Monde Russe* 55.3–4 (2014) at: http://journals.openedition.org/monderusse/8063 (accessed on 2 January 2017).

7. For those wanting greater detail on Mao's ideas, the analytical literature is vast. Stuart Schram's books and essays are a very good place to start. See also Benjamin Schwartz's writing, for example *Chinese Communism and the Rise of Mao* (Cambridge, MA: Harvard University Press, 1951), and Franz Schurmann's classic account of the Chinese Communist Party under Mao, *Ideology and Organization in Communist China* (Berkeley: University of California Press, 1968). Timothy Cheek, ed., *A Critical Introduction to Mao* (Cambridge: Cambridge University Press, 2010) offers an excellent selection of recent perspectives.

8. See the account in S. A. Smith, *A Road Is Made: Communism in Shanghai, 1920–1927* (Honolulu: University of Hawai'i Press, 2000), 168–89; statistics on weapons are on 173.

9. Christina Gilmartin, *Engendering the Chinese Revolution: Radical Women, Communist Politics, and Mass Movements in the 1920s* (Berkeley: University of California Press, 1995), 199.

10. Mao Zedong, 'Problems of War and Strategy', 6 November 1938, in *Mao's Road to Power: Revolutionary Writings 1912–1949* (Armonk, NY: M. E. Sharpe, 1992–), Volume 6, 552.

11. Mao, 'Letter to Xiao Xudong, Cai Linbin, and the Other Members in France', 1 December 1920, in ibid., Volume 2, 9.

12. Mao, 'Report on the Affairs of the New People's Study Society (No. 2)', summer 1921, in ibid., 66–75.

13. Hans van de Ven, *From Friend to Comrade: The Founding of the Chinese Communist Party, 1920–1927* (Berkeley: University of California Press, 1991), 37.

14. Ibid., 99.

15. Mao, 'Problems of War and Strategy', 553.

16. Anthony Sampson, *Mandela: The Authorised Biography* (London: Harper Collins, 1999), 149.

17. See, for example, comments in Andrew Walder, *China Under Mao: A Revolution Derailed* (Cambridge, MA: Harvard University Press, 2015).

18. Van de Ven, *From Friend to Comrade*, 162.

19. Mao, 'Report on the Peasant Movement in Hunan', February 1927, in *Mao's Road to Power: Revolutionary Writings 1912–1949*, Volume 2, 430.

20. Ibid., 430–1, 434, 436.

21. Ibid., 447, 435.

22. Ibid., 435, 432; translation adjusted with reference to the original.

23. Philip Short, *Mao: A Life* (London: John Murray, 2004), 222.

24. Ibid., 222, 237, 249, 252.

25. Mao Zedong, *Report from Xunwu*, trans. and ed. Roger R. Thompson (Stanford, CA: Stanford University Press, 1990).

26. Mao, 'Oppose Bookism', May 1930, in *Mao's Road to Power: Revolutionary Writings 1912–1949*, Volume 3, 419.

27. Short, *Mao*, 381.

28. Interview by Robert Gildea with Tiennot Grumbach, Paris, 18 May 2008.

29. Mao, 'Problems of Strategy in China's Revolutionary War', December 1936, translation slightly altered from *Mao's Road to Power: Revolutionary Writings 1912–1949*, Volume 5, 466–7.

30. Mao, 'How to Study the History of the Chinese Communist Party', 30 March 1942, in ibid., Volume 8, 68.

31. Mao, 'Interview with Edgar Snow on the United Front', 23 September 1936, and 'Interview with Edgar Snow on Japanese Imperialism', 16 July 1936, in ibid., Volume 5, 372, 272.

32. Jung Chang and Jon Halliday, *Mao: The Unknown Story* (London: Jonathan Cape, 2005), 154.

33. Gilmartin, *Engendering*, 57–9.

34. Chang and Halliday, *Mao: The Unknown Story*, 203.

35. Mao, 'The Question of Miss Zhao's Personality', 18 November 1919, in *Mao's Road to Power: Revolutionary Writings 1912–1949*, Volume 1, 423–4.

36. Mao, 'The Question of Love – Young People and Old People', 25 November 1919, and 'Smash the Matchmaker System', 27 November 1919, in ibid., 439–44.

37. Delia Davin, 'Gendered Mao: Mao, Maoism and Women', in Timothy Cheek, ed., *A Critical Introduction to Mao* (Cambridge: Cambridge University Press, 2010), 210.

38. Dennis O'Neil, interview, 23 March 2015, New York.

39. Zhisui Li, *The Private Life of Chairman Mao: The Memoirs of Mao's Personal Physician*, trans. Tai Hung-chao (London: Arrow Books, 1996), 364.

40. 'An Official Fund-Raising Letter', 13 February 1929, in *Mao's Road to Power: Revolutionary Writings 1912–1949*, Volume 3, 139.

41. Ma Mozhen, *Zhongguo jindu shi ziliao* (Materials from the History of Drug Prohibition in China) (Tianjin: Tianjin renmin chubanshe, 1998), 1611.

42. Chen Yung-fa, 'The Blooming Poppy Under the Red Sun: The Yan'an Way and the Opium Trade', in Tony Saich and Hans van de Ven, eds, *New Perspectives on the Chinese Communist Revolution* (New York: M. E. Sharpe, 1995), 263–98.

43. Dai Qing, *Wang Shiwei and 'Wild Lilies': Rectification and Purges in the Chinese Communist Party, 1942–1944*, ed. David E. Apter and Timothy Cheek (Armonk, NY: M. E. Sharpe, 1994), 110, 111, xxiv; Timothy Cheek, 'The Fading of Wild Lilies: Wang Shiwei and Mao Zedong's Yan'an Talks in the First CPC Rectification Movement', *Australian Journal of Chinese Affairs* 11 (January 1984): 46.

44. Short, *Mao*, 266–80.

45. Chang and Halliday, *Mao*, 100.

46. Merle Goldman, 'The Party and the Intellectuals', in Roderick MacFarquhar and John K. Fairbank, eds, *The Cambridge History of China, Volume 14, The People's Republic, Part 1: The Emergence of Revolutionary China, 1949–1965* (Cambridge: Cambridge University Press, 1987), 223.

47. Dai, *Wang Shiwei*, 20, 8.

48. For an excellent introduction to Ding Ling and her writing, see Tani Barlow and Gary Bjorge, eds, *I Myself Am a Woman: Selected Writings of Ding Ling* (Boston: Beacon Press, 1989).

49. Mao Zedong, 'Talks at the Yan'an Forum on Literature and Art', in Kirk A. Denton, ed., *Modern Chinese Literary Thought: Writings on Literature, 1893–1945* (Stanford, CA: Stanford University Press, 1996), 458–84.

50. Short, *Mao*, 388.

51. Dai, *Wang Shiwei*, 65.

52. For information about Kang Sheng, see David E. Apter and Tony Saich, *Revolutionary Discourse in Mao's Republic* (Cambridge, MA: Harvard University Press, 1994), 290; Dai, *Wang Shiwei*, 13; and Roger Faligot and Remi Kauffer, *The Chinese Secret Service*, trans. Christine Donougher (London: Headline, 1989).

53. Raymond Wylie, *The Emergence of Maoism: Mao Tse-tung, Ch'en Po-ta, and the Search for Chinese Theory, 1935–1945* (Stanford, CA: Stanford University Press, 1980), 163. See also Mark Selden, *China in Revolution: The Yenan Way Revisited* (Armonk, NY: M. E. Sharpe, 1995), and Pauline B. Keating, *Two Revolutions: Village Reconstruction and the Cooperative Movement in Northern Shaanxi, 1934–1945* (Stanford, CA: Stanford University Press, 1997).

54. Apter and Saich, *Revolutionary Discourse*, 164–5.

55. Ibid., 166, 292.

56. Mao, 'Resolution of the Central Committee of the Chinese Communist Party Regarding Methods of Leadership', 1 June 1943, in *Mao's Road to Power: Revolutionary Writings 1912–1949*, Volume 8 (New York: Routledge), 362.

57. For an excellent account of the personality cult after 1949, see Daniel Leese, *Mao Cult: Rhetoric and Ritual in China's Cultural Revolution* (Cambridge: Cambridge University Press, 2011).

58. Mao, *Mao's Road to Power: Revolutionary Writings 1912–1949*, Volume 1, xvii.

59. Wylie, *The Emergence of Maoism*, 41.

60. Ibid., 75.

61. Ibid., 125.

62. Ibid., 155.

63. Ibid., 169.

64. Ministry of Foreign Affairs Archive, Mongolian People's Republic, 5-2-360, 'Note of Examined Parcels Addressed to the Chinese Embassy', 11 March 1967 (obtained and translated by Onon Perenlei).

65. Wylie, *The Emergence of Maoism*, 162.

66. Ibid., 191–2.

67. Ibid., 192.

68. Apter and Saich, *Revolutionary Discourse*, 150.

69. Ibid., 33, and *passim* for the comparisons between the Greek philosophers and Mao – this is a hugely interesting book, built on interviews carried out in the 1980s with Yan'an veterans/survivors. My account of Mao's construction of philosophical authority has relied substantially on it and Wylie's book, cited above.

70. Ibid., 146.

71. Ibid., 86.

72. Mao, 'The Chinese Revolution and the Chinese Communist Party', 15 December 1939, in *Mao's Road to Power: Revolutionary Writings 1912–1949*, Volume 7, 290–1. See also Apter and Saich, *Revolutionary Discourse*, 73, for a development of this idea.

73. Apter and Saich, *Revolutionary Discourse*, 283.

74. Ibid., 307.

75. Chang and Halliday, *Mao*, 256.

76. Wylie, *The Emergence of Maoism*, 215–16.

77. Ibid., 159.

78. Ibid., 206–8.

79. Ibid., 274–6.

80. Odd Arne Westad, *The Global Cold War: Third World Interventions and the Making of Our Times* (Cambridge: Cambridge University Press, 2007), 51.

81. S. A. Smith, 'Issues in Comintern Historiography', in S. A. Smith, ed., *The Oxford Handbook of the History of Communism* (Oxford: Oxford University Press, 2014), 199.

82. Mao Zedong, 'Talk with the American Correspondent Anna Louise Strong', August 1946, at https://www.marxists.org/reference/archive/mao/selected-works/volume-4/mswv4_13.htm (accessed on 27 August 2018).

83. Mao Zedong, 'U.S. Imperialism Is a Paper Tiger', 14 July 1956, at https://www.marxists.org/reference/archive/mao/selected-works/volume-5/mswv5_52.htm; 'All Reactionaries Are Paper Tigers', 18 November 1957, at https://www.marxists.org/reference/archive/mao/selected-works/volume-5/mswv5_70.htm (both accessed on 27 August 2018).

84. Lin Biao, 'Long Live the Victory of People's War!', 1965, at https://www .marxists.org/reference/archive/lin-biao/1965/09/peoples_war/index.htm (accessed on 13 May 2015).

85. For another translation, see Mao Zedong, 'Reply to Comrade Guo Moruo', 17 November 1961, at https://www.marxists.org/reference/archive/mao/ selected-works/poems/poems31.htm (accessed on 27 August 2018).

86. Shaorong Huang, *To Rebel Is Justified: A Rhetorical Study of China's Cultural Revolution Movement, 1966–1969* (Lanham, MD: University Press of America, 1996), 88.

87. Quinn Slobodian, *Foreign Front: Third World Politics in Sixties West Germany* (Durham, NC: Duke University Press, 2012), 176.

88. John Bryan Starr, 'Conceptual Foundations of Mao Tse-Tung's Theory of Continuous Revolution', *Asian Survey* 11.6 (June 1971): 610–28.

89. Li, *The Private Life*, 120.

90. Conversation between Mao Zedong and S. V. Chervonenko, Beijing, 23 February 1963 (private collection).

91. Conversation between Mao Zedong and Aleksei Kosygin, Beijing, 11 February 1965 (private collection).

92. Conversation between Mao Zedong and Nicolae Ceaușescu, Beijing, 3 June 1971, at http://digitalarchive.wilsoncenter.org/document/117763 (accessed on 23 January 2018). Telegram 10353 from the American Embassy in Tokyo, 'Mao-Tanaka Meeting', 28 September 1972, at http://digitalarchive.wilson center.org/document/134380 (accessed on 23 January 2018).

93. *People's Daily*, 5 August 1966; Harry Harding, 'The Chinese State in Crisis', in Roderick MacFarquhar, ed., *The Politics of China: The Eras of Mao and Deng* (Cambridge: Cambridge University Press, 1997), 221. Although there is no clear written source for the 'chaos' quotation (widely attributed to Mao), it is highly plausible given his other utterances at the start of the Cultural Revolution. See, for example, Roderick MacFarquhar and Michael Schoenhals, *Mao's Last Revolution* (Cambridge, MA: Harvard University Press, 2009), 52.

94. Slobodian, *Foreign Front*, 177–8.

95. Sebastian Gehrig, '(Re-)Configuring Mao: Trajectories of a Culturo-political Trend in West Germany', *Transcultural Studies* 2 (2011): 203.

96. Harding, 'The Chinese State in Crisis', 223.

97. Stuart Schram, 'Mao Tsetung's Thought to 1949', in John K. Fairbank, ed., *The Cambridge History of China, Volume 13, Republican China 1912–1949, Part 2* (Cambridge: Cambridge University Press, 1986), 838.

98. Mao Zedong, 'On Contradiction', August 1937, at https://www.marxists .org/reference/archive/mao/selected-works/volume-1/mswv1_17.htm (accessed on 27 August 2018). Mao, of course, was not exceptional or original in his fascination with contradiction and strife. Humans have been preoccupied with these ideas since at least Heraclitus – see discussion in

G. S. Kirk and J. E. Raven, *The Presocratic Philosophers: A Critical History with a Selection of Texts* (Cambridge: Cambridge University Press, 1964), 195–6.

99. Christophe Bourseiller, *Les Maoïstes: La Folle Histoire des Gardes Rouges Français* (Paris: Plon, 1996), 300.

2 *The Red Star*

1. These details from Edgar Snow, *Red Star Over China* (New York: Random House, 1938), 73.

2. Jay Taylor, *The Generalissimo: Chiang Kai-shek and the Struggle for Modern China* (Cambridge, MA: Harvard University Press, 2009), 120.

3. Snow, *Red Star Over China*, 66.

4. S. Bernard Thomas, *Season of High Adventure: Edgar Snow in China* (Berkeley: University of California Press, 1996), 138.

5. Jung Chang and Jon Halliday, *Mao: The Unknown Story* (London: Jonathan Cape, 2005), 199.

6. Snow, *Red Star Over China*, 106.

7. Thomas, *Season of High Adventure*, 170–2.

8. John Maxwell Hamilton, *Edgar Snow: A Biography* (Bloomington: Indiana University Press, 1998), 94.

9. See https://www.nam.ac.uk/explore/malayan-emergency for estimate of deaths. For observation of copies in camps, see Karl Hack and Jian Chen, eds, *Dialogues with Chin Peng: New Light on the Malayan Communist Party* (Singapore: Singapore University Press, 2004), 66.

10. On Huk guerrillas, see Colleen Lye, *America's Asia: Racial Form and American Literature, 1893–1945* (Princeton, NJ: Princeton University Press, 2009), 224. For other references, see discussion below and Zhongguo Shimotelai-Sitelang-Sinuo yanjiuhui (Chinese Smedley-Strong-Snow Society), ed., *Xixingmanji he wo* (*Red Star Over China* and Me) (Beijing: Guoji wenhua chuban gongsi, 1999), *passim*.

11. Thomas, *Season of High Adventure*, 29.

12. Robert M. Farnsworth, *From Vagabond to Journalist: Edgar Snow in Asia, 1928–1941* (Columbia: University of Missouri Press, 1996), 20.

13. Thomas, *Season of High Adventure*, 48–9, 57.

14. Emily Hahn, *The Soong Sisters* (London: Robert Hale Limited, 1942), 47.

15. Chen Guanren, *Song Qingling dazhuan* (Biography of Song Qingling) (Beijing: Tuanjie chubanshe, 2003), 227.

16. Edgar Snow, *Journey to the Beginning* (London: Victor Gollancz, 1960), 82.

17. Farnsworth, *From Vagabond to Journalist*, 131.

18. Snow, *Journey to the Beginning*, 85, 95.

19. Ibid., 84.

20. Taylor, *The Generalissimo*, 122.

21. Farnsworth, *From Vagabond to Journalist*, 154.

22. Helen Foster Snow, *My China Years: A Memoir* (London: Harrap, 1984), 86, 152.

23. Farnsworth, *From Vagabond to Journalist*, 154.

24. Ibid., 201-2.

25. See Ruth Price, *The Lives of Agnes Smedley* (Oxford: Oxford University Press, 2005), 274-6, for more details.

26. Thomas, *Season of High Adventure*, 131.

27. Foster Snow, *My China Years*, 181-2.

28. Ibid, 197-8.

29. See Nicholas R. Clifford, 'White China, Red China: Lighting Out for the Territory with Edgar Snow', *New England Review* 18.2 (Spring 1997): 103-1, for a perceptive reading of the book.

30. Snow, *Red Star Over China*, 7, 3.

31. Thomas, *Season of High Adventure*, 133.

32. Frederic Wakeman, *Policing Shanghai, 1927-1937* (Berkeley: University of California Press, 1996), 154-9.

33. Snow, *Red Star Over China*, 23-4.

34. Ibid., 26.

35. Ibid., 45-8, 263-5, 355, 61.

36. Ibid., 43.

37. Ibid., 258-60.

38. Ibid., 279.

39. Ibid., 291.

40. Ibid., 66-9.

41. Ibid., 72-3.

42. Ibid., 363.

43. Ibid., 71, 73.

44. Ibid., 80, 82.

45. Ibid., 187-8.

46. Ibid., 196, 93. In Helen Snow's own account of her time in Yan'an, she carefully noted Mao smelling roses. See Nym Wales [Helen Foster Snow], *My Yenan Notebooks* (n.p., 1961), 63.

47. Snow, *Red Star Over China*, 60, 252, 106-7.

48. Ibid., 106.

49. David E. Apter and Tony Saich, *Revolutionary Discourse in Mao's Republic* (Cambridge, MA: Harvard University Press, 1994), 90.

50. Wales, *My Yenan Notebooks*, 165, 167, 170, 26, 168.

51. Snow, *Red Star Over China*, 365-7, 373, 390.

52. Anne-Marie Brady, *Making the Foreign Serve China* (Lanham, MD: Rowman & Littlefield, 2003), 47.

53. Ibid., 40-1.

54. Thomas, *Season of High Adventure*, 137.

55. Snow, *Red Star Over China*, 247.

56. Thomas, *Season of High Adventure*, 133; Snow, *Red Star Over China*, 31.

57. Taylor, *The Generalissimo*, 333–64, 359, 375; Chang and Halliday, *Mao: The Unknown Story*, 305, 242.

58. 'Memorandum from President Nixon to his Assistant for National Security Affairs (Kissinger)', 19 July 1971, at https://history.state.gov/historical documents/frus1969-76v17/d147 (accessed on 29 January 2018).

59. Brady, *Making the Foreign Serve China*, 52. See also Julia Lovell, 'The Uses of Foreigners in Mao-Era China: "Techniques of Hospitality" and International Image-Building in the People's Republic, 1949–1976', *Transactions of the Royal Historical Society* 25: 135–58.

60. See Yu You, *Hu Yuzhi* (Beijing: Qunyan chubanshi, 2011), 241, 214.

61. Ibid., 214, 240–1, 275–6; Christopher Bayly and Tim Harper, *Forgotten Wars: The End of Britain's Asian Empire* (London: Penguin Books, 2008), 198–9.

62. Chen Jian, *Mao's China and the Cold War* (Chapel Hill: University of North Carolina Press, 2001), 42.

63. Thomas, *Season of High Adventure*, 152.

64. John K. Fairbank, *China: The People's Middle Kingdom and the USA* (Cambridge, MA: Harvard University Press, 1967), 83; Mark Selden, *The Yenan Way in Revolutionary China* (Cambridge, MA: Harvard University Press, 1971).

65. Alex Hing, interview, 26 March 2015, New York.

66. Zhongguo Shimotelai-Sitelang-Sinuo yanjiuhui, *Xixingmanji he wo*, 147–50.

67. Ibid., 122.

68. Ibid., 35.

69. Nelson Mandela, *Long Walk to Freedom* (London: Little, Brown, 2010), 260–1.

70. Zhongguo Shimotelai-Sitelang-Sinuo yanjiuhui, *Xixingmanji he wo*, 33–5, 95; Robert P. Newman, *Owen Lattimore and the 'Loss' of China* (Berkeley: University of California Press, 1992), 31–2; Jack Belden, *China Shakes the World* (New York: Harper, 1949).

71. Hu Yuzhi, *Wo de huiyi* (My Memoirs) (Jiangsu: Jiangsu renmin chubanshe, 1990), 184–5.

72. Zhongguo Shimotelai-Sitelang-Sinuo yanjiuhui, *Xixingmanji he wo*, 90, 28–9.

73. Ibid., 165.

74. Ibid., 105–6.

75. Ibid., 124.

76. Ibid.

77. Ibid, 181.

78. Ibid., 194, 112–13, 171–2.

79. Ibid., 202–5.

80. This idea is nicely expressed in Lorenz Lüthi, *The Sino-Soviet Split: Cold War in the Communist World* (Princeton, NJ: Princeton University Press, 2008), 25–6.

81. See several accounts in Zhongguo Shimotelai-Sitelang-Sinuo yanjiuhui, *Xixingmanji he wo*.

82. Edgar Snow, *The Other Side of the River: Red China Today* (London: Victor Gollancz, 1963).

83. See comments in Hamilton, *Edgar Snow*, 90; Clifford, 'White China, Red China', 103; Zhongguo Shimotelai-Sitelang-Sinuo yanjiuhui, *Xixingmanji he wo*, 37.

3 The Brainwash

1. See document in Marcie Holmes, 'Edward Hunter and the Origins of "Brainwashing"', at http://www.bbk.ac.uk/hiddenpersuaders/blog/hunter -origins-of-brainwashing/ (accessed on 5 March 2018).

2. See the discussion of this term in David Seed, *Brainwashing: The Fictions of Mind Control – A Study of Novels and Films* (Kent, OH: Kent State University Press, 2004), 33.

3. Edward Hunter, *Brain-washing in Red China: The Calculated Destruction of Men's Minds* (New York: The Vanguard Press, 1951), cover and 302.

4. Edward Hunter, *Brainwashing: The Story of Men Who Defied It* (New York: Farrar, Straus, and Cudahy, 1956), 309.

5. See the excellent, lucid account in Hans van de Ven, *China at War: Triumph and Tragedy in the Emergence of the New China* (London: Profile, 2017), 221–55.

6. Mao Zedong, 'On the People's Democratic Dictatorship', 30 June 1949, at https://www.marxists.org/reference/archive/mao/selected-works/vol ume-4/mswv4_65.htm (accessed on 4 September 2018). See Chen Jian, *Mao's China and the Cold War* (Chapel Hill: University of North Carolina Press, 2001), 38–48.

7. Cited in Odd Arne Westad, *The Cold War: A World History* (London: Allen Lane, 2017), 157–8.

8. See discussion in Bruce Cumings, *The Korean War: A History* (New York: Modern Library, 2011).

9. David Halberstam, *The Coldest Winter* (London: Pan Macmillan, 2009), 306.

10. Cited in Sheila Miyoshi Jager, *Brothers at War: The Unending Conflict in Korea* (London: Profile Books, 2013), 130. This book offers a superb international history of the Korean War.

11. 'Oppose Bacteriological Warfare!', at https://www.youtube.com/watch ?v=Yb3s864MmXI (accessed on 30 January 2018). See also Mary Augusta Brazelton, 'Beyond Brainwashing: Propaganda, Public Health, and Chinese Allegations of Germ Warfare in Manchuria', at http://www.bbk.ac.uk/ hiddenpersuaders/blog/beyond-brainwashing/ (accessed on 30 January 2018).

12. William Brinkley, 'Valley Forge GIs Tell of Their Brainwashing Ordeal', *Life*, 25 May 1953, 107−8.

13. Charles S. Young, *Name, Rank and Serial Number: Exploiting Korean War POWs at Home and Abroad* (Oxford: Oxford University Press, 2014), 2, 143; Susan Carruthers, *Cold War Captives: Imprisonment, Escape and Brainwashing* (Berkeley: University of California Press, 2009), 302−3.

14. Hunter, *Brain-washing* (1951), 162−3.

15. 'A Report to the National Security Council by the Secretary of State on US Policy Towards Southeast Asia' (NSC 51), 1 July 1949, Digital National Security Archive, www.nsarchive.chadwyck.com/nsa/documents/PD/00145 /all.pdf, cited in Andrew Mumford, *Counterinsurgency Wars and the Anglo-American Alliance: The Special Relationship on the Rocks* (Washington, DC: Georgetown University Press, 2017), 64−5.

16. See, for example, 'Relations Between the Malayan Communist Party and the Chinese Communist Party', UKNA FO 371 84479; 'Communism: Federation of Malaya and Singapore', UKNA CO 537 4246.

17. 'The Cold War in the Far East', in 'Official Committee on Communism (Overseas)', UKNA CAB 134/3.

18. 'Singapore: Chinese Communist Party Aims in South East Asia; Joint Intelligence Committee Papers', UKNA FCO 141/14420.

19. Hunter, *Brainwashing* (1956), 3−4.

20. 'Communist Psychological Warfare (Brainwashing): Consultation with Edward Hunter', Committee on Un-American Activities, 13 March 1958, at http://www.crossroad.to/Quotes/globalism/Congress.htm (accessed on 30 January 2018).

21. Nasheed Qamar Faruqi, Marcie Holmes and Daniel Pick, *David Hawkins: A Battle of the Mind* (documentary).

22. See Timothy Melley, *The Covert Sphere: Secrecy, Fiction and the National Security State* (Ithaca, NY: Cornell University Press, 2012), 237; and 'Memorandum: Brainwashing from a Psychological Viewpoint', 25 April 1956, at https://www.cia.gov/library/readingroom/docs/DOC_0000886 487.pdf (accessed on 1 April 2018).

23. See, for example, Alfred McCoy, *A Question of Torture: CIA Interrogation, from the Cold War to the War on Terror* (New York: Henry Holt & Co., 2006); Timothy Melley, 'Brain Warfare: The Covert Sphere, Terrorism, and the Legacy of the Cold War', *Grey Room* 45 (Fall 2011): 18−41; Jane Mayer, *The Dark Side: The Inside Story of How the War on Terror Turned into a War on American Ideals* (New York: Anchor Books, 2009).

24. For these, and many more details, see Rebecca Lemov, *The World as Laboratory: Mice, Mazes and Men* (New York: Hill and Wang, 2005), 219; Dominic Streatfeild, *Brainwash: The Secret History of Mind Control* (London: Hodder & Stoughton, 2006); John Marks, *The Search for the 'Manchurian Candidate': The CIA and Mind Control* (London: Allen Lane, 1979).

25. Lemov, *The World as Laboratory*, 245; Melley, 'Brain Warfare', 28.

26. Marks, *The Search for the 'Manchurian Candidate'*, 73–86.

27. Lemov, *The World as Laboratory*, 215–16.

28. Streatfeild, *Brainwash*, 228, 241.

29. Mayer, *The Dark Side*, 170.

30. Ibid., 150.

31. Michael Welch, 'Doing Special Things to Special People in Special Places: Psychologists in the CIA Torture Program', *The Prison Journal* 97.6 (December 2017): 729–49.

32. Melley, 'Brain Warfare', 21; Melley, *The Covert Sphere*, 5.

33. Both cited in Mumford, *Counterinsurgency Wars*, 71.

34. Cited in ibid., 76.

35. Zhihua Shen and Yafeng Xia, 'Leadership Transfer in the Asian Revolution: Mao Zedong and the Asian Cominform', *Cold War History* 14.2 (2014): 202–3, 208.

36. Ibid., 205–6.

37. Mohit Sen, *A Traveller and the Road: The Journey of an Indian Communist* (New Delhi: Rupa & Co., 2003), 43.

38. Ibid., 83–5, 88.

39. Frederick C. Teiwes, 'The Establishment and Consolidation of the New Regime, 1949–57', in Roderick MacFarquhar, ed., *The Politics of China: The Eras of Mao and Deng* (Cambridge: Cambridge University Press, 1997), 36.

40. Sen, *A Traveller and the Road*, 99, 103.

41. Ibid., 106–7.

42. Chin Peng, *Alias Chin Peng – My Side of History: Recollections of a Revolutionary Leader* (Singapore: Media Masters, 2003), 47.

43. Ibid., 57.

44. Ibid., 48.

45. Ibid., 133.

46. Karl A. Hack and Jian Chen, eds, *Dialogues with Chin Peng: New Light on the Malayan Communist Party* (Singapore: National University of Singapore Press, 2004), 150.

47. Chin, *Alias Chin Peng*, 405.

48. Ibid., 254.

49. Ibid., 270, 278.

50. 'Functions and Activities of the Malayan Communist Party (MCP)', UKNA CO 1022/187; 'Recovered Documents of the Malayan Communist Party', UKNA CO 1022/46.

51. 'Malayan Communist Party', UKNA CO 1030/306.

52. 'Periodic Reports of Malayan Holding Centre: Interception of Post', UKNA CO 1035/7.

53. Chin, *Alias Chin Peng*, 367.

54. Ibid., 426–8.

55. Ah Cheng, *Wo jianfu de shiming: Magong zhongyang zhengzhiju weiyuan A Cheng huiyilu zhi si* (My Mission: Volume Four of the Memoirs of Ah Cheng, Member of the Politburo of the Malayan Communist Party) (Kuala Lumpur: Ershiyi shiji chubanshe, 2007), 21.

56. Ibid., 82–3.

57. Ibid., 105–8.

58. Chin, *Alias Chin Peng*, 429, 457.

59. Combination of private communication and remarks quoted in Yang Kuisong, 'Zhong-Mei hexie guochengzhong de zhongfang bianzou: "sange shijie" lilun tichu Beijing tanxi' (China's Reorientation During the Sino-American Rapprochement: An Exploration of the Background to the 'Three Worlds' Theory), *Lengzhan guojishi yanjiu* 4 (Spring 2007): 23.

60. Yang Meihong, *Yingsu huahong: Wo zai Miangong shiwu nian* (Red Poppies: The Fifteen Years I Spent in the Burmese Communist Party) (Hong Kong: Tiandi tushu, 2009); see also Maung Aung Myoe, *In the Name of Pauk-Phaw: Myanmar's China Policy Since 1948* (Singapore: Institute of Southeast Asian Studies, 2011), 79–83.

61. Zhihua Shen and Yafeng Xia, *A Misunderstood Friendship: Mao Zedong, Kim Il-sung and Sino-North Korean Relations, 1949–1976* (New York: Columbia University Press, 2018) (manuscript), 32–51.

62. Miyoshi Jager, *Brothers at War*, 62.

63. Shen and Xia, *A Misunderstood Friendship*, 55. For more on conversations between North Korea, the PRC and the USSR, see the invaluable collection of translated documents available at https://digitalarchive.wilsoncenter.org/collections/4?mode=list.

64. Zhihua Shen, *Mao, Stalin and the Korean War: Trilateral Communist Relations in the 1950s*, trans. Neil Silver (London: Routledge, 2012), 152.

65. Shen and Xia, *A Misunderstood Friendship*, 69.

66. Ibid., 57, 113–14.

67. Ibid., 127.

68. Ibid., 167–8, 131.

69. Ibid., 124–5.

70. See discussion in Zhihua Shen and Julia Lovell, 'Undesired Outcomes: China's Approach to Border Disputes During the Early Cold War', *Cold War History* 15.1 (2015): 89–111.

71. Shen and Xia, *A Misunderstood Friendship*, 134, 189–90; Charles Armstrong, *The Tyranny of the Weak: North Korea and the World 1950–1992* (Ithaca, NY: Cornell University Press, 2013), 103–34.

72. Shen and Xia, *A Misunderstood Friendship*, 200.

73. Armstrong, *The Tyranny of the Weak*, 55, 110, 122.

74. Dae-Sook Suh, *Kim Il-Sung: The North Korean Leader* (New York: Columbia University Press, 1988), 316.

75. Shen and Xia, *A Misunderstood Friendship*, 348.

76. See Julia Lovell, 'Soviets on Safari', *1843*, 23 February 2016, at https://www.1843magazine.com/culture/the-daily/soviets-on-safari (accessed on 30 January 2018).

77. Suh, *Kim Il-Sung*, 266.

78. Bernd Schaefer, 'North Korean "Adventurism" and China's Long Shadow, 1966–1972', Woodrow Wilson Center Working Paper 44, at https://www.wilsoncenter.org/sites/default/files/Working_Paper_442.pdf (accessed on 30 January 2018), 11, 13.

79. Shen and Xia, *A Misunderstood Friendship*, 156; Armstrong, *The Tyranny of the Weak*, 19.

80. Shen and Xia, *A Misunderstood Friendship*, 207–8.

81. Ibid., 210.

82. Schaefer, 'North Korean "Adventurism"', 9.

83. Robert A. Scalapino and Chong-sik Lee, *Communism in Korea, Volume 1* (Berkeley: University of California Press, 1972), 641. Among Korean specialists, the work of Robert Scalapino is somewhat controversial within the Cold War context, but these two volumes constitute very detailed, sourced scholarship.

84. Schaefer, 'North Korean "Adventurism"', 10.

85. Shen and Xia, *A Misunderstood Friendship*, 290–1.

86. 'Chaoxian shixisheng qingkuang jianbao' (Report on North Korean Vocational Students), 24 November 1966, SMA B103-3-730. See also, for example, 'Jiedai chaoxian shixisheng zongzuzhang Liang Zaiyi he ba wei shixisheng de gongzuo jihua' (Liang Zaiyi, Group Leader for Receiving North Korean Vocational Students, and the Work Plan for Eight Such Students), SMA B103-3-729.

87. See the lucid discussion in Glen Peterson, *Overseas Chinese in the People's Republic of China* (London: Routledge, 2013), 5.

88. Jin Li Lim, 'New China and Its Qiaowu: The Political Economy of Overseas Chinese Policy in the People's Republic of China, 1949–1959', unpublished PhD dissertation, London School of Economics, 2016, 273.

89. Peterson, *Overseas Chinese*, 32–6.

90. See discussion in ibid., 36–43, and Lim, 'New China', 113.

91. Peterson, *Overseas Chinese*, 59–60.

92. Ibid., 119, and Lim, 'New China', *passim*.

93. Lim, 'New China', 185.

94. Ibid., 260.

95. *Jiqing suiyue* (Times of Excitement) (Hong Kong: Jianzheng chubanshe, 2005), xi; *Manman linhai lu* (The Long Road Through Forest and Sea) (Hong Kong: Jianzheng chubanshe, 2003), 47.

96. On Burma, see Hongwei Fan, 'China-Burma Geopolitical Relations in the Cold War', *Journal of Current Southeast Asian Affairs* 31.1 (2012): 7–27. The case of Cambodia will be discussed in Chapter 7.

97. Ah Cheng, *Yilu jianxin xiangqian zou – wo fuze de shiming, xu* (A Tough Road Forward – My Mission, continued) (Johor: Hasanah Sin Bt. Abdullah, 2009), 97, 68, 87.

98. Chin, *Alias Chin Peng*, 467–9.

99. Ah Cheng, *Yilu*, 138–44, 154, 158.

100. Eugene Kinkead, 'A Reporter at Large: A Study of Something New in History', *New Yorker*, 26 October 1957, 102–53.

101. Ethan Young, interview, 24 March 2015, New York.

102. Clarence Adams, *An American Dream: The Life of an African American Soldier and POW Who Spent Twelve Years in Communist China* (Amherst: University of Massachusetts Press, 2007), 56.

103. Aminda Smith, *Thought Reform and China's Dangerous Classes: Reeducation, Resistance and the People* (Lanham, MD: Rowman & Littlefield, 2013), 96.

104. Mao Zedong, 'Analysis of the Classes in Chinese Society', March 1926, at https://www.marxists.org/reference/archive/mao/selected-works/volume-1/mswv1_1.htm (accessed on 4 September 2018).

105. Shuibo Wang, *They Chose China* (documentary).

106. Smith, *Thought Reform*, 146, 92, 158.

107. Young, *Name, Rank and Serial Number*, 80, 84.

108. Wang, *They Chose China*.

109. Mike Dorner, Max Whitby and Phillip Whitehead, *Korea: The Unknown War* (miniseries).

110. Extract of interview courtesy of Aminda Smith.

111. Adams, *An American Dream*, 34–40.

112. Ibid., 47, 51.

113. Ibid., 54.

114. Adam Zweiback, 'The 21 "Turncoat GIs": Non-repatriations and the Political Culture of the Korean War', *The Historian* 60:2 (Winter 1998): 358–9; Lewis Carlson, 'Preface', in Adams, *An American Dream*, xi.

115. Adams, *An American Dream*, 2.

116. Faruqi, Holmes and Pick, *David Hawkins: A Battle of the Mind*, and Chloe Hadjimatheou and Daniel Nasaw, 'The American POW who Chose China', 27 October 2011, at http://www.bbc.co.uk/news/magazine-15453730 (accessed on 31 January 2018).

4 World Revolution

1. See, for example, https://i.pinimg.com/originals/28/34/6c/28346cf211a817 7cfc2ec03334c8e645.jpg.

2. Sergey Radchenko, *Two Suns in the Heavens: The Sino-Soviet Struggle for Supremacy, 1962–1967* (Washington, DC: Woodrow Wilson Center, 2009), 212.

3. Lorenz Lüthi, *The Sino-Soviet Split: Cold War in the Communist World* (Princeton, NJ: Princeton University Press, 2010), 73.

4. For the full version of the speech, see: http://digitalarchive.wilsoncenter .org/document/121559 (accessed on 9 February 2018).

5. Nikita Khrushchev, *Khrushchev Remembers: The Last Testament*, Volume 2, trans. Strobe Talbott (London: Deutsch, 1974), 255; Zhihua Shen and Yafeng Xia, *Mao and the Sino-Soviet Partnership, 1945–1959: A New History* (Lanham, MD: Lexington Books, 2015), 265–6.

6. Shen and Xia, *Mao and the Sino-Soviet Partnership*, 267.

7. Martin McCauley, *The Khrushchev Era 1953–1964* (London: Routledge, 2014), 108.

8. Zhisui Li, *The Private Life of Chairman Mao: The Memoirs of Mao's Personal Physician*, trans. Tai Hung-chao (London: Arrow Books, 1996), 224.

9. Ibid., 220–2.

10. For excellent analyses of the Sino-Soviet relationship, see: Lüthi, *The Sino-Soviet Split*; Li Mingjiang, *Mao's China and the Sino-Soviet Split: Ideological Dilemma* (London: Routledge, 2012); Radchenko, *Two Suns in the Heavens*; Shen and Xia, *Mao and the Sino-Soviet Partnership*; Odd Arne Westad, ed., *Brothers in Arms: The Rise and Fall of the Sino-Soviet Alliance, 1945–1963* (Stanford, CA: Stanford University Press, 2000). On socio-economic inequalities within the day-to-day practice of the alliance, see Austin Jersild, *The Sino-Soviet Alliance: An International History* (Chapel Hill: University of North Carolina Press, 2014).

11. In this, I find Lüthi, *The Sino-Soviet Split*, persuasive.

12. Ibid., 63.

13. Ibid., 82, 85, 87, 89, 83.

14. Li, *The Private Life*, 453–4.

15. Ibid., 94.

16. Chen Jian, *Mao's China and the Cold War* (Chapel Hill: University of North Carolina Press, 2001), 186, 189.

17. Lüthi, *The Sino-Soviet Split*, 100.

18. Chen, *Mao's China*, 185–9.

19. Li, *The Private Life*, 262.

20. Lüthi, *The Sino-Soviet Split*, 88.

21. Hong Liu, *China and the Shaping of Indonesia, 1949–1965* (Singapore: NUS Press, 2011), 186.

22. Jiang Huajie, 'Lengzhan shiqi Zhongguo dui Feizhou guojia de yuanzhu yanjiu (1960–1978) (A Study of Chinese Aid to African Countries During the Cold War [1960–1978]), unpublished PhD dissertation, East China Normal University, 2014, 34.

23. Frank Dikötter, *Mao's Great Famine: The History of China's Most Devastating Catastrophe, 1958–1962* (London: Bloomsbury, 2010), 113.

24. See Elidor Mehili, *From Stalin to Mao: Albania and the Socialist World* (Ithaca, NY: Cornell University Press, 2018).

25. Zhang Fan, 'Jiu Zhongguo shehui wenti zhi Sugong zhongyang de yi feng xin' (A Letter About Socialism to the Central Committee of the Communist Party of the Soviet Union), reprinted in Song Yongyi et al., eds, *Zhongguo wenhua dageming wenku* (Collected Materials on the Chinese Cultural Revolution) (Hong Kong: Chinese University Press, 2013).

26. 'Long Live Leninism!' at https://www.marxists.org/history/international/comintern/sino-soviet-split/cpc/leninism.htm (accessed on 29 August 2018); Lüthi, *The Sino-Soviet Split*, 163, 274.

27. Jeremy Friedman, *Shadow Cold War: The Sino-Soviet Competition for the Third World* (Chapel Hill: University of North Carolina Press, 2015), 96.

28. Lüthi, *The Sino-Soviet Split*, 178.

29. Ang Cheng Guan, *Vietnamese Communists' Relations with China and the Second Indochina Conflict, 1956–1962* (London: McFarland, 1997), 162.

30. Lüthi, *The Sino-Soviet Split*, 269.

31. Ibid., 229–30, 235.

32. Ibid., 149, 162.

33. Ibid., 159.

34. Dikötter, *Mao's Great Famine*, 335–7.

35. Christopher Tang, 'Homeland in the Heart, Eyes on the World: Domestic Internationalism, Popular Mobilization, and the Making of China's Cultural Revolution, 1962–68', unpublished PhD dissertation, Cornell University, 2016, 53–7.

36. Lin Biao, 'Long Live the Victory of People's War!', at https://www.marxists.org/reference/archive/lin-biao/1965/09/peoples_war/index.htm (accessed on 13 May 2015).

37. Lin Biao, 'Foreword to the Second Edition of Quotations of Chairman Mao Tse-tung', at https://www.marxists.org/reference/archive/lin-biao/1966/12/16.htm (accessed on 13 May 2015).

38. 1966 nian Beijing huagong xueyuan *Hongse xuanchuanyuan* zhandouzu, Beijing jingji xueyuan wuchanjieji gemingtuan, Beijing shi dongfanghong yinshuachang geming zaofan lianluochu, huagongbu huaxue gongye chubanshe yinshuachang lianhe huibian *Wuchan jieji wenhua dageming canka-oziliao 2*, 'Ye Jianying zai quanjunyuanxiao wenhua dageming dongyuanhui shang de jianghua' (Ye Jianying's Speech at the All-Army College Mobilisation Meeting for the Cultural Revolution), October 1966, reprinted in Song et al., eds, *Zhongguo wenhua dageming wenku*.

39. Sidney Rittenberg and Amanda Bennett, *The Man Who Stayed Behind* (Durham, NC: Duke University Press, 2001), 277, and interview, 26 February 2013 (Skype).

40. See the excellent discussion in Tang, 'Homeland in the Heart', and Beijing Dizhi Xueyuan *Dongfanghong* bianjibu he *Wuhan gang er si* bianjibu, 'Zhongyang shouzhang zai Wuhan gemingpai zuzhi de zuotanhui shang de tanhua jihao'

(Abstract of a Central Leader's Talk to the Wuhan Revolutionary Group), 25 August 1967, reprinted in Song et al., eds, *Zhongguo wenhua dageming wenku*.

41. See examples in *Jianjue zhansheng meidiguozhuyi: zhichi Yuenan renmin kangmei jiuguo zhengyi douzheng gequ xuanji* (Resolutely Defeat American Imperialism: Selected Songs Supporting the Vietnamese People's Righteous Struggle to Resist America and Save Their Country) (Beijing: Yinyue chubanshe, 1965).

42. Tang, 'Homeland in the Heart', 70.

43. Ibid., 69.

44. Ibid., 71.

45. Ibid., 73.

46. Ibid., 125.

47. Ibid., 96–7.

48. Friedman, *Shadow Cold War*, 198.

49. Tang, 'Homeland in the Heart', 142.

50. Ibid., 171; on the latter phenomenon, see Zachary A. Scarlett, 'China After the Sino-Soviet Split: Maoist Politics, Global Narratives, and the Imagination of the World', unpublished PhD dissertation, Northeastern University, 2013, 115–21.

51. Tang, 'Homeland in the Heart', 192.

52. Ibid., 183, and Alexander C. Cook, 'Chinese Uhuru: Maoism and the Congo Crisis', unpublished paper.

53. Cook, 'Chinese Uhuru', 15, 17.

54. Li Xiangqian, 'The Economic and Political Impact of the Vietnam War on China in 1964', in Priscilla Roberts, ed., *Behind the Bamboo Curtain: China, Vietnam and the World Beyond Asia* (Stanford, CA: Stanford University Press, 2006), 186.

55. Jonathan Spence, *The Search for Modern China* (New York: Norton, 2013), 546.

56. Tang, 'Homeland in the Heart', 254, 267.

57. Ibid., 258.

58. Ibid., 277.

59. Yiyuan dazibao xuanbian xiaozu, 'Liao Chengzhi zai Beijing Daxue zuo guanyu guoji xingshi de baogao' (Liao Chengzhi Reports on the International Situation at Peking University), December 1966, reprinted in Song et al., eds, *Zhongguo wenhua dageming wenku*.

60. Friedman, *Shadow Cold War*, 198–9.

61. Radchenko, *Two Suns in the Heavens*, 178.

62. Li, 'The Economic and Political Impact', 178.

63. Barry Naughton, 'The Third Front: Defence Industrialization in the Chinese Interior', *China Quarterly* 115 (September 1988): 365.

64. Covell Meyskens, 'Third Front Railroads and Industrial Modernity in Late Maoist China', *Twentieth-Century China* 40.3 (October 2015): 240–1, 253.

65. Ibid., 251, 256.

66. Naughton, 'The Third Front', 376.

67. Ibid., 379.

68. Lüthi, *The Sino-Soviet Split*, 341–2.

69. Andrew Osborn and Peter Foster, 'USSR Planned Nuclear Attack on China in 1969', *Daily Telegraph*, 13 May 2010, at http://www.telegraph.co.uk/news/worldnews/asia/china/7720461/USSR-planned-nuclear-attack-on-China-in-1969.html (accessed on 10 February 2018).

70. Lüthi, *The Sino-Soviet Split*, 341.

71. Han Shaogong, *A Dictionary of Maqiao*, trans. Julia Lovell (New York: Columbia University Press, 2003), 301–6.

72. James Hershberg, Sergey Radchenko, Peter Vamos and David Wolff, 'The Interkit Story: A Window into the Final Decades of the Sino-Soviet Relationship', Cold War International History Project Working Paper, February 2011, 11, at https://www.wilsoncenter.org/sites/default/files/Working_Paper_63.pdf (accessed on 8 January 2018).

73. Radchenko, *Two Suns in the Heavens*, 193.

74. Friedman, *Shadow Cold War*, 105.

75. Radchenko, *Two Suns in the Heavens*, 83.

76. Friedman, *Shadow Cold War*, 197.

77. Christophe Bourseiller, *Les Maoïstes: La Folle Histoire des Gardes Rouges Français* (Paris: Plon, 1996), 70–1.

78. Jon Henley, 'Mr Chips Turns Out to Be 007', *Guardian*, 4 December 2004.

79. Friedman, *Shadow Cold War*, 102, 105.

80. Lüthi, *The Sino-Soviet Split*, 232.

81. Friedman, *Shadow Cold War*, 211.

82. Ibid., 112.

83. Ibid., 133.

84. Ibid., 218–19.

85. Ibid., 158.

86. See Hershberg et al., 'The Interkit Story'.

87. Frank Dikötter, *The Cultural Revolution: A People's History, 1962–1976* (London: Bloomsbury, 2016), 100; Friedman, *Shadow Cold War*, 176.

5 Years of Living Dangerously

1. Joshua Oppenheimer, *The Look of Silence* (film).

2. Adrian Vickers, *A History of Modern Indonesia* (Cambridge: Cambridge University Press, 2013), 144.

3. Bob Hering, *Soekarno: Founding Father of Indonesia, 1901–1945* (Leiden, NL: KITLV Press, 2002), 303.

4. Ibid., 314–15.

5. Vickers, *A History of Modern Indonesia*, 95.

6. Ibid., 105.

7. Hering, *Soekarno*, 352.

8. Vickers, *A History of Modern Indonesia*, 111.

9. Ibid., 114.

10. Ibid., 127, 138.

11. Mochtar Lubis, *Twilight in Djakarta*, trans. Claire Holt (London: Hutchinson, 1963).

12. See account in Robert Cribb and Colin Brown, *Modern Indonesia: A History Since 1945* (London: Longman, 1995), 74–81.

13. Hong Liu, *China and the Shaping of Indonesia, 1949–1965* (Singapore: NUS Press, 2011), 131.

14. See further discussion in Audrey Kahin and George Kahin, *Subversion as Foreign Policy: The Secret Eisenhower and Dulles Debacle in Indonesia* (Seattle: University of Washington Press, 1997), and Bradley R. Simpson, *Economists with Guns: Authoritarian Development and U.S.–Indonesian Relations, 1960–1968* (Stanford, CA: Stanford University Press, 2008).

15. Cribb and Brown, *Modern Indonesia*, 55.

16. David Mozingo, *Chinese Policy Toward Indonesia, 1949–1967* (Ithaca, NY: Cornell University Press, 1976), 148.

17. Liu, *China and the Shaping of Indonesia*, 211.

18. Ibid., 217–18.

19. Antonie C. A. Dake, *In the Spirit of the Red Banteng: Indonesian Communists Between Moscow and Peking, 1959–1965* (The Hague: Mouton, 1973), 299.

20. Ibid., 78.

21. Liu, *China and the Shaping of Indonesia*, 221.

22. Ibid., 223.

23. Ibid., 223–4.

24. Vickers, *A History of Modern Indonesia*, 148.

25. Liu, *China and the Shaping of Indonesia*, 229–30.

26. Taomo Zhou, 'China and the Thirtieth of September Movement', *Indonesia* 98 (October 2014): 47.

27. Sukarno, *Sukarno: An Autobiography, as Told to Cindy Adams* (Hong Kong: Gunung Agong, 1965), 5.

28. Liu, *China and the Shaping of Indonesia*, 75.

29. Hong Liu, 'The Historicity of China's Soft Power: The PRC and the Cultural Politics of Indonesia, 1945–1965', in Zheng Yangwen et al., eds, *The Cold War in Asia: The Battle for Hearts and Minds* (Leiden, NL: Brill, 2010), 162.

30. Lubis, *Twilight in Djakarta*, 57.

31. Liu, *China and the Shaping of Indonesia*, 86–7.

32. Abdul Haris Nasution, *Fundamentals of Guerrilla Warfare* (London: Pall Mall Press, 1965), 26–7.

33. Liu, *China and the Shaping of Indonesia*, 86.

34. Ibid., 134.
35. Ruth T. McVey, 'Indonesian Communism and China', in Tang Tsou, ed., *China in Crisis Volume 2: China's Policies in Asia and America's Alternatives* (Chicago: University of Chicago Press, 1968), 367.
36. See biographical accounts in *Tempo Magazine Special Issue: Aidit and the G30S*, October 2007, 15, 24.
37. See Larisa M. Efimova, 'Stalin and the New Program for the Communist Party of Indonesia', *Indonesia* 91 (April 2011): 131–63.
38. Jung Chang and Jon Halliday, *Mao: The Unknown Story* (London: Jonathan Cape, 2005), 389.
39. Donald Hindley, *The Communist Party of Indonesia, 1951–1963* (Berkeley: University of California Press, 1964), 32, 42.
40. See Robert Cribb, 'Indonesian Marxism', in Colin Mackerras and Nick Knight, eds, *Marxism in Asia* (Sydney: Croome Helm, 1985), 251–72.
41. Hindley, *The Communist Party of Indonesia*, 162.
42. John Roosa, 'Indonesian Communism: The Perils of the Parliamentary Path', in Norman Naimark, Silvio Pons and Sophie Quinn-Judge, eds, *The Cambridge History of Communism*, Volume 2 (Cambridge: Cambridge University Press, 2017), 476.
43. Hindley, *The Communist Party of Indonesia*, 90.
44. Ibid., 90–4; for numbers, see Vickers, *A History of Modern Indonesia*, 158, and Rex Mortimer, *Indonesian Communism Under Sukarno: Ideology and Politics, 1959–1965* (Ithaca, NY: Cornell University Press, 1974), 366–7.
45. Hindley, *The Communist Party of Indonesia*, 110.
46. Ibid., 113.
47. Mozingo, *Chinese Policy*, 209.
48. Hindley, *The Communist Party of Indonesia*, 100–1.
49. Vickers, *A History of Modern Indonesia*, 156.
50. Hindley, *The Communist Party of Indonesia*, 259.
51. Ibid., 262.
52. Doak Barnett, 'Echoes of Mao Tse-tung in Djakarta', 21 May 1955, at http://www.icwa.org/wp-content/uploads/2015/08/ADB-79.pdf (accessed on 1 February 2018).
53. Sukarno, *Sukarno: An Autobiography*, 267, 271.
54. J. D. Legge, *Sukarno: A Political Biography* (London: Allen Lane, 1972), 344.
55. Mortimer, *Indonesian Communism*, 179.
56. Ibid., 186.
57. Mozingo, *Chinese Policy*, 203.
58. Mortimer, *Indonesian Communism*, 197–8.
59. 'Zhongdian waibin zaijing canguan' (The Visits of VIP Foreign Guests to Beijing), 1961, BMA 1961 102-001-00190; D. N. Aidit, 'People's Republic of China Achieves Super-Abundance in People's Commune Production',

Harian Rakjat, 1 October 1963, in Joint Publications Research Service, *Translations on South and East Asia*, No. 43.

60. *Tempo Magazine Special Issue: Aidit and the G30S*, 15–18.

61. Sheldon W. Simon, *The Broken Triangle: Peking, Djakarta, and the PKI* (Baltimore: Johns Hopkins Press, 1969), 85, 101–2.

62. 'Intensify the Revolutionary Offensive on All Fronts', *Harian Rakjat*, 15 May 1965, in Joint Publications Research Service, *Translations on South and East Asia*, No. 91.

63. Mortimer, *Indonesian Communism*, 202, and D. N. Aidit, *Dare, Dare and Dare Again!* (Beijing: Foreign Languages Press, 1963).

64. Mortimer, *Indonesian Communism*, 276.

65. D. N. Aidit, *Set Afire the Banteng Spirit: Ever Forward, No Retreat!* (Beijing: Foreign Languages Press, 1964), 1–2, 4, 13, 29, 64, 102.

66. Ibid., 78, 87, 98.

67. Taomo Zhou, 'Diaspora and Diplomacy: China, Indonesia and the Cold War, 1945–1967', unpublished PhD dissertation, Cornell University, 2015, 191.

68. Mozingo, *Chinese Policy*, 217–18.

69. Mortimer, *Indonesian Communism*, 383–4.

70. Mozingo, *Chinese Policy*, 209, 212.

71. Ruth McVey, 'The Post-Revolutionary Transformation of the Indonesian Army: Part II', *Indonesia* 13 (April 1972): 176–7; Geoffrey Robinson, *The Killing Season: A History of the Indonesian Massacres, 1965–66* (Princeton, NJ: Princeton University Press, 2018), 45–7. See also Ulf Sundhaussen, *The Road to Power: Indonesian Military Politics 1945–1967* (Oxford: Oxford University Press, 1982).

72. Zhou, 'China': 33–7; Zhou, 'Diaspora and Diplomacy', 194.

73. Zhou, 'China': 38–9.

74. 'Southeast Asia: A World Center of Contradictions', *Harian Rakjat*, 26 September 1964, in Joint Publications Research Service, *Translations on South and East Asia*, No. 66.

75. Mortimer, *Indonesian Communism*, 381.

76. 'Intensify the Revolutionary Offensive on All Fronts', *Harian Rakjat*, 15 May 1965, in Joint Publications Research Service, *Translations on South and East Asia*, No. 91.

77. Simon, *The Broken Triangle*, 109.

78. 'Internal Political Situation: Attempted Coup Against Sukarno', 1965, UKNA FO 371/180324.

79. Vickers, *A History of Modern Indonesia*, 158.

80. Mary Ida Bagus, 'West Bali: Experiences and Legacies of the 1965–66 Violence', in Douglas Kammen and Katharine McGregor, eds, *The Contours of Mass Violence in Indonesia, 1965–68* (Copenhagen: NIAS Press, 2012), 213.

81. Dake, *In the Spirit of the Red Banteng*, 364.

82. Victor Fic, *Anatomy of the Jakarta Coup, 1 October, 1965: The Collusion with China Which Destroyed the Army Command, President Sukarno and the Communist Party of Indonesia* (New Delhi: Abhinav Publications, 2004), 86–9.

83. Vickers, *A History of Modern Indonesia*, 156.

84. John Roosa, *Pretext for Mass Murder: The September 30th Movement and Suharto's Coup d'État in Indonesia* (Madison: University of Wisconsin Press, 2006), 34–5; also John Hughes, *The End of Sukarno: A Coup that Misfired, a Purge that Ran Wild* (London: Angus & Robertson, 1968), 61.

85. Benedict R. Anderson, 'How Did the Generals Die?', *Indonesia* 43 (April 1987): 109–34.

86. Roosa, *Pretext for Mass Murder*, 51.

87. Ibid., 46.

88. Geoffrey Robinson, '"Down to the Very Roots": The Indonesian Army's Role in the Mass Killings of 1965–6', *Journal of Genocide Research* 19.4 (2017): 475.

89. Excellent histories of these events include: ibid. (and see other articles in this special issue on the killings); Robinson, *The Killing Season*; Robert Cribb, ed., *The Indonesian Killings 1965–1966: Studies from Java and Bali* (Melbourne, Aus.: Monash University, 1990); Kammen and McGregor, eds, *The Contours*; Jess Melvin, *The Army and the Indonesian Genocide: Mechanics of Mass Murder* (London: Routledge, 2018).

90. Cited in Robinson, *The Killing Season*, 10.

91. Oppenheimer, *The Look of Silence*.

92. Taufik Ahmad, 'South Sulawesi: The Military, Prison Camps and Forced Labour', in Kammen and McGregor, eds, *The Contours*, 180, 176.

93. Legge, *Sukarno*, 404.

94. Cited in Roosa, *Pretext for Mass Murder*, 24.

95. Ibid., 10.

96. Ibid., 24.

97. In Oppenheimer, *The Look of Silence*.

98. Roosa, *Pretext for Mass Murder*, 27.

99. Jess Melvin, 'Why Not Genocide? Anti-Chinese Violence in Aceh, 1965–1966', *Journal of Current Southeast Asian Affairs* 32.3 (2013): 71.

100. Roosa, *Pretext for Mass Murder*, 13.

101. Ibid., 195; Robinson, *The Killing Season*, 177–207; and https://nsarchive2 .gwu.edu/NSAEBB/NSAEBB52/.

102. Melvin, 'Why Not Genocide?', 72.

103. Ibid., 74.

104. Simon, *The Broken Triangle*, 154; Hughes, *The End of Sukarno*, 168–9.

105. Zhou, 'China': 49.

106. Benedict R. Anderson and Ruth T. McVey, *A Preliminary Analysis of the October 1, 1965, Coup in Indonesia* (Ithaca, NY: Modern Indonesia Project, 1971).

107. Roosa, *Pretext for Mass Murder*.

108. Fic, *Anatomy of the Jakarta Coup*, 96.

109. Zhou, 'China': 50–1.
110. Dake, *In the Spirit of the Red Banteng*, 407.
111. Roosa, *Pretext for Mass Murder*, 159.
112. Ibid., 144, 250.
113. Ibid., 122, 259.
114. Ibid., 247, 137, 211.
115. Ibid., 251, 229, 95.
116. Ibid., 232–3, 96.
117. Ibid., 229, 217.
118. Zhou, 'China': 55.
119. Dake, *In the Spirit of the Red Banteng*, 438.
120. Simon, *The Broken Triangle*, 141.
121. David Jenkins and Douglas Kammen, 'The Army Para-commando Regiment and the Reign of Terror in Central Java and Bali', 86, 88, and Vannessa Hearman, 'South Blitar and the PKI Bases: Refuge, Resistance and Repression', 199, both in Kammen and McGregor, eds, *The Contours*.
122. Cribb, *The Indonesian Killings*, 257.
123. Jenkins and Kammen, 'The Army Para-commando', 89, 93, and Bagus, 'West Bali', 217.
124. Melvin, 'Why Not Genocide?': 82.
125. Bagus, 'West Bali', 219, and Yen-ling Tsai and Douglas Kammen, 'Anti-communist Violence and the Ethnic Chinese in Medan, North Sumatra', in Kammen and McGregor, eds, *The Contours*, 146.
126. Jenkins and Kammen, 'The Army Para-commando', 95.
127. Ibid., 99, and Bagus, 'West Bali', 227.
128. Douglas Kammen and Katharine McGregor, 'Introduction: The Contours of Mass Violence in Indonesia, 1965–68', in Kammen and McGregor, eds, *The Contours*, 9.
129. Jenkins and Kammen, 'The Army Para-commando', 85.
130. Oppenheimer, *The Look of Silence*.
131. Adam Shatz, 'Joshua Oppenheimer Won't Go Back to Indonesia', *New York Times*, 9 July 2015.

6 Into Africa

1. John Cooley, *East Wind Over Africa: Red China's African Offensive* (New York: Walker & Company, 1965), 193.
2. Ibid., 7.
3. Kathleen Caulderwood, 'China Is Africa's New Colonial Overlord, Says Famed Primate Researcher Jane Goodall', *International Business Times*, at http://www.ibtimes.com/china-africas-new-colonial-overlord-says-famed-primate-researcher-jane-goodall-1556312 (accessed on 2 February 2018).

4. Lydia Polgreen and Howard W. French, 'China's Trade in Africa Carries a Price Tag', *New York Times*, 21 August 2007, at http://www.nytimes .com/2007/08/21/world/africa/21zambia.html (accessed on 2 February 2018).

5. See http://www.fmprc.gov.cn/mfa_eng/xwfw_665399/s2510_665401/t13 86961.shtml (accessed on 29 March 2018).

6. See http://www.fmprc.gov.cn/mfa_eng/xwfw_665399/s2510_665401/t14 67100.shtml (accessed on 29 March 2018).

7. Jiang Huajie places the yuan-dollar exchange rate during the Mao era at 2:1, in 'Lengzhan shiqi Zhongguo dui Feizhou guojia de yuanzhu yanjiu (1960–1978)' (A Study of Chinese Aid to African Countries During the Cold War [1960–1978]), unpublished PhD dissertation, East China Normal University, 2014, 19; http://www.usinflationcalculator.com holds that one dollar in 1975 was worth $4.56 in 2017.

8. For Chinese figures, see Jiang, 'Lengzhan shiqi Zhongguo', 18–20. On US figures, see http://archive.nytimes.com/www.nytimes.com/interac tive/2011/10/04/us/politics/us-foreign-aid-since-1977.html (accessed on 29 April 2018). On the USSR, see, for example, Quintin V. S. Bach, 'A Note on Soviet Statistics on Their Economic Aid', *Soviet Studies* 37.2 (April 1985): 269.

9. Cooley, *East Wind Over Africa*, 5.

10. Ali Mazrui 'Preface', in Robert Buijtenhuijs, *Mau Mau Twenty Years After: The Myth and the Survivors* (The Hague: Mouton, 1973), 7–13. See John Lonsdale's rebuttal in 'Mau Maus of the Mind: Making Mau Mau and Remaking Kenya', *Journal of African History* 31.3 (1990): 393. See also other, more recent works on Mau Mau, including: E. S. Atieno Odhiambo and John Lonsdale, eds, *Mau Mau and Nationhood: Arms, Authority and Narration* (Oxford: James Currey, 2003); S. M. Shamsul Alam, *Rethinking Mau Mau in Colonial Kenya* (New York: Palgrave Macmillan, 2007); David M. Anderson, *Histories of the Hanged: Britain's Dirty War in Kenya and the End of Empire* (London: Weidenfeld & Nicolson, 2005).

11. Elinor Sisulu, *Walter and Albertina Sisulu: In Our Lifetime* (London: Abacus, 2003), 166.

12. Walter Sisulu, *I Will Go Singing*, at http://www.sahistory.org.za/sites/ default/files/Sisulu%20bio%2C%20I%20will%20Go%20Singing%2C%20by %20George%20Houser%20and%20Herbert%20Shore.pdf (accessed on 29 March 2018), 90–3.

13. Nelson Mandela, *Long Walk to Freedom* (London: Little, Brown, 2010), 148. For details of Mandela's acquisition of Mao's works, see ibid., 112.

14. Cited in Jin Chongji and Pang Xianzhi, *Mao Zedong zhuan 1949–1976* (Biography of Mao Zedong, 1949–1976), Volume 2 (Beijing: Zhongyang wenxian chubanshe, 2003), 1695. Mao apparently said the same thing to

Kenneth Kaunda in 1974: see Philip Snow, *The Star Raft: China's Encounter with Africa* (London: Weidenfeld & Nicolson, 1988), 141.

15. J. C. Cheng, ed., *The Politics of the Chinese Red Army: A Translation of the Bulletin of Activities of the People's Liberation Army* (Stanford, CA: Hoover Institution, 1966), 315–17, 484–7. The report concludes: 'This material is for the study and reference of cadres at and above the regimental level. It is not allowed to spread knowledge of the contents outside or to quote or copy the same in public. Under no circumstance can this be lost or misplaced!'

16. Snow, *The Star Raft*, 73.

17. Ibid., 73–4.

18. Jiang, 'Lengzhan shiqi Zhongguo', 34.

19. Snow, *The Star Raft*, 74, 106, 120.

20. Cooley, *East Wind Over Africa*, 40.

21. G. Thomas Burgess, 'Mao in Zanzibar: Nationalism, Discipline, and the (De)Construction of Afro-Asian Solidarities', in Christopher J. Lee, ed., *Making a World After Empire: The Bandung Moment and Its Political Afterlives* (Athens: Ohio University Press, 2010), 207.

22. G. Thomas Burgess, Ali Sultan Issa and Seif Sharif Hamad, *Race, Revolution and the Struggle for Human Rights in Zanzibar: The Memoirs of Sultan Issa and Seif Sharif Hamad* (Athens: Ohio University Press, 2009), 60–1.

23. Ibid., 66.

24. Cooley, *East Wind Over Africa*, 41.

25. Burgess, 'Mao in Zanzibar', 224.

26. Alan Hutchison, *China's African Revolution* (London: Hutchinson, 1975), 95.

27. Ibid., 95, 62; Jiang, 'Lengzhan shiqi Zhongguo', 45–6; Cooley, *East Wind Over Africa*, 175, 172.

28. 'Kenya: Chinese Communist Activities in the Middle East and Africa', 1959–1962, UKNA FCO 141/7090.

29. Christopher M. Andrew and Vasili Mitrokhin, *The Mitrokhin Archive II: The KGB and the World* (London: Allen Lane, 2005), 442.

30. Priya Lal, 'Maoism in Tanzania: Material Connections and Shared Imaginaries', in Alexander C. Cook, ed., *Mao's Little Red Book: A Global History* (Cambridge: Cambridge University Press, 2014), 101.

31. Jamie Monson, *Africa's Freedom Railway: How a Chinese Development Project Changed Lives and Livelihoods in Tanzania* (Bloomington: Indiana University Press, 2009), 30.

32. Ibid., 7.

33. Hong Zhou and Hou Xiong, eds, *China's Foreign Aid: 60 Years in Retrospect* (Singapore: Springer, 2017), 116–17; Hutchison, *China's African Revolution*, 54.

34. Hutchison, *China's African Revolution*, 221–2.

35. Cooley, *East Wind Over Africa*, 224–5.

36. Cited in ibid., 143.

37. Snow, *The Star Raft*, 160.

38. Burgess et al., *Race*, 107.

39. Li Danhui, Liang Zhi and Zhou Na, 'Feizhou conglinzhong de xinshiming – Ma Faxian laoren fangtanlu (er)' (A New Mission in the African Bush: An Interview with Mr Ma Faxian, Part Two), *Lengzhan guojishi yanjiu* 8 (2009): 317.

40. Li Danhui, Chen Bo and Fan Baiyu, 'Feizhou conglinzhong de xinshiming – Ma Faxian laoren fangtanlu (san)' (A New Mission in the African Bush: An Interview with Mr Ma Faxian, Part Three), *Lengzhan guojishi yanjiu* 9 (2010): 265.

41. Jiang, 'Lengzhan shiqi Zhongguo', 174.

42. Ibid., 62.

43. Ibid., 70–1.

44. Snow, *The Star Raft*, 79–82.

45. Raymond Mhlaba, *Raymond Mhlaba's Personal Memoirs: Reminiscing from Rwanda and Uganda* (Johannesburg: HSRC Press, 2001), 112–17.

46. Paul S. Landau, 'The ANC, MK, and "The Turn to Violence" (1960–1962)', *South African Historical Journal* 64.3 (2012): 556–7.

47. Ibid., 560.

48. Snow, *The Star Raft*, 84–5.

49. Hutchison, *China's African Revolution*, 230.

50. Ibid.

51. Ibid., 243.

52. Snow, *The Star Raft*, 83.

53. 'Kenya: Chinese Communist Activities in the Middle East and Africa', 1959–1962, UKNA FCO 141/7090.

54. Jiang, 'Lengzhan shiqi Zhongguo', 85–6.

55. 'Africa: "Chinese Activities in Africa", Communist Propaganda in Africa and IRD Work in Nigeria, Ghana …', 1966, UKNA FO 1110/2073.

56. *Nkrumah's Subversion in Africa: Documentary Evidence of Nkrumah's Interference in the Affairs of Other African States* (Ghana: Ministry of Information, 1966), 7, 42 and *passim*.

57. Hutchison, *China's African Revolution*, 248.

58. Jiang, 'Lengzhan shiqi Zhongguo', 170.

59. Alaba Ogunsanwo, *China's Policy in Africa, 1958–1971* (Cambridge: Cambridge University Press, 1974), 193–4.

60. Ali Mazrui, 'Kenya: Global Africana – Kissinger and Nyerere Belonged to Two Cultures but Why Their Comparison?', *The Standard,* at http://allafrica.com/stories/200709230017.html (accessed on 4 February 2018).

61. Julius K. Nyerere, *Freedom and Socialism* (Dar es Salaam: Oxford University Press, 1968), 34.

62. South African Democracy Education Trust, *The Road to Democracy in South Africa*, Volume 5, Part 1 (Cape Town: Zebra Press, 2004), 202.

63. Hutchison, *China's African Revolution*, 5.

64. Nyerere, *Freedom and Socialism*, 137.

65. See, for example, 'The Arusha Declaration', in ibid., 246.

66. Priya Lal, *African Socialism in Postcolonial Tanzania* (Cambridge: Cambridge University Press, 2015), 56.

67. Ibid., 62.

68. Lal, 'Maoism in Tanzania', 96.

69. Julius K. Nyerere, *Freedom and Development* (Dar es Salaam: Oxford University Press, 1973), 42–4.

70. Lal, 'Maoism in Tanzania', 108; Snow, *The Star Raft*, 102.

71. Mu'ammar al-Gaddafi, 'The Social Basis of the Third International Theory', at https://www.marxists.org/subject/africa/gaddafi/ch03.htm (accessed on 4 February 2018).

72. Lal, 'Maoism in Tanzania', 104.

73. Snow, *The Star Raft*, 101–2.

74. Burgess, 'Mao in Zanzibar', 224.

75. Lal, *African Socialism*, 100, 181, 202.

76. 'Chinese Activities in Tanzania', 1964–1966, UKNA DO 213/100.

77. Jiang, 'Lengzhan shiqi Zhongguo', 169.

78. Ibid., 210.

79. Ibid., 215.

80. Ibid., 216, 236.

81. Bruce D. Larkin, *China and Africa, 1949–1970: The Foreign Policy of the People's Republic of China* (Berkeley: University of California Press, 1971), 167–8.

82. Cooley, *East Wind Over Africa*, 156.

83. Jiang, 'Lengzhan shiqi Zhongguo', 30.

84. Ibid., 158.

85. Hutchison, *China's African Revolution*, 111.

86. Snow, *The Star Raft*, 82.

87. Mohamed Heikal, *Nasser: The Cairo Documents* (London: New English Library, 1972), 285–6.

88. Snow, *The Star Raft*, 115.

89. Ibid., 146; Cooley, *East Wind Over Africa*, 102.

90. Snow, *The Star Raft*, 114.

91. Emmanuel John Hevi, *An African Student in China* (London: Pall Mall Press, 1963), 162–3.

92. Ibid., 48, 127.

93. Ibid., 204.

94. Ibid., 119.

95. Ibid., 34.

96. Lal, 'Maoism in Tanzania', 112.

97. 'Chinese Relations and Activities in Sierra Leone: In Particular Technical Assistance and Military Training', 1972, UKNA FCO 65/1242.

98. Hutchison, *China's African Revolution*, 99–100.

99. Ibid., 105; Larkin, *China and Africa*, 102.

100. See clipping in 'Chinese Activities', UKNA DO 213/100.

101. 'Kenya: Chinese Communist Activities', UKNA FCO 141/7090.

102. See title of report in UKNA FCO 65/1242.

103. Snow, *The Star Raft*, 110.

104. Nyerere, *Freedom and Socialism*, 51.

105. Hutchison, *China's African Revolution*, 94–5.

106. 'Chinese Activities', UKNA DO 213/100; Hutchison, *China's African Revolution*, 94.

107. Burgess, 'Mao in Zanzibar', 221.

108. Hutchison, *China's African Revolution*, 182–3.

109. Li Danhui, Li Xiufang and You Lan, 'Feizhou conglinzhong de xinshiming – Ma Faxian laoren fangtanlu (wu)' (A New Mission in the African Bush: An Interview with Mr Ma Faxian, Part Five), *Lengzhan guojishi yanjiu* 11 (2011): 180.

110. Snow, *The Star Raft*, 165.

111. From Cooley, *East Wind Over Africa*, 181, and Hutchison, *China's African Revolution*, 272.

112. Lal, 'Maoism in Tanzania', 112.

113. Larkin, *China and Africa*, 136–7.

114. Snow, *The Star Raft*, 119.

115. Ogunsanwo, *China's Policy in Africa*, 193.

116. Burgess et al., *Race*, 86, 61.

117. Ibid., 39, 41.

118. Ibid., 76.

119. Ibid., 119, 115.

120. Ibid., 11.

121. Li Danhui, 'Fu Feizhou xinshiming: Ma Faxian laoren fangtanlu' (To Africa on a New Mission: An Interview with Mr Ma Faxian), *Lengzhan guojishi yanjiu* 7 (2008): 253.

122. Cooley, *East Wind Over Africa*, 195.

123. Li et al., 'Feizhou', Part Three, 262–3.

124. Li et al., 'Feizhou', Part Five, 171.

125. Li et al., 'Feizhou', Part Three, 262; Li et al, 'Feizhou', Part Five, 151.

126. Li et al, 'Feizhou', Part Seven, 232, 235.

127. Li, 'Fu Feizhou', 255.

128. Ibid., 256–9.

129. Li et al., 'Feizhou', Part Two, 305–7.

130. Ibid., 324–5.

131. Li Danhui, Cui Haizhi and Jiang Huajie, 'Feizhou conglinzhong de xinshiming – Ma Faxian laoren fangtanlu (si)' (A New Mission in the African Bush: An Interview with Mr Ma Faxian, Part Four), *Lengzhan guojishi yanjiu* 10 (2010): 379, 381.

132. Li Danhui, Zhou Na and Cui Haizhi, 'Feizhou conglinzhong de xinshiming – Ma Faxian laoren fangtanlu (liu)' (A New Mission in the African Bush: An Interview with Mr Ma Faxian, Part Six), *Lengzhan guojishi yanjiu* 12 (2011): 243–4.

133. Li et al., 'Feizhou', Part Three, 266.

134. Jiang, 'Lengzhan shiqi Zhongguo', 120.

135. Li et al., 'Feizhou', Part Four, 390, 411; Li et al., 'Feizhou', Part Five, 168.

136. Li Danhui, Zhou Na and Cui Haizhi, 'Feizhou conglinzhong de xinshiming – Ma Faxian laoren fangtanlu (ba)' (A New Mission in the African Bush: An Interview with Mr Ma Faxian, Part Eight), *Lengzhan guojishi yanjiu* 14 (2012): 279.

137. Li et al., 'Feizhou', Part Four, 396–7.

138. Ibid., 402–4.

139. Ibid., 404–5; Li et al., 'Feizhou', Part Five, 156.

140. Li et al., 'Feizhou', Part Five, 198–9.

141. Conversation between Mao Zedong and PLO delegation, 24 March 1965 (private collection).

142. Lillian Craig Harris, 'China's Relations with the PLO', *Journal of Palestine Studies* 7.1 (Autumn 1977): 137.

143. Li et al., 'Feizhou', Part Three, 275–6.

144. Personal communication.

145. Snow, *The Star Raft*, 168.

146. Jiang, 'Lengzhan shiqi Zhongguo', 123.

147. Ibid., 160.

148. Ibid., 93–5.

149. Mao Zedong's conversation with Mobutu Sese Seko, 13 January 1973 (private collection); Jung Chang and Jon Halliday, *Mao: The Unknown Story* (London: Jonathan Cape, 2005), 593.

150. David Martin and Phyllis Johnson, *The Struggle for Zimbabwe: The Chimurenga War* (London: Faber and Faber, 1981), 12.

151. Munyaradzi Huni, 'Chimurenga II Chronicles: Zanu's Uncomfortable Truth', *Sunday Mail*, 8 May 2016, at http://www.sundaymail.co.zw/chimurenga-ii -chronicles-zanus-uncomfortable-truth/ (accessed on 5 February 2018).

152. Martin and Johnson, *The Struggle for Zimbabwe*, 83–4.

153. Paul Moorcraft and Peter McLaughlin, *The Rhodesian War: Fifty Years On* (Barnsley, UK: Pen & Sword, 2015), 33.

154. Ibid., 11.

155. Fay Chung, *Re-living the Second Chimurenga: Memories from the Liberation Struggle in Zimbabwe* (Stockholm: Nordic Africa Institute, 2006), 130.

156. Hildegarde Manzvanzvike, 'Fighting for the People, with the People', *Herald*, 10 December 2015, at http://www.herald.co.zw/fighting-for-the-people -with-the-people/ (accessed on 5 February 2018).

157. 'Murozvi: Rare Breed of Cadre', *Herald*, 11 April 2017.

158. Moorcraft and McLaughlin, *The Rhodesian War*, 73–4.
159. Pandya Paresh, *Mao Tse-tung and Chimurenga: An Investigaton into ZANU's Strategies* (Braamfontein, South Africa: Skotaville Publishers, 1988), 82–3.
160. Snow, *The Star Raft*, 84.
161. Paresh, *Mao Tse-tung and Chimurenga*, 128–9, 136–7.
162. Ibid., 135.
163. Moorcraft and McLaughlin, *The Rhodesian War*, 62.
164. Ibid., 64–75.
165. Ibid., 106.
166. Chung, *Re-living the Second Chimurenga*, 264.
167. Snow, *The Star Raft*, 230.
168. 'Statement by Chinese President Xi Jinping: Let the Sino-Zim Flower Bloom with New Splendour', *Herald*, 28 November 2015.
169. Christopher Farai Charamba, 'Party Principles Found in Song', *Herald*, 12 April 2016.
170. Snow, *The Star Raft*, 136; Zhang Yi, *Poxiao shifen* (When the Light Dawned) (Taibei: Zhongyang ribao chubanshe, 1985), 210–11.

7 Mao's Dominoes? Vietnam and Cambodia

1. *Red Chinese Battle Plan*, 1964, at https://archive.org/details/RedChine1964 (accessed on 23 January 2018).
2. *Why Vietnam?*, 1965, at https://www.youtube.com/watch?v=v1WzxlsOsjw (accessed on 23 January 2018).
3. Cited in Fredrik Logevall, 'The Indochina Wars and the Cold War, 1945–1975', in Melvyn P. Leffler and Odd Arne Westad, eds, *The Cambridge History of the Cold War: Crises and Détente*, Volume 2 (Cambridge: Cambridge University Press, 2010), 288.
4. Bruce D. Larkin, *China and Africa, 1949–1970: The Foreign Policy of the People's Republic of China* (Berkeley: University of California Press, 1973), 196.
5. Both quotations from Qiang Zhai, *China and the Vietnam War, 1950–1975* (Chapel Hill: University of North Carolina Press, 2005), 146.
6. Ibid., 147–8, 201.
7. The historical literature on the Vietnam and Indochinese wars is vast. See works listed in the bibliography by Mark Bradley, Christopher Goscha, Ben Kiernan and Marilyn Young, among others, and also Lien-Hang T. Nguyen, *Hanoi's War: An International History of the War for Peace in Vietnam* (Chapel Hill: University of North Carolina Press, 2012); Pierre Asselin, *Hanoi's Road to the Vietnam War, 1954–1965* (Berkeley: University of California Press, 2015).
8. See arguments in Sergey Radchenko, *Two Suns in the Heavens: The Sino-Soviet Struggle for Supremacy* (Washington, DC: Woodrow Wilson Center, 2009).

9. Cited in 'Office of the Historian', at https://history.state.gov/historical documents/frus1952-54v13p1/d716 (accessed on 23 January 2018).

10. Odd Arne Westad, Chen Jian, Stein Tønnesson, Nguyen Vu Tungand and James G. Hershberg, '77 Conversations Between Chinese and Foreign Leaders on the Wars in Indochina, 1964–1977', Woodrow Wilson International Center Working Paper No. 22, 91 and *passim.*

11. Ibid., 23, 154; Qiang, *China and the Vietnam War*, 135; Chen Jian, *Mao's China and the Cold War* (Chapel Hill: University of North Carolina Press, 2001), 227–9.

12. Westad et al., '77 Conversations', 85.

13. Ibid., 35.

14. William J. Duiker, *Ho Chi Minh: A Life* (New York: Hyperion, 2000), see chapters 3–4, and 274, 230.

15. Ibid., 210, 248–9.

16. Ang Cheng Guan, *Vietnamese Communists' Relations with China and the Second Indochina Conflict, 1956–1962* (London: McFarland, 1997), 57, 66.

17. Duiker, *Ho Chi Minh*, 255.

18. Bui Tin, *Following Ho Chi Minh: The Memoirs of a North Vietnamese Colonel* (London: Hurst, 1995), 29.

19. Guan, *Vietnamese Communists' Relations*, 37.

20. Luo Guibo, 'Shaoqi tongzhi paiwo chushi Yuenan' (Comrade Shaoqi Sends Me on a Mission to Vietnam), in He Jingxu et al., eds, *Mianhuai Liu Shaoqi* (Fond Memories of Liu Shaoqi) (Beijing: Zhongyang wenxian chubanshe, 1988), 234.

21. Ibid., 237; Qiang, *China and the Vietnam War*, 18–19.

22. Chen, *Mao's China*, 125.

23. Qiang, *China and the Vietnam War*, 35.

24. Ibid., 33.

25. Chen, *Mao's China*, 127, 130.

26. Bui, *Following Ho Chi Minh*, 24.

27. Ibid., 7–8.

28. Ibid., 14–16.

29. Ibid., 16; Hoang Van Hoan, *A Drop in the Ocean: Hoang Van Hoan's Revolutionary Reminiscences* (Beijing: Foreign Languages Press, 1988), 300.

30. Bui, *Following Ho Chi Minh*, 16.

31. Alex-Thai D. Vo, 'Nguyen Thi Nam and the Land Reform in North Vietnam', *Journal of Vietnamese Studies* 10.1 (Winter 2015): 30–9.

32. This is communicated by ibid. and by Bui, *Following Ho Chi Minh*.

33. Bui, *Following Ho Chi Minh*, 26.

34. Vo, 'Nguyen Thi Nam', 33.

35. Qiang, *China and the Vietnam War*, 230.

36. Vo, 'Nguyen Thi Nam', 1–2, 36.

37. Bui, *Following Ho Chi Minh*, 23–4.

38. Ibid., 28. For a discussion of the death toll, see Vo, 'Nguyen Thi Nam', 3–10, and Alec Holcombe, 'Socialist Transformation in the Democratic Republic of Vietnam', unpublished PhD dissertation, University of California, Berkeley, 2014, 2.

39. Bui, *Following Ho Chi Minh*, 35.

40. Ibid., 38.

41. Martin Windrow, *The Last Valley: Dien Bien Phu and the French Defeat in Vietnam* (London: Cassell, 2005), 205.

42. Chen, *Mao's China*, 134.

43. Windrow, *The Last Valley*, 624.

44. Huang Hua, *Memoirs* (Beijing: Foreign Languages Press, 2008), 149.

45. Qiang, *China and the Vietnam War*, 58.

46. Ibid., 61.

47. Guan, *Vietnamese Communists' Relations*, 102–3.

48. Bui, *Following Ho Chi Minh*, 52.

49. Qiang, *China and the Vietnam War*, 125.

50. Guan, *Vietnamese Communists' Relations*, 128.

51. *The Truth About Vietnam-China Relations over the Last Thirty Years* (Hanoi: Ministry of Foreign Affairs, 1979), *passim*; Luu Doan Huynh, 'Commentary: A Vietnamese Scholar's Perspective on the Communist Big Powers and Vietnam', in Priscilla Roberts, ed., *Behind the Bamboo Curtain: China, Vietnam, and the World Beyond Asia* (Stanford, CA: Stanford University Press, 2006), 443.

52. 'Yuenan dui wo dang bazhong quanhui deng wenti de fanying' (Vietnam's Reaction to the Eighth Plenum and Other Issues), 16 September 1959, AMFA 106-00444-04(1).

53. Westad et al., '77 Conversations', 112–19.

54. Duong Danh Dy, interview, carried out by Lucy Ha, 5 August 2015, Hanoi.

55. Nicholas Khoo, *Collateral Damage: Sino-Soviet Rivalry and the Termination of the Sino-Vietnamese Alliance* (New York: Columbia University Press, 2011), 37–8.

56. Westad et al., '77 Conversations', 63.

57. Sergey Radchenko, 'Mao Unplugged: the 1970s', unpublished paper.

58. Dan Levin, 'China Is Urged to Confront Its Own History', *New York Times*, 30 March 2015.

59. Dan Tong, '1960–70 niandai de Xihanuke, boerbute yu Zhongguo' (Sihanouk, Pol Pot and China in the 1960s–70s), manuscript copy provided by author.

60. Song Zheng, *Mao Zedong zhuyi de xingwang: Zhongguo geming yu Hong Gaomian geming de lishi* (The Rise and Fall of Maoism: A History of the Chinese and Khmer Rouge Revolutions) (US: Meiguo yangguang chubanshe, 2013), 555–7.

61. Rithy Panh, *The Missing Picture* (film).

62. Julio Jeldres, 'A Personal Reflection on Norodom Sihanouk and Zhou Enlai: An Extraordinary Friendship on the Fringes of the Cold War', *Cross-Currents: East Asian History and Culture Review* 4 (September 2012): 61.

63. Cited in Philip Short, *Pol Pot: The History of a Nightmare* (London: John Murray, 2004), 357.

64. Howard J. De Nike, John Quigley and Kenneth J. Robinson, eds., *Genocide in Cambodia: Documents from the Trial of Pol Pot and Ieng Sary* (Philadelphia: University of Pennsylvania Press, 2000), 550.

65. *People's Revolutionary Tribunal Held in Phnom Penh for the Trial of the Genocide Crime of the Pol Pot–Ieng Sary Clique, August 1979: Documents* (Phnom Penh: Foreign Languages Publishing House, 1990), 268, 246, 152, 131, 267, 244, 268.

66. Short, *Pol Pot*, 66–7, 70–1.

67. Ibid., 190.

68. David Chandler, *Brother Number One: A Political Biography of Pol Pot* (Boulder, CO: Westview, 1999), 37.

69. Short, *Pol Pot*, 96.

70. Ibid., 158.

71. Zhou Degao, *Wo yu Zhonggong he Jiangong: chise huaren jiemi* (The CCP, the CPK and Me: Revelations of a Red Chinese) (Hong Kong: Tianyuan shuwu, 2007), 75.

72. Short, *Pol Pot*, 159–61.

73. Ibid., 170, and 'Lettre du Comité Permanent du CC du CPK au bureau politique du CC du CPC', 6 October 1967, Doc TLM/175 VA (courtesy of Philip Short).

74. Chin Peng, *Alias Chin Peng – My Side of History: Recollections of a Revolutionary Leader* (Singapore: Media Masters, 2003), 454. Note, however, that Chin Peng's chronology is a little ambiguous. Note also Pol Pot's interesting comments about assistance given by the Chinese embassy in Phnom Penh in springing Khieu Samphan from Sihanouk's death row in ibid.

75. Short, *Pol Pot*, 177.

76. Song, *Mao Zedong zhuyi*, 129, 199–200.

77. Ibid., 124.

78. David Chandler, *Voices from S-21: Terror and History in Pol Pot's Secret Prison* (Berkeley: University of California Press, 1999), 4.

79. Song, *Mao Zedong zhuyi*, 199–200.

80. Zhou, *Wo yu Zhonggong*, 72.

81. Song, *Mao Zedong zhuyi*, 268.

82. Ibid., 206–7.

83. Zhou, *Wo yu Zhonggong*, for example 78, 81–2, 92, 63.

84. Ibid., 88–9.

85. Nayan Chanda, *Brother Enemy: The War After the War* (San Diego, CA: Harcourt Brace Jovanovich, 1986), 41.

86. Ben Kiernan, *How Pol Pot Came to Power: A History of Communism in Kampuchea, 1930–1975* (London: Verso, 1986), 276.

87. Short, *Pol Pot*, 167–8; Milton Osborne, *Sihanouk: Prince of Light, Prince of Darkness* (Honolulu: University of Hawai'i Press, 1994), 194.

88. See image in Jeldres, 'A Personal Reflection', 55.

89. Norodom Sihanouk and Julio A. Jeldres, *Shadow Over Angkor: Volume One, Memoirs of His Majesty King Norodom Sihanouk of Cambodia* (Phnom Penh: Monument Books, 2005), 81.

90. Zhou, *Wo yu Zhonggong*, 89–95.

91. Norodom Sihanouk and Wilfred Burchett, *My War with the CIA* (London: Penguin, 1973), 209–10.

92. Sihanouk and Jeldres, *Shadow Over Angkor*, 87.

93. Short, *Pol Pot*, 202.

94. Dan, '1960–70 niandai', 4.

95. Sihanouk and Jeldres, *Shadow Over Angkor*, 155.

96. Short, *Pol Pot*, 243–4.

97. 'Xihanuke qinwang shicha Jianpuzhai jiefangqu zhuanji' (Special issue on Prince Sihanouk's Inspection of Cambodia's Liberated Zone), *Renmin huabao*, June 1973.

98. Dan, '1960–70 niandai', 5.

99. Short, *Pol Pot*, 240.

100. Translation slightly altered; Ben Kiernan, *The Pol Pot Regime: Race, Power and Genocide in Cambodia under the Khmer Rouge* (New Haven, CT: Yale University Press, 2014), 326.

101. Harish C. Mehta, *Warrior Prince: Norodom Ranariddh, Son of King Sihanouk of Cambodia* (Singapore: Graham Brash, 2001), 54; see a similar version in Sophie Richardson, *China, Cambodia and the Five Principles of Peaceful Coexistence* (New York: Columbia University Press, 2010), 87–8: 'I must sacrifice my own views, out of consideration for China and His Excellency Zhou Enlai,' he declared in 1975, 'who have done so much for Cambodia and myself.'

102. See, for example, Song, *Mao Zedong zhuyi*, 489, 634.

103. Dan, '1960–70 niandai', 9.

104. See Henri Locard, *Pol Pot's Little Red Book: The Sayings of Angkar* (Chiang Mai, Thailand: Silkworm, 2004), 72, 69, 78, 97, 156; also see discussion in Ben Kiernan, 'External and Indigenous Sources of Khmer Rouge Ideology', in Odd Arne Westad and Sophie Quinn-Judge, eds, *The Third Indochina War: Conflict Between China, Vietnam and Cambodia, 1972–1979* (London: Routledge, 2006), 187–206.

105. De Nike et al., eds, *Genocide in Cambodia*, 292.

106. See Dan, '1960–70 niandai', 7, 9, for an expression of this idea by a veteran turned historian of the Mao era: 'Approved and encouraged by Mao and other Chinese leaders, Pol Pot rolled out policies even more radical than

China's Cultural Revolution. He unleashed upon an economically ravaged Cambodia a socialist line based on eradicating differences in class and between city and countryside, without currency, without trade; annihilating rich people, in a quest for equality; annihilating cities, moving residents to the countryside to work as peasants; destroying all "luxury items" such as furniture, televisions, fridges and cars; revolutionising street names; dissolving the family; setting up forced labour brigades, segregating the sexes; reforming intellectuals; those who would not be remoulded, would be annihilated ... The tragedy of China's Great Leap Forward was replayed in Cambodia.'

107. Haing Ngor with Roger Warner, *Survival in the Killing Fields* (London: Robinson, 2003), 3.
108. Andrew Mertha, *Brothers in Arms: Chinese Aid to the Khmer Rouge, 1975–1979* (Ithaca, NY: Cornell University Press, 2014), 99.
109. De Nike et al., eds, *Genocide in Cambodia*, 545.
110. Chanda, *Brother Enemy*, 85.
111. Song, *Mao Zedong zhuyi*, 481, 483, 551, 699.
112. Kiernan, *The Pol Pot Regime*, 129–30.
113. Chanda, *Brother Enemy*, 200.
114. Kiernan, *The Pol Pot Regime*, 133, 379.
115. Norodom Sihanouk, *Prisonnier des Khmers Rouges* (Paris: Hachette, 1986), 216.
116. De Nike et al., eds, *Genocide in Cambodia*, 81.
117. Kiernan, *The Pol Pot Regime*, 102.
118. Ibid., 108, 111, 148.
119. Chanda, *Brother Enemy*, 42, 44.
120. Kiernan, *The Pol Pot Regime*, 139.
121. Ibid., 380.
122. Dan, '1960–1970 niandai', 8; Chanda, *Brother Enemy*, 43; Song, *Mao Zedong zhuyi*, 638; Norodom Sihanouk, *War and Hope: The Case for Cambodia*, trans. Mary Feeney (London: Sidgwick & Jackson, 1980), 86.
123. Kiernan, *The Pol Pot Regime*, 135.
124. Mertha, *Brothers in Arms*, 55.
125. Song, *Mao Zedong zhuyi*, 636, 641. See also Kiernan, *The Pol Pot Regime*, 152–3.
126. David P. Chandler, *The Tragedy of Cambodian History: Politics, War and Revolution Since 1945* (New Haven, CT: Yale University Press, 1991), 240; Xu Yan, 'Boerbute: "zuohuo" de yi mian jing' (Pol Pot: A Mirror on the 'Leftist Disaster'), *Bainianchao* 3 (2001): 69.
127. Kiernan, *The Pol Pot Regime*, 295; Song, *Mao Zedong zhuyi*, 650.
128. Kiernan, *The Pol Pot Regime*, 155.
129. Chanda, *Brother Enemy*, 11–22.
130. Ibid., 23, 17.

131. Westad et al., '77 Conversations', 192.
132. Chanda, *Brother Enemy*, 28.
133. Ibid., 24.
134. Xiaoming Zhang, *Deng Xiaoping's Long War: The Military Conflict Between China and Vietnam, 1979–1991* (Chapel Hill: University of North Carolina Press, 2015), 36; see slightly different translation of the same idea in Westad et al., '77 Conversations', 192.
135. Chanda, *Brother Enemy*, 52–3.
136. Westad et al., '77 Conversations', 74.
137. Ibid., 182.
138. Chanda, *Brother Enemy*, 134.
139. Ibid., 34, 86, 194, 207–8.
140. Ibid., 213.
141. Ibid., 261, 325.
142. Ibid., 356–8, 361.
143. Short, *Pol Pot*, 396–7.
144. See evocation in Evan Gottesman, *Cambodia After the Khmer Rouge: Inside the Politics of Nation Building* (New Haven, CT: Yale University Press, 2004), 11, 50.
145. Dan, '1960–70 niandai', 10.
146. Short, *Pol Pot*, 421–3, 435, 442.
147. Zhou, *Wo yu Zhonggong*, 216, 229.
148. Cited in Mertha, *Brothers in Arms*, 1.

8 'You Are Old, We Are Young, Mao Zedong!'

1. Robert J. Alexander, *Maoism in the Developed World* (London: Praeger, 2001), 94.
2. Stephen Frank Rayner, 'The Classification and Dynamics of Sectarian Forms of Organisation: Grid/Group Perspectives on the Far-left in Britain', unpublished PhD dissertation, University College London, 1979, 141.
3. Robert Booth, 'Maoist Sect Leader Forced Woman into Sex Acts, Court Hears', *Guardian*, 16 November 2015.
4. Rayner, 'The Classification', 141–3.
5. Ibid., 143, 145.
6. Booth, 'Maoist Sect Leader Forced Woman into Sex Acts, Court Hears'.
7. Robert Booth, 'Cult Leader Comrade Bala's Daughter: 30 Years as a "Non-Person"', *Guardian*, 4 December 2015.
8. Robert Booth, 'The Brixton Sect Where Paranoia and Cruelty Reigned', *Guardian*, 4 December 2015.
9. Rayner, 'The Classification', 170.

10. Hans Petter Sjøli, 'Maoism in Norway: And How the AKP (m-l) Made Norway More Norwegian', *Scandinavian Journal of History* 33.4 (December 2008): 479.

11. See Frank Dikötter, *The Cultural Revolution: A People's History, 1962–1976* (London: Bloomsbury, 2016).

12. Robin D. G. Kelley and Betsy Esch, 'Black Like Mao: Red China and Black Revolution', *Souls: Critical Journal of Black Politics and Culture* 1.4 (Fall 1999): 7.

13. Shirley MacLaine, *You Can Get There From Here* (London: George Prior, 1975), 206, 213, 183–4, 223–4, 245, 247–8.

14. Christophe Bourseiller, *Les Maoïstes: La Folle Histoire des Gardes Rouges Français* (Paris: Plon, 1996), 64, 74.

15. Ibid., 73–8.

16. Ibid., 159.

17. 'Artists to Exhibit as Protest Against War', *New York Times*, 26 January 1967; Clive Barnes, 'Dance: "Angry Arts" at Hunter College', *New York Times*, 3 February 1967.

18. Jeremi Suri, 'Ostpolitik as Domestic Containment: The Cultural Contradictions of the Cold War and the West German State Response', in Belinda Davis, Wilfried Mausbach, Martin Klimke and Carlo MacDougall, eds, *Changing the World, Changing Oneself: Political Protest and Collective Identities in West Germany and the US in the 1960s and 1970s* (Oxford: Berghahn Books, 2013), 141.

19. Mark Kurlansky, *1968: The Year That Rocked the World* (London: Jonathan Cape, 2004), 202.

20. Max Elbaum, *Revolution in the Air: Sixties Radicals Turn to Lenin, Mao and Che* (London: Verso, 2006), 42–3.

21. Ibid., 45.

22. Ethan Young, interview, 24 March 2015, New York.

23. Muhammad Ahmad, interview, 25 March 2015, Philadelphia.

24. Dennis O'Neil, interview, 23 March 2015, New York.

25. Sebastian Gehrig, '(Re-)Configuring Mao: Trajectories of a Culturo-political Trend in West Germany', *Transcultural Studies* 2 (2011): 204; Quinn Slobodian, *Foreign Front: Third World Politics in Sixties West Germany* (Durham, NC: Duke University Press, 2012), 173.

26. Gerd Koenen, *Das Rote Jahrzehnt: Unsere kleine Deutsche Kulturrevolution 1967–1977* (Cologne: Kiepenheuer & Witsch, 2001), 46–7, 49.

27. Slobodian, *Foreign Front*, 194.

28. Aaron J. Leonard and Conor A. Gallagher, *Heavy Radicals: The FBI's Secret War on America's Maoists: The Revolutionary Union/Revolutionary Communist Party 1968–1980* (Winchester, UK: Zero Books, 2014), 25.

29. Bobby Seale, *Seize the Time: Story of the Black Panther Party and Huey P. Newton* (Baltimore: Black Classic Press, 1991), 82–3.

30. Muhammad Ahmad, *We Will Return in the Whirlwind: Black Radical Organizations 1960–1975* (Chicago: Charles H. Kerr, 2007), 292; see also 'Black Panther Greatest Threat to U.S. Security', *Desert Sun*, 16 July 1969, at https://cdnc.ucr.edu/cgi-bin/cdnc?a=d&d=DS19690716.2.89 (accessed on 10 May 2018).

31. Joshua Bloom and Waldo E. Martin, *Black Against Empire: The History and Politics of the Black Panther Party* (Berkeley: University of California Press, 2013), 60.

32. Kelley and Esch, 'Black Like Mao', 6.

33. Robeson Taj Frazier, *The East Is Black: Cold War China in the Black Radical Imagination* (Durham, NC: Duke University Press, 2015), 136.

34. Ibid., 136.

35. 'The Papers of Robert F. Williams', microfilm edn, University Publication of America, 2002.

36. Maxwell C. Stanford, 'Revolutionary Action Movement (RAM): A Case Study of an Urban Revolutionary Movement in Western Capitalist Society', unpublished MA dissertation, University of Georgia, 1986, 72.

37. Frazier, *The East Is Black*, 146.

38. See 'The Papers of Robert F. Williams', *passim*.

39. Frazier, *The East Is Black*, 183.

40. Stanford, 'Revolutionary Action Movement', 80, 83–4.

41. Ibid., 103.

42. Ahmad, interview.

43. Huey P. Newton, *To Die for the People* (San Francisco: City Lights Books, 2009), 234; Seale, *Seize the Time*, 113.

44. Seale, *Seize the Time*, 64.

45. Roberto Niccolai, *Quando la Cina era Vicina: La Rivoluzione Culturale e la sinistra extraparlamentare Italiana negli anni '60 e '70* (Pisa: Associazione centro de documentazione de Pistoia, 1998), 70.

46. Kurlansky, *1968*, 145.

47. Koenen, *Das Rote Jahrzehnt*, 148.

48. O'Neil, interview.

49. Young, interview.

50. O'Neil, interview.

51. Slobodian, *Foreign Front*, 178.

52. Ibid., 176.

53. Quinn Slobodian, 'The Meanings of Western Maoism in the Global 1960s', in Chen Jian et al., eds, *The Routledge Handbook of the Global Sixties* (London: Routledge, 2018), 72.

54. Gehrig, '(Re-)Configuring Mao', 201–2, 220.

55. Slobodian, *Foreign Front*, 176.

56. Uta G. Poiger, 'Generations: The "Revolutions" of the 1960s', in Helmut Walser Smith, ed., *The Oxford Handbook of Modern German History* (Oxford: Oxford University Press, 2011), 648.

57. Tony Judt, *Postwar: A History of Europe Since 1945* (London: Pimlico, 2007), 419.

58. Bourseiller, *Les Maoïstes*, 126.

59. Richard Wolin, *The Wind from the East: French Intellectuals, the Cultural Revolution and the Legacy of the 1960s* (Princeton, NJ: Princeton University Press, 2010), 4.

60. Bourseiller, *Les Maoïstes*, 65.

61. Niccolai, *Quando la Cina*, 146; Robert Lumley, *States of Emergency: Cultures of Revolt in Italy from 1968 to 1978* (London: Verso, 1990), 73.

62. Slobodian, *Foreign Front*, 185–6.

63. Lumley, *States of Emergency*, 87–8.

64. Ibid., 88; see also 121.

65. Niccolai, *Quando la Cina*, 237.

66. 'Interview on the Cultural Revolution with Chris Milton, a Participant', at https://www.marxists.org/history/erol/1960-1970/milton.pdf (accessed on 7 February 2018), 7.

67. O'Neil, interview.

68. See Ilaria Favretto, 'Rough Music and Factory Protest in Post-1945 Italy', *Past and Present* 228 (August 2015): 207–47; Ilaria Favretto and Marco Fincardi, 'Carnivalesque and Charivari Repertories in 1960s and 1970s Italian Protest', in Ilaria Favretto and Xabier Itçaina, eds, *Protest, Popular Culture and Tradition in Modern and Contemporary Western Europe* (London: Palgrave, 2017), 149–84.

69. Seale, *Seize the Time*, 395–401.

70. Jean Delavaud, 'De Choiseul-Praslin: de l'Ena … À l'usine', at http://www.nantes.maville.com/actu/actudet_-De-Choiseul-Praslin-de-l-Ena...-a-l-usine-_-625516_actu.htm (accessed on 7 February 2018).

71. Niccolai, *Quando la Cina*, 237.

72. Bourseiller, *Les Maoïstes*, 81, 49, 69.

73. Lisa Foa, 'Perché fummo maoisti: la Cina è un giallo', *Limes* (1995): 237–8. Jon Rognlien, the scholar of Norwegian Maoism, confirms this view: interview by author, 3 February 2014 (Skype).

74. Niccolai, *Quando la Cina*, 150–1.

75. Gerard Miller, *Minoritaire* (Paris: Seuil, 2001), 76, 80, 97.

76. Wolin, *The Wind from the East*, 207, 270–2, 274.

77. Young, interview.

78. See Andreas Kühn, *Stalins Enkel, Maos Söhne: Die Lebenswelt der K-Gruppen in der Bundesrepublik der 70er Jahre* (Frankfurt: Campus Verlag, 2005).

79. Niccolai, *Quando la Cina*, 116.

80. Ibid., 120–5.

81. 'Aldo Brandirali, storia di una conversione', at http://www.genteveneta.it/public/articolo.php?id=5553 (accessed on 10 May 2018).

82. Donald Reid, 'Etablissement: Working in the Factory to Make Revolution in France', *Radical History Review* 88 (2004): 86.

83. For an English translation, see Robert Linhart, *The Assembly Line*, trans. Margaret Crosland (London: Calder, 1981).

84. 'International Institute for Research and Education Archives', International Institute of Social History, Amsterdam.

85. Gehrig, '(Re-)Configuring Mao', 210.

86. Bourseiller, *Les Maoïstes*, 18.

87. Ibid., 154.

88. O'Neil, interview.

89. Young, interview.

90. See http://freedomroad.org/2000/02/family-tree-introduction/ for a visual guide to these parties. There is a 'basic' and a 'mega' family tree; visitors to the page are warned that their 'browser may have trouble' with the complexity of the latter. See Bourseiller, *Les Maoïstes*, 331, for a French counterpart.

91. Leonard and Gallagher, *Heavy Radicals*, 249.

92. 'You Don't Need a Weatherman to Know Which Way the Wind Blows', 1969, at https://archive.org/details/YouDontNeedAWeathermanToKnow WhichWayTheWindBlows_925 (accessed on 7 February 2018), 28.

93. Bourseiller, *Les Maoïstes*, 99.

94. Wolin, *The Wind from the East*, 32.

95. Slobodian, *Foreign Front*, 185–6.

96. Sebastian Gehrig, '"Zwischen uns und dem Feind einen klaren Trennungsstrich ziehen": Linksterroristische Gruppe und maoistische Ideologie in der Bundesrepublik der 1960er und 1970er Jahre', in Sebastian Gehrig, Barbara Mittler and Felix Wemheuer, eds, *Kulturrevolution als Vorbild? Maoismen im deutschsprachigen Raum* (Frankfurt: Peter Lang, 2008), 156.

97. Koenen, *Das Rote Jahrzehnt*, 174.

98. J. Smith and André Moncourt, *The Red Army Faction, a Documentary History: Volume 1, Projectiles for the People* (Oakland, CA: PM Press, 2009) 83–105, 122–59; Gehrig, '"Zwischen uns und dem Feind einen klaren Trennungsstrich ziehen"', 158.

99. Koenen, *Das Rote Jahrzehnt*, 367.

100. Alberto Franceschini, *Mara Renato e Io: Storia des Fondatori delle BR* (Milan: Arnoldo Mondadori, 1988), 19.

101. Ibid., 62–3.

102. Niccolai, *Quando la Cina*, 68.

103. Franceschini, *Mara Renato e Io*, 74–5.

104. Koenen, *Das Rote Jahrzehnt*, 453–4.

105. Akbar M. Ahmed, 'The World Black Revolution', 18, 26, at https://antiimperialism. files.wordpress.com/2012/10/ahmad-s.pdf (accessed on 7 February 2018).

106. Carol Hanisch, 'Impact of the Chinese Cultural Revolution on the Women's Liberation Movement', at http://www.carolhanisch.org/Speeches/ ChinaWLMSpeech/ChinaWLspeech.html (accessed on 7 February 2018).

107. Stanford, 'Revolutionary Action Movement', 87; Ahmad, *We Will Return*, xvii.

108. Wang Ning, 'Introduction: Global Maoism and Cultural Revolutions in the Global Context', *Comparative Literature Studies* 52.1 (2015), 2–3.

109. Wolin, *The Wind from the East*, 343, and 288–349 *passim*, on Foucault and French Maoism.

110. Sanjay Seth, 'From Maoism to Postcolonialism? The Indian "Sixties", and Beyond', *Inter-Asia Cultural Studies* 7.4 (2006): 602.

111. Kühn, *Stalins Enkel*, 288. For details on the overlap between Maoist and environmental movements in Western Europe, see Andrew S. Tompkins, '"BETTER ACTIVE TODAY THAN RADIOACTIVE TOMORROW!" Transnational Opposition to Nuclear Energy in France and West Germany, 1968–1981', unpublished PhD dissertation, University of Oxford, 2013.

112. Niccolai, *Quando la Cina*, 146.

113. Virginie Linhart, *Le jour où mon père s'est tu* (Paris: Éditions du Seuil, 2008).

114. Elbaum, *Revolution in the Air*, 321–3.

115. Young, interview.

116. Niccolai, *Quando la Cina*, 236.

117. See, for example, Karrin Hanshew, *Terror and Democracy in West Germany* (Cambridge: Cambridge University Press, 2012), 237. See Lumley, *States of Emergency*, 337–8, for similar remarks about the response of the Italian judiciary to left-wing terrorism.

118. Ward Churchill, '"To Disrupt, Discredit and Destroy": The FBI's Secret War Against the Black Panther Party', in Kathleen Cleaver and George Katsiaficas, eds, *Liberation, Imagination and the Black Panther Party: A New Look at the Panthers and Their Legacy* (New York: Routledge, 2001), 81.

119. Ibid., 86.

120. Muhammad Ahmad (Max Stanford), 'The Deeper Roots of the Black Activist Tradition "Know Your Local History"', at http://black2067.rssing.com/chan-6349830/all_p89.html (accessed on 7 February 2018).

9 Red Sun Over Peru

1. See https://www.opensocietyfoundations.org/moving-walls/8/yuyanapaq-remember.

2. Carlos Basombrío Iglesias, 'Sendero Luminoso and Human Rights: A Perverse Logic that Captured the Country', in Steve J. Stern, ed., *Shining and Other Paths: War and Society in Peru, 1980–1995* (Durham, NC: Duke University Press, 1998), 429.

3. Ton de Wit and Vera Gianotten, 'The Center's Multiple Failures', in David Scott Palmer, ed., *The Shining Path of Peru* (London: Hurst, 1992), 45.

4. Santiago Roncagliolo, *La cuarta espada: la historia de Abimael Guzmán y Sendero Luminoso* (Barcelona: Random House Mondadori, 2007), 82.

5. Matthew D. Rothwell, *Transpacific Revolutionaries: The Chinese Revolution in Latin America* (New York: Routledge, 2013), 30.

6. See, for example, ibid., 76–80. This is the best anglophone book on relations between the PRC and Latin America.

7. Ibid., 32–3.

8. Ibid., 81.

9. Ibid., 45.

10. Ibid., 53; Ernesto Toledo Brückmann, … *Y llegó Mao: Síntesis histórica de la llegada del Pensamiento Mao TseTung al Perú (1928–1964)* (Lima: Grupo Editorial Arteidea, 2016), 137–8.

11. Nandha Naidoo, 'The "Indian Chap": Recollections of a South African Underground Trainee in Mao's China', *South African Historical Journal* 64.3: 718.

12. Roncagliolo, *La cuarta espada*, 17.

13. Abimael Guzmán Reinoso and Elena Iparraguirre, *Memorias desde Némesis 1993–2000* (2014), 11, at http://bvk.bnp.gob.pe/admin/files/libros/801_digitalizacion.pdf (accessed on 14 January 2018); Roncagliolo, *La cuarta espada*, 33.

14. Guzmán Reinoso and Iparraguirre, *Memorias*, 17.

15. Gustavo Gorriti, 'Shining Path's Stalin and Trotsky', in Scott Palmer, ed., *The Shining Path of Peru*, 152.

16. Simon Strong, *Shining Path: The World's Deadliest Revolutionary Force* (London: Fontana, 1993), 25–6.

17. Ibid., 26–7.

18. Ibid., 26.

19. Ibid., 27.

20. Gustavo Gorriti, 'Documenting the Peruvian Insurrection', Reel 2 (microfilm collection, Princeton University).

21. Ibid.

22. Ibid.

23. Cynthia McClintock, 'Peru's Sendero Luminoso Rebellion: Origins and Trajectory', in Susan Eckstein and Manuel Antonio Garretón Merino, eds, *Power and Popular Protest: Latin American Social Movements* (Berkeley: University of California Press, 2001), 66.

24. Carlos Iván Degregori, *El Surgimiento de Sendero Luminoso: Ayacucho 1969–1979* (Lima: Instituto de Estudios Peruanos, 2010), 29, 33.

25. Jaymie Heilman, *Before the Shining Path: Politics in Rural Ayacucho, 1895–1980* (Stanford, CA: Stanford University Press, 2010), 12.

26. Degregori, *El Surgimiento*, 34.

27. Ibid., 36.

28. Roncagliolo, *La cuarta espada*, 48.

29. Strong, *Shining Path*, 31.

30. Roncagliolo, *La cuarta espada*, 56.

31. Carlos Iván Degregori, *How Difficult It Is to Be God: Shining Path's Politics of War in Peru, 1980–1999*, ed. Steve J. Stern, trans. Nancy Appelbaum (Madison: University of Wisconsin Press, 2012), 104, 108, 106.

32. Rothwell, *Transpacific Revolutionaries*, 27.

33. Gorriti, 'Shining Path's Stalin', 160–1.

34. Strong, *Shining Path*, 33.

35. See reminiscences in Guzmán Reinoso and Iparraguirre, *Memorias*, 48–50.

36. Strong, *Shining Path*, 33.

37. Guzmán Reinoso and Iparraguirre, *Memorias*, 32.

38. Ibid., 83, 82.

39. Ibid., 84–5.

40. Abimael Guzmán, 'Interview with Chairman Gonzalo', interview by Luis Arce Borja and Janet Talavera, *A World to Win* 18 (1992): 79, at http://bannedthought.net/International/RIM/AWTW/1992-18/GonzaloInterview-1988.pdf (accessed on 15 January 2018), 79.

41. Toledo Brückmann, . . . *Y llegó Mao*, 153.

42. Guzmán Reinoso and Iparraguirre, *Memorias*, 258, 220, 209, 193, 90; Antonio Zapata, 'Elena Yparraguirre: La Mirada de la Número Tres', unpublished paper given at the conference 'The Shining Path: Maoism and Violence in Peru', Stanford University, February 2016, 7.

43. Miguel La Serna and Orin Starn, *The Shining Path: Love, Madness, and Revolution in the Andes* (manuscript copy; forthcoming New York: Norton, 2019), 67.

44. Guzmán Reinoso and Iparraguirre, *Memorias*, 85, 98–9, 177, 169.

45. Michael L. Smith, 'Taking the High Ground: Shining Path and the Andes', in Scott Palmer, ed., *The Shining Path of Peru*, 27.

46. Zapata, 'Elena Yparraguirre', 10.

47. Degregori, *How Difficult It Is to Be God*, 22.

48. Rothwell, *Transpacific Revolutionaries*, 60. See also Colin Harding, 'Antonio Díaz Martínez and the Ideology of Sendero Luminoso', *Bulletin of Latin American Research* 7.1 (1988): 65–73.

49. La Serna and Starn, *The Shining Path*, 78.

50. Rothwell, *Transpacific Revolutionaries*, 61–2.

51. De Wit and Gianotten, 'The Center's Multiple Failures', 45.

52. Ronald H. Berg, 'Peasant Responses to Shining Path in Andahuaylas', in Scott Palmer, ed., *The Shining Path of Peru*, 98.

53. Rothwell, *Transpacific Revolutionaries*, 7.

54. De Wit and Gianotten, 'The Center's Multiple Failures', 46.

55. Gustavo Gorriti, *The Shining Path: A History of the Millenarian War in Peru*, trans. Robin Kirk (Chapel Hill: University of North Carolina Press, 1999), 91.

56. La Serna and Starn, *The Shining Path*, 71.

57. Heilman, *Before the Shining Path*, 182.

58. Zapata, 'Elena Yparraguirre', 7, 5 and *passim*.

59. Gorriti, *The Shining Path*, 63.

60. Heilman, *Before the Shining Path*, 180.

61. Ibid., 184.

62. Degregori, *How Difficult It Is to Be God*, 116, 136.

63. Ibid., 116.

64. Ibid., 125–31.

65. Guzmán Reinoso and Iparraguirre, *Memorias*, 408–9.

66. Abimael Guzmán Reinoso and Elena Iparraguirre, interview with the Commission for Truth and Reconciliation, 29 October 2002 (Cassette BN 29/X/02 – AGR –EI), available at http://grancomboclub.com/wp-content/uploads/2012/07/ABIMAEL-GUZMAN-REYNOSO-y-ELENA-IPARRA GUIRRE.pdf (accessed on 15 January 2018).

67. Gorriti, *The Shining Path*, 17–18, 65.

68. Ibid., 17–35.

69. Ibid., 76, 98.

70. Ibid., 104–5.

71. Ibid., 106.

72. Ibid., 223.

73. Ibid., 250–4.

74. Lurgio Gavilán Sánchez, *When Rains Became Floods: A Child Soldier's Story*, trans. Margaret Randall (Durham, NC: Duke University Press, 2017), 19–20.

75. Gorriti, *The Shining Path*, 117.

76. Ibid., 40–2, 202, 48.

77. Strong, *Shining Path*, 104.

78. Robin Kirk, *Grabado en piedra: las mujeres de Sendero Luminoso*, trans. Enrique Bossio (Lima: Instituto de Estudios Peruanos, 1993), 39–40.

79. José Luis Rénique, *La Voluntad Encarcelada: Las 'Luminosas trincheras de combate' de Sendero Luminoso del Perú* (Lima: Instituto de Estudios Peruanos, 2003), 58.

80. *State of Fear: The Truth About Terrorism* (documentary), at https://www.youtube.com/watch?v=WCıhAJOi6BE (accessed on 18 January 2018); Gavilán Sánchez, *When Rains Became Floods*, 55.

81. Orin Starn, Carlos Iván Degregori and Robin Kirk, eds, *The Peru Reader: History, Culture, Politics* (Durham, NC: Duke University Press, 2009), 358, 361.

82. Orin Starn, 'Villagers at Arms: War and Counterrevolution in the Central-South Andes', in Stern, ed., *Shining and Other Paths*, 237.

83. Gorriti, *The Shining Path*, 110.

84. Ibid., 108.

85. Ibid., 69.

86. Ibid., 132–7.

87. Zapata, 'Elena Yparraguirre', 22–3.

88. Marisol de la Cadena, 'From Race to Class: Insurgent Intellectuals *de provincia* in Peru, 1910–1970', in Stern, ed., *Shining and Other Paths*, 52–3.

89. La Serna and Starn, *The Shining Path*, 311.

90. James R. Mensch, 'Violence and Blindness: The Case of Uchuraccay', at https://www.opendemocracy.net/article/violence-and-blindness-the-case-of-uchuraccay (accessed on 18 January 2018); Ponciano del Pino H., 'Family, Culture, and "Revolution": Everyday Life with Sendero Luminoso', in Stern, ed., *Shining and Other Paths*, 163.

91. Combination of translations from Carlos Iván Degregori, 'Harvesting Storms: Peasant *Rondas* and the Defeat of Sendero Luminoso in Ayacucho', in Stern, ed., *Shining and Other Paths*, 143, and Guzmán, 'Interview with Chairman Gonzalo', 56.

92. Lewis Taylor, *Shining Path: Guerrilla War in Peru's Northern Highlands, 1980–1997* (Liverpool: Liverpool University Press, 2006), 106.

93. Ibid., 166.

94. Del Pino H., 'Family', 171.

95. Gavilán Sánchez, *When Rains Became Floods*, 15.

96. Del Pino H., 'Family', 181, 171.

97. See, for example, Edilberto Jiménez Quispe, 'Chungui: Ethnographic Drawings of Violence and Traces of Memory', in Cynthia E. Milton, ed., *Art from a Fractured Past: Memory and Truth Telling in Post-Shining Path Peru* (Durham, NC: Duke University Press, 2014), 87.

98. Nelson Manrique, 'The War for the Central Sierra', in Stern, ed., *Shining and Other Paths*, 214.

99. Del Pino H., 'Family', 186–7.

100. Billie Jean Isbell, 'Shining Path and Peasant Responses in Rural Ayacucho', in Scott Palmer, ed., *The Shining Path of Peru*, 74.

101. Starn, 'Villagers at Arms', 232.

102. Gavilán Sánchez, *When Rains Became Floods*, 61.

103. Starn, 'Villagers at Arms', 244.

104. Kirk, *Grabado en piedra*, 14, 18.

105. Heilman, *Before the Shining Path*, 101.

106. Kirk, *Grabado en piedra*, 70.

107. Zapata, 'Elena Yparraguirre', 21.

108. Ibid., 20.

109. See, for example, https://www.google.co.uk/search?hl=en&biw=1275&bih=854&tbm=isch&sa=1&q=sendero+luminoso+poster&oq=sendero+luminoso+poster&gs_l=psy-ab.12...70920.71418.0.73655.7.6.0.0.0.0.127.406.3j2.5.0....0...1.1.64.psy-ab..2.2.160...0j0i30k1j0i8i30k1.XoWlUH5tTnw#imgrc=HpeqoYK-AhU17M:

110. Starn et al., eds, *The Peru Reader*, 351.

111. Degregori, *How Difficult It Is to Be God*, 22.

112. See discussion in ibid., 77–81.

113. Gorriti, *The Shining Path*, 29–31.

114. Ibid., 127.

115. Cynthia McClintock, 'Theories of Revolution and the Case of Peru', in Scott Palmer, ed., *The Shining Path of Peru*, 232.

116. La Serna and Starn, *The Shining Path*, 92.

117. De Wit and Gianotten, 'The Center's Multiple Failures', 46.

118. McClintock, 'Theories', 232.

119. Isbell, 'Shining Path', 66.

120. Gorriti, *The Shining Path*, 188.

121. Degregori, *How Difficult It Is to Be God*, 24–5.

122. *State of Fear*.

123. Rénique, *La Voluntad Encarcelada*, 77.

124. See images and interviews in *People of the Shining Path* at https://www.youtube.com/watch?v=-HnH-MguElU (accessed on 19 January 2018) and *State of Fear*.

125. Gorriti, 'Shining Path's Stalin', 167.

126. Gabriela Tarazona-Sevillano, 'The Organization of Shining Path', in Scott Palmer, ed., *The Shining Path of Peru*, 179.

127. Kirk, *Grabado en piedra*, 58.

128. *State of Fear*.

129. Nathaniel C. Nash, 'Blow to Rebels in Peru: An Elusive Aura Is Lost', *New York Times*, 14 September 1992.

130. For an account of these events, see *Caretas*, 17 September 1992.

131. Robin Kirk, *The Monkey's Paw: New Chronicles from Peru* (Amherst: University of Massachusetts Press, 1997), 207.

132. See *People & Power – The New Shining Path*, at https://www.youtube.com/watch?v=oeyyENWusvo (accessed on 19 January 2018).

133. Paraphrase of Fujimori speech by General Rodolfo Robles, in *State of Fear* (53 minutes in).

134. Degregori, *How Difficult It Is to Be God*, 45–6.

135. Jiménez Quispe, 'Chungui', 88–9.

136. Gavilán Sánchez, *When Rains Became Floods*, 87, 3–6.

137. Ibid., 18, 119.

138. Ibid., 18, 36, 26, 39, 67.

139. Ibid., 88, 90.

140. Ibid., 93–7.

10 *China's Chairman Is Our Chairman*

1. See, for example, https://www.bricsmagazine.com/en/articles/the-dragon-vs-the-elephant.

2. See, for example, 'Naxalism Biggest Threat to Internal Security: Manmohan', *The Hindu*, 24 May 2010, at http://www.thehindu.com/news/national/naxalism-biggest-threat-to-internal-security-manmohan/article436781.ece (accessed on 9 January 2018).

3. 'Indian Minister: Maoists Are a Greater Threat Than Islamic Terrorists', *Foreign Policy* 12, March 2010, at http://foreignpolicy.com/2010/03/12/indian -minister-maoists-are-a-greater-threat-than-islamic-terrorists/ (accessed on 9 January 2018).
4. Private communication.
5. Sumanta Banerjee, *India's Simmering Revolution: The Naxalite Uprising* (London: Zed Books, 1984), 61.
6. Ibid., 62.
7. Jonathan Kennedy and Sunil Purushotham, 'Beyond Naxalbari: A Comparative Analysis of Maoist Insurgency and Counterinsurgency in Independent India', *Comparative Studies in Society and History* 54.4 (2012): 835–6.
8. Banerjee, *India's Simmering Revolution*, 22.
9. Ibid., 19.
10. Ibid., 23.
11. Ibid., 71.
12. Bappaditya Paul, *The First Naxal: An Authorised Biography of Kanu Sanyal* (Los Angeles: Sage, 2014), 80.
13. Ibid.
14. Ibid.
15. Ashoke Kumar Mukhopadhyay, *The Naxalites Through the Eyes of the Police: Select Notifications from the Calcutta Police Gazette (1967–1975)* (Kolkata: Dey's Publishing, 2007), 175.
16. Abhijit Mazumdar, interview, 4 December 2016, Siliguri.
17. Arun Mukherjee, *Maoist Spring Thunder: The Naxalite Movement 1967–1972* (Kolkata: K. P. Bagchi & Co., 2007), 11.
18. Henrike Donner, 'The Significance of Naxalbari: Accounts of Personal Involvement and Politics in West Bengal', Occasional Paper, Centre of South Asian Studies, University of Cambridge, 2004, 9; Paul, *The First Naxal*, 37–8.
19. Alan Truscott, 'The Naxalites, Whose Extremism Knows No Extremes, Are Indian Revolutionaries with a Chinese Accent', *New York Times*, 8 November 1970, at http://www.nytimes.com/1970/11/08/archives/the-naxalites -whose-extremism-knows-no-extremes-are-indian-indian.html (accessed on 9 January 2018).
20. Ibid.
21. Mazumdar, interview.
22. Dilip Simeon, interview, 3 December 2016, Delhi.
23. Truscott, 'The Naxalites'.
24. Charu Mazumdar, 'Eight Historic Documents', at https://ajadhind.word press.com/historic-documents-charu-mazumdar/ (accessed on 9 January 2018); Paul, *The First Naxal*, 85.
25. Banerjee, *India's Simmering Revolution*, 1–2.

26. Bela Bhatia, 'The Naxalite Movement in Central Bihar', unpublished PhD dissertation, University of Cambridge, 2000, 20–2.

27. Paul, *The First Naxal*, 96.

28. Ibid., 98.

29. Ibid., 98–103.

30. Dilip Simeon, 'Rebellion to Reconciliation', in B. G. Verghese, ed., *Tomorrow's India: Another Tryst with Destiny* (New Delhi: Penguin India, 2006) (manuscript copy obtained from author).

31. Paul, *The First Naxal*, 144.

32. *Liberation*, 3.7–9 (May–July 1970), 18, 20, 25, at http://www.bannedthought.net/India/CPI(ML)-Orig/Liberation/1970-MayJul/Liberation-v3n7-9-70 MayJul.pdf (accessed on 9 January 2018).

33. Mukhopadhyay, *The Naxalites*, 87.

34. Truscott, 'The Naxalites'.

35. Dilip Simeon, 'Permanent Spring,' at http://www.india-seminar.com/2010/607/607_dilip_simeon.htm (accessed on 9 January 2018).

36. Truscott, 'The Naxalites'.

37. Ibid.

38. Sreemati Chakrabarti, *China and the Naxalites* (London: Sangam, 1990), 61.

39. Mazumdar, interview.

40. My search was done on 18 January 2017.

41. 'Spring Thunder Over India', *Peking Review*, 14 July 1967, 22–3.

42. Ibid.

43. Paul, *The First Naxal*, 130.

44. Ibid., 129.

45. Minutes of Mao's conversation with the Indian Communist Party delegation, 13 December 1967, accessed through private archival collection.

46. Paul, *The First Naxal*, 131.

47. Simeon, interview.

48. Dilip Simeon, *Revolution Highway* (New Delhi: Penguin Books India, 2010), 154–60.

49. Paul, *The First Naxal*, 160.

50. Ibid., 148.

51. Banerjee, *India's Simmering Revolution*, 257.

52. Simeon, interview.

53. Ibid.

54. Paul, *The First Naxal*, 161; Amnesty International, *Short Report on Detention Conditions in West Bengal Jails*, September 1974, 3.

55. Amnesty International, *Short Report*, 4.

56. Ibid., 6–7.

57. Chakrabarti, *China and the Naxalites*, 107.

58. Bidyut Chakravarty and Rajat Kumar Kujur, *Maoism in India: Reincarnation of Ultra-Left-Wing Extremism in the Twenty-first Century* (London: Routledge, 2009), 50.

59. Ibid., 48.

60. Ibid., 49.

61. Ibid., 53.

62. Supriya Sharma, 'Guns and Protests: Media Coverage of the Conflicts in the Indian State of Chhattisgarh', Reuters Institute Fellowship Paper, University of Oxford, 2012, 17, at https://reutersinstitute.politics.ox.ac.uk/sites/default/files/Guns%20and%20Protests%20Media%20coverage%20of%20the%20conflicts%20in%20the%20Indian%20state%20of%20Chhattisgarh.pdf (accessed on 9 January 2018).

63. Rahul Pandita, *Hello Bastar: The Untold Story of India's Maoist Movement* (Chennai: Tranquebar, 2011), 39.

64. Rahul Pandita, interview, 3 December 2016, Delhi.

65. Ibid.

66. Satnam, *Jangalnama: Travels in a Maoist Guerilla Zone*, trans. Vishav Bharti (New Delhi: Penguin India, 2010), 93.

67. Pandita, *Hello Bastar*, 53–6.

68. Pandita, interview.

69. Pandita, *Hello Bastar*, 62–4.

70. 'The Lady Naxals', at http://naxalrevolution.blogspot.co.uk/2010/09/lady-naxals-open-magazine.html (accessed on 9 January 2018).

71. Pandita, *Hello Bastar*, 67.

72. P. Kesava Kumar, 'Popular Culture and Ideology: The Phenomenon of Gaddar', at http://untouchablespring.blogspot.co.uk/2006/11/song-of-gaddar.html (accessed on 9 January 2018).

73. Syed Amin Jafri, 'India's Subalterns Too Have a Poet', 2 September 2005, at https://www.countercurrents.org/india-jafri020905.htm (accessed on 9 January 2018).

74. Ajith Pillai, 'Songs of a Revolution', *Outlook*, 29 November 1995, at http://www.outlookindia.com/magazine/story/songs-of-a-revolution/200309 (accessed on 9 January 2018).

75. Pandita, *Hello Bastar*, 127.

76. Constitution of the CPI (Maoist), at http://www.bannedthought.net/India/CPI-Maoist-Docs/#Founding_Documents (accessed on 9 January 2018).

77. Party Programme Central Committee CPI (Maoist), 26, at http://www.bannedthought.net/India/CPI-Maoist-Docs/Founding/Programme-pamphlet.pdf (accessed on 9 January 2018).

78. Pandita, *Hello Bastar*, 134.

79. Ibid., 123; see Alpa Shah, *Nightmarch: Among India's Revolutionary Guerrillas* (London: Hurst, 2018).

80. Supriya Sharma, interview, 2 December 2016, Delhi.

81. 'Development Challenges in Extremist Affected Areas: Report of an Expert Group to Planning Commission', at http://planningcommission.nic.in/reports/publications/rep_dce.pdf (accessed on 9 January 2018).

82. Nandini Sundar, *The Burning Forest: India's War in Bastar* (Delhi: Juggernaut, 2016), 354.

83. Ibid., 28.

84. Ibid., 32–3.

85. Ibid., 33.

86. Ibid., 13.

87. Ibid., 102–3.

88. Ibid., 108–17.

89. Pandita, interview.

90. Arundhati Roy, *Broken Republic: Three Essays* (London: Hamish Hamilton, 2012), 37, 50.

91. The essays are collected together in ibid.

92. Sundar, *The Burning Forest*, 303.

93. Roy, *Broken Republic*, 134.

94. Ganapathi, 'Open Reply to Independent Citizens' Initiative on Dantewada', *Economic and Political Weekly*, 6 January 2007, 71.

95. Pandita, interview.

96. Roy, *Broken Republic*, 208–9.

97. Ibid., 93, 117.

98. For just a sample of Shah's prolific and remarkable writing on this topic, see *Nightmarch* and the essays and articles listed in the bibliography.

99. Aditya Nigam, 'The Rumour of Maoism', Seminar #607, March 2010, at http://www.india-seminar.com/2010/607/607_aditya_nigam.htm (accessed on 9 January 2018).

100. Pandita, *Hello Bastar*, 115.

101. Jason Miklian and Scott Carney, 'Fire in the Hole: How India's Economic Rise Turned an Obscure Communist Revolt into a Raging Resource War', *Foreign Policy*, September/October 2010, 110.

102. Sundar, *The Burning Forest*, 65.

103. Pandita, interview.

104. Simeon, 'Rebellion to Reconciliation'.

105. Simeon, interview.

106. Ibid.

107. Pandita, interview.

108. Sundar, *The Burning Forest*, 45.

109. See, for example, ibid., 343.

110. Pandita, interview.

111. Sundar, *The Burning Forest*, 257.

11 Nepal

1. See Binaj Gurubacharya, 'Opposition Turns Violent Inside Nepal Parliament, on Streets', at https://www.dailystar.com.lb/News/World/2015/Jan-20/284700-opposition-turns-violent-inside-nepal-parliament-on-streets.ashx.

2. Aditya Adhikari, *The Bullet and the Ballot Box: The Story of Nepal's Maoist Revolution* (London: Verso, 2014), 91.

3. Ibid., 37–8.

4. John Whelpton, *A History of Nepal* (Cambridge: Cambridge University Press, 2005), 142; Laxman Kumar Regmi, 'An Overview of Population Growth Trends of Nepal', *Journal of Institute of Science and Technology* 19.1 (2014): 61.

5. Jeevan Raj Sharma and Sanjay Sharma, 'Enumerating Migration in Nepal: A Review', 32 and 46, at https://www.ceslam.org/files/Eumerating%20Migration%20in%20Nepal.pdf (accessed on 10 January 2018).

6. 'Labour Migration for Employment: A Status Report for Nepal, 2014–15', 1, at http://www.ilo.org/wcmsp5/groups/public/-asia/-ro-bangkok/-ilo-kathmandu/documents/publication/wcms_500311.pdf (accessed on 15 May 2018).

7. Whelpton, *A History of Nepal*, 165, 137.

8. Krishna Hachhethu, interview, 13 December 2016, Kathmandu.

9. Whelpton, *A History of Nepal*, 176.

10. Comrade Rohit, interview, 11 December 2016, Kathmandu.

11. C. K. Lal, interview, 9 December 2016, Kathmandu.

12. Baburam Bhattarai and Hisila Yami, interview, 9 December 2016, Kathmandu.

13. Adhikari, *The Bullet and the Ballot Box*, 4–5.

14. Khagendra Sangroula, interview, 9 December 2016, Kathmandu.

15. Michael Hutt, 'Ganga Bahadur's Books: Landmark Proletarian Novels and the Nepali Communist Movement', *Inter-Asia Cultural Studies* 17.3 (2016): 365.

16. Sangroula, interview.

17. Hutt, 'Ganga Bahadur's Books', 365.

18. Ibid., 363.

19. Adhikari, *The Bullet and the Ballot Box*, 1; Sanjay Upadhya, *Nepal and the Geo-strategic Rivalry Between China and India* (London: Routledge, 2012), 87.

20. Adhikari, *The Bullet and the Ballot Box*, 1.

21. See *Peking Review*, 1 November 1963, 4.

22. Nanda R. Shrestha, *Historical Dictionary of Nepal* (Lanham, MD: Rowman & Littlefield, 2017), 63.

23. Sangroula, interview.

24. Hutt, 'Ganga Bahadur's Books', 365.

25. Prashant Jha, *Battles of the New Republic: A Contemporary History of Nepal* (London: Hurst, 2014), 25.

26. Hutt, 'Ganga Bahadur's Books'. For the first analysis of the importance of Gorky's *Mother* within Nepal, see David Gellner and Mrigendra Bahadur Karki, 'The Sociology of Activism in Nepal: Some Preliminary Considerations', in H. Ishii, David Gellner and K. Nawa, eds, *Political and Social Transformations in North India and Nepal (Social Dynamics in Northern South Asia)*, volume 2 (Delhi: Manohar, 2007), 361–97.

27. See the exposition of this idea in Benedict Anderson, *Imagined Communities: Reflections on the Origins and Spread of Nationalism* (London: Verso, 1991). I owe this insight to Ina Zharkevich, 'Learning in a Guerrilla Community of Practice: Literacy Practices, Situated Learning and Youth in Nepal's Maoist Movement', *European Bulletin of Himalayan Research* 42 (2013): 116.

28. Surendra Kumar Karki, interview, 10 December 2016, Nepal.

29. Yami, interview.

30. Sangroula, interview.

31. Mohan Bikram Singh, interview, 12 December 2016, Kathmandu. For an excellent biographical analysis of Mohan Bikram Singh, see Benoît Cailmail, 'A History of Nepalese Maoism since Its Foundation by Mohan Bikram Singh', *European Bulletin of Himalayan Research* 33–34 (2008–2009): 11–38; 'Le Mouvement Maoiste au Nepal, 1949–2008: La tentation de la révolution internationale', unpublished PhD dissertation, Panthéon-Sorbonne University – Paris 1, 2015.

32. Singh, interview.

33. Cailmail, 'A History of Nepalese Maoism', 30.

34. Ibid., 25.

35. Deepak Thapa with Bandita Sijapati, *A Kingdom Under Siege: Nepal's Maoist Insurgency, 1996 to 2003* (London: Zed Books, 2004), 43–5.

36. Kiran, interview, 13 December 2016, Kathmandu.

37. Lal, interview.

38. Marie Lecomte-Tilouine, *Hindu Kingship, Ethnic Revival and Maoist Rebellion in Nepal* (Oxford: Oxford University Press, 2009), 219, 230.

39. Singh, interview.

40. Thapa and Sijapati, *A Kingdom Under Siege*, 59.

41. David Seddon, Ganesh Gurung and Jagannath Adhikari, 'Foreign Labour Migration and the Remittance Economy of Nepal', *Himalaya, the Journal of the Association for Nepal and Himalayan Studies* 18.2 (1998): 5, at http://digitalcommons.macalester.edu/cgi/viewcontent.cgi?article=1598&context=himalaya (accessed on 10 January 2018).

42. Adhikari, *The Bullet and the Ballot Box*, 20–1.

43. Ibid., 141.

44. Ibid., 29.

45. Ibid., 32.
46. Ibid., 33.
47. Ibid., 34–5.
48. Ibid., 35.
49. Thapa and Sijapati, *A Kingdom Under Siege*, 91–2.
50. For just one egregious example, see Amnesty International documentation on the death of Maina Sunuwar, for instance at https://www.amnesty.org.uk/press-releases/nepal-authorities-must-provide-justice-torture-and-murder-15-year-old-girl-maina (accessed on 6 March 2018).
51. Thapa and Sijapati, *A Kingdom Under Siege*, 49.
52. Mandira Sharma and Dinesh Prasain, 'Gender Dimensions of the People's War: Some Reflections on the Experiences of Rural Women', in Michael Hutt, ed., *Himalayan 'People's War': Nepal's Maoist Revolution* (London: Hurst, 2004), 157.
53. Interviews, 10–11 December 2016, Kathmandu.
54. Lal, interview.
55. Marie Lecomte-Tilouine, 'Maoist Despite Themselves: Amid the People's War in a Maoist Model Village, Northern Gulmi', in Marie Lecomte-Tilouine, ed., *Revolution in Nepal: An Anthropological and Historical Approach to the People's War* (New Delhi: Oxford University Press, 2013), 226.
56. Satya Shrestha-Schipper, 'Women's Participation in the People's War in Jumla', *European Bulletin of Himalayan Research* 33–34 (2008–2009): 108.
57. Sharma and Prasain, 'Gender Dimensions', 163.
58. Michelle J. Lee, 'Nine Years Later, Still in Shock,' *Nepali Times*, 27 June–3 July 2014, at http://nepalitimes.com/article/nation/madi-bus-bomb-blast-nine-years-later,1474 (accessed on 12 January 2018).
59. See Sudheer Sharma's analysis in 'The Maoist Movement: An Evolutionary Perspective', in Hutt, ed., *Himalayan 'People's War'*, 51–3.
60. 'One Year of the People's War in Nepal', in Arjun Karki and David Seddon, eds, *The People's War in Nepal: Left Perspectives* (Delhi: Adroit Publishers, 2003), 220.
61. Jha, *Battles*, 27; Thapa and Sijapati, *A Kingdom Under Siege*, 98.
62. Lecomte-Tilouine, *Hindu Kingship*, 226.
63. Adhikari, *The Bullet and the Ballot Box*, 108.
64. Lecomte-Tilouine, 'Maoist Despite Themselves', 224–5, 233.
65. Satya Shrestha-Schipper, 'The Political Context and the Influence of the People's War in Jumla', in Lecomte-Tilouine, ed., *Revolution in Nepal*, 273.
66. Adhikari, *The Bullet and the Ballot Box*, 43–4.
67. Lecomte-Tilouine, 'Maoist Despite Themselves', 232–3.
68. Adhikari, *The Bullet and the Ballot Box*, 126.
69. Ibid., 106–7.
70. Shrestha-Schipper, 'Women's Participation': 107.

71. Lecomte-Tilouine, 'Maoist Despite Themselves', 235–6.

72. Ibid., 236–7.

73. Kiyoko Ogura, 'Maoist People's Governments 2001–2005: The Power in Wartime', in David N. Gellner and Krishna Hachhethu, eds., *Local Democracy in South Asia: Microprocesses of Democratization in Nepal and Its Neighbours*, Volume 1 (New Delhi: Sage, 2008), 212.

74. Judith Pettigrew, *Maoists at the Hearth: Everyday Life in Nepal's Civil War* (Philadelphia: University of Pennsylvania Press, 2013), 78, 82.

75. Carine Jaquet, '"One Should Not Cut the Blossom in the Bud": Voices of Nepalese Child Soldiers', *European Bulletin of Himalayan Research* 33–34 (2008–2009): 175–85.

76. Lecomte-Tilouine, 'Maoist Despite Themselves', 247–8.

77. Ogura, 'Maoist People's Governments', 210.

78. Pustak Ghimire, 'The Maoists in Eastern Nepal: The Example of Khotang', in Lecomte-Tilouine, ed., *Revolution in Nepal*, 125.

79. Adhikari, *The Bullet and the Ballot Box*, 149.

80. Ibid., 112. See also Kiyoko Ogura, 'Reality and Images of Nepal's Maoists After the Attack on Beni', *European Bulletin of Himalayan Research* 27 (September 2004): 67–25.

81. Adhikari, *The Bullet and the Ballot Box*, 73–6.

82. Ibid., 69–70.

83. Jha, *Battles*, 144.

84. Adhikari, *The Bullet and the Ballot Box*, 168–9.

85. Adhikari, *The Bullet and the Ballot Box*, 175.

86. Kåre Vollan, 'Group Representation and the System of Representation in the Constituent Assembly and Future Parliaments of Nepal', at http://www.follesdal.net/projects/ratify/nepal/Vollan-2011-The-development-of-an-electoral-system.pdf, 8 (accessed on 16 February 2018).

87. Mahendra Lawoti, 'Ethnic Politics and the Building of an Inclusive State', and Catinca Slavu, 'The 2008 Constituent Assembly Election: Social Inclusion for Peace', both in Sebastian von Einsiedel and David M. Malone, eds, *Nepal in Transition: From People's War to Fragile Peace* (Cambridge: Cambridge University Press, 2012), 139, 244, 249.

88. Human Rights Watch, '"Like We Are Not Nepali": Protest and Police Crackdown in the Terai Region of Nepal', at https://www.hrw.org/report/2015/10/16/we-are-not-nepali/protest-and-police-crackdown-terai-region-nepal (accessed on 16 February 2018).

89. Charles Haviland, 'Why Is Nepal's New Constitution Controversial?', 19 September 2015, at http://www.bbc.co.uk/news/world-asia-34280015 (accessed on 12 January 2018).

90. Bhadra Sharma and Nida Najar, 'Amid Protests, Nepal Adopts Constitution', *New York Times*, 20 September 2015, at https://www.nytimes.com/2015/09/21/world/asia/amid-protests-nepal-adopts-constitution.html?action

=click&contentCollection=Asia%20Pacific&module=RelatedCoverage& region=EndOfArticle&pgtype=article (accessed on 12 January 2018).

91. Thomas Bell, *Kathmandu* (London: Haus, 2016), 63.

92. See, for example, Kamal Dev Bhattarai, 'The Geopolitics of Nepal's Federal Structure', *The Diplomat*, 27 October 2014, at https://thediplomat.com /2014/10/the-geopolitics-of-nepals-federal-structure/ (accessed on 12 January 2018).

93. See Jha, *Battles*, 277, for a version of this.

94. Personal communication.

95. Adhikari, *The Bullet and the Ballot Box*, 229.

96. Sudheer Sharma, interview, 13 December 2016, Kathmandu.

97. Hachhethu, interview.

98. Lal, interview.

99. Aditya Adhikari, 'The Communist Dream', *Kathmandu Post*, 18 October 2017, at http://kathmandupost.ekantipur.com/news/2017-10-18/the -communist-dream.html (accessed on 31 July 2018).

100. Lal, interview.

101. Yami, interview.

102. Kiran, interview.

12 Mao-ish China

1. Ruru Li, 'Sino the Times: Three Spoken Drama Productions on the Beijing Stage', *Drama Review* 45.2 (Summer 2001): 137–40.

2. Wu Hung, *Remaking Beijing: Tiananmen Square and the Creation of a Political Space* (Chicago: University of Chicago Press, 2005), 34.

3. *Jianzhu xuebao* 4 (1977), 4.

4. See Frank Dikötter, *The Cultural Revolution: A People's History, 1962–1976* (London: Bloomsbury, 2016), 276.

5. Geremie R. Barmé, *Shades of Mao: The Posthumous Cult of the Great Leader* (New York: M. E. Sharpe, 1996), 5.

6. Alexander C. Cook, ed., *Mao's Little Red Book: A Global History* (Cambridge: Cambridge University Press, 2014), xiii.

7. Barmé, *Shades of Mao*, 6–11.

8. Richard Bodman, 'From History to Allegory to Art: A Personal Search for Interpretation', in *Deathsong of the River: A Reader's Guide to the Chinese TV Series Heshang,* trans. and eds. Richard W. Bodman and Pin P. Wan (Ithaca, NY: Cornell University, 1991), 34.

9. John Pomfret, *Chinese Lessons: Five Classmates and the Story of New China* (New York: Henry Holt, 2006), 66.

10. See conversation in Lee Kuan Yew, *From Third World to First: Singapore and the Asian Economic Boom* (New York: Harper, 2011), 599–600; Chin Peng,

Alias Chin Peng–My Side of History: Recollections of a Revolutionary Leader (Singapore: Media Masters, 2003), 458–9.

11. Ah Cheng, *Yilu jianxin xiangqian zou – wo fuze de shiming, xu* (A Tough Road Forward – My Mission, continued) (Johor: Hasanah Sin Bt. Abdullah, 2009), 300.

12. Yang Meihong, *Yingsu huahong: Wo zai Miangong shiwu nian* (Red Poppies: The Fifteen Years I Spent in the Burmese Communist Party) (Hong Kong: Tiandi tushu, 2009), 276–8.

13. Private communication.

14. Zhisui Li, *The Private Life of Chairman Mao: The Memoirs of Mao's Personal Physician*, trans. Tai Hung-chao (London: Arrow Books, 1996), 17.

15. Oriana Fallaci, 'Deng: Cleaning Up Mao's "Feudal Mistakes"', *Washington Post*, 31 August 1980. Cited in Jude Blanchette, *Under the Red Flag: The Battle for the Soul of the Communist Party in a Reforming China* (Oxford: Oxford University Press, forthcoming), Chapter One.

16. Blanchette, *Under the Red Flag*, Chapter One; Robert Suettinger, 'Negotiating History: The Chinese Communist Party's 1981', 11, at http://www.project 2049.net/documents/Negotiating%20History%20CCP_Suettinger%20 2049%20Institute.pdf (accessed on 8 January 2018).

17. Suettinger, 'Negotiating History', 13.

18. Ibid., 13.

19. 'Resolution on Certain Questions in the History of Our Party Since the Founding of the People's Republic of China', at https://www.marxists.org/ subject/china/documents/cpc/history/01.htm (accessed on 8 January 2018).

20. Suettinger, 'Negotiating History,' 17.

21. Blanchette, *Under the Red Flag*, Chapter One.

22. Ibid.

23. James Hershberg, Sergey Radchenko, Peter Vamos and David Wolff, 'The Interkit Story: A Window into the Final Decades of the Sino-Soviet Relationship', Cold War International History Project Working Paper, February 2011, 27, at https://www.wilsoncenter.org/sites/default/files/ Working_Paper_63.pdf (accessed on 8 January 2018).

24. Barry Naughton, 'Deng Xiaoping: The Economist', *China Quarterly* 135: 491–514. Cited in Blanchette, *Under the Red Flag*, Chapter Two.

25. Zhao Ziyang, *Prisoner of the State: The Secret Journal of Chinese Premier Zhao Ziyang* (London: Pocket Books, 2010), 163.

26. Christopher S. Wren, 'China Honors Mao with Selective Fanfare', *New York Times*, 25 December 1983, at http://www.nytimes.com/1983/12/25/world/ china-honors-mao-with-selective-fanfare.html (accessed on 8 January 2018). See also Blanchette, *Under the Red Flag*, Chapter Two.

27. Orville Schell, *Discos and Democracy: China in the Throes of Reform* (New York: Pantheon Books, 1988), 14.

28. Zhao, *Prisoner of the State*, 11.

29. For these, and further details, see the account in Geremie R. Barmé, *In the Red: On Contemporary Chinese Culture* (New York: Columbia University Press, 1997), 20–37.

30. Barmé, *Shades of Mao*, 9.

31. Ibid., 23.

32. Ibid., 25.

33. Ibid., 37.

34. Ching Kwan Lee, 'What Was Socialism to Chinese Workers? Collective Memories and Labor Politics in an Age of Reform', in Ching Kwan Lee and Guobin Yang, eds, *Re-envisioning the Chinese Revolution: The Politics and Poetics of Collective Memories in Reform China* (Stanford, CA: Stanford University Press, 2007), 158; Philip Pan, *Out of Mao's Shadow: The Struggle for the Soul of a New China* (London: Picador, 2008), 120–46.

35. Personal communication.

36. Blanchette, *Under the Red Flag*.

37. Andy Yinan Hu, 'Swimming Against the Tide: Tracing and Locating Chinese Leftism Online', unpublished MA dissertation, Simon Fraser University, 2006, 80–1.

38. Ibid., 81.

39. As an indication of how sensitive the topic of post-2003, popular Maoism is, I have only found one PRC master's dissertation on the subject: Cui Jinke, 'Dangdai "Mao Zedong zuopai" sixiang fenxi – yi "wuyouzhixiang wangzhan weili' (An Analysis of Contemporary Maoist Thought, Focused on Utopia Website), unpublished MA dissertation, Beijing University, 2013. I am grateful to Daniel Leese for sending this to me.

40. Hu, 'Swimming Against the Tide', 161.

41. Ibid., 130.

42. Cui, 'Dangdai "Mao Zedong zuopai"', 11.

43. Ibid., 13.

44. Ibid., 14.

45. Ibid.

46. Ibid., 15–20.

47. Ibid., 24, 21.

48. Ibid., 20.

49. Ibid., 18.

50. Oiwan Lam, 'China: Hang the Slaves of the West', 30 November 2010, at https://globalvoices.org/2010/11/30/china-hang-the-slaves-of-the-west/ (accessed on 8 January 2018).

51. David Bandurski, 'Heckled by the Left, Again', 26 April 2013, at http://cmp.hku.hk/2013/04/26/heckled-by-the-left-again/ (accessed on 8 January 2018).

52. David Bandurski, 'Forum Denounces Economist Mao Yushi', 30 May 2011, at http://cmp.hku.hk/2011/05/30/forum-denounces-economist-mao-yushi/ (accessed on 8 January 2018).

53. Jude Blanchette, 'Still Holding High Mao's Banner', *China Economic Quarterly*, June 2017, 51.

54. Cui, 'Dangdai "Mao Zedong zuopai"', 32, 9.

55. David Bandurski, 'Rare Essay Humbles Mao Zedong', 28 April 2011, at http://cmp.hku.hk/2011/04/28/chairman-mao-humbled-in-rare-essay/ (accessed on 8 January 2018).

56. 'Boundlessly Loyal to the Great Monster', *The Economist*, 26 May 2011, at http://www.economist.com/node/18744533?story_id=18744533 (accessed on 8 January 2018).

57. John Garnaut, *The Rise and Fall of the House of Bo: How a Murder Exposed the Cracks in China's Leadership* (Beijing: Penguin China, 2012), loc 577.

58. 'Biggest Mao Zedong Statue Unveiled in China: Report', at http://www.sinodaily.com/reports/Biggest_Mao_Zedong_statue_unveiled_in_China_report_999.html (accessed on 23 July 2018).

59. Garnaut, *The Rise and Fall of the House of Bo*, loc 602.

60. Xujun Eberlein, 'On Bo Xilai's "Chongqing Model"', 20 March 2012, at https://insideoutchina.blogspot.co.uk/2012/03/bo-xilais-chongqing-model.html (accessed on 8 January 2018).

61. Kathrin Hille and Jamil Anderlini, 'China: Mao and the Next Generation', *Financial Times*, 7 July 2011, at http://www.ftchinese.com/story/001039457/en?page=2 (accessed on 8 January 2018).

62. John Garnaut, 'Profound Shift as China Marches Back to Mao', *Sydney Morning Herald*, 9 October 2011, at http://www.smh.com.au/world/profound-shift-as-china-marches-back-to-mao-20111008-1lewz.html (accessed on 8 January 2018).

63. 'Understanding Chinese President Xi's Anti-corruption Campaign', *The Conversation*, 27 October 2017, at http://theconversation.com/understanding-chinese-president-xis-anti-corruption-campaign-86396; 'China Murder Suspect's Sisters Ran $126 Million Business Empire', Bloomberg, 14 April 2012, at https://www.bloomberg.com/news/articles/2012-04-13/china-murder-suspect-s-sisters-ran-126-million-business-empire (accessed on 8 January 2018).

64. See https://www.youtube.com/watch?v=6AcSEaOBrng&t=131s (accessed on 8 January 2018).

65. Tom Phillips, 'Xi Jinping Becomes Most Powerful Leader Since Mao with China's Change to Constitution', at https://www.theguardian.com/world/2017/oct/24/xi-jinping-mao-thought-on-socialism-china-constitution; https://twitter.com/xinwenxiaojie/status/929705310230478848; 'Xi Jinping: Xinshidai de lingluren' (Xi Jinping: Pathfinder for the New Era), at http://www.xinhuanet.com/2017-11/17/c_1121968350.htm (all accessed on 16 May 2018).

66. See https://twitter.com/XHNews/status/931333019020951552.

67. See Tom Phillips, 'Singing Xi's Praises: Chorus of Chinese Pop Songs Celebrate President', at https://www.theguardian.com/world/2016/mar

/30/xi-jinping-chorus-of-chinese-pop-songs-celebrate-president (accessed on 8 January 2018).

68. Sangkuk Li, 'An Institutional Analysis of Xi Jinping's Centralization of Power', *Journal of Contemporary China* 26.105 (2017): 325–36.

69. *Yongyuan zai lushang* (Always on the Road) at https://www.youtube.com/watch?v=qbgsWn5gMDs (accessed on 8 January 2018).

70. 'Xi: Holding High Banner of Mao "Forever",' *Xinhua*, 26 December 2013, at http://www.china.org.cn/china/2013-12/26/content_31015643.htm (accessed on 29 July 2018).

71. Kerry Brown, *The New Emperors: Power and the Princelings in China* (London: I. B. Tauris, 2014), 134.

72. David Bandurski, 'China's Political Discourse in 2013', 6 January 2014, at http://chinamediaproject.org/2014/01/06/chinas-political-discourse-in-2013/ (accessed on 8 January 2018).

73. Damien Ma, 'Can China's Xi Pivot From Disrupter-in-Chief to Reformer-in-Chief?', *World Politics Review*, 15 November 2016, at http://www.worldpoliticsreview.com/articles/20460/can-china-s-xi-pivot-from-disrupter-in-chief-to-reformer-in-chief (accessed on 8 January 2018).

74. 'Han Deqiang chuangban de Zhengdao Nongchang zhengshi xuangao: dao niandi tingban' (Han Deqiang's Righteousness Farm Formally Announces That It Will Close Down at the End of the Year), 26 August 2016, at http://www.szhgh.com/Article/health/food/2016-08-26/120019.html (accessed on 8 January 2018).

75. See https://www.youtube.com/watch?v=cm5w3bCpbQg.

76. Chen Yizhong, 'Yongyuan de zaofanpai – Yuan Yuhua xiansheng fangtanlu' (The Eternal Rebel: A Conversation with Mr Yuan Yuhua) at http://www.wengewang.org/read.php?tid=30237 (accessed on 8 January 2018).

77. Kerry Brown and Simone van Nieuwenhuizen, *China and the New Maoists* (London: Zed Books, 2016), 66.

78. Zhang Chengzhi, *Koueihei no jidai* (The Red Guard Era), trans. Kojima Shinji and Tadokoro Takehiko (Tokyo: Iwanami shoten, 1992), 70, 188, 193.

79. Barmé, *Shades of Mao*, 274.

80. Zhang Chengzhi, 'Yisilan yao nuli yu Zhongguo wenming jiehe' (Islam Must Strive to Unite with Chinese Civilization), 2005, at http://history.sina.com.cn/idea/rw/2014-03-17/104185358.shtml (accessed on 26 January 2016).

81. Zhang Chengzhi, *Wuse de yiduan* (Five Colours of Heresy) (Hong Kong: Dafeng chubanshe, 2007) 223–30; Zhang Chengzhi, *Zhi Riben: jingzhong yu xibie* (Japan: To Cherish and Respect) (Shanghai: Shanghai wenyi chubanshe, 2015), 107–53.

82. William R. Farrell, *Blood and Rage: The Story of the Japanese Red Army* (Lexington, MA: Lexington Books, 1990).

83. Hai Pengfei, 'Zhang Chengzhi: Zoubuchu wutuobang' (Zhang Chengzhi: Forever in Utopia), *Nanfang renwu zhoukan*, 30 June 2014, at http://www .nfpeople.com/story_view.php?id=5532 (accessed on 26 January 2016).

84. See, for example, Zhang Chengzhi, *Jinmuchang* (The Golden Pasture) (Beijing: Zuojia chubanshe, 1987); Zhang Chengzhi, *Beifang de he* (Rivers of the North) (Beijing: Zuojia chubanshe, 2000).

85. Zhang, *Wuse*, 53.

86. Zhang, *Koueihei no jidai*, 102.

87. Zhang, *Wuse*, 281–2.

88. Zhang Chengzhi, 'Wenxue yu Zhengyi: zai Zhongguo Renmin Daxue wenxueyuan de yanjiang' (Literature and Righteousness: A Lecture Given at the Institute of Literature at People's University), *Dangdai wentan* 6 (2013): 6.

89. For more details, see Julia Lovell, 'From Beijing to Palestine: Zhang Chengzhi's Journeys from Red Guard Radicalism to Global Islam', *Journal of Asian Studies* 75.4 (November 2016): 891–911.

90. Lucy Hornby and Tom Hancock, 'China Cracks Down on Mao Critics', *Financial Times*, 22 January 2017; Raymond Li, 'Liberal Economist Mao Yushi Warns of a "Leftist Revival" in China', *South China Morning Post*, 26 May 2013.

91. Tom Phillips, 'China Breaks Official Silence on Cultural Revolution's "Decade of Calamity"', *Guardian*, 17 May 2016.

92. Nectar Gan, '"Whole World Should Unite to Defeat the American Invaders and Their Lackeys": Controversy Sparked Online by "Red Songs" at Concert in Beijing', *South China Morning Post*, 6 May 2016, at http://www.scmp .com/news/china/policies-politics/article/1941686/whole-world-should -unite-defeat-american-invaders-and (accessed on 9 January 2018).

93. Chun Han Wong, 'Maoist Overtones in Beijing Concert Raise Red Flags', *Wall Street Journal*, 8 May 2016, at https://blogs.wsj.com/ chinarealtime/2016/05/08/maoist-overtones-in-beijing-concert-raise-red -flags/ (accessed on 9 January 2018).

94. Zheping Huang, 'Introducing China's Totally Wholesome 56-Member Patriotic Girl Pop Group', *Quartz*, 3 July 2015, at https://qz.com/444680/ introducing-chinas-totally-wholesome-56-member-patriotic-girl-pop-group/ (accessed on 9 January 2018).

Conclusion

1. 'A New Form of Totalitarianism Takes Root in China', *Washington Post*, 26 February 2018.

2. Charles Lane, 'We Got China Wrong. Now What?', *Washington Post*, 28 February 2018.

3. The *locus classicus* of this is Bill Clinton's 2000 speech concerning PRC accession to the WTO. See, for example, https://archive.nytimes.com/www.nytimes.com/library/world/asia/030900clinton-china-text.html?mcubz=2 (accessed on 30 July 2018).

4. See, for example, Wang Xiaohong, '"2018 Liang Hui – gaige xin zhengcheng" xinxing zhengdang zhidu wei shijie zhengdang zhengzhi fazhan gongxian zhongguo zhihui' ('Two Conferences – A New Journey in Reform': The New-Style Party System Contributes Chinese Wisdom to the Global Development of Political Parties), at http://news.cri.cn/20180308/962b9850-3a41-45ac-57c0-a4afdaa2d9e4.html (accessed on 15 March 2018).

5. See, for example, https://hrichina.us9.list-manage.com/track/click?u=be7 1fffd3e2fea33689a7d0d8&id=a94125227e&e=1bd184054a.

SELECT BIBLIOGRAPHY

Archives

People's Republic of China
Archives of the Ministry of Foreign Affairs
Beijing Municipal Archives
Shanghai Municipal Archives
Contemporary Documentation Centre, East China Normal University

UK
National Archives
Society for Anglo-Chinese Understanding, Oundle
Special Collections, School of Oriental and African Studies

US
Papers of Robert F. Williams, University of Michigan (microfilm consulted)
'Documenting the Peruvian Insurrection', Princeton University (microfilm
    consulted)
Tamiment Library and Robert F. Wagner Archives (New York)
Joint Publications Research Service Reports (database consulted)
Foreign Broadcast Information Service (database consulted)

Continental Europe
International Institute of Social History, Amsterdam
APO-Archiv, Berlin
Bibliothèque de Documentation Internationale Contemporaine, Paris
Archives Nationales, Paris

Mongolia
Archives of the Ministry of Foreign Affairs

Peru
Defensoría del Pueblo, Lima

Other Sources

Adams, Clarence, *An American Dream: The Life of an African American Soldier and POW Who Spent Twelve Years in Communist China*, Amherst: University of Massachusetts Press, 2007.

Adhikari, Aditya, *The Bullet and the Ballot Box: The Story of Nepal's Maoist Revolution*, London: Verso, 2014.

Ah Cheng, *Wo jianfu de shiming: Magong zhongyang zhengzhiju weiyuan A Cheng huiyilu zhi si* (My Mission: Volume Four of the Memoirs of Ah Cheng, Member of the Politburo of the Malayan Communist Party), Kuala Lumpur: Ershiyi shiji chubanshe, 2007.

———, *Yilu jianxin xiangqian zou – wo fuze de shiming, xu* (A Tough Road Forward – My Mission, continued), Johor: Hasanah Sin Bt. Abdullah, 2009.

Ahmad, Muhammad, *We Will Return in the Whirlwind: Black Radical Organizations 1960–1975*, Chicago: Charles H. Kerr, 2007.

Ahmad, Taufik, 'South Sulawesi: The Military, Prison Camps and Forced Labour', in Douglas Kammen and Katharine McGregor, eds, *The Contours of Mass Violence in Indonesia, 1965–68*, 156–81, Copenhagen: NIAS Press, 2012.

Aidit, D. N., *Dare, Dare and Dare Again!*, Beijing: Foreign Languages Press, 1963.

———, *Set Afire the Banteng Spirit: Ever Forward, No Retreat!*, Beijing: Foreign Languages Press, 1964.

Alexander, Robert J., *International Maoism in the Developing World*, New York: Praeger, 1999.

———, *Maoism in the Developed World*, New York: Praeger, 2001.

Anderson, Benedict, 'How Did the Generals Die?', *Indonesia* 43 (April 1987): 109–34.

———, *Imagined Communities: Reflections on the Origins and Spread of Nationalism*, London: Verso, 1991.

Anderson, Benedict R., and Ruth T. McVey, *A Preliminary Analysis of the October 1, 1965, Coup in Indonesia*, Ithaca, NY: Modern Indonesia Project, 1971.

Anderson, David M., *Histories of the Hanged: Britain's Dirty War in Kenya and the End of Empire*, London: Weidenfeld & Nicolson, 2005.

Andrew, Christopher M., and Vasili Mitrokhin, *The Mitrokhin Archive II: The KGB and the World*, London: Allen Lane, 2005.

Apter, David E., and Tony Saich, *Revolutionary Discourse in Mao's Republic*, Cambridge, MA: Harvard University Press, 1994.

Armstrong, Charles, *The Tyranny of the Weak: North Korea and the World 1950–1992*, Ithaca, NY: Cornell University Press, 2013.

Asselin, Pierre, *Hanoi's Road to the Vietnam War, 1954–1965*, Berkeley: University of California Press, 2015.

Aust, Stefan, *The Baader–Meinhof Complex*, trans. Anthea Bell, London: Bodley Head, 2008.

Bach, Quintin V. S., 'A Note on Soviet Statistics on Their Economic Aid', *Soviet Studies* 37.2 (April 1985): 269–75.

Badiou, Alain, 'The Cultural Revolution: The Last Revolution?', *Positions* 13.3 (Winter 2005): 481–514.

Bagus, Mary Ida, 'West Bali: Experiences and Legacies of the 1965–66 Violence', in Douglas Kammen and Katharine McGregor, eds, *The Contours of Mass Violence in Indonesia, 1965–68*, 208–33, Copenhagen: NIAS Press, 2012.

Banerjee, Sumanta, *India's Simmering Revolution: The Naxalite Uprising*, London: Zed Books, 1984.

Barlow, Tani, and Gary Bjorge, eds, *I Myself Am a Woman: Selected Writings of Ding Ling*, Boston: Beacon Press, 1989.

Barmé, Geremie R., *Shades of Mao: The Posthumous Cult of the Great Leader*, New York: M. E. Sharpe, 1996.

———, *In the Red: On Contemporary Chinese Culture*, New York: Columbia University Press, 1997.

Basombrío Iglesias, Carlos, 'Sendero Luminoso and Human Rights: A Perverse Logic that Captured the Country', in Steve J. Stern, ed., *Shining and Other Paths: War and Society in Peru, 1980–1995*, 426–46, Durham, NC: Duke University Press, 1998.

Bayly, Christopher, and Tim Harper, *Forgotten Wars: The End of Britain's Asian Empire*, London: Penguin Books, 2008.

Becker, Jasper, *Hungry Ghosts: China's Secret Famine*, London: John Murray, 1996.

———, *Rogue Regime: Kim Jong Il and the Looming Threat of North Korea*, New York: Oxford University Press, 2005.

Belden, Jack, *China Shakes the World*, New York: Harper, 1949.

Bell, Thomas, *Kathmandu*, London: Haus, 2016.

Berg, Ronald H., 'Peasant Responses to Shining Path in Andahuaylas', in David Scott Palmer, ed., *The Shining Path of Peru*, 83–104, London: Hurst, 1992.

Berger, Dan, 'Rescuing Civil Rights from Black Power: Collective Memory and Saving the State in Twenty-First-Century Prosecutions of 1960s-Era Cases', *Journal for the Study of Radicalism* 3.1 (2009): 1–27.

Bhatia, Bela, 'The Naxalite Movement in Central Bihar', unpublished PhD dissertation, University of Cambridge, 2000.

Bianco, Lucien, *La Récidive: Révolution Russe, Révolution Chinoise*, Paris: Gallimard, 2014.

Blanchette, Jude, *Under the Red Flag: The Battle for the Soul of the Communist Party in a Reforming China* (manuscript copy consulted), Oxford: Oxford University Press.

Bloom, Joshua, and Waldo E. Martin, *Black Against Empire: The History and Politics of the Black Panther Party*, Berkeley: University of California Press, 2013.

Bodman, Richard W., and Pin P. Wan, trans. and eds, *Deathsong of the River: A Reader's Guide to the Chinese TV Series Heshang*, Ithaca, NY: Cornell University, 1991.

Bourseiller, Christophe, *Les Maoïstes: La Folle Histoire des Gardes Rouges Français*, Paris: Plon, 1996.

Bradley, Mark Philip, *Vietnam at War*, Oxford: Oxford University Press, 2009.

Brady, Anne-Marie, *The Friend of China: The Myth of Rewi Alley*, London: Routledge, 2002.

———, *Making the Foreign Serve China: Managing Foreigners in the People's Republic*, Lanham, MD: Rowman & Littlefield, 2003.

Brazinsky, Gregg, *Winning the Third World: Sino-American Rivalry During the Cold War*, Chapel Hill: University of North Carolina Press, 2017.

Brown, Archie, *The Rise and Fall of Communism*, London: Vintage, 2010.

Brown, Kerry, *The New Emperors: Power and the Princelings in China*, London: I. B. Tauris, 2014.

———, *CEO China: The Rise of Xi Jinping*, London: I. B. Tauris, 2017.

———, *The World According to Xi*, London: I. B. Tauris, 2018.

———, and Simone van Nieuwenhuizen, *China and the New Maoists*, London: Zed Books, 2016.

Buchanan, Tom, *East Wind: China and the British Left, 1925–1976*, Oxford: Oxford University Press, 2012.

Bui, Tin, *Following Ho Chi Minh: The Memoirs of a North Vietnamese Colonel*, London: Hurst, 1995.

Buijtenhuijs, Robert, *Mau Mau Twenty Years After: The Myth and the Survivors*, The Hague: Mouton, 1973.

Burgess, G. Thomas, 'Mao in Zanzibar: Nationalism, Discipline, and the (De) Construction of Afro-Asian Solidarities', in Christopher J. Lee, ed., *Making a World After Empire: The Bandung Moment and Its Political Afterlives*, 263–91, Athens: Ohio University Press, 2010.

———, Ali Sultan Issa and Seif Sharif Hamad, *Race, Revolution and the Struggle for Human Rights in Zanzibar: The Memoirs of Sultan Issa and Seif Sharif Hamad*, Athens: Ohio University Press, 2009.

Cailmail, Benoît, 'A History of Nepalese Maoism since Its Foundation by Mohan Bikram Singh', *European Bulletin of Himalayan Research* 33–34 (2008–2009): 11–38.

_____, 'Le Mouvement Maoïste au Népal, 1949–2008: La tentation de la révolution internationale', unpublished PhD dissertation, Panthéon-Sorbonne University – Paris 1, 2015.

Carruthers, Susan, *Cold War Captives: Imprisonment, Escape and Brainwashing*, Berkeley: University of California Press, 2009.

Chakrabarti, Sreemati, *China and the Naxalites*, London: Sangam, 1990.

Chakravarty, Bidyut, and Rajat Kumar Kujur, *Maoism in India: Reincarnation of Ultra-Left-Wing Extremism in the Twenty-first Century*, London: Routledge, 2009.

Chanda, Nayan, *Brother Enemy: The War After the War*, San Diego, CA: Harcourt Brace Jovanovich, 1986.

Chandler, David, *The Tragedy of Cambodian History: Politics, War and Revolution Since 1945*, New Haven, CT: Yale University Press, 1991.

_____, *Voices from S-21: Terror and History in Pol Pot's Secret Prison*, Berkeley: University of California Press, 1999.

_____, *Brother Number One: A Political Biography of Pol Pot*, Boulder, CO: Westview, 1999.

_____, Ben Kiernan and Chanthou Boua, trans. and eds, *Pol Pot Plans the Future: Confidential Leadership Documents from Democratic Kampuchea, 1976–1977*, New Haven, CT: Yale Center for International and Area Studies, 1988.

Chang, Jung and Jon Halliday, *Mao: The Unknown Story*, London: Jonathan Cape, 2005.

Cheek, Timothy, 'The Fading of Wild Lilies: Wang Shiwei and Mao Zedong's Yan'an Talks in the First CPC Rectification Movement', *Australian Journal of Chinese Affairs* 11 (January 1984): 25–58.

_____, *The Intellectual in Modern Chinese History*, Cambridge: Cambridge University Press, 2015.

_____, ed., *A Critical Introduction to Mao*, Cambridge: Cambridge University Press, 2010.

Chen Guanren, *Song Qingling dazhuan* (Biography of Song Qingling), Beijing: Tuanjie chubanshe, 2003.

Chen Jian, *Mao's China and the Cold War*, Chapel Hill: University of North Carolina Press, 2001.

_____, et al., eds, *The Routledge Handbook of the Global Sixties*, London: Routledge, 2018.

Chen Yung-fa, 'The Blooming Poppy Under the Red Sun: The Yan'an Way and the Opium Trade', in Tony Saich and Hans van de Ven, eds, *New*

Perspectives on the Chinese Communist Revolution, 263–98, New York: M. E. Sharpe, 1995.

Cheng, J. C., ed., *The Politics of the Chinese Red Army: A Translation of the Bulletin of Activities of the People's Liberation Army*, Stanford, CA: Hoover Institution, 1966.

Cheng Yinghong, *Mao zhuyi geming: Ershi shiji de Zhongguo yu shijie* (Maoist Revolution: China and the World in the 20th Century), Hong Kong: Tianyuan shuyuan, 2008.

_____, 'Beyond Moscow-Centric Interpretation: An Examination of the China Connection in Eastern Europe and North Vietnam during the Era of De-Stalinization', *Journal of World History* 15.4 (December 2004): 487–518.

Chin Peng, *Alias Chin Peng – My Side of History: Recollections of a Revolutionary Leader*, Singapore: Media Masters, 2003.

Chung, Fay, *Re-living the Second Chimurenga: Memories from the Liberation Struggle in Zimbabwe*, Stockholm: Nordic Africa Institute, 2006.

Churchill, Ward, '"To Disrupt, Discredit and Destroy": The FBI's Secret War Against the Black Panther Party', in Kathleen Cleaver and George Katsiaficas, eds, *Liberation, Imagination and the Black Panther Party: A New Look at the Panthers and Their Legacy*, 78–117, New York: Routledge, 2001.

Cleaver, Kathleen, and George Katsiaficas, eds, *Liberation, Imagination and the Black Panther Party: A New Look at the Panthers and their Legacy*, New York: Routledge, 2001.

Clifford, Nicholas R., 'White China, Red China: Lighting Out for the Territory with Edgar Snow', *New England Review* 18.2 (Spring 1997): 103–11.

Cook, Alexander C., 'Chinese Uhuru: Maoism and the Congo Crisis', unpublished paper.

_____, ed., *Mao's Little Red Book: A Global History*, Cambridge: Cambridge University Press, 2014.

Cooley, John, *East Wind Over Africa: Red China's African Offensive*, New York: Walker & Company, 1965.

Craig Harris, Lilian, 'China's Relations with the PLO', *Journal of Palestine Studies* 7.1 (Autumn 1977): 123–54.

Cribb, Robert, 'Indonesian Marxism', in Colin Mackerras and Nick Knight, eds, *Marxism in Asia*, 251–72, Sydney: Croome Helm, 1985.

_____, ed., *The Indonesian Killings 1965–1966: Studies from Java and Bali*, Melbourne, Aus.: Monash University, 1990.

_____, and Colin Brown, *Modern Indonesia: A History Since 1945*, London: Longman, 1995.

Cui Jinke, 'Dangdai "Mao Zedong zuopai" sixiang fenxi – yi "wuyouzhixiang" wangzhan weili' (An Analysis of Contemporary Maoist Thought, Focused on Utopia Website), unpublished MA dissertation, Beijing University, 2013.

Cumings, Bruce, *The Korean War: A History*, New York: Modern Library, 2011.

Dai Qing, *Wang Shiwei and 'Wild Lilies': Rectification and Purges in the Chinese Communist Party, 1942–1944*, ed. David E. Apter and Timothy Cheek Armonk, NY: M. E. Sharpel, 1994.

Dake, Antonie C. A., *In the Spirit of the Red Banteng: Indonesian Communists Between Moscow and Peking, 1959–1965*, The Hague: Mouton, 1973.

Degregori, Carlos Iván, 'Harvesting Storms: Peasant *Rondas* and the Defeat of Sendero Luminoso in Ayacucho', in Steve J. Stern, ed., *Shining and Other Paths: War and Society in Peru, 1980–1995*, 129–57, Durham, NC: Duke University Press, 1998.

_____, *El Surgimiento de Sendero Luminoso: Ayacucho 1969–1979*, Lima: Instituto de Estudios Peruanos, 2010.

_____, *How Difficult It Is to Be God: Shining Path's Politics of War in Peru, 1980–1999*, ed. Steve J. Stern, trans. Nancy Appelbaum, Madison: University of Wisconsin Press, 2012.

Del Pino H., Ponciano, 'Family, Culture and "Revolution": Everyday Life with Sendero Luminoso', in Steve J. Stern, ed., *Shining and Other Paths: War and Society in Peru, 1980–1995*, 158–92, Durham, NC: Duke University Press, 1998.

De Nike, Howard J., John Quigley and Kenneth J. Robinson, eds, *Genocide in Cambodia: Documents from the Trial of Pol Pot and Ieng Sary*, Philadelphia: University of Pennsylvania Press, 2000.

Denton, Kirk A., ed., *Modern Chinese Literary Thought: Writings on Literature, 1893–1945*, Stanford, CA: Stanford University Press, 1996.

De Sales, Anne, 'Thabang: The Crucible of Revolution', in Marie Lecomte-Tilouine, ed., *Revolution in Nepal: An Anthropological and Historical Approach to the People's War*, 165–206, New Delhi: Oxford University Press, 2013.

De Wit, Ton, and Vera Gianotten, 'The Center's Multiple Failures', in David Scott Palmer, ed., *The Shining Path of Peru*, 45–57, London: Hurst, 1992.

Dikötter, Frank, *Mao's Great Famine: The History of China's Most Devastating Catastrophe, 1958–1962*, London: Bloomsbury, 2010.

_____, *The Cultural Revolution: A People's History, 1962–1976*, London: Bloomsbury, 2016.

Donner, Henrike, 'The Significance of Naxalbari: Accounts of Personal Involvement and Politics in West Bengal', occasional paper, Centre of South Asian Studies, University of Cambridge, 2004.

Duiker, William J., *Ho Chi Minh: A Life*, New York: Hyperion, 2000.

Efimova, Larisa M., 'Stalin and the New Program for the Communist Party of Indonesia', *Indonesia* 91 (April 2011): 131–63.

Elbaum, Max, *Revolution in the Air: Sixties Radicals Turn to Lenin, Mao and Che*, London: Verso, 2006.

Fairbank, John K., *China: The People's Middle Kingdom and the USA*, Cambridge, MA: Harvard University Press, 1967.

Faligot, Roger, and Remi Kauffer, *The Chinese Secret Service*, trans. Christine Donougher, London: Headline, 1989.

Fan, Hongwei, 'China-Burma Geopolitical Relations in the Cold War', *Journal of Current Southeast Asian Affairs* 31.1 (2012): 7–27.

Farnsworth, Robert M., *From Vagabond to Journalist: Edgar Snow in Asia, 1928–1941*, Columbia: University of Missouri Press, 1996.

Farrell, William R., *Blood and Rage: The Story of the Japanese Red Army*, Lexington, MA: Lexington Books, 1990.

Favretto, Ilaria, 'Rough Music and Factory Protest in Post-1945 Italy', *Past and Present* 228 (August 2015): 207–47.

————, and Marco Fincardi, 'Carnivalesque and Charivari Repertories in 1960s and 1970s Italian Protest', in Ilaria Favretto and Xabier Itçaina, eds, *Protest, Popular Culture and Tradition in Modern and Contemporary Western Europe*, 149–84, London: Palgrave, 2017.

Fei Xiaotong and Xia Yan, eds, *Hu Yuzhi yinxiang ji zengbuben* (Impressions of Hu Yuzhi: enlarged edition), Beijing: Zhongguo youyi chuban gongsi, 1996.

Fic, Victor, *Anatomy of the Jakarta Coup, 1 October, 1965: The Collusion with China Which Destroyed the Army Command, President Sukarno and the Communist Party of Indonesia*, New Delhi: Abhinav Publications, 2004.

Fields, A. Belden, *Trotskyism and Maoism: Theory and Practice in France and the United States*, New York: Praeger, 1988.

Foster Snow, Helen (see also Nym Wales), *My China Years: A Memoir*, London: Harrap, 1984.

Franceschini, Alberto, *Mara Renato e Io: Storia des Fondatori delle BR*, Milan: Arnoldo Mondadori, 1988.

Frazier, Robeson Taj, *The East Is Black: Cold War China in the Black Radical Imagination*, Durham, NC: Duke University Press, 2015.

Friedman, Jeremy, *Shadow Cold War: The Sino-Soviet Competition for the Third World*, Chapel Hill: University of North Carolina Press, 2015.

Garnaut, John, *The Rise and Fall of the House of Bo: How a Murder Exposed the Cracks in China's Leadership*, Beijing: Penguin China, 2012.

Garver, John, *China's Quest: The History of the Foreign Relations of the People's Republic of China*, Oxford: Oxford University Press, 2016.

Gavilán Sánchez, Lurgio, *When Rains Became Floods: A Child Soldier's Story*, trans. Margaret Randall, Durham, NC: Duke University Press, 2017.

Gehrig, Sebastian, '"Zwischen uns und dem Feind einen klaren Trennungsstrich ziehen": Linksterroristische Gruppen und maoistische Ideologie in der Bundesrepublik der 1960er und 1970er Jahre', in Sebastian Gehrig, Barbara

Mittler and Felix Wemheuer, eds, *Kulturrevolution als Vorbild? Maoismen im deutschsprachigen Raum*, 153–77, Frankfurt: Peter Lang, 2008.

_____, '(Re-)Configuring Mao: Trajectories of a Culturo-political Trend in West Germany', *Transcultural Studies* 2 (2011): 189–231.

Gellner, David, and Mrigendra Bahadur Karki, 'The Sociology of Activism in Nepal: Some Preliminary Considerations', in H. Ishii, David Gellner and K. Nawa, eds, *Political and Social Transformations in North India and Nepal (Social Dynamics in Northern South Asia)*, Volume 2, 361–97, Delhi: Manohar, 2007.

Gildea, Robert, James Mark and Anette Warring, eds, *Europe's 1968: Voices of Revolt*, Oxford: Oxford University Press, 2013.

Gilmartin, Christina, *Engendering the Chinese Revolution: Radical Women, Communist Politics, and Mass Movements in the 1920s*, Berkeley: University of California Press, 1995.

Goldman, Merle, 'The Party and the Intellectuals', in Roderick MacFarquhar and John K. Fairbank, eds, *The Cambridge History of China, Volume 14, The People's Republic, Part 1: The Emergence of Revolutionary China, 1949–1965*, 218–58, Cambridge: Cambridge University Press, 1987.

Gorriti, Gustavo, 'Shining Path's Stalin and Trotsky', in David Scott Palmer, ed., *The Shining Path of Peru*, 149–70, London: Hurst, 1992.

_____, *The Shining Path: A History of the Millenarian War in Peru*, trans. Robin Kirk, Chapel Hill: University of North Carolina Press, 1999.

Goscha, Christopher, *The Penguin History of Modern Vietnam*, London: Penguin, 2017.

Gottesman, Evan, *Cambodia After the Khmer Rouge: Inside the Politics of Nation Building*, New Haven, CT: Yale University Press, 2004.

Guan, Ang Cheng, *Vietnamese Communists' Relations with China and the Second Indochina Conflict, 1956–1962*, London: McFarland, 1997.

Guzmán Reinoso, Abimael, and Elena Iparraguirre, *Memorias desde Némesis 1993–2000* (2014), http://bvk.bnp.gob.pe/admin/files/libros/801_digitalizacion.pdf.

Hack, Karl, and Jian Chen, eds, *Dialogues with Chin Peng: New Light on the Malayan Communist Party*, Singapore: Singapore University Press, 2004.

Hahn, Emily, *The Soong Sisters*, London: Robert Hale Limited, 1942.

Halberstam, David, *The Coldest Winter: America and the Korean War*, London: Pan Macmillan, 2009.

Hamilton, John Maxwell, *Edgar Snow: A Biography*, Bloomington: Indiana University Press, 1998.

Han Shaogong, *A Dictionary of Maqiao*, trans. Julia Lovell, New York: Columbia University Press, 2003.

Hanshew, Karrin, *Terror and Democracy in West Germany*, Cambridge: Cambridge University Press, 2012.

He Jingxu et al., eds, *Mianhuai Liu Shaoqi* (Fond Memories of Liu Shaoqi), Beijing: Zhongyang wenxian chubanshe, 1988.

Hearman, Vanessa, 'South Blitar and the PKI Bases: Refuge, Resistance and Repression', in Douglas Kammen and Katharine McGregor, eds, *The Contours of Mass Violence in Indonesia, 1965–68*, 182–207, Copenhagen: NIAS Press, 2012.

Heikal, Mohamed, *Nasser: The Cairo Documents*, London: New English Library, 1972.

Heilman, Jaymie, *Before the Shining Path: Politics in Rural Ayacucho, 1895–1980*, Stanford, CA: Stanford University Press, 2010.

Heilmann, Sebastian, and Elizabeth Perry, eds, *Mao's Invisible Hand: The Political Foundations of Adaptive Governance in China*, Cambridge, MA: Harvard University Press, 2011.

Hering, Bob, *Soekarno: Founding Father of Indonesia, 1901–1945*, Leiden, NL: KITLV Press, 2002.

Hershberg, James, Sergey Radchenko, Peter Vamos and David Wolff, 'The Interkit Story: A Window into the Final Decades of the Sino-Soviet Relationship', Cold War International History Project Working Paper, February 2011.

Hevi, Emmanuel John, *An African Student in China*, London: Pall Mall Press, 1963.

Hindley, Donald, *The Communist Party of Indonesia, 1951–1963*, Berkeley: University of California Press, 1964.

Hoang Van Hoan, *A Drop in the Ocean: Hoang Van Hoan's Revolutionary Reminiscences*, Beijing: Foreign Languages Press, 1988.

Holcombe, Alec, 'Socialist Transformation in the Democratic Republic of Vietnam', unpublished PhD dissertation, University of California, Berkeley, 2014.

Hollander, Paul, *Political Pilgrims: Western Intellectuals in Search of the Good Society*, Oxford: Oxford University Press, 1981.

Hong Zhou and Hou Xiong, eds, *China's Foreign Aid: 60 Years in Retrospect*, Singapore: Springer, 2017.

Hu, Andy Yinan, 'Swimming Against the Tide: Tracing and Locating Chinese Leftism Online', unpublished MA dissertation, Simon Fraser University, 2006.

Hu Yuzhi, *Wo de huiyi* (My Memoirs), Jiangsu: Jiangsu renmin chubanshe, 1990.

Huang Hua, *Memoirs*, Beijing: Foreign Languages Press, 2008.

Huang, Shaorong, *To Rebel Is Justified: A Rhetorical Study of China's Cultural Revolution Movement, 1966–1969*, Lanham, MD: University Press of America, 1996.

Hughes, John, *The End of Sukarno: A Coup That Misfired, a Purge That Ran Wild*, London: Angus & Robertson, 1968.

Hunter, Edward, *Brain-washing in Red China: The Calculated Destruction of Men's Minds*, New York: The Vanguard Press, 1951.

———, *Brainwashing: The Story of Men Who Defied It*, New York: Farrar, Straus, and Cudahy, 1956.

Hutchison, Alan, *China's African Revolution*, London: Hutchinson, 1975.

Hutt, Michael, 'Reading Nepali Maoist Memoirs', *Studies in Nepali History and Society* 17.1 (June 2012): 107–42.

———, 'Ganga Bahadur's Books: Landmark Proletarian Novels and the Nepali Communist Movement', *Inter-Asia Cultural Studies* 17.3 (2016): 357–74.

———, ed., *Himalayan 'People's War': Nepal's Maoist Revolution*, London: Hurst, 2004.

Isbell, Billie Jean, 'Shining Path and Peasant Responses in Rural Ayacucho', in David Scott Palmer, ed., *The Shining Path of Peru*, 59–81, London: Hurst, 1992.

Jaquet, Carine, '"One Should Not Cut the Blossom in the Bud": Voices of Nepalese Child Soldiers', *European Bulletin of Himalayan Research* 33–34 (2008–2009): 171–90.

Jeldres, Julio, 'A Personal Reflection on Norodom Sihanouk and Zhou Enlai: An Extraordinary Friendship on the Fringes of the Cold War', *Cross-Currents: East Asian History and Culture Review* 4 (September 2012): 52–64.

Jenkins, David, and Douglas Kammen, 'The Army Para-commando Regiment and the Reign of Terror in Central Java and Bali', in Douglas Kammen and Katharine McGregor, eds, *The Contours of Mass Violence in Indonesia, 1965–68*, 75–103, Copenhagen: NIAS Press, 2012.

Jersild, Austin, *The Sino-Soviet Alliance: An International History*, Chapel Hill: University of North Carolina Press, 2014.

Jha, Prashant, *Battles of the New Republic: A Contemporary History of Nepal*, London: Hurst, 2014.

Jiang Huajie, 'Lengzhan shiqi Zhongguo dui Feizhou guojia de yuanzhu yanjiu (1960–1978)' (A Study of Chinese Aid to African Countries During the Cold War (1960–1978)), unpublished PhD dissertation, East China Normal University, 2014.

Jianjue zhansheng meidiguozhuyi: zhichi Yuenan renmin kangmei jiuguo zhengyi douzheng gequ xuanji (Resolutely Defeat American Imperialism: Selected Songs Supporting the Vietnamese People's Righteous Struggle to Resist America and Save Their Country), Beijing: Yinyue chubanshe, 1965.

Jiménez Quispe, Edilberto, 'Chungui: Ethnographic Drawings of Violence and Traces of Memory', in Cynthia E. Milton, ed., *Art from a Fractured*

Past: Memory and Truth Telling in Post-Shining Path Peru, 75–102, Durham, NC: Duke University Press, 2014.

Jin Chongji, *Mao Zedong zhuan, 1893–1949* (Biography of Mao Zedong, 1893–1949), Beijing: Zhonggong zhongyang wenxian yanjiushi, 2004.

———, and Pang Xianzhi, *Mao Zedong zhuan 1949–1976* (Biography of Mao Zedong, 1949–1976), Beijing: Zhongyang wenxian chubanshe, 2003.

Jiqing suiyue (Times of Excitement), Hong Kong: Jianzheng chubanshe, 2005.

Johnson, Cecil, *Communist China and Latin America 1959–1967*, New York: Columbia University Press, 1970.

Johnson, Matthew, 'From Peace to the Panthers: PRC Engagement with African-American Transnational Networks, 1949–1979', *Past and Present* 218 (special supplement) (January 2013): 233–57.

Joiner, Lynne, *Honorable Survivor: Mao's China, McCarthy's America, and the Persecution of John S. Service*, Maryland: Naval Institute Press, 2009.

Judt, Tony, *Postwar: A History of Europe Since 1945*, London: Pimlico, 2007.

Kahin, Audrey, and George Kahin, *Subversion as Foreign Policy: The Secret Eisenhower and Dulles Debacle in Indonesia*, Seattle: University of Washington Press, 1997.

Kammen, Douglas, and Katharine McGregor, eds, *The Contours of Mass Violence in Indonesia, 1965–68*, Copenhagen: NIAS Press, 2012.

———, 'Introduction: The Contours of Mass Violence in Indonesia, 1965–68', in Douglas Kammen and Katharine McGregor, eds, *The Contours of Mass Violence in Indonesia, 1965–68*, 1–24, Copenhagen: NIAS Press, 2012.

Karki, Arjun, and David Seddon, eds, *The People's War in Nepal: Left Perspectives*, Delhi: Adroit Publishers, 2003.

Keating, Pauline B., *Two Revolutions: Village Reconstruction and the Cooperative Movement in Northern Shaanxi, 1934–1945*, Stanford, CA: Stanford University Press, 1997.

Kelley, Robert D. G., and Betsy Esch, 'Black Like Mao: Red China and Black Revolution', *Souls: Critical Journal of Black Politics and Culture* 1.4 (Fall 1999): 6–41.

Kennedy, Jonathan, and Sunil Purushotham, 'Beyond Naxalbari: A Comparative Analysis of Maoist Insurgency and Counterinsurgency in Independent India', *Comparative Studies in Society and History* 54.4 (2012): 832–62.

Khoo, Nicholas, *Collateral Damage: Sino-Soviet Rivalry and the Termination of the Sino-Vietnamese Alliance*, New York: Columbia University Press, 2011.

Khrushchev, Nikita, *Khrushchev Remembers: The Last Testament*, Volume 2, trans. Strobe Talbott, London: Deutsch, 1974.

Kiernan, Ben, *How Pol Pot Came to Power: A History of Communism in Kampuchea, 1930–1975*, London: Verso, 1986.

_____, 'External and Indigenous Sources of Khmer Rouge Ideology', in Odd Arne Westad and Sophie Quinn-Judge, eds, *The Third Indochina War: Conflict Between China, Vietnam and Cambodia, 1972–1979*, 187–206, London: Routledge, 2006.

_____, *The Pol Pot Regime: Race, Power, and Genocide in Cambodia Under the Khmer Rouge, 1975–79*, New Haven, CT: Yale University Press, 2008.

Kirk, G. S., and J. E. Raven, *The Presocratic Philosophers: A Critical History with a Selection of Texts*, Cambridge: Cambridge University Press, 1964.

Kirk, Robin, *Grabado en piedra: las mujeres de Sendero Luminoso*, trans. Enrique Bossio, Lima: Instituto de Estudios Peruanos, 1993.

_____, *The Monkey's Paw: New Chronicles from Peru*, Amherst: University of Massachusetts Press, 1997.

Koenen, Gerd, *Das Rote Jahrzehnt: Unsere kleine Deutsche Kulturrevolution 1967–1977*, Cologne: Kiepenheuer & Witsch, 2001.

Kühn, Andreas, *Stalins Enkel, Maos Söhne: Die Lebenswelt der K-Gruppen in der Bundesrepublik der 70er Jahre*, Frankfurt: Campus Verlag, 2005.

Kurlansky, Mark, *1968: The Year that Rocked the World*, London: Jonathan Cape, 2004.

Lal, Priya, 'Maoism in Tanzania: Material Connections and Shared Imaginaries', in Alexander C. Cook, ed., *Mao's Little Red Book: A Global History*, 96–116, Cambridge: Cambridge University Press, 2014.

_____, *African Socialism in Postcolonial Tanzania*, Cambridge: Cambridge University Press, 2015.

Landau, Paul S., 'The ANC, MK, and "The Turn to Violence" (1960–1962)', *South African Historical Journal* 64.3 (2012): 538–63.

Larkin, Bruce D., *China and Africa, 1949–1970: The Foreign Policy of the People's Republic of China*, Berkeley: University of California Press, 1971.

La Serna, Miguel, *The Corner of the Living: Ayacucho on the Eve of the Shining Path Insurgency*, Chapel Hill: University of North Carolina Press, 2012.

_____, and Orin Starn, *The Shining Path: Love, Madness, and Revolution in the Andes* (manuscript copy consulted), New York: Norton, 2019.

Lawoti, Mahendra, 'Ethnic Politics and the Building of an Inclusive State', in Sebastian von Einsiedel and David M. Malone, eds, *Nepal in Transition: From People's War to Fragile Peace*, 129–52, Cambridge: Cambridge University Press, 2012.

Lecomte-Tilouine, Marie, *Hindu Kingship, Ethnic Revival and Maoist Rebellion in Nepal*, New Delhi: Oxford University Press, 2009.

_____, ed., *Revolution in Nepal: An Anthropological and Historical Approach to the People's War*, New Delhi: Oxford University Press, 2013.

_____, 'Maoist Despite Themselves: Amid the People's War in a Maoist Model Village, Northern Gulmi', in Marie Lecomte-Tilouine, ed.,

Revolution in Nepal: An Anthropological and Historical Approach to the People's War, 213–53, New Delhi: Oxford University Press, 2013.

Lee, Ching Kwan, and Guobin Yang, eds, *Re-envisioning the Chinese Revolution: The Politics and Poetics of Collective Memories in Reform China*, Stanford, CA: Stanford University Press, 2007.

Lee Kuan Yew, *From Third World to First: Singapore and the Asian Economic Boom*, New York: Harper, 2011.

Leese, Daniel, *Mao Cult: Rhetoric and Ritual in China's Cultural Revolution*, Cambridge: Cambridge University Press, 2011.

Legge, J. D., *Sukarno: A Political Biography*, London: Allen Lane, 1972.

Lemov, Rebecca, *The World as Laboratory: Mice, Mazes and Men*, New York: Hill and Wang, 2005.

Leonard, Aaron J., and Conor A. Gallagher, *Heavy Radicals: The FBI's Secret War on America's Maoists: The Revolutionary Union / Revolutionary Communist Party 1968–1980*, Winchester, UK: Zero Books, 2014.

Li Danhui, 'Fu Feizhou xinshiming: Ma Faxian laoren fangtanlu' (To Africa on a New Mission: An Interview with Mr Ma Faxian), *Lengzhan guojishi yanjiu* 7 (2008): 249–64.

———, Liang Zhi and Zhou Na, 'Feizhou conglinzhong de xinshiming – Ma Faxian laoren fangtanlu (er)' (A New Mission in the African Bush: An Interview with Mr Ma Faxian, Part Two), *Lengzhan guojishi yanjiu* 8 (2009): 299–348.

———, Chen Bo and Fan Baiyu, 'Feizhou conglinzhong de xinshiming – Ma Faxian laoren fangtanlu (san)' (A New Mission in the African Bush: An Interview with Mr Ma Faxian, Part Three), *Lengzhan guojishi yanjiu* 9 (2010): 255–87.

———, Cui Haizhi and Jiang Huajie, 'Feizhou conglinzhong de xinshiming – Ma Faxian laoren fangtanlu (si)' (A New Mission in the African Bush: An Interview with Mr Ma Faxian, Part Four), *Lengzhan guojishi yanjiu* 10 (2010): 377–412.

———, Li Xiufang and You Lan, 'Feizhou conglinzhong de xinshiming – Ma Faxian laoren fangtanlu (wu)' (A New Mission in the African Bush: An Interview with Mr Ma Faxian, Part Five), *Lengzhan guojishi yanjiu* 11 (2011): 147–213.

———, Zhou Na and Cui Haizhi, 'Feizhou conglinzhong de xinshiming – Ma Faxian laoren fangtanlu (liu)' (A New Mission in the African Bush: An Interview with Mr Ma Faxian, Part Six), *Lengzhan guojishi yanjiu* 12 (2011): 197–251.

———, 'Feizhou conglinzhong de xinshiming – Ma Faxian laoren fangtanlu (qi)' (A New Mission in the African Bush: An Interview with Mr Ma Faxian, Part Seven), *Lengzhan guojishi yanjiu* 13 (2012): 223–77.

_____, 'Feizhou conglinzhong de xinshiming – Ma Faxian laoren fangtanlu (ba)' (A New Mission in the African Bush: An Interview with Mr Ma Faxian, Part Eight), *Lengzhan guojishi yanjiu* 14 (2012): 273–90.

Li Mingjiang, *Mao's China and the Sino-Soviet Split: Ideological Dilemma*, London: Routledge, 2012.

Li, Ruru, 'Sino the Times: Three Spoken Drama Productions on the Beijing stage', *Drama Review* 45.2 (Summer 2001): 129–44.

Li, Sangkuk, 'An Institutional Analysis of Xi Jinping's Centralization of Power', *Journal of Contemporary China* 26.105 (2017): 325–36.

Li, Zhisui, *The Private Life of Chairman Mao: The Memoirs of Mao's Personal Physician*, trans. Tai Hung-chao, London: Arrow Books, 1996.

Lim, Jin Li, 'New China and Its Qiaowu: The Political Economy of Overseas Chinese Policy in the People's Republic of China, 1949–1959', unpublished PhD dissertation, London School of Economics, 2016.

Linhart, Robert, *The Assembly Line*, trans. Margaret Crosland, London: Calder, 1981.

Linhart, Virginie, *Le jour où mon père s'est tu*, Paris: Éditions du Seuil, 2008.

Liu, Hong, 'The Historicity of China's Soft Power: The PRC and the Cultural Politics of Indonesia, 1945–1965', in Zheng Yangwen, Hong Liu and Michael Szonyi, eds, *The Cold War in Asia: The Battle for Hearts and Minds*, 147–82, Leiden, NL: Brill, 2010.

_____, *China and the Shaping of Indonesia, 1949–1965*, Singapore: NUS Press, 2011.

Locard, Henri, *Pol Pot's Little Red Book: The Sayings of Angkar*, Chiang Mai, Thailand: Silkworm, 2004.

Logevall, Fredrik, 'The Indochina Wars and the Cold War, 1945–1975', in Melvyn P. Leffler and Odd Arne Westad, eds, *The Cambridge History of the Cold War: Crises and Détente*, Volume 2, 281–304, Cambridge: Cambridge University Press, 2010.

Lonsdale, John, 'Mau Maus of the Mind: Making Mau Mau and Remaking Kenya', *Journal of African History* 31.3 (1990): 393–421.

Lovell, Julia, 'The Uses of Foreigners in Mao-Era China: "Techniques of Hospitality" and International Image-Building in the People's Republic, 1949–1976', *Transactions of the Royal Historical Society* 25 (2015): 135–58.

_____, 'The Cultural Revolution and Its Legacies in International Perspective', *China Quarterly* 227 (September 2016): 632–52.

_____, 'From Beijing to Palestine: Zhang Chengzhi's Journeys from Red Guard Radicalism to Global Islam', *Journal of Asian Studies* 75.4 (November 2016): 891–911.

Lubis, Mochtar, *Twilight in Djakarta*, trans. Claire Holt, London: Hutchinson, 1963.

Lumley, Robert, *States of Emergency: Cultures of Revolt in Italy from 1968 to 1978*, London: Verso, 1990.

Lüthi, Lorenz, *The Sino-Soviet Split: Cold War in the Communist World*, Princeton, NJ: Princeton University Press, 2010.

Luu Doan Huynh, 'Commentary: A Vietnamese Scholar's Perspective on the Communist Big Powers and Vietnam', in Priscilla Roberts, ed., *Behind the Bamboo Curtain: China, Vietnam, and the World Beyond Asia*, 433–49, Stanford, CA: Stanford University Press, 2006.

Lye, Colleen, *America's Asia: Racial Form and American Literature, 1893–1945*, Princeton, NJ: Princeton University Press, 2009.

Ma Mozhen, *Zhongguo jindu shi ziliao* (Materials from the History of Drug Prohibition in China), Tianjin: Tianjin renmin chubanshe, 1998.

McCauley, Martin, *The Khrushchev Era 1953–1964*, London: Routledge, 2014.

McClintock, Cynthia, 'Theories of Revolution and the Case of Peru', in David Scott Palmer, ed., *The Shining Path of Peru*, 225–40, London: Hurst, 1992.

———, *Revolutionary Movements in Latin America: El Salvador's FMLN and Peru's Shining Path*, Washington, DC: United States Institute of Peace Press, 1998.

———, 'Peru's Sendero Luminoso Rebellion: Origins and Trajectory', in Susan Eckstein and Manuel Antonio Garretón Merino, eds, *Power and Popular Protest: Latin American Social Movements*, 61–101, Berkeley: University of California Press, 2001.

McCoy, Alfred, *A Question of Torture: CIA Interrogation, from the Cold War to the War on Terror*, New York: Henry Holt & Co., 2006.

MacFarquhar, Roderick, ed., *The Politics of China: The Eras of Mao and Deng*, Cambridge: Cambridge University Press, 1997.

———, and Michael Schoenhals, *Mao's Last Revolution*, Cambridge, MA: Harvard University Press, 2009.

MacLaine, Shirley, *You Can Get There From Here*, London: George Prior, 1975.

McVey, Ruth T., *The Rise of Indonesian Communism*, Ithaca, NY: Cornell University Press, 1965.

———, 'Indonesian Communism and China', in Tang Tsou, ed., *China in Crisis Volume 2: China's Policies in Asia and America's Alternatives*, 357–94, Chicago: University of Chicago Press, 1968.

———, 'The Post-Revolutionary Transformation of the Indonesian Army: Part II', *Indonesia* 13 (April 1972): 147–81.

Mandela, Nelson, *Long Walk to Freedom*, London: Little, Brown, 2010.

Manman linhai lu (The Long Road Through Forest and Sea), Hong Kong: Jianzheng chubanshe, 2003.

Manrique, Nelson, 'The War for the Central Sierra', in Steve J. Stern, ed., *Shining and Other Paths: War and Society in Peru, 1980–1995*, 194–223, Durham, NC: Duke University Press, 1998.

Mao Zedong, *Report from Xunwu*, trans. and ed. Roger R. Thompson, Stanford, CA: Stanford University Press, 1990.

———, *Mao's Road to Power: Revolutionary Writings 1912–1949* (seven volumes), eds Stephen C. Averill, Timothy Cheek, Nancy Jane Hodes, Stuart Schram and Lyman Van Slyke, Armonk, NY: M. E. Sharpe, 1992–.

———, *Mao's Road to Power: Revolutionary Writings 1912–1949*, ed, Timothy Cheek, Nancy Jane Hodes and Stuart Schram, Volume 8, New York: Routledge, 2015.

Marks, John, *The Search for the 'Manchurian Candidate': The CIA and Mind Control*, London: Allen Lane, 1979.

Martin, David, and Phyllis Johnson, *The Struggle for Zimbabwe: The Chimurenga War*, London: Faber and Faber, 1981.

Mayer, Jane, *The Dark Side: The Inside Story of How the War on Terror Turned into a War on American Ideals*, New York: Anchor Books, 2009.

Mehili, Elidor, *From Stalin to Mao: Albania and the Socialist World*, Ithaca, NY: Cornell University Press, 2018.

Mehta, Harish C., *Warrior Prince: Norodom Ranariddh, Son of King Sihanouk of Cambodia*, Singapore: Graham Brash, 2001.

Melley, Timothy, 'Brain Warfare: The Covert Sphere, Terrorism, and the Legacy of the Cold War', *Grey Room* 45 (Fall 2011): 18–41.

———, *The Covert Sphere: Secrecy, Fiction and the National Security State*, Ithaca, NY: Cornell University Press, 2012.

Melvin, Jess, 'Why Not Genocide? Anti-Chinese Violence in Aceh, 1965–1966', *Journal of Current Southeast Asian Affairs* 32.3 (2013): 63–91.

———, *The Army and the Indonesian Genocide: Mechanics of Mass Murder*, London: Routledge, 2018.

Mertha, Andrew, *Brothers in Arms: Chinese Aid to the Khmer Rouge, 1975–1979*, Ithaca, NY: Cornell University Press, 2014.

Meyskens, Covell, 'Third Front Railroads and Industrial Modernity in Late Maoist China', *Twentieth-Century China* 40.3 (October 2015): 238–60.

Mhlaba, Raymond, *Raymond Mhlaba's Personal Memoirs: Reminiscing from Rwanda and Uganda*, Johannesburg: HSRC Press, 2001.

Miles, James, *China: Rising Power, Anxious State*, London: Penguin, 2012.

Miller, Gerard, *Minoritaire*, Paris: Seuil, 2001.

Milton, Cynthia E., ed., *Art from a Fractured Past: Memory and Truth Telling in Post-Shining Path Peru*, Durham, NC: Duke University Press, 2014.

Miyoshi Jager, Sheila, *Brothers at War: The Unending Conflict in Korea*, London: Profile Books, 2013.

Monson, Jamie, *Africa's Freedom Railway: How a Chinese Development Project Changed Lives and Livelihoods in Tanzania*, Bloomington: Indiana University Press, 2009.

Moorcraft, Paul, and Peter McLaughlin, *The Rhodesian War: Fifty Years On*, Barnsley, UK: Pen & Sword, 2015.

Mortimer, Rex, *Indonesian Communism Under Sukarno: Ideology and Politics, 1959–1965*, Ithaca, NY: Cornell University Press, 1974.

Mozingo, David, *Chinese Policy Toward Indonesia, 1949–1967*, Ithaca, NY: Cornell University Press, 1976.

Mukherjee, Arun, *Maoist Spring Thunder: The Naxalite Movement 1967–1972*, Kolkata: K. P. Bagchi & Co., 2007.

Mukhopadhyay, Ashoke Kumar, *The Naxalites Through the Eyes of the Police: Select Notifications from the Calcutta Police Gazette (1967–1975)*, Kolkata: Dey's Publishing, 2007.

Mumford, Andrew, *Counterinsurgency Wars and the Anglo-American Alliance: The Special Relationship on the Rocks*, Washington, DC: Georgetown University Press, 2017.

Myoe, Maung Aung, *In the Name of Pauk-Phaw: Myanmar's China Policy Since 1948*, Singapore: Institute of Southeast Asian Studies, 2011.

Naidoo, Nandha, 'The "Indian Chap": Recollections of a South African Underground Trainee in Mao's China', *South African Historical Journal* 64.3: 707–36.

Nasution, Abdul Haris, *Fundamentals of Guerrilla Warfare*, London: Pall Mall Press, 1965.

Naughton, Barry, 'The Third Front: Defence Industrialization in the Chinese Interior', *China Quarterly* 115 (September 1988): 351–86.

Newman, Robert P., *Owen Lattimore and the 'Loss' of China*, Berkeley: University of California Press, 1992.

Newton, Huey P., *To Die for the People*, San Francisco: City Lights Books, 2009.

Ngor, Haing, with Roger Warner, *Survival in the Killing Fields*, London: Robinson, 2003.

Nguyen, Lien-Hang T., *Hanoi's War: An International History of the War for Peace in Vietnam*, Chapel Hill: University of North Carolina Press, 2012.

Niccolai, Roberto, *Quando la Cina era Vicina: La Rivoluzione Culturale e la sinistra extraparlamentare Italiana negli anni '60 e '70*, Pisa: Associazione centro de documentazione de Pistoia, 1998.

Nkrumah's Subversion in Africa: Documentary Evidence of Nkrumah's Interference in the Affairs of Other African States, Ghana: Ministry of Information, 1966.

Nyerere, Julius K., *Freedom and Socialism*, Dar es Salaam: Oxford University Press, 1968.

_____, *Freedom and Development*, Dar es Salaam: Oxford University Press, 1973.

Odhiambo, E. S. Atieno, and John Lonsdale, eds, *Mau Mau and Nationhood: Arms, Authority and Narration*, Oxford: James Currey, 2003.

Ogunsanwo, Alaba, *China's Policy in Africa, 1958–1971*, Cambridge: Cambridge University Press, 1974.

Ogura, Kiyoko, 'Reality and Images of Nepal's Maoists After the Attack on Beni', *European Bulletin of Himalayan Research* 27 (September 2004): 67–125.

_____, 'Maoist People's Governments 2001–2005: The Power in Wartime', in David N. Gellner and Krishna Hachhethu, eds, *Local Democracy in South Asia: Microprocesses of Democratization in Nepal and Its Neighbours*, Volume 1, 175–231, New Delhi: Sage, 2008.

_____, *Seeking State Power: The Communist Party of Nepal (Maoist)*, Berlin: Berghof, 2008.

Osborne, Milton, *Sihanouk: Prince of Light, Prince of Darkness*, Honolulu: University of Hawai'i Press, 1994.

Pan, Philip, *Out of Mao's Shadow: The Struggle for the Soul of a New China*, London: Picador, 2008.

Pandita, Rahul, *Hello Bastar: The Untold Story of India's Maoist Movement*, Chennai: Tranquebar, 2011.

Paresh, Pandya, *Mao Tse-tung and Chimurenga: An Investigation into ZANU's Strategies*, Braamfontein, South Africa: Skotaville Publishers, 1988.

Passin, Herbert, *China's Cultural Diplomacy*, New York: Praeger, 1962.

Paul, Bappaditya, *The First Naxal: An Authorised Biography of Kanu Sanyal*, Los Angeles: Sage, 2014.

People's Revolutionary Tribunal Held in Phnom Penh for the Trial of the Genocide Crime of the Pol Pot–Ieng Sary Clique, August 1979: Documents, Phnom Penh: Foreign Languages Publishing House, 1990.

Peterson, Glen, *Overseas Chinese in the People's Republic of China*, London: Routledge, 2013.

Pettigrew, Judith, *Maoists at the Hearth: Everyday Life in Nepal's Civil War*, Philadelphia: University of Pennsylvania Press, 2013.

Poiger, Uta G., 'Generations: The "Revolutions" of the 1960s', in Helmut Walser Smith, ed., *The Oxford Handbook of Modern German History*, 640–62, Oxford: Oxford University Press, 2011.

Pomfret, John, *Chinese Lessons: Five Classmates and the Story of New China*, New York: Henry Holt & Co., 2006.

Price, Ruth, *The Lives of Agnes Smedley*, Oxford: Oxford University Press, 2005.

Priestland, Robert, *The Red Flag: A History of Communism*, London: Penguin, 2010.

Radchenko, Sergey, *Two Suns in the Heavens: The Sino-Soviet Struggle for Supremacy, 1962–1967*, Washington, DC: Woodrow Wilson Center, 2009.

Rayner, Stephen Frank, 'The Classification and Dynamics of Sectarian Forms of Organisation: Grid/Group Perspectives on the Far-left in Britain', unpublished PhD dissertation, University College London, 1979.

Regmi, Laxman Kumar, 'An Overview of Population Growth Trends of Nepal', *Journal of Institute of Science and Technology* 19.1 (2014): 57–61.

Reid, Donald, 'Etablissement: Working in the Factory to Make Revolution in France', *Radical History Review* 88 (2004): 83–111.

Ren Xiaosi, *The Chinese Dream: What It Means for China and the Rest of the World*, Beijing: New World Press, 2013.

Rénique, José Luis, *La Voluntad Encarcelada: Las 'Luminosas trincheras de combate' de Sendero Luminoso del Perú*, Lima: Instituto de Estudios Peruanos, 2003.

Richardson, Sophie, *China, Cambodia and the Five Principles of Peaceful Coexistence*, New York: Columbia University Press, 2010.

Rittenberg, Sidney, and Amanda Bennett, *The Man Who Stayed Behind*, Durham, NC: Duke University Press, 2001.

Roberts, Priscilla, ed., *Behind the Bamboo Curtain: China, Vietnam, and the World Beyond Asia*, Stanford, CA: Stanford University Press, 2006.

Robinson, Geoffrey, '"Down to the Very Roots": The Indonesian Army's Role in the Mass Killings of 1965–6', *Journal of Genocide Research* 19.4 (2017): 465–86.

———, *The Killing Season: A History of the Indonesian Massacres, 1965–66*, Princeton, NJ: Princeton University Press, 2018.

Roncagliolo, Santiago, *La cuarta espada: la historia de Abimael Guzmán y Sendero Luminoso*, Barcelona: Random House Mondadori, 2007.

Roosa, John, *Pretext for Mass Murder: The September 30th Movement and Suharto's Coup d'État in Indonesia*, Madison: University of Wisconsin Press, 2006.

———, 'Indonesian Communism: The Perils of the Parliamentary Path', in Norman Naimark, Silvio Pons and Sophie Quinn-Judge, eds, *The Cambridge History of Communism*, Volume 2, 441–66, Cambridge: Cambridge University Press, 2017.

Rothwell, Matthew D., *Transpacific Revolutionaries: The Chinese Revolution in Latin America*, New York: Routledge, 2013.

Roy, Arundati, *Broken Republic: Three Essays*, London: Hamish Hamilton, 2011.

Sampson, Anthony, *Mandela: The Authorised Biography*, London: Harper Collins, 1999.

Satnam, *Jangalnama: Travels in a Maoist Guerilla Zone*, trans. Vishav Bharti, New Delhi: Penguin India, 2010.

Scalapino, Robert A., and Chong-sik Lee, *Communism in Korea*, 2 volumes, Berkeley: University of California Press, 1972.

Scarlett, Zachary A., 'China After the Sino-Soviet Split: Maoist Politics, Global Narratives, and the Imagination of the World', unpublished PhD dissertation, Northeastern University, 2013.

Schell, Orville, *Discos and Democracy: China in the Throes of Reform*, New York: Pantheon Books, 1988.

Schram, Stuart, *The Thought of Mao Tse-Tung*, Cambridge: Cambridge University Press, 1989.

Schurmann, Franz, *Ideology and Organization in Communist China*, Berkeley: University of California Press, 1968.

Schwartz, Benjamin, *Chinese Communism and the Rise of Mao*, Cambridge, MA: Harvard University Press, 1951.

Scott, David, *China Stands Up: The PRC and the International World*, London: Routledge, 2007.

Scott Palmer, David, ed., *The Shining Path of Peru*, London: Hurst, 1992.

_____, 'The Influence of Maoism in Peru', in Alexander C. Cook, ed., *Mao's Little Red Book: A Global History*, 130–46, Cambridge: Cambridge University Press, 2014.

Seale, Bobby, *Seize the Time: Story of the Black Panther Party and Huey P. Newton*, Baltimore: Black Classic Press, 1991.

Seed, David, *Brainwashing: The Fictions of Mind Control – A Study of Novels and Films*, Kent, OH: Kent State University Press, 2004.

Selden, Mark, *The Yenan Way in Revolutionary China*, Cambridge, MA: Harvard University Press, 1971.

_____, *China in Revolution: The Yenan Way Revisited*, Armonk,, NY: M. E. Sharpe 1995.

Sen, Mohit, *A Traveller and the Road: The Journey of an Indian Communist*, New Delhi: Rupa & Co., 2003.

Service, Robert, *Comrades: Communism – A World History*, London: Pan, 2008.

Seth, Sanjay, 'From Maoism to Postcolonialism? The Indian "Sixties", and Beyond', *Inter-Asia Cultural Studies* 7.4 (2006): 589–605.

Shah, Alpa, *In the Shadows of the State: Indigenous Politics, Environmentalism and Insurgency in Jharkhand, India*, Durham, NC: Duke University Press, 2010.

_____, 'The Intimacy of Insurgency: Beyond Coercion, Greed, or Grievance in Maoist India', *Economy and Society* 42.3 (2013): 480–506.

_____, 'The Agrarian Question in a Maoist Guerrilla Zone: Land, Labour and Capital in the Forests and Hills of Jharkhand, India', *Journal of Agrarian Change* 13.3 (2013): 424–50.

————, '"The Muck of the Past": Revolution, Social Transformation, and the Maoists in India', *Journal of the Royal Anthropological Institute* 20 (2014): 337–56.

————, *Nightmarch: Among India's Revolutionary Guerrillas*, London: Hurst, 2018.

————, and Judith Pettigrew, eds, *Windows into a Revolution: Ethnographies of Maoism in India and Nepal*, New Delhi: Social Science Press, 2012.

Shamsul Alam, S. M., *Rethinking Mau Mau in Colonial Kenya*, New York: Palgrave Macmillan, 2007.

Sharma, Mandira, and Dinesh Prasain, 'Gender Dimensions of the People's War: Some Reflections on the Experiences of Rural Women', in Michael Hutt, ed., *Himalayan 'People's War': Nepal's Maoist Revolution*, 152–65, London: Hurst, 2004.

Sharma, Sudheer, 'The Maoist Movement: An Evolutionary Perspective', in Michael Hutt, ed., *Himalayan 'People's War': Nepal's Maoist Revolution*, 38–57, London: Hurst, 2004.

Shen Zhihua, *Mao, Stalin and the Korean War: Trilateral Communist Relations in the 1950s*, trans. Neil Silver, London: Routledge, 2012.

————, *Sulian zhuanjia zai Zhongguo (1948–1960)* (Soviet Experts in China [1948–1960]), Beijing: Shehui kexue wenxian chubanshe, 2015.

————, and Danhui Li, *After Leaning to One Side: China and Its Allies in the Cold War*, Washington, DC: Woodrow Wilson Center, 2011.

————, and Julia Lovell, 'Undesired Outcomes: China's Approach to Border Disputes During the Early Cold War', *Cold War History* 15.1 (2015): 89–111.

————, and Yafeng Xia, 'Leadership Transfer in the Asian Revolution: Mao Zedong and the Asian Cominform', *Cold War History* 14.2 (2014): 195–213.

————, and Yafeng Xia, *Mao and the Sino-Soviet Partnership, 1945–1959: A New History*, Lanham, MD: Lexington Books, 2015.

————, and Yafeng Xia, *A Misunderstood Friendship: Mao Zedong, Kim Il-sung and Sino-North Korean Relations, 1949–1976*, New York: Columbia University Press, 2018.

Short, Philip, *Mao: A Life*, London: John Murray, 2004.

————, *Pol Pot: The History of a Nightmare*, London: John Murray, 2004.

Shrestha-Schipper, Satya, 'Women's Participation in the People's War in Jumla', *European Bulletin of Himalayan Research* 33–34 (2008–2009): 105–122.

————, 'The Political Context and the Influence of the People's War in Jumla', in Marie Lecomte-Tilouine, ed., *Revolution in Nepal: An Anthropological and Historical Approach to the People's War*, 259–92, New Delhi: Oxford University Press, 2013.

Sihanouk, Norodom, *Prisonnier des Khmers Rouges*, Paris: Hachette, 1986.

_____. *War and Hope: The Case for Cambodia*, trans. Mary Feeney, London: Sidgwick & Jackson, 1980.

_____, and Wilfred Burchett, *My War with the CIA*, London: Penguin 1973.

_____, and Julio A. Jeldres, *Shadow Over Angkor: Volume One, Memoirs of His Majesty King Norodom Sihanouk of Cambodia*, Phnom Penh: Monument Books, 2005.

Simeon, Dilip, 'Rebellion to Reconciliation', in B. G. Verghese, ed., *Tomorrow's India: Another Tryst with Destiny*, New Delhi: Penguin India, 2006 (manuscript copy obtained from author).

_____, *Revolution Highway*, New Delhi: Penguin Books India, 2010.

Simon, Sheldon W., *The Broken Triangle: Peking, Djakarta, and the PKI*, Baltimore: Johns Hopkins Press, 1969.

Simpson, Bradley R., *Economists with Guns: Authoritarian Development and U.S.–Indonesian Relations, 1960–1968*, Stanford, CA: Stanford University Press, 2008.

Sing, Manfred, 'From Maoism to Jihadism: Some Fatah Militants' Trajectory from the Mid 1970s to the Mid 1980s', in Rüdiger Lohlker and Tamara Abu-Hamdeh, eds, *Jihadi Thought and Ideology*, 55–82, Berlin: Logos Verlag, 2014.

Sisulu, Elinor, *Walter and Albertina Sisulu: In Our Lifetime*, London: Abacus, 2003.

Sjøli, Hans Petter, 'Maoism in Norway: And How the AKP (m-l) Made Norway More Norwegian', *Scandinavian Journal of History* 33.4 (December 2008): 478–90.

Slavu, Catinca, 'The 2008 Constituent Assembly Election: Social Inclusion for Peace', in Sebastian von Einsiedel and David M. Malone, eds, *Nepal in Transition: From People's War to Fragile Peace*, 232–64, Cambridge: Cambridge University Press, 2012.

Slobodian, Quinn, *Foreign Front: Third World Politics in Sixties West Germany*, Durham, NC: Duke University Press, 2012.

_____, 'The Meanings of Western Maoism in the Global 1960s', in Chen Jian et al., eds, *The Routledge Handbook of the Global Sixties*. London: Routledge, 2018, 67–78.

Smith, Aminda, *Thought Reform and China's Dangerous Classes: Reeducation, Resistance and the People*, Lanham, MD: Rowman & Littlefield, 2013.

Smith, J., and André Moncourt, *The Red Army Faction, a Documentary History: Volume 1, Projectiles for the People*, Oakland, CA: PM, 2009.

Smith, Michael L., 'Taking the High Ground: Shining Path and the Andes', in David Scott Palmer, ed., *The Shining Path of Peru*, 15–32, London: Hurst, 1992.

Smith, S. A., *A Road Is Made: Communism in Shanghai, 1920–1927*, Honolulu University of Hawai'i Press, 2000.

———, ed., *The Oxford Handbook of the History of Communism*, Oxford: Oxford University Press, 2014.

Snow, Edgar, *Red Star Over China*, New York: Random House, 1938.

———, *Journey to the Beginning*, London: Victor Gollancz, 1960.

———, *The Other Side of the River: Red China Today*, London: Victor Gollancz, 1963.

———, *The Long Revolution*, London: Hutchinson, 1973.

Snow, Philip, *The Star Raft: China's Encounter with Africa*, London: Weidenfeld & Nicolson, 1988.

Song Yongyi et al., eds, *Zhongguo wenhua dageming wenku* (Collected Materials on the Chinese Cultural Revolution), Hong Kong: Chinese University Press, 2013.

Song Zheng, *Mao Zedong zhuyi de xingwang: Zhongguo geming yu Hong Gaomian geming de lishi* (The Rise and Fall of Maoism: A History of the Chinese and Khmer Rouge Revolutions), US: Meiguo yangguang chubanshe, 2013.

South African Democracy Education Trust, *The Road to Democracy in South Africa*, Volume 5, Part 1, Cape Town: Zebra Press, 2004.

Spence, Jonathan, *The Search for Modern China*, New York: Norton, 2013.

Stanford, Maxwell C., 'Revolutionary Action Movement (RAM): A Case Study of an Urban Revolutionary Movement in Western Capitalist Society', unpublished MA dissertation, University of Georgia, 1986.

Starn, Orin, *Nightwatch: The Politics of Protest in the Andes*, Durham, NC: Duke University Press, 1999.

———, Carlos Iván Degregori and Robin Kirk, eds, *The Peru Reader: History, Culture, Politics*, Durham, NC: Duke University Press, 2009.

Starr, John Bryan, 'Conceptual Foundations of Mao Tse-Tung's Theory of Continuous Revolution', *Asian Survey* 11.6 (June 1971): 610–28.

Stern, Steve J., ed., *Shining and Other Paths: War and Society in Peru, 1980–1995*, Durham, NC: Duke University Press, 1998.

Streatfeild, Dominic, *Brainwash: The Secret History of Mind Control*, London: Hodder & Stoughton, 2006.

Strong, Simon, *Shining Path: The World's Deadliest Revolutionary Force*, London: Fontana, 1993.

Suh, Dae-Sook, *Kim Il-Sung: The North Korean Leader*, New York: Columbia University Press, 1988.

Sukarno, *Sukarno: An Autobiography, as Told to Cindy Adams*, Hong Kong: Gunung Agong, 1965.

Sundar, Nandini, *The Burning Forest: India's War in Bastar*, Delhi: Juggernaut, 2016.

Sundhaussen, Ulf, *The Road to Power: Indonesian Military Politics 1945–1967*, Oxford: Oxford University Press, 1982.

Suri, Jeremi, *Power and Protest: Global Revolution and the Rise of Détente*, Cambridge, MA: Harvard University Press, 2003.

————, 'Ostpolitik as Domestic Containment: The Cultural Contradictions of the Cold War and the West German State Response', in Belinda Davis, Wilfried Mausbach, Martin Klimke and Carlo MacDougall, eds, *Changing the World, Changing Oneself: Political Protest and Collective Identities in West Germany and the US in the 1960s and 1970s*, 133–52, Oxford: Berghahn Books, 2013.

Tang, Christopher, 'Homeland in the Heart, Eyes on the World: Domestic Internationalism, Popular Mobilization, and the Making of China's Cultural Revolution, 1962–68', unpublished PhD dissertation, Cornell University, 2016.

Tarazona-Sevillano, Gabriela, 'The Organization of Shining Path', in David Scott Palmer, ed., *The Shining Path of Peru*, 171–90, London: Hurst, 1992.

Taylor, Jay, *The Generalissimo: Chiang Kai-shek and the Struggle for Modern China*, Cambridge, MA: Harvard University Press, 2009.

Taylor, Lewis, *Shining Path: Guerrilla War in Peru's Northern Highlands, 1980–1997*, Liverpool: Liverpool University Press, 2006.

Thapa, Deepak, with Bandita Sijapati, *A Kingdom Under Siege: Nepal's Maoist Insurgency, 1996 to 2003*, London: Zed Books, 2004.

Thomas, S. Bernard, *Season of High Adventure: Edgar Snow in China*, Berkeley: University of California Press, 1996.

Toledo Brückmann, Ernesto, *. . . Y llegó Mao: Síntesis histórica de la llegada del Pensamiento Mao TseTung al Perú (1928–1964)*, Lima: Grupo Editorial Arteidea, 2016.

Tompkins, Andrew S., '"BETTER ACTIVE TODAY THAN RADIOACTIVE TOMORROW!" Transnational Opposition to Nuclear Energy in France and West Germany, 1968–1981', unpublished PhD dissertation, University of Oxford, 2013.

The Truth About Vietnam–China Relations over the Last Thirty Years, Hanoi: Ministry of Foreign Affairs, 1979.

Tsai, Yen-ling, and Douglas Kammen, 'Anti-communist Violence and the Ethnic Chinese in Medan', in Douglas Kammen and Katharine McGregor, eds, *The Contours of Mass Violence in Indonesia, 1965–68*, 131–55, Copenhagen: NIAS Press, 2012.

Ungor, Cagdas, 'Reaching the Distant Comrade: Chinese Communist Propaganda Abroad (1949–1976)', unpublished PhD dissertation, Binghamton University, 2009.

Upadhya, Sanjay, *Nepal and the Geo-strategic Rivalry Between China and India*, Abingdon: Routledge, 2012.

Van de Ven, Hans, *From Friend to Comrade: The Founding of the Chinese Communist Party, 1920–1927*, Berkeley: University of California Press, 1991.

_____, *China at War: Triumph and Tragedy in the Emergence of the New China*, London: Profile, 2017.

Van Ness, Peter, *Revolution and Chinese Foreign Policy: Peking's Support for Wars of National Liberation*, Berkeley: University of California Press, 1970.

Varon, Jeremy, *Bringing the War Home: The Weather Underground, the Red Army Faction, and Revolutionary Violence in the Sixties*, Berkeley: University of California Press, 2004.

Vickers, Adrian, *A History of Modern Indonesia*, Cambridge: Cambridge University Press, 2013.

Vo, Alex-Thai D., 'Nguyen Thi Nam and the Land Reform in North Vietnam', *Journal of Vietnamese Studies* 10.1 (Winter 2015): 1–62.

Von Einsiedel, Sebastian, and David M. Malone, eds, *Nepal in Transition: From People's War to Fragile Peace*, Cambridge: Cambridge University Press, 2012.

Wakeman, Frederic, *Policing Shanghai, 1927–1937*, Berkeley: University of California Press, 1996.

Walder, Andrew, *China Under Mao: A Revolution Derailed*, Cambridge, MA: Harvard University Press, 2015.

Wales, Nym (see also Helen Foster Snow), *My Yenan Notebooks*, n.p., 1961.

Wang Jiarui, ed., *Zhongguo gongchandang duiwai jiaowang 90 nian* (A History of the Chinese Communist Party's Interactions with the Outside World over the Past Ninety Years), Beijing: Dangdai shijie chubanshe, 2013.

Wang Ning, 'Introduction: Global Maoism and Cultural Revolutions in the Global Context', *Comparative Literature Studies* 52.1 (2015): 1–11.

Wang Zhichun, *Qingchao rouyuanji* (A Chronicle of the Qing Dynasty's Policy of Cherishing Distant Lands), Beijing: Zhonghua shuju, 1989.

Welch, Michael, 'Doing Special Things to Special People in Special Places: Psychologists in the CIA Torture Program', *The Prison Journal* 97.6 (December 2017): 729–49.

Westad, Odd Arne, *The Global Cold War: Third World Interventions and the Making of Our Times*, Cambridge: Cambridge University Press, 2005.

_____, *The Cold War: A World History*, London: Allen Lane, 2017.

_____, ed., *Brothers in Arms: The Rise and Fall of the Sino-Soviet Alliance, 1945–1963*, Stanford, CA: Stanford University Press, 2000.

_____, Chen Jian, Stein Tønnesson, Nguyen Vu Tungand and James G. Hershberg, '77 Conversations Between Chinese and Foreign Leaders on the Wars in Indochina, 1964–1977', Woodrow Wilson International Center Working Paper No. 22.

_____, and Sophie Quinn-Judge, eds, *The Third Indochina War: Conflict Between China, Vietnam and Cambodia, 1972–1979*, London: Routledge, 2006.

Whelpton, John, *A History of Nepal*, Cambridge: Cambridge University Press, 2005.

Windrow, Martin, *The Last Valley: Dien Bien Phu and the French Defeat in Vietnam*, London: Cassell, 2005.

Wolin, Richard, *The Wind from the East: French Intellectuals, the Cultural Revolution and the Legacy of the 1960s*, Princeton, NJ: Princeton University Press, 2010.

Wu, Hung, *Remaking Beijing: Tiananmen Square and the Creation of a Political Space*, Chicago: University of Chicago Press, 2005.

Wylie, Raymond, *The Emergence of Maoism: Mao Tse-tung, Ch'en Po-ta, and the Search for Chinese Theory, 1935–1945*, Stanford, CA: Stanford University Press, 1980.

Yang, Guobin, 'Mao Quotations in Factional Battles and Their Afterlives: Episodes from Chongqing', in Alexander C. Cook, ed., *Mao's Little Red Book: A Global History*, 61–75, Cambridge: Cambridge University Press, 2014.

Yang Kuisong, *Mao Zedong yu Mosike de enen yuanyuan* (The Grudges Between Mao Zedong and Moscow), Nanchang: Jiangxi renmin chubanshe, 2002.

_____, 'Mao Zedong and the Indochina Wars', in Priscilla Roberts, ed., *Behind the Bamboo Curtain: China, Vietnam, and the World Beyond Asia*, 55–96, Stanford, CA: Stanford University Press, 2006.

_____, 'Zhong-Mei hexie guochengzhong de zhongfang bianzou: "sange shijie" lilun tichu Beijing tanxi' (China's Reorientation During the Sino-American Rapprochement: An Exploration of the Background to the 'Three Worlds' Theory), *Lengzhan guojishi yanjiu* 4 (Spring 2007): 1–24.

_____, *Zhonghua renmin gongheguo jianguoshi* (History of the Founding of the People's Republic of China), two volumes, Nanchang: Jiangxi renmin chubanshe, 2009.

Yang Meihong, *Yingsu huahong: Wo zai Miangong shiwu nian* (Red Poppies: The Fifteen Years I Spent in the Burmese Communist Party), Hong Kong: Tiandi tushu, 2009.

Young, Charles S., *Name, Rank and Serial Number: Exploiting Korean War POWs at Home and Abroad*, Oxford: Oxford University Press, 2014.

Young, Marilyn, *The Vietnam Wars, 1945–1990*, New York: HarperPerennial, 1991.

Yu You, *Hu Yuzhi*, Beijing: Qunyan chubanshi, 2011.

Zapata, Antonio, *La Guerra Senderista: Hablan los Enemigos*, Lima: Taurus, 2017.

Zhai, Qiang, *China and the Vietnam War, 1950–1975*, Chapel Hill: University of North Carolina Press, 2005.

_____, 'China and the Cambodian Conflict, 1970–1975', in Priscilla Roberts, ed., *Behind the Bamboo Curtain: China, Vietnam, and the World Beyond Asia*, 369–404, Stanford, CA: Stanford University Press, 2006.

Zhang Chengzhi, *Jinmuchang* (The Golden Pasture), Beijing: Zuojia chuban-she, 1987.

_____, *Koueihei no jidai* (The Red Guard Era), trans. Kojima Shinji and Tadokoro Takehiko, Tokyo: Iwanami shoten, 1992.

_____, *Beifang de he* (Rivers of the North), Beijing: Zuojia chubanshe, 2000.

_____, *Wuse de yiduan* (Five Colours of Heresy), Hong Kong: Dafeng chubanshe, 2007.

_____, 'Wenxue yu zhengyi: zai Zhongguo Renmin Daxue wenxueyuan de yanjiang' (Literature and Righteousness: A Lecture Given at the Institute of Literature at People's University), *Dangdai wentan* 6 (2013): 4–11.

_____, *Zhi Riben: jingzhong yu xibie* (Japan: To Cherish and Respect), Shanghai: Shanghai wenyi chubanshe, 2015.

Zhang, Xiaoming, *Deng Xiaoping's Long War: The Military Conflict Between China and Vietnam, 1979–1991*, Chapel Hill: University of North Carolina Press, 2015.

Zhang Yi, *Poxiao shifen* (When the Light Dawned), Taibei: Zhongyang ribao chubanshe, 1985.

Zhao Ziyang, *Prisoner of the State: The Secret Journal of Chinese Premier Zhao Ziyang*, London: Pocket Books, 2010.

Zharkevich, Ina, 'Learning in a Guerrilla Community of Practice: Literacy Practices, Situated Learning and Youth in Nepal's Maoist Movement', *European Bulletin of Himalayan Research* 42 (2013): 104–32.

Zheng Yangwen, Hong Liu and Michael Szonyi, eds, *The Cold War in Asia: The Battle for Hearts and Minds*, Leiden, NL: Brill, 2010.

Zhongguo Shimotelai-Sitelang-Sinuo yanjiuhui (Chinese Smedley-Strong-Snow Society) ed., *Xixingmanji he wo* (*Red Star Over China* and Me), Beijing: Guoji wenhua chuban gongsi, 1999.

Zhou Degao, *Wo yu Zhonggong he Jiangong: chise huaren jiemi* (The CCP, the CPK and Me: Revelations of a Red Chinese), Hong Kong: Tianyuan shuwu, 2007.

Zhou, Taomo, 'China and the Thirtieth of September Movement', *Indonesia* 98 (October 2014): 29–58.

_____, 'Diaspora and Diplomacy: China, Indonesia and the Cold War, 1945–1967', unpublished PhD dissertation, Cornell University, 2015.

Zweiback, Adam, 'The 21 "Turncoat GIs": Non-repatriations and the Political Culture of the Korean War', *The Historian* 60:2 (Winter 1998): 345–62.

PICTURE CREDITS

Section 1

Mao and Zhou Enlai at Yan'an, *c.*1936 (Pictures from History / akg-images).

Mao and Jiang Qing (reproduced from *The Challenge of Red China* by Gunther Stein, Pilot Press, London, 1945).

Woodcut of Mao (courtesy of Shanghai Library).

Agnes Smedley, George Bernard Shaw, Song Qingling, Cai Yuanpei, Harold Isaacs, Lin Yutang and Lu Xun (reproduced from *Lu Xun's Revolution* by Gloria Davies, Harvard University Press, Cambridge, MA, 2013).

Edgar and Helen Snow (reproduced courtesy of Brigham Young University).

Jacket of the first edition of *Red Star Over China*, Random House, 1938.

Edgar Snow with Mao in north-west China, October 1936 (Pictures from History / akg-images).

Hu Yuzhi on way to Singapore (reproduced from *Wo de huiyi* by Hu Yuzhi, Jiangsu renmin chubanshe, Jiangsu, 1990).

Chin Peng (reproduced from *My Side of History* by Chin Peng, Media Masters, Singapore, 2003).

Two Malayan guerrillas (courtesy of Roy Follows and Norman W. Doctor).

Captured and deported MCP guerrillas and underground members aboard a steamer on its way to China, late 1950s (courtesy of C.C. Chin).

Mao welcomes Kim Il-sung, October 1954 (Sovfoto / UIG / Getty Images).

Edward Hunter (AP Images).

Clarence Adams (courtesy of Della Adams).

World map (Ditu chubanshe, 1966).

Poster of the peoples of the world waving Little Red Books (courtesy of Dong Zhongchao).

Mao and Khrushchev at Tiananmen Square (*People's Daily* / Cambridge University Library).

Kang Sheng and Deng Xiaoping returning from the USSR (*China Pictorial* / Cambridge University Library).

'Brave the wind and the waves, everything has remarkable abilities' (courtesy of IISH / Stefan R. Landsberger Collections; chineseposters.net).

'Hold high the great red banner of Mao Zedong Thought to wage the Great

Proletarian Cultural Revolution to the end – revolution is no crime, to rebel is justified' (courtesy of IISH/Stefan R. Landsberger Collections; chineseposters.net).

Section 2

Sukarno with Mao (reproduced from *Presiden Sukarno Mengundjungi Tiongkok*, Kedutaan Besar Republik Rakjat Tiongkok di Indonesia, Jakarta, 1956).

Aidit with Mao (*China Pictorial*/Cambridge University Library).

Group of Indonesian anti-Communist youths helping the army with the search for the Communist leader, D. A. Aidit, and his followers, 1965 (Getty Images/Bettman).

Mao with visitors from Africa and the Middle East (author's collection).

Julius Nyerere with Zhou Enlai (*China Pictorial*/Cambridge University Library).

Scene from *War Drums on the Equator* (*China Pictorial*/Cambridge University Library).

Chinese instructors in Ghana demonstrate how to lay anti-personnel mines (reproduced from *Nkrumah's Subversion in Africa: Documentary Evidence of Nkrumah's Interference in the Affairs of Other African States*, Ministry of Information, Accra-Tema, Ghana, 1966).

Chemicals from Shanghai used for military training in Ghana (reproduced from *Nkrumah's Subversion in Africa: Documentary Evidence of Nkrumah's Interference in the Affairs of Other African States*, Ministry of Information, Accra-Tema, Ghana, 1966).

Josiah Tongogora (reproduced from *Re-living the Second Chimurenga: Memories from the Liberation Struggle in Zimbabwe* by Fay Chung, The Nordic Africa Institute, Stockholm, 2006).

Ho Chi Minh with Zhou Enlai (*China Pictorial*/Cambridge University Library).

Anti-American board game (courtesy of IISH/Stefan R. Landsberger Collections; chineseposters.net).

Sukarno, Zhou Enlai, Chen Yi, Norodom Sihanouk at the tenth anniversary of the Bandung Conference (courtesy of Julio Jeldres).

Zhou Enlai welcomes Norodom Sihanouk to Beijing airport, 25 April 1973 (Keystone/Hulton Library/Getty Images).

Mao with Pol Pot and Ieng Sary in Beijing, June 1975 (API/Gamma-Rapho/Getty Images).

Jubilant Khmer Rouge guerrillas pose for the cameras after the fall of Phnom Penh, 17 April 1975 (Roland Neveu/LightRocket/Getty Images).

Phnom Penh deserted (courtesy of Documentation Center of Cambodia Archives).

Vietnamese militiawoman with captured Chinese soldier (reproduced from *Brother Enemy: The War After the War* by Nayan Chanda, Harcourt Brace Jovanovich, San Diego, New York and London, 1986).

Li Fanwu punished for bearing a resemblance to Mao (Li Zhensheng/Contact Press Images; from *Red Color News Soldier*, Phaidon, 2003).

'Revolution is not a dinner party', *Lui* magazine, 1967, photograph by Frank Gitty (Francis Giacobetti).

Robert F. Williams with Mao (Robert F. Williams papers; Bentley Historical Library, University of Michigan).

Portrait of Mao at the Sorbonne, May 1968 (AFP/Getty Images).

Section 3

Aravindan Balakrishnan (London Metropolitan Police).

Idalgo Macchiarini kidnapped by the Red Brigades, 3 March 1972 (Archivo Mondadori; reproduced from *Mara Renato e 10: Storia dei fondatori delle BR* by Alberto Franceschini, Pier Vittorio Buffa and Franco Giustolisi, Arnoldo Mondadori Editore, Milan, 1991).

Dead dog hung from Lima lamppost by Shining Path militants (Carlos Bendez, *Caretas* magazine; courtesy of Peru's Truth and Reconciliation Commission).

Photograph of Abimael Guzmán, probably from the 1960s (Archivo Baldomero Alejos).

Female Shining Path prisoners sing and march towards a mural of Abimael Guzmán (by kind permission of the photographer, Oscar Medrano).

Anguish of a Peruvian Quechua mother searching for her dead son (by kind permission of the photographer, Oscar Medrano).

Charu Mazumdar and comrades (reproduced from *The Naxalites: Through the Eyes of the Police – Select Notifications from the Calcutta Police Gazette, 1967–1975*, ed. Ashoke Kumar Mukhopadhyay, Dey's Publishing, Kolkata, 2006).

Communist pantheon in Naxalbari (author's photograph).

Naxalites in the jungle today (Communist Party of India (Maoist); reproduced from *Hello Bastar: The Untold Story of India's Maoist Movement* by Rahul Pandita, Tranquebar, Chennai, 2011).

Environmental destruction in Orissa (reproduced by kind permission of Sanjay Kak).

Nepali Maoist leadership in the 1990s (reproduced by kind permission of Kunda Dixit from *A People War: Images of the Nepal Conflict 1996–2006*, Publication Nepalaya, Kathmandu, 2006).

Baburam Bhattarai, Hisila Yami and Manushi in front of picture of Abimael Guzmán (reproduced by kind permission of Manushi Bhattarai-Yami).

Victims of Maoist bus bombing (reproduced by kind permission of Kunda Dixit from *A People War: Images of the Nepal Conflict 1996–2006*, Publication Nepalaya, Kathmandu, 2006).

Comrade Kiran (author's photograph)

Sentencing of Chinese politician Bo Xilai, 22 September 2013 (Feng Li/Getty Images).

Broadcast of Gu Kailai giving recorded testimony at Bo Xilai's trial, 23 August 2013 (Mark Ralston/AFP/Getty Images).

Xi Jinping and Mao trinkets (Reuters/Thomas Peter).

Mao with pigtails, detail of *Chairmen Mao* by Zhang Hongtu, 1989 (reproduced by kind permission of the artist).

Giant statue of Mao under construction in Zhushigang village, Henan province, January 2016 (STR/AFP/Getty Images).

Every effort has been made to trace and contact copyright holders. The publishers will be pleased to correct any mistakes or omissions in future editions.

INDEX

RED CHINA BLUES
My Long March From Mao to Now
by Jan Wong

Jan Wong, a Canadian of Chinese descent, went to China as a starry-eyed Maoist in 1972 at the height of the Cultural Revolution. A true believer—and one of only two Westerners permitted to enroll at Beijing University—her education included wielding a pneumatic drill at the Number One Machine Tool Factory. *Red China Blues* is Wong's startling—and ironic—memoir of her rocky six-year romance with Maoism; her dramatic firsthand account of the devastating Tiananmen Square uprising; and her engaging portrait of the individuals and events she covered as a correspondent in China during the tumultuous era of capitalist reform under Deng Xiaoping. In a frank, captivating, deeply personal narrative she relates the horrors that led to her disillusionment with the "worker's paradise." And through the stories of the people, Wong reveals long-hidden dimensions of the world's most populous nation.

Memoir

CHINA WITNESS
Voices from a Silent Generation
by Xinran

Xinran, acclaimed author of *The Good Women of China*, traveled across China, seeking out the nation's grandparents and great-grandparents, the men and women who experienced firsthand the tremendous changes of the modern era. Although many of them feared repercussions, they spoke with stunning candor about their hopes, fears, and struggles, and about what they witnessed: from the Long March to land reform, from Mao to marriage, from revolution to Westernization. In the same way that Studs Terkel's *Working* and Tom Brokaw's *The Greatest Generation* gave us the essence of very particular times, *China Witness* gives us the essence of modern China—a portrait more intimate, nuanced, and revelatory than any we have had before.

History

EVERYTHING UNDER THE HEAVENS
How the Past Helps Shape China's Push for Global Power
by Howard W. French

For many years after its reform and opening to the world in 1978, China maintained an attitude of false modesty about its ambitions. That façade, reports former *New York Times* Asia correspondent Howard W. French, has now been cast off. China is increasingly asserting its place among the global powers, signaling its plans for pan-Asian dominance by building its navy, increasing territorial claims to areas like the South China Sea, and diplomatically bullying smaller players. Underlying this attitude is the millennia-old concept of *tian xia*, which held that "everything under the heavens" fell within the influence of the Chinese empire. If we understand how this historical identity continues to color current actions, in ways ideological, philosophical, and even legal, we can learn to forecast just what kind of global power China stands to become—as the world order is poised to shift.

Political Science

.MAO
The Unknown Story
by Jung Chang and Jon Halliday

The most authoritative life of the Chinese leader ever written, *Mao: The Unknown Story* is based on a decade of research and on interviews with many of Mao's close circle in China who have never talked before — and with virtually everyone outside China who had significant dealings with him. It is full of startling revelations, exploding the myth of the Long March and showing a completely unknown Mao. After Mao conquered China in 1949, his secret goal was to dominate the world. In chasing this dream he caused the deaths of nearly 38 million people in the greatest famine in history. In all, well over 70 million Chinese perished under Mao's rule — in peacetime.

Biography